THE LEVELLER REVOLUTION

THE LEVELLER
REVOLUTION

Radical Political Organisation in England,
1640–1650

John Rees

VERSO

London • New York

First published by Verso 2016
© John Rees 2016

The moral rights of the author have been asserted

3 5 7 9 10 8 6 4 2

Verso
UK: 6 Meard Street, London W1F 0EG
US: 20 Jay Street, Suite 1010, Brooklyn, NY 11201
versobooks.com

Verso is the imprint of New Left Books

ISBN-13: 978-1-78478-388-4
eISBN-13: 978-1-78478-391-4 (US)
eISBN-13: 978-1-78478-390-7 (UK)

British Library Cataloguing in Publication Data
A catalogue record for this book is available from the British Library

Library of Congress Cataloging-in-Publication Data
Names: Rees, John, 1957– author.
Title: The Leveller Revolution : radical political organisation in England,
 1640–1650 / John Rees.
Description: Brooklyn, NY : Verso, 2016. | Includes bibliographical
 references and index.
Identifiers: LCCN 2016039447| ISBN 9781784783884 (hardback : alk. paper) |
 ISBN 9781784783914 (eISBN)
Subjects: LCSH: Levellers. | Great Britain – History – Civil War, 1642–1649. |
 Great Britain – Politics and government – 1642–1660.
Classification: LCC DA405 .R429 2016 | DDC 941.06/2 – dc23
LC record available at https://lccn.loc.gov/2016039447

Typeset in Minion Pro by Hewer Text UK Ltd, Edinburgh
Printed and bound by CPI Group (UK) Ltd, Croydon, CR0 4YY

It must be the poore, the simple and meane things of this earth that must confound the mighty and strong.

Richard Overton, 1647

And well he therefore does, and well has guest,
Who in his Age has always forward prest:
And knowing not where Heavens choice may light,
Girds yet his Sword, and ready stands to fight

Andrew Marvell, 1655

In the 'most spontaneous' movement it is simply the case that the elements of 'conscious leadership' cannot be checked, have left no reliable document.

Antonio Gramsci, 1927–37

Contents

Acknowledgements		ix
A Note on the Text		xiii
Introduction		xvii
1.	'The Maddest Christmas That Ever I Saw'	1
2.	The First Leveller, John Lilburne	23
3.	London, the Great Leveller	43
4.	Levelling by Print	67
5.	Civil War	77
6.	The War, the Church and the State	106
7.	The Coming of the Levellers	128
8.	Petitions and Prison	156
9.	Agitators	172
10.	Putney Church and Corkbush Field	198
11.	Counterrevolution	221
12.	Revolution	250
13.	Defeat in Victory	280

14. Lieutenant Colonel John Rede's Last Stand   311

15. The Levellers and the English Revolution   334

Notes   349

Select Bibliography   445

Index   471

Acknowledgements

The English Revolution has been with me for as long as I can remember. On the desk in front of me now is the magnificent colour programme available to cinema-goers when the film *Cromwell* was released in 1970. Beside it is the facsimile reprint of the Levellers' *Agreement of the People* from the Jackdaw education pack Number 33 on the English Civil War published in 1975. Over the intervening years since I acquired those publications I have accumulated many debts that I should acknowledge now. First I should pay tribute to some friends and teachers who are no longer here to read this book, much as I wish that they were. My old friend and comrade Paul Foot was one of the few whose own interest in the English Revolution was as compulsive as my own. I well remember trips to the bookshops of Charing Cross Road, when there were more of them than there are now, looking for rarities related to the English Revolution. For my fortieth birthday he gave me a copy of an 1843 edition of Clarendon's *History of the Rebellion* with an inscription which read, 'Hope this helps with the definitive study of the Revolution by J Rees, pubn. date 1999?' I am afraid I've missed his deadline and even more afraid that it will fall even farther short of being definitive for the lack of his criticism. I have also missed the intellectual stimulation of knowing Brian Manning, with whom I worked in arranging the republication of his unrivalled *The English People and the English Revolution* and the publication of his impressive body of subsequent work. I was not a personal friend of Christopher Hill but I did work with him in publishing and republishing some of his work late in his life. My view of the Revolution differs from Hill's, but no one writing about the seventeenth century, however critical some revisionist historians may have been, has anything but an enormous debt to his magnificent body of work.

More recently I had the considerable piece of good fortune to find myself quite by accident sharing a platform with Ariel Hessayon at the Institute of Historical Research in a seminar organised by the London Socialist Historians some years back. I decided afterwards to write asking him if he would supervise doctoral research on the Levellers. From that moment on he has been encouraging, intellectually stimulating, and supportive far beyond any professional obligation. His careful supervision and generous assistance during my research were invaluable in the completion of that work. I am also grateful to the History Department at Goldsmiths, University of London, for awarding me a bursary during my study and for extending the courtesy of making me a visiting research fellow during the completion of this book. Not every doctoral candidate enjoys their viva. That I did is accounted for by that fact that Jason Peacey and Rachel Foxley had an engaged and constructive approach that after four years of research every candidate hopes for from their examiners.

I have some more specific thanks to record as well. I am grateful to Justine Taylor, the archivist at the Honourble Artillery Company, and to Tim Wells for sharing the results of his work in the same archive. Norah Carlin and Jordan Downs were both kind enough to share very useful unpublished papers with me. Stephen Freeth, the archivist of the Vintners Company, was helpful in respect of material on the Saracen's Head tavern and other matters to do with the history of the City. Dr Alastair Massie at the National Army Museum was of considerable assistance in locating the standards of the London Trained Bands. Frances Henderson, who I came across by chance in Worcester College, was helpful in respect of the discussion of John Rede's links with the Levellers, as was family historian Gordon Rede. At Verso, Leveller enthusiast Rowan Wilson has always been supportive of any scheme involving the recovery of the English Revolution. Special thanks are due Leo Hollis, who has been a magnificent, enthusiastic and engaged editor. The book would be so much the poorer without his efforts.

Some friends have heard more detail about the Levellers than can conceivably have been good for them. So thanks for patience are due to Chris Nineham, Feyzi Ismail, Sam Fairbairn, Jane Shallice, Andrew and Anna Murray, Clare Solomon, John Westmoreland, Mike Simons, Andrew Burgin and Kate Hudson, Shelia Wiggins and Haydn Wheeler (whose skills as a landscape gardener helped uncover the graves of John Rede's family and friends one sunny day in the Baptist burial ground in Porton, Wiltshire). David Shonfield is one of that remarkable generation of secular Jewish intellectuals who just seem to know something interesting about practically everything, including the seventeenth century. I'm grateful for his company and for his hospitality at his house near San Leolino, Tuscany, where part of what follows was written. But the longest and deepest debt of all is to Lindsey German.

John Rees, May 2016

A Note on the Text

In quoting from seventeenth-century documents I have retained the original spelling and punctuation except in a small minority of cases where to do so would seriously impair the reader's chances of making sense of the text. I have done this not merely for the sake of accuracy but because I think it helps us in some way I still cannot quite define to better understand the thoughts of those living over 300 years ago if the spelling and punctuation are retained.

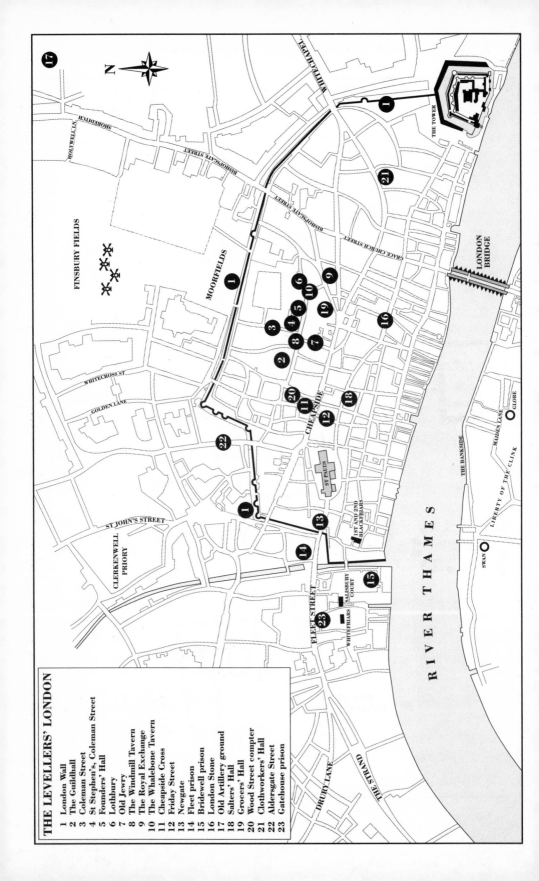

THE LEVELLERS' LONDON

1 London Wall
2 The Guildhall
3 Coleman Street
4 St Stephen's, Coleman Street
5 Founders' Hall
6 Lothbury
7 Old Jewry
8 The Windmill Tavern
9 The Royal Exchange
10 The Whalebone Tavern
11 Cheapside Cross
12 Friday Street
13 Newgate
14 Fleet prison
15 Bridewell prison
16 London Stone
17 Old Artillery ground
18 Salters' Hall
19 Grocers' Hall
20 Wood Street compter
21 Clothworkers' Hall
22 Aldersgate Street
23 Gatehouse prison

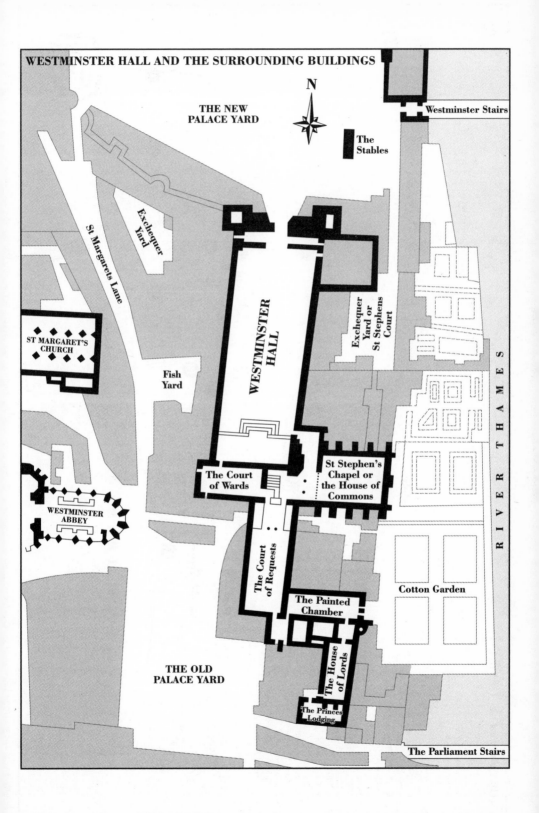

WESTMINSTER HALL AND THE SURROUNDING BUILDINGS

N

THE NEW
PALACE YARD

Westminster Stairs

The
Stables

Exchequer
Yard

St Margarets Lane

WESTMINSTER HALL

Exchequer
Yard or
St Stephens
Court

ST MARGARET'S
CHURCH

Fish
Yard

RIVER THAMES

St Stephen's
Chapel or
the House of
Commons

The Court
of Wards

WESTMINSTER
ABBEY

The Court
of Requests

The Painted
Chamber

Cotton Garden

THE OLD
PALACE YARD

The House
of Lords

The Princes
Lodging

The Parliament Stairs

Introduction

In 1649 the English people did something that had never been done in the entire millennia-long history of the existence of kings and their related titles of caesar, kaiser, tsar or shah. At the culmination of a popular revolution they put their monarch on public trial and found him guilty of treason against the people. Charles I was then executed on a platform built outside Banqueting House in London's Whitehall. Kings had lost their lives before—in battle, at the hands of rivals, even killed by members of their own family. But never like this. Never had an armed people, called to battle by a parliament, defeated their sovereign and created a court to find him guilty of crimes against them. 'It was not', as the Regicide Thomas Harrison later told his own trial for his part in killing the king, 'a thing done in a corner'.[1] The greatest poet of the age, John Milton, wrote the *The Defence of the English People* so that in every nation on the continent it would be known that it was an act of justice.

At the same time the Revolution abolished the House of Lords and declared the Commonwealth of England to be a republic. This was not unique, for the Netherlands was already a republic, but in the world of the seventeenth century it was remarkable that a second European country should do so amidst the almost universal order of monarchy. And it was not just that England had become a republic, but *how* it had become a republic. Nearly a decade of political upheaval, popular mobilisation, and Civil War had indeed 'turned the world upside down', in the phrase contemporaries used. The entire national church, a pillar of government as well as a religious institution, had been torn down and the archbishop of Canterbury tried and executed. Censorship had collapsed and tens of thousands of pamphlets, newspapers, broadsheets and ballads had poured from printing presses in an uncontrollable and unprecedented torrent of free speech. An entire army had, in another historical first, elected its own representatives from every regiment, challenged their commanders, and altered the entire political direction of the Revolution. The war that they had fought was, and remains, proportionally one of the most destructive of human life that the British Isles has ever experienced.[2] A considerable part of the wealth and land of the defeated cavaliers was taken from them, sequestrated and used to pay for the war and given to the victors. It is hard to think of another decade in English history, with the possible exception of the 1940s, which saw so much political and social change.

On the king's scaffold on that cold January day in 1649 stood John Harris and Richard Rumbold.[3] The two men were from a political movement called the Levellers. It was entirely fitting that they should be there, for the movement they were part of had played a crucial role in the developing political crises of the previous decade. From the earliest days of the Revolution, and long before they were known as Levellers, the radicals of this movement were at the forefront of events. John Lilburne, the best-known Leveller leader, was already famous to the London crowd after he was imprisoned by Charles I for distributing illegal pamphlets in the late 1630s. Richard Overton was operating a secret press that produced incendiary texts from the very earliest days of the Revolution. The steadfast parliamentary ally of the Levellers, Henry Marten, shocked the king's future political adviser by being the first MP he ever heard to advocate a republic. As these and many other activists came to meet and organise together, they produced a torrent of the most radical literature that the Revolution witnessed, often from illegal presses. They petitioned and demonstrated, fought in the war, agitated in the ranks, became spokesmen for the elected soldiers' representatives and were often imprisoned for their pains. There were, of course, many other political factions at work during the Revolution. And some of them used the same organisational tools as the Levellers. But none used all of them so consistently and effectively through the successive crises of the Revolution. And while much other political organisation focussed on the political elite, the Levellers were unique in systematically focussing on popular politics and popular mobilisation. It was this focus which, unable to rely on existing institutional networks of power, required them to develop their own organisational capacities.

The Revolutionaries of the seventeenth century had enough support in society to pull down the ages-old institution of monarchy. But they were still a minority. Their enemies were a substantial part of the whole society, and a very substantial part of the old ruling order. The Revolutionaries could find allies lower down the social strata among the working poor. These could be engaged against this old regime, but they were not themselves part of the 'middling sort' of lesser gentry, merchants and craftsmen that were at the heart of the parliamentary cause. Among this minority that made the Revolution, the Levellers were themselves a minority. But they were, when the decisive crisis of the Revolution arrived, a minority sufficiently bold in their ideology and effective in organisation that they could make the difference between revolution and counterrevolution.

The Levellers were first and foremost an organised group of political activists. This is perhaps a more contentious judgement than it might sound. Much interest in the Levellers has focussed on the novelty of their democratic ideology. There has also been much debate about their social origins and class location. These are, of course, vital and engaging areas of study. Henry Brailsford's magisterial study and the earlier historians of the Levellers had much to say about both.[4] I have some things to say about this as well, particularly in the final chapter, but I also agree with Jason Peacey's observation that in recent studies of the Levellers,

> the context explored has tended to be an intellectual, rather than a political one, and authors' aims are assumed to have been intellectual, philosophical and theoretical, rather than polemical and propagandistic . . . few works have sought to interpret non-intellectual motivations for the composition and publication of books and pamphlets, or the interaction of political writers with the day-to-day political life of the times.[5]

So this book is primarily a political history that focusses on the construction of Leveller organisation. This is, after all, how they themselves confronted political problems and sought to develop their ideas in response to them. And in any case, political organisation can never be seen as immediately reducible to class locations in either appeal, membership or ideology. This is, not least, because any class, or even a subsection of a class, can support more than one political organisation and more than one variant of an ideology. And, for this reason, exactly which organisation, and which ideology, becomes decisive at a particular historical juncture is contested and not predetermined.

In describing what kind of political organisation the Levellers were I have gone back to the original of all exchanges on this issue. When Baptist and Leveller Henry Denne was captured at the Burford mutiny in 1649 he appeared before the firing squad in his winding sheet. He was so penitent that Oliver Cromwell reprieved him when he recanted his Leveller views. Soon after, he wrote that the Levellers were too disparate to be an effective political organisation: 'We were an Heterogenial Body consisting of parts very diverse from another, setled upon principles inconsistent one with another'.[6] Historians sceptical of the effectiveness of the Levellers as an organisation have been making the same case ever since.[7] But the Levellers responded directly to Denne in their own pamphlet. They made the obvious point that it was not 'impossible that this Hetergenerall body, these severall parts, so diversified by light and darknesse, good and evil, should be concentrick, as to joynt pursuance of publique ends'.[8] I have tried to follow this thought through and to examine the Levellers as a political movement integrating activists from different constituencies, and creating still broader alliances with other political currents, for the joint pursuance of revolutionary ends. Indeed, to be effective such a movement must pursue a strategy based on this understanding.

In order to make this argument I have tried to take up a challenge that Ian Gentles laid down many years ago. In his article on the Leveller activists, mother and son Katherine and Samuel Chidley, he suggested,

> The four or five individuals who formed the first rank of Leveller leadership have been intensively studied; the tens of thousands of men and women who signed Leveller petitions and participated in Leveller demonstrations will never be studied because they have nearly all vanished without trace. If we wish to increase our knowledge of the social and intellectual context of the Leveller movement, the most fruitful field of study will be the second rank of leadership who left some evidence behind of their activities.[9]

I have tried to follow this suggestion because to do so gives some deeper sense of the Levellers as an effective and socially rooted organisation. In a chronological study it has not always been possible to halt the narrative to talk about these individuals as they emerge as political activists. Nevertheless, I have tried to do justice to their often considerable contributions. The long-time Leveller printer William Larner or the General Baptist Thomas Lambe, whose activity was 'scarcely less important' than Lilburne's work, probably made greater contributions to the Leveller organisation than the much better known John Wildman.[10] The same might be said of Captain William Eyre and Captain William Bray. But I have also tried to catch sight of figures who were much less central, so far as we know, to the Levellers, but whose activity, for that very reason, tells us about how far the influence of Leveller organisation and ideas might travel: the bookseller William Browne and his daughter caught distributing John Lilburne's pamphlets, John Rede the governor of Poole accused of sheltering Leveller mutineers, for instance.

I have chosen to present this account of the Levellers as a chronological narrative.[11] Despite being aware of the limitations of this approach, this is the easiest way that readers new to this era can enter the other country of England in the seventeenth century. Further, so much of recent research on the Levellers exists as essays in scholarly journals where the analytical form is dominant. This has obvious strengths but the individual trees of academic journal articles do not amount to a wood. Without a synoptic account of the Levellers it is impossible to properly weigh the contributions of those historians who have made enormous efforts to illuminate particular aspects of Leveller history. Finally, and most importantly, a chronological narrative allows us to trace the historical process of the Levellers coming to be. My case is that the Levellers arose out of wider currents of radicalism and that through a process of differentiation with both opponents and allies they came to form a distinctive political organisation. It is a history of what natural scientists call emergent properties—at certain critical moments pre-existing strands of development fuse into something novel and re-enter the chain of historical causation in a new form, and so alter its course.[12] To illuminate this process a narrative form is the most suitable.

The great Victorian Civil War historian Samuel Gardiner is said to have refused to read the relevant source material until he reached the point in the story when it was produced. I have not emulated his discipline but I am sensitive to Gardiner's fear that hindsight would prejudice his judgement of the actors themselves. So I have tried to see the alternatives and opportunities, and the strategic and organisational choices made by the Levellers, as they would have appeared to them. Historians do well to remember Kierkegaard's injunction that 'life can only be understood backwards; but it must be lived forwards'. But activists like the Levellers know that, fundamentally, it is untrue. The Levellers understood life around them well enough. They had to: they were trying to change it, often enough with their lives at stake.

CHAPTER 1

'The Maddest Christmas That Ever I Saw'

The Christmas of 1641 started well enough for Colonel Thomas Lunsford. King Charles had appointed him lieutenant of the Tower of London. It was an important post giving him control of the fortress dominated the eastern fringe of the capital. The Tower was also the home of the Mint and the depository of much of the City's merchant wealth. The new role was a political appointment of considerable significance, at a time of heightened crisis. In the already highly charged political atmosphere of late 1641, Charles was determined to regain political control of London, and saw Lunsford's appointment as an ideal opening gambit.

Charles needed a dramatic change in his fortunes. The year had already been scarred by rebellion in Ireland, causing something close to political panic among both the political elite and the population across Britain. Tales of massacres of Protestants and imminent Catholic invasion circulated like wildfire. In January 1641, Charles's key minister, the earl of Strafford, had been charged before the Commons and, later, convicted and executed as a traitor in front of a huge crowd at the Tower. In February charges of impeachment were brought against Archbishop Laud, the clerical mainstay of the Stuart government. He in turn had been imprisoned in the Tower. The Commons then dismantled the Courts of Star Chamber and High Commission that had been used to enforce Laud's regime of religious intolerance in July. In November the catalogue of Charles's failures in the eyes of Parliament, the Grand Remonstrance, was passed and then, later, printed.

Even Charles's one success, the ending of the Bishops' Wars with Scotland, a disastrous product of the king's attempt to impose a new church structure north of the border, had left demobbed soldiers, known as refor-madoes, adrift in the streets of London looking for pay and employment in Ireland. Thomas Lunsford was one of them. At the same time the Tower remained the site of continual conflict throughout the year. When the Commons had imprisoned the earl of Strafford in the Tower in May ahead of his execution the king sent soldiers to try and affect a rescue. But the then lieutenant of the Tower, Sir William Balfour, had barred them from entering. Charles now aimed to strike a bold blow in the battle to control London by removing Balfour and putting the Tower in the hands of a figure of unquestioning loyalty.

Thomas Lunsford's loyalty to the king was beyond question, but everything else about him was less impressive. Perhaps the only bad thing to have been said about Lunsford which was *untrue* was the accusation of cannibalism; even if he himself did claim that he was 'fierce enough to eat children'. Lunsford was the very picture of a cavalier. Red-haired and short-tempered, even his own cousin, Lord Dorset, described Lunsford as 'a young outlaw who neither fears God nor man, and who, having given himself over to all lewdness and dissoluteness, only studies to affront justice, [taking] glory to be esteemed . . . a swaggering ruffian'. In 1633 he made an attempt on the life of his Sussex neighbour Sir Thomas Pelham after Lunsford's family were found guilty of poaching Pelham's deer. Lunsford fired his pistol at Sir Thomas's coach as it left East Hoathly Church after Sunday morning service. The bullet passed through the coach and lodged in the church door. Lunsford was imprisoned in Newgate but escaped to France, where he became a soldier of fortune and colonel of a regiment of foot that he raised himself. Lunsford owed a fine of £8,000 imposed by order of the Court of Star Chamber. In 1639 Lunsford returned to England to offer his services to King Charles in the Bishops' Wars. Consequently, Charles pardoned him and dismissed the fine. Lunsford was a loyal soldier and this further recommended him to the king, despite Lunsford's claim to have killed two mutineers out of hand. So it was that on 22 December 1641 Charles appointed Lunsford to the Tower, apparently on the advice of one of his more irascible courtiers, Lord Digby.[1]

Every element of the parliamentary opposition to Charles, and their wider circles of support across the City, reacted with fierce disapproval to Lunsford's appointment. The City complained and petitioned the Commons, demanding Lunsford be removed. Future Leveller leader Richard Overton was one of the signatures on the City petition which described Lunsford as 'a man outlawed and most notorious for outrages' who was 'fit for any dangerous Attempt' and who had put the City in the 'Height of Fear'.[2] The majority in the Commons agreed and demanded that the Lords join them in protesting at the appointment. The Lords refused on the grounds that it was 'in his Majesty's power to make choyce of his own Officers'. The Commons insisted that Lunsford was 'of a decayed and desperate fortune' and of a 'desperate condition' and could not be trusted with the Mint or the merchants' money. They recalled his attack on Sir Thomas Pelham and added to it Lunsford's threat to a Captain Buller that he would 'cut his throat'. In debate the Commons heard that when on the Continent Lunsford was so 'given to drinking and quarrelling that all civill and sober men avoided his company', that he had fled the Low Countries to escape debt, that he had stolen money from his own troops, and that he was 'debauched' and unfit to control the Tower. Respectable citizens and less respectable apprentices came to the doors of Westminster demanding that Lunsford be dismissed. Republican MP and future Leveller ally Henry Marten was instructed to seize the arms of Lunsford's supporters. London, particularly the City, was now arming itself. One newsletter from the capital issued this call the day after Lunsford's appointment: 'I say still, provide weapons, get muskets, powder and shot. Let not the Popish party surprise us with a riding rod only in our hands'. The cry was not in vain: 'There is a great ado made for arms . . . there is not any muskets or other guns to be bought, not iron to make them of, so great is the fears of the people here, especially about the Tower'. Even late on Christmas Day 'there were hundreds watching voluntarily to prevent some income of the soldiers, the Lieutenant being sworn in. All the merchants have taken out their bullion out of the Tower which was to be coined'. The outcry was so great that on Sunday 26 December the lord mayor visited Charles in Whitehall on two occasions to tell him of the 'tumultuous rising of the Prentices and other inferior persons of London' who had warned that if Lunsford were not removed there would be 'some further inconvenience happen upon it'. This 'further inconvenience', the Commons heard, would be 'an attempt on the Tower' to force Lunsford out. This did the trick and later the same day the King retreated and removed Lunsford. But this proved to be too small a retreat, too late.[3]

The crowds still swarmed to Westminster Yard outside Parliament on the following day, Monday 27 December. The news of Lunsford's removal, far from pacifying the crowd, seemed to 'increase the uproare'. Some of the crowd were armed with clubs and they called out to the members of both houses, 'No bishops, no popish lords!' But the citizens were not the only ones to arrive at Westminster that day. So did the freshly humiliated Colonel Lunsford with about thirty or forty supporters. Neither he nor they were in an even temper. In fact Lunsford was 'resolved to be revenged upon those which first went about to withstand him'.[4]

Lunsford and his supporters swaggered into Westminster Hall and began abusing the London citizens gathered there. They repeatedly taunted the people, asking, 'I wonder which of you dare speake against Bishops'. One 'country gentleman' stepped forward and told them that 'my conscience doth tell me that Bishops are no law full'. Swords were drawn but the crowd intervened and parted them. In another incident Captain David Hide, a demobilised soldier from the army, drew his sword and said he would 'cut the throats of those Round headed Dogs that bawl against the Bishops'. It was said to be the first time that 'roundhead' was used as a term of abuse. In the midst of this was a figure already familiar to radical Londoners. This was the future leader of the Levellers, John Lilburne. Lilburne was leading a crowd of apprentices and sailors who confronted Hide. With his own sword drawn Lilburne disarmed Hide 'and brought both him & his sword up to the House of Commons door'. Astoundingly Hide was immediately released and rejoined Lunsford in Westminster Hall. Then Lunsford's party 'all drew their swords and Rapiers, and fell upon the people with great violence'. Lilburne recorded that the cavaliers 'fell to slashing and cutting' the crowd, driving them in panic 'up the very Parliament staire'. Some fled into the adjacent Court of Wards and some up the stairs to the Court of Requests. There they found parliamentarian stalwart Sir Richard Wiseman, who, 'perceiving how it went, spoke most bravely to animate them to return with such weapons as they had'. Lilburne recalled 'Sir Richard Wiseman, my selfe, and divers other Citizens with our swords in our hands freely adventured our lives' to drive back Lunsford's cavaliers. Wiseman fought two or three of Lunsford's gang, breaking the rapier of one into two pieces. He was joined by some sailors with clubs. But they were outnumbered until more apprentices and sailors arrived and began to fight back using tiles prised from the floor or walls. A running fight was now in process across Westminster Hall.

News of this was abroad in the City and hundreds of apprentices arrived at Westminster armed with swords and staves. As Lilburne later recalled, 'I fought with C. Lunsford, and divers others at Westminster (who drew first) with my sword in my hand, to save the Parliament men throats from being cut'. The 'citizens . . . fought like enraged lions' and Lilburne and his supporters got the better of Lunsford and 'his crue of ruffians', as they were later to describe them. Half the gentlemen ran away at the first volley of stones, and eventually all the gentlemen of the Court scattered or were 'beat down'. Lunsford himself had to escape the crowd by wading into the Thames until the water came over the tops of his boots in order to make his getaway in a boat.[5]

That night the lord mayor and sheriffs rode around the City attempting to calm the mood. The City gates were locked, and the watch was strengthened. The next morning, the Trained Bands, the local militia, were called out to defend the City. The king demanded that Trained Bands also be deployed to 'Guard his Royal person, and his Consort and Children at Whitehall'. Charles was unnerved by the 'disorderly and tumultuous conflux of people at Westminster and Whitehall'. His courtiers were disquieted and he had heard the 'most seditious language being uttered under His own windows'. Furthermore, punishment of these offenders had been 'interrupted and stopped'. It was to no avail. Fighting broke out again the following day, Tuesday 28 December.[6]

The crowds now seem to have turned their attention from Westminster Hall to nearby Westminster Abbey. The archbishop of York had to be rescued by Lord Dover and Lord Faulconbridge from a hostile crowd that thronged the Yard. The protestors were intent on rescuing fellow apprentices who had been detained and were being examined by the archbishop. The apprentices cried 'a Bishop, a Bishop' when they saw the clerics approach the palace on the Thames and prevented them from coming ashore. The bishops had to keep 'rowing up and down for about an hour, and at last went back'. One of their number 'thanked God they knew not me to be a Bishop'.

As night fell the crowd attempted to force an entrance into the abbey but only succeeded in bursting 'part of the door to pieces'. They threatened to pull down the organ and altar. But the doors were held against them. Meanwhile, the abbey's defenders, including some scholars from the nearby Westminster College, got up onto the roof of the building and 'endeavoured to beat them off with Stones'. It was also reported that shots were fired at the crowd. As the battle turned, some thirty or forty of the abbey defenders rushed out and charged at the crowd 'pell mell with pistols and swords drawn' in a 'cruell and most Butcherly manner'. Several protestors were hurt. John Lilburne, once again in the thick of the fighting, was 'very sorely wounded', according to one contemporary report.

Another injury, even more serious than Lilburne's, was sustained by his ally in the fight the previous day in Westminster Hall, Sir Richard Wiseman, who in the end received such serious injury that he later died of his wounds. He was a hero among the apprentices and elegies at his death were printed and distributed by his supporters. The apprentices collected the money that paid for Wiseman's funeral. The funeral procession wound from Westminster to the radical heart of the City, St Stephen's in Coleman Street. It was composed of 200 apprentices and another 400 citizens decked in black ribbons and with their swords at their sides.[7]

One of the elegies produced for Richard Wiseman, *The Apprentices Lamentation*, was printed by William Larner.[8] In the same year, Larner also printed the early pamphlets of both John Lilburne and fellow future Leveller Katherine Chidley. He was also printing material by William Kiffin, then a key supporter of Lilburne and a leading religious radical. Larner was to become a mainstay of Leveller printing throughout the movement's existence.[9]

On the same day that Wiseman was killed Charles issued a proclamation that all citizens should cease their assemblies. He also instructed the lord mayor to tell the captains of the Trained Bands that they should shoot to kill the crowds. Charles directed that if the crowd

> shall refuse to retire to their homes peaceably, that then for the better keeping of the peace and preventing of further mischiefs, you command the captains and officers of the train bands by shooting with bullets or otherwise to slay and kill such of them as shall persist in their tumultuary and seditious ways and disorders.[10]

The following day, Wednesday 29 December, no doubt taking the lead from his king, one MP was in such a state of panic at the 'riotous and tumultuous Assembly of vaine and idle persons who presume to begirt our House' that he also proposed that if they could not be persuaded to disperse then the best course was to 'shoot at them' as 'it will bee the best and speediest means to repell them'.[11]

This was just the kind of talk to warm Thomas Lunsford's heart. Charles had been forced to remove him as lieutenant of the Tower but he was certainly not out of favour. The king had knighted him and awarded him £500 a year for life. He also appointed him to guard duties in Whitehall. Charles had ordered that all courtiers wear swords and that a guardhouse be built in Whitehall. Lunsford's soldiers were on guard duty on the afternoon of Wednesday 29 December when they were at the heart of yet another attack on a large crowd that had been gathering since early morning. That day there were 10,000 'mechanic citizens and apprentices' in Whitehall south of Charing Cross. They were armed with halberds, staves and some swords. The earl of Huntington reported to his son, 'They stood so thick that we had much ado to pass with our coaches . . . They cried "No Bishops, no papist lords", looked in our coaches where [whether] any bishops were therein . . . we went in great danger'. Inevitably, the soldiers became involved in an argument with some of the crowd and one of the protestors threw a clump of mud at the officers. In response the officers came out of Whitehall and 'cut and hacked the apprentices that were passing to Westminster'. In the affray there 'much hurt ensued, very many wounded on both sides, some hands cut off, others arms, others sides of their faces cut off'. Again the insults 'cavalier' and 'roundhead' were bawled across Whitehall. Some thirty or forty of the apprentices 'were wounded, and lost their hats and cloaks'.[12] But the crowd remained densely packed at nightfall and 'though it were a dark night their innumerable links made it as light as day'. Constable Peter Scott 'tried to appease the prentices by promising to release their fellows detained in the Mermaid tavern'. But when he arrived at the door of the tavern one of his fellow constables was attacked with a sword from within. This enraged the apprentices and they broke into the tavern. The keeper of the Mermaid was later charged with riot.[13]

The House of Commons supported the crowds against their attackers, telling the Lords that protestors had committed 'no offence at all' and that criticism of them was 'a true violation of the liberty of the subject, and an affront to parliament'. The Commons then dispatched MP and Alderman Isaac Pennington at the head of a delegation of three other MPs to free those apprentices that had earlier been jailed in the Gatehouse prison. The Commons were treading a fine line. They knew that they relied on the London crowd as a bulwark against the king, but they were also nervous that the crowd might take measures they could not support. So it was that on the same night Captain John Venn MP, though he was one of the parliamentary organisers of the protests, attempted to calm a crowd of 2,000 apprentices who were roaming the City armed with clubs, swords and halberds. They were intent on freeing apprentices who had been arrested earlier and who they thought were being held in the White Lion prison. Venn told them that the apprentices in the Gatehouse had already been freed by the Commons and pleaded with them to return to their homes. He was only partially successful. Some dispersed, crying 'Home, home, home' with a 'mighty noise'. But others headed for the Woodstreet prison, and fought with the warders, eventually breaking into the cells. Only when they were satisfied that there were no apprentices being held captive did they go on their way. Nor was this the only kind of action being taken in the City. By this time shopkeepers and other traders were closing their businesses in a rudimentary kind of strike. Such action, of course, freed both citizens and apprentices of their daily occupation and made them more likely to join the protesting crowds.[14]

At the end of three feverish days, the crowds emerged with a signal victory. The crowd's chant of 'No bishops, no popish lords' had never been mindless anti-episcopalianism or even anti-Catholicism. The bishops and their allies in the Lords had for some time been blocking legislation sent to them by the Commons. Some, but not all, of this was to do with the sending and provisioning of troops for Ireland where the rising had killed thousands of Protestants (though not the hundreds of thousands sometimes exaggeratedly reported) and was threatening invasion. Other legislation included bills directed at limiting the king's power. 'The Bishops [are] continually concurring with the Popish Lords against the passing of any good bills sent thither from the House of Commons', wrote Thomas Smith. 'Their last plot was to make this Parliament no Parliament, and so overthrow all Acts passed and to cause dissolution of it for the present'. This was a reference to an attempt by Lord Digby on 28 December to declare that this was 'no free parliament' because of the protests in the streets. This had been defeated, ironically, because the crowd had prevented the bishops from being able to sit.[15]

Twelve bishops, led by the archbishop of York, renewed this line of attack by delivering a complaint to Charles that the violent menace of the crowd had prevented them from attending the Lords. For fear of their lives they could not carry out their duty. Then they added a fateful rider arguing that no vote taken since 27 December should therefore be considered valid.[16] This was obviously designed to give Charles the excuse to dissolve Parliament. Charles sent the complaint to the Lords and the Lords sent it to the Commons. When the protestation was read in the Commons, Denzil Holles delivered a damning response accusing the bishops of high treason. The bishops were, said Holles, instruments of the Devil bent on aiding rebellion in Ireland and undermining the Church at home with Romish practices. They were sowing division between Lords and Commons and between the king and Parliament. Their traitorous actions were paving the way for arbitrary government and they were 'unfit and unworthy' to bear office. Not least, argued

Holles, the bishops' protestation 'may cause great uproars and tumults in the City, and about Westminster, of the Citizens who are altogether set against the Bishops'.

The Commons promptly impeached the twelve bishops and sent them to prison, a decision which seemed to hearten Henry Marten. The archbishop of York and nine others were sent to the Tower, and three who were too infirm were imprisoned elsewhere. In the City the church bells rang to celebrate the popular victory and bonfires blazed in the street. At the start of the protests the complaint was made that 'every tinker and tapster called for Justice'. Now they, and many others, felt they had had a measure of it. Looking back over the December Days, Thomas Coke wrote to his family that it was the 'most tumultuous Christmas that in all my life I ever yet knew'. Captain Robert Slyngesbie wrote to the lord mayor of London, 'I cannot say we have had a merry Christmas, but the maddest one that ever I saw'.[17]

The birds have flown

The bishops had miscalculated, acting too early, but they were not wrong in sensing that the Court was beginning to reinforce itself as the protests in the yard subsided. Charles was gathering an augmented guard around him and preparing a new political offensive against the parliamentary opposition. Some 500 gentlemen of the Inns of Court marched to Whitehall and swore allegiance to their king, promising to protect him and his family. Ever more cavaliers of Lunsford's stamp were drawn to Whitehall and feasted by the king. Westminster Abbey remained under permanent guard. 'I never saw the Court so full of gentlemen,' wrote Captain Slyngesbie, 'everyone comes thither with his sword'.[18] He thought the demonstrators had been 'terrified by the multitude of gentry and soldiers who flock to the court . . . and the rough entertainment that was like to be given them if they came again'. Prophetically, he observed that

> the citizens for the most part shut up their shops, and all the gentlemen provide themselves with arms as in time of open hostility. Both factions talk very big, and it is a wonder there is no more blood spilt, seeing how earnest both sides are. There is no doubt but if the King do not comply with the Commons in all things they desire, a sudden civil war must ensue, which every day we see approaches nearer.[19]

But Charles not only felt that the armed force at his disposal was growing, he also felt that he was able to make a political thrust which would behead the parliamentary opposition once and for all.

The Common Council of the City, even with its newly elected more radical members, was in a conciliatory mood. On 31 December Charles sent Lord Newburgh to the City to deliver a carefully phrased message demanding loyalty from the Common Council assembled in the Guildhall. The king's message reminded the officials, though doubtless they did not need it, of the 'many tumultuary and riotous Assemblies about Our Palaces of Whitehall and Westminster'. Whether or not he actually believed it, the king was careful not to find fault with the City but instead put the blame on the 'mean and unruly people of the Suburbs'. But he did demand that the Council bend their every effort to stop any 'ill-affected persons' from inciting more protests. The response of the Council bordered on grovelling. They assured the king that 'neither this Court, nor any particular member thereof, hath had any hand in these Tumultuous and Riotous proceedings'. They went on to promise their best efforts to 'prevent and suppress in time to come ... the like Tumultuous Assemblies, and all Mutinous and rebellious persons'. If they apprehended any troublemakers they swore to make sure that they would 'receive condign punishment'. The watch was strengthened for this purpose and the Trained Bands were admonished for laxity.[20]

Then Charles acted. On 3 January 1642 the king charged five members of the Commons—John Pym, John Hampden, Denzil Holles, Arthur Haselrig and William Strode—with high treason. One of their key allies in the Lords—Lord Mandeville, the future earl of Manchester—was also charged. Charles simultaneously moved to prevent the lord mayor from sending the Trained Bands to protect the Commons and reissued his command to have protestors shot. The king then instructed the sergeant-at-arms to seal the rooms and trunks of the five members. The five members were, Charles insisted, traitors who had attempted to 'deprive the King of his Royal Power' and who had 'actually levied War against the King'. The Commons bluntly refused to deliver the five members. Both Houses in conference decided that the king's accusation was made without due legal procedure and was a breach of the privileges of Parliament. They replied to the king with a message saying they would examine his accusations in due course.[21]

That night there seems to have been another attempt by forces loyal to the king to gain control of the Tower. The MP Simonds D'Ewes records that at about 10 p.m. the Tower Hamlets men who normally guarded the Tower were refused arms and thirty or forty well-armed 'Bishops men' replaced them. Later, Isaac Pennington reported the dismissal of the Tower Hamlets forces to the Commons and some of them gave testimony that they had been replaced by cavaliers. They had been prevented from getting into the Tower and the moat had been kept flooded.[22]

The hue and cry over this new attempt on the Tower came from William Larner's secret press. It produced a broadsheet that was not only remarkable for its political radicalism but also notable because it was a direct intervention in the controversy over control of the Tower. It came in the name of the inhabitants of Stepney, Shoreditch, Whitechapel, Aldgate and St Katherines. The places are significant. They were the areas adjacent to the Tower and yet beyond the walls, and partly the jurisdiction, of the City. These were precisely the areas that the king had identified as most responsible for the riotous mobilisations of the recent days. Larner's petition spoke in the name of the mariners, trained soldiers and 'handy-craftsmen' of the districts. Their complaint was that alehouse keeper Richard Cray, constable of Stepney and newly appointed warden of the Tower, was obstructing the work of the local 'well affected', the Puritan supporters of Parliament.

Cray, in the eyes of the petitioners, was a petty Lunsford who had pushed aside these traditional defenders of the Tower. In their place he had substituted personnel who may have 'some bloody design in hand against the well affected of the Kingdome'. The petition goes on particularly to indict Cray for his hostility to the radical religious congregations, including Baptists in Tower Hamlets. Cray, the petition says, had said that he hoped that all Puritans and Baptists would be 'tortured and torne' and that 'he himselfe would helpe to do it'. Cray's associates, Mathew Owen, Thomas Bungie and a John Walter of Limehouse, had variously said that Mr Pym 'carried two faces under one hood', that they would join with papists against Puritans and, in the case of John Walter, that he had on 27 December gone around beating a drum and crying out that he hoped before long to see the 'damned Puritan-whores and rogues' with 'all their throats cut, or they hang'd, as those are in Ireland'.[23]

Specifically the pamphlet taxed Cray with opposing 'two worthy preachers' from Stepney, Mr Burroughs and Mr Greenhill. These were the radical preachers Jeremiah Burroughs and William Greenhill. Referring in all likelihood to the events in the City following the king's attempt to arrest the five MPs, the petitioners say:

on Thursday night last, when the Citizens of London were up in Armes, for their defence upon rumour of approaching danger, divers of the petitioners having Armed themselves also, for their own defence, . . . the said Cray in a violent manner tooke the Armes from some of the Petitioners, threatened the rest, and said, if he had known, he would have been better provided for them, meaning (as they conceive) either to hurt, or unarme, or oppose them.[24]

Larner's petitioners had some direct and radical remedies to propose: Cray should be charged and subject to 'such condign punishment' as the Commons should see fit, the petitioners should have the liberty to choose their own officers, they should be able to carry out military exercises at their own discretion, and they should be provided with arms and ammunition.[25] The petitioners' view of Cray seems to have been more widely shared. Certainly he was, at about this time, bound over for good behaviour and judged not fit to keep a victualling house after he made 'some scandalous speeches' against the Commons. In July, Parliament had to free recruiters for its army that Cray had jailed when they appeared in Stepney.[26]

It was precisely to stem the rising tide illustrated by Larner's petition that, on Tuesday 4 January, Charles moved to execute what he must have hoped would be a decisive blow against the parliamentary opposition. On hearing that Parliament had ordered the seals he placed on the rooms of the five members to be broken open, Charles 'came out of his chamber immediately and proceeding to the guard room said in a loud voice, My most loyal subjects and soldiers, follow me'.[27] He arrived unannounced in the Commons, having rushed there in a hackney coach. He was attended by between 200 and 500 armed men; 'cavaliers, which were that day feasted at Court, his Guard of yeomanry, Gent. Petitioners, his Serjeants at Armes, and divers others'. They had been armed with 100 muskets, bullets and powder brought from the Tower to Whitehall and had instructions to take the five members by force should that be required. Among them were both Thomas Lunsford and Captain Hide, who stood at the door with his sword raised in its scabbard. Charles approached the Speaker's chair and said, 'by your leave Mr Speaker I must borrow your Chair a little'. Standing before the Speaker's chair he said that when he issued the warrant for the five members on the day before, 'I did expect Obedience, not a Message'. He told the Commons that while he was aware of their privileges, 'in cases of treason no person hath a privilege'. Charles then demanded to know where John Pym was, but he was met with silence from MPs. Charles for 'a long time together cast his eyes round about the House' but 'could not discern any of these five Members there'. At the end of a short speech the king announced, 'What are all the birds flown, well, I will find them'. The soldiers at the door had their swords drawn and their pistols cocked as Charles then demanded that the Speaker point out the five MPs. The Speaker fell on his knees and humbly beseeched 'his Majesty to excuse him' because 'I Have neither Eyes to see, nor Tongue to speak in this Place, but as the House is pleased to direct me'. Defiance worked and the King left the hall 'in great disorder', with many MPs crying out 'Privilege! Privilege!' As Charles walked out of the chamber Simonds D'Ewes thought 'he went out of the howse in a more discontented and angry passion than he came in'. His soldiers cursed 'fearfull Oaths', bemoaning that they had lost both their quarry and a chance of 'cutting . . . the throats of all those men of the House of Commons'.[28]

The five members had been warned of the king's approach and the Commons had instructed them to flee. Four of the five did so but William Strode, being young and unmarried, wanted to stay and defend his innocence with his life's blood. Only as the king's soldiers were coming across New Palace Yard did his friend and fellow MP Sir Walter Earle manage to pull Strode out of the building by his cloak.[29] The five had flown to the safety of the very epicentre of radical Puritanism, the St Stephens Ward of Coleman Street, in all likelihood to the house of Isaac Pennington. The Commons made attempts to have Trained Bands placed on guard at Westminster. But when they did not muster as instructed the Commons as a whole moved to the City and went into session at the Guildhall and the Grocers' Hall until the following Tuesday.[30]

The Common Council was already looking to the defence of the City when, the following day, the king arrived at its meeting in pursuit of his quarry. Captain Slyngsbie had met with the king's party on the way to the City and was an eyewitness to the confrontation that followed. The king told the Council he had only gone to the House of Commons the previous day with armed men to protect himself from the mob, that the six men would have a fair trial, and that he would restore traditional Church government by cracking down on papists and Baptists and separatists. The response of the Common Council was significantly different to that which they had given Lord Newburgh a few days earlier.

> After a little pause a cry was set up amongst the Common Council, 'Parliament! Privileges of Parliament!' and presently another, 'God bless the King.' These two continued both at once a good while. I know not which was

loudest. After some knocking for silence the King commanded one to speak, if they had anything to say. One said, 'It is the vote of this Court that your Majesty hear the advice of your Parliament;' but presently another answered, 'It is not the vote of this Court; it is your own vote.' The King replied, 'Who is it that says I do not take the advice of my Parliament? I do take their advice, and will; but I must distinguish between the Parliament and some traitors in it'. Another bold fellow in the lowest rank stood upon a form, and cried, 'The privileges of Parliament!' Another cried out, 'Observe the man; apprehend him!' The King mildly replied, 'I have and will observe all privileges of Parliament, but no privileges can protect a traitor from a legal trial,' and so departed.[31]

But if the Common Council had divided opinions, the crowd outside were of one mind. As the king passed through the outer hall 'a multitude of the ruder people . . . set up a great cry, The privileges of Parliament!' Charles was hurried off for lunch at the house of Alderman Garrett, the sheriff, and was waited upon by the lord mayor. But the popular mood once again broke into the proceedings. As soon as the king had departed, 'citizens wives fell on the lord mayor, and pulled his chain from his neck, and called him a traitor to the city, and to the liberties of it, and had like to have torn him and the Recorder in pieces'. As he left the City, the king's coach was besieged by an angry crowd of thousands. They cried 'the privileges of Parliament'. Surging forward in the crowd, parliamentary polemicist and tub preacher Henry Walker threw the pamphlet *To Your Tents, O Israel* into the King's coach. Walker was arrested; he escaped, but eventually ended up in the pillory. The City's shops were again closed and citizens stood at their doors with swords and halberds in their hands. As one newsletter said, 'The King had the worst day in London . . . that he ever had'.[32] But worse still was to come for the Crown.

On the night of 6 January the news spread through the City that the king was being advised to raise a force to take the City and apprehend the five members.[33] The speed and scale of the popular response was impressive. 'The Cittie and the suburbs were almost wholly raised, soe as within as little more then an houres space there were about 40000 men in complete armes and neare upon an hundred thousand more that had halberds swords clubs and the like'. Even if the true figures are a mere 20 per cent of those claimed they are still an impressive mobilisation. A general cry of 'Arm, Arm' thundered through the streets. Every door was knocked to turn inhabitants out into the street—some with such force that 'some women being with childe were so affrighted therewith they miscarried'. The gates and portcullis were shut. 'The lowest of the people', complained the Venetian ambassador, 'are provided with arms'. It all turned out to be a false alarm and the streets cleared again within an hour. 'Every hour', wrote Thomas Coke to his family in Derbyshire, 'threatens public insurrection and confusion'.[34]

The mobilisation of the night of 6 January terrified the Court. Captain Hide, at dinner the following night in lodgings in St Martins Lane with Lord Blayny, boasted that 'he himself was one of the first to draw his Sword on the apprentices in White-Hall-Gate', and that if they did come again to guard MPs returning to Westminster,

> it would be the Bloodiest day that was seen in England these many Years, and that for his part he would kill as many of them as he could, and that they were a company of prick-eared and crop-eared Rascals, and that he would believe a Papist before a Puritan.

And with that thought he drew a loaded pistol on his listeners.[35] More seriously, the mayor and Common Council received an angry communication from the king: 'his Majesty has taken notice of a great disorder within the City, where many thousands of men, as well of the Trained Bands as others, were in arms last Thursday night, without any lawful authority, to the great disturbance and affright of the inhabitants'. The king denied knowing 'any cause given nor danger threatened to the City by any person whatsoever'. Charles demanded to know how it had happened. He wanted to know why the Trained Bands had been raised without the lord mayor's permission. And he wanted 'the names of those who at first importuned you to put the trained bands in arms', and the 'punishment of the offenders'. Clearly Charles could see that not only were Parliament refusing to hand over the five members, and not only was the City harbouring them, but, in addition, control over the military forces in the capital was falling into the hands of the rebellion.

On 8 January the Committee of the House at the Grocers' Hall decisively put itself at the head of a popular movement to return the five members and the Commons to Westminster the following Tuesday, 11 January. This time it would not simply be crowds coming to Westminster under their own direction or partly under the leadership of the more radical City MPs. Now there would be a full-blown mobilisation to resist the king. A *posse comitatus* was ordered giving the sheriff the power to conscript a military force in addition to the mobilisation of the Trained

Bands. Philip Skippon, a highly reliable officer with strong parliamentarian sympathies, was given the task. John Hampden said thousands would come up from Buckinghamshire with a petition. The committee received a petition from 1,000 mariners and seamen offering to protect MPs on their return to Westminster. The committee accepted the offer and ordered that

> they should provide such Artillery as was necessary on *Tuesday* Morning, and to rendezvous so as to go through Bridge with the Tide; and that all great Guns and Musquets in their Vessels should be cleared before-hand, to the end there might be no shooting that Day, except in case of great Necessity.[36]

A great number of apprentices then came before the committee and offered to mobilise 10,000 of their number armed with 'warlike weapons'. But the MPs, while 'sensible of their former readiness to guard the Parliament', asked them to remain at home 'whilst ther Masters did guard us at the Parliament'. The apprentices were 'wounded' by this rebuff but reluctantly agreed. Clearly the parliamentary leaders were themselves more organised now and, equally clearly, they were still unsure of their ability to direct the crowd.[37] Viewing these preparations the Venetian ambassador recorded,

> in order to render more evident the power of parliament the commissioners are devoting the most skilful efforts so that when the session is reopened on Tuesday there may be a numerous gathering of country people as well as of citizens to assist and acclaim the defence of parliament. To this end they sent letters to the neighbouring counties relating what had happened and asking them to send a certain number of troops on that day. They made known their intentions also to the heads of the guilds and to all others, ostensibly for the sake of upholding the privileges of parliament. Incited by this the simple minded folk vied with one another in offering their services. The commissioners being thus assured of having at their disposal a body of 20,000 persons, comprising countrymen, citizens and sailors, announced that they would proceed with that following to the Houses of Parliament.[38]

Just two days later, at 3 p.m. on 10 January, Charles left Whitehall for Hampton Court. He was only to return to his palace when he was put on trial for his life. The prospect of the show of force by Parliament the following day persuaded Charles to flee London. As the Venetian ambassador observed, 'The king, hearing of these preparations, and possibly fearing some enormity such as fanatical tongues are discussing freely at the moment, decided to withdraw to Hampton Court'.[39]

The following day the MPs, including the five members, returned to Westminster amidst a huge show of force, but this was a much more organised and disciplined affair than had been the case in the December Days. Eight companies of the Trained Bands with eight cannon and a mounted guard were sent to watch over MPs and peers 'from the Grocers-Hall . . . to Westminster'. On the Thames, 'Sea-Captaines, Masters of ships, Mariners, with small Barges, and long Boates, sufficiently man'd and Armed' with cannon and 'with Musquets and halfe-pikes, to the number of 2,000 persons, have engaged to Guard the Parliament by water'. The Southwark Trained Bands were watching the south bank of the Thames. Bargemen ferried MPs to Westminster for their own safety. Some 4,000 horsemen attended the MPs at Westminster as they returned. The apprentices did not wholly obey the command to stay in their homes. Indeed they

> gathered in great numbers . . . and all carried upon banners, pikes and sticks a printed paper protesting that at any price they would preserve inviolable the laws of the realm, the liberties of the country and the observance of the Protestant religion. They accompanied the members to the Houses at Westminster, acclaiming their entry by firing guns and muskets and the greatest applause for those of the six accused by the king in particular.

Though the 'City and the people in the adjacent parts are so much moved in this business' because they fear 'some sudden execution may be done upon the Parliament', this was now a task being taken in hand much more by parliamentary leaders. It was wholly successful.[40]

On the same day the king left Hampton Court for Windsor Castle, 'perhaps not considering himself sufficiently safe at Hampton Court, which is an open place'.[41] Sir John Hotham and his son already had orders not to surrender Hull without parliamentary permission. Similar orders were issued to the Portsmouth garrison. Colonel Lunsford and Lord Digby tried, but failed, to seize the arsenal at Kingston-on-Thames for the king. The Commons had Lunsford arrested and brought to London 'with his hands bound behind him'.[42] Civil war was now inevitable.

The sinews of resistance

The great political crisis that precipitated civil war, lasting from the December tumults at Westminster Yard to the king's departure from London, bore first witness to characteristics that recur time and again in the history of the Levellers and the English Revolution. The first of these is the centrality of London and its suburbs to popular protest in the revolutionary era. By far the largest urban area in the country, both the City itself and its suburbs uniquely concentrated radical sentiment and popular political organisation. The five members fled to Coleman Street near the Guildhall because it was a home and centre to radical religion and politics. But the suburbs, rapidly expanding in the years before the Civil War, were also a home to radicalism. The king may have been conniving at the goodwill of the Common Council when he forgave the City any role in the tumults and blamed them all on the suburbs, but Tower Hamlets and Southwark were nonetheless renowned for their militancy, as Larner's petitions underlined.

Regardless of which part of London it came from, it was the sight of mass, popular mobilisation that horrified many observers, especially those loyal to the bishops and the king. The protests had brought out 'the *basest* and refuse of all men, watermen, porters, and the *worst* of all the apprentices, with threats and menaces, to thunder forth *death* and destruction' on the bishops. Parliamentary leaders like John Venn, Isaac Pennington 'and others of the same Sect' were despised in these quarters for daring 'to gather together the *scum* of all the prophanest rout, the *vilest* of all men, and the *outcast* of the People'.[43] The Venetian ambassador thought the crowds at Westminster on the first of the December Days were apprentices, shop boys and their masters who were 'Puritans for the most part'.[44] The apprentices were also perfectly aware of the social profile of their opponents, whom they described thus: 'Delinquents and roaring Cavaliers . . . decayed and indebted persons, are ranked together, with a multitude of drunken idle persons, and giddy brain'd Gentlemen, and lastly, the ambitious Clergie'.[45]

The explosion of popular print was also a component in the crisis of the December Days. Parliament's decision, just before the crisis erupted, to have the Grand Remonstrance printed and circulated to the public was taken, at the time, as a watershed moment. But it was not just pro-Parliament words that were in circulation. The press was by now so influential that the king was careful to ensure that his words reached the street in print as fast as those of his opponents. When parliamentary secretary John Rushworth took down the king's speech to the Commons about the five members in shorthand he was summoned that evening to an interview with the king. Charles made him copy it out in longhand there and then. The king corrected it and it was in print and on the street the following morning.[46]

Nonetheless, nearly all control over what was permissible in print was lost. The marks of illegal printing and secret presses are also clearly to be seen in these early mobilisations. Henry Walker's striking intervention is one example of the impact of the growth in radical pamphleteering. Larner's petitions were calling for popular action as well as expressing radical views. Lilburne was already known as a popular leader partly because of his own previous exploits, described in the next chapter. News of these deeds had been made widely available by secret presses, one of which was William Larner's. The appeals of the apprentices found a large audience never before addressed in this way.

Even before the December Days the growth of radical, sometimes separatist, religion was widely remarked on as one important element in the emerging political crisis. Then and later, gathered churches were blamed for the outcry against the bishops.[47] The novelty of women 'tub preachers' was noted and denounced, for, among other things, sermonising to the effect that 'the Devill was the father of the Pope, The Pope the father of those that did weare Surplices, whereof consequently the Devill was the Father of all those that did not love Puritans'. Many of these women were Londoners and lower-class, like Mary Bilbrowe from St Giles in the Fields who reportedly preached from a pulpit made of brick by her husband, 'a good honest Bricklayer'.[48]

Between 1640 and 1642 separatist communities could be found led by Henry Jessey in the Tower Liberty; by future Leveller Thomas Lambe in Whitechapel; by John Spilsbury in Ratcliffe, Stepney; by Praise-God Barebone in Fleet Street; and by John Dart in his house in Southwark. There were two more in St Saviour's, Southwark, and Goat Alley off Whitecross Street.[49] When Spilsbury's congregation was arrested in September 1641, John Lilburne, his wife Elizabeth Lilburne and his sister, also Elizabeth, who lived in Wapping, were among those brought before the authorities.[50] William Larner was also a religious radical printing the work of other religious radicals—Lilburne himself, the future Leveller and separatist Katherine Chidley and Lilburne's associate and a central figure in

London's radical religious landscape, William Kiffin. Larner's broadsheet also defended independent church preachers Jeremiah Burroughs and William Greenhill. It was because of the mobilisation of the gathered churches, thought some, that 'the Bishops . . . might passe with more honour, and lesse contempt at Constantinople among the Turkes, or in Jerusalem among the Jewes, than in the Citie of London among this brood of Anabaptists'.[51] Again Venn and Pennington were blamed for 'the multi-tude of zealous Sectaries, the rabble of ignorant people', who 'cry Justice, Justice, and, No Bishops, No Bishops' outside Westminster.[52]

Armed force became an issue in this period as the Parliament and City on one side, and the king on the other, battled to take control of the key elements of military power: the Tower and the Trained Bands. One reason why the king could not rely on the Trained Bands was, as the Venetian ambassador saw it, because 'these troops are for the most part the masters of these very apprentices' and so 'the latter do not fear punishment from them'.[53] This element assumed much greater significance as the Civil War erupted, of course. In the end, many years later, the battle for political influence in the army would be decisive both for the fate of the king and for the Levellers.

Crucially emerging in this period is a level of political organisation among the crowd. The December Days should not be seen as simply a spontaneous reaction to a political crisis. All such events require some kind of organisation even if they are not wholly choreographed. And often the kind of political organisation that emerges is partly from the political elite and partly from the popular mass, sometimes working in concert, some-times contradicting each other. Such was the case in the December Days and the crisis around the five members. No one single political faction caused these protests, and while there was a degree of spontaneity about them there was also an important degree of political organisation both from the political leaders in Parliament and the City and from emerging popular leaders much lower down the social scale. John Venn, for instance, 'sent tickets by Porters and Emissaries to raise these Mirmidons' from the City, 'where they were bid to come like men, that is with swords' to 'cry for Reformation at the Parliament doores'. But, as we have seen, neither Venn nor the whole Parliament, in the case of the demonstration that returned the five members to Parliament, were able to completely control the crowd once it was summoned.

There was an important degree of continuity among the activists involved in successive riots, demonstrations and petitions. Men like John

Lilburne, Nehemiah Wallington and Henry Boyse were often at the head of the crowds, and at a more senior level Isaac Penington and John Venn are names that constantly recur. Moreover, these figures remained central in the next set of confrontations between king and Parliament. Historians Keith Lindley and Brian Manning both agree that the presence of Lilburne, Boyse and others points to a continuity of leadership of the London crowd in the years 1641 and 1642,[54] while Robert Brenner argues,

> What especially needs emphasizing is the fact of broader political organisa-tion—the existence of some sort of 'party'—which is manifest in this series of actions, and particularly in the ability of London oppositionists to respond, sometimes within hours of an event, with significant numbers of signatures on a petition or with a mass demonstrations.[55]

For the future Levellers like John Lilburne, William Larner and Richard Overton, these were formative experiences in organised politics rather than mere atomistic participation in spontaneously occurring events.

The success of these popular mobilisations encouraged the militants. Organisation begat more organisation. At the end of January, two more incendiary petitions came out bearing Larner's name. The first was addressed to the Lords in the name of the youngmen, apprentices and seamen of London. It demanded effective action to suppress not only the rebellion in Ireland and but also 'domestique plots and conspiracies of Papists'. In more threatening tone it continued, 'if present remedie be not afforded from the hands of this honourable Parliament . . . multitudes will be ready to take hold upon that remedy which is next at hand: *Oppression* (as *Solomon* saith) *making wise men mad*'. In a postscript printed at the foot of the page we can glimpse the popular organisation that lay behind the presentation of these petitions. It tells us that it was delivered to the Lords by a delegation of three freemen, five apprentices and five seamen who were 'chosen by the rest for that purpose'.[56] The second petition was addressed to the Commons but not, significantly, to the Lords. This peti-tion is remarkable as a plea 'from many thousand poor people . . . who are of the meanest rank and quality being touched by penury'. It is directed against the 'Bishops and the Popish Lords', whom it accuses of obstructing the relief of Ireland, disturbing the peace of the kingdom, and obstructing the passage of legislation proposed by the Commons. In this it echoed much widespread argument among supporters of Parliament during this period. But it then goes on to propose that the Lords who are in agreement with the Commons' majority merge with the lower house to form a single-chamber legislature 'to sit and Vote as one intire body'. This effective abolition of the Lords was a proposal well in advance of any contemporary thinking on the parliamentary side. Moreover, the petitioners threaten that, if the Commons does not act, 'your Petitioners shall not rest in quietness, but shall be inforced to lay hold on the next remedy which is at hand, to remove the disturbers of our peace, want, and necessity, breaking the bounds of modesty'. And in a declaration of their intention to take matters into their own hands the printed instruction at the foot of this petition says, 'For the use of the Petitioners who are to meet this present day in Moor Fields, and from thence to go to the house of Parliament with it in their hands'.[57]

Larner's petition had such an impact on the radicals that even after the passage of six years it was being cited by John Wildman when the Leveller movement was at its height. Indeed, in his *Truths Triumph* Wildman quoted precisely those passages that called for the abolition of the Lords, and cited the fate of Cray, in defence of his right to petition the Commons.[58] But in 1642 Wildman was unknown. One figure above all others embodied the growing confidence and organisation among the popular element of the London crowd: John Lilburne. He had been a cornerstone of every radical development from long before the December Days. It is to his early career that we must now turn.

CHAPTER 2

The First Leveller, John Lilburne

Long before the Levellers were called Levellers there was John Lilburne. Lilburne was already famous before the English Revolution began. What made him famous at first was persecution and his resistance to persecution. John Lilburne was, as he said himself, 'the second Son of a Gentleman in the North parts of England'. His family came from Thickley Punchardon in County Durham, where his father held land. His mother and father had both been courtiers and he was probably born in London. He was brought up in the North East but came back to the capital at the age of fourteen as an apprentice to cloth merchant Thomas Hewson. Hewson's premises were in the heart of the walled City of London at Londonstone in what is now Cannon Street. Lilburne's first political experiences, and among of his first political audiences, were the London apprentices. His political engagement would soon alienate him from his family who were, Lilburne said, afraid of the great power of his adversaries.[1]

The London apprentices

The London economy was dominated by the great trading companies, often described as 'livery companies', although not all of them had a privileged section of the membership who wore a special uniform at feast days and celebrations. These seventy or so corporations were granted a charter to regulate and control the production and sale of goods and services. The lord mayor of London was chosen from among the 'Twelve Great

Companies' of the City, the largest and most prestigious of the corporations. The livery men of the companies sat together in the Common Hall and chose the candidates for mayor, one of London's two sheriffs and two of the City's four MPs. To become a member of a company required serving a seven-year apprenticeship under an existing master, although it was also possible to buy in to membership in some cases. In most cases masters could only take on one apprentice at a time, institutionalising the small household economy. At the end of the apprenticeship period some companies required the apprentice to produce their 'masterpiece' in order to gain admittance. Once one was a member, certain civic privileges and rights within the company could be claimed, as well as the right to trade. In many corporations the 'commonalty'—the ordinary members—had some say over the running of the company and some rights to elect its officers. But more often than not the leading figures, the master and his Court of Assistants, were a largely self-perpetuating oligarchy. The rights and privileges of company self-government were, however, fiercely guarded against royal, or any other, interference.[2]

The London apprentices were a key social force in the City and one of the incubators of the Revolution, especially in its early stages. They existed in vast numbers. Exactly how great a proportion of the adult male population were apprentices is a matter of considerable debate among historians. But, in general, the lowest estimates are above 10 per cent and the highest credible figures are above 20 per cent.[3] It is likely true that apprenticeship in London 'made the capital into the largest educational site that existed in England before compulsory basic schooling was introduced in the late nineteenth century. The share of the population who were trained in the city exceeded the proportion going to university before the 1980s'.[4]

The apprentices were young, on average eighteen or nineteen years of age when they began their seven-year indenture. Many came from outside the City, as Lilburne had done. Teenage boys in Yorkshire were as likely to be apprenticed to a London master as were their fellows in the Home Counties. The cost of an apprenticeship, to be paid to the master, varied according to the prestige of the trade. The great trading companies would demand a small fortune, coopers or cutlers rather less.[5] Drapers such as Hewson were about the middle of this range. But in general the amounts were considerable, perhaps the same as a proportion of income as modern student fees—but without the capacity to loan the fee in advance. The payment of an up-front premium meant, in turn, that few of the poor or labouring classes had the backing or capital to become apprentices.

Apprentices came from the middling sort—already established merchant families, lawyers or other professions, yeomen farmers, and lesser gentry, often second sons who would not inherit.[6] Indeed, one apprentices' petition described themselves as having 'bloods mingled with the nobility, although it were our fortune to be younger brothers'.[7]

In return for the fee, apprentices received bed and board in the master's household and, of course, instruction in the trade. Masters varied in diligence. Some trained their apprentices well and treated them as members of the family. Some treated them as servants, gave poor instruction and exploited their labour. But apprentices too were a mixed bunch. Some applied themselves; others spent money sent by their parents on drinking, gambling and mistresses.

Apprentices faced a repressive environment with long working days. Even the leisure time of the apprentice was policed by the master. Physical punishment was not unusual. But there was some greater flexibility than the formal arrangement of the seven-year contract might imply. Apprentices sometimes changed masters and trades. Contracts were frequently terminated after a few years, often by agreement but sometimes not. These disputes were settled by the City's chamberlain. Apprentices who left their masters would not then qualify or become freemen of the City, foregoing civic rights and the right to trade within City walls. But they were able to begin earning money years earlier than those who stayed the full course. And the fast-growing suburbs of Tower Hamlets and Southwark provided trading opportunities beyond the City.

In general apprentices were boisterous, often meeting on the open spaces of the City on holidays and sometimes rioting or laying siege to bawdy houses. In the early stages of the Revolution a significant section of apprentices could be mobilised for the parliamentary cause. It was claimed that 8,000 London apprentices joined the parliamentary army in the summer of 1642.[8] But they were not politically homogeneous and, later, apprentices could be found among 'peace party' protests of 1642–43, as well as among those protests that urged a more decisive war against the king. In 1647–48 they provided a decisive element of the Presbyterian push for a Personal Treaty with the king. Later still they could be found petitioning both in favour of, and against, the Levellers. Much depended on the wider correlation of political forces. In this sense the apprentices were not independent of wider social layers.[9]

There was much about the household economy of the apprentice–master relationship which tended to conservatism. But there were also elements of the apprentices' experience in the mid-seventeenth century that could be appealed to by radicals. Puritanism was one factor, providing youthful and social discontent with an image of a New Jerusalem, often promoted among them by preachers and more prominent London citizens. Norah Carlin has suggested that the notions of fraternity and brotherhood commonly expressed in the corporations created some fertile ground for Leveller ideas. Certainly when the democratic impulses of the Revolution fused with challenges to the oligarchic hierarchy of the corporations in the later 1640s the Levellers took up the cause of the 'commonalty'. The political affiliations of the apprentices were also influenced by local leadership. A number of prominent Levellers were members of the London corporations and had, therefore, served as apprentices: William Walwyn was a member of the Merchant Adventurers, Thomas Prince of the Tallow Chandlers, the Chidley family were Habedashers, and both Maximillian Petty and Edward Sexby were of the Grocers. But it was John Lilburne who became one of the first figureheads among the 'apron youths'.[10]

Lilburne's experience as an apprentice was in some ways typical. He was brought to London by his father and settled in Hewson's household in 1629. He quickly became a trusted figure who had substantial responsibilities in running the Hewson warehouse. He served Hewson for six years and was given his liberty when it looked as if his master might quit the trade. Lilburne never 'gave nor took a box on the eare'. Hewson had 'sometimes offered me some abuse' for which Lilburne 'carryed him before the Chamberlain of London'. As in other cases, this dispute was settled amicably and Lilburne 'ever after lived in peace' with Thomas Hewson. Indeed Hewson supported his former apprentice during his first imprisonment and punishment.[11]

But in other ways Lilburne's experience was, while by no means unique, less typical. Lilburne had come from a Puritan family background and when he came to London he entered the Hewson's Puritan household. Not all masters were Puritans and not all apprentices were godly. But Lilburne was. He, at least on his own account, 'never misspent' his free time. He used it 'continually reading . . . books that I bought with my own money'. These included 'the Bible, the Book of Martyrs, Luthers, Calvins . . .' and history books. Moreover, he met some key Puritan radicals at Hewson's house. He was conversant with fellow clothier Edmund Rosier 'at my Master's house from the beginning of my coming to him'. And not long after he met with William Kiffin, who, like Rosier, was a central figure in the development of separatist churches in London.

Hewson was also a friend of Henry Jessy, another key figure in the emerging separatist opposition to royal church policy. Tantalisingly, Hewson was also a friend of the Winthrop family into which future Leveller Thomas Rainsborough's sisters, Judith and Martha, were both to marry. It was also from around this time that Lilburne knew Katherine and Samuel Chidley, also to become Levellers. But it was through Edmund Rosier that in 1636 Lilburne had himself introduced to John Bastwick, already a prisoner in the Gatehouse jail.[12]

The Puritan underground

The national church, the Church of England, was an institution of considerable social and economic weight in the seventeenth century. The Church was a huge landowner, and payment of tithes compulsory. Church attendance was a legal requirement and absenteeism was punishable by fines and, ultimately, imprisonment. Nor could worshipers attend any other church except the one in their parish. The content and form of church services were determined by government policy, transmitted to the local parish by the hierarchy of archbishops and bishops. The Church as well as the state was the licenser and censor of printed material, and the enforcer of conformity. The country was, of course, a theocracy: the monarch was the head of the Church. In short, the Church performed some of the social functions which in modern society are performed by a combination of property owners, the education system, the civil service, the police and the media. Naturally, any challenge to religious authority was also a challenge to wider social hierarchy. If there were just four words that could encapsulate the English Revolution they would be those uttered by King Charles's father, James VI: 'No bishop, no king'.

The Church of England broke from Rome in the Reformation of the mid-sixteenth century. But how far reformation should go had been debated ever since. Should many of the outward forms of religious submission—the icons and stained glass, the reignments and prelates—of Catholicism be retained? Or should religious worship be a plainer, more individual relationship between worshipper and God, unmediated by religious hierarchy? Charles, his Catholic queen, and his archbishop, William Laud, thought reformation had gone too far and were, in the 1630s, trying to turn back the clock. Puritans, whether they still thought there should be a national church structure or whether they thought that churches should be free of national direction, or even simply gathered assemblies of believers, were increasingly persecuted.

The tradition of Puritan martyrdom is much longer and deeper than the Levellers' political usage. John Lilburne recalled during his first imprisonment that he, like many Puritans of his generation, had read John Foxe's *Book of Martyrs*.[13] This book had long since become a significant part of national consciousness. Since its original publication in 1563 it had run to many editions and been abridged, and its contents had been reproduced in broadsheets and ballads. Its anti-papist message was gathering a new urgency during Laud's rule. But Foxe's was not the only literature of this kind. In 1639 John Taylor produced his own *Booke of Martyrs*.[14] The Lollards, Luther, Calvin, William Tyndale, Thomas Cromwell and bishops Latimer and Ridley are all celebrated. The glory of Elizabethan Protestantism is trumpeted, the virtues of James I enumerated and the 'damn'd powder plot' cursed. And that is, significantly perhaps, where Taylor's long litany of praise and the poem end.[15] Charles I's rule is not mentioned. This is a telling, if necessary, omission since the public to which this book was likely to appeal were well aware that Puritan martyrs were still being created in the 1630s.

John Lilburne's entrance on the political stage was as an understudy to the Puritan martyrs Henry Burton, John Bastwick and William Prynne. As a young apprentice in London in the 1630s he absorbed the message of opposition to the Laudian church and its bishops, accused of putting themselves beyond the reach of the law, of sheltering behind the royal prerogative and riding roughshod over the liberties of the subject. In 1624 and again in 1637 control over printing was tightened and invested in the hands of the two archbishops, the bishop of London, and the vice chancellors of Oxford and Cambridge. No foreign book could be imported without approval. Similarly so with any reprinted book.[16] But secret Puritan presses and the importation of tracts from Holland continued to furnish the reading appetite of the godly.

In the mid-1630s Lilburne was already moving in these circles. He was an associate of William Kiffin, soon to be a leader of the gathered churches of London. Another close associate, the preacher Edmund Rosier, introduced Lilburne to John Bastwick in 1636. They met in the Gatehouse Prison where Bastwick was being kept for printing anti-episcopal tracts in 1633–4. Lilburne made many subsequent visits to Bastwick. And this growing friendship led to another with William Prynne. From the later 1620s to the early 1630s Prynne had repeatedly attacked the bishops in print. In his *Histrio-Mastix* of 1633 he attacked stage plays and actors. This was taken as an attack on the Court. Prynne was hauled before the royal prerogative court of Star Chamber in 1634. He was deprived of his academic degrees and of his living as a lawyer in Lincoln's Inn, and given a considerable fine. More seriously, he was deprived of his ears while in the pillory and then his freedom for life by imprisonment in the Tower. Lilburne was a frequent visitor to Prynne. As he wrote later, 'I accounted it my duty to do William Prynne and Dr Bastwick all the free offices of love and service that lay in my power, during all the time that I conceived they stood either for God, Goodnesse or Justice'.[17]

Prynne continued his attacks on the bishops from his imprisonment. In March 1637 he was back before the Star Chamber, this time with Burton and Bastwick for company. On 14 June they were all convicted of seditious writing, fined £5,000 each, and sentenced to life imprisonment at, the authorities hoped, the safe distances of Lancaster for Prynne, Launceston for Bastwick and Carnarvon for Burton. All three were to lose their ears. In the case of Prynne this meant the removal of the stumps that remained after his first mutilation. He also had the letters SL, for 'seditious libeller', branded on his cheek. While they were in the pillory it was obvious, at least to the perspicacious Venetian ambassador, that public sympathy was with the victims:

> The king, seeing this poison spreading, tries to keep it far from his heart and to pull out its roots, but the more he tries to extirpate them the stronger they become. They do not care about their goods or esteem their lives when efforts are made to moderate their doctrines, or rather their ignorance. When the sentence in question was being executed, one could see even women and children collecting the blood of the victims, exalting their punishment and ignominy with tears and cries to the most exalted martyrdom. In short this pest may be the one which will ultimately disturb the repose of this kingdom.[18]

The martyr John Lilburne

John Lilburne was around twenty years old at the time of the persecution of Burton, Bastwick and Prynne. He was about to undergo a formative experience.[19] And the pattern of this experience—defiance of authority; imprisonment and torture; legal challenge backed by popular protest, vindication and popular acclaim—was to be repeated until his death some twenty years later. Lilburne was so close to the martyrs, and known by the authorities to be so, that he found it prudent to bolt to Holland in the summer of 1637. Lilburne seems to have had it in mind to have Bastwick's English-language tirade against episcopacy, the *Letany*, printed in Holland for distribution in England. His associates in this scheme were Edmund Chillenden, a button seller from Cannon Street, and John Chilliburne, a servant to another Puritan martyr, John Wharton. Chillenden was meant to distribute the pamphlets but was arrested, and the contraband was seized. To save himself, Chillenden gave up Lilburne's name.

Chilliburne was even less trustworthy than Chillenden. When Lilburne returned to London in December 1637 he was wary enough to go about armed. But by Chilliburne's treachery he was seized by agents of Archbishop Laud on Tuesday 11 December.[20] Lilburne was pushed into a shop and held over a sugar chest, and his sword taken from him. His captors were over-joyed at having taken 'one of the most notoriousest dispersers of scandalous bookes that was in the kingdom'. Lilburne's account of his capture, published in 1641, contained a foreword by William Kiffin. It was printed by future Leveller printer William Larner, whom Lilburne had probably met through Kiffin in the 1630s.[21]

Lilburne found himself back in the familiar surroundings of the Gatehouse prison, not this time as a visitor to Bastwick but as a prisoner in his own right. Lilburne also found himself before the Star Chamber, a court without a jury in which the examination of the defendant was the primary method of obtaining a conviction. Lilburne refused cooperation with the court in every particular: he objected that he had not been subpoenaed and that he could not afford the clerk of the court's fee, and finally he refused to take the oath until he had had time to consider its 'lawfulness'.[22] It was his from refusal, as a 'free-born Englishman', to bow to the court that his popu-lar nickname, Freeborn John, first derived.[23] He was then told that he would be imprisoned until he conformed to court procedure, be fined £500 and suffer physical punishment.

Lilburne did not know what this punishment would be until, on 18 April 1638, he was told by the prison porter that he was to be tied to the back of a cart and whipped from the Fleet Bridge to Westminster, where he would then be put in the pillory. Lilburne claimed that the man who was to inflict this punishment told him that he had 'whipped many a Rogue, but now I shall whip an honest man'. And so he did.[24] On an unusually hot day Lilburne was lashed by a corded and knotted three-thonged whip every three or four paces. One of Lilburne's supporters, Mary Dorman, saw the whipping and thought Lilburne's shoulders 'swelled almost as big as a penny loaf'. Lilburne's surgeon thought that 'the wheales on his back . . . were bigger than Tobacco-pipes'. After 500 blows Lilburne was dragged into New Palace Yard and put in the stocks. He had been supported by the crowd along the route and had periodically called out to them. But now, when the crowd was greatest, he began a full-blown speech from the pillory. Invoking the memory of Bastwick, Burton and Prynne, Lilburne denounced the Star Chamber, the Court of High Commission, Archbishop Laud and the 'prelates' and their abuse of authority.[25] He refused to stop speaking and then his mouth was gagged so roughly by the warden of the Fleet 'as if he would have torne his jaws in peeces, in so much as the blood came out of his mouth'. Lilburne then reached into his pockets and threw Bastwick's pamphlets into the crowd.[26] When this was done he continued to stamp his feet until the two hours allotted for his time in the pillory had passed. He was ordered back to the Fleet and as he went through the streets, Lilburne recorded, 'a greate store of people stood all along to behold me, and many of them blessed God for enabling me to undergoe my sufferings with such cheerfulnes and courage'.[27] We can gain some insight into the political impact of Lilburne's punishment from Rushworth's reaction:

> Whipping was painful and shameful, Flagellation for Slaves. In the Eleventh of Elizabeth, one Cartwright brought a Slave from Russia, and would scourge him, for which he was questioned; and it was resolved, That England was too pure an Air for Slaves to breath in. And indeed it was often resolved, even in Star-Chamber, That no Gentleman was to be whipt for any offence whatsoever; and his whipping was too severe.[28]

Even after the whipping Lilburne was again cross-questioned by the Star Chamber about his conduct, where he obtained the pamphlets, and which pamphlets they were. Outraged that he had continued to distribute the very pamphlets he was being punished for importing, Lilburne's jailer was told to use exemplary methods of imprisonment.[29]

Lilburne was denied food, linen and medical treatment. He was kept in heavy chains in solitary confinement. Visitors were either denied access or beaten for their pains. His jailers sent assassins to murder him and he had to fight them off in a struggle that lasted two hours and almost cost him his hand. A beggar at the gate and fellow prisoners had to smuggle food to him through holes in the wall and by taking up the floorboards. But, remarkably, Lilburne not only claims to have survived but also managed to continue to smuggle out pamphlets describing his trial and imprisonment.[30] The *Christian Man's Triall* came out before his whipping. But even after this he produced *A Worke of the Beast* and *Come Out of Her My People*, 'which I writ', Lilburne claimed, 'when my hands were fettered together with Irons'. These and others were sent to Holland to be printed.[31] But the pamphlet that had most immediate political effect was *A Cry for Justice*.

The apprentices' riot

In the Whitsun holidays in June 1639 Lilburne's *Cry for Justice* and another letter addressed to apprentices were 'thrown abroad in Moor Fields'. They had been smuggled out and distributed by Katherine Hadley, who had visited and cared for Lilburne during his imprisonment. Hadley herself was then thrown into jail for this act. The pamphlet had contributed, or so the authorities believed, to one of the first riots against Archbishop Laud in the opening phase of the Revolution. The letter was a direct appeal to the apprentices, particularly those of Lilburne's own trade, the clothworkers: 'To all the brave, courageous, and valiant Apprentices of the honourable City of London, but especially those that appertain to the worshipful Company of Cloth workers (of which company, if I live I hope to be a Free man).'[32] The paper incited the apprentices to go 'by hundreds of thousands' and 'in a faire and peaceable way' to demand Lilburne's freedom from the mayor of London. But it's most bitter invective was reserved for Archbishop Laud, whom Lilburne describes variously as 'the devil', 'that devouring Lyon', the 'guilty Traytor', the prelate of Canterbury. Hardly surprisingly, Laud wrote in his diary that these two publications 'both subscribed by John Lilburn a Prisoner in the Fleet' were 'very Seditious papers' and designed to 'excite the Apprentices'.[33]

The very fact that Lilburne told the apprentices to avoid 'tumult' and 'uproar' means that he was in little doubt that this might be one outcome of his appeal. The letter was certainly phrased in Lilburne's characteristically incendiary prose. It appealed to the apprentices to act before the harsh conditions of imprisonment took away his life. Addressing 'you stout and valiant Prentizes', Lilburne wrote, 'I cry out murther, murther, murther'. He called on them to act for the glory of God and 'in courage and boldness to stand for the liberties and privileges which are granted to us by Parliament laws of this land, against the wicked Prelates'. This was a powerful combination of the two elements which had shaped Lilburne's life up to this point: his experience as an apprentice and his opposition to Laudian Church government. The pamphlets hit their mark and the apprentices responded with public protests to such a degree that, as Lilburne later observed, they almost saved the hangman a job as far as Laud was concerned.[34]

Lilburne remained in jail, but less than twelve months later, on 5 May 1640, the Privy Council learned that there were plans to attack and burn Archbishop Laud's Lambeth Palace if the king attempted to dissolve Parliament. Then broadsides started to appear calling on apprentices to attack Lambeth Palace. The words 'bishops devils', exactly the terms Lilburne had used of Laud, were scrawled on the Royal Exchange on 8 May. The next day a placard appeared calling on 'all gentlemen prentices that desire to kill the bishops, who would fain kill us, our wives, and children' to assemble at St George's Fields on the following Monday. The crowds did indeed assemble on Monday 11 May, armed and summoned by the beat of drums. But the authorities had been able deploy the Trained Bands. Laud had fled the palace by river and taken sanctuary in Whitehall. The crowds waited out the Trained Bands and attacked after they stood down for the night. Around midnight the apprentices attacked for two hours but failed to gain entrance to the palace and so vented their anger on the gardens and orchards. On Thursday of the same week crowds attacked the White Lion Prison in Southwark in an attempt to free those arrested for the attack on the palace. They succeeded in freeing the prisoners and also attacked three other Southwark jails. As the Venetian ambassador reported, 'At this moment other bands of the same proceeded to the prisons, knocked down the gates, slew the keepers and released all the prisoners, especially those in custody for the riot of Monday'. They demanded one of the City aldermen who had been imprisoned by Charles be freed and he quietened the crowd on the day he walked free. The authorities did, however, manage to spirit one of the leaders of the revolt, John Archer, away to the Tower. He was tortured and later executed.[35]

This attack on the prisons came after the king had instructed the lord mayor that 'double watches are to be kept within the city and liberties' in response to 'the late tumultuous assembly in and about Lambeth'. Every householder was 'to be answerable for the quiet behaviour of all his apprentices and servants' and to 'prevent any concourse of people to pass in or out of the city'. The Justices in Westminster were similarly ordered to 'prevent disorders and tumultuous assemblies'. The earl of Dorset and the earl of

Holland, the lords lieutenant of Middlesex, were ordered to 'double watches kept in and about St Giles and Tuttle [Tothill] fields, and all other passages and places near London and Westminster to prevent tumultuous assemblies'. They were also 'to give order that there be boats provided to be in readiness to transport horse and men at Lambeth ferry and elsewhere upon any occasion for the better suppressing of such disorders and tumults as may happen'. This too was unpopular and ineffective. The Trained Bands had been unwilling to act decisively against the rioters. One apprentice in Whitefriars said he would 'turn rebel with the rest of my fellow apprentices' if he was forced to act as watch after the May riots.[36]

More orders demanding action were issued by Charles 'for punishing and repressing the late traitorous and rebellious assemblies in Lambeth and Southwark'. These were to be 'proclaimed in the market-places and chief streets of the city, and . . . in the suburbs and adjacent places'. Indeed the king now feared for the lives of his family. On 15 May he announced that 'the traitorous insolences lately practised by some base people near Southwark give us occasion to take care of the persons of the Prince and their Majesties' other children at Richmond'. A 200-strong force of the Trained Bands was sent to guard them. The Venetian ambassador reported, 'The archbishop and other ministers, who are the objects of the popular hatred, have abandoned their own dwellings and retreated to the palace, while no little confusion reigns everywhere'.[37]

The moment was approaching where Charles would no longer be safe in his own capital. So too was the moment of Laud's execution. Lilburne's early acts of religious dissent and his agitation among the apprentices had played their part in creating that situation.

Lilburne at liberty

The Long Parliament sat for the first time on 3 November 1640. Among the MPs elected to it was a man who described his background as being 'by birth a gentleman, living neither in considerable height, nor yet in obscurity'.[38] His maiden speech came on 9 November and it was a demand that John Lilburne be set free. As he spoke he appeared to the royalist Sir Philip Warwick 'very ordinarily apparelled' in a 'plain cloth suit, which seemed to have been made by an ill country-tailor'. His linen shirt was also plain and 'not very clean', with 'a speck or two of blood' on the collar. His hat was without a hat band. His countenance was 'swoln and reddish, his voice

sharp and untunable', but 'his eloquence full of fervour'. He took his
complaint about Lilburne's imprisonment to such a height 'that one would
have believed the very Government itself had been in danger by it'. In fact
the speaker made such a poor impression on Warwick that it lowered his
opinion of Parliament as a whole because 'this gentleman was very much
hearkened unto'. The speaker was a yeoman farmer from Huntingdon and
his name was Oliver Cromwell. And he was indeed hearkened to: on 13
November the doors of the Fleet opened and Lilburne was set free to argue
his case to Parliament. Lilburne did not, in his moment of triumph, forget
Katherine Hadley, who had distributed his appeal to the apprentices at
Moorfields. He claimed against the lord mayor for her wrongful imprisonment and, with the help of Lord Brooke, won her case and reparations of
ten pounds.[39]

Two weeks later William Prynne and Henry Burton returned to London
from their imprisonment. A week after that John Bastwick was treading the
streets of the City a free man. Huge crowds in coaches, on horseback and in
carriages accompanied their return. Some said 5,000 met Prynne and Burton,
others said 10,000. Flowers were strewn in the streets ahead of them. Charles
tried to limit the numbers that met Bastwick in the City to 800 horse. On the
day there were twenty-seven coaches, 1,000 horse and huge crowds on foot.
Trumpets sounded as Bastwick approached. The earl of Clarendon
complained that no 'minister of justice or the State itself' had 'courage
enough to prosecute . . . any persons who were part of that riotous assembly . . . so low was the reputation of the government fallen'. Another week
passed and a petition with 15,000 names was brought to the House demanding the 'root and branch' abolition of the bishops. Large crowds came to
Westminster to present the petition. On 18 December Archbishop Laud was
charged with treason. In the new year huge crowds forced on the impeachment of the earl of Strafford, already a target during the previous year's May
Day riots. The City delayed its loan to the king because Strafford's trial was
not making rapid progress. In March Laud was committed to the Tower. As
his carriage moved through the City mobs tried to haul him out of it.[40]

In May 1641, when crowds several thousand strong gathered to press the
Lords for the execution of Strafford, Lilburne, now at liberty, was an identified ringleader. When one of the crowd asked Lilburne why such numbers
had turned out he told them that they came for justice and that although
there were 6,000 or 7,000 present now there would be 40,000 or 50,000 the
next day. When asked how matters would end he was reported to have
replied, 'If we do not have the Lieutenants life, we will have the King's'.[41]

This speech landed Lilburne in trouble. Charles directed that Lilburne be apprehended and brought in front of the House of Lords, but the witnesses could not agree an account of the events and Lilburne remained at liberty.[42] Perhaps it was coincidence but on the very same day the Commons voted that Lilburne's previous imprisonment by the Star Chamber was 'illegal, and against the Liberty of the Subject; and also, bloody, wicked, cruel, barbarous, and tyrannical', and agreed he should be awarded compensation. Henry Marten was on the committee that was appointed to prepare the case for reparations.[43] Lilburne was, as we have seen in the previous chapter, in action again when crowds besieged Westminster in late December 1641, protesting at the king's attempt to secure the Tower by the appointment of Colonel Thomas Lunsford.

Lilburne was not, even at this early stage, acting alone. He was clearly in touch with a network of radicals, including printers and religious sects. Some of these would become Levellers, others not, though many of them came from similar social and religious backgrounds. One outstanding figure of the early radical religious circle was Katherine Chidley. She and her son Samuel would both become Levellers and stayed with the movement until its last days.

The remarkable Katherine Chidley

Katherine Chidley was an early associate of John Lilburne's and a religious dissenter long before she met him. So was her son, Samuel Chidley, later treasurer of the Leveller organisation. Their association with Lilburne, and with future Leveller printer William Larner, was to last from the 1630s to the very end of organised Leveller activity in the 1650s.

Katherine Chidley's political activity would be worthy of comment in any age. But given the position of women in seventeenth-century England her career is truly striking. It was almost universally held that women were the inferior sex, destined to marriage and multiple childbirth at an early age. A married woman could own no property and she was to be represented in Church and state by her husband. All this was bolstered by the fact that for many the family and the household economy were substantially the same. Puritans had to a limited degree begun to recognise that women might be worth more than this. Puritan family relations were supposed to be based on love, at least after marriage. The woman was meant to be a partner, albeit a junior partner. Wife beating and sexual double standards were denounced. But still, the family was regarded as the basic unit of the society. Like the state, it rested on order and hierarchy. 'To question the family, the place of women, or any other part of the social order', writes Keith Thomas, 'was to flaunt nature, reason and, above all, the will of God. It could only result in chaos and anarchy'.[44]

The Revolution and Civil War did disrupt this social structure and women in all walks of life and on both sides of the conflict began to step outside their compass. Royalists like Lady Bankes defended their castles alone. So did moderate parliamentarians like Lady Brilliana Harley.[45] But it was among the radical religious sects, with their emphasis on church democracy and the responsibility of all to testify, that this development was most marked. 'Women preachers', prophetesses and women petitioners became more common, and were widely remarked on. They were still a minority of women and, in some quarters, much reviled. Women protestors were variously described as 'Amazons, Oyster-wives, whores, bawds, beggar-women, kitchenstuffe women' and 'the very scum of the Suburbs'. Leveller women were 'Mealymouth'd Muttonmongers wives', 'holy sisters', 'a company of Gossops', and 'Levelling sea-greene Sisters'.[46] Katherine Chidley emerged from this environment. Indeed she was an early pioneer of women's engagement in Church and state politics.

We first hear of the Katherine Chidley, her husband Daniel, and their seven children in Shrewsbury in the 1620s. It was there that they set up an independent church and became locked in a battle with Peter Studley the staunchly royalist rector of St Chads, Shrewbury. In 1626 Katherine Chidley, alongside eighteen others, was charged with refusing to attend church. She was also in trouble because she declined to come to church for the 'the obligatory cleansing of a woman for the "taint of childbirth"'.[47] Perhaps we can catch something of the tenor of this dispute from Peter Studley's later pamphlet *The Looking-Glasse of Schisme*, a long denunciation of dissenters, in which he describes Nonconformists as 'painted strumpets'.[48] But before Studley burst into print the Chidleys had left Shrewsbury for London.

They arrived in the capital in 1629, the same year that John Lilburne arrived from the North East. Daniel and Samuel, after apprenticeship, became members of the Haberdashers Company. In 1630 father and son help establish one of the first dissenting congregations, the separatist church headed by John Duppa. The congregation claimed the right to choose its own pastor who was not paid from Church funds. Katherine Chidley was probably the most forceful member of the congregation, though as a woman she was unable to hold church office. Other members included Wiltshire radical Rice Boye, Sabine Staresmore, who had spent time in Holland, and, later, Thomas Pride, whose name would be eventually linked with the purge of Parliament that he led in 1648. Duppa was listed as a 'tub-preacher' in 1647.[49] The churches were illegal; their congregations faced harassment, arrest and imprisonment. Katherine Chidley said that members often went about in disguise, even wearing periwigs, to 'blinde the eyes of the Bishops blood-hounds', when they come to take them'.[50] Two years after the Duppa church was founded, twenty-six of its members were arrested. When two more years had passed, in 1634, some thirty of its members left for New England.[51]

This was, as we have seen, precisely the milieu in which Lilburne was moving. And indeed Samuel Chidley records that he knew Lilburne for a 'long time, even from the time of his sufferings by the bloody Bishops' in the 1630s.[52] And, since Katherine and Samuel Chidley were working as a writing team, Lilburne will have known the mother as well as the son. And they were soon to have another vital ally in common, the printer William Larner. In 1641, the same year that Larner printed Lilburne's *The Christian Mans Triall*, he also printed Katherine Chidley's impressive first pamphlet *The Justification of the Independent Churches*. Both came from Larner's press and were sold at his shop 'at the sign of the Golden Anchor, neere Pauls-Chaine'.[53]

Katherine Chidley's *The Justification of the Independent Churches* was a response to Thomas Edwards's attack on separatism and toleration, *Reasons against the Independent Government of Particular Congregations*. Edwards was to become one of the most famous controversialists defending the idea of a uniform Presbyterian national church. But long before his *Gangraena*, a mammoth three-part attack on separatists and Levellers, began publication in 1646, Chidley had identified him as an important opponent. She was the first to contest him in print. This in itself was a considerable act of political prescience. For a woman to mount such a challenge was unusual, if not unique. The main burden of Chidley's response was a defence of separate churches and an attack on Edwards's vision of a hierarchical and centralised Church government. Her concept of toleration was extensive, including Jews and Anabaptists. Her arguments involved a justification of those from humble origins, whether they be 'taylors, feltmakers, butttonmakers, tentmakers, shepherds or ploughmen, or what honest trade soever', organising their own churches.[54] This freedom to choose Church government tends to be extended by Chidley into the civil sphere. She certainly defends the right of independent churches to petition government in their own defence, a right that was to become central to Leveller argument and action.

Chidley's defence of the capacities of those usually socially excluded from church leadership was necessarily extended to the role of women. This is not always immediately obvious from Chidley's text because she uses a number of stock phrases about women being the weaker vessel and her own subordinate position as a woman. But closer analysis reveals a different aspect. For instance, having cited St Paul's examination of the problem of a devout woman married to an unbelieving husband, Chidley asks, 'I pray you tell me what authority this unbeleeving husband hath over the conscience of his beleeving wife. It is true he hath authority over her in bodily and civill respects, but not to be Lord over her conscience'.[55] And, in general, the image of God using socially inferior or weaker forces to defeat the ungodly and powerful is a recurrent theme. David's battle with Goliath is an obvious device in this respect. The title page of Chidley's pamphlet cites the biblical reference to the story of Jael, the woman who takes a hammer in her hand and kills Sisera, the enemy of the Israelites, by driving a tent peg through his skull while he sleeps.[56]

Edwards ignored Katherine Chidley's response, later complaining that in order to 'weaken my esteem, credit and authority with the people' the Sectaries had wanted to portray him 'as a man so weak that a Woman can answer my writing'.[57] Certainly when preacher John Goodwin came to make his own reply to Edwards, *Anapologesiates Anapologias*, he noted, 'this piece of his hath [already] been convicted, and baffled by the pen of a woman, and was never yet relieved by him with any REJOYNDER'.[58] Undeterred Chidley returned to the attack in 1645, writing both *A New-Yeares-Gift to Mr. Thomas Edwards* and a broadsheet, *Good Counsell to the Petitioners for Presbyterian Government*. But, as we shall see when we examine this work below, the political context was now very different from that in 1641 when she made her original reply to Edwards. The First Civil War was drawing to a close and the split, both political and religious, between the Independents and the Presbyterians was now a gaping chasm. Gathered churches were more numerous and their adherents operating more openly. But they were not legal and Presbyterian ascendency meant they were under increasing attack. Chidley's work established her as a key proto-Leveller controversialist.

Katherine and Samuel Chidley were now at the heart of the emerging Leveller movement. In the following year, for instance, Samuel would become treasurer of the Leveller organisation and be present at the Leveller-inspired army mutiny at Corkbush field in Ware. Katherine was one of the organisers of, and probable author of, the women's petitions to free the Leveller leaders from the Tower in 1649. Certainly the figure of Jael reappears in those petitions.[59] Both Samuel and Katherine Chidley remained actively in support of John Lilburne until his final trial for treason in 1653. On that final occasion we hear of Katherine Chidley as she headed a group of twelve women who presented Parliament with a petition signed by 6,000 women demanding Lilburne's release.[60]

But we will return to these events later. The interesting point about the early public career of Katherine Chidley is that it illustrates a number of significant issues in the prehistory of the Leveller movement. Her work highlights that the early networks of dissenting churches were a vital point of contact for activists who would become Levellers. It shows that underground printing was a key part of this political education and organisation. It illustrates the democratic impulse that could be derived from independent congregations. And in Katherine Chidley we have one of the earliest and foremost examples of the participation of women in public affairs in general and in the Leveller movement specifically. It was not usual for women to play any role in politics but more did during the Revolution. Some became prophetesses, seemingly a semi-accepted form of politico-religious expression for women. But few were as Kathernine Chidley was, a published and engaged activist, a religious and political leader.[61]

These elements were not sufficiently well defined in the earliest years to be a self-conscious radical movement. Both Chidley's and Lilburne's first pamphlets, for instance, assume the continued existence of the monarchy and are mostly concerned with church, not civil, government. Chidley was a separatist but not a Baptist in 1641, though she had become one by 1645. She and Lilburne at first formed part of the wider stream of Independency. But as events unfolded, and as their opponents defined their positions, some of this early cadre of radicals began to develop both their political thought and their political organisation in more radical directions. Lilburne and the Chidleys were activists among that plebeian social layer which sustained the popular mobilisations of the first phase of the revolution and which continued to do so in the first years of the Civil War. Their actions existed in symbiotic relationship with the parliamentary and City leaders of the revolution. The parliamentary leaders needed the support of mass mobilisation and were influenced by it as well as attempting to lead it. The poetical impulse travelled from the top to the base and back again, creating political escalation.[62] For the future Levellers these were formative experiences in organised politics.

Lilburne's reputation in 1641

Without the calling of the Long Parliament it is not easy to see the conditions under which Lilburne or Katherine Hadley could have obtained their freedom.[63] After Oliver Cromwell made his speech in the Long Parliament in defence of Lilburne his case was referred to a committee that included John Pym, John Hampden, Denzil Holles and Oliver St John. Reparations were ordered, although they took four years to be granted. Lilburne was a national political figure who had attracted the support of the most powerful moving forces of parliamentary politics and a significant degree of popular support.

Lilburne's subsequent actions in the first phase of the Revolution enhanced this already considerable reputation. He had already helped to organise a demonstration of apprentices from his prison cell. He was already 'Freeborn John' as a result of his defiance at his trial. Lilburne's rhetoric never lost the dimension of religiously inspired resistance to persecution. But, as the experience of participation in the Civil War and the Revolutionary mass movement accumulated, other themes emerged. The notion of freedom and equality under and in the law quickly became a central concern. Joined to this was the matter of legal precedent and, to demonstrate this, Lilburne relied on copious citation of Coke's *Institutes*. Then there was the historical argument that this notion of freedom had been lost under the Norman yoke. And, as experience accumulated, there was an increasing reliance on citing the Long Parliament's and the army's previous acts and engagements as a precedent for Leveller actions.

Lilburne's early career allowed him to develop his capacity to use the court and the prison as a political platform. He had need of this skill. In the twenty years between 1637 and 1657 there were only four in which Lilburne did not spend some time behind bars. From the mid-1640s Lilburne wrote as a prisoner or under the imminent threat of arrest and imprisonment.[64] His bravery commended him to many who were not wholly sympathetic to his cause. And Lilburne was mindful of the need to present his suffering as an example of wider social injustice. But all of this could only have the effect it did because Lilburne had organised access to print. However, all the pamphlets and petitions that flowed from Lilburne's pen, even from the closest imprisonment, were a political intervention which mere personal resistance to injustice in prison and courtroom could not have achieved. One of Lilburne's earliest Leveller-to-be associates was the printer William Larner, who produced the *Christian Man's Triall*. So was Katherine Hadley, who smuggled the pamphlet from Lilburne's cell. So were Katherine and Samuel Chidley. These were associations deeply rooted in the Puritan underground and networks in the City. They all lasted until Lilburne's death. The intersection where these lives met was one of the nodal points around which the Leveller movement would emerge.

CHAPTER 3

London, the Great Leveller

London was the incubator and mainstay of the Leveller movement. Its streets and alleys, its teeming suburbs, its taverns and churches, were where the radicals first met, first petitioned and protested, and built their organisation. To understand what made the Levellers we must understand London in the mid-seventeenth century. London was by far the largest city in the country at the time of the Revolution and it was expanding rapidly. The population of the old walled City and its associated parishes was 135,000 in 1640. But the population of the suburbs was already larger still, giving a total of over 350,000. Within the walls the skyline above the tightly packed narrow streets with their overhanging gabled houses was dominated by the spires of the many churches, as prominent then as the corporate towers are today. St Pauls, already much in need of repair before the fire of 1666 made rebuilding a necessity, was the centre of the book trade. Stalls and shops selling everything from Bibles to revolutionary pamphlets dominated the churchyard. The Tower of London anchored the eastern end of the wall. London Bridge was the only crossing of the Thames and it was built along its entire length with shops and houses. A castle-like gatehouse on the bridge could be closed against hostile forces. So could the gates in the City wall: Aldgate, Bishopsgate, Moorgate, Newgate, Aldersgate, Cripplegate and Ludgate. The Guildhall was the centre of City government, and the Exchange and the halls of the great City corporations the centre of its economic management.[1]

London was, however, much more than the walled City. Ribbon development spread out in all directions. To the west over the historic limit of the Fleet river there was now continuous building along Fleet Street, the

Strand and Charing Cross all the way to the separate jurisdiction and centre of national government at Westminster. North of this line building only reached the new, and fashionable, Covent Garden. The City was a great port and, in the east, shipbuilding yards and docks stretched along the Thames to Blackwall, Wapping and Limehouse. Whitechapel and Bishopsgate, the Tower Hamlets, were growing, but open field was still between them and the village of Hackney. South of the river in Southwark food and drink businesses concentrated in Boroughside, watermen in Clink Liberty and Paris Garden, and seamen in St Olave's, along with leather-makers, tanners, candlemakers and soap boilers. Dutch immigrants with new or specialised trades—brewing, felt and hat making, dyeing and glass making—settled in east Southwark.[2]

The laws and regulations of the City of London governed life within the walls and their jurisdiction had expanded irregularly beyond the wall. But here the City writ was less than absolute and often contested. The Liberties, based on old ecclesiastical rights that pre-dated the dissolution of the monasteries, whether inside or, mostly, outside the wall, were literally a law unto themselves. But, to a degree, so were Southwark and the Tower Hamlets where the Liberties had been attenuated or contested.[3] This is where many theatres and bawdy houses were located to escape the attention of the City authorities and the bishop of London. The names of these areas constantly recur in the story of the Levellers as locations of gathered churches, the homes of revolutionaries and the hiding places of secret presses. Also outside the walls were the open areas of Finsbury Fields, Moorfields, Spitalfields, and, south of the river, St George's Fields. Here apprentices gathered on holidays and the militia companies practised martial manoeuvres.

Manufacture engaged 40 per cent of the working population, retail another 36 per cent. The main trades were clothing, metalwork and leather working, and building. In one parish, St Botolph Aldgate, the proportion of manufacturing workers increased from 48 per cent to 72 per cent between 1600 and 1640. The London economy was dominated by the City companies, whose members provided the government of the City. There was a great variation in the membership of these companies. Many might have served the obligatory seven-year apprenticeship (although some might have bought their way in) to become freemen of the City with the right to trade within the walls and to vote in elections, but there was all the difference in the world between the great merchants and the ordinary masters, tradesmen and shopkeepers.

City government contained a weak democracy and a strong hierarchy. The Common Hall was the most popular institution, meant to include all 4,000 of the liverymen of the City. Edward Hyde, later earl of Clarendon and Charles I's key adviser, thought that this 'most general assembly of the City' admitted 'the meanest sort of person'. But the powers of the Common Hall were limited. The lord mayor called and dismissed the Common Hall as he chose. Then came the much smaller Common Council, chosen by election at a meeting of the wardmote, the old Saxon term for a meeting of the inhabitants of a ward. Attendance was compulsory and the usual business was the election of ward officers, beadles and constables. However, in elections for the Common Council only freemen could vote. The Common Council only sat five or six times a year. Real decision-making power rested with the third tier of City government, the mayor and the Court of Aldermen. These met twice a week. Again election was from the wardmote, but the aldermen had the right to reject candidates and so elections were often nominal. Office holding was both a self-perpetuating oligarchy and financially rewarding. This does not mean that the City did not have its own conflicts with the Crown over the rules and regulations governing trade or that it did not guard its privileges with care. But many merchants were also dependent on the Crown and the Court for their charters, for the granting of trading monopolies, and as a lucrative market.[4]

Many kinds of public political activity mushroomed when the Long Parliament met. Street protests were an important factor in the early history of the Revolution and remained so for its duration. Protest within the national Church and the growth of alternatives to it took on a new significance. Unsurprisingly, political meetings in taverns became both more frequent and more open.[5] There were precedents in all these cases. Street protest did not begin with the meeting of the Long Parliament, disputation in the national Church went back to its foundation, and political discussion had often taken place in taverns, some of which was oppositional. But the scale, breadth and, in some cases, radicalism of these phenomena grew beyond all historical precedent when the Revolution broke out, as contemporaries noted.[6]

London, even including its rapidly growing suburbs, was a walkable city in the 1640s. Its narrow streets were crammed with churches and taverns. John Venn could send a note to the apprentices of the walled City to bring them down to Westminster while a protest was going on.[7] In the heart of the City it would only take about 10 minutes to walk from John Goodwin's church or Samuel How's preaching place at the Nags Head, both in Coleman

Street, past the Levellers' taverns of the Windmill and the Whalebone, both in Lothbury, to John Wildman's lodging at the Saracen's Head in Friday Street. A visit to a secret press in Bishopsgate or Southwark might take no more than twenty minutes. Proximity can produce political intensity and is a facilitator of political organisation. The Levellers emerged from this environment. This is where they learnt organisational methods which would later be practised in the Leveller movement.

In the streets and localities

Town squares, streets and open spaces, churches and taverns were appropriated for public political use as the Revolution developed, and nowhere more so than in London. But even before the Revolution some urban areas were associated with radicalism. The Coleman Street Ward of the City is one of the best-known examples. Like no other area in the country its narrow alleys around the Guildhall harboured religious radicals, tub preachers, secret printing presses and politicians who were to be at the heart of the coming Revolution. The St Stephen's parish of Coleman Street was noted for disorders in 1617, 1636 and 1642. The St Stephen's parishioners had gained the unusual right to elect their vicar at the dissolution of the monasteries, one of only thirteen London parishes that could do so. Nearby St Mary's, Aldermanbury, elected Edmund Calamy. St Annes, Blackfriars, elected William Gouge in 1608.[8] In 1624 Puritan John Davenport was elected to the living in St Stephens by sixty-five votes to five against the archbishop of Canterbury's chaplain Aaron Wilson. Davenport was reported to the High Commission in 1631 and again in in 1632. When Laud became archbishop of Canterbury in 1633 Davenport went into hiding for three months. He then resigned at a secret meeting of vestry members and fled to Amsterdam just before the five men sent to arrest him arrived.[9] He was replaced by another Puritan preacher, John Goodwin, elected at a large general vestry meeting in December 1633. To royalist waterman and poet John Taylor he was 'the red dragon of Coleman Street'.[10] Among Goodwin's supporters was Coleman Street newcomer Isaac Penington, future MP and lord mayor, and a key figure in the opening phase of the Revolution. When the five members flew from the king's grasp they headed to Penington's house in Coleman Street.[11] Independent printer Henry Overton, publisher of Goodwin's pamphlets, owned a bookshop at the entrance to Popes Head Alley, off Lombard Street.

Several inhabitants of the parish were involved in the New England Company and the Massachusetts Bay Company. Francis Bright of St Stephens, the first minister to agree to emigrate, was elected to the Colony council in 1629, quarrelled with his fellow emigrants and returned to be Goodwin's curate at St Stephens from 1631 to 1640. Sir Nathaniel Barnardiston bought a house in Coleman Street in 1633. He was a friend of John Winthrop, the first governor of Masschusetts, who married into the family of Thomas Rainsborough. In 1633 Henry Overton was acting as an intermediary between preacher Henry Jessey and John Winthrop.[12] John Davenport returned secretly to Coleman Street to organise thirty-three families to emigrate to New England. Among them was Nathaniel Rowe, son of future Regicide Owen Rowe. They founded New Haven as a 'Bible Commonwealth . . . of the extremest type'.[13]

John Goodwin was radical but not as radical as some of those in the gathered churches in his parish. Sectarians appeared in the ward in the 1630s. There were Baptists in White's Alley off Coleman Street, plus two other sectarian congregations in the parish some time before 1639. Samuel How, of whom more later, took over John Canne's conventicle in 1633. Some years before Goodwin and Thomas Edwards became major disputants across the Independent–Presbyterian divide, Goodwin was worried enough about the gathered congregations to get Edwards to preach against 'Apostacie and falling into Errors' in St Stephens in 1638.[14] In 1646 Edwards reported that William Walwyn's friend and a leading Leveller, Thomas Lambe, was a soap boiler whose Church 'meets in Bell-Alley in Colemanstreet'. He could be also found preaching as far afield as Surrey, Essex and Hampshire.[15] Another Coleman Street stalwart separatist with associations with John Lilburne, William Kiffin, could be found in Kent, where he 'did a great deal of hurt'.[16] Worse still, as far as Edwards was concerned, 'there are women . . . who have preached weekely', including 'one Lace-woman, that sells Lace in Cheapside, & dwells in Bel-Alley in Colemanstreet'.[17] This was the Baptist preacher Mrs Attaway from Lambe's church.[18]

Two of John Goodwin's parishioners were secret printers. Henry Overton was hauled before the Ecclesiastical Commission in 1632 and 1633 for printing Rome's Ruin. Rice Boye, the second printer, was charged before the High Commission alongside Prynne, Bastwick and Burton in 1637. Edmund Chillenden, future Agitator and sometime Leveller ally, was involved with a secret press in 1637. Future Levellers Nicholas Tue and Richard Overton ran presses in Coleman Street. Goodwin was said to be a close associate of those who controlled the secret presses. Goodwin was, by 1645, meeting Walwyn and Lilburne on an almost daily basis.[19]

Coleman Street may have been the single most radical area of London. But it was not the only one. The parishes adjoining the City had grown enormously in the seventeenth century to the point where their population equalled that within the walled City. Thomas Rainsborough's family owned houses in Southwark as well as Wapping. His father was buried in the local church, St Johns, Wapping. Wapping was the site of Lilburne and Wildman's meeting with their supporters in Well Yard. Thomas Edwards complained of Sectaries in Stepney—among them Katherine Chidley.[20] Chillenden, Overton and Samuel Chidley were all active in Southwark at one time or another. Chillenden and sixty others were taken by the constables and churchwardens of St Saviour's, Southwark, for worshiping at the house of Richard Sturges in January 1641. They said they would not go to their parish church and that they recognised 'no true Church but where the Faithful met'. Further, they thought 'the King could not make perfect Law, for He was not a perfect Man', and they would not obey him in religious matters. They also threatened the constables and churchwardens 'that they had not answered for this Day's Work'. They were brought before the Lords, admonished as Sectaries, instructed to attend their parish church and told they would be 'severely punished' if they did not obey. The Lords also ordered that a warning to all who 'disturb' the 'wholesome order' of the Church should be read in every parish church in London.[21] In 1654 Samuel Hyland and Robert Warcup were said not to be qualified to sit as burgesses for Southwark because, among other crimes, they did not observe the Sabbath and they favoured the Levellers. Lilburne and Overton had both lived in the area in the 1640s.[22]

There are some indications that even before the outbreak of the Revolution the open spaces around the City were being used for oppositional political purposes. The author of *Persecutio Undecima* thought that from the early 1630s 'so many Military yards in London, Westminster and Southwark, and other places' were being used by 'Sectaries in London' to draw others into those 'Artillery Gardens' to exercise 'feates of armes'. Some came as a pastime, but the 'Brethern' saw this as preparation 'against a time of need'. Indeed,

> above a yeare before any face of war appeared . . . its well knowne scarce a
> Sectary in London but had stored himself with armes, to furnish each boy
> in his house; and many Porters loaded with Muskets, have beene seene

carried in the Evenings, into the Houses of men, notoriously disaffected in Religion, who conveied Armes, and Trayterous Libels, and Observations, printed at publick charge to their Countrey Chapmen.[23]

Even more directly, one royalist newsbook looking back at the origins of the Rebellion recalled that at first 'you may well remember when the Puritans here did much abominate the military-yard or Artillery Garden, as . . . they would not mingle with the Profane'. But 'at last when it was instill'd into them that the blessed Reformation could be effected by the sword, these places were instantly filled with few or none but men of that Faction'. For some two years they were said by this account to be 'very merry at their training' and 'could not be brought to discharge a Musket without winking'. Over time the winking Puritans took over the chief offices of command, 'so that when any prime Commanders dyed new men were elected, wholly devoted to that Faction'.[24]

The Honourable Artillery Company (HAC) was certainly a home for many radicals. The company had been incorporated under Henry VIII in 1507 to train men for the defence of the realm. It originally mustered on the Old Artillery ground in Spitalfields and did not acquire its home at the New Artillery Ground at Bunhill Fields until 1641. The company declined after the defeat of the Armada, but was rebuilt in the years 1611–44, holding continuous annual parades, feast days and sermons at City churches.[25] The HAC had royal patronage but it also contained a remarkable radical presence which ultimately decided its allegiance in the Civil War. The admissions book of the company records an impressive number of radicals who joined before the Revolution. The extravagantly named radical preacher Praise-God Barebone was a member. In 1631 Henry Overton joined. Thomas Pride learnt his military trade in the company, joining in August 1640. George Joyce joined in 1642, possibly the later Cornet Joyce.[26] John Bradley was admitted to the Honourable Artillery Company in 1626, becoming a captain in the Trained Bands in 1639. In April 1641 he and John Venn were two of the three City captains who presented citizens' petitions to Parliament against the earl of Strafford.[27] William Shambrooke joined the company in 1641 and in 1643 became a major of the Tower Hamlets Auxiliary Regiment and later its colonel. He was a member of Henry Jessey's semi-separatist (later Baptist) Congregation by 1640, and in 1644 was host to a meeting debating the validity of infant baptism. In August 1647 he was appointed lieutenant-colonel of the Tower Guards under Robert Tichborne. He died from a poisoned bullet at the siege of Colchester.[28]

Future members of the Levellers may also have been members of the Artillery Company. In 1640 Francis White, perhaps the future major who was central to events at Burford, joined. William Allin (*sic*) was a member, possibly the future Agitator. Allen's later presence in Holles's and Skippon's regiments may suggest this connection.[29] Leveller connections with the Massachusetts Artillery Company set up by former HAC members in New England in 1637 are considerable.[30] William Rainsborough and his brother-in-law both joined.[31] Their first military involvement was a naval expedition to Ireland in 1642 to suppress Irish rebels, in which both William Rainsborough and preacher Hugh Peter were involved. In 1643 Israel Stoughton, a major general of the Bay Colony and a veteran of battles with the Pequot Native Americans, led a party back across the Atlantic to join Thomas Rainsborough's regiment. Stoughton became Rainsborough's lieutenant colonel. Nehemiah Bourne came back as well. He had a past in Wapping like the Rainsboroughs, and became a major in Rainsborough's regiment. Stephen Winthrop, brother-in-law to Thomas Rainsborough, became a captain in his regiment in 1646. Winthrop was part of the Burford mutinies in 1649. Preacher Richard Baxter thought it was returning New Englanders that disturbed the peace of the New Model Army.[32]

In the 1630s in St Stephen's parish almost a third of householders appear to have been members of the HAC. Four HAC officers lived in the parish, including future Regicide and one of the main armours of Parliament's army Owen Rowe, and Robert Tichborne, also a future Regicide. So did John Venn. In 1629 John Davenport preached to the HAC. So did John Everard and William Gouge.[33] John Goodwin became a member on 19 April 1642.[34] One of Godwin's general vestrymen, Caleb Cockcroft, was brought before Star Chamber for the illegal import of gunpowder.[35] In the year before the Civil War began, 300 new members joined the HAC.

The company provided the overwhelming majority of the officers for the Trained Bands. Among those listed in the 'joyful' homecoming of the Trained Bands after the battle of Newbury in 1643 were Captain Walter Lee, a haberdasher of Ludgate, who had broken 'the windows on Westminster Abbey', and Captain William Coleson, who 'with his company carried the statues in the church of Allhallows to ye parliament'.[36] John Warner was, according to a royalist observer, a 'most violent' roundhead. Warner was to play a key role in the Revolution. He was not in the Artillery Company but was a colonel of the Green Regiment of the Trained Bands whose catchment area was the Coleman Street and Lothbury area. He oversaw the destruction of the stained glass at St

Stephens, Walbrook, and presented a petition against scandalous ministers to Parliament in 1641.[37]

A contemporary royalist account of the Southwark regiment lists officers and describes some as 'violent O', meaning 'violent roundhead'. Among the violent roundheads in Southwark are Captains Hobson, 'a grocer'; Captain Sowton, 'a woodmonger'; Captain John Thorton, 'a fishmonger'; and Captains Hobland (or Holland), a dyer, and Luke Bradby, a woolstapler, both from St Olaves.[38] Clarendon thought that 'all the factious and schismatical people about the City and suburbs would frequently . . . convene themselves, by the sound of a bell or other token, in the fields, or some convenient place, and receive orders from those by whom they were to be disposed'. He, too, mentions Southwark as 'a place where arms and magazine . . . were kept'. This is a reference to St George's Fields. And there was indeed, as we have seen, in May 1640 a great meeting of apprentices, glovers, tanners, sailors and dockhands held on what was to become a familiar rallying point for radical protest.[39]

Not all those who were radicals in the early years of the Revolution remained so during later political divisions. In the battle for control of the Militia Committee later in the Revolution some of those mentioned above were supporters of, and supported by, the Presbyterians. Others remained on the most radical wing of the Revolution supported by the Independents. Some went on to play a critical role both in Pride's Purge and the execution of the king. Some were Leveller supporters. John Warner was excluded from the Militia Committee in April 1647 in the Presbyterian purge of Independents. In June William Shambrooke was put out of his command. But Walter Lee, despite being jeered by peace petitioners in December 1642 as a 'roundhead rogue', was promoted to lieutenant colonel by the Presbyterian-controlled committee in 1647, although he was displaced when the Independents regained control later in the year.[40] None of this, however, detracts from the impact which the radical forces in the Artillery Company and the Trained Bands had on the early stages of the Revolution.

Taverns and alehouses

In the seventeenth century, as now, taverns and alehouses performed a variety of functions well beyond that of selling drink. Some were also a place to stay. They could act as a bank, a warehouse, an exchange, a scrivener's office or a place to trade goods and hire carriers. Some were used as wool markets, operating outside the regulations of the official market. Inns were an increasingly important centre of trade, business, administration, politics and social activity in the fifty years before the calling of the Long Parliament.[41] But inns, taverns and alehouses were not all the same. Inns were extensive establishments with guest rooms, stables and warehouses. They sold food and wine as well as ale and beer. Taverns, especially in London, were also fairly large establishments with a number of drinking rooms furnished with panelling, paintings and plate. Alehouses were poorer establishments with rudimentary furnishing located in back alleys, back rooms and cellars. They mainly sold ale and beer. Alehouses served the poorest and there was a considerable increase in their numbers in the century before the Civil War. Contemporary complaints about disorder and political opposition being associated with alehouses may be overstated in the period before the Revolution, especially since there is little evidence that radicalism first grew among the very poorest sections of the population. But in the 1640s there is considerable evidence of radical use of at least some taverns.[42]

The king was denounced in an Oxfordshire victualling house in 1625, in a Hereford alehouse in 1628, at the King's Head in London's New Fish Street in 1631, at the Angel Inn in Stilton in 1633, in an Essex tavern in 1634, and at both the Lion and Greyhound in Lavenham and the Three Horseshoes in London's Fetter Lane in 1637. In 1641 the alehouse keeper Joan Allen of Pleshey in Essex said 'she knew not the King, nor cared not for him ... nor would not obey his authority'. She was sentenced to a month in prison, whipped and sent home to her husband.[43] There must have been enough social or religious disputation going on in the taverns for playwright William Rowley to assume that his audience would know what a 'Taverne Accademian' was when he mentioned one in his 1633 *A Match at Midnight*.[44] Henry Wilkinson's sermon to the House of Commons in 1646 said that 'alehouses generally are the Devil's castles, the meeting places of malignants and sectaries'.[45] The widow that Isaac Penington married kept a tavern in White Friars where the 'scouts' of the Puritan underground could report and where Puritan ministers would lodge so that 'when they preached in London, or there abouts, they wanted not a crowd of Followers'.[46]

When the Revolution broke out, printed texts provoked discussion, sometimes tending to violence, in taverns like the Angel in Norwich, the Crown in Boston and the Three Trumpets at Dover.[47] From the early days of the Revolution petitions were on display for subscription in taverns. In December 1641 Edward Curie told the lord mayor that John Greensmith, a tobacconist, came to his shop and asked if he had signed a petition to Parliament that was available for subscription at the White Lion tavern, Canning Street. When Curie replied that 'he was busy and could not go then conveniently, but however, he would not subscribe against Bishops', Greensmith told him '"then you are like to have your throat cut," and went away in a discontented manner'.[48] The Puritan faction were reported as having 'dayly Taverne clubs in each Ward' of the City. To and from these meetings information was transmitted to gatherings in private houses and 'to report to Mr. Pym and his close committee'.[49] News-sheets could be read aloud and discussed in taverns. Pamphlets, news-sheets and petitions could be collected and returned to taverns using 'Bible carriers' who ferried messages to and from 'brethern' in the country.[50]

As we shall see below, the gathered churches were also providing a base for political activity, but we should not see taverns and churches as being as distinct as they are today or as the stereotype of Puritan attitudes might lead us to imagine. For instance, in 1640, at the 'Nags-head Taverne neare Coleman-Street in the presence of about a hundred people', the cobbler Samuel How of Long Ally in Moorfields preached a sermon on the theme that 'such as are destitute of Human learning, are the learned ones and truely understand the Scriptures' and that 'Jesus Christ was destitute of Human learning, and so his Servants ought to be also'. The five ordained ministers who were present were outraged, especially by How's decision to vindicate himself by having his sermon printed. He described ministers as 'men of the Throne'. He also declared his intention to cast down the throne and 'grind it to Powder'.[51]

John Taylor's pamphlet attacking How and other separatists contains a woodcut on its cover that pictures How preaching from a barrel in the first-floor room of the Nags Head.[52] John Goodwin was challenged to attend the sermon by How after he said that a man could not preach without learning. Goodwin heard How preach but then stopped the sermon from being printed. How's supporters had it printed in Amsterdam and distributed in London.[53] How's pamphlet was a best seller that ran through many reprints. The second of these came from future Leveller Richard Overton's secret press and the edition of 1655 was printed by William Larner.[54] How was supported by Edmund Chillenden.[55] When John Lilburne was in prison in 1640 he threatened to have his letters printed in Holland and 'if it be possible, it may be claimed upon the Posts, and made as publique as the Cobler's

Sermon, that so you may if you will read it in the Streets, as you go to the Parliament house'. How died during the prison term he was given for the sermon and buried in unconsecrated ground. Lilburne said that when he died he wanted to be buried 'beside the Cobler in Finsbury Fields'.[56] William Walwyn told John Goodwin, after he became a separatist, that he had moved towards the Cobler's views since they first debated.[57]

A year later another gathered church was reported meeting in a tavern. This time in the 'signe of the Locke in Fleet-street'. A 'congregation of sedition' was said to flower there. It was raided by a constable and some watchmen who found a 'Teacher was prating, his Pulpit was made of half a tub, having a black velvet cloath hanging down'. The constable left them in peace but later in the evening after a hostile crowd gathered he returned and made some arrests.[58] Few, however, would have supported Lawrence Clarkson's view that 'Tavernes I called the house of God', that those drawing the beer were messengers of God, and that sack was a divinity. Ironically, Clarkson was arrested when he was lured to a meeting in the Four Swans in Bishopsgate.[59]

The Levellers emerged from this milieu and the movement was associated with particular taverns, often with sympathetic landlords, although of course brewers and tavern keepers could be found among royalists and moderate parliamentarians as well.[60] The Windmill in Lothbury was a London landmark long before it became a Leveller centre. It was recorded as 'the Wyndemylne in Old Jury' when in 1522 the house was named in the list of inns and taverns viewed prior to the visit to England of Charles V. It was 'able to supply "fourteen feather-beds, and stabling for 20 horses"'. A plan of 1720 shows that the main entrance to Windmill Court is in Old Jewry and there is a long rambling back way from the court into Lothbury on its south side, almost opposite Founders' Hall.[61]

John Lambe, astrologer to the deeply unpopular George Villiers, duke of Buckingham, had temporary cause to be grateful to the Windmill. On 18 June 1628 he was returning from a playhouse through the City when he was set on by a crowd of 'ordinary People and the Rabble' who called him 'a Witch, a Devil' and 'the Duke's Conjuror'. The crowd grew to 500 strong and 'pelted him with rotten eggs, stones, and other riffraff'. He was chased from street to street until he took refuge in the Windmill. But the crowd found out the 'two Doors opening to several Streets' and secured both of them. The vintner then threw Lambe out for fear that the crowd would pull down the tavern and that the wines in his cellar would be 'spoiled and destroyed'. The lord mayor sent the Guard to rescue Lambe, but when the crowd saw them coming they beat Lambe so severely that he later died of the injuries. Despite Charles I's personal concern to apprehend the killers no one was willing to give up the rioters. The killing of Lambe coincided with the presentation of the remonstrance against Buckingham and 'so high was the Rage of the People . . . they would ordinarily utter these Words': 'Let Charles and George do what they can, / The Duke shall die like Doctor Lambe'.[62] Both the Windmill's size—it is a relatively large tavern at a time when the largest held no more than 200 people—and its notoriety probably served the Levellers well.

Thomas Edwards thought John Lilburne 'a great stickler in the meetings at the Windmill Tavern, and drawing up petitions for the Parliament', and that he was 'a player at Cards, who will sit long with company at Wine and Tippling'.[63] However that may be, on 31 May 1644 Lilburne was elected to a committee of sixteen at a meeting at the Windmill to decide action against the king.[64]

In 1646, at similar meeting at the Windmill to organise a petition, William Walwyn confronted one of his critics in the hearing of six or seven others and compelled him to apologise for spreading rumours that Walwyn was, variously, 'a dangerous man, a Jesuite, an Anti-scripturist' and a tempter of women into 'lewdness'.[65] One of those who had told Walwyn of the slander against him was Peter Cole, Richard Overton's early collaborator in secret printing in the very earliest days of the Revolution.[66] The centre of the movement in 1645 and 1646 was the Windmill Tavern.[67] At the time of the Ware mutiny in 1647 the Levellers were organising large meetings with the new Agitators and their supporters, like Henry Marten, in the Windmill and the Mouth taverns.[68]

The Windmill also had a role to play in the final act of Lilburne's public political career, his treason trial in 1653. When the jury found him not guilty they were hauled before the Council of State to account for their verdict. One juror denied it, but most admitted that on the morning of the day they gave their verdict they had met at the Windmill Tavern before coming to court. Some jurors admitted that they had decided their verdict in the Windmill, though another, William Hitchcock, a woollen draper from Watling Street, said they had simply met to 'drink a pint of wine' together. They were all insistent that no attempt had been made by others to influence them in Lilburne's favour. Given the history of the Windmill Tavern this may not be a wholly credible claim. At any rate William Hitchcock also said they came back to the Windmill after they had given the verdict to enjoy another pint of wine.[69] Hitchcock had been a member of the Honourable Artillery Company.[70] He was one of three captains in the Yellow Regiment of the Trained Bands at the muster in 1643. His fellow captains were Regicide Robert Tichborne and Walter Lee, the man who broke the windows at Westminster Abbey. Lee's and Hitchcock's standards are reproduced together on facing pages of William Lovell's contemporary watercolours of the Trained Bands' insignia.[71]

Even more prominent than the Windmill as a centre for the Levellers was the nearby Whalebone tavern. In two broadsides of July 1649 designed to hurl defiance at the authorities and raise the spirits of the 'brethren of the Sea-green order', Richard Overton addressed 'the citizens of London usually meeting at the Whale-bone in Lothbury behind the Royal Exchange, commonly (though unjustly) styled Levellers'. The Whalebone is by this stage so well known as a Leveller centre that it is mentioned by Overton on the title page of both pamphlets.[72] In the same month John Lilburne wrote from the Tower to 'my true Friends, the Citizens of London . . . usually meeting at the Whalbone in Lothbury, behind the Royal Exchange, commonly (but most unjustly) stiled Levellers'.[73] 'The Whaleboners' became a popular nickname for the Levellers. And the Whalebone and the Mouth were referred to as 'the Levellers two new Houses of Parliament' in *Mercurius Pragmaticus*, which it said the 'Juncto' of Lilburne, 'Southwarkian Rabbi Overton' and Tobias Box, agitator and London agent, met with their 'ravening Representatives'.[74]

In 1649, Henry Ireton, Cromwell's son-in-law, 'imployed many Spies at severall meetings (especially) at the Whale-bone in Lothbury' to gather intelligence on Leveller plans to oppose the Cromwellian regime.[75] The Mouth inn was in Aldersgate, recorded as kept near Bishopsgate in 1641.[76] Tobias Box had been arrested leaving the Mouth on 10 November 1647 and accused of having 'severall Papers about him'. Three days later, 150 weavers met at the Mouth. They spoke of coordinated action with the army. One of them suggested they follow the example of Naples, where, he understood, 'if any Person stand up for Monarchie there, he is imme-diately hanged at the Doore'.[77] It was to the Mouth that the body of John Lilburne was taken in 1657 before burial in the Bethlem new churchyard the following day.[78]

In 1647 another tavern, the Saracen's Head in Friday Street, was at the heart of a campaign to win affiliation to the Levellers' first *Agreement of the People*. This was a national campaign organised from London. It involved the dispatch of copies of the *Agreement of the People* to 'all quarters of the army, [and] the countries abroad'.[79] John Wildman's lodgings were at the

Saracen's Head. Subscribed copies of the *Agreement of the People* were brought back to London by agents and taken to the Saracen's Head.[80] In November 1647 a royalist claimed to have come across instructions issued by the army Agitators to the 'Agents of the City of London for the more orderly carrying, and the more speedy effecting and bringing in the subscriptions'. These instructions speak of a high level of organisation. The papers were to be delivered to 'such faithful persons, as will be vigilant and active in the prosecution of them'. There would then be places chosen where they could meet which would be 'most convenient, to take Subscriptions of the City or place where they reside'. One 'active and faithfull man' or more should be appointed 'for each County, City, or Place'. The petitions should be brought 'as soon as possibly they can, to the *Saracen's Head* in Friday-street in London, where there will be Agents to receive them, or the Master of the House . . . will direct them where they shall be received'.[81] In the same month the Speaker acquainted the Lords with the news that 'he hath received from *Nottingham* a Letter, with "*The Agreement of the People*" inclosed, sent down thither by an Agent, from *The Saricen's Head*, in *Friday Street, London*; stirring up the People to subscribe the Agreement; and to send the same up to *London*, to *The Saricen's Head*'.[82] The activities at the Saracen's Head were described in 1648 as like those in the Puritan Tavern clubs at the outbreak of the Revolution.[83]

The Saracen's Head was a large inn. Merchant Taylors' records from 1656 and later plans show it as a long, narrow building running most of the width of the block from Friday Street to Bread Street and with a substantial yard.[84] It was from here that the coaches to Wiltshire, Somerset and other parts of the West Country departed.[85] It was a great centre for carriers from all over the country, it was recorded in 1637.[86] In 1642 craftsman Nehemiah Wharton was writing that every Wednesday those who wanted news of the fate of the parliamentary army could find a post at the Saracen's Head.[87] It was in the Saracen's Head that Wildman overheard Wiltshire cloth workers complaining of the dearth of work and telling that they had gathered in groups of ten to thirty and seized corn on its way to market. They then 'divided it among themselves before their owners faces, telling them they would not starve'. Retelling this tale was part of what got Wildman into trouble when the Levellers' Well Yard meeting was reported to the Commons in January 1648.[88] Wildman may have been acting in concert with Henry Marten at this point and the Saracen's Head's coaching routes to the west that ran through Marten's home territory in Berkshire may have been convenient for that reason.[89]

Other taverns associated with the Levellers include the Nags Head 'by Blackwell Hall' where, on 15 November 1649, the preliminary meeting to draft the final *Agreement of the People* took place. Although there was more than one Nags Head tavern in close proximity in the City at this time, this seems to have been the same tavern at which Samuel How preached.[90] Mark Hildesley was a member of John Goodwin's congregation and owned the Star Inn located in St Stephens. From early 1645 Goodwin and Hildesley were holding daily meetings and 'intimate discourse' with Lilburne, Walwyn, Henry Burton and Hugh Peters. In June 1647 Peters, Cromwell and others met at the Star before the seizure of the king. In December 1647 Hildesley was one of those chosen to organise the implementation of the *Agreement of the People*. Cromwell, Pride, Peters and others also met at the Star before the king's trial.[91] In the 1650s the Leveller leader John Wildman himself bought Nonsuch House in Bow Street, Covent Garden. It was run by his servant William Parker, who had acted as a courier between Wildman and Leveller agitator Edward Sexby. Described both as a tavern and later as a coffee house, the Nonsuch marks a transition from the tavern culture of the 1640s to a later form of radical gathering place.[92] Leveller printer William Larner operated from the Blackamore in Bishopsgate.

The churches

In 1641 there were complaints about separatists giving the impression to 'every Ploughman' and 'every Tradesman' that they could pronounce on religion. These were once 'but a handful' that had now become so bold that they might 'overthrow the whole Land'. Indeed, it was claimed, 'They are now growne to that height of impudence, that it is a common thing for them to command the preacher what he shall say, and no more'. Just as the anti-bishop protests were gathering in late 1641, this included thrusting a note into the hand of the minister at Christchurch in London and insisting that he read it to the congregation. It told him to 'move the Congregation of Saints here met, to joyne with you, that would be pleased to assist the Apprentices and others with strength and power and to blesse their undertakings, which are speedily to root out . . . all innovations of Bishops, and Clergie'.[93] Such complaints reached flood tide in the mid-decade work of Thomas Edwards. His three-part *Gangraena* contained over 600 pages of outrage at Sectaries, Independents, gathered churches, the New Model

Army, and political radicals. Other prime targets were women, the young and mechanic preachers.[94] But Edwards was not alone in objecting to 'Insolent' orders about protests that were 'throwne into Church-wardens houses by unknown hands'. From Sunday sermons or lectures the congregation learnt 'not only what was done the weeke before, but also what was to be done in Parliament the weeke following; besides the information, which their Pulpits gave the people, for comming in tumults to the House for justice'.[95] The royalist *Mercurius Elencticus* complained that papers had been pasted up 'in many Churches, and upon severall Gates and Posts throughout the City, inciting the People to rise up as one Man'. When this was reported to the Commons, Henry Marten defended the protestors' right to do so, 'wondering why anyone should want to restrain the people from seeking redress for their grievances'.[96]

Part of the upheaval that the Revolution produced in the Church was the campaigns, often supported by petitioning, to have insufficiently Puritan ministers replaced by more godly preachers. In December 1640 a Commons committee was established with this aim in mind; its members included Isaac Penington and Oliver Cromwell.[97] Its aims were broadcast in a pamphlet from Henry Overton's secret press.[98] One hostile account records that the 'Puritan Faction in the House of Commons' encouraged 'any Knave, or Foole in the Parish' to oppose their minister and that 'in a short space above two thousand Petitions were brought in against the Clergy'. Petitioning was augmented by direct action: 'its too well known how a few . . . zealous . . . young fellowes with their wenches rushing into any Church in London could . . . sing a whole parish out of their Religion (a trick they had from the Dutch rebels and Anabaptists . . .)'.[99]

Gathered churches also multiplied once the Revolution broke out. From 1640 to 1642 separatist communities could be found in the Tower Liberty, Whitechapel, Ratcliffe, Stepney and Fleet Street in Southwark. There were two more in St Saviour's Southwark and Goat Alley off Whitecross Street.[100] Lilburne was arrested for his part in one such church.[101] In a long diatribe against Overton's and Lilburne's work, Prynne complained that the gathered churches are 'sending out the Emissaries, Captaines and Souldiers everywhere to preach in corners and giving tickets of the time and place of their conventicles'.[102] The future Leveller leaders came of age politically in this environment. Indeed it is possible to see a direct line of descent from this type of organisation to the kind of organisation the Levellers became.

Walwyn was deeply engaged with the Independents and the gathered churches. Richard Overton was a Baptist, wavering between Goodwin's church and Lambe's in 1643.[103] John Lilburne was already a hero of the sectarian churches for his persecution by the Star Chamber. He was a member of Edmund Rosier's separatist church.[104] Samuel Highland was a Leveller in the 1640s and he had a congregation in Southwark in 1654 that supported the Fifth Monarchists. These may have been the semi-separatists recorded in Southwark in the 1640s. Certainly the Levellers had a base in the area. Katherine and Samuel Chidley, the future Leveller treasurer, ran their own separatist congregation in the Coleman Street area. The Leveller printer William Larner was a separatist.[105] Some church-learnt methods of association were transferred into political life.[106]

Some continuity exists between the gathered churches as an early incubator of radicalism and the army as a later incubator. William Allen the agitator was a Southwark felt maker and a Particular Baptist serving first in Holles's regiment and later in Skippon's. He was captured once and wounded twice. He was, with Sexby and Thomas Shepard, questioned by the Commons for his actions as an agitator.[107] His fellow agitator Edmund Chillenden was also from a separatist church, and became a Baptist. Army chaplain Edward Harrison was a Leveller. Robert Lockyer may well have been a Baptist. Henry Denne was a Leveller and a Baptist. In a certain sense the army made preaching to 'gathered churches' a necessity as well as the choice for many, though it also meant that formal separation was not an option since military discipline held all soldiers in one unit.[108] This may, paradoxically, have enlarged the audience for separatist preachers since their listeners would be a cross section of soldiers, not a self-selecting gathered church. In the series of chaplains which served Colonel Whalley—Richard Baxter, Henry Steevens, Hanserd Knollys and Jeremiah Ives—each new appointment was progressively more radical.[109] Ives was an associate of Henry Denne and Leveller printer Henry Hills. In 1647 he was imprisoned with William Larner in the Gatehouse, and at the same time as Thomas Prince and Samuel Chidley, for defending the *Agreement of the People*.[110] The questions of political freedom and religious freedom were, of course, intertwined. Richard Baxter found many in Whalley's regiment arguing 'sometimes for state-democracy, sometimes for church-democracy'.[111] But to be in the parliamentary army was a radicalising experience for many in and of itself.

There is one impact of the Independent and gathered churches on the future Levellers that is perhaps too-little commented on—their role as a

school of autonomous, collective organisation. The churches were a voluntary association in which congregations met to pursue religious aims
outside the established framework. This in itself required self-organisation,
often of an oppositional nature. Spaces to meet had to be located, congregations gathered, money raised. In some churches 'scruplers' were
encouraged to question the preacher, just as they were later to do in Leveller
meetings. Lay members might be encouraged to speak and preach, again
developing leadership capacities and independence of mind. Notes might
be taken in shorthand, a technique later used, for instance, to record *The
Triall of Lieut. Collonell John Lilburne*, which was described on its front
cover 'as being exactly pen'd and taken in short hand'.[112] Reading and study
of biblical texts was encouraged, an enthusiasm that translated into the
study and discussion of political pamphlets and broadsheets. We can see
how the gathered churches could function as a support base for radical
politics in the career of Thomas Lambe.

A Leveller leader: Thomas Lambe

Thomas Lambe was an important figure in the Leveller movement. He
provided a vital link between the political mobilisations of the Levellers
and the Baptist congregations. He was himself the leader of one of the
largest such congregations in London. In Murray Tolmie's judgement,
Lambe's activity was so extensive that it was 'scarcely less important' than
Lilburne's work.[113]

Like Katherine Chidley's, Thomas Lambe's first confrontation with
authority was not in London. In Lambe's case it was in Colchester, where he
had married Dorcas Prentice on 23 March 1619 and lived in the St Giles
parish of the town. In 1629 he was, again like Chidley, accused of not attending church and of failing to receive communion at Easter. Lambe vowed 'he
would be burned before he would receive the holy sacrament after this
manner'. In July 1636 Thomas and Dorcas Lambe were excommunicated for
not attending church and for refusing to have their child baptised. The
following year he was reported for breaking the Sabbath by 'boyling of sope
on a Sunday'. And a year after that, on 26 April 1638, the churchwardens
reported that when they asked Lambe for money to repair the church he
told them 'he did wish that all churches were layd in the dust'.[114]

It was imprisonment that brought Thomas Lambe to London just as
the Revolution began. On 6 February 1640 he was accused by the High

Commission of keeping a conventicle. He was thrown in the Fleet prison, where the warders were told to prevent him organising another conventicle. In June he successfully petitioned for his release on condition that he would not organise a gathered church or baptise children. Lambe does not seem to have had much intention of meeting these conditions. He was back before the High Commission again in October 1640, and in January 1641 he was organising a gathered church in Whitechapel. Even more seriously, he was at the heart of a riot in the area and was arrested along with sixty others. On a Sunday in mid-January Thomas Lambe gathered a congregation at a house in Whitechapel. The local Justice of the Peace, a Mr Gibbs, arrived with the constables and 'divers . . . rude Persons' and 'furiously beat and broke in Pieces the Door'. They then 'violently entered the House' and threatened the worshippers with 'Swords, Halberts, and Clubs'. The Justice then encouraged a mob numbering 'scores of Persons' to 'beat down the Windows with Stones'. A child was injured and one of the mob threatened to slit the throat of a worshipper. This was the account of Lambe and his fellow prisoners. Justice Gibb and the constables had a different story. They claimed, in a manner still familiar in police testimony today, that they were attacked first and only entered the house to protect those inside from the mob. But when Justice Gibbs entered the house, he told the House of Lords, 'upon Search' to he happened to find 'divers Persons gathered together; and he, being informed they were Sectaries, did examine them when they did receive Communion in the Parish Church. They said, They had not for a long Time, neither would they. After this, for the present, he committed them to Prison'. Interestingly, Lambe and his congregation had contested the Justice's right to do this in terms familiar from Lilburne's trials: they complained that Gibbs had proceeded 'contrary to the Laws and Statutes of the Land' and that he had not shown them any warrant for his actions.[115]

From this point on Lambe's activity revolved around two great projects: the building of his gathered church in London and itinerant evangelical preaching. Later in the same year as the Whitechapel riot, 1641, we catch sight of Lambe proselytising in Gloucestershire, where he baptised new followers in the Severn. He offered to preach in nearby Cranham in the temporarily vacant parish minister's place. This offer being refused he preached in private houses. Back in London Lambe's church was meeting in the very centre of the Revolutionary maelstrom, Bell Alley, off Coleman Street. 'Mr Lambe's Congregation' became, in the words of Scottish Commissioner Robert Baillie, 'the greatest, as they say, and most fruitful of all their societies without comparison'. Lambe's house would fill with listeners and so would the yards outside. The church was especially attractive to 'young youths and wenches' who 'flock thither'.[116]

Everything about Lambe's church, unsurprisingly, outraged Presbyterian heresy hunter Thomas Edwards. He didn't like Lambe's General Baptist preaching that all could be saved. He didn't like the fact that the church debated theological questions. He hated the fact that 'mechanicks' and women were allowed to preach. He didn't like that the congregation would cry out for which preacher they wished to hear next. And he particularly didn't like the fact that this was sometimes put to the vote. He didn't like that a preacher might be interrupted by 'some standing up and objecting', which would then result in 'pro and con for almost an hour'. Neither did Edwards like the fact that some of his own supporters were drawn to 'this Lambs Church for Novelty'.[117]

Edwards was really only inaccurate in one respect—he oversimplified Lambe's theological position. Lambe was a indeed a General Baptist but he actually held to an amalgam of general salvation and particular predestination. This seems to have armed him with a specific and popular combination of the motivational aspects of election with the broad appeal of general absolution.[118] However this may be, Lambe's church drew around it a remarkable collection of radicals. Samuel Oates was an even more incendiary preacher than Lambe and accompanied him on some of his journeys outside the capital. Oates was a future Leveller and distributed the *Agreement of the People* through a network of agents in Rutland, Lincolnshire and Northamptonshire. Henry Denne was a member of the Lambe church and one of the Leveller mutineers at Burford before he recanted when captured. Nicholas Tue may well have been associated with Lambe from the Whitechapel days, before the church moved to Bell Alley. Tue worked in association with Richard Overton on a Leveller press in Coleman Street and was arrested for the production of a broadside attacking the earl of Manchester and the earl of Essex in 1644. Jeremiah Ives, another Leveller, was a confidant of Lambe who accompanied him on his evangelical tours. Richard Overton was a member of Lambe's church. Indeed every preacher that came out of Lambe's church is identifiable as a Leveller committed to the organisational core of the movement and not a mere sympathiser or fellow traveller.[119]

In 1645 Parliament passed a law against lay preaching. Presbyterians postered the City calling for a demonstration to 'suppress conventicles'. The lord mayor utilised the legislation to move swiftly against Lambe that spring. But when the mayor's officers came to Lambe's church in Bell Alley the congregation called them 'persecutors and persecuting rogues'. Lambe himself offered them 'better words' and asked that they be allowed to finish prayer. Lambe then went to the mayor's house the same evening and told him that he had not broken the law as he was 'a preacher called and chosen of a Reformed Church as any was in the world'. It didn't wash. Lambe was jailed, though soon released. This affair and another test case convinced the mayor that he could not make more arrests, 'feeling it is in vain'. Lambe continued to preach even 'more openly and frequently than before'.[120]

Leveller leader Richard Overton was a member of Lambe's church and he organised and participated in debates on the 'mortalist' heresy that the soul died with the body. This debate took place on 5 February 1646 at Lambe's residence, now in Spitalfields. The mayor sent 'two of the Marshall's men' to break up the 'great concourse of people'. Lambe met the officers and seems to have been willing to halt the meeting. But Overton was for defiance and 'stood up and said, Brother Lamb, had Paul done well if he had desisted from preaching in the name of Jesus if he had been commanded by the High priests to forbear, had he done well or not?' Lambe agreed that he would not. Overton 'replied in a scornful and proud manner, nor ought we to obey Master Mayor'. And so it was, for the meeting stayed in session for in excess of four hours.[121]

Lambe continued to travel and preach throughout this time. He was in Terling in Essex in 1643 debating in front of a 'great concourse of people', in Guildford and Portsmouth with Samuel Oates in 1645, and later the same year in Kent with Henry Denne. Lambe and Jeremiah Ives were in Devizes, Wiltshire, in September 1646 meeting with radicalised soldiers. Together with Captain Henry Pretty and other soldiers from Ireton's regiment they disrupted a church service and expelled the preacher from both pulpit and church. Lambe, Ives and Pretty were reported to Parliament by angry congregants who said they were 'armed in the most irreverent manner, to the abominable disturbance of the whole congretion'.[122]

Lambe was at the heart of many of the Leveller petitioning campaigns.[123] Leveller leaders John Lilburne and William Walwyn testified to the central role that Lambe played in the Levellers 1647 petitioning campaign.[124] Later the same year Lambe was also involved in distributing the *Agreement of the*

People. And it was alleged that Lambe had a hand in producing the papers worn in the soldiers' hats at the Ware Mutiny.[125]

Lambe had become increasingly central to Leveller organisation as the movement grew. But, in 1649, at the very peak of the Revolutionary wave, there was a division among Baptist supporters of the Levellers. Thomas Lambe remained loyal to the Levellers. He offered to defend them in public debate but, according to William Walwyn, his opponents 'were asham'd, and durst not, for none of them would undertake him'.[126] His association with the Levellers, like that of the Chidleys and William Larner, lasted into the 1650s. In 1656 his pamphlets, always theological in content, were still being printed by the old operator of the army press, Henry Hills, and sold by William Larner.[127]

City Levellers

What emerges from this overview is a sense of the dense fabric of political opposition in the capital during the early days of the Revolution, and in some cases from before that, from which the Levellers emerged as an organised current. Underground activity in churches and taverns, combined with the secret printing and petitioning activity analysed in other chapters, provided a schooling in organised politics which would feed into the foundations of the Leveller movement. The point where meetings in churches and taverns spill over into mass street demonstrations is possibly an early decisive moment of transition. This is the point where clandestine or semi-clandestine activity becomes irrefutably public opposition to established authority. Later mutinies in the army were to provide another moment of open defiance to the established order. The Levellers became a unique current within the English Revolution by being able to maintain a mass, public presence through petitioning, printing and street demonstrations. Such work required collective organisation, action and leadership. London was a unique environment which facilitated such activity.

The trust essential to such leadership could only be established over time in joint activity. To an important degree the Levellers acquired this ability through a concentrated course of oppositional activity on the streets, in taverns and churches. As John Lilburne, Richard Overton, William Walwyn, Samuel Chidley, Thomas Lambe and others moved in the same circles, met and cooperated, they came to form the core of an identifiable current with its own profile. This led both to a distinct series of ideological and political positions about the course of the Revolution and to the creation of an organised movement capable of conducting political campaigns and seeking alliances with other radical forces. This was the Levellers' singular contribution to the Revolution, and the dense urban environment, the internet of the alleyways, the churches as a focal point of opposition, were London's contribution to the birth of the Levellers.

CHAPTER 4

Levelling by Print

In any age, political activity is, in part, shaped by the means of communication available. The future leaders of the Levellers began to meet and cooperate in the gathered churches and the apprentice networks of the City of London. But this was true only in a general way. It was print that brought John Lilburne and his supporters together in closer and specifically organised relationships long before they became known as Levellers. At the time, print was a relatively new technology; the ability to use this technology for oppositional purposes was more recent still. The opportunity to use it on a mass scale was almost unknown in England. Yet the political crisis of the 1640s produced the breakdown of pre-publication censorship as well as widespread opposition that would make this new weapon central to their armoury.[1] Print, and the ability to use it on a mass scale, were not the sole determinant creating Leveller organisation, but they are central to its creation. No political organisation that mobilised beyond the political elite had done this before and no other organisation that did these things existed at the time. It is the Levellers' coordinated use of print for political purposes that is one of the things that marks them out as an effective organisation. The prehistory of Leveller organisation is found in the writing, production and distribution of printed material in which we see some of the earliest and longest-lasting political relationships being formed.

'The persecutors of the Saints':
censorship and the Stationers' Company

In 1637 the Star Chamber cut the number of authorised printers in London to twenty. Meanwhile, imported books were controlled by the bishops. To print domestic news was an offence. No book in English could be legally printed abroad. Authors and printers of unlicensed books could be pilloried and whipped. The 'Puritan martyrs' Henry Burton, John Bastwick and William Prynne had their books burnt before them as they stood in the pillory before having their ears severed. Prynne had the initials 'SL', standing for 'seditious libel', branded on his face.[2] The work of apprehending offenders was mainly in the hands of the body that had a monopoly of legal printing, the Stationers' Company. When John Lilburne was first arrested in December 1637 for distributing the pamphlets of the Puritan martyrs he was seized by members of the Stationers' Company.[3] In 1639 Richard Overton had the speaker in *Vox Borealis* say that the 'Search at London was hotter then the Presse at Paris', and so though 'I had once a good store of newsbooks in my pocket-book' he burnt them 'else the hangman had done it for me, and perhaps burned me with it'.[4]

Sir John Lambe, Archbishop Laud's enforcer, was certainly energetic in his efforts to supress separatist booksellers. His notes submitted to the High Commission identify 'one Fisher, a barber in Old Bailey'; Woulston, a scrivener in Chancery Lane; Edward Hill, a tailor, and his wife, in Seething Lane; Stephen Proudlove of Bishopsgate, who 'travels up and down to fairs'; 'one Harford, a bookbinder in Paternoster Row'; and 'Abbott, a bookseller in Whitechapel'. One of these, 'Callo, a perfumer in Cloth Fair, near Smithfield, and his wife, an Antinomian', had already been caught by an agent of the High Commission in the company of Sir Henry Marten, father of the Leveller ally Henry Marten.[5]

The degree to which effective censorship had grown under Charles I is disputed by historians. Some argue that 'fear of the courts had virtually no impact on the economy of the book trade'.[6] But a larger body of opinion holds that while the Caroline state cannot be seen as having totalitarian powers it was effective, if erratic, in enforcing censorship. Jason McElligott rightly emphasises four points. First, the early modern state could enforce its will upon the press when it chose to do so. Second, censorship is not reducible to statistics of licensing evasion or prosecutions. Third, 'censorship is also a pragmatic, contingent and grubby process dependent on the actions of individuals, which often defies idealised, abstract notions of how it should operate'. Finally, 'there were a variety of factors which might make censorship of a particular item more or less likely, but it was almost impossible for contemporaries to judge in advance how any or all of these might interact with each other'.[7] It is true that censorship was less a part of the routine machinery of an authoritarian state than an ad hoc authoritarian response to particular texts that the state perceived to endanger the exercise of its power. But this is exactly how the state *did* frequently see Leveller activity.[8]

Censorship and the ability to enforce it received a huge blow in the opening months of the Long Parliament, even before the Courts of Star Chamber and High Commission were abolished in 1641. Printed titles of all kinds rose from 600 to 700 a year in the 1630s, to 900 in 1640, to more than 2,000 in 1641, and to over 3,500 in 1642. The number of newspapers alone grew from three in 1641, to fifty-nine in 1642, to seventy in 1648. The number of print shops rose from twenty-four, containing fifty presses in 1640, to more than forty shops with some seventy presses in 1649. The traditional system of press licensing by the episcopal authorities and the Privy Council and managed through the Stationers' Company all but collapsed. In its place there emerged a freewheeling and mostly unregulated market of print.[9] But as the political situation became ever more polarised, both Parliament and the king urged on repeated attempts by the Stationers to stem the tide of unlicensed pamphlets.[10] From this moment on there were repeated attempts to reimpose censorship. This created a running battle between the Stationers' Company and other authorities and the secret presses. Historian Ariel Hessayon notes that Leveller works were among those burnt by the authorities and that between 1640 and 1660 Lilburne had more of his works consigned to the flames than any other author. Despite erratic state policy and internal company divisions between 1644 and 1649 the Stationers' Company did hunt down the presses of Levellers Nicholas Tue, William Larner and Richard Overton. Henry Hills had to vow not to produce scandalous material.[11]

Almost as soon as censorship broke down there were calls for it to be restored and repeated attempts by the authorities to do so, in part encouraged by the Stationers' Company.[12] Something of the atmosphere of this conflict can be gained from *The Humble Remonstrance of the Company of Stationers* issued in April 1643 requesting greater powers from the government.[13] This prolonged defence of the Stationers' monopoly is justified by the argument that 'commonly where Printing droops, and Printers grow poor by neglect of Government, there errors and heresies abound'. The 'late decay of the Stationers' is blamed on the 'want of Politick regulation' and this has 'emboldened Printers to run into enormous disorders' since the abolition of the Star Chamber and High Commission. New regulation is needed because, say the Stationers, 'within these last four yeers, the affairs of the Presse have grown very scandalous and enormious, and all redresse is almost impossible, if power be not given to reduce the Presses'.[14]

The work of reducing the number of presses and apprentices is all the more important, according to the Stationers, because

> the same disorder which undoes the Stationers . . . causes also Strangers, as Drapers, Carmen, and others to break in upon them, and set up Presses in divers obscure corners of the City, and Suburbs; so that not onely the ruine of the Company is the more hastened by it, but also the mischief, which the state suffers by irregularity of all is the less remediable . . . Where Delinquents grow too numerous, they grow out of the Eye of government.[15]

Indeed the entire Civil War, they suggested, had been fuelled by uncontrolled printing that 'by deceiving the multitude' has 'brought into both Church and State . . . mischiefs and miseries'.[16] If only the government gave the Stationers the power 'all odious opprobrious Pamphlets of the incendiaries, Printed and invented in London . . . would be quashed'.[17]

Two months later, on 14 June 1643, the government did indeed grant the Stationers more power. But the Stationers did not manage to 'quash' the printing of odious pamphlets. Not for the want of trying. The 'Ordinance for correcting and regulating the Abuses of the Press' was draconian in intent. It echoed the Stationers' *Remonstrance* in denouncing the setting up of 'sundry private Printing Presses in Corners, and to print, vend, publish, and disperse, Books, Pamphlets, and Papers, in such Multitudes, that no Industry could be sufficient to discover, or bring to Punishment, all the several abounding Delinquents'. It sought to reimpose licensed printing under the control of the Stationers' Company. It gave power to the Committee of the House of Commons for Examinations to search 'for all unlicensed Printing Presses, and all Presses any Way employed in the Printing of scandalous or unlicensed Papers, Pamphlets, Books, or any Copies of Books'. They were empowered to seize presses and take them to 'the Common Hall of the said Company, there to be defaced and made unserviceable'.[18]

Print and the origins of the Levellers

Richard Overton was, amongst other things, one of the main printers and writers in the Leveller cause. Exemplary research by David Como has demonstrated how early Overton was engaged in underground printing and his connections with other future Levellers.[19] Como's close analysis of the type used in various radical pamphlets at the start of the 1640s has managed to significantly revise the history of the 'Cloppenburg Press'. This secret press, producing unlicensed and therefore illegal material, was first thought to have been based in the Netherlands. But Como has shown that it was based in London and that Richard Overton, in partnership with Peter Cole, was likely its owner.

In 1640 a series of pamphlets began to roll off the Cloppenburg Press. Some were the official propaganda of the Scottish Covenanters, others were books of well-known English 'Puritan martyrs' and lesser-known Puritan radicals. Among the material produced was *A Copy of a Letter Written by John Lilburne*. Another of the pamphlets was a reprint of one of the late sixteenth-century Marprelate Tracts.[20] In 1641 Richard Overton was already appropriating the Martin Marprelate persona, the pseudonym used for anti-episcopal tracts in the late 1580s, for his own use in the tract signed Margery Marprelate.[21] But more definite proof of Overton's involvement comes from the records of the Stationers' Company, soon urged by the authorities to close down the press producing these pamphlets. The records of the company show that they seized the press and that it was 'taken at Bell alley over against Finsbury'. Nearly two years later they returned it to Peter Cole and 'the owner thereof', Richard Overton.[22] Overton and Cole parted company at some point in 1644. But Cole was printing Henry Marten's *The Independency of England* in 1648.[23]

What is important here is not just the involvement and contact between the future Leveller leaders. Equally important is the level of political organisation that was necessary to sustain a secret press. Como notes that

someone had to secure the press and letter, a location (or locations) needed to be found, copyists, compositors and printers identified, editorial decisions made, material secured, and a distribution network established; moreover, it is difficult to imagine a complex operation of this nature existing without some collusion from sympathetic fellow-travellers, whose silence, if not participation, would have been necessary to protect the press.[24]

Samuel Chidley recalled the close involvement that he and John Lilburne had in the process of illegal printing. He remembered being 'out of purse' through paying printers. And he records his and Lilburne's battles with one particular printer who insisted on 'foysting in his own tedious stuffe' and 'whimes of his owne braine' into the text. This 'mad stuffe' would make 'honest Liburne very much vexe . . . and he would put it out again'. Chidley recalls that he would never pay out money 'contrary to the order of those who instructed me'. His whole account is permeated with a sense of organised politics. Even when he disagreed with the title of one Leveller petition, because it described the Commons as the 'Supreame Authority' at a time when the Commons were acknowledging the king and the Lords, he still defended the petition to the Commons from 'the latter end of the title to the end of the petition'.[25]

Richard Overton was not alone in being an early printer of illegal pamphlets who went on to become a mainstay of Leveller organisation. William Larner was much more than the printer of both John Lilburne's and Katherine Chidley's early pamphlets. He stands at the centre of the network that connects the radicals of the gathered churches with the early popular mobilisations of the Revolution and the secret presses producing illegal pamphlets, petitions and broadsheets. In a long printing career he remained loyal to the Levellers and, even after their defeat, to what became known as 'the Good Old Cause'. Like Lilburne, Thomas Lambe and the Chidleys, Larner was not a Londoner. He was born to a father of the same name in Little Rissington, Gloucestershire. Larner left his parents and arrived in London in 1630, about the same time as Lilburne and the Chidleys. He was first apprenticed to the Merchant Taylors' Company. In 1633, however, he transferred his apprenticeship to a London stationer, beginning a lifelong career as a printer and bookseller.[26]

William Larner was deeply involved in printing and selling tracts for separatist churches. William Kiffin, a leader of the gathered churches, provided an introduction for Lilburne's *Christian Man's Triall*, printed by Larner, in 1641. In the same year Kiffin also provided an introduction to Thomas Goodwin's *A Glimpse of Sion's Glory*, again printed by Larner. Kiffin was himself printed by Larner the following year. Larner also printed radical preacher Hanserd Knollys.[27] But more than this, Larner's press was, from the earliest days of the Revolution, intimately involved in printing directly political petitions and broadsides with the specific aim of mobilising popular protest. We have seen the first fruit of this at the time when Lilburne was at the forefront of mass protests in Westminster in 1641, when Larner printed the apprentices' eulogy to Sir Richard Wiseman. In the same year he printed a one-page appeal to the Commons that was specifically designed 'for the use of Petitioners who are to meet this present day in More Fields, and from thence to go to the house of Parliament with it in their hands'. This, as we have seen, called for the Lords to be dissolved into the Commons, creating a single-chamber parliament which would 'sit and Vote as one intire body', and was issued in the name of 'many thousand poore people' who are 'of the meanest rank and quality, being touched by penury'. And in 1642 it was again Larner distributing a petition against a 'bloody designe in hand, against the well affected of the Kingdome, under the names of Puritans and Brownists'. This clearly formed part of the agitation of the 'war party' at this time against more conservative forces in the parliamentary camp.[28] This, then, is an early appearance of calls for mobilisation and of democratic themes that later become a staple of Leveller agitation.[29]

Larner's career also provides us with a link to another, vital, emerging constituency for radical, later Leveller, activity: the army. Larner joined Lord Robartes's regiment in the First Civil War. He served as a sutler, or civilian supplier in the field. This regiment fought at both Edgehill and Brentford, as did John Lilburne, and at the first battle of Newbury in 1643 where Larner's fellow future Leveller, Thomas Prince, was injured and invalided out of the army. Larner, too, left the army at some point before 1645 as a result of illness, possibly the typhus that decimated his regiment in 1643. The regiment still owed Larner the considerable amount of over forty-six pounds at the time of his later arrest in 1646. Back in London, Larner was at the heart of the new pamphlet wars between the Presbyterians and the Independents, centrally involving future Levellers. He was imprisoned in 1647 for presenting a Leveller petition in favour of the *Agreement of the People*, was briefly reimprisoned in August 1648 and released again, and faced yet another warrant for his arrest in April 1649 as the final crackdown on the Levellers was beginning.[30]

Larner's career after the defeat of the Levellers in 1649 demonstrates a sustained loyalty to the radical ideas he had done so much to pioneer during the Revolution. He and his wife were ordered to answer charges before the Council of State in 1653. This is unsurprising given that he was still printing a remarkable stream of radical pamphlets in the 1650s. The pamphlet output shows not just Larner's continuing willingness to propagate radical ideas but also the persistence of radical networks established during the preceding decade. In 1650 Larner printed *The Light and Dark Sides of God* by Ranter Jacob Bothumley and is most likely the 'W.L.' who printed Digger Gerrard Winstanley's *England's Spirit Unfolded*. He was one of those named as a seller of *The Beacons Quenched*, a wholesale attack on Presbyterianism, in 1652. Among the tract's six authors were Colonel Thomas Pride and Larner's old associate William Kiffin. The printer was another old Leveller and an early Lilburne associate, Henry Hills. The following year, again in association with Hills, he was back in the territory of radical religion with *Baby-Baptism meer Babism*. In 1656 Larner printed a pamphlet called *The Relief of the Poore*, demanding action by the government to remedy the condition of destitute former soldiers. In the same year, once again with Henry Hills as the printer, he was selling *Absolute Freedom from Sin by Christs Death* written by Leveller stalwart Thomas Lambe. As late as 1660 he was publishing work by Muggletonian mystic Lawrence Clarkson.[31] Larner's life carries us from the very earliest associations of the gathered churches and illegal printing through to the aftermath of defeat. Even more than Thomas Lambe, and like Samuel and Katherine Chidley, he sustained a central organisational commitment over more than two decades.

These accounts of the working of the secret presses are a direct challenge to some conclusions of revisionist writing because they demonstrate that in London an organised and ideologically motivated group of activists were illegally seeking, sometimes alongside the Scots, sometimes alone, to promote parliamentary authority over royal authoritarianism and the replacement of the Church of England with a regime of gathered voluntary churches. Moreover, they illustrate the early emergence of a proto-Leveller network, the continuity of personnel, tactics and political approach.[32] At the same time that Larner was in contact with future Levellers Richard Overton and John Lilburne and other radical figures, he was also printing work by Katherine Chidley.[33] Another future Leveller printer, Thomas Paine, printed the first edition of John Milton's *The Doctrine and Discipline of Divorce* in 1643.[34] The second edition, to which Milton put his name, was printed by Gregory Dexter, who had already produced a pamphlet for Larner in 1641.[35] Larner was already known to William Walwyn and printed his work. It was John Lilburne who originally arranged future Leveller Henry Hills's apprenticeship in the printing trade in 1642, drawing him away from his previous calling as a postilion for future Regicide Thomas Harrison. Hills was at first apprenticed to Thomas Paine. Harrison later made Hills printer to the army.[36] And Hills's co-printer at the army press was John Harris, who edited the most radical of the Leveller news-heets, *Mercurius Militaris*, in 1648.[37]

Much would change in the ensuing decade. The allies of 1640–1 would fall away and some, like Prynne and Bastwick, would become enemies. New allies from the gathered churches and the army would replace them. Ideology was sharpened by further thought and by the impact of events. Organisation became more extensive. But an irreducible core of the organisation from the early 1640s, much of it revolving around the production of printed material, remained through the peak of Leveller influence late in the decade.

Spreading the word

The writers of pamphlets and their printers and booksellers are not easy to identify, but the wider networks of distribution are even more difficult to re-create. From the glimpses that we do catch, it can be seen that these networks organised around the distribution of printed material were far wider than those established around the actual printing of the material itself. Samuel Chidley said that 'if a man print an Impression of fifteen hundred books, peradventure they be spread to 15000. persons, and leven them all'.[38]

We know that some printed material was simply scattered in the streets. On the night of 8–9 December 1644, the Overton printed broadsheet *Alas Pore Parliament how Art thou Betrai'd?* was posted in the streets at night.[39] Women street sellers of pamphlets were widespread. The Stationers' Company petition of 1643 complained of 'the shamefull custome of selling Pamphlets by Sempsters [seamtresses], &c. and dispersing them in the streets by Emissaries of such base condition'.[40] Broadsheets could be bought for a penny, and an eight-page pamphlet for a penny or twopence, approximately the price of a drink.[41] Thomas Edwards was particularly alarmed that one of Overton's anti-Presbyterian pamphlets had proved so popular that it was turned into a two-part printed ballad to be sung to the tune of 'the merry Souldier, or the joviall Tinker'.[42] These were not methods of distribution found only in London: even early Cloppenburg pamphlets were found as far afield as Cambridge, Hertfordshire, Sussex and Northamptonshire.[43]

Pamphlets were sold in the bookshops and bookstalls, the greatest concentrations of which were around St Pauls. The most detailed picture of this trade in respect of Leveller pamphlets comes from the House of Lords examinations of Giles Calvert, Henry Cripps and William Larner concerning the sale of the pamphlet *The Last Warning to All the Inhabitants of London*, which the Lords thought printed by Overton.[44] Under examination by Thomas Atkins, the lord mayor, it emerged that Overton had sold 100 copies of this pamphlet to both Giles Calvert and Henry Cripps at his shop in Pope's Head Alley. Larner refused to say where he had got his copies when they were seized at his 'dwelling at The Blackimore, in Bishoppsgate Streete'. A third party present at the examination did, however, volunteer that more copies of *The Last Warning* had been 'seized upon in the Shop of one Woodnett, living in Cornhill; who confessed that he received them from the said William Lerner'.[45] That was enough to see Larner imprisoned. Overton printed the tracts in his defence.

A core of Leveller activists remained engaged in writing, printing and distributing material throughout the 1640s. Lilburne, Overton, Walwyn, Larner, Prince, the Chidleys and those who worked with and around them sustained the production of revolutionary publications in illegal conditions for a decade. They were hunted, prosecuted and imprisoned throughout. They printed everything from single-sheet petitions and leaflets to substantial books and, eventually, weekly newspapers. They organised distribution by giving away material in the street and at political gatherings; by selling it in bookshops, on stalls and in the street; by having it passed from hand to hand in the army; or by sending in packages around the country. If this is all they had done it would have been a remarkable feat of sustained organisation.

This core of activists drew around themselves very substantially greater numbers. Printed material was essential to communicating ideas to and organising these forces. And in the process the core of writers, printers and those involved in the organisation grew. But none of this happened outside a wider balance of forces, especially those within the parliamentary camp itself. The course of defining Leveller ideas and organisation can be seen as a process of coming to terms with a series of crises among parliamentarians: the split between, for the sake of simplicity, the Presbyterians and the Independents, the division between the Silken Independents and the Agitators and London Levellers at Putney and after, the final reformation of the Independent–Leveller alliance that prevented the Personal Treaty with the king. In each of these crises it was the Levellers' ability to define the political tasks in print and to use printed material to organise their followers that made them able to play a significant part in shaping the eventual outcome of the English Revolution.

CHAPTER 5

Civil War

The king never came so close to regaining his capital as he did in late 1642. The first major battle of the Civil War at Edgehill had proved indecisive. But it had cleared the way for the royalists to move on London. In the aftermath of the battle the earl of Essex, Parliament's commander, returned to London to replenish a battered army. Edgehill polarised the parliamentary camp. For some it reinforced the idea that the king could only be negotiated with from a position of strength and therefore it hardened their resolve. For others the inconclusive nature of the clash highlighted the fact that the war might well be lengthy, costly and disruptive to trade and stable government. Seized by such premonitions a peace party formed which was determined to find a speedily negotiated settlement with Charles. In the meantime the king moved his army towards the capital, reaching the edge of the city by November. Here, at Brentford and Turnham Green, the fate of the city was to be decided. In this battle John Lilburne played a role as decisive as any single soldier.

John Lilburne goes to war

Lilburne enlisted to fight as soon as war broke out, taking up 'Arms in Judgement and Conscience against the King'.[1] He became a captain in Lord Robert Brooke's purple-coated regiment and marched with it to Edgehill, where both he and the regiment distinguished themselves. Elizabeth Lilburne went to war with John and may have been with the baggage train at Edgehill when it was plundered by Prince Rupert's cavalry. John Lilburne's belongings were certainly lost in that raid.[2]

In dispatches it was reported that Lilburne had fought with such 'valour at the batell of Kenton', as Edgehill was also known, that the City's Militia Committee had issued an order for him to raise a troop of horse. This order was issued the very day that the king began to advance on London. But Lord Brooke himself begged Lilburne not to act on the commission. Brooke had only two days since made a speech at the Guildhall calling on Londoners to march out and face the king's army. Meeting Lilburne at Essex's house in the Strand he told him that the king was advancing on the capital and that 'we shall speedily have another fight with him, and therefore I intreat thee doe not leave me, and my Regiment now'.[3] Brooke continued to persuade Lilburne by telling him that if he did not stay with the regiment he might think that Lilburne had become 'covetous' and that he would 'have a troop of horse for a little more pay' or that he had 'turned Coward' because he was leaving his foot company 'now when we are going to fight'. Brooke must have known his man, for nothing was so likely to elicit a positive response from Lilburne as a simultaneous appeal to his high moral sense and his bravery. Lilburne told Brooke that he was 'as free from covertousness or cowardlinesse as yourselfe'. He got straight on his horse and rode to Brentford, then a single street of shops and houses, arriving at nine that evening.[4]

That night, 11 November 1642, a heavy mist hung along the banks of the Thames west of London. And as Lilburne rode west Prince Rupert brought a sizable detachment of the king's army in a 'close and still march' through the night to the outskirts of Brentford where Denzil Holles's regiment of redcoats were stationed.[5] The regiment, like Brooke's, had been one of the most stalwart at Edgehill. William Eyre, a figure central to the development of the Levellers, had, like Lilburne, fought at Edgehill. He was a seargent in Holles's redcoats and when his officers deserted in the middle of the battle and the soldiers began to retreat Eyre 'ran beyond them, telling them I would die before them, if they would not face about'. When the deserters told him they had no one to lead them, Eyre volunteered and led them back to the fight, making 'Officers of their file leaders'. Now, at Brentford, Eyre was leading the 'forlorn hope' of skirmishers as the royalists attacked. Rupert's forces arrived undetected and emerged from the morning mist of 12 November to attack with considerable ferocity. The redcoats were outnumbered but their defence was 'vigorous and obstinate', despite being low on ammunition. Eyre was in the thick of the fighting all day.[6]

Holles's regiment were forced back into Brentford, sustaining more heavy losses. Lilburne heard the alarm in the morning but found that a large part of Brooke's regiment had, without their officers, started marching off the battlefield and back to London. Lilburne then took action that played a considerable role in salvaging the parliamentary cause that day:

> I galloped after them, and put them to a stand, at the head of whom I made the best incouraging speech I could and tooke those Colours that were mine into mine owne hands and desired all those that had the spirits of men, and the gallantry of Souldiers, and willing resolutely to spend their bloud for their Country, and to preserve the honour that they had lately gained at Kenton battell, to follow mee.[7]

Lilburne 'promised not to leave them, so long as I was able to fight with them'. The speech hit its mark: 'they all faced about without any more dispute, and I led them up to the field where their fellow Souldiers the Red Coates were, which ground with them we maintained divers hours together in a bloudy fight'.[8]

It was indeed a bloody fight. Lilburne estimates that the parliamentary forces numbered no more than 700 and were short of match, powder and bullets. They had to ransack the houses around them to supply themselves. They fought without trenches or breastworks, taking what cover they could behind houses, walls and the hedges. The fighting was, Lilburne recalled, 'to the sword point' and 'the butt end of our Musquets'. It was an exaggeration that they fought, as Lilburne claimed, 'the Kings whole Armie', but they were bearing the brunt of the whole of Rupert's advance guard of perhaps 4,500 infantry and cavalry with the rest of the king's forces advancing towards their position. Certainly they endured musket and cannon fire on their flanks as well as a frontal assault.

Lilburne's action prevented a breakthrough that might, at least, have resulted in the loss of the parliamentary artillery train then guarded by a mere seventy-five soldiers at Hammersmith. It was not a boast for Lilburne to claim that 'I dare say of that peece of service, that Parliament and the Citie, and the whole Kingdome, owes not more to any one particular number of Commanders and Souldiers . . . then they doe to my selfe and the rest that was in that at Branford'.[9] Hampden's greencoats came up late in the battle and only in time to cover the retreat of their comrades. By the time they had arrived, Rupert's troops had ransacked and pillaged Brentford, taking from the residents 'all that ever they had'. Brentford suffered and so did Lilburne. As his regiment was forced to retreat many of the troops around him were forced back to the river and drowned, a fate that Lilburne just managed to escape. But though he escaped death he did not escape capture. He was taken prisoner and transported to Oxford jail.[10]

While Lilburne was on his way to prison, the news of the surprise of Brentford reached MPs in the Commons, even then debating the king's peace proposals, and the earl of Essex as he sat in the Lords. Overnight a mass mobilisation of the London populace, led by the Trained Bands, turned imminent defeat into a parliamentary victory. Londoners had plenty to fear if the king's victory in Brentford were to be translated into a triumphant attack on London. The reputation of Rupert's troops as sackers and looters of anything they could conquer was already well established. 'The terror of Rupert's name did far more to quicken the ardour of the City than the eloquence of the members of Parliament', wrote S. R. Gardiner in his timeless account of the Civil War.[11] It was at this moment that John Milton wrote a verse that he imagined being pinned to the door of his house in Aldersgate Street:

> Captain or Colonel, or knight in arms,
> Whose chance on these defenceless doors may seize,
> If deed of honour thee did ever please,
> Guard them, and him within and protect from harms.[12]

The MP Dudley North thought these fears were artificially exaggerated and 'yet they were some way tending to the great design of raising the terror to a height, and putting the arms into the hands of Schismatical people under the name of volunteers'. The volunteers certainly did come. The remains of the Essex army in London were joined by fresh levies and by the Trained Bands under the command of the experienced Philip Skippon. All night the roads leading west to the rendezvous at Turnham Green were packed with armed men and their supporters. When day broke on 13 November some 24,000 parliamentary troops stood arrayed in battle order between the king and the capital. After a tense stand-off, some cannon fire was exchanged but there was no more fighting that day. The parliamentary forces outnumbered the king's by two to one. The odds were simply too daunting for Charles to attempt to capitalise on the advantage gained at Brentford. This impressive emergency mobilisation blocked any attempt on the capital but it was not a disciplined enough force to go on the offensive. Twice the politicians in attendance, including John Hampden, recommended moving to the attack and twice the professional soldiers countermanded the order. Some in the ranks felt the same way as the politicians. According to MP Walter Yonge they 'were full of courage and sange psalms all day; and did even weepe because they could not fall on'. Thus the king's army slipped away westward. As the Londoners stood guard, five miles to their backs, their relatives and friends, wives, daughters and apprentices poured out of the Sunday sermons and brought their dinners and other food to the Guildhall, where it was loaded on some 100 wagons and taken to the front line. There was bread and cheese, 'meate, baked, bouled and roasted', 'Pyes pyping hot', beer and hogsheads of sack and burnt claret to ensure the defenders were 'made merry; and the more so when they understood the king and all his army were retreated'.[13]

The political effect of the retreat was, back in Westminster, to put even greater distance between the emerging peace party and the war party. The king had ordered the attack on Brentford at exactly the same moment that he was entertaining parliamentary overtures for a treaty. Rupert's sacking of the town offered a very visceral account of what might happen if the royalists were victorious. All this was grist to the war party's mill. Speaking of Parliament's most determined supporters, Clarendon said that the popular mobilisation to defend the city had 'extremely puffed them up'. But the great fear that had seized London also had a contrary effect. Merchants feared for trade and there was, diarist John Evelyn recorded, 'greate consternation in the City' that the king might occupy London. As Gardiner observes, 'to the wealthy merchant and the wealthy landowner the prospect of a long interruption of commerce, of plunderings in town and country, was appalling'. In addition, Denzil Holles's political trajectory seems to have been permanently altered by the events. His redcoats had been badly mauled at Edgehill and were effectively destroyed at Brentford. The regiment never again appeared on parliamentary order of battle after Brentford. Holles himself, one of the original five members whom the king had charged with treason only months earlier, from this point on became an unstinting advocate of a compromise peace.[14]

Honest John in the court of the cavaliers

John Lilburne's first imprisonment under Charles's regime had been brutal. His second imprisonment in Oxford was not less so. And this time he was brought to trial for his life. Lilburne's jailer, the king's provost Marshall Smith, was a zealot who seems to have taken a particular pleasure in humiliating prisoners. Lilburne was kept in wrist and ankle irons, denied food, robbed and abused as a 'Roundhead' and 'parliament-dog'. Prisoners were tied together at the ankle and the neck. But even under these conditions Lilburne's powers of persuasion did not fail him. Smith thought any 'timorous Prisoner' that might convert to the royalist cause should be 'got way from Lilburne for if he comes to discourse with him he will seduce him from . . . taking the King's Covenant'.[15]

One small consolation for Lilburne was to be found in the company of some notable fellow radicals among the prisoners. One of these Lilburne could be forgiven for not welcoming. Edmund Chillenden had been the very turncoat who had betrayed him to the bishop's men when he was first arrested. Yet Lilburne made common cause with Chillenden and lent him money to save him from starvation, although he complained later that the debt was never fully repaid.[16] After the fall of Marlborough in early December Lilburne was joined by prisoners taken by the royalists after the battle. The town's MP, John Franklin, was one of them. Another was radical and future Ranter Francis Freeman, who had already spent time in jail for refusing to collect ship money. Freeman had commanded a company in the battle at his home town and was described by royalist Lady Seymour as a traitor to the king whom she would see hanged at his own door. 'There is not', she added, 'such a rogue in the country'. For good measure Lord Seymour told the magistrates of Marlborough that if they got their hands on Freeman 'they should bring him to Oxford, dead or alive, or else they must expect no favour from his Majesty'. In fact the Marlborough prisoners had been marched without food to Oxford in leg irons. When some stopped to drink they were struck in the face by their drivers. On one occasion during their imprisonment Smith brought them down to the prison yard to be harangued by the king's advocate, Dr Beeves, who tried to intimidate them into signing the Royalist Wiltshire Protestation. The prisoners refused, claiming their rights as citizens. Smith responded by calling out, 'Hark ye I hark ye! thy axe a preaching!' When the prisoners complained of starvation Beeves put on his spectacles and said, 'Why, ye are all as fat as conies'. Francis Freeman was singled out to be bound 'at the neeke and heales . . . for not taking the Protestation'. Lilburne himself became so ill that all his hair fell out.[17]

Lilburne was quick to protest at these conditions. Through the efforts of a parliamentary intelligencer in Oxford employed by the earl of Essex and Isaac Pennington, Lilburne smuggled a letter out and it was printed by supporters, as was the joint complaint he made with Francis Freeman, John Franklin and other prisoners.[18] But while the Marlborough prisoners were subjected to a lecture by Dr Beeves, Lilburne was treated to a higher level of royalist solicitation. No less than four royalist lords—Dunsmore, Maltravers, Kingston and Andover—tried 'to woo' Lilburne with 'large proffers of the honour and glory of Court preferment' if he would 'return to obedience'.[19] But Lilburne was having none of it: 'I was then knowingly ingaged . . . to make the people of England free and happy . . . and in whose quarrel I would them have laid down a thousand lives (if I had had them)'.[20]

If their Lordships thought they were in for a short discussion they did not know Lilburne. The argument continued for 'the greatest part of an hour'. The lords moved from bribery to threats, telling Lilburne he was on trial for his life as a traitor. He replied that he could not be since, under martial law, they had given him quarter when he was captured at Brentford. Frustrated in this argument the lords said, 'Well . . . we have two strings to our bow'. The royalists had not forgotten his part in the December Days. They told Lilburne, 'we will arraign you for a Traitor for being the chief or General of the Prentices that came down to Westminster and Whitehall and forced the House of Peers and drove away the King from his Parliament, and so begun the Warres'. Quick-witted as ever, Lilburne told them that this would not work either since he had already been acquitted on that charge in May 1641, while the king still sat in London. This left the lords calling down a pox on Lilburne as a 'cunning, subtle rogue', but it did not halt Lilburne's treason trial for being in arms against the king.[21]

Lilburne could not halt the proceedings, but he could delay them. He objected to the indictment on the basis that it described him as a 'yeoman' when in fact he was from a gentry family. This was the kind of objection that might appeal to Lord Justice Robert Heath and indeed Lilburne won his point and the charge was duly amended. Then the trial resumed its inevitable course. Lilburne attempted to deploy the widely held argument that he only took up arms against the king's evil counsellors. But that was never going to detain the prosecution for long.[22]

But then, as he was forced to answer his enemy, Lilburne found himself face to face not only with the earl of Northampton and Earl Rivers, but also with Prince Rupert himself. Northampton demanded whether Lilburne's conscience had yet convicted him of that crime by which he stood condemned in law. Lilburne asked by return 'whether the abuse of the law had convicted their consciences'. Rupert interrupted to ask what death he would choose, since being a soldier gave him that right. Lilburne 'demanded a sword telling them he desired to die in single opposition man to man with any there, or if they feared the trial, any two so he might die with honour'. Rupert ignored the challenge and asked if it were honourable that Lilburne had shed innocent blood. Lilburne asked Rupert 'if it were lawful to shed innocent blood by abuse of the law'. The exchange ended with the royalists concluding 'the fellow is mad' and sending Lilburne back to jail.[23] Lilburne had done all that could be done by delay, debate and procrastination. But in the end the inevitable verdict was pronounced: he was found guilty of treason and sentenced to death.

Lilburne was a high-profile prisoner, one of only three mentioned by name in a royalist account of events at Brentford. In his own letter from jail to London supporters he had already raised the question of asking Essex to get him freed in a prisoner exchange.[24] But it took the extraordinary efforts of Elizabeth Lilburne to set these wheels in motion. The wife of Lilburne's fellow prisoner, Captain Primrose, took a letter that Elizabeth addressed to the Speaker of the Commons. She lobbied 'daily and hourly' at the bar of the Commons to get the MPs to support her plea to save John Lilburne's life. With only two days before Lilburne's execution the Commons agreed that if Lilburne were executed 'the like Punishment shall be inflicted by Death or otherwise upon such Prisoners as have been or shall be taken by the Forces raised by both Houses of Parliament'.[25]

But for this threat to have effect the news of the decision had to reach Oxford—and so Elizabeth herself, though heavily pregnant, took to the road. Passing through checkpoints of friend and foe she made a journey that few had even attempted. She arrived just in the nick of time and saved her husband's life, handing a letter from the Commons directly to Judge Heath. Much as Heath resented it, Lilburne was indeed later exchanged for royalist prisoners. After months in the Oxford jail Lilburne returned to London to receive, for the second time, a hero's welcome from the well affected of the capital. Even Clarendon had heard that he was greeted 'with public joy, as a champion that had defied the King in his own court'.[26]

Lilburne already had a reputation as Puritan martyr, a radical pamphleteer, and a leader of street protests long before he fought at Brentford. To these achievements he now added those of a courageous leader of troops and a man who had faced down the chief royalists in the heart of their new capital. He was, as he said, exchanged well above his social station. The earl of Essex gave him £300 for his troubles, but politically he was more aligned with Cromwell and the emerging war party. As soon as he was free he joined Cromwell, 'having some invitation to goe downe to Lieu. Gen. Cromwell (my old friend that got me my libertie from the Bishops Captivitie)'.[27]

Henry Marten, William Walwyn and the Committee for the General Rising

In the aftermath of Turnham Green the campaign for peace with the king grew to new heights. It lasted into the autumn of the following year, 1643, framing all other political developments. The peace party were dominant in the Commons from late November 1642 until February 1643. The Treaty of Oxford, a series of negotiations between the king and Parliament, lasted from the beginning of February until mid-April. But the agitation for a settlement did not end with the treaty, persisting through the summer. And all through this period Parliament was losing battles and territory to the royalists, most notably at Adwalton Moor, Roundway Down and in the surrender of the second city, Bristol.[28]

The City throughout this time was alive with petitions and protests both for and against the war. In early December 1642 radicals Hugh Peter, Captain Randall Mainwaring, preacher John Goodwin and others demanded 'a more speedy and effectuall prosecution of the Warres', including by means of 'seizing and securing malignant persons and estates'. The Commons told them it would not consider the petition without the support of the City. Lord Mayor Isaac Pennington tried to get the petition adopted by the Common Council but it was voted down. On 7 December another petition specifically proclaimed that it was designed to counter this petition which it belittled as 'by some few Inhabitants of London not exceeding the number of a Hundred, against an Accommodation for Peace'. As the peace petitioners were gathering support it was seized from them under a warrant from the lord mayor and one of their number was imprisoned. The next day when a group of the petitioners gathered in protest outside the Guildhall it was broken up by a troop of cavalry, swords drawn.[29]

When the peace petitioners returned on 12 December to try to convince the City aldermen and the Common Council to support the petition, some twenty soldiers, again with drawn swords, rushed at them inside the Guildhall, crying, 'Let us destroy these Malignant Doggs that would have PEACE, let us cut the throats of these Papist rogues'. The petitioners managed to disarm the soldiers and then closed the Guildhall doors against other soldiers outside. A troop of horse, swords and pistols in hand, then unsuccessfully tried to force the door. One of the petitioners was shot in the face through the keyhole of the door. Other petitioners outside the hall were attacked by the troopers. The petitioners were besieged for hours, and though they called out to the mayor and aldermen for help 'a strange deafenesse possessed them, and the Petitioners remained remedylesse'. Meanwhile the soldiers outside brought up two cannon. The petitioners fled up to the Common Council chamber and forced their way in. They were then told they could leave in safety. But once outside they were 'pursued . . . with drawne Swords, and bitter execrations, many of the rude multitude taking advantage, did kicke, beate, reproach, and inhumanely abuse them, crying out, *hang them, cut their throates*'. One of the petitioners had to flee to the roof of a house and only escaped by 'leaping from one house top to another'.[30] Two days later it was reported that there were 5,000 peace protestors at Westminster.[31] By 17 December the Common Council had agreed a peace proposal to be put to the king. Two days later Parliament endorsed it and messengers were sent to the king at Oxford. The peace party had won a victory.

In early January 1643 the king replied and, not for the first or last time, his response was more useful to the war party than to those closest to him. As 4,000 peace protestors marched from Covent Garden to Westminster, the king complained of those who had raised tumults against him and driven him from London, and accused Pennington, Mainwaring, John Venn and John Fowke of high treason.[32] The war party's response was unbending. The king's answer was read in the Common Hall, where it was met with loud cries from the crowd that they would 'live and die' with the accused Londoners. Parliament set up a 'Committee for the Vindication of the Parliament from the Aspersions thrown on them in the King's Answer to the London Petition'. Its members from the Commons were a roll call of the war party: Pym, Hampden, Ludlow, Vane and John Franklin, now free from the king's jail he had shared with Lilburne. In addition Henry Marten and his ally Peter Wentworth were members.[33] By 15 January Mainwaring was leading soldiers on raids of delinquents avoiding requisition and the City's Militia Committee were empowered to disarm all those who would not pay money towards the war effort. The war party had begun to fight back.

Two figures central to future Leveller organisation were active in the campaign to defeat the peace party, William Walwyn and Henry Marten. In his social and economic background William Walwyn was typical of London revolutionaries in the 1640s. He was the second son of a country gentleman apprenticed into trade. Born in Newland in Worcestershire in 1600 he came to London to learn silk weaving in the house of his master in Paternoster Row. He married Anne Gundell when he completed his apprenticeship in 1627 and lived in her father's house in Thames Street. He was father to, by his own account, some twenty children, although many died in infancy. Nevertheless it was a happy marriage blighted only by his wife's regular illness. Walwyn was a success in his trade, becoming a master weaver and merchant and, by 1632, a member of the Merchant Adventurers' Company. He lived 'in a middle and moderate but contentful condition', recorded a contemporary.[34] In the fateful year of 1643 the Walwyn family moved to Moorfields, just outside the city walls.

Walwyn was older than most of the Leveller leaders and more contemplative by nature. 'The most of my recreation' he wrote, 'being a good Book, or an honest and discoursing friend'. He did not have an Oxford education like his elder brother and neither did he have a very high opinion of the teachers he did have. But he read voraciously and had an autodidact's veneration for self-enlightenment. He was not, like many Levellers, a member of a dissenting church but a believer in a more fundamental Christian sense of love. Walwyn would walk between church meetings looking for the most interesting preacher. This approach gave him an extensive network of contacts across the gathered churches which he was able to use in his political projects. Walwyn was a radical tolerationist, bordering on deist rationalism. There was no injunction ever 'given by Christ or his Apostles for the extirpation of the Romans or any others that denied our God', he wrote. Jesus used 'no other meanes but argument and persuasion to alter or controle'. He carried this belief in the power of argument over into his political practice. When the Presbyterian heresy-hunter Thomas Edwards was railing against Walwyn his reply had the brilliantly understated title *A Whisper in the Eare of Mr. Thomas Edwards*. Indeed, just to read the titles of Walwyn's pamphlets is to have some measure of his approach: *The Power of Love, Good Counsell to All, Toleration Justified, A Word in Season, A Still and Soft Voice from the Scriptures*. But we should not conclude from this that Walwyn was not as resolute or as determined as other Levellers.

Before the Long Parliament met, Walwyn described himself as 'sensible to the oppressions of the times' but in such 'great uncertainty' and 'affliction of the mind' that he 'tooke not boldnesse to judge . . . things morall, politque and religious'. But study of the Scriptures 'void of any glosse' gave him confidence to engage politically 'in a more publick way then formally'. He was first active at parish level, where he 'moved for reformation' in the running of the church that was previously 'quite out of order'. His next moves were 'for the whole ward, wherein after much labour, we so prevailed, that the well affected carried the choice of Aldermen and common-coun-cell men and all other officers of the Ward'. Walwyn was among those petitioning against peace party critics of the Militia Committee in March 1642. Walwyn's pamphlet later in the year had a typically pacific title, *Some Considerations Tending to the Undeceiving of Those, Whose Judgements are Misinformed*. But its message to the peace party was uncompromising:

> Another villainous worke they have in hand, is to take away our courages and dull our resolutions by commending peace unto us, when we are neces-sitated to take up our Swords; what fooles they imagine us to be, as if we did not know what were the sweets of peace, but them it must be accompanied with liberty.

In an unjust peace, Walwyn argued, the bondsman is still in chains and the prisoner still in his dungeon. 'I thinke no man can bee heartily in love with such kinde of peace', and until these liberties are attained, says Walwyn, 'our swords are drawn for them, and so long as they are violated, what peace? what peace?' Against the 'sweet words and smooth faces' of the peace party Walwyn both worked on the Salters' Hall committee and backed the revolutionaries' petition that established the Committee for the General Rising. And here his path crossed that of Henry Marten.[35]

Henry Marten was one of the most astounding, attractive and humane of the seventeenth century's revolutionaries.[36] Born in Oxford, his father, also Henry Marten, was first-generation gentry. Marten himself graduated from Oxford, and inherited the family estates in Berkshire. He was returned from there to both the Short and Long Parliaments. When he inherited, 'the whole county of Berkshire rang with the festivities of the Vale of the White Horse; and his personal courtesies to all classes of men gave him unprecedented popularity there'. What is politically astounding is that he stepped onto the political stage of the 1640s as a fully convinced republi-can. That was practically unique, certainly among MPs.[37]

Edward Hyde, long before he became either the king's most senior adviser or was ennobled as the earl of Clarendon, moved in the same parliamentary circles as Marten. We can still sense the shock Hyde felt at an exchange he had with Marten when walking from the Commons one day before the war began. Marten told him he 'would undo himself by adhering to the court'. When Hyde asked Marten what his thoughts were about the Parliament and the king he was told, 'I do not think one man wise enough to govern us all'. This was, remembered Hyde, 'the first word he had ever heard any man speak to that purpose'. He was to hear many more such words in the years to follow, but he may well have been right that in 1641 'if it had been then communicated' it would have been 'abhorred by the whole nation'.[38]

It was, as Marten later noted, not the personality of the king he opposed, but the office. Yet the significance of Marten's view was not lost on the monarch. The king knew an enemy when he saw one. Coming across Marten in Hyde Park, where he was attending a horse race, he said, loud enough for Marten to hear, 'let that ugly rascal be gone out of the park, that whoremaster, or I will not see the sport'. John Aubrey, the Wiltshire antiquarian and contemporary of Marten, thought that the king's remark that day 'raised the whole county of Berkshire against him' when war was declared.[39]

Marten held the governorship of Reading when war broke out and set about raising his own regiment of cavalry. After attempting to defend the garrison with a force of dragoons, Marten had to abandon Reading as the king advanced on London in 1642. When it was advised by some that the king should remove himself from the military struggle 'for the preservation of his person', Marten scandalised the royalists by insisting 'that if the King would not withdraw, but put his finger to be cut, they could not helpe it; what was it to them?'[40] Marten argued that the king owed the nation protection and if he should 'desert us' why should the Commons continue to 'defend the kinges person?'[41] He thought that 'if the King should take the advice of his gun-smiths and powdermen he would never have peace'. When the king offered a general pardon to the members of the Lords and Commons he specifically excluded only eighteen members of both Houses from the roll call. Marten was one of them, alongside Pym, Hampden, Pennington, Venn and Strode.[42] In fact Charles paid Marten the compliment of excepting him from pardon on an additional two occasions. By 1643 Marten was, alongside other leaders of the war party, the regular target of royalist broadsheets and satiric verses.[43]

But it was not simply that Marten was a republican. He was also a constant champion of plebeian mobilisation in defence of parliamentary sovereignty. He was, wrote Aubrey, not only a great cultivator of justice, but also 'did always in the house take the part of the oppressed'.[44] Sir John Maynard accused Marten of 'bringing in the democraticall eliment' and putting himself 'at the head of the skumme of the people'.[45]

As an MP Marten operated with a constituency and allies different to any other Leveller, but he was of their movement. He had known Lilburne since he sat on the Commons committee to settle reparations for his Star Chamber imprisonment. It was to Marten that Lilburne turned when he needed help right up to his exile in the 1650s. He thought Marten the 'best friend' the Levellers had. Marten was on even closer political and personal terms with another Leveller leader, John Wildman, to whom he sold part of his estate when debt caught up with him after the war. And Leveller William Eyre was both a Berkshire neighbour and Marten's confederate in raising a regiment in the Second Civil War. Indeed in the secret code found in Henry Marten's papers the individuals listed fall into two categories. The first were prominent individuals: the king and army leaders like Cromwell, Ireton and Fairfax. Of the others only Colonel Overton is not a Leveller supporter. The rest are all Levellers: Marten himself (code letter O); John Wildman (A); William Walwyn (B); 'Petter', presumably Maximillian Pettus or Petty (E); Thomas Rainsborough (W); and William Eyre (AA). Indeed, Marten may well have been one of the authors of the Levellers' manifestos.[46]

Marten's politics were not the only thing that marked him out. So did his personality. John Aubrey recalled him as 'not at all covetous; humble, not at all arrogant, as most of them were'. He was a 'great lover of pretty girls' and Sir Edward Baynton, the Wiltshire MP and parliamentary soldier, thought 'his company was incomparable, but that he would be drunk too soon'. He certainly was no Puritan in the accepted sense. After the Revolution he was one of those who moved to repeal the banishment of the Jews from England and he was on principle opposed to the invasion of Ireland. Aubrey thought him 'as far from a Puritan as light is from darkness'. When a godly member of the Commons proposed that all profane and unsanctified persons should be put out of the House, Marten rose and proposed that if all the fools were put out as well it would be a thin House. Indeed Marten's wit was one of his best weapons, though it could also get him into trouble. His speeches in the House were 'not long, but wondrous poignant, pertinent and witty'. Marten was apt to catnap in the House and so Thomas Atkins, the City MP, proposed that all the 'Nodders' be expelled for not minding the business of the House. Marten was instantly on his feet to propose that the 'Noddees', the bores that sent them to sleep, should also be put out. When, at the height of the Revolution, the motion was proposed to abolish the House of Lords as 'useless and dangerous', Marten said it should read 'useless but not dangerous'. It was said that he would rather lose a friend than lose a joke. But in John Lilburne he had a friend that could take a joke. Marten commented on Lilburne's famously argumentative character, 'That if there were none living but himself, John *would be against* Lilburne, *and* Lilburne *against* John'. To honest John's credit he repeated the same joke against himself, and in print. Marten's enemies, as we shall see, were not so content to be skewered by his wit. Yet it was not personal insult they feared but political effect. The MP Dudley North recalled that in 1641 though the leaders of the House thought it 'unseasonable' to propose the Protestation oath requiring loyalty to the Protestant religion and to Parliament, Marten nevertheless moved it in the Commons and won the vote. Marten, said Aubrey, 'alone has sometimes turned the whole house'.[47]

What was the mood of Marten, Walwyn and their fellow radicals over the spring of 1643? The pamphlet *Remonstrans Redivivus* gives us some indication. The pamphlet, printed in July, recalled the campaign around the radical war party petition first issued in March. It called on the well affected to bear arms and make contributions towards the war effort. But more than this it insisted that 'the safety of the people is the Supreme Law', that 'originally Supreme power being in the whole people, Parliaments were by them constituted to manage the same for the preservation and well-being of the Commonwealth', and that the king was not necessary for Parliament to enact laws. These were mainstays of future Leveller thought and, at this time, only articulated in Parliament by Henry Marten and his few supporters. William Walwyn was one of the promoters of the March petition. He made it his 'public business' in 'a remonstrance of the Common Council, to move the Parliament to confirm certain infallible maxims of free Government: wherein the power of Parliament was plainly distinguished from the Kings Office'. *Remonstrans Redivivus* was printed by 'T.P. and M.S.', almost certainly Thomas Paine and Matthew Simmons. Thomas Paine would become a Leveller printer, especially of William Walwyn's pamphlets. He was already a printer of Milton and moving in same circles as, and known to, other future Levellers.[48] Henry Marten was certainly of one mind with the pamphlet's assertion of popular sovereignty. He had already told his fellow MPs that they 'ought to receive instructions for our proceedings from the people' when some objected to the activities of petitioners.[49]

The opposition to the peace party ran across a wide spectrum. Pym's 'middle group' of MPs and supporters of the earl of Essex were its moderate wing. Soon-to-be political Independents like Pennington and his supporters were radicals driving the war party. But more radical still were some of those allied to them, like Henry Marten and William Walwyn. In general this broad alliance held together until late 1643, but long before then tensions were emerging. The City was a radical stronghold after Pennington became mayor in August 1642. The Militia Committee was at the centre of operations. Its members, precisely those people who had authorised John Lilburne to raise his own troop of horse on the eve of the battle of Brentford, were some of Pennington's most active supporters: the merchants and brothers John and Samuel Warner, Thomas Atkin, Thomas Andrews and John Towse.[50] In March 1643 the more radical members established their own subcommittee within the Militia Committee in an attempt to gain greater control over the war effort. This sub-committee for volunteers met at the Salters' Hall in Bread Street. The Salters' Hall committee, as it became known, set itself the task of raising a 10,000-strong force to bolster the war effort by acting as auxiliaries to the Trained Bands.

William Walwyn was central to the work of this committee.[51] The Salters' Hall committee began to enlarge its remit. In early May it launched the 'Weekly Meal' initiative that asked citizens to donate the cost of one meal a week to the war effort. The broadsheet announcing the weekly meal aimed to set up local parish organisations for the collection of money on every Monday night, money then to be brought to the Salters' Hall every Wednesday.[52] A supportive pamphlet encouraged women to take a lead in the organisation of the project. It suggested that 'a few of the wisest of them here in London' should appoint 'some of their sex, fittest and most active in every parish', to 'carry this work through' and so 'ease the men of this labour'.[53]

The Salters' Hall committee now posed a threat to the more mainstream radical Militia Committee in two ways. It was raising money and an armed force under its own jurisdiction. And it was doing this not only in the City but in the more radical suburbs where the City's jurisdiction was contentious. On 7 June the Militia Committee sought a Common Council decision to reinforce its dominance. In response the Salters' Hall committee protested to the same Common Council that the Militia Committee should not be allowed to 'obtain a sole power'.[54] Weeks of wrangling only ended with a parliamentary ordinance in late July reinforcing the Militia Committee's claim to control all forces raised in the City and suburbs. In essence this moderate reassertion of control had only been possible by an alliance of the war party moderates and the peace party in the Commons.[55]

While Walwyn was about the business of the Salters' Hall committee, Henry Marten was conducting his own war party operations against royalists and peace party sympathisers in Parliament. Unfortunately, his ideological republicanism was shared by few and his militancy only by a minority. But he kept up an irregular political warfare designed to undermine the king's party, thwart moves for a compromise peace, promote the power of the Commons, and defend the actions of extra-parliamentary protestors.

Beyond Westminster, Marten was at the heart of Parliament's operations to 'seize and sequester' the estates of all those royalists who had taken up arms. A lengthy ordinance published on 30 March went into ten printed pages of detail itemising the 'Money, Goods, Chattells, Debts, and person-all Estate; as also all and every the Mannors, Lands, Tenements, and Heriditaments, Rents, Arrerages of Rents, revenues, and profits of all the said Delinquents'. Every county in the country had appointed agents to carry out this declaration of economic warfare. Marten was named seques-trator for both Reading and Poole, but was, as *Mercurius Aulicus* reported, 'to be the general collector for the two Houses of Parliament'. He was also 'to have ten Troopes of Horse with him to attend the business, with which he is commissioned to to goe into all parts to collect the same, or else force by distresse'.[56]

At the same time, from this position of authority, Marten moved for the impeachment of Queen Henrietta Maria, then attempting to land ship-loads of arms for the king on the east coast. He insisted that she should not even be addressed as 'Majestie' because she 'was no other then their fellow Subject'. In a spectacular proof of how ideas can lag behind reality, other MPs, with a civil war surrounding them, opposed the queen's impeach-ment on the unlikely grounds that it was 'no time to stirre up controversie'. But eventually the Commons came to take Marten's view and indicted the queen for high treason.[57]

On 3 April Marten and three other MPs were sent to the queen's resi-dence and private church at Somerset House to deface papist idols they found there and seize the Catholic Capuchin friars who had served Henrietta Maria. Soldiers from the Trained Bands who accompanied the MPs found that the friars, warned of the raid, had removed the most expen-sive furniture. But Marten and his colleagues, undeterred, spent all afternoon and evening searching the place from the vaults to the roof. In the end the Capuchins were arrested and shipped to France.[58]

On the same day Marten and his allies Peter Wentworth, Henry Hayman and William Strode were pushing for fellow MP Sir Hugh Cholmley to be thrown out of the House and tried for treason after he defected to the king.[59] During the debate Marten told the Lords that they had no jurisdic-tion over the raising of money as this was the sole province of the Commons. This was a thought that would not be accepted by the Lords until 1911 and so, unsurprisingly, in 1643 it was met with outrage. The Lords complained that their privileges were being trampled on and appointed a committee of a dozen to defend themselves. A conference of both Houses was necessary to smooth things over.[60]

More seriously for Marten, on 18 April he was involved in a physical fight with the earl of Northumberland, the leading peer in the peace party and part of the parliamentary delegation then discussing the Treaty of Oxford with the king. Marten had some responsibility for parliamentary security and had opened a letter sent to Northumberland from Oxford. No doubt he suspected the earl of being sympathetic to the peace party and was looking for proof. If so it was a gamble that backfired. An enraged Northumberland caught up with Marten in the painted chamber as he returned from a conference with the Lords. The confrontation ended with the earl punching and striking the MP over the head with his stick. Bystanders, including Pym, had to draw their swords before the fight was stopped. The Commons complained that the assault on an MP was a breach of privilege. The Lords complained that the opening of the letter was a breach of privilege. The earl of Manchester was deputised to draw up an account of the whole affair and, again, a conference of both Houses was called.[61]

Marten's next action again called into question the right of the Lords to have any say over the behaviour of members of the Commons. Marten had sent De Luke, the quartermaster of his regiment, to the king's stables and requisitioned two of the king's horses. The Lords instantly demanded that the horses be returned but when the order reached De Luke at Smithfield where he was keeping the horses the matter was referred to Marten, who refused to return them. He told the Lord's messenger that 'we had taken the king's ships, and Forts, for the Defence of the Kingdom, and might as well take his horses, lest they might be employed against us'. That response produced uproar. On 3 May the earl of Manchester was again on his feet in the Lords demanding the horses be returned and that Marten's commission as colonel be revoked. They deplored Marten's 'disrespect to their Lordships' and his 'abuse of power'.[62] Marten replied simply that he would 'make the House of Commons . . . acquainted with the whole case'.

The incident was another stark test of where power lay in Parliament, with the Lords or with the Commons. And, on this occasion, Marten won handsomely. The Commons voted that he 'did well, in not delivering these two horses, til he had made this House acquainted therewith'. It further decided that Marten should keep both the horses and his colonel's

commission. Thus emboldened, Marten embarked on an even more audacious scheme: requisitioning the Crown's coronation regalia. At first the
Commons voted down the plan but, the following day, gave its permission.
At the head of 300 soldiers Marten broke into the Westminster Abbey
depository where the crown, sceptre and royal robe for the king's coronation were held. Not much was found, but this did not prevent Marten from
encouraging the parliamentary poet, journalist and soldier George Wither
to dress up in the regalia. Wither first marched 'about the room with a
stately garb, and then afterwards with a thousand apish and ridiculous
actions exposed those sacred ornaments to contempt and laughter'. Marten
declared that 'there should be no further use of these toyes and trifles'.
According to the Venetian ambassador, when the Lords got wind of this
they 'hastened thither before the things were taken away, and tried to stop
it, in which with some difficulty they succeeded'. But the Commons once
again backed Marten and took possession of the regalia and ordered that
new keys be cut and given over to the House.[63] Marten was beginning to
build wider support in the Commons.

The London in which Marten and Walwyn were operating now bore
the aspect of an armed camp. There were guardhouses throughout the
City and Westminster and along the river. New barricade posts were in
place and 'the opening passages and street ends for the fields and road-
wayes' were 'girded with great chaines of iron' to prevent sudden cavalry
incursions. The Trained Bands guarded them at night.[64] But this was an
armed camp in which the popular mobilisation of the kind seen in the
December Days and at Turnham Green was taking a new and even more
dramatic form. In October 1642 work began on an ambitious and dramatic
plan to encircle the whole of London and Westminster with a ring of forts
connected by reinforced earthworks and fronted by a deep ditch. Work on
this eleven-mile circuit of defences, known as the 'lines of communication', lasted until the summer of 1643.[65] With more than twenty forts
defended by over 200 cannon the defences were certainly formidable. But
it was the popular mobilisation of Londoners that was necessary to build
them that was really striking.

Month after month, mostly organised by their trade guilds, thousands
upon thousands of the commonalty of London poured out to construct the
defences of their city. Visiting London from Scotland, the much-travelled
former tailor William Lithgow walked the whole circuit of the lines of
communication and saw the work that constructed them. He thought the
'daily musters of all sorts of Londoners here were wonderous

commendable in marching to the fields and outworks (as Merchants, Silk-men, Macers, Shopkeepers, &c.) with great alacritie, carrying on their shoulders iron Mattocks, wooden shovels, with roaring Drummes, flying colours, and girded swords'. Lithgow records 8,000 tailors marching with forty-six flags, 7,000 watermen with thirty-seven colours, 5,000 shoemakers with twenty-nine banners, and porters marching to Tyburn fields with twenty-three colours. Lithgow had a reputation for exaggeration but his account is born out by the newsbook *Mercurius Civicus*. It recorded 800 porters going out 'in clean white Frockes, with Spades and Pick-axes', with 'Drums beating, and Colours flying', on Tuesday 9 May 1643. The next day the porters from Billingsgate and other wharves did the same. On Monday of the next week the butchers were out. On 30 May it was the turn of 1,000 glovers with their colours. And on 12 June 9,000 weavers with forty-eight colours marched out.[66]

During the Revolution, any profound movement like this involved women to a degree that astounded contemporaries. Lithgow took special notice that 'most companies' were 'interlarded with Ladies, women and girls: two and two carrying baskets for to advance the labour'. They worked 'till they fell sick of their pains'. On the same day that the porters marched to Tyburn, 'a thousand Oyster wives advanced from Billingsgate through Cheapside to Crabtree Field all alone, with drummes and flying colours, and in a civil manner, their goddess Bellona leading them in a martial way'. On 25 May the shoemakers' mobilisation was accompanied by 'about 400 Women who imitating those ancient British Viragos of their Sex, appointed Commanders and Officers among themselves, and went in compleat Rancke and File, one of them (like a stout Amazonian) triumphantly carried a black Ensigne', according to *Mercurius Civicus*.[67]

Lithgow catalogued a total of over fifty trades that took the work in hand, including boxmakers, turners, goldsmiths, brewers, coblers, horologiers, tinkers, watchmakers, chimney-sweeps and printers. He thought that in all 100,000 citizens were involved, which seems an exaggeration. But the Venetian ambassador's figure of 20,000 seems on the low side. But whatever the exact figure, this was a terrific popular outpouring of support, as even the ambassador admitted,

The forts round this city are now completed and admirably designed. They are now beginning the connecting lines. As they wish to complete these speedily and the circuit is most vast, they have gone through the city with drums beating and flags flying to enlist men and women volunteers for the

work. Although they only give them their bare food, without any pay, there
has been an enormous rush of people, even of some rank, who believe they
are serving God by assisting in this pious work, as they deem it.

The Common Council complained of the damage to trade caused by the
constant mobilisation needed to build the lines of communication, but the
work went ahead anyway. It was in this atmosphere that the radicals
embarked on their most ambitious project so far.[68]

By midsummer the partial eclipse of the Salters' Hall committee in their
contest to control the military forces of the City did not stop the radicals
from attempting to exercise greater control over the war as a whole, not
least because of two developments that strengthened the war party. On 6
June a royalist plot led by Edmund Waller was announced in the Commons
to maximum effect by Pym. The plot had the support of some of London's
wealthiest merchants and customs farmers. The news that active preparations were being made to surprise the capital was a devastating blow to the
peace party. The pro-treaty forces never regained their previous momentum.[69] Then on 9 July a considerable political blunder by the earl of Essex
disconcerted both the whole peace party and Pym's moderate wing of the
war party.[70] Essex wrote a letter which seemed to say that Parliament's army
was unfit for service and that peace negotiations with the king should be
reopened. The Commons reacted sharply by resolving that no such overtures could be made without their explicit agreement. Essex's reputation
plummeted. He had become 'of little trust and credit in the House of
Commons'. Marten's wit had already found Essex a fitting target. As the
royalists advanced in the North and West, Essex's army was inert at
Windsor. Why, asked Marten, was it 'summer in Devonshire, summer in
Yorkshire, and onlie winter at Windsor'?[71] Even Pym had to abandon Essex
for the moment and bend to the popular pressure to appoint William
Waller commander of the new army being proposed by the radicals.

An even more ambitious attempt to mobilise mass participation in the
war effort was afoot. On 20 July an extraordinary petition from the well
affected of the City and suburbs arrived at Parliament. It was raised by radicals including Henry Marten and William Walwyn and printed by Peter
Cole and John Sweeting. Peter Cole was Richard Overton's partner in
running the underground Cloppenburg Press, and two months later John
Sweeting would be the printer of William Walwyn's pamphlet *The Power of
Love*. As Walwyn recalled, 'when the common enemy was at the highest,
and Parliaments forces at the lowest, I and many others petitioned

Parliament for a general raising and arming of all the well affected in the Kingdom'.[72] The popular campaign behind this petition for a Committee of the General Rising was clearly extensive. Single-sheet leaflets were strewn around the streets on at least two occasions requesting citizens to subscribe to the petition at the Merchants' Hall and the Grocers' Hall in support 'of raising the whole People of the Land as one Man'. 'Great sums of money' arrived at the Grocers' Hall and many thousands signed the petition on 19 July at Merchant Taylors' Hall. The petition gained a total of 20,000 signatures and was presented to Parliament by a group that included John Norbury, later a defender of those refusing to pay tithes, a close associate of William Walwyn and other Leveller leaders, and a 'pernicious man' according to the royalists.[73]

The petition took the highly unusual step of naming the committee that should undertake this work. The thirteen named included Lord Mayor Pennington, William Strode, Alexander Rigby, Henry Hayman and Henry Marten—in short, the radical wing of the war party. A royalist account complained, 'they not so much Petition, as Command' the House of Commons and 'limit them to a committee of their own nomination'. Most MPs were astonished at this presumption. The House voted that it 'conceived [it] to be irregular, and contrary to the Proceedings and Privilege of Parliament'. But the crisis facing the parliamentary cause, and the strength of feeling behind the petition, meant that they did not have the luxury of standing on ceremony. The MPs did not like doing it, but they approved the proposed committee exactly as it appeared in the petition, warning that they acted only out of 'the Urgency of the Necessities at this time and to prevent the drawing of it into Example for the future'. Nevertheless, the decision gave the committee wide-ranging powers to raise regiments 'in a warlike manner', to appoint commanders, and to 'receive all Contributions and Subscriptions for Monies, Ammunition, Arms, Horses, and any other necessary Provisions, for strengthening and maintaining the said Forces'. Royalists were aghast that 'Plunder-Master Generall' Henry Marten was a moving force on the committee.[74]

The campaign swung into action. A meeting was called at Common Hall in the City and it was addressed by a platform encompassing the entire breadth of the war party: the earl of Manchester, John Pym and Henry Marten. The speakers were united in a common cause, but the differences between them must have been clearly visible at least to those who knew the political context in which they spoke. Manchester's short speech restricted itself to advocating the Militia Committee's control over the forces in

London and announcing the decision that Pennington had been made Lieutenant of the Tower. Pym's was by far the longest speech, cleverly constructed and persuasive. Before he had spoken more than a few opening sentences, Pym stopped to allow the reading of the king's recent proclamation banning trade between London and other parts of the country. Nothing else was likely to get the audience in the mood Pym wanted. Charles's statement railed at the very people now listening to it. London was, it said, 'that City formerly famous for their loyalty and love to their Sovereign', but 'is now become the head of that traitorous faction' that leads a 'horrid rebellion'. Until the City 'return to their due obedience' all trade with the capital was outlawed and both goods and traders would be seized where possible by royalist forces. If any peace party supporters were present it is hard to see how their hearts were not sinking into their boots at this point. Pym rose to continue his speech and he was not slow to profit from the king's alarming statement. He told the crowd that they were being insulted as 'a Den, a Receptacle of Rebels and Traitours', and that while the Parliament wanted peace the king clearly did not. And in a striking passage Pym reveals his own fears about the king's move to cut off trade:

> Farmers will not be able to pay their rents; the Gentry and Nobility will be brought into as necessitous condition as the rest, because they will be able to make nothing of their own . . . it will also put you into a general combustion, because the poor will rise, and the rich made poore, and none shall know his friends, and we shall fight over a morsel of bread, which God (I hope) will avert.

Pym was doing more than putting his hopes in God to avoid a social conflagration, which the activities of the radicals must have made him fear all the more immediately. He called for 'us to unite ourselves, with all our strength and means to defend our Religion, and to defend our Liberties, and to defend the publique safetie'.[75]

Henry Marten's speech struck a more urgent note. He was the only one to mention the mass petitioning that had resulted in the setting up of the Committee for the General Rising, saying that 'the principle cause why this meeting was desired, was to communicate unto you, a Petition of many thousands of well affected persons of this Citie, and other parts of the Kingdome'. He stressed that William Waller was to be commander of the newly raised forces. He insisted that the Commons 'conceive that there shall be a general and unanimous rising of the people both in this Citie and in other parts of the Kingdome'. 'Your enemies', said Marten, 'will spare none of you, their bullets doe not distinguish you, they would starve you all'. And he ended with a ringing call to arms: 'certainly I am of the opinion, that either you must goe forth all, and meete the enemy as Vassalls with Ropes about your neckes, or like men with swords in your hands'. The speeches were quickly printed up, once again by Peter Cole, and issued as a pamphlet.[76] In early August another account of the Committee for the General Rising hit the streets. Once again the printer was future Leveller Thomas Paine.[77]

Historian Jordan Downs has noted that the popular mobilisations of the winter of 1642–43 reveals 'a history from below that travels to the top and back down again' in which 'the actions of petitioners *and* the subsequent manipulations of politics' led to political escalation. We can see this process at work in the radical ascendancy of the summer of 1643. On 25 July Waller arrived in London and was welcomed as a conquering hero especially by 'multitudes of factious people', or so a royalist newsbook complained. Preachers gave thanks from the pulpits for Waller's return, despite his crushing defeat at Roundway Down on 13 July. This was conveniently blamed on lack of support from Essex. On 27 July the Commons recommended Waller as commander of the new army, though Essex delayed the appointment. Two days later the Common Council also approved Waller as the leader of the new forces being raised in the capital. This was the high point of the radicals' influence in the war party. Waller was a compromise candidate and there were rumours circulating that the radicals would have preferred Marten himself to take command.[78]

In August Pym began to reassert the dominance of the moderates. The radicals were in the midst of a new push to reject peace proposals coming from the Lords that had been taken into consideration by the Commons at Holles's insistence. Marten and Strode were at the centre of the attempt to have the peace proposal rejected immediately. A petitioning campaign was organised over the weekend of 5–6 August. Printed bills were pinned to church doors calling on 'all such as desire there maybe a general raising of the people' to meet at Westminster Hall 'to move the Parliament that this may be put in speedy execution'. For peace party MP Sismond D'Ewes it was all the work of 'schismatical persons in the Citty of London' and 'violent and ill disposed persons meeting together on the said Saturday night' who organised for 'Libellous and scandalous writing' to be 'dispersed up and down the Citty'. The mobilisation was certainly effective. By one o'clock on

Monday 7 August Old Palace Yard 'was filled with a seditious multitude'. The radicals mobilised 5,000 people to prevent Parliament voting for peace. Peers arriving at Westminster were met with 'affronts and violence . . . yet that was nothing in comparison of the insolent violence they offered them at their departure'. D'Ewes thought that some peers were in danger of their lives as they passed through Old Palace Yard. The royalists complained that the radicals 'brought down their City Club-men to awe the members of both Houses'. Some MPs stayed away from the House that day, others fled to Essex and the army quartered at Kingston, but were rebuffed. The peace party in the Lords led by Northumberland demanded that these demonstrations be halted, but to no avail. D'Ewes recorded, 'I assure you that if you will but inquire into those actions of this very forenoon you shall finde that the Privileges of Parliament have been absolutely broken and violated'. On the following day women peace petitioners organised by royalist Lady Brouncker and adorned with white ribbons were at the doors of Westminster. They were back in larger numbers, perhaps 6,000 strong, the next day. Blank shots failed to move them and they replied by pelting the Trained Bands with stones. Only when Waller's troops actually shot several of the protestors did they disperse. The following day another radical protest of 5,000 returned to Westminster chanting 'No Peace!' Pym was facing a first-class political crisis. He was losing influence in the Commons to Marten, and losing the streets to the radicals on one side and the peace protestors on the other.[79]

Pym moved to rebuild the moderate war party's control. He could make the best of the difficulties that the radicals were facing. Marten wanted Waller to take the field and confront the king's forces but was stymied by John Glyn, the City recorder. And the Committee for the General Rising did not have the funds independently under its control to raise new troops. The volunteer principle that some, but not all, radicals favoured worked well for the defence of the city, but was of less worth in raising forces for an offensive. The radicals were divided over the volunteer principle, though the committee was unanimous that if this did not work quickly funds would be needed for enlistment. The problem was that Pym's supporters held the purse strings and would not release money except to Essex. Lack of progress made Waller vacillate.[80] Pym created a new Council of War on 2 August to replace the Committee for the General Rising. It retained Pym's supporters but excluded Marten and the radicals. Essex complained bitterly that he was 'abused in Pictures, censured in Pulpits' and 'dishonoured in the table-talke of the common people'. Essex approved Waller's commission but limited his command to the London militia. Pym had already tried twice to get Marten out of London and returned to his regiment. Both times he had failed.[81]

Now Pym seized a moment to remove Henry Marten from Parliament for the foreseeable future. It happened like this. The belongings of preacher John Saltmarsh had been searched and some private papers taken in which he had raised profound criticisms of the monarchy. Saltmarsh had written that 'all means should be used to keep the king and his people from a sudden union' and that 'if the king would not grant their demands, then they should root him out and the royal line' and give the crown to someone else. This caused uproar but Marten rose to defend Saltmarsh, saying 'that it were better if one family should be destroyed than many'. Neville Poole, Pym's ally, immediately challenged him to say which family he meant. Marten interrupted him and said, 'The king and his family'. The House erupted around his ears. Pym denounced Marten in a speech that made use of all his oratorical skills. He 'fell foul upon Martin with a long speech saying he was a man extremely guilty of injustice and lewdness', according to a royalist news-sheet.[82] Marten was expelled from the House and imprisoned in the Tower. He was quickly released but did not return to the Commons until after the war. Marten's regiment was taken from him.[83]

Pym was aiming not just at Marten but also at breaking the influence of the Committee for the General Rising and its promotion of Waller over Essex. Pym was also constructing an agreement with the Scots, which would mean accepting a Presbyterian church settlement. Marten had opposed him on this, as on much else, telling the Commons that 'idolatry is a national sinne of this kingdome' and so 'would have noe power att Courte to dispence religion'. Even peace party MP Sismond D'Ewes wrote that 'the tru and onlie cause why hee was at this time putt out of the house was by reason of the almost constant opposing and often wittile ierking at old John Pym'.[84] It was a signal victory for the moderates in the war party. They could now take firm action against both the king and the peace party without the fear that such action would embolden the radicals in their own ranks. In short, an elite pro-war policy could be pursued without the danger of it empowering a radical and plebeian pro-war strategy.

What did the radicals achieve in 1643?

Historians of the parliamentary cause are divided on the effectiveness of the radicals during this crucial year. In many ways, J. H. Hexter's narrative *The Reign of King Pym*, published in 1941, still holds sway. It is certainly a powerful, complex and persuasive account of parliamentary politics. But in its eagerness to promote the reputation of John Pym it is unremittingly dismissive of the radicals in general and of the role of Henry Marten in particular. At points Hexter simply descends into retelling the gossip of the royalist newsbooks at Marten's expense. And no one actually reading Marten's speech at the Common Hall could be convinced that its brief two pages were 'a grandiose speech in the old Roman style, full of the very best bombast'.[85] Consequently Hexter's handling of the radical threat contains an unresolved paradox. He admits on the one hand that the radical threat was real and effective, on the other that the people responsible were incompetent.

Thus Hexter admits that 'Essex's peace letter wrenched control of the House from Pym and put it in the hands of the fiery spirits' and that by July 'it seemed that Martin and the fiery spirits would absorb the militant section of the middle group, leaving impotent Pym and his personal following'.[86] Pym's recovery and his ability to 'pluck from his side—his left side—a thorn that for a long time had bothered him and had once spread poison and threatened him with political extinction' he attributes to the ineffectiveness of the Committee for the General Rising, Pym's loyalty to Essex, and his quiet management of the infrastructure of the war effort. In a modern twist on this argument, Ian Gentles, in an otherwise insightful account of the peace campaigns of 1643, is dismissive of radical attempts at popular mobilisation and concludes that the royalists were defeated neither by the strategy of the radicals or by that of Pym, but by 'the Solemn League and Covenant that produced 21,500 able Scottish troops' at Marston Moor in 1644.[87]

There are a number of reasons for thinking that Hexter's account is inadequate, not least those in the more recent accounts of this period by Valerie Pearl and Keith Lindley.[88] To begin, with the Committee for the General Rising and the Salters' Hall committee were not weak. Amidst constant peace party activity at both elite and popular level, and at a time when all Parliament had to show on the battlefield was a nearly unbroken series of defeats, the radicals' activities 'replaced commanders in a way that

was least destructive to the war-effort, undermined the Oxford peace negotiations, and had a temporarily unifying effect on London'.[89] More than
this, the success of Pym's strategy depended, as did the entire parliamentary cause, on a mobilised population, especially in London. This is what
had made the December Days and the defence of the five members, Pym
included, possible. This is what had delivered the victory at Turnham
Green. It is what had defeated the peace party protests in the capital. And
all the while this had been going on it had provided the enormous outburst
of sustained plebeian enthusiasm that had built the eleven miles of the lines
of communication which now ran all around the City and Westminster.
Even coercive orders to pay the excise tax, introduced by Pym, or shut the
shops and join the Trained Bands, could not be effective without a substra-
tum of popular enthusiasm.[90]

This elemental force was to rebuild Essex's army and mobilise the
Trained Bands to march across the country and confront the king, just as
Marten had argued it should. That force relieved the siege of Gloucester,
giving the parliamentary cause a talisman victory. It went on immediately
to defeat the king at the first battle of Newbury, ending any attempt on the
capital. Marching with the City's Blue Regiment to lift the siege of Gloucester
and until he was seriously wounded at Newbury was Thomas Prince, the
future treasurer of the Levellers. City radicals who worked with Pym but
who were also open to the arguments of the 'fiery spirits'—Pennington,
Mainwaring, Atkins, John Warner, Towse—were all colonels or senior
officers in the Trained Bands.[91] Their forces began to turn the tide against
the king long before the alliance with the Scots had any significant effect
the following year. The royalist historian John Spelman, commenting
directly on the effect of the meeting at the Common Hall on 29 July 1643,
wrote, 'By all of which it is most evident that this *Languishing Rebellion* had,
before this day, gasp'd its last and given up the ghost, had not this rebellious
Citie by its *wealth* and *multitudes* fomented it, and given it life.'[92] Pym's
victory was not in spite of the popular mobilisation that the radicals cham-
pioned, but because of it. What Pym needed was the popular mobilisation
without the radical leadership, and this is what removing Marten gave him.

Pym's victory had a cost. The moderates were ultimately incapable of
finally defeating the king politically even after he had been eventually
defeated militarily in 1645. It was Marten's vision of what victory entailed
that eventually came to pass, not Pym's more moderate course. As it
happened, war and disease were taking their toll on the moderate war party
and the original five members themselves. Lord Brooke, Pym's ally and

Lilburne's commander, was shot dead by a sniper at the siege of Lichfield in March. John Hampden was dead from wounds inflicted on Chalgrove Field in June and, by December, Pym had died of cancer. Denzil Holles was now leading the peace party. Marten's ally William Strode and Arthur Haselrig were of the war party. The centre was not going to hold. Eventually, as C. M. Williams's defence of Marten concludes, it was 'the logic of his resistance to King Charles and King Pym that would be vindicated'. In the end Walwyn was not far from the truth when he wrote that from the radical's efforts of 1643 'much good issued to the whole City and Kingdom'. Walwyn thought that even though the project 'was stifled at birth' and did 'not come to perfection: yet it mated the common enemy and set all wheels at work at home' and 'was the spring of more powerful motions and good successes'.[93]

Some crucial aspects of what would become Leveller organisation began to emerge in this period.[94] Whether or not they knew each other, Marten and Walwyn were both closely engaged in the same radical project. The presses, especially those run by Thomas Paine and Peter Cole, were to be mainstays of Leveller organisation even though they also printed material for other war party strands of opinion. The conflict within the war party was the first time that the radicals as a whole saw the full willingness for compromise among the moderates and found themselves, on some crucial issues, in political formations opposed to them. They could mobilise protests on these issues as well as those where they made common cause with those who would become Independents. The Levellers-to-be shared a social location with their sometime allies. All were part of the 'middling sort', although the Levellers tended to be the second sons of gentry and less wealthy merchants.[95] But the future Levellers, Marten by ideological predisposition, Walwyn and Paine by experience, tended to look more to popular mobilisation under its own direction, as opposed to under elite influence, than did other radicals.

CHAPTER 6

The War, the Church and the State

John Lilburne and Oliver Cromwell had known each other since Cromwell used his first speech in the Long Parliament to help free Lilburne from his Star Chamber imprisonment. When Cromwell began to recruit at the start of the Civil War, though an MP, he was a mere captain of a troop of sixty cavalry. Lilburne was a captain famous for having escaped execution at the king's hand in Oxford. Cromwell's original force, troop sixty-seven out of seventy-five in Essex's army, was present at Edgehill and they appear to have seen some action late in the battle.[1] Cromwell was also present at Turnham Green, according to Gardiner.[2] What he saw already convinced him that the current ways of organising the parliamentary army would not be sufficient to beat the royalists. He told his cousin John Hampden,

> Your troops are most of them old decayed serving men and tapsters, and such kind of fellows; and their troops are gentlemen's sons and persons of quality. Do you think the spirits of such base and mean fellows will ever be able to encounter gentlemen that have honour and courage and resolution in them? . . . You must get men of spirit, and, take it not ill what I say—I know you will not—of a spirit that is likely to go on as far as gentlemen will go, or else you will be beaten still.[3]

Cromwell's point was that, faced with an ideologically motivated, militarily confident royalism set upon victory, Parliament must dig deep into the social layers that supported it most fully, the religiously radical middling sort, and create an even more effective military force from this material.

Cromwell was about the business of forming exactly this kind of force in East Anglia. As one contemporary noted, 'most of them were freeholders, or freeholders' sons, and who upon a matter of conscience engaged upon this quarrel, and under Cromwell'.[4] These troops were committed to taking whatever action was necessary for victory.

By February 1643 Cromwell had been so successful that he was made a colonel of the regiment he had raised, soon to be known as the Ironsides. It was natural that Cromwell should invite Lilburne to join the Eastern Association forces and natural that Lilburne would enthusiastically accept. And so it was that John and Elizabeth Lilburne moved to Boston in Lincolnshire. The move took the Lilburnes from one centre of radical resistance, London, to another, the army of Parliament's Eastern Association.[5] Militarily the forces of Parliament were distributed among four different armies which became five when the Scottish army when it crossed the Tweed in January 1644. The English parliamentary armies were those of the earl of Essex and Sir William Waller in the South, the army under Lord Fernando and Sir Thomas Fairfax in the North, and the Eastern Association. The earl of Manchester became commander of the Eastern Association in August 1643. Manchester was a powerful Presbyterian figure, one of only ten lords to sit as lay members of the Assembly of Divines, the body charged with creating a new national religious settlement. He was one of seven lords appointed to Parliament's joint executive with the Scots, the Committee of Both Kingdoms.[6] Cromwell's force, raised in the fenlands of East Anglia around his home town of Huntingdon, was the heart of the Eastern Association.

In both London and East Anglia a somewhat similar conflict was being played out. At its core was the issue of popular participation in the leadership of the Revolution. In London this was a broad political, social and organisational issue being fought out everywhere from the streets, through Salters' Hall and the Merchant Taylors' Hall, to the floor of the Commons. In the Eastern Association it was in the first instance a matter of recruitment, the appointment of officers, and military strategy. Cromwell, above and beyond any other soldier, grasped two things. The first was that the war should be fought until victory. The second was that respect for social or religious convention, or hereditary entitlement, were no way to win a war. These were not majority views among parliamentarians. In every respect Cromwell's methods would have appealed to Lilburne. But they were also initially shared by the earl of Manchester. He and Cromwell were agreed on the project of raising a disciplined and godly force. And at this stage Lilburne saw Manchester and Cromwell as his 'familiar friends' and his 'two Darlings'.[7]

Cromwell's forces grew rapidly by recruiting religiously motivated troopers loyal to the parliamentary cause. By March 1643 he had five troops, by September ten. Cromwell's second in command in his own troop was James Berry, derided because he had been a clerk in a Shropshire ironworks before the war. But Berry proved his worth at the Battle of Gainsborough in July 1643, slaying royalist general Charles Cavendish, the king's godson, 'with a thrust under his short ribs'. He rose to be a colonel in his own right. In the first instance Cromwell relied on his relatives to captain the other new troops in his regiment. After his own troop, the next four troops were all commanded by members of the 'great cousinage': Edward Whalley was Cromwell's cousin and captain of the second troop; John Disbrowe, who married Cromwell's sister, was in charge of the third troop; the commander of the fourth troop was Cromwell's son, also Oliver; and Valentine Walton, the son of Cromwell's sister Margaret, commanded the fourth. As the regiment grew to become a double regiment, Henry Ireton, Cromwell's future son-in-law, became commander of the final fourteenth troop.[8] Some of these men were lesser gentry like Cromwell himself, close to the middling sort from which others came. But in pursuit of victory no barrier which excluded those of lowly origin or radical religion was to be tolerated. It is in this truly revolutionary approach that all Cromwell's greatness lies. When young men and maids in Norwich offered to raise money for an infantry regiment Cromwell encouraged them instead to give the funds to a troop of horse and vowed he would make up the difference in cost. 'Pray raise godly men and I will have them in my regiment', he told them. They did. And under Captain Swallow they became the eleventh troop, called the 'Maiden Troop' after their original supporters.[9]

The words Cromwell used at this time to encourage his supporters still carry urgency. Writing to supporters in Cambridge he directed them, 'I beseech you be careful what Captains of Horse you choose . . . a few honest men are better than numbers . . . If you choose godly honest men to be Captains of Horse, honest men will follow them'. And in the same letter, 'I had rather have a plain russet-coated Captain that knows what he fights for, and loves what he knows, than that which you call a gentleman and is nothing else'.[10] And in the same month, September 1643,

Gentlemen, it may be it provokes some spirits to see such plain men made Captains of Horse. It had been well that men of honour and birth had entered these employments: but why do they not appear? Who would have hindered them? But seeing it was necessary the work must go on, better plain men than none.[11]

Much of this was written in defence of Captain Ralph Margery, to whom the local authorities objected both because he was low-born and because he was busy requisitioning horses. Cromwell's defence of Margery ran to the heart of his policy at this time: radicalism born of military necessity as much as political affinity.

Cromwell's attitude to religious radicalism was more complex. Though never a member of a gathered church or sect, he was a committed opponent of the Laudian church and its ceremonial practices. The Reverend Hitch of Ely Cathedral found this to his cost after he refused an order to desist holding a choir service that Cromwell found 'unedifying and offensive'. Cromwell, his hat still on his head, came into the cathedral 'with a rabble at his heals', approached the reverend in his pulpit and told him, 'Leave off your fooling, and come down, Sir!' Hitch obliged and he and the congregation filed from the cathedral.[12]

When Scots Presbyterian Major General Laurence Crawford wished to rid himself of the Anabaptist William Packer from his ranks, Cromwell wrote to him insisting that 'you are not well advised to turn off one so faithful to the cause'. To Crawford's reply that the 'the man is an Anabaptist', Cromwell responded, 'Are you sure of that? Admit he be, shall that render him incapable to serve the Public? . . . Sir, the State, in choosing men to serve it, takes no notice of their opinions; if they be willing faithfully to serve it,—that satisfies'. Crawford was later to complain of Lilburne petitioning, with Cromwell's support, to advance the interests of religious radicals in the army. No wonder Robert Baillie, the Scots commissioner, thought that Cromwell was not only 'a known Independent' but also a 'favourer of Sects'. The Presbyterian preacher Richard Baxter, who refused when asked to become a chaplain in the regiment, later singled out Captain Christopher Bethel's twelfth troop as a home of Anabaptists and Levellers.[13]

Lilburne certainly was not the only radical working with Cromwell; indeed he was not even the only future Leveller. The sixth troop of Cromwell's Ironsides was captained by William Eyre, who, as we have seen, had also fought at Edgehill and Brentford. Cromwell sent for Eyre after Holles's regiment was destroyed at Brentford and asked him to become quartermaster in his troop, promising that he would later make him a captain of his own troop. Eyre was exactly the kind of man for which Cromwell looking. He was of proven bravery in battle but, more than this, he was a man with 'the root of the matter in him'. Eyre had emigrated to New England in the 1630s in protest at Laud's imposition of the service book. He returned with the calling of the Long Parliament, 'hoping to have seen more done by them for the Freedom of the People'. He was hounded out of Dorset where he was living after denying the service book was of divine inspiration. Eyre was befriended by Philip Skippon in London before volunteering for Holles's redcoats. Cromwell asked for his help in raising troops because 'he would fain see what a Troop of godly men could do; for he said, That, under God, it must be honest men that must deliver the People from their Oppressions'. Eyre recruited for Cromwell and was duly made a captain in Cromwell's regiment. Indeed he was something of a favourite of Cromwell's for, as Eyre recalled, 'he would often (when he was low) stroke me on the head, saying, The nation was bound to bless God for me'.[14]

Another trooper in Cromwell's regiment destined to play a central role in the future of the Leveller movement was Edward Sexby. Like Lilburne he was a second son of gentry apprenticed to trade, in this case to Edward Price of the Grocers' Company in 1632. His apprenticeship would have therefore ended in 1640 and by 1643 he was enrolled in the Eastern Association. Sexby was one of the key organisers of the army revolt of 1647 and spoke in favour of liberty of conscience at the Putney debates. We can safely assume he held these views while under Cromwell's command. Sexby, like Eyre, was a favourite of Cromwell, who would share his sleeping quarters with Sexby so that they could talk privately in the late hours. We do not know if Sexby first met Lilburne during their time in the Eastern Association, but if he did it would explain why Lilburne entrusted messages of special importance to Sexby to take to Cromwell in 1648.[15]

Lilburne was cut from the same cloth as Eyre and Sexby, though he was not in fact in Cromwell's own regiment. Having come to the Eastern Association at Cromwell's request Lilburne at first joined in action at Lincoln although he had no commission. This was just the moment when Cromwell was joined by the forces Sir Thomas Fairfax brought across the Humber to drive the royalists out of Lincolnshire and annex that disputed county to the Eastern Association. Cromwell then used his influence in the Eastern Association to get Lilburne appointed, in October 1643, to the rank of major in the regiment of Colonel Edward King. But Lilburne was actually working more closely politically with Cromwell than if he had been in his own regiment. For at this time, and for two years hence, Lilburne was essentially furthering the political project that Cromwell was engaged in as well as attending to his military duties.[16]

Cromwell not only organised Lilburne's military post but made an essentially private arrangement with Lilburne about his political activities. The gist of the matter was this: Cromwell supported the appointment of Edward King to a number of influential commands in the contested county of Lincolnshire because of his local popularity. King had originally been a supporter of Lord Willoughby of Parham, the first parliamentarian commander in Lincolnshire. But under Willoughby Parliament's forces suffered defeat, demoralisation, dissention and desertion. With Manchester's arrival in the Eastern Association, King switched allegiances and worked to strip Willoughby of all authority. Manchester and Cromwell were in alliance in the early phase of Manchester's command because they both sought religious tolerance in the name of military effectiveness. But the seeds of future division existed because, while Cromwell sought toleration for Independents and Sectaries against the prevailing Presbyterian majority, Manchester came to the same conclusion from the opposite direction, hoping that the Independents 'should close with the honest Calvinist and Scot and go on unanimously against the common enemy'. Thus both Manchester and Cromwell supported King in becoming not only colonel of his regiment but also governor of both Boston and Lincoln.[17] But Cromwell distrusted King and charged Lilburne, and John Berry, with reporting directly to him about any disloyalty on King's part. Lilburne's 'particular instructions and private directions from Lieut. General Cromwell' were to report 'information and intelligence of the state and condition of Lincolnshire, under the command of the said Col King, and of the carriage and behaviour of the said Col King, towards the Country and Solderie'. More generally, Cromwell asked Lilburne to complain of 'whomsoever I groundedly knew, did any actions to the ruin of Salus Populi, the Saftey of the People'.[18]

At first Lilburne simply laboured to keep the peace. When he returned from a visit to London, Lilburne found that King had 'imprisoned divers of his Officers, and divers townes people, and some of Lieu. Gen. Cromwells Troopers, for assembling together in a private meeting'. Lilburne rode to Sleaford and reported to Cromwell and they worked to restore relations between the men and the colonel. Cromwell was sufficiently grateful that he immediately issued a commission to Lilburne's elder brother Robert.[19]

But an unravelling of this relationship was inevitable. Since 6 March 1644 Sir John Meldrum had been besieging the royalists in Newark, a territorial possession of the queen that commanded the road north from London to York. Rupert arrived to lift the siege on 21 March, striking swiftly with his cavalry in advance of his foot regiments. Lilburne had already faced down Rupert in the court room at Oxford when he was the king's captive after Brentford. Now, in the first stages of the fight at Newark, he achieved the distinction of defeating Rupert in the field:

> Prince Rupert, with a great body of horse, came unexpectedly upon the parliaments forces before Newark, so that they had no time to prepare to receive him; yet colonel Rossiter, major Lilburne, captain Bethel, and Hunt, gallantly charged and routed the right wing led by the prince.[20]

But not all the parliamentary forces were so determined and 500 of them deserted before the great fort was assaulted, leaving Rupert master of the field.[21] It was agreed in the surrender that the parliamentarians could march away without their arms. But, Lilburne alleged, King forced the troops to march with their arms and this resulted in their being attacked by the royalists.[22] While King 'shifted for himself', Lilburne's force was plundered. He had to make his way to safety over hedge and ditch stripped of everything he had—horse, bag, papers, hat, doublet, boots, even the periwig he was wearing to cover the fact that his hair had not grown back after his illness in jail. Lilburne alleged, as did others, that it was division among the officers that caused the loss of the battle. Newark was a serious defeat causing demoralised parliamentarians to evacuate Lincoln, Gainsborough and Sleaford.[23]

There was a religious dimension to this quarrel which mirrored the emerging national divisions between Independents and Presbyterians. This involved the discussions aimed at resettling a national church, and the agreement of a military pact with Scotland. An early consequence of the Revolution had been to destroy the old state policy of the Church under Charles I. Archbishop Laud, the author and enforcer of that policy, was in the Tower awaiting trial. The Root and Branch petition of 1640 had been unequivocal in its first lines: 'the government of archbishops and lord bishops, deans and archdeacons, &c., with their courts and ministrations in them, have been proved prejudicial and very dangerous both to Church and Commonwealth'. The Act based on the petition that would have legally abolished Prelacy, as the Puritans called the Church hierarchy, did not pass the Commons in 1641, but an Act to exclude bishops from the Lords was passed later in the year. After the December Days, twelve bishops were impeached, the majority joining Laud in the Tower. As fundamentally, the Church's very powerful role as a censor of printed material, particularly enumerated in the Root and Branch petition as one of the 'manifold evils' practised by the Laudian church, had gone the way of all flesh.[24]

As early as June 1643 Parliament had moved to try and reimpose some degree of control over unlicensed printing, as we have seen. It could only ever be partially successful and so it was intermittently repeated. A month later the project to reform the national church was begun in earnest. In July 1643 the Westminster Assembly of Divines met for the first time, tasked by Parliament with agreeing a new national church to replace the discredited episcopacy of Laud. The churchmen of the assembly were in their majority Presbyterians with a small number of Independents in opposition, the so-called 'Dissenting Brethren'. The majority favoured a legally enforced, all-inclusive, national church. This would be governed by a hierarchy of elders. The pact agreed with Scotland by Parliament in September 1643, the Solemn League and Covenant, swore, in return for a Scottish army that was to march to the aid of Parliament, that the Presbyterian model of Church government would be implemented in England. From February 1644 the war was managed by the Committee of Both Kingdoms, an executive composed of English MPs and peers, and Scottish commissioners in London. These measures—censorship, Presbyterian Church government, and the pact with Scotland—were coercive and divisive. The long radical reaction to these policies would determine the course of the Revolution.[25]

These developments were directly reflected in the Eastern Association. Lilburne thought that dissension with Colonel King was stirred up by 'Priests' that 'fomented our differences', in particular King's Presbyterian chaplains, Lee and Garter. 'Bishop Lee', as Lilburne called him, encouraged King to behave as 'imperious as an Emperor' and to 'set us together by the eares'. Lilburne also thought that one reason why the earl of Manchester was reluctant to move against King was that King's chaplains prevailed upon the Earl's chaplains, Simeon Ashe and William Goode, to 'cast a Scotch-clergy mist over their Lords eyes'. Ashe and Goode were certainly acting as political agents of Manchester, and were both members of the Westminster Assembly and strong advocates of the Solemn League and Covenant.[26]

These religious dispositions could never sit well with Cromwell's officer corps, which now included such Independent luminaries as Charles Fleetwood, Thomas Harrison and Robert and John Lilburne. Joining these was the future Leveller Thomas Rainsborough, who was about to make his reputation with the daring capture of Crowland Abbey. Rainsborough's new regiment was officered by a large number of returning New Englanders, including members of Rainsborough's own family, habituated to the norms of the radical religion on the other side of the Atlantic. These were the kind of men especially targeted for criticism by Presbyterians, and King himself thought all right-minded people should report to the authorities 'all Papists, Anabaptists, Brownists, Separatists, Antinomians, and Hereticks, who take upon them boldness to creep into houses, and lead captive silly women laden with sinnes; Prophaners of the Sabboth, Swearers, Drunkards, Fornicators, Idolators, Adulterers, abasers of themselves with mankind, or with beast'.[27]

Lilburne's contest with King was to have consequences as he attempted to have the colonel removed from his posts and pursued the case through appeals to Parliament. In this long wrangle he had the support of Parliament's Lincolnshire committee, not all of whom were of the same mind politically as Lilburne.[28] At the outset the contest with King did Lilburne's military career no immediate harm and on 16 May 1644 he was made lieutenant colonel of dragoons in Manchester's regiment.[29] Six weeks later his regiment were in the thick of one of the decisive battles of the Civil War, Marston Moor. Here he and his force seemed to have served bravely. But it was the political aftermath of the parliamentary victory that was to engage Lilburne in a conflict much more serious than the one with Colonel King.

Manchester and Cromwell

The Battle of Marston Moor was a signal parliamentary victory in which Cromwell, now risen to the rank of lieutenant general, played a crucial role. His cavalry charged with the same ferocity as Rupert's cavalry but, having the discipline that the cavaliers lacked, they reformed to attack Charles's forces in the rear. This victory was Cromwell's to claim since Manchester and the other senior commanders had fled the field of battle, convinced the day was lost. The victory cost the royalists any hope of holding the North. But the Presbyterians were 'grieved and angry' that Independents 'trumpet over all the city their own praises to our prejudices, making all believe that Cromwell alone, with his unspeakably valorous regiments, had done all that service'. But that was the truth of it.

Manchester's failure to follow up the victory earned him Cromwell's settled enmity. Cromwell was now less concerned to defend the participation of all the godly in the army and more concerned to see the army as the force that might prevent a peace settlement on royalist terms.[30] In August Cromwell pursued this plan by, unsuccessfully, attempting to have Manchester's ally Major General Crawford cashiered from the army. This change of mood was further bolstered by Cromwell's growing antipathy towards Presbyterian intolerance. This was part of a wider strategy by the Independents. The five Dissenting Brethren in the Assembly of Divines, realising they were unable to prevent the establishment of a national Presbyterian church, focussed their efforts on gaining toleration for those opposed to such a settlement. Cromwell was soon to take the Scots and Presbyterians by surprise by moving for toleration in the Commons. His troopers were already actively petitioning in London for liberty of conscience.[31] Lilburne was to experience this entire political situation in the microcosm of his own relations with Manchester.

In the wake of Marston Moor, on Cromwell's orders, Lilburne's dragoons were set down before the royalist held Tickhill Castle on the border between Nottingham and the West Riding of Yorkshire. It was not a major military engagement but it did have some important political consequences that made Lilburne even more central to the Independent attack on Manchester than he might otherwise have been. Lilburne was tasked with keeping the royalists penned up in the castle. And so he sent a party of horse across the drawbridge, getting between it and the town. Lilburne followed up, taking prisoners and horses. On the night of the following day Lilburne led a party of musketeers and seized the town mill, letting out the mill dam. This clearly rattled the town's garrison, who did not seem to have the appetite for a fight. Their commanding officers insisted on meeting Lilburne 'to be merrie at the Ale-house' and made it clear that, if summoned, they would surrender on terms.[32]

Lilburne rode to meet Manchester, Cromwell and other senior officers at Doncaster with the proposal that he be allowed to summon the castle and take the surrender. He was clearly stunned when Manchester told him 'it cannot be done'. Lilburne continued to make his case but Manchester said that the castle was a 'scurvie strong place' and upbraided Lilburne for thinking it 'was nothing to summon a Castle and take it'. Manchester said he would not risk ten men in taking it and that if it were attempted the reputation of his whole army might be damaged. This clearly was nonsense. Lilburne, not long on patience at the best of times, offered to take it on his own authority if Manchester would 'winke at me'. Manchester simply replied, 'get thee gone, thou art a mad fellow'. Lilburne, on a very wide interpretation of Manchester's words, took this as permission to act.

Perhaps sensing trouble he asked Henry Ireton if this was a plausible inter-pretation of the exchange. Ireton thought it was.[33]

Lilburne lost no time, rode back to Tickhill, wrote out a summons and sent it with his drummer to the castle. The garrison surrendered and Lilburne returned, two captive royalist officers along with him, to present his prize to Manchester. He found him on horseback with a crowd of officers heading out to take the air. Manchester immediately exploded in front of the royalists and the other officers, calling Lilburne a 'Rogue, Rascall, and a base-fellow'. He demanded to know whether Lilburne thought he or the earl were in command, and insisted that the army was 'much troubled' with rogues like Lilburne who deserved to be hanged. Without suffering Lilburne to speak he then turned away 'in a greater fury than ever I see him in my dayes'. Cromwell had to intercede to ensure that the surrender of the castle took place at all. Astoundingly, Manchester then claimed full and exclusive credit for the surrender, writing to the Committee of Both Kingdoms that he had freed

> these parts from the violence and oppression which they suffered under the garrisons of the enemy. Tychill castle being the nerest and most prejudi-ciall . . . I summoned at my first coming, and sent into the towne three hundred dragoones. Whereupon those of the place desired a parley, and have rendered the place unto mee.[34]

Manchester may not have shown much audacity in the field but, even in the long history of senior officers taking the credit for the acts of those under their command, these claims probably deserve special mention. The whole incident profoundly affected Lilburne. He said that his soul was so vexed that he could never, after that, 'draw my sword, nor engage my life in the way of a Souldier, with that freshness, alacrity, and cheerfullnesse, as formalie I had done'. He recalled that 'Manchester's baseness spoiled a Souldier of me'. He thought many times of leaving the army but Cromwell persuaded him to remain. It was from about this time that Lilburne detected that 'Manchester visibly degenerated'.[35]

Manchester's behaviour on the field at Marston Moor and at Tickhill Castle was only the beginning. In September 1644 Cromwell and Manchester, supported by Major General Crawford, were in London argu-ing their opposing cases with MPs and at the Committee of Both Kingdoms. The committee told Manchester to compose the differences, at least until the troops were in winter quarters. Baillie, the Scottish commissioner, recorded that Crawford had 'got a great hand with Manchester, and with all the army that were not sects'. By contrast Baillie thought that the 'Independents' great plot by this army' was to 'counterbalance us, to over-awe the Assembly and Parliament both to their ends'.[36] On 1 October the Committee of Both Kingdoms ordered Manchester to rally all the forces he could and march speedily west to assist Waller and Essex. Manchester told his subordinates that if any of them tried to persuade him to 'goe westward he would hange him'. A dozen more letters, three orders from the Commons, and nearly three weeks passed and Manchester's forces had still only reached Reading. But it was Manchester's disastrous decision to allow the king's army to escape and to evacuate the royalist artillery train from Donnington Castle after the Second Battle of Newbury that brought the conflict to a head. One contemporary supporter of Parliament thought that 'neglect and treachery' of the 'great officers' had resulted in 'the greatest affront that ever we received' and that 'the fault is chiefly laid upon the Lord Manchester and Crawford and Balfour'.[37]

Manchester had originally enjoyed the support of the war party MPs that placed their hopes in the Eastern Association. That support was now weakening. Manchester's increasing hostility to the role of the Independents and Sectaries in his army bolstered his fear that outright victory over the king would result in a politically and religiously unac-ceptable settlement of the nation. This was the root of his military sloth. On 23 November the Commons instructed the Committee of Both Kingdoms to bring forward 'a frame or model of the whole militia'. The wholesale reconstruction of Parliament's army was now in train. This decision also signalled the start of a competition among the senior commanders to escape blame for the military reverses since Marston Moor and to stake a claim to generalship in the new force. Essex as well as Manchester was now jockeying for position.[38]

In the thick of this commotion Cromwell took the bold step of a full-scale denunciation of Manchester and Essex to the House of Commons on 25 November. On the night before he spoke, the Countess of Manchester invited Cromwell and Sir Henry Vane to dine and pleaded that her husband 'did exceedingly honour and respect' Cromwell. But the die was cast. Cromwell replied, 'I wish I could see it'.[39] In the Commons the next day Cromwell accused Manchester of 'backwardness to all action' and attributed this to 'unwllingness in his Lordshipp to have this warre prose-cuted unto full victory'. Rather, Manchester would prefer 'it ended by accommodation'. And for this purpose it would be 'disadvantageous to bring the King too lowe'. Manchester, Cromwell insisted, had expressed 'much contempt and scorne for the commands from the Parliament'.[40] Second among Cromwell's specific charges of military incompetence against Manchester was the fact that 'he was very unwilling to the summoning of Tickhill Castle, and expressed much anger and threats against him that (being sent to quarter in the towne) did summon it, though upon the summons it was surrendered'. Cromwell told the Commons that 'his judgement was for Independency' and he said that although 'there might be some were Anabaptist' among his troops it was 'not for that he chose them but because they were honest and gallent men; men that were faithful in their duties and would fight'. The speech rang through the City and, according to Thomas Juxon, most men cried up Cromwell and cried Manchester down.[41]

Manchester replied to Cromwell both in a letter to the Lords and in a speech in the Upper House. He asserted that the privileges of the Lords had been traduced, not just his reputation. Cromwell, said Manchester, had said 'he hoped to live never to see a Nobleman in England, and that he loved such better than others because they did not love lords'. Moreover, Cromwell had 'expressed himself with contempt of the Assembly of Divines' as a 'company of persecutors' and wanted to be rid of 'this synod tyrannising over consciences'. Manchester objected to Cromwell's 'animos-itie against the Scottish Nation' and he told the Lords that Cromwell had said that he 'would be the first to draw his sword against the Scots who wanted to introduce Presbyterianism, and in a short time he hoped to destroy the nobility of England, composed of so many traitors'. Cromwell, Manchester alleged, had said that 'he hoped to see the day when there should not be a lord in England'. He accused Cromwell of proposing 'to form an army of Independent sectaries' that could 'lay down the law not only to the king but to the parliament' in case there was 'any conclusion of a peace such as might not stand with the these ends that honest men should aim at'. If such a peace was proposed 'this army might prevent such a mischeife'. But what really perturbed Manchester about Cromwell's views, though only some of them were aired in public, was that 'I saw they had a publique influence in the army'.[42]

On 25 November 1644 a Commons committee under Presbyterian MP Zouch Tate was appointed to examine Cromwell's accusations against Manchester.[43] A second committee was established to examine whether the privileges of the Lords had been abused. Lilburne gave evidence against Manchester to this committee. The two camps were now contesting the future direction of the war. On the one side were Cromwell, the Independents and the radical religious sects. On the other side were Essex, Manchester, Holles and the Presbyterians in the Commons, and the Scots. The political alliances were complex but the issue was not. Indeed, this great contest could be summed up in a single exchange. Manchester thought that 'if we beate the King 99 times he would be King still, and his posterity, and we subjects still; but if he beate us but once we should all be hang'd, and our posterity undone'. Cromwell damned this thought as being 'against fighting hereafter'.[44]

The Presbyterians were ready to move against Cromwell as 'an Incendiary'. The Scots 'endeavoured to turn the stream of all upon him and his party, for they say, "ruin him, for he's the head, and you ruin all"'. The MPs Bulstrode Whitelocke and Sir John Maynard were summoned to a private meeting at Essex's house in the Strand. Gathered there were the Scots commissioners, Holles, and his allies Sir Philip Stapleton and Sir John Meyrick. Whitelocke recalled the conversation, even reproducing the dialect of Scottish Chancellor Loudoun, who said: 'Ye ken vary weele that Lieutenant-General Cromwell is not friend of ours; he not only is no friend to us and to the government of our Church, but he is also no well-wisher to his Excellency [Essex], whom you and we have cause to love and honour'. The plan was that 'we will clept his wings from soaring to the prejudice of our cause'. And he continued, 'It is thought requiste for us, and for the carrying on of the cause of the tway kingdoms, that this obstacle or remora may be moved out of our way'. By 'moved out of our way' the company meant put on trial. Holles and his company 'spake smartly' against Cromwell, but Whitelocke advised that such a plan would be politically impossible even if legally valid. Cromwell, warned Whitelocke, 'hath (especially of late) gained no small interest in the House'. The significance of the meeting, which did not finally break up until two in the morning, is that it marked a transition in the loyalties of the Scots. They, like Manchester, had first been promoted by the war party MPs; now, like Manchester, they feared the rise of Independents and their tolerationist stance and swung behind the peace party.[45]

The contest between Independents and their allies and Presbyterians and their allies was reaching the point of meltdown. Cromwell's speech against Manchester was considered so controversial that John Dillingham's *Parliamentary Scout* simply refused to divulge the details to its readers, hoping that they would be 'buried in the grave of oblivion'. Some MPs were busy trying to halt what they saw as an imminent implosion of the military leadership. 'The leading parliamentarians', reported the Venetian ambassador, 'who were zealous on this point when it served their purpose, do not appear so at present but are trying to smoothe matters with unsubstantial expedients and to bring about unity'. Cromwell and others then moved the entire contest into a different register by proposing that all Members of Parliament, MPs and peers alike, should lay down their military commands. Presbyterian Zouch Tate pushed through the proposal, seconded by Independent Henry Vane. This drive was the root of the Self-Denying Ordinance and would clear the army of the moderates, albeit at the cost of Cromwell and his supporters also being required to resign. This was to go hand in hand with the army being reorganised, or 'new modelled'. It was a plan that had, at least at this stage, something for everyone and it avoided a disaster that no one wanted. Some MPs opposed the ordnance but it passed with considerable support in the Commons. In Thomas Juxon's judgement,

> This vote, though upon the face seem to confound all our armies and militia, yet indeed it is the way to lay a good foundation for them. It stills all differences between lord general and Waller, and between Lord Manchester and Cromwell . . . 'Tis a very strange piece of providence, and being but now so divided that wise men knew not what to say or do, or could see to the end of it.

The MPs had been staring into the abyss and were happy to have a new prospect to gaze on. The press gave the plan a very favourable reception. Lilburne distrusted Cromwell's manoeuvre, believing that Manchester should have been prosecuted as Strafford had been before him. Whatever the disappointments of the most radical supporters of the Independents this struggle had ended very differently than the previous contest within the war party. Then Pym, defending Essex, had vanquished Henry Marten. Now the momentum lay with those most determined to inflict a decisive military defeat on the king.[46]

Popular politics

These political differences were not just fought out among MPs, lords and the senior officers of the army. Battles involving more junior officers in Manchester's army were common as Presbyterians tried to rid the army of Independents and Sectaries, and vice versa. One supporter of Manchester was horrified that soldiers 'have gonn up into the pulpits . . . and preached to the whole parish'. The baptism of a horse in urine in Yaxley church in East Anglia by dragoons from radical Captain Beaumont's company was abhorred by Presbyterian heresy hunter Thomas Edwards.[47] The Venetian ambassador reported,

> Serious quarrels have occurred this week between Manchester and Cromuel, chief commanders of the army, about religion and church government, in which many of the soldiers have taken sides, and I hear there has been some fighting. This is most carefully concealed in order not to stir up worse humours in the body of this city, which is seriously affected.[48]

Even before the Solemn League and Covenant had taken full effect, William Lithgow, the Scottish tailor whom we last met traversing the lines of communication, was recording the ambiguous attitudes of hundreds of Londoners that he met towards Scots military assistance. Although Londoners were 'praying for our help', the name of the Scots was nevertheless as 'odious amongst Londoners as the name of Satan is to the soule of a Saint'. Lithgow defended his countrymen, 'Scotland hath done for them (said I) which they could not do for themselves which you acknowledge and are yet ungrateful'. For Lithgow, Scotland's continued support depended on Presbyterian reform: 'cast away your ceremonies, your holy days, superstitious rights, your Romeish letanie, and upbraiding our cavaliers, and then will Scotland prove a true sister to England; which if not, why should they go fight to maintain your Fopperies'. The Venetian ambassador reported, 'This canker of division about church government keeps spreading in London, and the more it is kept under by orders which do not destroy it, the worse, the poison grows'. Parliament's attempt to ban preaching except in the public churches was 'not obeyed and they do not venture to treat those who infringe it with severity'.[49] Essex certainly expressed antipathy towards the rude multitude invading the political sphere:

> General Essex . . . turning towards his colleagues said, Is this the liberty which we claim to vindicate by shedding our blood? This will be the reward of all our labours and our posterity will say that to deliver them from the yoke of the king we have subjected them to that of the common people. If we do this the finger of scorn will be pointed at us, and so I am determined to devote my life to repressing the audacity of the people.[50]

The whole of society was certainly alive with the debate over the conduct of the war, the future of Church government, and the freedom of the press. John Milton's *Areopagitica*, published in November 1644, was a direct response to the censorship laws of the previous year. Its subtitle was 'For the liberty of unlicence'd printing'. In prose often as evocative as the poetry of *Paradise Lost* it pictured the 'vast City' of London as 'the mansion house of liberty' in which

> the shop of warre hath not there more anvils and hammers waking to fashion the plates and instruments of armed Justice in defence of beleaguer'd Truth, then there be pens and heads there, sitting by their studious lamps, musing, searching, revolving new notions and ideas wherewith to present, as with their honour and their fealty the approaching Reformation: others as fast reading, trying all things, assenting to the force of reason and convincement.

This newly awakened popular consciousness was at risk from the censors and their Presbyterian backers. 'No man of worth' would be a licenser in Milton's view since it is 'as good almost kill a Man as kill a good Book'. The 'project of licencing crept out of the Inquisition, was catcht up by our Prelates, and hath caught some of our Presbyters'. If the licencing regime continues it 'will soon put it out of controversie that Bishops and Presbyters are the same to us both name and thing'. Milton would 'endure not an instructor that comes to me under the wardship of an overseeing fist'. Censorship was 'to the common people nothing less than a reproach' since it demonstrates that the government 'dare not trust them with an English pamphlet'.[51]

Right at the critical moment of the crisis between Cromwell and Manchester one such English pamphlet was being scattered through the streets of London. This stinging one-paragraph broadsheet was distributed on the night of 8–9 December 1644, two days before the Self-Denying Ordinance was voted on for the first time in the Commons. Entitled *Alas Pore Parliament how Art thou Betrai'd?*, it was printed by Richard Overton.[52] And, if the style is anything to go by, it was almost certainly written by him as well. Aimed at the Earls Manchester and Essex it complained, 'We have brave Generalls who fight for the King, and make pore people pay for their own destructions. One of them hath wrought finely in the darke all this while like a Divell, but the other hath shew'd himselfe an open enemie'. One of them, Manchester surely, 'hath culd out all the honestest Youth in the

Kingdome to keep them from Action, or for slaughter'. And it concluded, in what would become hallmark Leveller style,

> Neither of them worke, but make worke; when they should doe, they undoe, and indeed to undoe is all the marke they aim at. Do yee thinke that Greatnesse without Goodnesse can ever thrive in excellent actions? no, Honour without honesty stinkes: away with't. no more Lords and yee love me, they smell o' the Court.[53]

Perhaps it was Overton's broadside that the Venetian ambassador had seen when he reported 'seditious pamphlets reviling Essex and Manchester, demanding the dissolution of the Upper House because it always resists the popular will', had been scattered in the streets. Certainly the Lords were alarmed enough to demand that those responsible were apprehended. The Lords hauled in George Jeffery, an apprentice of Cornhill hosier Joseph Blackwell, who had found twenty-two copies stuffed into his master's stall boards. Jeffery took them to show his master at his shop but 'some of the unruly Neighbours came in, and got some of them away', leaving him only eight to take to the lord mayor. One of those named as distributing Overton's broadsheet was Thomas Lambe. Overton was a by this time a member of Lambe's congregation. Despite repeated demands from the Lords the Stationers' Company were no nearer catching Overton by the end of the year.[54]

Overton's broadsheet was by no means the only invention in these debates by a future Leveller. William Walwyn, though never formally part of a separatist congregation, was in principle a tolerationist and had been making this case in language very similar to that of Milton since the very earliest days of the Revolution. *The Humble Petition of the Brownists* of 1641 was, confusingly, also issued as *A New Petition of the Papists*. The former is a more accurate title because although the pamphlet argues for the extension of toleration to Catholics its main argument is a defence of the radical religious sects.[55] The following year *Some Considerations Tending to the Undeceiving of Those, Whose Judgements are Misinformed* put the same argument in the form of an appeal for Puritan unity in the face of the royalist threat:

> Wee heare of daily plunderings, rapes, and murthers of the Cavaliers, women and children runne through, and many other butcheries, and yet wee passe by these, as if by no interest they concerned us, and let flie our

speeches only against the Puritan for plucking a raile down, or a paire of Organs, a Surplice, Crucifix, or painted window, which are indeed no way conducible to the substantial worship of God.[56]

In early 1644 the five Dissenting Brethren in the Assembly of Divines set out a moderate Independent position in their *Apologetical Narration*. This triggered a widespread political and ecclesiastical debate among Independents. By mid-1644 Walwyn's arguments had become much more sharply focussed because the rise of the Presbyterians and the attempted imposition of censorship provided visible anti-tolerationist targets. *The Compassionate Samaritane*, addressed to the Commons of England, immediately takes aim at the Assembly of Divines and the licensers who have 'stope the mouthes of good men'.[57] Like Milton a few months later, Walwyn sees the Presbyterians returning to the practice of trying to unite Protestants by means of 'Fines Imprisonments, Pillories, &c. used by the Bishops'. Thus the actions of the Divines mean that 'the tyrannie over conscience that was exercised by the Bishops, is like to be continued by the Presbyiters'. It is unacceptable that the Divines 'should take the same course of prohibitions with the Bishops, locke up the Presse, and then vent themselves in a furious way . . . in their late preachings and Pamphlets against the Anabaptists'. Such people, who 'echo the Kings words and take the Bishops course', are doing the king's work. Walwyn 'cannot blame the Separatists now for crying out, they feare your Club more than your Reason'. This is all the more unworthy since the separatists' political views are at the heart of the parliamentary project: representative government, supremacy of Parliament and opposition to the royal veto.[58]

Richard Overton had also long been in the lists as an illegal printer and pamphleteer. By 1644 he was a Baptist in Thomas Lambe's church. This was exactly the kind of congregation that was the target of so much Presbyterian ire. Overton had already developed an almost surreal style of satirical commentary written in verse. In 1642, when, as part of its campaign against idolatrous monuments, Parliament had ordered Cheapside Cross demolished, Overton wrote and printed *Articles of High Treason Exhibited against Cheap-side Crosse*.[59] In an imaginary dialogue between Master Papist and Master Newes, the articles of treason against the Cross, its last will and testament, and its epitaph are all laid before the reader. In the same year Overton also wrote *New Lambeth Fayre*, in which, again in verse, he imagines all the belongings of the old church up for sale at Lambeth fair. The bishops are also busy selling their wares: the Book of Common Prayer, crucifixes, bishops' gowns, and wedding and burial licenses. But eventually Parliament catches up with the bishops:

> With that the Bishops cri'd we are undone,
> we are so fatt, alas we cannot run,
> But unto them a lustie Porter struts,
> Sirs here's a Basket that will hold your Guts,
> Take my advice, (the knave have Halters plenty)
> You'l run the better when your bellie's emptie.[60]

The developing political crisis focussed Overton's writing, as it had done Walwyn's. In 1644 Overton published a longer pamphlet with a wholly different kind of originality. *Mans Mortalitie* was a philosophical and theological treatise designed to prove, as its subtitle spelt out, 'that whole Man (as a rationall Creature) is a Compound wholly mortall, contrary to that common distinction of Soule and Body'. The notion that the soul as well as the body ceased to exist at the point of death remains a contested notion in our century, and in the seventeenth century it was an extreme doctrine even among separatists. Overton thought that 'Mans Foundation to be wholly Dust' meant that only God was immortal and supernatural. But the arguments from 'natural reason' in the *Mans Mortalitie* were longer still and this put Overton at the leading edge of mid-seventeenth-century thought. So it is not fanciful of one historian to judge that this work both 'reaches back to the long tradition of scepticism, and forward, through Hobbes, to the materialism of Marx'. The pamphlet was condemned by Parliament in August 1644 and the Stationers' agents were sent to track down its author in the same order that sent them after John Milton, who had just anonymously published the *Doctrine and Discipline of Divorce*.[61]

Overton was already an accomplished illegal printer; from his writing over this period it is clear that he also had an unsurpassed popular style of writing and an intellect as curious as Walwyn's. Both were intellectually more radical that Lilburne at this point. But whether from the writings of Overton and Walwyn, or from the actions of Lilburne, it can be no surprise that as the year turned they would all find themselves increasingly at odds with the defenders of Presbyterianism. And their opposition would be mounted from a platform different to that of mainstream Independency in some important, though as yet not obvious, respects.

The Independents: unity and difference

After Pym's defeat of Henry Marten and the radicals in late 1642, the Independents, broadly the inheritors of the mantle of the war party, remained united in the face of the growing challenge of the Presbyterians, broadly the inheritors of the peace party. Modern historians have rightly pointed to the fact that future Levellers were part of the Independent alliance in this phase of the Revolution.[62] But there is also an important truth contained in the older claim that in fact three parties existed at this time: Presbyterians, Independents and sects.[63] And while it was true that the Independents and the sects remained united against the Presbyterians there were also differences in the ways in which they fought a common enemy.

Milton's *Aeropagitica* addressed the 'Lords and Commons', while the title of Walwyn's pamphlet addressed the Commons alone as the arbiter of the nation's fate, a presumption for which Levellers were soon to be attacked. Overton thought it better, as we have seen, if there were 'no more Lords'. Milton argued that stable government would be better served by toleration, but he did not advocate the positive value of the separatists' political programme, as did Walwyn. For Walwyn, in the times of the bishops, many Independents 'fled to places where they might live at ease, and enjoy their hundred pounds a yeare, without danger', while 'the Brownist and Anabaptist endured the heate and brunt of persecution'. And he was disappointed that the Independents in the Assembly of Divines justified toleration for themselves on the basis of 'the nearnesse between them and the Presbyterians', not on a wider defence of toleration for all separatists. In short, says Walwyn, the Independents left the separatists 'in the lurch'.[64]

And then there is the question not simply of what was said but of how it was articulated, by whom, and to whom. Milton was arguing for freedom to pamphleteer. But Walwyn, Overton, Lilburne and their printers, including the printer of Milton's divorce pamphlet, were systematically and repeatedly producing illegal pamphlets. Cromwell may have been making the same points about Essex and Manchester in the Commons, and expressing anger at the nobility privately, as Overton was in his broadsheet *Alas Pore Parliament*, but the context was very different. It is one thing to move against a political opponent within the confines of the Commons' chamber, quite another to broadcast the conflict abroad in the streets of London and thereby invite the mass of the population to join in the argument. It is exactly this aspect of events to which Essex objected so violently. Manchester was clear in his attack on Cromwell that it was 'the publique influence on the army' that 'made me jealous of his intencions'.[65] And Cromwell could swiftly alter course when he found a less damaging way of obtaining the removal of Manchester through the adoption of the Self-Denying Ordinance. Lilburne thought the attack on Manchester should have been continued. One does not have to agree with the Machiavellian explanations, then or by later historians, of Cromwell's actions for he certainly could not have foreseen that he would escape the conditions of the Self-Denying Ordinance. It is simply that he and Lilburne occupied different positions within the Independent camp. Lilburne had little to lose in pursuing Manchester. Cromwell had a great deal to lose if the pursuit was unsuccessful, or produced a backlash, or provoked his enemies—some or all of which were possible.

In origin and orientation the future Levellers focussed on popular politics and popular mobilisation. They certainly aimed to alter the course of national politics but they were not themselves, with the exception of Henry Marten and Thomas Rainsborough, either MPs or senior army commanders. There were some gentry figures among them, though usually second sons sent into trade, but they were more likely to be in the middle to lower ends of the 'middling sort'. They were certainly either more radical separatists, or sympathetic to radical separatists, than mainstream Independents. They had seen action, and often been injured. Lilburne and Eyre were veterans of Edgehill and Brentford before they joined the Eastern Association. Sexby and Eyre were, presumably, veterans of the Ironsides' decisive charge at Marston Moor. Lilburne had been shot through the arm at Walton Hall in June 1644. Thomas Prince marched to the relief of Gloucester and had been so badly injured at Newbury that he was two years in the care of a surgeon and had thirty-six bone fragments taken from his body. William Larner fought in Lord Robartes's regiment, but illness brought him back to London by 1645.[66] These were men who were unlikely to yield when they thought they were in the right, even to their allies.

At this stage in the struggle, however, the differences between the future Levellers and the Independents existed only in embryo and had little practical effect. But over the next eighteen months they were to become active elements in the divisions within the Independent alliance and to play their part in the emergence of the future Levellers as an identifiable current in their own right.

CHAPTER 7

The Coming of the Levellers

John Lilburne, William Larner and Thomas Prince were all home from the war by 1645. Lilburne did not formally leave the army until in April he refused to swear the Covenant, a precondition of remaining in the New Model. He was the only senior officer to refuse to do so, although it is clear from his own writings that it was his disillusion with the earl of Manchester that was a large part of the reason he declined to serve any longer. When the future Levellers arrived back in the capital they found that the long-rumbling arguments both between Presbyterians and Independents, and within the Independent camp, about Church and state were about reach a new intensity. The Venetian ambassador thought, 'In spite of the efforts to settle the differences between Manchester and Cromuel these sectaries keep them up in order to keep their party to the fore'.[1] But in reality every party to the argument was now fighting tooth and nail to establish their view of how the nation should be governed both ecclesiastically and temporally. An extensive pamphlet war between the radical sects, the Independents and the Presbyterians stoked the flames.

Three of the Presbyterian champions in this war of 'paper-bullets' were well known to radicals. William Prynne and John Bastwick were the Puritan martyrs who had first drawn Lilburne into politics in the 1630s. It had been for distributing Bastwick's pamphlets that Lilburne had been imprisoned by the Star Chamber before the Revolution. But Prynne and Bastwick were now staunch Presbyterians and Prynne had recently acted as Colonel Edward King's lawyer when he was brought before a Commons committee.[2] Moreover, Prynne had now turned gamekeeper and was legal counsel for the Stationers' Company, now once again being asked to stem the tide of unlicensed pamphlets.[3]

The third champion, Thomas Edwards, had long been a supporter of increased censorship. He was just about to make his name as the best-known heresy hunter of the Revolutionary decade. Back in 1641 he had been the first Presbyterian to be engaged by a future Leveller, Katherine Chidley, in print. Edwards had never replied to her initial attack, in part because it was seen as demeaning to debate a woman and in part because, shortly after he wrote his first work, Presbyterians under preacher Edmund Calamy's guidance had decided to avoid print controversy as a danger to parliamentary unity. That agreement had broken down when the Independents in the Assembly of Divines had issued an *Apologetical Narration*, their call for toleration, in January 1644.[4]

Edwards returned to the attack in *Antipologie*, a blast against the Dissenting Brethren's *Apologetical Narration*. Katherine Chidley was again the first future Leveller into print with a new response, *A New-Yeares-Gift to Mr Thomas Edwards*. This was followed at the end of the year by a second broadsheet, *Good Counsell to the Petitioners for Presbyterian Government*.[5] Here Chidley gave Edwards a dressing-down for failing to respond to her first reply, for the 'frothinesse' of his reasoning, and for the 'rangling-insinuating-contradictory-revengeful' nature of his tract. Her only hostage to fortune was to repeatedly mock Edwards for not producing the 'large tractates' that he had promised would follow his first book. The following year Edwards certainly met that challenge with the three-part encyclopedia of sectarian errors, *Gangraena*. But even in the single month of January 1645 the Chidley–Edwards exchange was only one of many.

Three days after Chidley delivered *New-Yeares-Gift*, the second edition of Walwyn's tolerationist pamphlet *The Compassionate Samaritane* rolled from Richard Overton's secret press.[6] That same month John Lilburne was drawn into the controversy when William Prynne published *Truth Triumphing*, a 156-page response to Independent preacher John Goodwin's *Innocencies Triumph*, which was itself a reply to a previous tract by Prynne.[7] Lilburne's reply came out on 7 January 1645. It was the first political or religious tract Lilburne had written since his release from prison in November 1640. Lilburne complained that, though they had both suffered at the hands of the bishops, now Prynne 'and the Black-Coates in the Synod have not dealt fairly with your Antagonists in stopping the Presse against us'. The Presbyterians are, Lilburne says, proving more cruel than the bishops. Like Chidley, Lilburne favoured the gathered churches' convention of refusing to maintain the 'Blacke-coates with Tythes'. And though one of Prynne's friends had told Lilburne that he was like a small shrub in comparison to Prynne's great cedar, Lilburne replied, 'goe you and tell the tall Cedar, the little Shrub have a bout with him'. Prynne's supporters then, among other things, judged it 'an act of wisdom' to close the presses to Lilburne and his associates, arguing that otherwise every 'Church and State disturber' would print 'what the madness of his brain' dictates and there 'would be no end to strife'. Lilburne was perhaps unwise to taunt Prynne by saying that 'I weigh it not' if 'you'll run to Parliament and presse them upon their Covenant to take vengeance upon on me', since that is exactly the course Prynne took.[8]

In a pattern to be much repeated, the authorities, Prynne among them, invoked legal sanction and on 17 January the Commons ordered Lilburne brought before the Committee of Examinations, the body charged with enforcing censorship. As it happened, Lilburne's case was not heard until May because, while walking in Moorfields, he was accidently struck in the eye by a pike. He was seriously hurt, his face was slightly disfigured and he was left in need reading glasses for the rest of his life. But while action against Lilburne was delayed the Stationers were busy tracking down other radcials. On the same day that the Commons ordered action be taken against Lilburne the Stationers reported to the Lords that they had at last found the press they thought might be responsible for the attack on Essex and Manchester, *Alas Poore Parliament*. They had arrested Nicholas Tue at his house in Coleman Street. Tue was a member of Thomas Lambe's General Baptist Church, now moved from Whitechapel to Bell Alley, off Coleman Street. In 1643 Tue had already been arrested for 'admitting assemblies into his private house' and 'confessing himself to be of the separation'. The Coleman Street press had produced Lilburne's *An Answer to Nine Arguments*, an old tract dating from Lilburne's persecution in the late 1630s. This had as its cover the same George Glover engraving of Lilburne that William Larner had used on the front of *The Christian Mans Triall* in 1641. Tue also admitted that the press had produced Lilburne's letter to Prynne and that Overton ran the press in his house. But he claimed not to know Overton well. This seems to have been a device to say just enough to get out on bail and he was duly released on 10 February. From this evidence it seems highly likely that Larner already knew Tue and, quite possibly, Overton. Tue and Overton will have known Walwyn since their Coleman Street press printed his *The Compassionate Samaritane*. Tue must have gauged his confession correctly as Overton was not arrested. But the press was seized and Overton was out of action as a printer until March.[9]

The rise of Martin Marpriest

Overton's return to the fray in early spring caused a publishing sensation. In a series of wildly satirical pamphlets he ripped into Presbyterian rule as it was entrenching itself. In quick succession he produced *The Arraignment of Mr Persecution* on 8 April 1645, with a second edition coming out either later in April or in May; a sequel, *A Sarcred Decretall*, published on 7 June; then, on the 27th of the same month, *Martin's Eccho*; and on 2 July *The Nativity of Sir John Presbyter*.[10] Thomas Edwards and John Bastwick are targets throughout this series of tracts. All these pamphlets were signed with the pseudonym Martin Marpriest. This was a brilliant conceit designed to recall memories of the Elizabethan anti-episcopal tracts written under the name Martin Marprelate in 1588–9. Overton's style, already established in the Cheapside Cross pamphlet, was perfectly suited to reviving the irreverent, not to say abusive, attacks on the clergy that characterised the seven Marprelate tracts. But 'Younge Martin Mar-priest, Son to old Martin', took aim not just at the clergy but also at the entire governing structure of Presbyterianism: the Solemn League and Covenant, the recent ordinance reinforcing tithes, print censorship, the ban on unordained preachers and, of course, the Assembly of Divines. This necessarily, and as one of its prime purposes, was not just a defence of toleration but a positive assertion of the virtues of the radical sects.

Overton's style alone would have placed the Marpriest pamphlets on the very radical end of the Independent alliance. The sheer force of expression denoted militancy. Overton created a cast of characters to represent the ideological positions in the battles taking place around him. Martin Marpriest himself is aided by his cousin Martin Claw-Clergy, Bartholomew Bang-Priest, Christopher Scale-Sky and Rowland Rattle-Priest. Their enemies are Sir Symon Synod and Sir John Presbyter. *The Arraignment of Mr Persecution* is written as a play-script in which Mr Persecution is brought to trial before the Judge, Parliament, and the Justices of the Peace, Reason, Humanity, and Conformity. Sir Symon Synod and Sir John Presbyter speak in defence of Mr Persecution. Sir Simon Synod tries to empanel a fresh jury to acquit Mr Persecution and this includes Mr Satan, Mr Antichrist, Mr Spanish Inquisition, Mr High Commission, Mr Assembly-of-Divines, Mr Scotch-Government, Sir John Presbyter, Mr Ecclesiastical-Supremacy and Mr Pontificall-Revenue. But the Judge and Justices strike down the proposal.

As the trial of Mr Persecution continues he is accused of suffering 'nothing to be Licenced, Printed, Preached, or otherwise published, but himself alloweth, and having thus bound the hands of, and stopt the mouthes of all good men, then comes forth in print against them like an Armed man'. Despite the best efforts of Symon Synod and John Presbyter, Mr Persecution is found guilty on the evidence of Mr Liberty of Conscience and by a jury which includes Mr Politick Power, who insists that Mr Persecution is a danger to the maxim that 'the safety of the people is the Sovereign Law'. Another juryman is named Mr Compassionate Samaritane, as was Walwyn's pamphlet. A third jury member, Mr Truth-and-Peace, says, 'I commend unto you, and to the necessary perusall of the Commons and Nobles of England, that most famous peece, called, *The Compassionate Samaritane*, as a most exact modell of rationality'.[11]

Overton's next tract, *A Sacred Decretall*, where *The Compassionate Samaritane* is again promoted, parodies the Presbyterian defence of tithes by adopting their own voice:

If the People once understand their owne Rights, and that the exaction of Tythes, is mere Theft and Robbery, they'l have the wit (if they be wise) to keep their own, cease hiring us to cheate and delude them to their faces, while they want to supply their owne necessities, and cashiere us, as they did the Bishops; then the parliament will regaine their Power, and the People their native Liberties from our divine usurpation, and we will be laid levill with the Mechannik illiterate Laicks, (a wickedness not to be mentioned in the Church of God) this is MARTINS drift, the great Anti-Clergie; O that profane Martin! that cursed Martin! that wicked Martin! wring of his neck, for ever and ever!, And let the people say, AMEN.[12]

But there are passages where the satire halts and straightforward political analysis takes over. For instance, there is an account of the decision, led by Edmund Calamy, not to pursue religious debates with Anabaptists and Brownists until the Presbyterians were in the ascendant. Then the Presbyterians 'changed our posture' and made 'all the pulpits in London . . . ring against the Anabaptists, Brownists &c., so lowd that the Divine Eccho might easily be heard beyond the River Tweed'. And so battle was joined, and again adopting he Presbyterians' voice, Overton writes,

like Noble renegadoes, wee quickly plac'd Jockey in the right wing, Sir John in the left wing, and OLD NICK in the Battalia, and seeing the Sectaries had Toleration in their right wing, no Tythes in their left wing and Christ in the Battalia; wee wheel'd both wings into the Battalia, and facing our Leader, discharged all in triplicity upon them bravely resolving to take Christ Prisoner, make him a Presbyter, kill all his Sectaries, rout the Independents, and make them runne before the Wolfe.[13]

This is a fairly accurate account of the disposition of political forces, and interesting in that Overton sees Independents and Sectaries as allied but distinct forces. Indeed the text goes on to warn of the extirpation of the sects from the New Model as a trap set for Cromwell. A similar warning in *The Nativity of Sir John Presbyter* blames the Presbyterians for the argument between Manchester and Cromwell.[14] In *Martin's Eccho* Overton feared an England in which the clergy would

shine most gloriously in their Sattin doublets, and cloakes lin'd with Plush, their Wives and Children Flourish like young Princes, their spits fill'd with Pigges, Geese and Capons, their Caldrons with beefe, their barnes with Corne, their pastures with sheep, their Prisons with Hereticks; Widows, Orphanes, and Lame Souldiers, standing with their Pitchers, begging Pottage at others doors, and the Independents, Brownists and Anabaptists driven into Augure-holes, as it was in Primative times.[15]

This characteristically powerful passage, with its sharp contrasts between the fate of rich and poor, draws our attention to the popular audience to which Overton addressed the Marpriest tracts. This was not learned theological disquisition, though it was intelligent and informed. This was popular politics of a kind in which the Levellers were to specialise. Indeed *Martins Eccho* ends with an address 'to the Common People, as you call them', in which Overton contrasts the situation during the first years of the Revolution with the conditions under Presbyterian rule. 'Before the Synod was Assembled, the cryes of the people were heard, their Petitions answered, miseries redress'ed, Monopolies removed, Oppressions eased, tender Consciences respected, and servants of God delivered out of Prisons, Courts of Tyranny and Oppression supresse'd &c'. But now things are 'quite altered'. Now there are 'thousands of petitions of poor Widdows, Orphans, and all manner of distressed, oppressed persons who Cry daily, and cannot be heard'. Overton once again strikes the note of class difference:

the fatt Priests can have Ordinance upon Ordinance for their ends, they have the sweat of other mens browes confine'd on them by an Ordinance, while others cannot have their just requests or their owne Rights answered, though their wives and children perish, our Presbyters wives must goe like Ladies, with their silkes and Taffety, some with their Fans, and silver Watchers forsooth hang by their girdles, to please the Pretty sweet-faced Mopphets withal; prittie Things, 'tis a pittie there's not an Ordinance al this while for them to wear Rattles.

And then Overton asks his readers to contrast this with their own condition:

consider . . . for what your Estates and blood hath been engag'd, The Liberties of the Subject, and the Protestant Religion, now how much after this vast expense, this sea of blood, of the Subjects Liberties, have you obtained? Even this much; hee that shall open his mouth freely for the vindications of your Native Liberties, cannot doe it without the hazard of his owne, yea of his life.[16]

This pamphlet skirmish bears testimony to an emerging group of radical voices including Lilburne, Chidley, Overton and Walwyn, united in opposition to Presbyterian hierarchy. Lilburne's and Walwyn's pamphlets had been produced on Overton's press in Tue's Coleman Street house while, after this press was seized, the Marpriest pamphlets were being printed by Larner's press in its hiding place off Bishopsgate Street.

John Lilburne had, since his recovery from the accident in Moorfields, been travelling to Lincolnshire in pursuit of his old Presbyterian quarry Colonel King. But when he returned to London he was once again before the Committee of Examinations on 16 May. About this time he was confronted by Prynne himself in Westminster Hall. Lilburne tried to ignore him but Prynne touched Lilburne on the sleeve and attempted to tax 'the obscure apprentice' with 'forgetting his duty to Parliament' and other shortcomings. Lilburne, at least according to Prynne, 'fell into an angry fit' and said, 'A turd in your teeth; if you were out of the Hall I would teach you to lay your hand on mine'. After Lilburne published an account of his time at the Committee of Examinations, he was arrested on 18 June, but was released without charge. At this point he could still rely on the support of Cromwell and other Independents.

Lilburne had also been pursuing his claim for reparations for his Star Chamber imprisonment, including by journeying to the army to get a letter from Cromwell to intercede on his behalf. In the course of this he witnessed at close quarters the parliamentary victory at the battle of Langport and was charged with bringing the news to the House of Commons. This he did in a long report that included praise for Rainsborough's part in the engagement. A few days later, on 19 July, Lilburne was again about the business of extracting his Star Chamber award in Parliament when he met William Walwyn and others telling four MPs that they had heard that Speaker of the House William Lenthall had been sending money and information to the king at Oxford. Unfortunately for Lilburne, two of his greatest enemies, Bastwick and Colonel King, overheard the discussion and sent a note to the Speaker informing him that Lilburne had libelled him. Lenthall, without calling Lilburne, got the House to vote to imprison him for further questioning. The Committee of Examinations' case against Lilburne from January had not got anywhere and so it seems that Lilburne's Presbyterian foes contrived other means to silence him, especially as they feared he might be about to give evidence against Denzil Holles implicating him in links with royalists.[17]

Within five days of Lilburne's arrest, Prynne was firing another paper-bullet aimed at justifying the suppression of Lilburne and his associates, *A Fresh Discovery of some New Wandering-Blazing-Stars and Firebrands*. At this stage, Prynne and his allies are struggling to bring the radical underground into exact focus. Overton's Marpriest pamphlets took centre stage, condemned by Prynne as 'compiled, published, printed, vended, dispersed, by Independent Sectaries, who highly applaud them'. In particular he is horrified by the final oration of *Martin's Eccho* because it is 'directed to the common people, to excite them to mutiny and Rebellion against the Assembly, Parliament, their Military, Civill and Ecclesiasticall present proceedings'. But *A Fresh Discovery* wrongly identifies Independent Henry Robinson as author of the Martin pamphlets. More accurately, Prynne identifies John Lilburne as 'the Ringleader of this New Regiment of Firebrands'. He accuses Lilburne of chairing a meeting at the Windmill Tavern to frame a petition to disperse the Assembly of Divines to 'country cures' to prevent them settling Church government. Lilburne later disputed the details of the meeting, but not that it took place. And Prynne probably had Lilburne in mind when he attacked those who refuse to take the Solemn Covenant because 'they fear to disengage the considerable party they have in the Army'. Prynne seems to have had a pretty clear idea where Larner's press was, possibly through his Stationers' Company links, when he identifies 'Mr. Printer of all these new Seditious Libels, in an Alley in

Bishopsgate Street'. Indeed it may have been this identification of the location of the press by Prynne that caused its hasty removal from Larner's Bishopgate premises to a then more remote, semi-rural house in Goodman's Fields beyond Aldgate.[18]

On the very day that *A Fresh Discovery* appeared, Lilburne was hauled before the Committee for Examinations and imprisoned. The following day, 25 July, Lilburne responded with a recapitulation of the whole story of his current imprisonment in *The Copy of a Letter from Lieutenant Colonell John Lilburne to a Friend*. Again this came from Larner's press. On 9 August 1645 the Committee of Examinations committed Lilburne to Newgate for writing a seditious book.[19]

As Lilburne lay in prison, John Bastwick contributed *A Just Defence of John Bastwick* to the pamphlet war. Here Lilburne is portrayed as part of the Independent party, but with a distinct organised group of supporters.[20] Bastwick's pamphlet is a reply to a printed letter of Lilburne's attacking the Presbyterians. Bastwick says that Lilburne's 'Letter is now as publike as weekly newes, and in every bodyes hands'. It is the 'ordinary practice' of Lilburne 'and those in his society', says Bastwick, 'to abuse such in tongue and in print' in this and 'his many other Pamphlets'. Bastwick directly refers to organised efforts by Lilburne's supporters to distribute printed material 'through the kingdome, that so they may with more facility spread abroad and publish the sentence given by the Lieutenant against the whole Parliament'.[21] Lilburne's doctrines have been causing divisions as far afield as Boston and 'through Lincolnshire'.[22] From this it seems that Lilburne was continuing to make use during his recent visit to Lincolnshire of contacts made during his time in the Eastern Association to ensure that printed material was distributed in the area.

Bastwick clearly sees Lilburne as the leader of a group of 'Rabble rout, tagragge and bobtaile' that he encountered at the Committee of Examinations. Walwyn (or 'Worly', as Bastwick and Lilburne both spell the name) is specifically referred to in this context as the only gentleman among Lilburne's followers. Bastwick sees this as an organised, self-sustaining group.[23] Lilburne 'is but the mouth, and the foreman of that Tribe, and what he did, they all owne', as the 'champion' of the Independents who are 'applauding all his actions'. Lilburne, he says, is 'upheld by that party'. Thus far Bastwick portrays Lilburne and his supporters as a group within the Independents.[24] But Bastwick also clearly sees from the behaviour of Lilburne's supporters at the Committee for Examinations that they have a distinctive set of ideas and allegiances against which he warns the Independents. Lilburne's supporters, says Bastwick,

> gave laws to the Committee, and would not be examined but upon their own tearmes, crying out of injustice, and threatening that they would bring up the whole City, and a thousand such insolencies they used there for many dayes together; all of which doe manifest, that if in time their party grow a little stronger, they will give laws to Parliament . . . or else they will take authority into their own hands; for Lieutantant-Colonell John Lilburne hath plainly taught his Disciples, that the power that now resides in Parliament, is inherent in the people . . . and affirmes, that the power is the people's birth-right.[25]

'No men, not even the Independents themselves', says Bastwick, should be 'abetting with Lieutentant-Colonell Lilburne'. For once the power of Parliament is destroyed 'you shall shortly see . . . every servant become a Master and a Mistris, and cast off the yoke of obedience to their Superiours, whether Parents, Masters or Governours . . . for I well perceive the poore people are all deluded by his false information'.[26]

Undeterred by these attacks, the future Levellers remained in the field. On 10 October, Walwyn published *Strong Motives, Or Loving and Modest Advice Unto the Petitioners for Presbyterian Government*, which caused something of a sensation by reproducing a paragraph from the conclusion to Cromwell's report to Parliament on the capture of Bristol that had been censored from the officially printed copy. This paragraph had been removed by the Presbyterian majority because it was a renewed call for religious toleration.[27] Yet again we see the radicals in alliance with Cromwell, but in their own way and with their own methods.

On the same day appeared *Englands Birth-Right Justified*, written by Richard Overton and John Lilburne, despite the latter's incarceration. The next day *England's Lamentable Slavery*, written by William Walwyn 'after discussions with his friend Lilburne', was published. The Overton–Lilburne pamphlet is much longer and contains a number of additional letters and petitions that support its argument. Nevertheless there are significant similarities between the contents of the two publications. In both Cromwell is advised to circumvent orders that are seen to keep him out of London and to return to the Commons, where his political value would outweigh his military value in the field. No doubt the decisive victory over the king at the battle of Naseby in June encouraged the view that the crucial struggle was now over the future political settlement of the nation. Consequently, *Englands Birth-Right Justified* argues that the charges that Cromwell brought against Manchester are unfinished business: 'let him perfect what he began' and 'lay Manchester flat on his back'. Both pamphlets also claimed that the supporters of the parliamentary cause had undergone much hardship and deprivation during the war and were now disappointed by the slowness of Parliament to meet their grievances. There are specific complaints in both pamphlets that Parliament was not above the law and should be subordinate to the people who elected it. But the two pamphlets also contain information about organisational cooperation between the future leaders of the Levellers.[28]

Walwyn's pamphlet is a protest at Lilburne's imprisonment and insists that there is little progress if the Star Chamber is abolished but the 'imprisoning of men' continues 'contrary to law, equitie, and justice'. In a direct reference to Lilburne's case it concludes, 'All the Art and Sophisterie in the world, will not availe to perswade you, that you are not in New gate, much less that you are at libertie'.[29] Moreover in the postscript, 'The Printer to the Reader', Walwyn again urges support for Lilburne's cause. And in the final sentence of the pamphlet Walwyn 'desires thee to read' Overton and Lilburne's *England's Birth-Right Justified*. Here we see again direct collaboration and mutual support between Overton, Lilburne and Walwyn some two years before the Levellers were called such.[30]

But once Lilburne was freed on 14 October Prynne was again in print to assail him. In the preface to *The Lyar Confounded* Prynne describes 'notorious lyes' against Parliament spread by Lilburne 'and his confederates' in 'seditious Printed Papers' which are 'scattered abroad by one Leaner and others, among Kentish Malignants and Male-contents in other parts'.[31] Prynne, again wrongly, attributes the Martin Marpriest pamphlets to Lilburne, alleging, correctly, that they have the 'self same Letter and Presse' as Lilburne's letters. It is perhaps indicative of the close relationship among the core group of future Levellers that Prynne thought he detected Lilburne's 'very Expressions and Phrases' in Overton's work. Prynne goes on to describe how Lilburne 'after his old manner' had his *Copy of a Letter* 'sent to a private Unlicensed Presse (alwaies ready at his command) where being speedily Printed, he dispersed the printed Copies thereof every where by his Agents among his Friends, and Confederates, who vented them underhand for money'.[32] Here we begin to see, from the point of view of their enemies, how the future Levellers appeared as a distinct group with its own organisation and aims within the broader current of Independency.

The attempts to repress Lilburne's supporters did not diminish with his own release. Prynne, as chair of the committee appointed to consider Lilburne's Star Chamber reparations, tried to block his settlement. He also had a hand in briefly returning Lilburne to jail over accusations against Colonel King in April 1646. Even more seriously, the Stationers were hunting down the secret presses. Joseph Hunscot of the Stationers' Company had long been on the trail of printers of anti-Presbyterian tracts. Embittered after losing his preferred government post while fighting for Parliament he was a man with a grudge.

However, his petition for redress provides valuable evidence of proto-Leveller organisation. Hunscot claims to have got on to the trail of his quarry by cross-examining a woman, the daughter of a William Browne, a bookseller, whom he found selling seditious pamphlets in the street. Before he revealed his identity as a Stationer, she told Hunscot that she had got the pamphlets from 'one Lilburne in Newgate'.[33] Hunscot searched Browne's house and found a 'great store' of printed material. He then went and searched Lilburne's chambers without success. At this moment *Englands Birth-Right* hit the streets and it complained bitterly of Hunscot as a robbing thief and rogue who had, while Elizabeth Lilburne was lying pregnant alongside her husband in Newgate, raided their house and stolen their goods, including their child-linen. Lilburne and Overton also complained of Hunscot's raids on other friends of Parliament, presumably the Browne family, where he 'doe rob all choice old books as well as new'. This simply enraged Hunscot, who then returned with a new warrant to arrest Browne at his house. But Browne gave the constable the slip and left Hunscot with only the daughter and another haul of 'scandalous Bookes and Pamphlets'. Shortly after, William Browne was arrested, but, much to Hunscot's dismay, he was acquitted. Browne told Hunscot that if he ever came to search his house again he would 'knock out his braines'. The hapless Hunscot then moved against Larner and his press at Goodman's Fields.[34]

On the day after *The Lyar Confounded* appeared Hunscot seized the very press that might answer Prynne.[35] But as Stationers' Company men tried to break into the Goodman's Fields house they found that the printers held the door against the raiding party. Eventually the door gave way but by then the illegal printers had managed to descend down a rope from an upper window and escape through the garden. Nevertheless, the press and a store of books were seized by Hunscot. But this had little impact for, with remarkable persistence, a new press and type were set up again in

Larner's Bishopsgate headquarters, with Lilburne living close by. This press ran until it too was seized in 1646. Not entirely surprisingly, Hunscott said he would like to see Larner 'whipt once a day, for six weeks . . . and then to be hanged'.[36]

The coming of the Levellers and Thomas Edwards's *Gangraena*

The battle of Naseby in June 1645 was the final turning point of the war, but it was not until the following year that the conflict was finally fought to a conclusion. In the course of 1646 the Scottish army was paid off and ushered back to its homeland. A moderated form of Presbyterianism was adopted as orthodoxy within the established Church. This was made clear in April when the Commons adopted a declaration running counter to Scottish proposals, allowing for a Presbyterian church that was subservient to Parliament and encompassed some toleration of the Independent churches. These developments somewhat attenuated the debates over Church government but the polarisation over religion fed into the polarisation over state modelling. Presbyterian conservativism in religion might not always mean conservatism in politics, but there was a significant overlap as the Presbyterians came increasingly to take their stand for the old constitution of king, Lords and Commons.

In February 1646 the Scots commissioners were given a warm welcome at the Common Council, cementing a political bloc with the Presbyterians in the City. The City and the Lords argued for the militia to be under the control of the City. In May the king surrendered to the Scots, a fact which encouraged the radicals' view that the Scots were no longer needed south of the border. In April, MP Thomas Juxon recorded, the City decided to 'pay no more taxes or excise, yet cry for the king and wish him with them, condemn the House of Commons or the godly party of men of no conscience or honesty, no king, no church government'. He recounts one contemporary describing the balance of political forces moving against the Independents and radicals:

There was one that said, they had drawn the Lords, the Scots, the assembly and now the City about their ears and had only got Oliver Cromwell to their friend. The honest party in the House begins now (though never before) to fail them [i.e. the godly party] and to be jealous. The Scots, the assembly, City, Lords, Stapilton's party, and malignant so, their interests all meet upon several considerations against the godly party and are resolved to get the mastery and to try how they can steer the commonwealth.

This was the context of the debates that followed between the radicals and the Presbyterian ideologues in the course of 1646.[37]

The radicals' forces were enhanced by Henry Marten's return to his Commons seat in January 1646, the record of his expulsion expunged from the Commons' journal. Marten was immediately at the heart of that group of radical MPs that wanted the Scots and their Presbyterian influence removed from England as fast as possible.[38] At the same time the future Levellers were continuing to form an identifiable group, especially in the eyes of their enemies. Over the course of 1646 Thomas Edwards's compendium of sectarian error, *Gangraena*, was published in three parts in February, May and December. While Lilburne remains a constant target throughout, the future Levellers emerge as a more central concern in the final part, which contains 'A Relation of the names and Speeches, and doings of the principall Independents and Sectaries', naming over seventy individuals. Only Hugh Peter and John Goodwin have more citations than Lilburne and Overton. Also included were William Walwyn, Thomas Lambe, Henry Denne, Katherine Chidley and Clement Wrighter.[39] Larner does not appear in the index but he is attacked in the text of Part III, his name linked to Overton and Lilburne.[40]

By this time the Lilburnes, William Larner and the Chidleys were all living close by each other in Bishopsgate.[41] Edwards had disdainfully ignored Katherine Chidley's first attack on him in 1641, but now he was certainly not ignoring her any longer. Never short of invective, Edwards described Katherine Chidley as 'an old Brownist' who, with her son 'a young Brownist', was 'not content with spreading their poison in and about London' and so had been travelling the country. She was, said Edwards, a 'brasen-faced audacious old woman' who 'resembled unto Jael'.[42] But this repetition of Chidley's own Biblical reference to Jael, obnoxious to Edwards, was considered praise by Chidley's allies. In the summer of 1646 Katherine Chidley and Samuel Chidley were in Bury St Edmunds in Suffolk, where they assisted John Lanseter and seven others in setting up a gathered church.[43] John Lanseter travelled to London in an attempt to get Edwards to retract his attack on him in the second part of *Gangraena*, not least the accusation that he was a peddler when he was actually a mercer. When Edwards, refused Lanseter made his own reply, *Lanseter's Lance for Edwards'es Gangrene*. In the foreword Lanseter recalled,

> When Mr Thomas Edwards his book against Independencie and Tolera-
> tion, came forth, about foure years agoe, O what boasting there was among
> the Prelaticall party, and Temporizers, as if the day had been their own! But
> when a woman came and strook the naile of Independency into the head of
> Sisera, with the Hammer of Gods holy word; then their sport was spoyled
> and quasht . . .[44]

The hunt for Larner's press

Over the course of 1646, arguments over the future of the state ran in
tandem with discussion of Church government. In the first six months of
1646 the bookseller George Thomasson collected over 140 tracts relating to
the war and the diplomatic manoeuvres arising from the war. The number
of pamphlets relating to Church government and related theological
debates are equal in number to those concerned with secular matters of
state.[45] These included Lilburne's and Walwyn's responses to *Gangraena*,
Lilburne's lengthy summary of his trials, *Innocency and Truth Justified* and
A true Relation of the material passages of Lieut. Col. John Lilburne. Walwyn
was more focussed in two pamphlets published in quick succession on 13
and 19 March, *A Whisper in the Eare of Mr. Thomas Edwards* and *A Word
More to Mr. Thomas Edwards*.[46]

Overton's *The Last Warning to the Inhabitants of London* brought the
Stationers' beagles back on the trail of the future Levellers. *The Last Warning*
is Overton's prose at its best: clear, concise, conversational and convincing,
targeting monarchy and Presbyterian intolerance. Adopting the tone of a
friend, he advises those misled by 'Oylie tongues, and flattering long
Speeches', not to turn away from their principles or their 'constant and
sted-fast friends' among the Sectaries. No one can show you, says Overton,
'one good act that ever any King did voluntarily for the Good of the People:
though yourselves, if you will examine Storyes, or your own experience,
may produce thousands of Oppressions, Murthers and other tyrannyes'.
Enforced ecclesiastical uniformity will cause 'rents and Divisions'. And
these will be worse because 'nothing tendeth more to the dissolving of that
Army, that under God that been your preservation'. The Presbyterian
government of the City and the petitions emanating from it are warned
against, tithes are condemned, the Lords are dismissed, and toleration is
upheld. The Presbyterian reply to Overton thought all this 'subtile sophes-
try' spun by a 'canting Fortune teller, that tells you you are neer an ill turne'

when 'he is picking your pocket'. It insisted that the order of nationally enforced Church government must be upheld and that Sectaries were not to be suffered.[47] But, as before, it was not Presbyterian argument that was to be feared but the actions of the Stationers' Company agents.

William Larner was arrested on 21 March and imprisoned in Poultry Counter for having *The Last Warning* in his possession. Joseph Hunscot had eventually run Larner to ground on the basis of information provided by Prynne. Larner was successively cross-examined by Thomas Adams, the lord mayor of London, the Committee of Examinations, and the earl of Manchester in the Lords. Manchester's questioning introduced the additional charge that Larner had bought a secret press. Larner's brother John and his servant Jane Hales were examined, and both were jailed for refusing to testify against him. Larner petitioned on his own behalf, and so, on at least two occasions, did his wife Ellen Larner. In the second of these petitions she tells of William Larner's service in Lord Robartes's regiment and that 'since his return home the Wardens and Beadle of the Company of Stationers, did sundry times search, ransack and break open your petitioners trunks, and injuriously carry away her goods' in their search for her husband's printed material. Ellen Larner's petition, plus three petitions from Larner himself, plus a letter from Larner to Sir Henry Vane, and an account of his persecution by Larner, were all bound together and published in May 1646 as a pamphlet with the formidable title *A True Relation of all the Remarkable Passages, and Illegall Proceedings of some Sathannical or Doeg-like Accussers of their Brethern Against William Larner, A Free-man of England*. The same month a single printed sheet, *Every Man's Case*, was issued anonymously in 'brotherly support to Mr Larner'. It denounced the Stationers as 'Setting Dogges' who, in the 'Bishops times', used to 'hunt Good Men and Women into the *Star-Chamber* and *High-Commission* netts'. In June Larner himself produced a second letter to Vane and a short second petition appeared from Ellen Larner. They were again printed together in a pamphlet. Larner's household, which included Ellen, an earlier child, his brother, an 'ancient Maide, neer 60 yeers of age' and Jane Hales, were reduced to destitution. Larner's parents in Gloucestershire were financially affected because they were dependent on him after they were plundered by cavaliers. Ellen was pregnant at the time of the Stationers' raid. Her petition records that she is 'with child' and that seeing the 'violent apprehension of her husband' made her fall 'into a dangerous sickness'. The shock resulted in a prolonged illness and a miscarriage.[48]

Hunscot recounts that he and the warden for the Stationers' Company went to see Larner in prison and found him with 'divers papers of his own hand writing . . . which about a week after came forth in print, called, *A True Relation of all the Remarkable Passages, and Illegall Proceedings of some Sathannical or Doeg-like Accussers of their Brethern Against William Larner, A Free-man of England*'.[49] Larner's *A Vindication of Every Free-mans Libertie*, addressed to Vane, is a succinct but effective use of Leveller rhetoric. It demands Parliament stand by their previous declarations guaranteeing freedom from arbitrary laws. Larner cites Magna Carta in his defence and he insists that it is only by the will of the people that MPs sit in Parliament. He threatens that 'the people begin already look upon you, as men carrying on your own designes and peculiar and private interests'. If this course continues, Larner argues, the MPs 'will make the people hate you'. This, in June 1646, was accurate prophecy. But it was to no immediate avail. Larner did not emerge from jail until October, whereupon Leveller material began to be produced in greater quantities.[50]

The postscript to the pamphlet version of Larner's *Every Man's Case* and Overton's *An Alarum to the House Of Lords* urged readers to consult *England's Birth-Right Justified*. The postscript to *An Alarum*, which the Lords set up a special committee to investigate, also urged the reading of the petition *A Remonstrance of Many Thousand Citizens*, Walwyn's *Just Man in Bonds* and *The Pearle in the Dunghill*, and 'Larner's Bookes'.[51] Walwyn's May 1646 pamphlet *A Word in Season* appeared in two editions printed by Leveller Thomas Paine. One conventionally tells us that it is to be sold by 'Edward Blackmoore at his shop in Pauls Churchyard'.[52] The other contains the printed information that Paine dwells in 'Red-Crosse Street, in Goldsmith's Alley, over against the signe of the Sugar-loaf', where, presumably, copies could be purchased. But this edition also contains Thomason's handwritten annotation telling us that on 26 May it was handed out by John Lilburne at Westminster Hall.[53] What has now quite clearly emerged, both in the eyes of their opponents and in the internal ideological and practical support they deliver to each other, is a functioning collective organisation.

The battle of the churches

The struggle over political and religious freedom between Presbyterians and Independents and the sects was not merely waged in an exchange of pamphlets. It was also a struggle in the churches, streets and neighbourhoods concerning the right to preach. Katherine and Samuel Chidley ran their own separatist congregation in the Coleman Street area.[54] In August 1645 she had already drawn people to become Baptists in Stepney. She then confronted orthodox minister William Greenhill in his own church, telling him that 'he might as lawfully baptise a dog as a beleevers childe'. Greenhill attempted to answer her 'and laboured to reduce to a short head all that she spoke'. But he did not get very far because 'instead of being satisfied or giving any answer, shee was so talkative and clamorous, wearying him with her words, that he was glad to go away, and so left her'.[55]

In the same month the popular Independent preacher Hanserd Knollys was encouraging his congregation to pray for John Lilburne to be delivered out of jail.[56] But Knollys could not always be guaranteed such a sympathetic audience. While proselytising in Suffolk a 'malignant High-Constable' encouraged a 'rude multitude' to oppose him while he preached. The encounter ended with Knollys being 'stoned out of the Pulpit' and having the church doors shut against him.[57] At the end of 1645, Knollys, Lilburne's old confederate William Kiffin, and Benjamin Coke attempted to organise a public debate about the validity of infant baptism with Edmund Calamy. At first the lord mayor gave permission. Then he reversed the decision, banning the meeting until the Commons had given agreement on the grounds that it 'might be hazard of the disturbance of the publike peace'. This was in response to rumours that the separatists meant to manage the dispute 'with our Swords, Clubs and Staves', and that 'if Mr. Callamy escaped with his life, it would be well'. The Baptists protested their peaceable intentions and objected to the use of 'Club-law instead of Arguments', but they had to be content with setting out their views in print.[58]

Thomas Lambe, though a Baptist, regarded himself as a lawfully ordained minister and therefore claimed the right to preach in parish churches. His sermon at St Bennet Gracechurch in November 1644 drew 'a mighty great audience'.[59] Overton describes an attack on a gathered church where Presbyterians had stuck

Bills upon the posts to assemble the rude Multitude in Bell-Ally in Cole-man Street . . . to pull downe their place of meeting, stone them, commit outrage upon them, drag them tumultuously to prison, stop their mouthes with violence and cruelty, and seeing this took little effect, caused the discharge of Five or Six Bullets, while they were at the Service of God into one of their meeting houses.

This in all probability was Overton's own church, Thomas Lambe's congregation in Bell Ally.[60]

In 1645 the most famous woman preacher in London, the lace seller from Cheapside, Mrs Attaway, began weekly Tuesday meetings for women. Attaway was a graduate of Lambe's church and her lectures were a runaway success, drawing 'a world of people, to the number of a thousand first and last to Bell Alley' in Coleman Street. But success brought discussion punctuated by 'laughing, confusion and disorder', plus dissention among the women who formed the core of the congregation, about whether there had been agreement to make the lectures public events. By February 1646 Mrs Attaway told her audience she was 'in the wilderness'. But at least she was not alone for she shortly disappeared with another woman's husband.[61]

The influence of Lambe's church was not limited to London. Two preachers associated with Lambe, Jeremiah Ives and Samuel Oates, carried both the Baptist creed and the Leveller message far and wide. Ives was a cheesemonger by trade associated with Baptism from early in the Civil War. He may have fought in the parliamentary army and certainly preached to soldiers. In 1646 he toured mid-Wales with lay Baptist preacher Hugh Evans. Later the same year Ives was with Lambe in Devizes, Wiltshire, where they caused 'an abominable disturbance of the whole congregation' and, with the help of soldiers led by Captain Pretty of Ireton's regiment, they forced the local minister to come down out of the pulpit and depart his own church. The following year Ives was charged with sedition, promoting Leveller material in the army.[62]

Samuel Oates came from Norwich, where he became known as a 'notorious anabaptist'. He was a weaver by trade. Lambe probably re-baptised him on a visit to the city in 1642. Oates was in London in 1645 preaching to Lambe's Bell Alley congregation. Later that year he was with Lambe on a preaching tour that took in Guildford and Portsmouth. In spring 1646 he was preaching in Essex, where he was said to have baptised hundreds and 'dipped many in Bocking River'. He was hauled before the Essex quarter sessions at Colchester in March and imprisoned in Colchester jail for some weeks. Here he was visited by many friends from London, some travelling by coach. In April Oates was acquitted of having caused the death of Anne Martin, a girl he baptised in the river. The following year he was in Rutland agitating against tithes, proclaiming against infant baptism, and denying, as Overton did, the immortality of the soul. The following that he attracted resulted in a complaint to Parliament against him by nineteen parish ministers. Like Ives he was accused of being 'a great dispenser' of Leveller pamphlets. This he did by his own efforts and by 'his agents brought or sent to several towns in the countie'.[63]

Church congregations could be mobilised behind political campaigns, but this was also a contested process. The authorities did all they could to suppress support for radical petitions. On 26 May 1646 a Remonstrance from the lord mayor, aldermen and Common Council called for a 'strict course for suppressing all private, and separate congregations'. It demanded that 'all Anabaptists, Hereticks, and Sectaries, &c. as not conformed to the publick Discipline, may be declared and proceeded against', and that 'none disaffected to the Presbyterian government maybe imployed in any place of publick Trust'. Furthermore it advocated that 'the propositions of Peace may be hastened' and that 'the Union maybe preserved'. The Lords welcomed this intervention but in the Commons 'many expressed great offence at it', seeing it as 'wholly a design of the Presbyterian Party, and it was not liked'.[64] On 2 June there was a counterpetition from 'many thousands of free born people of this Kingdom'.[65] These were precisely the battles that Walwyn, Lilburne and other future Levellers were engaged in, not least among the congregations of the City.

Support for Walwyn and Lilburne was stronger among the mass of the congregation than it was among the preachers. In 1646 Walwyn reported both the support for radical petitions among the gathered churches and the divisions among them. Walwyn cited support from 'Anabaptist and Brownists congregations', but opposition, on this occasion, from 'Master Goodwin's people, and some of the other Independent churches'.[66] John Goodwin's congregation had supported Lilburne during his imprisonment. In a letter to Goodwin at his house in Swan Alley, Coleman Street, Lilburne thanked them for 'large kindnesses manifested unto me in this my present imprisonment in supplying my necessities', but he also upbraided some members of the same congregation for blocking petitions by his supporters.[67]

In the face of Presbyterian intolerance, radical Independents and the Lilburne group came together at meetings in the Windmill Tavern. This assisted the future Levellers in mobilising wider support from the churches. Goodwin's congregation raised fifty shillings to print Walwyn's *A Word in Season* and assisted in the distribution of this counterblast to the Presbyterian City petition.[68] The print run was 10,000.[69] There were, as we have seen, two editions of the pamphlet, one of which was given out at Westminster Hall by Lilburne.[70] Overton relied on members of his congregation to distribute pamphlets that were too hot for booksellers to handle. *The Last Warning to the Inhabitants of London*, the pamphlet that was to get Overton and Larner arrested and Larner jailed, was also distributed by Henry Overton of Goodwin's church.

The *Remonstrance of Many Thousand Citizens*

After Larner's arrest in March, Thomas Paine and Richard Overton remained in command of functioning presses. They had already been at work with Walwyn's pamphlets and other material. But they were about to become busier still. Lilburne's uncanny ability to find himself in circumstances that dramatised the key political issue of the day was again on display. In mid-1646 he was in the cross hairs of two legal proceedings. The first was his ongoing suit against Colonel King that he took up once more with the Commons after his release from prison in October 1645. King countersued for slander in April 1646 in the court of Common Pleas. This, argued Lilburne, was an inferior court and therefore could not intervene while he was prosecuting King's case in front of the Commons. His letter to this effect, addressed to Justice Reeves, was published as *The Just Mans Justification*. In this Lilburne recounted his belief that King's Presbyterian chaplains had influenced the earl of Manchester's judgement for the worse. This was enough to trigger the second and more serious legal action. On 10 June Lilburne was summoned to appear before the House of Lords to answer for his criticisms of the earl of Manchester himself. Manchester had been bearing a grudge from the time of the clash over the taking of Tickhill Castle and later had been heard complaining of Lilburne to two other Lords and five MPs at a meeting at the Beare tavern at Bridgefoot.[71]

Lilburne would have preferred to avoid this conflict with the Lords, but when he came face to face with his accusers he denied their authority to judge him. The Lords demanded he answer the question whether he knew of *The Just Mans Justification*. Lilburne countered with a demand to know if there were any charges against him. He then handed in his own protestation. The clerk refused it and threw it after Lilburne as he left the proceedings. On the following day he was committed to Newgate for contempt. A flock of pamphlets defending Lilburne immediately flew from the presses. In late June Lilburne himself published *The Freemans Freedom Vindicated*, and a broadsheet addressed to one of his jailers, *A coppy of a letter sent by Lieu. Col. John Lilburne to Mr. Wollaston*. Walwyn also brought out his defences of Lilburne, *The Just Man in Bonds* and *A Pearle in a Dounghill*.[72] The Lords took *The Freemans Freedom Vindicated* as a new affront and on 22 June they issued a new writ demanding that the warder at Newgate bring Lilburne before them the next day. In response Elizabeth Lilburne took a letter to the authorities from John refusing to attend unless compelled by force. When the warders broke down his door and brought him to the Lords he appeared, hat on head, and refused to kneel at the bar. When asked why he would not kneel he replied, 'he had learned both better Religion and manners then to kneele to any humane or mortal power how great so ever'.[73] When he was brought to trial on 11 July he told their Lordships, 'He would not hear' the charge and 'stopped his Ears with his Fingers, and would not hear it read'. The Lords considered this as great an affront as they had ever suffered and commanded him to listen to the charges. Lilburne stopped his ears for a second time and when asked what he said to the charges, he replied,

> He heard nothing of it; he had nothing to do with it; he took no Notice of it; but would stand to his Protestation, and having appealed from their Lordships, and protested against them, as unrighteous Judges, to those Judges who are to judge him and their Lordships, the House of Commons assembled in Parliament; and did render up his Body to their Lordships Fury.[74]

The charges were entirely concerned with the contents of *The Just Mans Justification*, *The Freemans Freedom Vindicated* and other recent pamphlets. The copies of these pamphlets still held in the Parliamentary Archives have those passages underlined that were used to condemn Lilburne. The tracts were all ordered burnt at the old Exchange in London and in New Palace Yard at Westminster. The Lords were enraged that Lilburne had repeated the charges against Manchester over the taking of Tickhill Castle, had renewed his attack on Colonel King, and had denied their authority on the grounds that they were a mere prerogative assembly. On the same day that Lilburne was charged the Lords immediately ordered the public burning of

Cromwell's speech against Manchester. Lilburne was sentenced to a fine of £2,000, a prison sentence of seven years, and a ban from all public employment. He was sent to the Tower with the instruction that the warder should ensure he wrote no more pamphlets. This was interpreted by the authorities as a ban on all visitors, including Elizabeth Lilburne. The effect of this was to deny Lilburne both food and the money necessary to pay his jailers, a requirement for even minimally humane treatment in seventeenth-century prisons. Indeed, so close was the imprisonment that Lilburne was not permitted even to speak with Elizabeth in the prison yard. The couple were forced to shout to each other, Lilburne from his cell window, Elizabeth from the window of a house forty yards away. Even then the jailer threatened to board up the casement in the cell. Lilburne told him to 'doe his worst, for I would pull them down as fast as he nailed them up' and that he would speak to his wife until they 'sewed up my lips, or cut out my tongue'.[75]

In September, 'A petition of lieutenant-colonel Lilburne's wife, accompanied with many women at the door of the house, and mentioning the tyranny of the lords by their imprisoning of her husband' was just one of 'multitudes' of protests, including by other women petitioners, that 'proved very troublesome and impetuous to the parliament'. This account, by MP Bulstrode Whitelocke, is a rather sanitised telling of Elizabeth Lilburne's treatment at Westminster, at least if John Lilburne's more detailed account is true. Standing on the steps of the Court of Requests in Westminster, Elizabeth Lilburne was approached by Richard Vaughan, the ensign of the guard. Having ascertained that she was John Lilburne's wife he told her that he wished that her husband had been thrown out of the country at the start of the war. He then tried to push her down the three or four steps into the Court of Requests but here friends prevented her from falling. Vaughan then followed her into the court and caught her by the throat, calling for the guard to arrest her. Elizabeth managed to free herself and deliver her petition demanding Lilburne's freedom. In it she insisted, in words that prefigure Rainsborough's famous speech at Putney the following year, that 'the meanest of the Commonalty may enjoy their own birth-right, freedom and liberty of the lawes of the land; being equally (as you say) intiteld thereunto with the greatest subject'. And she repeated Cromwell's charge against Manchester as of 'a higher nature then the Earle of Straffords, for which he lost his head'. Small wonder, perhaps, that she overheard one Lord say, 'a Plague on him for a Rogue; how are we troubled by him? But if the Lords would be ruled by me, and be all of my mind, we would dispatch him, and stretch him up without any more adoe'. But at least Elizabeth Lilburne's efforts were not totally in vain: the bar on her visiting John in the Tower was removed. Lilburne had good reason to praise his wife's 'resolution, wisdome and courage'. John himself had already appealed to the Commons to intervene against the Lords persecution of a commoner. The lower house appointed Henry Marten to head a committee to hear Lilburne's plea, which it did on two occasions on 27 October and 6 November. But this did no good. Lilburne remained in the Tower.[76]

In the midst of Lilburne's contest with the Lords, on 7 July, George Thomasson collected what is widely accepted as the Leveller's founding manifesto, *A Remonstrance of Many Thousand Citizens, and other Free-born People of England*. It was unsigned but it bears the unmistakable style of Overton, repeating tone, arguments and phrases of *The Last Warning to the Inhabitants of London*. But its content is likely to have been collectively agreed and the pamphlet also contains the influence of Walwyn's tolerationism and Henry Marten's overt republicanism.[77]

A Remonstrance of Many Thousand Citizens certainly came from Overton's press since it bears on its opening page the same crude dropped capital surrounded by small printer's decorations as all his other work. But though the print might be basic, it contained a brilliantly effective engraving of Lilburne. Overton took the original George Glover depiction of Lilburne that first appeared in Larner's edition of *The Christian Mans Triall* and engraved over the top a set of vertical and horizontal prison bars. At the top of the page a band bearing the words 'The Liberty of the The Freeborne English-man, conferred on him by the house of lords, June 1646' has been added. The meaning of this inventive 'engravo-montage' and its sarcastic title could not be clearer: John Lilburne, the popular hero of the struggle against the bishops, was now enduring the same punishment by the House of Lords. Nothing about the content of the pamphlet was less impressive that its frontispiece. In any age it would be a supremely effective example of popular political writing, both immediately of its moment and embodying fundamental political principles.

A Remonstrance of Many Thousand Citizens is addressed to the Commons. The tone is forthright and uncompromising but not clamorous or insulting, and so never risks alienating even unsympathetic readers. The very first sentence established the principle that the Commons sit at the pleasure of the people, since 'we possessed you with the same Power that was in our selves, to have done the same; For wee might justly have done it our selves without you, if we had thought it convenient'. This power 'is ever revocable, and cannot be otherwise', because 'Wee are your Principalls, and you our Agents'. *A Remonstrance* then makes it clear that the primacy of the people and their representatives is radically incompatible with kingship: 'the continuall Oppressours of the Nation have been Kings, which is so evident that you cannot denie it'. The MPs have been too lenient with the king and their talk of fighting for 'King and parliament', their excusing the king by blaming evil counsellors, and their 'frequent treating' with the king, have all been serious errors. By extension the Commons have also been wrong in defending the Lords 'negative voice'. The Lords 'Act and Vote in our affaires but as intruders, or as thrust upon us by Kings, to make good their Interests, which to this day have been to bring us into slavish subjection to their wills'. These are precisely the sentiments Henry Marten had been advancing in 1643. But now the imprisonment of Lilburne and Larner are cited as evidence that the Lords, 'being not Chosen thereunto by the People', are using the people as 'vassalls and servants'.[78]

Then the *Remonstrance* moves to a fascinating account of the history of the Revolution that lays bare the political dynamic between the leaders of the revolt and their popular supporters. 'Time hath revealed hidden things unto us', the *Remonstrance* says. The lords of both Scotland and England began the struggle with the king in order to 'exclude all those from managing State-affaires that hee had advanced thereunto, and were grown so insolent and presumptuious, as these discontented ones wee lyable to continuall molestations from them, either by practices at the Counsel-table, High Commission, or Starre-chamber'. But this 'mighty worke' that aimed to 'abate the Power of the King' the Lords 'were no wise able to effect it for themselves'. And 'therefore (say they) the generality of the People must be engaged'. But what was to be the mechanism by which the people could be drawn into the struggle?

> Why, say they, wee must associate with that part of the Clergy that are now made underlings, and others that have been oppressed, and with the most zealous religious Non-conformists, and by the helpe of these we will . . . be sure to get into our party the generality of the Citie of London, and all the considerable substantiall People of both Nations.

This was a history of the Civil War from below of considerable sophistication. But there was an even more potent sting in the tail. Once the war became necessary the Lords were required to 'hold all at our Command' for 'once if this People thus stirred up by us, should make an end too soon of the King and his party', they would put all power in the hands of the

Commons. And so the Lords reasoned that 'as we have a care the King and his Lords must not prevail, wee must be carefull the Supreme Power fall not into the People's hands, or House of Commons'. For this reason there must be no 'end with the King' until war has wearied the people by degrees so that 'they shall not be able to contest or dispute with us, either about Supreme or inferiour Power; but we are able, afore they are aware, to give them both Law and Religion'.[79] Moreover, this is why 'yee have never made that use of the People of the Nation in your warre as you might have done'. The Lords preferred to bring in the Scots than to mobilise the people, 'Whereas yee might have ended the Warre long ere this, if by Sea or Land you had shewed your selves resolved to make us a Free-People, but as it is evident, a change of our bondage is the uttermost is intended us, and that too for the worse'.[80] This was the experience of the mass mobilisations that began the Revolution, the work of the Committee for the General Rising and the Salters' Hall committee, the raising of the Eastern Association, the conflict with Manchester, and the struggle against Presbyterianism all condensed into a political programme.

Within the framework of this analysis all else was located: the stopping of the presses, the suppression of the right to petition, the coercive nature of Presbyterianism, the prerogative power of the Lords. Historical perspective was added by the invocation of the Norman yoke as the moment when kingly and lordly power was established. Magna Carta, being 'but a beggarly thing, containing many markes of intolerable bondage', was only a partial and inadequate defence. The laws of England were 'unworthy of a Free-People'. Imprisonment for debt is un-Christian and unjust. Forced military service is intolerable, and not used by the admirable Dutch Republic. The faithfulness of the New Model Army was being abused by those that 'love their Kings more than all this Nation'. Uniformity was being enforced by those who are practising Machiavelli's principle of divide and rule. Foreshadowing the reserved powers of *The Agreement of the People*, matters of conscience should not be enforced by Parliament. Nor is the principle of the sovereignty of the Commons to be confused with approval for the actions of those MPs now sitting. 'Have you shoke this Nation like an Earth-quake, to produce no more than this for us', asked *The Remonstrance*. The MPs have 'now sate a full five years, which is foure yeers longer then wee intended', and have for a 'long time acted more like a House of Peers then a House of Commons'. The Commons should be subject to annual elections 'for wee must not loose our free choice of a parliament once every year', for, the MPs are warned, 'The Worke yee must note is ours, and not your owne'. In many of its essentials this is the Leveller programme of years to come. It was rarely stated with such clarity, depth, force and brevity as it was on that day in July 1646 when George Thomasson took it into his hand.[81]

Levellers in fact if not in name

The Levellers as an organised and distinct current were now a fact of political life even if they were not to be named until late in 1647. Any birth is a story of emerging properties which at a certain point condense into a recognisably new entity. The Levellers had by 1646 a long history of radical politics behind them both as individuals and, in some combinations, as small collectives. In 1645–6 these began to amalgamate. The process by which they did so, as often in politics, was by differentiating themselves from opponents. Opposition to compromise in the conduct of the war and opposition to Presbyterianism shaped them. The appeal to popular support and the doctrine of popular sovereignty were mutually reinforcing practical and ideological formative experiences for them to a greater degree than they were for other sections of the Independent alliance.

For Cromwell and the other Independent Grandees, both popular mobilisation and popular sovereignty were much more pragmatic and instrumental stances, useful in some contexts and at some times, but not at others. And it is precisely the Lilburne group's capacity for mobilisation that meant that they were not mere instruments in the hands of the Independent Grandees. The Independent leaders, as historian Jason Peacey has pointed out, were 'prepared to sanction the use of mass demonstrations as a political tool' and therefore found Lilburne indispensable as 'a man with influence among the sectarian churches in London'.[82] And if we read this relationship from the other side it means that Lilburne had a base of his own and was not wholly reliant on the Grandees' support.

We should also be wary of assuming that Lilburne's relationship with Cromwell can stand as a full representation of the future Levellers' relationship with all the Independent leaders. Lilburne and Cromwell had a long-standing personal association, but even Lilburne did not feel as warmly about Oliver St John or Henry Vane. William Larner, despite two appeals, got no relief from Henry Vane during his imprisonment. It was this, among more general concerns, that led him to warn MPs that 'it is utterly a fault in many of you, of no little blemish and shame on you', that

'so long as your selves fare well' you do not care if you actions are 'exasper-
ating our spirits' and 'alienating our affections from you'. This is precisely
the fault to which the authors of *A Remonstrance of Many Thousand Citizens*
were referring in those passages that urged the Commons not to disappoint
the hopes of their best supporters.[83]

The Leveller leaders tended to come from the centre and lower end of
the middling sort. Even when they were gentry they tended to be second
sons apprenticed to trade. The Independents were more likely to be from
the centre and upper reaches of the middling sort, with levers of power
and influence available to them that the Leveller leaders did not have. And
the more the Revolution developed, the more this was true. The Levellers
only really had the continuous support of one MP, Henry Marten. When
Cromwell looked out from his own seat in the Commons he could see
eighteen family relatives sitting on the benches. Rainsborough was the
only senior officer of the New Model Army to support the Levellers, but
large numbers of the senior officers were Independents. It was the same in
the City. The Independents had support at various times of the mayor and
significant numbers of aldermen; the Levellers campaigned on behalf of
the commonalty locked out of City government by the oligarchy. When
the Levellers appealed to their core constituency they appealed down to
those whose lives were wrecked by war and taxes, oppressed by tithes and
monopolies, leeched on by lawyers and prelates. This was not language
used by other Independent writers, even those who might hold political
views consonant with the future Levellers, like Henry Parker or
Marchamont Nedham in his time as editor of parliamentary newspaper
Mercurius Britanicus.[84]

Not all Independents were activists and organisers, fusing theory and
action, as were the future Levellers. So even while the future Levellers were
emerging as a current within Independency, they were a visibly distinct
grouping in their radicalism, their popular orientation and their collective
organisation. This long preparation came into the open in the course of the
winter of 1645 and the spring of 1646, as their enemies among the
Presbyterians and in the House of Lords recognised full well.

CHAPTER 8

Petitions and Prison

By 1646 London was more divided then ever. The City Presbyterians were pushing for a conservative settlement with the king and by the following year they were able to mobilise 'Kirk and King' mobs. The higher reaches of City governance had become a Presbyterian stronghold, though MP Thomas Juxon thought this as much a product of the intensity of the Presbyterian minority's activity and of the cowing of a majority on Common Council. In February 1646 he recorded that the Presbyterians were a thirty- to forty-strong faction in a Common Council of 250 members, facing opposition from only five diehard Independents, but that the majority 'are silent, as either not willing or not daring to appear'. In the same month the Presbyterians began pressing to get control of the London militia. In April the City resolved to 'pay no more taxes or excise' to Parliament, and, wrote Juxon, they 'condemn the House of Commons or the godly party of men' as 'of no conscience or honesty' who would have no king and no Church government. In May 1646 a City remonstrance circulated for a month before it was presented to the House. This remonstrance, 'whipped up by the high Presbyterian divines of Sion College', demanded a swift peace with the king and the enforcement of religious conformity. In June some 20,000 copies of another conservative petition were circulated for subscription. By September divisions between Presbyterians and Independents over their candidates for mayor, respectively John Langham and John Warner, had become so great that they actually resulted in a third candidate, crypto-royalist John Gayre, taking the office. Essex, until his death in September, led a sympathetic majority in the Lords and, from December 1646, the peace party led by Denzil Holles and Philip Stapleton was dominant in the Commons.[1]

It had not always been this way. In the first phase of Revolutionary mobilisation between 1640 and 1642 the political line of differentiation between the camps was not drawn primarily on this religious line. Former lord mayor Isaac Pennington and Alderman John Fowke were both leading lights in the mobilisations of the December Days and future supporters of the republic. Both were also religious Presbyterians and both were now being marginalised by the political conservatives in the City. But the 'new Presbyterianism' that grew from the time of the calling of the Assembly of Divines and the Scottish Covenant in 1643 had evolved, first, into a conservative movement and then, second, into an openly counterrevolutionary movement acting in concert with royalists. This long Presbyterian ascendancy incorporated the old peace party and allied them to the Scots as they became disillusioned with the Independent's attitudes to Church government and religious toleration.[2]

The Presbyterian movement was top-heavy, dominated by the City oligarchy, the High Presbyterians of Sion College, the Scots commissioners, and the peace party in the Commons. But it did also have a popular base. Its intermediate ranks were populated by some of the middling sort of domestic traders and the bottom ranks by demobilised soldiers (the reformadoes), and by seamen, watermen and labourers. Among these layers there were concerns about taxation, free quarter of the army, and the need for a stable political settlement. The same issues were of concern to the potential audience for Leveller and radical ideas and so there was a struggle over which political force could effectively address these issues.[3]

While the Presbyterians were dominant their grip on power was nevertheless contested. The Eastern Association had been the bulwark of Independency and the establishment of the New Model Army was both the condition of Parliament's military victory and a political victory for the Independents. The Commons was divided and it frustrated the desires of the most extreme Presbyterians by retaining a degree of parliamentary control over the national Church, the so-called Erastian settlement named after the sixteenth-century theologian Thomas Erastus, who argued that it was the task of the state to set the limits of Church rule. But, paradoxically, the more certain victory over the king became, the less powerful the Independents appeared, because the question now seemed to be less how to win the war against the king and more what kind of settlement could be made with him. In early 1646 Juxon recorded, 'each faction labours to engage the king . . . and to be the means of his reconciliation'. And Charles was, naturally, happy to play this game. If, as seemed possible, the

Independents would suffer the return of the bishops in return for a modicum of toleration, then the king would deal with them and 'in time work out the rest'.[4]

This situation, in turn, produced a differentiation within the Independent camp. Some were happy with mild tolerationism, others held out for freedom of worship. Some Independents, having lost their popular base at the time of Pym's triumph over Henry Marten in late 1643, were more minded to compromise with moderates in Parliament and less likely to antagonise them with renewed attempts at popular mobilisation. Others, often coming from more humble backgrounds, were 'more willing to risk reliance on the populace and alliance with the separatist congregations'. These figures included John Goodwin, thrown out of his church by the Presbyterian settlement, and Hugh Peter, preacher and propagandist for the New Model Army. But even these radicals combined moments of courage with moments of caution. The most consistently militant were the Levellers.[5]

Little Martin caught by the feathers

By mid-1646 the Leveller organisation was beginning to draw itself to its full height as the *Remonstrance of Many Thousand Citizens* was issued that summer. Its political enemies reacted accordingly and the Presbyterian polemicists, Thomas Edwards in the vanguard, were in full cry against them. By this time Lilburne and Larner were already in jail. Richard Overton was still at large and at the end of July he issued another tract in defence of Lilburne, *An Alarum to the House of Lords Against their insolent Usurpation of the Common Liberties and Rights of this Nation*. In a sign of the increasingly closely coordinated efforts of the emerging Leveller leadership, Overton recommended that his readers also obtain *The Remonstrance of Many Thousand Citizens*, Walwyn's *Just Man in Bonds* and *Pearle in a Dounghill*, Lilburne's *Just Mans Justification* and *Englands Birth-Right*, and William Larner's books.

The substance of Overton's text recited Lilburne's long service in the parliamentary cause and complained of his imprisonment. He questioned the preferment of titles on the Lords, accusing the earl of Middlesex of being advanced for 'devising ways to sharke the People', the earl of Coventry for 'heaping up Masses of wealth by extremity of Bribery, Extortion', and the earl of Manchester of gaining his title by 'the most palpable corruption'. Overton did not limit himself to criticism of particular Lords but broadened his attack to include the whole titled aristocracy: 'by what means some of you came by yours, is very uncertaine, but this is certaine, that most you gained no part of it your selves: and the common wayes your Auncesters gained it for you, was generally adhering to kings, in subduing and oppressing the Commons'. This literary slap in the face was not something the Lords were likely to ignore, and neither did they.[6]

On 11 August 1646 a dawn raid on Overton's house in Southwark was led by Robert Eeles and Abraham Eveling of the Stationers' Company. In the early hours Eeles, 'commonly known by the name of Robin the Divell', surrounded the house with a company of musketeers. They broke into the house and came into the bedchamber, Eeles with his sword drawn and Eveling with a cocked pistol in his hand. Eeles held his sword against Overton as he lay in his bed and said 'Tut, tut, tut, rise up and put on your clothes'. Overton's wife Mary, lying in bed with her newborn baby and close to fainting, looked on in terror as the Stationer's men picked the pockets of their clothes and ransacked their belongings. As he went downstairs Overton attempted to make an escape through the front door but ran into the troops waiting outside, who advanced on him, threatening to run him through. Overton was 'struck into a sudden fear of my life' and retreated into the house again.[7]

Overton was dragged away and initially taken to the Bull tavern in St Margarets Hill, Southwark. He turned the arrest into a public platform, forcing Eveling to read the warrant 'for Printing of seditious and scandalous books' and appealing to the growing crowd that he was being unjustly arrested. While Overton was being held in the Bull, Eeles and some musketeers went to search for his printing press, and when he returned he told Overton that he had taken his press and other materials. Confined, Overton refused to answer questions, and he reports that Eeles 'led me through the streets' in a 'contemptuous and disgraceful manner amongst my neighbours, being strongly guarded by armed men, as if I had been a Traytor, or a Fellon'. En route he was abused by bystanders in 'base and evill language'. The captive responded by telling the crowd that he was not arrested under any proper legal authority but merely by violence and force of arms. Eeles tried to shut Overton up, telling him that he was a 'Tub-preacher' who 'preached in the streets . . . on purpose to raise a mutiny'. The guard eventually got Overton into a boat at St Mary Overies stairs and took him to Westminster.[8]

Here he was brought before the earl of Essex and Lord Hunsdon and was questioned about his printing activities, but in the manner perfected by Lilburne and already duplicated by Larner, he refused to incriminate himself and challenged the Lords' right to examine a commoner. Eeles interjected that Overton was 'one of Lilburns Bastards'. Hunsdon told Eeles to keep quiet, but later, when Overton said he would appeal to the House of Commons, Hunsdon himself said this was 'Lilburn like'. Overton was then brought before the whole House of Lords and again refused to answer questions about his activity, at which 'in a most scornful and deriding manner' the chamber 'laughed at me'. He told them that it did not become them to deride a prisoner at the bar. Meanwhile, he had refused to remove his hat and when Essex complained he took it off and 'in a most courteous lowe manner gave him an other salute; that done I put on my hat again'. Essex commanded that Overton's hat be plucked from his head, and so it was. The Lords found that 'Overton carried himself in an insolent Manner, both by Words and Gestures'. He was quickly ushered away to Newgate for contempt. As Overton was quick to point out, 'Little Martin' had now joined John Lilburne and William Larner under lock and key. Overton, like Lilburne, appealed to 'his honoured friend' Henry Marten and appeared before his committee on 3 November 1646. Marten was unable to free Overton but he did make it clear that he was not held by any command of the Commons. Overton, having left Marten in the Palace Yard, refused to walk back to prison. He told his guards, 'My Leggs were borne as free as the rest of my Body, and therefore I scorne that Leggs, or Armes, or hands of mine should do them any villiene-Service, for I am a Freeman by Birth'. His jailers took him to Blackfriars by boat and then attempted to force him to walk up the hill to Newgate. Overton refused and let his legs hang 'as if they had been none of my own, or like a couple of farthin Candles dangling at my knees'. Undeterred his captors carried him bodily back to prison, taking care to throw him in the mud en route and pull him by the hair 'just as if the John of all Sir Johns had got little Martin by the feathers'. Back in Newgate he was clapped in irons and his copy of Magna Carta taken from him.[9]

Worse was to follow. In early January 1647 a copy of Lilburne's *Regall Tyrannie Discovered* came into the Lords' possession. They ruled it 'full of Treason and Scandal' and ordered the Stationers to hunt down the printer and 'any Person they shall suspect to have any Hand in the said Pamphlet'. It is hard to argue with the judgement since Lilburne described the king as 'the greatest Delinquent in the three Kingdoms' and the Lords as perpetrators of 'Tyrannie and Injustice'. To this was 'annexed a little touch' describing 'some palbable miscarriages of some rotten Members of the House of Commons'. On 5 January the Stationers raided Overton's house for a second time and caught Mary Overton and her family in the very act of 'binding up' scandalous books. The stationers found 'Thomas Johnson sitting, with divers Books before ready bound up, and a Bodkin sticking in One of the said scandalous Pamphlets, having Holes in it ready to be made up'. If this was indeed *Regall Tyrannie Discovered* one sympathises with Johnson; Lilburne's book ran to 108 pages cataloguing royal oppression from William the Conqueror to Charles I. Mary Overton and Thomas Johnson, who was in fact Richard Overton's brother under a pseudonym, were taken to Maiden Lane prison and then brought before the Lords. The following day another raid on the house just failed to capture Mary's sister and her husband, who fled into hiding. The house was nevertheless boarded up and neighbours took in the Overton's children, except for the six-month-old baby who went with Mary into Maiden Lane.[10]

When that same afternoon Mary was brought before the Lords she refused to give evidence against her own family. Thomas Johnson, in answer to the question 'who brought those Books into that House?' gave the unlikely reply, 'He did not know; he found them there'. The Lords found Mary Overton guilty of contempt and ordered that she be moved from Maiden Lane to the Bridewell prison, notorious as the jail for prostitutes. Mary refused to go and told the City marshall 'in plaine down-right termes' that she would not obey the order or 'set one leg before another' to execute it unless she were ordered to do so by the Commons as 'Englands legitimate lawfull authority'. The marshall attempted to get porters and cabmen to carry her but they refused on the grounds that they were not jailers. The marshall then had to break into Mary Overton's room and, strutting toward her 'like a Crow in a gutter', attempted to pull her child from her arms. Failing this, the guards dragged her and the child to the Bridewell, abusing her as a wicked whore and a strumpet. The baby was taken from her and given into her sister's care. It died before the mother was eventually released. Meanwhile, Mary petitioned for her own release, citing Magna Carta and previous parliamentary acts. She castigated the Commons for freeing royalists before its best supporters, for suppressing petitions, for keeping the laws in 'Pedlars French and Latine', and seeking to destroy the religiously well affected, 'the very props and pillars of your house'. She concluded 'instead of one Tyrant we have got three or foure hundred'. Leveller patience with the Commons was quickly evaporating.[11]

Before 1646 some future Levellers—Lilburne and, more briefly, Lambe, Tue, and Henry Marten—had been imprisoned. But in 1646 the intensity of the Lords campaign affected a wider circle of the leadership and certain offences were now designated joint enterprises. When we examine why the Levellers fought with such tenacity against arbitrary power, for legal and prison reform, for the sovereignty of the people represented in Parliament, this experience stands in the rank of first causes. Few things directly generate radicalism in both the immediate victims and their supporters as unjust imprisonment. Historians underplay this brute experience to the detriment of our ability to understand what moved the radicals of the seventeenth century. This was why the Levellers spent so much time publicising and explaining what had happened to them and the causes that had occasioned their imprisonment. As the movement grew it was an important act of conscious political direction by its leading figures that it searched out new constituencies that might be convinced to lend support to the cause.

Democracy and the City

One such campaign can be seen in the City of London. The Levellers always had close links with the City institutions and had been intimately associated with oppositional politics even before the outbreak of the Revolution. Lilburne had been closely involved with the mobilisations of the apprentices; Walwyn had been instrumental in ward, vestry and City-wide agitation. Many other Levellers had been apprenticed and become freemen. Opposition to the monopolies of the great trading companies had been a frequent motif of Leveller pamphleteering. Lilburne had borne a particular animus against the greatest of these, the Merchant Adventurers, since their monopoly had prevented his entry into trade at the end of his military service. The irregular constitution of the City and its corporations had long contained elements of democracy, in which freemen could elect officers from ward level to the lord mayor, though not in the upper reaches by direct election. But equally time-worn was the actual oligarchic management of the City thinly glossed with a restricted democratic element. The wider debates about Church and state were bound to destabilise this paradox further. The recent Presbyterian dominance in the City made it more unstable still. One moment of crisis occurred as Lilburne was in the Tower.[12]

On 29 September 1646 a group of freemen attempted to assert their right to elect the lord mayor directly. They came, led by their preferred candidate, Major Henry Wansey, to the Guildlhall to participate in the election but found the door barred against them. The marshall of London was outside the door at the head of a group of men with staves, bills and halberds. In the ensuing rumble the conservative candidate, Thomas Adams, denied them the right to participate, and when Wansey began to read a protest to the crowd of citizens who had gathered he was laid hold of 'with force, and much violence', dragged into the Guildhall and held for an hour. Wansey was examined the following day by the mayor. The marshall urged Wansey's imprisonment but he was eventually released.[13]

Thomas Adams was a leading alderman who had first become mayor the previous year. It was Adams who cancelled the discussion between Baptists and Presbyterians examined in the previous chapter. During the Civil War he had been one of the conservative figures on the Militia Committee who had worked to undermine Walwyn's Salters' Hall committee. It was Adams who examined William Larner on his arrest the previous year. He was a key organiser of the Presbyterian faction and had some royalist sympathies. In April 1646 he had been woken at midnight and questioned on a false report that he was hiding the king—an incident about which Adams remained 'extremely nettled'. Henry Wansey was a man of a different stripe. A watchmaker by trade with a residence in Cornhill, he seems on Lilburne's account to be the same Henry Wansey who fought first as a captain in Lord Robartes's regiment, the same regiment as Larner, and then in Waller's regiment. He served with considerable bravery in Wiltshire as a major at the right hand of republican and future Regicide Edmund Ludlow and alongside future Leveller John Rede. Like Rede, Wansey's family were prominent Wiltshire dissenters. Wansey, himself a member of the Goldsmiths' Company, was to be involved a conflict with the Clockmakers' Guild the following month as they tried to make all members of the profession join their guild.[14]

Wansey was a man to whom Lilburne warmed. And his cause was close to Lilburne's heart. He could not stand 'the boylings' of his own conscience if he did not act to aid Wansey. So Lilburne lost no time in paying William Colet, the record keeper at the Tower, to bring him all the information he had on the charters of the City; the parts in Latin and French were translated by a friend. The fruit of Lilburne's study emerged in two publications, *Londons Liberty in Chains Discovered* and *The Charters of London*, published in October and December 1646 respectively. The aim was simple: to prove by copious and lengthy citation of original charters that the freemen of London had the right to elect the lord mayor and senior officials of the City. Clearly this was a matter of some intrinsic importance to Lilburne because of his own experience at the hands of the City authorities and the Merchant Adventurers. But Lilburne was also clear that the battle with the mayor and his supporters was part of the wider struggle in which his enemies had spread lies about Anabaptists and Separatists and that his bitter 'Presbyterian Adversaries', Prynne in particular, were attempting 'to make me and my friends odious to the people'. And in the midst of this Lilburne came back to the fundamental principle. Repeating the words of Elizabeth Lilburne's petition he wrote, 'the only and sole legislative Law making power is originally inherent in the people . . . in which the poorest that lives, hath as true a right to give a vote, as well as the richest and greatest'.[15]

Lilburne's aim was, as historian Philip Baker has argued, to mobilise one traditional democratic sentiment about City governance in support of the Leveller cause. But it would be a mistake to think that the Levellers were merely appealing to tradition. They were deliberately stressing the most democratic elements of the City's past. But where even this interpretation of the City's charters fell short of a fuller conception of democracy, they opted for democracy over tradition, as Baker acknowledges. The Levellers were quite clear that the argument they were having in the City in 1646 took place in a national political context which made it wholly more explosive than in the past. Finally, to take up this argument was clearly a strategic choice made by Lilburne and his allies in order to renew and deepen support among the citizens of the City.[16]

The petition campaign of 1647

Undaunted by imprisonment, Overton organised a petition setting out the case for a far-reaching overhaul of government. On 11 February 1647 Parliament received a petition in the name of 'the inhabitants of Buckinghamshire and Hartfordshire'. When they came to London these petitioners had sought out Overton and Lilburne in spite of their imprisonment. At the foot of the petition's single printed page is a note 'To the Reader' which explains that 'This petition was with almost ten thousand names, and was brought to Parliament . . . with about 500 Gentlemen and yeoman'. But this considerable delegation 'did not find that fair access to Parliament that they expected'. Most of them then left London but they chose six 'Commissioners' to stay behind and try to get the petition read and answered. But though they waited until 18 February they 'could not prevail'. This failure was attributed to the fact that 'those they had to deal with' had 'a greater affection for the House of Lords, then to the Liberties and Freedoms of those that choose and trusted them'. The commissioners then 'were forced in great discontent to return to their several dwellings, and truly to acquaint the rest of their fellow-Petitioners, what hard dealings they had found from the hands of the peoples great Trusties at Westminster'. Lilburne and Overton reprinted the petition in their *Out-Cryes of oppressed Commons*, but this pamphlet was declared 'obnoxious' by the Commons and a committee appointed to track down those who produced it.[17] But this was as nothing compared to the treatment meted out to the petitioners who supported the so-called Large (meaning comprehensive) Petition of March 1647.

The petition originally came from joint work by Independents and Lilburne's group and aimed at fending off the Presbyterian offensive. This new and broad-based audience for the Levellers provided considerable support for Lilburne in the early months of his imprisonment. But there were also constantly recurring tactical and strategic differences. Walwyn reported arguments with John Price of Goodwin's church about 'our different judgement for seasons of petitioning'. This resulted in a previous petition not being delivered despite support from the gathered churches. A second petition, more limited in scope, was proposed and Walwyn had 'multitudes with me for the presenting', but the Independents were 'against it'. The meeting where this was discussed, probably at the Windmill, exploded in uproar as attacks on Walwyn caused 'clamour and discontent' and 'he that had the petition and hands in keeping, rent it in peeces, and so the meeting ended'. The conflicts between Walwyn and the Independents were, at this point, so intense that when he was charged with being an atheist a meeting was arranged at the Dolphin inn where he could clear his name. The Independents failed to attend but, under advice from his friend Henry Brandiff, Walwyn pulled back from further controversy. Indeed he appeared in defence of Goodwin and his supporters when they were brought before Colonel Leigh's Committee for Examinations. It was this continued persecution that in March 1647 brought the Independents around to agreeing that a new petition should be presented.[18]

The Leveller Petition of March 1647 was an extensive political programme that foreshadowed the *Agreement of the People*. In, probably, Walwyn's measured prose the document paid tribute to the Long Parliament's achievements to date, but went on to complain that 'we still find this Nation oppressed with grievances of the same destructive nature as formerly, though under different notions'. It then listed a thirteen-point programme to halt this backsliding. The first three of these grew directly from the Levellers' recent experience of persecution by the Lords: an end to the negative voice, or veto, over bills sent from the Commons; an end to commoners' prosecution by the Lords; and an end to examinations designed to illicit self-incriminating testimony. The next two points aimed at establishing religious toleration by calling for the repeal of laws insisting on conformity or punishing those who printed or preached heretical opinions. Point six called for the abolition of the Merchant Adventurers and similar monopolies. In the next two clauses law reform was demanded by an insistence that the laws should be published in English and that speedy trials should be mandatory. To this, prison reform was added. Point nine demanded an end to tithes—an act which would have removed livings from 9,000 Presbyterian ministers. Alleviation of prisoners of debt and the poor generally was advocated in two other clauses. The final, and least practical, thirteenth demand was to 'restraine and discountenance the . . . reviling and reproaching' of the 'well-affected with ignominious titles of Round-heads, factious, seditious and the like'.[19]

The Large Petition was circulated for subscription in and around London. Walwyn recorded 'Divers printed coppies thereof being sent abroad to gain subscriptions'. Lambe was clearly central to the subscription campaign. It was in his house that the City recorder, John Glyn, seized it and took it to the Commons, which 'in a great heat' voted it a seditious paper. The Commons heard testimony from a Mr Boys, who had been in Lambe's congregation when the petition was read at the end of the sermon. He reported that someone read the petition while Lambe 'corrected him in reading it, in many Places'. He saw 'divers People subscribed it: Some Six subscribed it in his Presence: That there was some Hundred or Sixscore Hands subscribed'. Boys had got a 'printed Copy of the Petition from a Woman that was reading it'. The matter was referred to Colonel Leigh's committee, which already had responsibility for suppressing dissenting preachers. This order was reissued immediately after the Levellers' petition was condemned.[20]

On 17 March the mayor and aldermen brought their own demands to the Commons and also appended the Levellers petition, clearly expecting action to be taken to suppress it. On 19 March Lambe was brought before Colonel Leigh's committee. He was accompanied by 'divers hundreds' of the petition's supporters bringing a certificate asserting that the original petition was genuine and not seditious. But they were not allowed to deliver the certificate and were 'with violence thrust out of the Committee-Chamber, and a Guard called for to set them packing with a vengeance'. Instead they gathered near the Court of Requests to hear the petition read aloud by Nicholas Tue, who was promptly arrested by the sergeant-at-arms and imprisoned. Colonel Leigh's committee numbered the leaders of the Presbyterian faction—Denzil Holles, Philip Stapleton and Walter Earle—among its members. As the meeting rose they tangled with the petitioners, calling them 'rogues, villains and seditious'. They 'laid violent hands upon them'. Philip Stapleton took Leveller stalwart Major Alexander Tulidah by the throat and dragged him to the door. There were attempts to carry some petitioners off as prisoners. Walter Earle raised his cane at the protestors and Holles threatened to draw his sword. The next day Holles and his supporters reported the petitioners to the Commons and Tulidah was arrested. In consequence, the Levellers returned the next day with a petition demanding Tulidah be released. Holles and Stapleton acquiesced; according to Lilburne's account, they wanted to prevent him giving his account of their behaviour towards the protestors.[21]

The petitioners returned on two subsequent occasions to protest this treatment. On both occasions printed versions of the petitions were handed to MPs at the door of the Commons. On 4 May the House voted down the latest petitions. On the second occasion, on 20 May, the House voted to have the petition burnt by the common hangman. On that day William Browne, the Leveller bookseller, was at the head of a group of petitioners outside Parliament that also included Southwark Leveller Samuel Highland. Some MPs clearly remembered an equally pugnacious exchange they had with Browne at the end of April when he had said that 'they had waited many days' for an answer to the petitions, 'and would wait no longer'. For good measure he added that 'now they see they shall have none, and take it for a flat Denial; therefore, now we are resolved to take another Way'. Asked for his name by an MP he retorted that the 'time may come when I may ask you for your name in another Place'. The MPs had him kneel at the bar and told him that he was a delinquent and that his words were not 'fit Language to be given at the Door of the Parliament'. Browne denied the charges but was packed off to Newgate in any case. He was defended by Walwyn in *Gold Tried in the Fire* and by Overton in *An Appeale*. In consultation with Lilburne more protests were called, demanding whether the Commons could tell them why their petitions had been burnt and 'how and in what manner' they would be allowed to petition. A final petition was presented to the House by William Waller but it was voted by 128 votes to 112 not to answer it. All such Leveller efforts were rebuffed and in the end they issued a statement that they 'discharged themselves of further attendance for the present'. In an intense campaign lasting less than ten weeks the Levellers had appealed to the House *six* times, with four petitions, a certificate of avowal, and finally a declaration announcing their withdrawal in disgust.[22]

The Levellers' experience at the hands of the Presbyterian faction in the Commons fundamentally shifted their perspectives towards revolution. The change of temper can be seen in Lilburne's review of the campaign, *Rash Oaths Unwarrantable*. This lengthy account of the spring petitioning campaign was addressed to Henry Marten as chair of the Commons committee charged with reviewing Lilburne's ongoing imprisonment in the Tower. The publication marks the only time a breach might have opened up between Lilburne and Marten. Lilburne is clearly distressed not only at his treatment but also at the similar treatment of Overton, Larner, Tue and Tulidah. He also records that Thomas Paine, Walwyn's printer, had recently been jailed. Lilburne is certainly concerned at what he regards as Marten's negligence in not bringing his committee's report to the Commons. But before he makes this case he goes out of his way to pay tribute to Marten and to record their close cooperation. Lilburne writes that he regards Marten as one whose name is 'extraordinary famous' as a great pillar of the Liberties of the Commons of England. He reports approvingly that another MP has said that 'England were more beholden unto Mr. Henry Marten for his sincerity, uprightnesses, boldnesse and gallantry, then to halfe, if not all those that are called conscientious men in the House'. Lilburne records his 'happinesses (for so I esteemed it) often to be in your company' and to have participated in 'those gallant discourses for the Liberty of this Nation'. It is only out of sheer desperation at the current course of the Commons that Lilburne, 'in a friendly way before we fall out', moves beyond private messages to a printed public appeal. This was followed up in July, after Lilburne had been incarcerated for a year, with a sharp one-page printed appeal to Marten.

The MP was clearly disconcerted by Lilburne's criticism. His manuscript reply, *Rash Censures Uncharitable*, is revealing about his relationship with the Levellers. He writes that he has often 'seen my name bespattered in songs ballads and pamphlets, yet never troubled myself with framing of any counter-song, anti-ballad, or vindication till I found Lieut. Col. John Lilburne firing upon Henry Marten'. Marten says he had only thought to reply now because if he remained 'very quiet' then 'my silence would give you what never have you yet, just cause of offence'. Marten contrasts

Lilburne's decision to go into print with contact he has had with William Larner's still imprisoned household members. 'John Larners & Jane Hales', he writes, 'who perhaps have no better company in the Fleet than you have in the Tower', have been 'so civil' as to send 'a letter sealed and left at my house not in a printed epistle'. Marten is nevertheless full of praise for Lilburne, who has, he writes, 'allways been true & steadfast to the common interest, allways active industrious in promoting it & gallant in all conditions temperate sober & discreet, carrying before you whatsoever you undertake'. And he concludes that he would have 'submitted my selfe to your sentence of my guilt' if he had been 'careless of you and your sufferings' or omitted any 'opportunity of doing you service'.[23]

The potential breach was in fact soon closed between Marten and Lilburne, who even offered to pay for the publication of Marten's manuscript. Overton, in a postscript to his *An Arrow Against All Tyrants*, had already said he had been wrong to think that Marten had been absent from the House and had not pursued Elizabeth Lilburne's petition either by negligence or because of pressure from the Lords. He wrote that 'for my over-hasty censorious esteem of you I humbly crave your excuse, hoping you will rather impute it to the fervency of my faithful zeal for the common good than to any malignant disposition or disaffection in me towards you'. What these exchanges reveal is that, despite the occasion of the dispute, a close relationship remained between Marten and the Levellers and a mutual admiration existed between Marten and Lilburne. But it also reveals that the Levellers' patience with the existing House of Commons was reaching an end.[24]

Marten's inability to do more for Lilburne and the other Leveller prisoners had less to do with his personal and political sympathies and more to do with the fact that as the Presbyterian offensive drew to its height, the radical Independents became less willing to cooperate with the Levellers. Goodwin's congregation wavered in its support for Leveller petitions. Walwyn reported that in the conflicts that followed the attempt to present the Large Petition, 'most Independents stood aloof, and looked on', leaving Thomas Lambe, Samuel Highland and others to organise support at the Commons. As even Lilburne recognised, Marten may have been unwilling to bring his report to the Commons for fear of it being rejected and so resulting in Commons approval for the Lords' verdict against Lilburne. Overton later accepted that this was the reason why Marten had not acted. The success of the agitation around the Large Petition did, however, offer some support to the Levellers. First, it dramatized the impending threat, 'all men evidently seeing, that we were likely, though the Common Enemy was vanquish'd, to be liable to the same, or worse bondage'. Second, according to Walwyn, this caused some Independents 'to approve of our motions, and they and I began to come a little nearer together, and had joynt meetings and debates'. However, it was not until the Presbyterian push became a definite attempt at counterrevolution that the Independents as a whole were willing to countenance outright resistance.[25]

Lilburne made the breach with the Commons explicit in *Rash Oaths Unwarrentable* when he insisted that 'I am now in good sober resolved earnest, determined to appeale to the whole kingdome and Army against them, and it may be thereby come quitance with them, and measure unto them as they have measured unto me'. *Rash Oaths* reproduced one of the first petitions of the newly arising army revolt. Lilburne immediately sensed the strategic necessity of making common cause with the petitioners among the soldiers. He told the Commons 'that though some of your members call the Army Rebells and Traitors, for contesting with those that gave them their power and authority', it was actually the MPs who were the 'reall Rebells and Traitors to the trust reposed in them by the free people of England'. The answer to the political crisis was that the army should refuse to disband, and that the 'everlasting parliament' should be replaced by a system in which

> every freeman of England, as well poore as rich, whose life, estate, &c., is to be taken away by the law, may have Vote in chusing those that are to make the law, it being a maxim in nature, that no man justly can be bound without his own consent, and care taken that this may be once every year without fail.[26]

The Levellers held to the notion of the sovereignty of the Commons but now found themselves branded disturbers of the state for being in opposition to the conservative domination of the House. To appeal beyond the Commons to the original power of the people was the next logical step. But merely because it was a logical step did not mean that even all the Independents were willing to take it. The revolutionary implications were too much for some, even under the growing threat of counterrevolution.

The Levellers were equipped and ready to take this step. Their struggle in the campaign for the Large Petition had raised their collective profile among radical supporters of Parliament, the congregations of the gathered churches and the citizenry of the City. But even so it was a strategic choice of some bravery to act on this new opportunity. Similarly, just because the army radicals and the Levellers faced analogous problems did not mean that an alliance between them was inevitable. Nevertheless, the Levellers took the strategic gamble to attempt such an alliance.

CHAPTER 9

Agitators

In 1647 the soldiers of the New Model Army did something truly revolutionary. They refused to disband when commanded to do so by Parliament. This alone was mutiny. But they then proceeded to directly elect their own representatives from the ranks. The organisation of these Agitators became so powerful that the most senior officers of the New Model, Sir Thomas Fairfax and Oliver Cromwell, had to share command of the army with them. This created an entirely new centre of Revolutionary activity and fundamentally altered the course of the Revolution.[1] All this happened just as the Levellers fought the battles of the Large Petition of March 1647.

As is often the case in revolutions, this new development was a reaction to a counterrevolutionary thrust by the opponents of the radicals. The most immediately contentious part of this planned coup was reduction of the New Model Army by disbandment or the transfer of forces to fight in Ireland. But this was only the most visible aspect of the counterrevolution being planned by parliamentary moderates and the Presbyterian party. The second, equally important, element of the plan was to create a new military force loyal to the conservative faction and capable of confronting the shrunken New Model. The aim was to bring the king to London and resettle the nation on the basis of its old tripartite constitution of king, Lords and Commons, and to reinforce the Presbyterian church settlement. This move would quash the demand for toleration for good. But had this counterrevolution worked it is unlikely that it would have halted at the political settlement hoped for by moderates. A full-scale reaction would have been a more likely result.[2]

The Presbyterian counterrevolution

By spring 1647 the faction led by Denzil Holles and Philip Stapleton dominated the Commons, making effective alliances with the ascendant
Presbyterians in the City. Neither Holles nor Stapleton was a religious
Presbyterian, but they shared common conservative political goals that
bound them together in a powerful bloc. In contrast, as a Scottish commissioner observed, 'the Independent party is for the present sunk under
water in Parliament and runne down'. The conservative alliance was
strengthened in March when a petition by Presbyterians to the Common
Council, the latest in a year-long petitioning campaign, asked for the King
to be brought from the Isle of Wight to London. In the City a secret
committee instructed Thomas Adams and Thomas Skinner to draw up a
complimentary petition for presentation to Parliament. This was then sent
to the Commons with a copy of the Levellers' Large Petition attached,
clearly in the expectation it would be condemned. At the same time
progress was made creating a military force to counter the New Model
Army. During these tense weeks disbanded officers and soldiers, the
so-called reformadoes, were recruited by the City authorities. Meanwhile
regiments of the New Model Army that might be sympathetic to the
Presbyterian cause were suborned, and there was a systematic attempt to
put control of the Northern Army, other forces not part of the New Model,
and the Trained Bands into in safe Presbyterian hands. The Militia
Committee, always a weathervane, was the first to fall. In April,
Independents such as Isaac Pennington, John Fowke, John Estwicke and
Colonel Player—stalwarts of the Revolution from its early days—were
voted off and replaced by loyal Presbyterians, often officers in the Trained
Bands. Thomas Adams was among their number and most were prosper-
ous or wealthy Common Council members. The committee quickly got to
work overhauling the Trained Bands and adding to it a force of 500 cavalry,
an offensive military arm that it had not previously possessed. Elsewhere,
militants controlling the suburban Trained Bands, like that in Tower
Hamlets, were purged and subordinated to the City. New Model guards on
the City fortifications were replaced by the Trained Bands. These forces
numbered about 12,000 men at a time when the scheme to reduce the
New Model would have left it with about half that number. Two army
commanders of known hostility to the New Model were at the heart of this
project, Sir William Waller and Edward Massey.[3]

In tandem with this move the Presbyterians on the Militia Committee took control of the financial committees disbursing arrears to the New Model Army. In May a £200,000 loan was agreed with the City for the payment of arrears. In June £10,000 of this was released for the payment of reformadoes. One of the venues for payment was Thomas Edwards's Christ Church at Newgate. As Valerie Pearl notes in her exemplary account of the counterrevolution, 'rarely can pulpit, party headquarters, army pay centre and recruiting office have been so effectively combined as they were here'. At the heart of this operation was the agreement that the king, who had fled to the Scots after the military defeat of royalism, should be handed over to the care of Parliament and the Scottish army should leave England. It was argued that while Scottish soldiers were still on English soil the case for the disbandment of the New Model was not likely to prosper. As Scottish commissioner Robert Baillie recalled, 'Stapleton and Hollis . . . had been the maine persuaders of us to remove out of England, and leave the King to them, upon assurance, which was most lykelie, that this was the only means to gett that evill army disbanded, the King and peace settled according to our minds'. Across January and February 1647 the king was given into the charge of parliamentary commissioners and taken to Holmby House in Northamptonshire. In return the Scots were paid two instalments of the money due to them, totaling £200,000, and the last of their forces left England. Six days later, on 18 February, Presbyterian MPs proposed the disbanding of the New Model Army.[4]

William Walwyn's *The Poore Wise-mans Admonition* captures this moment, articulating an urgent call for unity with the army against the imminent Presbyterian coup. Its force derives from the masterly enumeration of the elements combining against the radicals. Modern historians have added much detail but, even though they are not writing in the very heat of events, they have not bettered his account. Walwyn describes the rise of the conservatives in the Commons and their plan to 'embroyle us in a new warre'. In order to do this they sow division between the army and the common people by abusing Sectaries and burning petitions. The 'corrupt men in the House of Commons' are assisted by the mayor and 'many of the Aldermen and great men of the Citie'. To this end they have taken control of the militia by expelling 'the former men who shewed themselves faithful to the Common-wealth and City' but who are now not 'judged fit instruments for this secret work'. To this end, 'The Scots will be ingaged, and forraigne Forces called in'. The excise tax is being abused to pay for this and customs are as great a tax as ever, leaving 'poore seamen and mariners wrack'd to the utmost point of extremity'.[5]

The only way to defeat this threat, Walwyn proposes, is to stand by the army and then to demand reform of Parliament to end 'corrupt elections' in which 'the one part of the Parliament procure the election of the other' and so the Commons is no longer 'freely made by the people'. Revolt against the corrupted Parliament is justified in the same way that the Parliament justified the revolt against the king: trust has been betrayed and public safety is at risk. The right to oppose such a Parliament exists 'by the same rule of right reason, and law of equity, as the souldiers of an Army may oppose the general, when he turneth the mouth of his Cannon upon them'. The Levellers hoped to form a common front with army radicals against the looming Presbyterian coup.[6]

The rise of the Agitators

The army revolt unfolded at the same time the Levellers were doing battle over the Large Petition. Both campaigns coincided on 4 March 1647 when the Lords voted against raising any more taxes to pay the army. Essex petitioners called for the disbandment of the army a week later, as did Presbyterian petitioners in the City a week after that. The plan for disbandment at first found no resistance from the army's commander. Fairfax wrote to Parliament agreeing to cooperate with the plan to send troops to Ireland. He had already agreed that the army would not come closer than twenty-five miles from London. On 21 March over forty officers met a delegation of parliamentary commissioners, led by Sir John Clotworthy and Sir William Waller, at Saffron Walden in Essex to agree the process of disbandment and the formation of an Irish expedition. However, the officers resisted and on the following day a second meeting drew up a petition refusing to enlist for Ireland without assurances that their arrears of pay would be met. In addition they demanded indemnification against prosecution for acts carried out during the war, that there should be a statement of which regiments would remain in service in England, and that the commander of forces in Ireland be named. Fairfax, under pressure from the commissioners, prevailed on twenty-nine of the officers to withdraw their names from the petition.[7]

Cromwell was of the same mind as Fairfax in all this. He told the Commons, 'In the presence of Almighty God, before whom I stand, I know the army will disband and lay down their arms at your door, whenever you will command them'. The MP Thomas Juxon records that 'Cromwell and their friends in the House' acted on the assumption that if the soldiers did not 'content themselves with what's proper to them as soldiers, but go about to confound and disorder the whole business, they would certainly desert them'. Cromwell believed that though 'there were many miscarriages in the parliament' they must be borne with, because

> though the people were rationally the supreme power, yet parliament legally was and therefore were bound to submit to them. Nay, though they should do things that tended apparently to the prejudice of the common good, rather to suffer and wait for a better time than to resist. The common people never were fit for government.

This was, of course, precisely the opposite view to the popular-sovereignty theory that the Levellers had now developed in response to the same political crisis. In their eyes the only thing that could put a stop to what would have an easy first victory for the Presbyterian coup was a widespread mutiny by the officers and men of the New Model Army.[8]

The soldiers took matters into their own hands as the officers' petition stalled, and drew up a separate petition of their own. Lieutenant Colonel Thomas Pride was accused of calling a rendezvous of his regiment and getting some 1,100 to sign the petition, but denied it when examined by the Commons. The soldiers' petition was more forcefully expressed; it was only with difficulty that the officers got them to moderate it. At just this point Lilburne was writing to Cromwell from the Tower threatening to break off all relations because he had heard from two informants, an officer and another soldier, that Cromwell was attempting to prevent the circulation of the petition. But Cromwell's efforts were overtaken by events. On 29 March John Clotworthy and William Waller alerted Parliament that a petition listing army grievances was circulating among the troops. The MPs immediately demanded its suppression. The Commons summoned Commissary-General Ireton, Colonel Hammond, Colonel Grimes, Colonel Robert Lilburne (John's brother) and Thomas Pride to answer charges that they had been intimidating soldiers into signing petitions. On 1 April the officers were called in and told that 'the House had received Information of a Petition that was going on in the Army' and that the House 'had expressed a very great Dislike of it'. Holles quickly scribbled these sentiments out as a motion and Parliament took the extraordinary step of declaring the petitioners 'enemies of the State and disturbers of the public peace'. The so-called Declaration of Dislike was then ordered to be printed. No attempt was made to meet the soldiers' concerns, even over the eighteen weeks of back pay then owning, and the officers were told to get back to their regiments and put a stop to the petitions. The confrontation was so heated that William Waller and others had to prevent Denzil Holles and Henry Ireton from fighting a duel.[9]

The reaction in the army was equally strong. Letters phrased in Leveller-inflected language sent from Saffron Walden to the Commons defended the soldiers' right to petition, saying that they 'had fought for the Liberty of the Subjects of England' and should not 'be denied the Liberty of the Subject to Petition', especially since a recent Essex petition and others had been critical of the army. It concluded, 'And what (says the Souldier) makes the Army lyable to these Reproaches, unless it be for finishing their Work so soon? And have they sought to maintain the Petition of Right, and be denied a right of Petitioning themselves?' The attack on the Essex petition was taken up in the pamphlet *A New Found Stratagem*, which bore all the hallmarks of being a Leveller production. It contends that the Essex petition was sent from London and promoted by ministers, and that few in the locality signed it. It refers directly to the recent conflict in the Commons between Denzil Holles, Walter Earle and Leveller Major Tulidah. In language repeated across Leveller literature at this time it argues that there is more 'injustice, cruelty, and oppressions exercised by the Parliament, then ever was by the King', and argues against tithes. It warns that forces previously commanded by the earl of Essex and Edward Massey will make up 'an Army of wicked men' who will impose a new tyranny and a 'Presbyterian yoake'. The pamphlet has a detailed knowledge of the events surrounding the officers' being called to the bar of the Commons. Thomason's note on the cover records that it was 'scattered about in the Armie when the Commissioners were sent from Parliament to disband'. Major Robert Saunders, Captain Styles, and his sergeant, Roger Crafts, were sent to be examined by the Commons for distributing it.[10]

Lilburne had been actively engaged in the petitioning process in the army from as early as February, complaining to John Goodwin that Colonel Sadler had informed him that members of Goodwin's congregation had been blocking a radical petition at a rendezvous at St Albans. And Gilbert Mabbott, part of clerical staff of the army but based at Fairfax's house in London, was keeping the army informed about the course of the Levellers' March petitioning campaign and the arrest of Major Tulidah. Indeed, as Gardiner observes, 'for some weeks the names of Tew and Tulidah are of constant occurrence in the various petitions and declarations of the soldiers, who appear to have taken alarm at their treatment, as if it were a warning of the fate likely to befall themselves if they were once disbanded'. Further evidence of Leveller influence in the army comes from exactly this period. On 20 April a letter from Suffolk reported that some soldiers quartered there 'do not stick to call the Parliament men tyrants' and that 'Lilburne's books are quoted by them as statute law'. These remarks were reported to the Commons. The same letter detailed the first stirrings of Agitator organisation. It reported that the soldiers were circulating a petition which they intended to send up to London with 'two out of every troope' even though, perhaps with an eye on the recent arrest of Leveller petitioners, 'they expect the parliament should clap them up whoe goe up with it'. Another letter dated six days later from Saffron Walden described the troops as 'one Lilburne throughout, more likely to give than to receive laws'. On 20 May a letter to the Agitators reported 'a long debate' in the Commons on the Levellers' petition and the arrest of William Browne. It reported that the Commons had hit on 'a new way to answer Petitions'— burning by the common hangman. This all accompanied the first emergence of the Agitators' organisation.[11]

The election of the Agitators is a momentous turning point in the Revolution. No army, ever, had done this before. The election of directly accountable agents, for this was what the term 'Agitators' then meant, from regiments across the face of the army stymied compromise by the army commanders and, ultimately, both prevented the Presbyterian coup and provided a new popular impetus to the Revolution. The Agitators emerged because, on the one hand, the force of the Presbyterian reaction demanded active resistance if the army was to be preserved, and because, on the other hand, some senior officers, Fairfax and Cromwell in particular, were unwilling to confront this threat effectively. Soldiers in Presbyterian Colonel Sheffield's regiment cashiered their officers and seized their horses and weapons. Sir Robert Pye and a loyal captain drew their swords on mutineers in his regiment, but 'the Souldiers hem'd round, made him putt up . . . dismounted the Captaine, and beat him out of their Quarters'. Other officers, including Ireton, Robert Lilburne, and Thomas Pride, were more supportive of the soldiers. And this was important in opening a space into which the Agitators could emerge. For the Levellers it hugely enlarged their audience in the army and won them new adherents. It was a constituency that they would never wholly lose until the moment of their final defeat.[12]

The Agitators first emerged in eight cavalry regiments, but they were soon elected in the foot regiments as well. This is of some social significance. The cavalry were usually men of higher social standing, paid more (perhaps two shillings rather than eight pence a day for the foot), and more likely to be ideologically motivated volunteers than pressed men. In unofficial meetings where they were quartered the troops elected their representatives. William Rainsborough, in a sharp exchange with Colonel Sheffield, bore witness that when the men chose 'two out of a troope' to represent them they did so in a disciplined way and that they 'did nothing that did not become them as souldiers'. When troopers met in Bury St Edmunds, representatives of the foot regiments came to meet them 'and every Foot Soldier gave four Pence a piece, towards defraying of the Charges of that meeting'. The Agitators were so numerous that they could not sensibly form a deliberative body and so Agitators from each regiment chose two of their number to represent the regiment.[13]

The officer-written *Vindication* of the army was due to be discussed by the Commons in late April. But on 30 April, as the House was about to begin this business, it had the *Apologie* of some Agitators brought to its attention by Major General Philip Skippon. Three Agitators—Edward Sexby, William Allen and Thomas Shepherd, part of a larger group standing at the Commons door—were brought to the bar. They refused to answer questions about their tract, replying that it was the joint work of the regiments and that all questions would have to be addressed to them in writing. The Presbyterians moved to have the Agitators committed. Holles later said he thought one of them should have been shot as a lesson to the army. But something of the depth of the crisis was beginning to transmit itself to the Commons. One MP said he 'would have them committed indeed, but it should be to the best inn of the town, and good sack and sugar provided'. In the event the day resulted in two victories for the soldiers. The House voted to pay arrears and prepare an indemnity ordinance. In addition the old Presbyterian commissioners to the army were replaced with Cromwell, Ireton, Fleetwood and Skippon in the hope that they would have more luck restoring order.[14] The commissioners and army officers met on 7 May in Saffron Walden and again on 15 May, this time in a long conference with the Agitators. The following day, 223 officers signed a *Representation of the Army*, a declaration of the grievances, for presentation to Parliament.[15]

All this, including the belated conciliatory gestures, had little effect on the Holles–Stapleton faction in the Commons. On 18 May Parliament voted to accept a letter from the king as the basis for a settlement, and two days later the Lords invited the king to negotiate at his Oatlands Palace, near London. They ignored the *Representation of the Army*. Nevertheless, on 21 May Cromwell assured MPs that the soldiers would remain loyal if treated respectfully and fairly. Four days later the Commons voted in favour of immediate disbandment of the army in an atmosphere where the sentiments 'of the Parliament and the City against the army are very violent'.[16] The New Model Army now stood on the verge of destruction. Its most senior and respected commanders were unhappy, but unwilling to confront Parliament directly. Its wider officer corps was divided, although many opposed disbandment, some actively. This minority of officers were working with the emerging organisation within the ranks which was quickly developing its own momentum. One vital element of this organisation was the establishment of an army printing press by two radicals working in the orbit of the Levellers, Edward Sexby and John Harris.

Edward Sexby, John Harris and the army press

The army printing press was set up by Agitator Edward Sexby in May 1647. Sexby was, like Lilburne, a veteran of the Eastern Association. He established the press at the very height of the crisis resulting from Parliament's attempt to disband the army.[17] Two letters concerning the establishment of the army press exist in the Clarke manuscripts. The one dated 17 May 1647 is definitely from Sexby. It is a short urgent note to the Agitators insisting, 'If there is not [*s] a presse got into the Army we shall be att a losse, there want nothing butt Mony therefore tell the Officers they must disburse the Mony'. Sexby's urgency is a product of the fact that he thinks, 'The King will it is verily thought come and joyne with' the army's parliamentary enemies. He encourages the Agitators to spread their grievances rapidly and instructs them to send messengers to 'Rainsborowe's Regiment' and 'two more to London to Convey newes'.[18] In the second letter, which historian Charles Firth attributes to Sexby although it is not signed, and dates on internal evidence as written on 18 May, the author insists that the Agitators' previous 'Printer is taken and undone', and that unless another press is found 'wee are undone'. The letter continues by recommending 'one perfect' workman.[19] It is unlikely to be a coincidence that John Harris arrived with the army on that very day. Harris would go on the following year to produce the most outspoken of Leveller publications, the news-sheet *Mercurius Militaris*, aimed at the army.[20]

Sexby's hopes for funding from the officers were only partially fulfilled. Some payments were made to Harris, but the press seems to have remained a rudimentary operation.[21] Its type was limited and its productions of poor quality. But it produced a stream of soldier-inspired documents, beginning with *A True Declaration of the Present Proceedings of the Army*.[22] Others included *A Declaration of Master William Lenthall*, printed in 'Oxford by J Harris and H Hills', *A Letter Sent from the Agitators of the Army* and *The Resolutions of the Agitators of the Army*.[23] John Harris's association at this early stage with Henry Hills is instructive. Baptist Henry Hills was also the printer of Walwyn's pamphlets. But it was John Lilburne who originally arranged his apprenticeship in the printing trade in 1642, drawing him away from his previous employment by Thomas Harrison. Hills was at first apprenticed to Leveller printer Thomas Paine. Harrison later made Hills printer to the army. Hills was an associate, like Lilburne, of William Kiffin and was later attacked as a 'fanatic' alongside Richard Overton and Leveller Jeremy Ives.[24]

The extent and seriousness of the organisation among the Agitators becomes clear in Sexby's directions for 'Managing the Councels of the Army' from May 1647. This is a devastating series of organisational measures for radical political work. From initiating committees to running printing presses, from keeping in correspondence with 'wel-affected friends' around the country to avoiding delay in action, from preventing disbandment to the importance of framing arguments 'for the good of the people'—Sexby's advice is sophisticated, practical and clear. Sexby and other Agitators were especially keen on sustaining civilian support for the army and kept in close contact with radicals who were petitioning in their favour. The Levellers were the primary group that had this capacity.[25] An examination of the accounts of army payments from 1647 to 1650 underlines the degree to which Sexby's recommendations were reflected in practice and, critically, of Leveller involvement in them. The records show payments to Agitators, although the word 'Agitators' is later crossed through or replaced by another term. Something in excess of £1,800 is paid to unnamed and named Agitators between June 1647 and May 1649, although there are only four payments after May 1648. There are some group payments such as the ninety-six pounds paid to the 'Agitators towards their charges at Putney'. Of the fifteen named individuals receiving payment, at least eight are Levellers, including Sexby himself, William Bray, John Rede, Alexander Tulidah, and printers Henry Hills and John Harris. Two of these payments, those to Bray and Tulidah, are for arrears.

Of those named Agitators who are are paid more than once all are Levellers except for Cornet Joyce, paid the substantial sum of £100 for 'extra charges' in the week after he seized the king at Holmby House in June 1647. Remarkably since he had left the army in 1645, John Lilburne is also paid ten pounds in August 1647, sent to him by army messenger. A number of payments are for printing, including a payment of nine pounds to 'Mr. Hills printer for 5000 of the Agreement' in February 1649.[26]

The Agitators represented a substantial, new and effective political force erupting into the political scene. Over eighty officers and some 229 named Agitators or sympathisers of the Agitators who were not officers have been identified. This compares with some 450 officers who sided with Parliament or whose views are not known. The extent to which the rise of Agitators in 1647 provided a new cohort of future Levellers with a model, and direct experience, of widespread and effective political organisation should not be underestimated.[27]

The revolt in the army

Sexby's letter to Rainsborough's regiment was a portent of things to come. On 28 May the regiment mutinied when it was directed to Portsmouth to embark for the recapture of the last royalist stronghold in Jersey. Rainsborough's men drove off their officers and took command regiment for themselves. Their great fear was that the army would lose control of its artillery train then at Oxford. And who would know better the importance of artillery than the regiment of the New Model Army's most experienced and renowned siege master? Directed only by the Agitators, Rainsborough's regiment began marching to Oxford. Rainsborough was not with the regiment but Parliament immediately ordered him to return to it and get it under control. Rainsborough eventually caught up with his troops at Abingdon on 30 May and managed to get them to halt their progress on promises that the army would take care to preserve their control of the artillery.

The day after Rainsborough's regiment mutinied, but before their colonel caught up with them, Fairfax and his council of war ordered a general rendezvous of the army at Newmarket, as the Agitators had demanded. On the day after Rainsborough met his regiment at Abingdon, Parliament attempted to have the artillery train brought from Oxford to London. In Chelmsford the parliamentary commissioners began disbanding Fairfax's foot regiment. The regiment mutinied and began marching to Newmarket to join the rendezvous. Presbyterian Lieutenant Colonel Jackson and Major Goody caught up with about 1,000 of them who cried, 'There comes our Enimies'. The officers demanded to know on whose command they marched. They told them they had 'received orders from the Agitators'. Asked if they had heard the declarations of Parliament the soldiers told them, 'what doe you bringing your two-penny pamphlets to us?' In a masterpiece of understatement Rushworth recorded, 'you see then the Officers do not altogether lead them'. Events had now reached crisis point. The Presbyterian majority in the Commons and their allies in the City, supported, militarily if needs be, by the Scots, were now on the verge of disbanding the army and constructing their own military force with which to impose a settlement of the nation. This would certainly involve bringing the king from Holmby House, where he was guarded by a force under the command of Presbyterian stalwart Colonel Graves. The essentially defensive reactions of the Agitators had slowed but not halted the Presbyterian offensive. Something more was now needed.[28]

Cromwell's house in Drury Lane was where such a move was planned. Cromwell's residence had become a centre of radical activity. As the Levellers' spring petitioning campaign unfolded it had created a dynamic which drew support from initially sceptical Independents. As a result William Walwyn records that he visited Cromwell 'often in Drury-lane about that time'. On at least one occasion he was joined by John Price, a leading member of John Goodwin's Coleman Street congregation. Much of the discussion was about the state of the army. Cromwell, as we have seen, had until this point insisted to the Commons that the army would remain subordinate to Parliament. Walwyn clearly played a role in persuading Cromwell that this would lead to disaster:

> And the Lieutenant General also knows, upon what grounds I then perswaded him to divide from that Body, to which he was united; and that if he did not, it would be his ruine, and the ruine of the General, and all those Worthyes that had preserved us; that if he did do it in time, he should preserve himself and them, and all conscientious people, but he should do it without spilling one drop of bloud; professing, that if it were not evident to me that it would be so, I would not perswade him.

Similar meetings were also being held at Walwyn's own house with radical Independents through 'all the time the Army disputed with the Parliament'.

A later account thought that Cromwell only joined 'that violent and rash party of the Army' after the third letter from them came to Cromwell telling him, 'if you would not forthwith, nay presently, come and head them, they would go their own way without you'.[29]

The pressure from Agitators and Levellers seems to have eventually moved Cromwell, for it was at one such meeting in Drury Lane, though not with Walwyn present, that a plan was devised to act on this advice. At a meeting on the night of 31 May Cromwell gave his cautious assent to a plan that originated with the Agitators. Agitator Cornet George Joyce would take a body of horse and seize the artillery train in Oxford. He would then go to Holmby House and ensure that the Presbyterians could not remove the king or act on Parliament's declared scheme of taking him to Scotland. Cromwell told Joyce that he believed that Holles and his supporters were set on removing the king themselves and that Joyce should 'secure the person of the King from being moved by any other, or if occasion were, to remove him to some place of better security'. Leveller John Harris is the only source for what transpired at the meeting and it is likely that he had the information from Joyce himself. When Joyce arrived in Oxford on 1 June he found the garrison, held by Ingoldsby's regiment, already determined to retain the artillery train for the army. The next day, as Joyce turned his troopers towards Holmby House, William Walwyn laid the last petition of the Leveller's spring campaign at the door of the Commons, where, predictably, it was rejected with many 'villifying and disgracefull speeches from severall Members of the House'. On 3 June Joyce arrived at Holmby House and, in a justly famous exchange, confronted the king.[30]

When Joyce's troopers arrived the soldiers of the existing garrison embraced them and swore that no 'sword should be drawn in wrath, or a musquet fired in anger'. Nevertheless Colonel Graves and the commissioners sent by Parliament to treat with Charles confronted Joyce. Graves cross-questioned one of Joyce's troopers, asking if he were not satisfied with Parliament's recent concessions. The trooper replied,

> no, and that it would in no way secure them . . . because many of their Fellow Soldiers, and those that had acted for the Parliament, were molested notwithstanding it; and what a sad thing will it be to consider, that the Soldiery shall taste of the Parliament's Judges Cruelty, notwithstanding their good Services, and the preserving of the Heads of some Men in the Parliament.

On behalf of the commissioners a Captain Middleton demanded to know who was in command. The answer was unanimous: 'All commanded'. Joyce told the commissioners that they came 'to secure his Majesty's Person . . . there being a secret design, as they were informed, to convey or steal away the King, and to raise another Army to suppress this under his Excellency Sir Thomas Fairfax'.[31]

An uneasy peace reigned at Holmby until Joyce discovered that Colonel Graves and the Scottish commissioners had fled. Joyce, fearing that Graves might return with a larger military force, decided on taking the king away from Holmby. He insisted on raising Charles from his bed at half-past ten that night and getting him to agree to this course of action on promises that he would not be harmed, that he would not be forced to anything against his conscience, and that his servants could come with him. So it was that at six the following morning the king emerged to see Joyce's 500 troopers ready mounted to escort him away. Charles attempted one last evasion. He demanded under what commission Joyce was acting. Joyce said he was acting to prevent another war. Charles again asked for Joyce's commission. Joyce said his commission came from 'the Soldiery of the Army'. This did not satisfy Charles any more than the first answer and he asked one more time whether Joyce had anything in writing from Sir Thomas Fairfax. Joyce recorded the exchange which followed:

> Then said the King, I pray Mr. Joyce deal ingeniously with me, and tell me what Commission you have? The Cornet's Answer was, Here is my Commission. Where, said the King? He answered, Here. His Majesty again asked, Where? He answered, Behind me: pointing to the Soldiers that were mounted; and desired his Majesty that that might satisfie him. Whereupon the King smiled, and said, It is as fair a Commission, and as well written as he had seen a Commission written in his life; a Company of handsom proper Gentlemen as he had seen a great while.[32]

This rightly celebrated exchange is as emblematic of the Revolution as any single event can be, for it would have previously been unthinkable that a mere cornet, the lowest-ranking officer in the army, and a tailor by trade could on the authority of having been elected by his fellow troopers take the king of England into custody. But the exchange that immediately followed between the troopers and Parliament's commissioners is also of the greatest interest because it shows both the balance of forces within the parliamentary camp and the degree of politicisation in the most advanced sections of the army.

After a brief discussion of whether the king should go to Oxford, Cambridge or Newmarket the commissioners made one last attempt to prevent Charles being taken by Joyce. Lord Montague waived their parliamentary warrant in the faces of the troopers and demanded if they were all agreed with Joyce. The reply was a resounding 'All, all'. Another commissioner said that, had he the forces with him, he would defy Joyce's troopers 'with his life'. Major Browne said that though they cried 'All, all' there was not two of them that understood what they did. He ended by saying, 'all that are willing the King shall stay with us, the Commissioners of Parliament, let him speak'. The troopers cried, 'None, none', and told him, 'We understand well enough what we do. Now let the World judge what is done, and who is at fault, and who they are that seek War, and no Peace nor Justice'. And so Joyce's troopers escorted the king from Holmby 'sounding their Trumpets, with ecchoes of tryumph' as they rode out. In Newmarket the king was 'well guarded more than regarded', as John Rushworth wrote. Within days the pamphleteers had Joyce's account of his exploits circulating on the streets.[33]

Inevitably Joyce's actions caused a political crisis. Fairfax, truthfully, and Cromwell, untruthfully, denied all knowledge of Joyce's actions. The harsh interpretation of Cromwell's denial is that he was perfidious, and many made that claim. The benign interpretation is that he had agreed that Joyce's force should secure the king at Holmby but not that it should remove him elsewhere. But even on this favourable reading, since Joyce had acted in good faith and under the realistic assumption that if he sat still at Holmby he might be surprised by a larger force rallied by Colonel Graves, it was less than heroic of Cromwell to distance himself from Joyce's decision. But however we may judge Cromwell's reaction to Joyce's capture of Charles there can be little doubt that in origin and execution the initiative lay with the rank and file. Cromwell was, at best, late in endorsing their actions and, at worst, merely pragmatically adjusting his position to the facts that the radicals were creating. In the minds of the Presbyterians, however, no such shades of grey existed. They already suspected Cromwell and, fearing imminent impeachment, he rode from London to join the army rendezvous at Newmarket.[34]

The Presbyterian coup

The crisis caused by the seizure of the king resulted in a further polarisation between the army and the Presbyterians. The rendezvous of the army at Kentford Heath near Newmarket over the two days of 4 and 5 June was a turning point in the development of political organisation in the New Model. At Newmarket Fairfax was presented with two remarkable documents. The first had been 'unanimously agreed upon, and subscribed by the Officers and Soldier's of the several Regiments at the Rendezvous'. This was *An humble Representation of the Dissatisfactions of the Army*. It listed at length the soldier's grievances and prominent among these was the right to petition. In defence of this right the *Representation* was clearly concerned with the recent fate of civilian petitioners since this might also be the soldier's fate after disbandment. This led the soldiers to object to the treatment of the Levellers, though they are not named: 'there have been of late, in other Cases, too much dangerous Precedents of suppressing Petitions, and punishing or censuring the Petitioners'. The second and shorter document, *A Solemn Engagement of the Army*, reiterated army grievances but also initiated the setting up of the Council of the Army, a body composed of senior officers plus two commissioned officers and two private soldiers delegated from each regiment.[35] When it was read to the assembled soldiers they chanted, 'Justice, Justice'. The remarkable advance of the Agitators had now created a body in which they jointly debated the actions of the army with its senior commanders. At another general rendezvous of the whole army at Triploe Heath near Cambridge the Council of the Army rejected Parliament's latest offer. Fairfax, Cromwell and Ireton signed a letter listing the soldiers' grievances addressed to the City. On 16 June the army demanded the impeachment of the eleven MPs at the heart of the Presbyterian operation and this was bolstered by a similar demand from the Council of the Army on 23 June. The political mood of the army may be judged from the justly famous statement of its Declaration of 14 June: 'we were no mere mercinary Army, hired to serve any Arbitrary power of a State; but called forth and conjured, by the severall Declarations of Parliament, to the defence of our owne and the peoples just rights, and liberties'.[36] Meanwhile the army was advancing ever closer to London, moving to Royston and St Albans, and reaching Uxbridge on 25 June.[37]

The direction of the Presbyterian camp was in all fundamentals set for further conflict, though there were signs of weakness and internal division.

On 6 June the Scottish commissioners, who were willing to attempt to rescue Charles, stoked anger in the army by issuing a condemnation of the army's capture of the monarch. The following day reformadoes organised a violent demonstration at Westminster demanding back pay. They dispersed only after the MPs voted them £10,000. On 8 June the Commons voted for the creation of the cavalry force to augment the Trained Bands. But when the Trained Bands were ordered to a muster on 12 June only the Westminster force turned out in any number. The City, beginning to waver in its commitment to the planned coup, asked Parliament that they be allowed to send a deputation to Fairfax. And although the MPs refused to suspend the eleven members, further army pressure forced them to withdraw themselves from the Commons. They did not go far, only moving to their allies in the City.[38]

At the start of July 1647 it looked as if the political initiative was in the hands of the army and the radicals. William Walwyn was at army headquarters in Reading, where 'eminent persons of the Army' were asking his advice about how to proceed for 'the good of the people'. In the name of officers and Agitators, including Thomas and William Rainsborough and Edward Sexby, the eleven members were accused of trampling the rights and freedoms of the subject underfoot and of raising an army to crush the New Model. In the Northern Army, which the conservatives had hoped would join with the Scots and the City forces to confront the New Model, Agitators were making a bold move. Their general, firm Presbyterian Sydenham Poyntz, was losing control. Agitators from the New Model had travelled to the Northern Army and received a warm welcome. Poyntz wrote to the Commons that the Houses' instructions were being ignored by the troops as 'there is such distemper in several of their regiments as that we find no authority or power we have, to recall them to their former obedience'. Indeed the troops desired to join the New Model and 'have selected two out of every assenting troop or company who now reside at Pontefract, advising and acting with some come from the southern army what they think fit in pursuance of their aforementioned end'. Poytnz would have liked to arrested them but 'did conceive it of dangerous consequence to apprehend them'. The soldiers were not suffering from the same fear in regard of their general. The Agitators arrested Poyntz and sent him as a prisoner to Fairfax. Fairfax denied he had sent the Agitators north, but did not repudiate their actions. Instead he appointed John Lambert to Poyntz's command. The revolt was now nationwide. In the West the 'agitators do tread in the steps of the Northern'. They cashiered Colonel Birch and his major for merely suggesting that they could not communicate with the New Model. They also seized Hereford Castle and £2,000 they found in it. They let the colonel go, but kept the regiment's major, the castle and the money. In Bristol the new governor tried to take his place with a warrant signed by leading Presbyterian MPs. But when a Captain Sampson 'saw the names Holles, Stapleton, Waller, Lewis, Clotworthy, Massey were at it' he told him that, unlike the army, these MPs had not acted with 'fidelity to the public' and he would therefore not obey the commission. And 'so the new intended Governor was dismissed'.[39]

The Levellers were certainly bending their best efforts to support the army against the Presbyterians, to rally support for the army in London, and to assist the Agitators in the army. In early July *Plain Truth Without Feare or Flattery* argued over more than twenty pages the case against the Presbyterians. It was issued in two editions, one of which carried the obvious alias 'Amon Wilbee'. In the second the author was identified by the initials 'JL', which Thomason took to be John Lilburne. From the clear and disciplined style this seems unlikely, but the content was wholly in line with Leveller thinking. Richard Overton insisted that he did not know who Amon Wilbee was but thought the pamphlet 'a most excellent and worthy treatise' whose author 'deserves to weare the laurel from all that have writ . . . since the Parliament began'. Overton said he would own the 'charge therein contain'd against Denzill Hollis & the rest of that traitrious Faction' as if it had been 'writ by myself'. It would be very like Overton's humour if he were indeed the author.[40] The close organisational cooperation of the Levellers working with the army and the older core of London activists can be seen with the publication on 12 and 15 July respectively of *A Cleere and Full Vindication of the late Proceedings of the Armie* and *The Grand Informer*. The first came from Larner's operation in Bishopsgate, the second was printed by Harris and Hills in Oxford. In content they are identical; only the title and title page are different. The text is a sustained defence of the proposition that 'the safety and prosperity of the People is the supreme law' and that betrayal of trust by the legislature licences the right to revolt.[41] On 14 July Larner printed the pro-army *Humble Petition of Many Thousands of young men and Apprentices*, which immediately called forth a Presbyterian counterpetition. Harris was back in print in mid-July with *The Antipodes or Reformation with its Heeles Upward*.[42] Here was the evidence to prove Lilburne's later claim that he 'applied myself vigourously unto . . . the private soldiers' and with the 'expence of a great deale of money . . . and industry . . . acted both night and day to settle the Souldiers in a complete and just posture by their faithful agitators'. Lilburne's ever-vigilant enemy, William Prynne, thought he was having some success. Prynne's attack on the Agitators variously cites the influence of Lilburne's *Regal Tyranny Discovered*, *England's Birth-Right Justified*, Larner's *Vindication* and apprentices' petition, Overton's Marpriest pamphlets, and the Hertfordshire petition that had begun the Levellers' petitioning campaign earlier in the year. These 'have a great influence on the Agitators and the Army', says Prynne. Lilburne's 'brothers are chief sticklers in the Armies Treasonable proceedings', so readers can 'judge what condition the King, Kingdome, and Parliament now are in, under the power of men of Lilburns Spirit and Principles'. Both Lilburne and Prynne may have overestimated the degree to which the army was acting under the direct influence of Leveller writings rather than coming to adopt similar ideas through the force of circumstance. But, however that might be, neither were wrong to see a mutually reinforcing convergence between radicals in the army and Leveller politics.[43]

This dynamic can be seen from Overton's most dramatic and direct intervention in the debates in the army, *An Appeale From the degenerate Representative Body the Commons of England*. This pamphlet, signed by Overton on 10 July, in part rehearses the case against his continuing imprisonment, but its real interest lies elsewhere. First, it contains a substantial political theory justifying the right to appeal to the people in cases where political power in Parliament has degenerated into tyranny. In keeping with recent Leveller and army experience Overton identifies the Holles–Stapleton faction as having usurped parliamentary power for their own purposes. This fact justifies an appeal both to the people at large and to the army specifically to act to restore fully representative rule. Second, the *Appeale* concludes with strategic advice to the 'right worthy and faithful Adjutators'. It warns them to 'trust no man, whether he be officer or Souldier, how religious soever appearing, further than he act apparently for the good of the Army and the Kingdome'. He warns to 'marke them which would and doe bring you into delayes and demurres, let their pretences be what they will be, their councels are destructive'. And he continues,

I am afraid, that your Officers are not too forward to interpose all delayes; therefore as I dare not totally condemne them, but do honour them so farre as they have dealt honourably in your engagement, I only warn you to be cautious and wary; and keep up your betrusted power and authority, and let nothing be acted, done, or concluded, without your consent.

Overton warned not to allow 'the power of all Adjutation' to be taken from 'the hand of the private Souldier'. Why, he asked, had recent papers been issued in the name of Fairfax and 'the Councell of Warre' and not as they previously were in the name of Fairfax 'with the officers and Souldiers of the Armie'? He concluded,

> Sure I cannot judge that you will bee befooled of your power; if you doe, I am sure we shall all bee befooled with you . . . then farewell our hopes in the Armie; for I am confident that it must be the poore, the simple and meane things of this earth that must confound the mighty and strong.

These were well-aimed darts and they found their mark in the deliberations of the Council of the Army that met the following week.[44]

On 16 July Agitators at the Council of the Army called for a march on London unless Parliament met their demands. In addition to the Agitators there were about 100 officers and the debate lasted until midnight. The Agitators were more militant than the officers, John Rushworth noted. The Agitators presented five main demands. The first was that the London Militia Committee be returned to the control of the Independents. The second was that the Commons should repudiate any invasion by foreign forces. The third demand was that there should be an investigation of why funds released for arrears had not reached the army. The fourth demand was a reiteration of a call that the Agitators had already made on 6 July: freedom for the imprisoned Leveller leaders. On this occasion the language was unmistakable:

> That all Prisoners that have been illegally committed . . . may forthwith be sett at liberty, and reparation given them for their false imprisonment, as namely:– Lieutenant Colonell John Lilburne, Mr. Musgrave, Mr. Overton's wife and brother, Mr. Larner, his two Lieutenants, Mr. Tew, Mr. Prest, and all the others which have been in like manner wrongfully imprisoned.

The Agitators also demanded that a declaration to this purpose be published throughout the country so that no Justices, officers or ministers of state could 'upon pain of the severest punishment . . . neglect to putt the same in execution'. A final demand restated the call for arrears to be paid.[45]

In the debate that followed, the Levellers had some potential allies in the room among the officers: Thomas Rainsborough and his brother William, sometime Leveller ally Lieutenant Chillenden, the signatories of the document, plus Major Daniel Abbot and Captains Edmund Rolf and John Clarke. Most promisingly Major Tulidah was there. Cromwell argued he had not had time to consult about the paper and moved that a committee consider it. This was agreed and it reported to the full meeting later. Cromwell moved that the freeing of the prisoners was a new issue not yet proposed to Parliament and then proceeded to ignore the matter. Lieutentant Scotton tried to return to the issue and Chillenden, in his familiar manner, said that while the matter of the prisoners 'lies soe weighty uppon my spirit . . . at this juncture of time . . . I should nott trouble your Excellency and this Councill of Warre concerning itt'. Most of the debate concerned the insistence, in a long appendix to the Agitators' document, on a 'speedy march towards London'. In this Major Tulidah, Edward Sexby and Cornet Joyce were the most insistent that the army should advance immediately. Cromwell wanted to conclude the terms of a treaty with Parliament before any advance and remained steadfast in opposition to any march on London. Tulidah was forceful and clear in reply: 'nothing will expedite them to putt them into the same way of boldly speaking for the Kingdomes interest like our advance towards the City'. It was only 'by the sword' that 'wee may take the sword out of the hands that are enemies to justice. Wee cannot any thinge unlesse by way of advancing to London'. Cromwell accused Tulidah of wanting to 'quarrell with every dogge in the streete that barkes att us' and so 'suffer the Kingdome to bee lost with such fantastical thinge'. Tulidah was supported by Sexby and Joyce, but Cromwell's caution won the day. But the Agitators had the firmer grasp of what would soon be necessary. The demand to free the Leveller leaders was quickly reinforced by a pamphlet elaborating the same cause. *The Just Request* came in the form of a petition from officers and soldiers to 'their free elected Councell Agitators'. It noted the decision of the Council of Agitators to take up the imprisoned Levellers' cause and urged Fairfax to act on 'behalfe of Lieutenant Colonell John Lilburne, Richard Overton (this Kingdomes and the Armies Appellant) his Wife, Brother and others'. These, it says, are victims of the 'traitorous party in the House' who are acting in a destructive, anti-parliamentary and illegal manner. A handwritten note on the front of *The Just Request* adds, 'It is no wonder if such an army as this then was do undertake ye defence of such rogues as John Lilburne, Richard Overton &c'.[46]

The intensification of resistance in the army was so inimical to Presbyterian interests that Scottish commissioner Robert Baillie was close to despair:

These matters of England are so extremely desperate, that now twyse they have made me sick . . . The impudence and cowardice of the better part of the City and Parliament, which was triple or sextuple the greater, has permitted a company of silly rascalles, which calls themselves no more than fourteen thousand, horse and foot, to make themselves masters of King, and Parliament, and City, and by them all of England.

Baillie thought that 'no humane hope remaines but in the King's unparalleled wilfulness' and that 'the finger of God in their spirits should so farr dement them as to disagree'. In these hopes he was not disappointed for, with or without divine intervention, the counterrevolution had one more roll of the dice. On both 13 and 21 July mass demonstrations by apprentices, watermen and reformadoes called for the return of the king and the disbandment of the army. Lords and Commons had to make a show of disapproval. But it was to be the counterrevolutionary mass that had the last word. The eleven members might have been out of the House but they were not down. They were holding private meetings in the City and still doing everything in their power to undermine the army and bring the king to the city. They sent a proclamation around the City and, records Thomas Juxon, 'The conspiracy was so strong that as 'twas cried in the streets'.[47]

When the Independents tried to restore their supporters to the Militia Committee its first meeting at the Guildhall was invaded by a 'company of young men, who came boldly into them and wished them to begone and not to sit there'. The crowd told them 'if they caught them there again they would hang their guts about their ears'. The crowd 'compelled them to rise, and, as they went, followed them with ill language'. The lord mayor refused to restore the Independent Militia Committee. The Common Council petitioned in favour of a Presbyterian Militia Committee. The face-off was resolved by force. On 26 July there occurred one of the most immediately successful mass demonstrations of the entire Revolution, and it came from the conservative forces. The Common Council presented a petition for the existing Presbyterian militia committee to continue. Apprentices, seamen and reformadoes broke into Westminster and, first, forced the Lords to repeal their vote of the previous day which had repudiated the earlier demonstrations. Having given the demonstrators what they wanted, the Lords chose to 'shift for themselves out the back door' and 'thought themselves well they had got so away'. Then the crowd went to the Commons but the Lower House held out from four in the afternoon until seven at night. They repeatedly sent messengers to the mayor and sheriffs to send troops to their aid but, apart from the late and ineffective arrival of a small number of halberdiers, these calls went unanswered. The mob seized New Model scout-master Watson after he told them that if they carried on in this course the City would be plundered. He was carried away and imprisoned in the City. The 'servants of some in the army were abused by pulling them by the ears and noses, and so leading them up and down, saying "These are the Independents"'. The crowd proceeded to 'knock, hoote and hollow at the Parliament doores'. The protestors then broke into the chamber and, around eight o'clock they forced the Speaker, William Lenthall, back into the chamber as he attempted to leave. He was forced to shout 'God save the King' and to call a vote returning the Militia Committee to Presbyterian control. When the MPs voted 'the prentices voted with them'. The mob remained until the vote was entered in the Commons' journal. All this while, records Thomas Juxon, Alderman Bunce and Common Council men were in Palace Yard 'to give direction for the management of the business . . . This force upon the House remained till nine at night'. The Speaker was chased out of the chamber and had to clamber into the first coach he could find to escape. Levellers John Harris and Henry Hills printed Lenthall's complaint at the abuse of Parliament.[48]

The following day, fifty-eight Independent MPs, including Lenthall, were joined by Manchester, the Speaker of Lords, as they fled Westminster and hurried to join the army. The eleven members retook their places in the Commons. The Common Council ordered the strengthening of the City defences and Edward Massey was appointed commander of all the forces raised by the City. Fairfax was ordered to keep the New Model at least thirty miles outside the capital. On 2 August the Commons voted to invite the king to return to London and Massey's troops attacked petitioners against a second war. This was a coup. The army's reaction was immediate. Even Fairfax declared that the Parliament was no longer a free parliament and the army advanced on London with the intention of restoring the MPs who had fled to them for protection. It sent forces south, swinging around the capital towards Southwark and London Bridge. Here the Southwark men held the bridge against the City and only opened it when the New Model arrived. On 4 August it was Thomas Rainsborough's regiment that led the New Model into London. Though much feared, the army's entry into the City was disciplined in the way that only a highly politicised force could be. According to the admittedly sympathetic Thomas Juxon, ''Twas not heard that so much as an apple taken by any of them—to the great admiration of all that beheld them'.[49]

The failure of the Presbyterian coup

Fortunes were now reversed. The eleven members fled to the Continent with the assistance of Vice Admiral William Batten. Stapleton was shortly to die in Calais. The Independents were in the ascendancy now. Eventually, in September, Overton was freed and even Lilburne was bailed from the Tower in November. So why did the Presbyterian coup fail? The internal weaknesses of the Presbyterian party and its errors in the course of its attempted coup have rarely been analysed more effectively or with such brevity than they were by Robert Baillie. 'The follie of our friends was apparent', wrote Baillie, when at

> the armie's first back-march, and refusall to disband, they recalled their declaration against their mutinous petitions. Easily might their designes have been crushed at that nick of tyme, with one stout look more; but it was dementation to sitt still amazed at the taking of the King, the accusation of the eleven members, the armie's approach to the city.

If, he believed, the City had agreed at this point and 'our friends in Parliament shewed any resolution', they could have arrested the 'chief of the Sectarian partie in both Houses, and stopped their flight to the armie'. It was all a 'rarely paralleled' example 'of childish improvisation and base cowardice'.[50] But while Baillie is clear-sighted enough about the fragilities on his own side he says too little about the strength of his opponents.

The Presbyterian coup failed not only because of the divisions and weaknesses among the conservative forces—divisions between Scots and those in London, between the City and the hard core of the Holles–Stapleton party, and among MPs themselves. They lost, crucially, because although they commanded a popular base it was neither as well organised, in military or civilian terms, nor as ideologically coherent as that of the radicals. Nor was the coup driven from below in the way that the radicals drove the Revolution for much of this period. Certainly there was widespread discontent to which the Presbyterian leadership could appeal, and there were plebeian forces that shared their political aims. But the independent organisational and political dynamic that informed the Agitators' movement was weak or non-existent among the popular forces supporting the coup. This is not to suggest that the Agitators did not have a political relationship with the army Grandees and officers. They did, and they understood the political value of that relationship. But Fairfax and Cromwell, until Joyce seized the king, were opposed to political action by the army. Some officers were more sympathetic and moved with the men. But the dynamic came from below. The plans to resist disbandment, the initial refusal to disband, the conscious organisation of the Agitator movement, the creation of the army press, the formation of radical demands, and the conscious links with the Levellers, were all things that originated in the ranks, even if they later secured support from officers and Grandees. As one letter from an Agitator, welcoming officer support for calling a general rendezvous, put it, if they 'scruple itt, itt will be done however'.[51]

What drove this radicalism was primarily the need to resist Presbyterian plans for disbandment. As Juxon wrote when the army entered London, ''Tis remarkable that it was never in the minds of the army to carry it on so far, but were brought to it, one thing after another, and that by the design of their enemies'. What made this a rank-and-file-driven movement was the initial unwillingness of Fairfax and Cromwell to countenance active resistance to Parliament. What facilitated it was both the direct participation of a small number of activists with Leveller connections and the previous widely disseminated ideological positions which could be used to justify such actions. Of these two elements the second was the more important. The radical ideology which the Levellers had embodied in petitions and pamphlets for some years before the army revolt had made its mark. The army had long since complained about Edwards's *Gangraena* where the views of Liburne, Overton and their associates were well advertised. A pamphlet from one of Baillie's countrymen, published less than two weeks after Rainsborough had led the New Model into London, was clear on this point. It railed at Lilburne and Lambe by name as Sectaries whose pamphlets and petitions were destructive to the monarchy and the House of Lords. It damned Leveller pamphlets going back to 1644—Overton's *Remonstrance of Many Thousand Citizens*, and Walwyn's *The Pearle in the Dounghill*, *The Just Man in Bonds* and *The Compassionate Samaritane*—for inciting the 'over-awing tyrannical Army'. When poet George Wither, whom we last saw dressed in the sequestrated royal regalia by Henry Marten, published a broadsheet ridiculing the City's defeat by the New Model, the only figures named that were not Presbyterians were Fairfax, Overton and Lilburne:

> Overton now may walke abroad,
> Stone walls are weak to hold him;
> As Lilburne that fame Demie-god,

Propheticakly hath told him:
And you may goe, and shake your eares,
Who had, and could not hold it,
What you had stove for many yeares,
And got; you now have sold it.

Of course it was not literally true that the army was 'one Lilburne through-out', but it was true that a significant minority, the yeast which allowed the mix of the soldiery to rise, had absorbed these ideas and they quickly adapted them to justify their actions. In doing so some of the Agitators and even officers who were not previously Levellers began to adhere to the movement and its leaders. At important moments the whole Agitator movement made declarations in favour of the Leveller leaders. Lilburne, Overton, Walwyn, John Harris and others had made common cause with the Agitators. It was a strategic orientation that had paid off handsomely. But after the watershed created by Joyce's seizure of the king and Cromwell's decision to join the army the influence of the Grandees was amplified. Cromwell repeatedly urged caution on the Agitators and those officers sympathetic to them. Writing about the Council of the Army on 16 July, John Rushworth reassured Lord Fairfax that 'although the agitators were higher in their proposals than the officers . . . you may be assured the infe-rior, upon good reasons, submitted to the superior, so that it is not will but reason that guides the proceedings of the army'. This judgement might have been a little sanguine both as a description of the debates and as a predic-tion about the necessity of the march on London, but it was entirely accurate in delineating the fault line that would shape the events of the rest of the Revolution in general and the debate in the army in particular.[52]

CHAPTER 10

Putney Church and Corkbush Field

Each successive revolutionary wave was more powerful than the last but there was still an ebb once each wave had reached its peak. And just at the moment when the more radical leaders were swept to positions of greater authority they became more cautious. It is testimony to how deeply the old constitution of king, Lords and Commons was imprinted on most seventeenth-century minds that few could think outside this frame, even if they might differ over the relative weight of the components. But in the period after the army marched into London in August 1647 there was a more pressing tactical consideration that bolstered adherence to the old constitution in the minds of the dominant political factions. For the recently rebuffed Presbyterians, including their Scottish variant, it had always been a maxim that striking a deal with the king was a sure method of isolating the radicals and the army. For many leading Independents and the Grandees of the army the equal and opposite maxim applied: coming to a compact with the king would put the royal seal on the defeat of the Presbyterians. Among the royalists this allowed the belief to flourish that the king might triumph because he was indispensable and that he could achieve the best possible terms for his return by playing his suitors against each other.

Once the army entered London and defeated the Presbyterian coup the Independents were in the saddle. In the New Model, Independents replaced Presbyterians among the senior officers. The Tower was in the hands of Fairfax himself and Robert Titchborne. All of the Commons decisions taken during the absence of the Independents after the 26 July coup were struck down in the Null and Void Ordinance. Six of the eleven members fled abroad, and Vice Admiral William Batten resigned his post rather than face charges over facilitating their flight to the Continent. Thomas Rainsborough was appointed in his place. In the City the lord mayor and five prominent aldermen were impeached and long-standing Independent John Warner was chosen as mayor. The lines of communication were ordered pulled down so that the City could never again rise against the army.[1]

But at the moment of victory the Independent leaders became overwhelmed by caution. They used the prestige of their victory to attempt to close an agreement with the king based on Ireton's *The Heads of Proposals*. The king was moved to Hampton Court and the headquarters of the army were moved to Putney, midway between Westminster and Charles's new home. But for this scheme to proceed, the radicals among the Agitators, especially those influenced by the Levellers, had to be defeated. A few days after the army marched into London, Sir Lewis Dyve, a royalist fellow prisoner of Lilburne's in the Tower, wrote to the king,

> The General and Cromwell and all the grandees both in the army and the two Houses, are as egarly bent to destroy the agitators as to suppresse their greatest adversarys, the Presbiterian faction, which I am perswaded they will hardly be able to effect without dangerous distempers in the army.[2]

So it was that the joint meetings of officers and Agitators, the Council of the Army, were suspended and Cromwell and Ireton became willing to amended *The Heads of Proposals* to accommodate a recalcitrant king. The stage was set for confrontation.

Oliver Cromwell, Thomas Rainsborough and John Lilburne

Thomas Rainsborough became central to Leveller hopes at Putney. His string of military successes—at Crowland, in the storming of Bristol, in taking the surrender of royalists across the West Country—made him a hero of the army. His regiment was officered by returning New Englanders schooled in the Independent churches of the Americas. His family were intermarried with the colonies elite. His brother William was already a radical. Thomas had been returned as a recruiter MP for Droitwich in the summer of 1646 and joined Henry Marten's group of republicans in the

Commons. In the very first negotiations with Charles in late July 1647, just ahead of the army's entry into London, Rainsborough had joined Ireton and Colonels Hammond and Rich as part of the army's delegation at Woburn.[3]

During the talks Rainsborough was repelled both by the king's declaration that 'you cannot be without me; You will fall to ruin if I do not sustain you', and by Ireton's willingness to compromise. Rainsborough left the negotiations halfway through in order to report his fears to the army. It was no doubt this difference of opinion that was revived during the discussions of the cabal around Cromwell when they attempted to oppose Rainsborough's appointment as vice admiral in place of the disgraced Presbyterian William Batten. This is the origin of Sir Lewis Dyve's view that some 'looke with an eye of jealously upon Rainsborough as haveing too great a power in their melitia, who knowing him to be a man of such a temper as would rather act according to his owne then other mens' principles'. Cromwell's opposition to Rainsborough had, however, to be mounted covertly because Rainsborough's 'credit with the common soldiers' was 'not inferior to any officer in the army' and because Cromwell did not wish to open a public breach with a former ally. Instead Cromwell and his allies, Lord Say, Oliver St John and Sir Henry Vane the younger, came up with a plan in which Lord Northumberland was to propose an alternative candidate for vice admiral. Cromwell would then publicly defend Rainsborough, but, on pretence of not offending the House of Lords at a difficult political moment, 'mediate with his friend Rainsborough to rest satisfied in the busines'.[4]

This scheme might have worked, had not Rainsborough learnt of what was afoot. On the day before Batten resigned at the meeting with the Admiralty commissioners, Cromwell, Ireton, St John and Henry Vane were meeting, no doubt to discuss their tactics. But Rainsborough arrived as they were meeting with a young captain from his regiment, Thomas Creamer. Rainsborough went into the room leaving Creamer sitting outside the door. Creamer reported that after a long period of quiet 'Crumwell was heard to be very loud . . . and Rainsborough therupon clapping his hand upon the table with violence rose from the bord, and tould Crumwell aloud that he would not longer be abused by him under the colour of friendship'. Behind the closed doors Rainsborough vowed he would have the vice admiral's post or make Cromwell regret it. Meanwhile, the others intervened and quietened things down. But then 'Rainsborough againe flew from the bord and told Crumwell flatly that it should cost one of them their lives but that he should have the place, and that he better deserved it then Crumwell had done the honour hee tooke upon him'. The rest of those at the meeting had to impose peace once more. Rainsborough got his way and the post of vice admiral, and the meeting broke up in 'seeming friendship on all sides', or at least so Creamer thought. This dispute was about more than Rainsborough's desire to hold the vice admiral's post. Five days later a motion was on the floor of the Commons that no more addresses should be made to the king. The tellers against any more negotiations with the king were Henry Marten and Thomas Rainsborough. Those for the motion in favour of treating with the king were Henry Ireton and Oliver Cromwell. The vote of no addresses was defeated by eighty-four votes to thirty-four, the Presbyterians and the Cromwellian Independents voting together to defeat Marten and Rainsborough's republicans.[5]

During the same period the conflict between Cromwell and Rainsborough was coming to a head, Cromwell was practising the arts of flattery to try and neutralise the opposition of John Lilburne. On 6 September Cromwell visited Lilburne in the Tower aiming to 'qualifie the heate of his distemper against him by faire words and large promises'. Lilburne himself relayed the discussion to Sir Lewis Dyve immediately after it took place. The meeting started well enough with Cromwell using expressions of great kindness to Lilburne. But then Cromwell asked Lilburne how 'it had come to passe that he had fallen out with his best friends, and was become great an enemy to Parliament, advising him to patiens and moderation, and not to speake with so much bitterness of Parliament'. Lilburne replied 'that he neither had, nor ever would, fall out with his friends, but he saw with much greefe of heart that these who he esteemed for his friends had fallen of both from him and their first principles'. And he told Cromwell that 'the greatest crimes' of the king 'was in comparison of the best of there actions both glorious and righteous'. Cromwell answered that Charles's government was tyrannical by habit, but the Parliament's only by 'accident and necessity'. To this Lilburne suggested that 'the best way whereby to preserve themselves would be impartially to doe right and equaly to administer justice to all men'. Cromwell, perhaps unadvisedly since he was addressing a man who had been in prison for a year, told Lilbune that his 'feares were vaine' and that he was too much influenced by the royalists with whom he had been talking. Lilburne retorted that Cromwell 'mistooke him, for he had not vanished at all from his first principles', and then said 'in plaine English' that 'he would by all the wayes he could possible invent, labour to destroy them as he had formerly done the bishops, rather then that thay should destroy him, his wife and children by keeping him longer in prison'.

Cromwell then moved from argument to bribery, asking Lilburne 'in case they should set him at liberty, whether he would then be quiet'. He must have known that the likely reply would be 'no', and so it was. Cromwell again counselled patience and offered Lilburne employment in the army. Lilburne gave him thanks but said he would have no employment in Parliament or army unless he was 'satisfied with the justice of their wayes'. Cromwell admitted defeat, saying that 'though you have given me little encouragement, yet such is the affection I beare you, as you shall see I will not be wanting in my best endeavours to procure your liberty'. Lilburne thanked him and said he had little doubt he would then be free, 'well knowing it is in your power to do it'. After this the two went to dinner with the lieutenant of the Tower, over which Lilburne continued to protest about the prisoners' conditions. It may have been as a result of this conversation that Overton was freed ten days later. Nonetheless, Cromwell did not give up urging moderation on Lilburne or attempting to get him to abandon his work with the Agitators. Until the very eve of the Putney debates in late October, Cromwell 'employed severall agents to deale with Mr. Lilbourne to perswade him to imploy his interest in the army, which he conceives to be powerfully to divert the storme, makeing many large and faire promises to him'. These attempts fared no better than the first. But at least Lilburne did eventually get to make his case once again to Henry Marten's committee in mid-October. John Rushworth recorded, 'Freeborn John Lilburne . . . this Day attended the Committee about his Business, made a long Speech . . . complaining against the Lords as Accusers and Judges against him, declaring their Proceedings illegal, and gave in many Precedents, which he undertakes to prove. His Expressions were in Law very high'. High, but still unsuccessful.[6]

Lilburne's strategy in the face of the attempts by the Grandees to come to an agreement with the king was to redirect the Agitators to frustrate these plans. Three days after Cromwell's visit to Lilburne the Army Council discussed the terms of the king's restoration. Major Francis White was expelled from the Council for suggesting that the army was the dominant power in the land and that the old constitution was at an end. At the same time five cavalry regiments elected new Agitators because they thought the existing ones too moderate. Sir Lewis Dyve reported that the new Agitators were meeting in London with radicals from the City and that 'Mr. Lilborne set this busines first on foote and hath great influence upon their counsels'.

A week later he wrote to the king, 'Those new agitators . . . have everyday constantly mett together and I am told by Mr. Lilborne that they are resolved to doe their utmost for suppressing of Crumwell's faction and put a period to this Parliament'. On 6 October 1647 *Mercurius Pragmaticus* reported, 'What Lilburne says must be done, the adjutators will do'. And a month later it reinforced the point:

> John keeps a weekly rendezvous in the way of edification over Capen and Cook-broth, at close meetings with the venerable agents and ambassadors from the high and mighty adjutators, who if they could once be weaned from that learned opinion that monarchical government is Anti-Christian, are resolved to have no King but John; and then we shall have a John a London as famous as John a Leyden.

The emergence of the new Agitators heralded the first line of attack against Cromwell and his faction. And it 'infused the like sperit into a great part of the foot, which begins to break forth in divers regiments'. The regiment of Independent stalwart Paul Hobson, for instance, 'being commanded to Newcastle and being in their way beyond Dunstable one Satterday last, positively refused to march one foot farther'. Earlier troops destined for Ireland had revolted against their officers.[7]

This mood found its expression in *The Case of the Army Truly Stated*, printed in October 1647. The accompanying letter to Fairfax told him that 'the Meanest Vassal in the Eyes of the Lord, is equally oblig'd and account-able to God with the greatest Prince or Commander under the Sun', and it was their duty 'when we see our Neighbour's Houses on fire, to wave all Forms, Ceremonies, or Complements forthwith (not waiting for order or leave) to attempt the quenching thereof', and so how much more were they obliged to act 'when we behold the great Mansion-House of this Commonwealth, and of this Army . . . on fire all ready to be devoured with Slavery, Confusion and Ruin'. The defence of their actions, they argued, was that 'the Safety of the People is above all Forms and Customs, &c. And the Equity of Popular Safety is the thing which justifieth all Forms . . . and no Forms are lawful longer than they preserve or accomplish the same'.[8] *The Case of the Army Truly Stated* certainly caught the attention of the Venetian ambassador, who reported,

> The new faction in the army which has caused some regiments to separate from the others, bears the title of the Levellers (Ugualità) and demands that

the state shall be formed without king, princes or nobles, but all equal, as men were after the Creation. The excitement over a small book published last week has not died down. It bears the title 'The Case of the Army' and since it tends to encourage disorder, they are making careful enquiry for the author.[9]

The pamphlet was a collaborative document, and one of the collaborators was John Wildman, who would soon be central to the defence of its contents at the Putney debates. We know relatively little about Wildman before he stepped forward at Putney – he was a mere twenty-four years old; had been at Cambridge University; was probably not of gentry origin; had some legal training, as his pseudonym John Lawmind suggests; and was acting as a solicitor by the late 1640s. He came from the same part of Berkshire as Henry Marten. They were closely related later, and may have been before the Putney debates. He may have been a major in Fairfax's Lifeguard, but had not seen action in the war. He was often referred to as Major Wildman, but not usually until after the Putney debates. But if there were some earlier connection with the army it would explain why the Agitators asked him to come to Putney to help present their case to the Council of the Army.[10]

It was perfectly obvious that no criticism of the discussions with the king in *The Case of the Army* was going to deflect Cromwell from his course. Midway between the appearance of the *The Case of the Army* and the beginning of the Putney debates, on 20 October, Cromwell rose from the benches to address the Commons. For the next three hours the steadfast and disciplined MPs were treated to a speech in praise of monarchy and in opposition to the demands of the Levellers. The scene was set for the confrontation at Putney.[11]

The Putney debates and the man of blood

The meeting of the Council of the Army in Putney was remarkable in so many ways. It was remarkable because of the make-up of this ruling body of the army. It was composed of the high command of the New Model Army, junior officers, elected Agitators and civilian Levellers. No such body had ever been, even temporarily, in charge of a victorious army before. The questions it addressed were even more remarkable: how should a revolution in progress deal with a defeated king and what new constitution should it adopt? But these, amounting to no less than the fate of the nation, were the issues addressed on the first day of debate in St Mary's Church, Putney, and on subsequent days in the nearby lodgings of the quartermaster of the New Model in late October and early November 1649. No less remarkable are the means by which we know so much of these debates.

William Clarke was secretary to the Council of the Army. He took down the debates at Putney in his newly acquired shorthand, itself a technique pioneered by Puritans whose stress on the individual relationship between the worshipper and God led them to want to take down notes of sermons as they were delivered, for further study.[12] Clarke prospered into the Restoration and his manuscripts were deposited, some translated into longhand, others not, in the library of Worcester College, Oxford. And there they stayed for more than 200 years until the librarian H. A. Pottinger drew them to the attention of the great Civil War historian Charles Firth, who published them in two volumes in 1891 and 1894. It is hard to argue with Austin Woolrych's more recent judgement that 'one may well wonder whether there has ever been a more exciting archival discovery in any field of British history'.[13] Of all the turning points in the English Revolution there can be no other that has been analysed so thoroughly by modern historians.[14] But the very excitement over Clarke's transcription of the debates has sometimes encouraged historians to adopt a narrow focus both on the few days of the debates themselves and on close textual analysis. Both have their value, but not to the exclusion of the political context that allows us to see clearly what was at stake.

In late October, Fairfax called this meeting of the Council of the Army in order to discuss *The Case of the Army*.[15] Yet, in response, at the start of the proceedings, the Agitators and Levellers produced the *Agreement of the People*, a much-condensed version of their programme. The *Agreement of the People* is a brilliantly simple document. But its brilliant simplicity could only come from a long process in which the demands and attitudes it embodies had first been canvassed and refined through the years of petitioning and pamphleteering by the Levellers. That experience was now applied to a particular political moment. So the short preamble insists on the desire to 'avoid both the danger of returning into a slavish condition, and the chargeable remedy of another war'. The current crisis is a result of an undemocratic Parliament and therefore the *Agreement* makes five proposals: more equal electoral constituencies, the dissolution of the current Parliament, annual Parliaments, the supremacy of the people, and the sovereignty of the Parliament they choose in election. It then adds five reserved powers which Parliament has no capacity to alter: freedom of religious worship, freedom from military conscription, indemnity for acts carried out in wartime, equality before the law, and that no law should 'be destructive to the safety and well-being of the people'. The concluding paragraph insisted that these rights were inalienable, but once again returned to current politics as their driving necessity:

> These things we declare to be our native Rights, and therefore are agreed and resolved to maintain them with our utmost possibilities, against all opposition whatsoever, being compelled thereunto, not only by the examples of our Ancestors, whose bloud was often spent in vain for the recovery of their Freedomes, suffering themselves, through fraudulent accommodations, to be still deluded of the fruit of their Victories, but also by our own woeful experience, who have long expected, & dearly earned the establishment of these certain rules of Government are yet made to depended for the settlement of our Peace and Freedome, upon him that intended our bondage, and brought cruell Warre upon us.[16]

But why were the radicals in such a hurry to establish a rudimentary written constitution? It was the political crisis caused by Cromwell, and the majority in Parliament, attempting to arrange a treaty with the king before any settlement had been agreed that was fuelling the urgency of the Levellers. So the debates at Putney were not simply or mainly a constitutional discussion of the finer details of a parliamentary regime. In fact, the Levellers were attempting to shut the door on any return of the king and the Cromwellians were seeking to keep it open. In the course of debate, between 28 October and 8 November, much else was discussed. But the threat of a revived monarchy was never far from the surface. On the very first day, 28 October, the debate immediately ignited on this issue.

No sooner had it been proposed by Edward Sexby, and agreed by Henry Ireton, that John Wildman and Maximillian Petty, the two representatives of the Levellers, be invited to join the meeting, than Sexby launched a broadside against the king and against Cromwell for negotiating with the king. Sexby's speeches at Putney are always short, urgent and pointed. He told the meeting, 'Wee have bin by providence putt upon strange thinges, such as the ancientist heere doth scarce remember'. He reminded the officers, 'The Kingdomes cause requires expedition', and that they had 'resolv'd if anything [reasonable] should be propounded to you, you would joyne and goe alonge with us'. And then he moved to 'the cause of our misery', which was 'uppon two thinges':

Wee have labor'd to please a Kinge, and I thinke, except that wee goe about to cutt all our throats, wee shall nott please him; and wee have gone to support an house which will prove rotten studs, I meane the Parliament which consists of a Company of rotten Members.[17]

Sexby then turned to Cromwell and Ireton and told them, 'Your credits and reputation hath bin much blasted uppon these two considerations'. It was relations with the king and Parliament that were the causes of 'all those blemishes' cast on Cromwell and Ireton. For these reasons, Sexby concluded, 'I desire you should consider those thinges that shall be offer'd to you'. This was the radicals' programme in short: neither the king nor the Parliament could be trusted to deliver liberty and justice, Cromwell and Ireton were endangering the Revolution by compromise with both, and therefore a new settlement embodied in the *Agreement of People* must be speedily adopted.[18]

Cromwell, chairing the meeting while Fairfax was absent through illness, replied that he did not know why Sexby had named him and Ireton since they had only carried out the resolutions of the General Council. This was patently untrue in regard of his recent three-hour speech in favour of monarchy in the Commons, so that had to be excused on the basis that it was 'spoken in another capacitie, as a Member of the House' and he was 'nott ashamed' of proposing 'a second addresse to the Kinge'.[19] For his part, Ireton professed that he 'doe detest and defie the thought . . . of any indeavor, or designe, or purpose, or desire to sett uppe the Kinge'. The debate then moved on to the *Agreement of the People*.[20]

Cromwell immediately began to prevaricate. The *Agreement* had many good things in it, he said, but it was new to them, and another group of men might even now be coming up with an equally good proposal, and, anyway, there might be 'great difficulties' in getting the nation to go along with it. Finally, he added, the army had already made a number of declarations and it had to be seen whether these were compatible with the *Agreement*. Ireton, at length, backed up this last objection. This is the point at which Thomas Rainsborough entered the debate. Rainsborough's reply to Cromwell, despite the passage of hundreds of years, crackles with the suppressed antagonism between them. Rainsborough's regiment had been taken away from him on his elevation to vice admiral, no doubt as a rearguard action by Cromwell's faction after they were forced to grant him the navy. Rainsborough is referring to this when he complains that this may be 'the last time I shall speake heere' as he has recently received a letter telling him that 'my Regiment should bee immediately disposed from mee'. He would, he says, rather lose his seat in the House or be imprisoned than 'loose this Regiment of mine . . . for truly while I am [employed] abroad I will nott be undone at home'. Turning to the substance of the debate he makes a biting reply to Cromwell's point that they would face difficulties in getting the nation to accept the new proposal:

> if ever wee [had] look't uppon difficulties I doe nott know that ever wee should have look't an enemy in the face. Truly I thinke the Parliament were very indiscreete to contest the Kinge if they did not consider difficulties . . . truly I thinke that let difficulties bee round about you, have you death before you, the sea on each side of you, and behind you, are you convince't the thinge is just I thinke you are bound in conscience to carry itt on . . .[21]

Cromwell's unctuous reply was that he was glad 'wee shall enjoy his company longer than we thought we should have done'. Rainsborough shot back, 'If I should nott be kick't out'.[22]

The debate wound on with frequent detours: whether the *Agreement* was compatible with previous army declarations; whether such declarations could be abandoned or superseded if judged unjust or inadequate. Colonel Goffe, more religiously zealous than most even in this company, was moved to seek God's guidance at length. In difficult moments Cromwell was always content to move from politics to prayer. Wildman spoke on the matter of breaking engagements, saying, in a metaphor first deployed by Walwyn and later incorporated into the *Declaration of the Army*, that it was always justified in intervening if a 'General . . . would destroy an army'. And he applied a similar argument to the threat of royal restoration:

> The Agents thinke that delay is to dispose their enemy into such a capacitie as hee may destroy them . . . .I doe apply this to the case in hand: that itt might bee consider'd whether itt bee just to bringe in the Kinge in such a way as hee may been in capacity to destroy the people. This paper may be applied to itt.

Captain Audley backed up Wildman: 'if we tarry longe the kinge will come and say who will be hang'd first'.[23]

Ireton replied that there was no parallel with the situation where a general was turning his cannon on his own troops. Rainsborough answered that in fact a general turning his cannon on his own troops was entirely an apt metaphor since 'the Kinge and his partie could nott have come in uppon those termes that he is come in, if this very army did nott engage for him'. Here Rainsborough is no doubt taxing Ireton with his weakness in the nego-tiations with the king, and Cromwell with his Commons speech in support of the monarchy. Captain Merriman had the truth of the debate when he interjected that 'one partie feares, That the Kinge will rise by the proposals, another that he will lose'. Eventually Cromwell began to give ground, claim-ing not to be fixed or glued to specific forms of government, and the day's business ended with a committee chosen to consider the proposals.[24]

The Levellers were not content to keep discussion within the confines of the council. Overnight a response to the day's proceedings, *A Call to all the souldiers of the Armie*, was put into print.[25] It brought news that in the council Cromwell and Ireton 'held forth to you the bloody flagge of threats and terrous, talk't of nothing but Faction, dividing-principles, Anarchy . . . and impudently maintatined that your Regiments were abused, and the aforementioned Case, not truly subscribed'. It warned the Agitators, 'be not frighted by the word Anarchy, unto to love of Monarchy, which is but the gilded word for Tyranny'. It urged distrust of the army leaders in the House of Commons—both Ireton and Cromwell 'doe earnestly and palpably carry on the Kings designe'. It urged support for the *Agreement* and pleaded the cases of Larner, Lilburne, Overton and Tue. *A Call* became one of the first printed attacks on Charles as 'a man of blood'. It concluded by lambasting 'Say, Wharton, Fines, Vaine, St John' as neuters and urged that the soldiers tell Cromwell, if he does not alter his course,

> that ye loved and hounoured just, honest sincere and valiant Cromwell, that loved his Country, and the liberties of the people above his life, yea, and hated the King as a man of blood, but that Cromwell ceasing to be such, he ceaseth to be the object of your love.[26]

On the second day the debaters, now in the nearby quartermaster's lodg-ing, focussed on who should be able to vote in elections. Should it be, as it was then, property owners only, or should there be a much wider fran-chise? And, if so, how wide? From the Levellers and their supporters this drew some of the most celebrated expressions of popular sovereignty to emerge in the whole of the English Revolution. Rainsborough's words, though oft repeated, have lost none of their grandeur:

> For really I think that the poorest hee that is in England hath a life to live as the greatest he; and therefore truly, Sir, I think itt's cleare, that every

man that is to live under a Government ought first by his owne consent to putt himself under that Government; and I doe thinke that the poorest man in England is nott att all bound in a strict sense to that government that he hath not had a voice to put himself under.[27]

In truth this was not a new thought for the Levellers. Elizabeth and John Lilburne had both previously made similar declarations in not dissimilar words. And in the course of the debate at Putney Rainsborough elaborated this argument, as did others. Wildman argued, 'Every person in England hath as cleere a right to Elect his representative as the greatest person in England. I conceive that's an undeniable maxime of Government: that all government is in the free consent of the people'. Sexby thought that 'the poore and meaner of this Kingdome' could not be denied a vote because they 'have bin the meanes of the preservation of the Kingdome'. Lieutenant Colonel Reade could see 'noe reason why any man that is a native ought to bee excluded' from the vote 'unless from voluntarie servitude'.[28]

Ireton took on this argument, supported from time to time by Cromwell. Ireton's chosen ground was the defence of a property qualification. He insisted that only those with 'a permanent fixed interest' should be able to vote. There was no sense that birthright alone entitled an individual to the vote. If the poor had the vote they would take away the property of the rich and this would, as Cromwell put it, 'tend to anarchy'. No one spoke at greater length at Putney than Ireton, but no one provided a summary of their argument with as much brevity as he did when he announced, 'All the maine thinge I speake for is because I would have an eye to propertie . . . lett every man consider with himself that hee doe nott goe that way to take away all propertie'.[29] Ireton's defence pushed the discussion to consider social inequality and its relation to the vote in a way that might not otherwise have been true. Rainsborough thought that if only the rich have the vote, 'Then I say the one parte shall make hewers of wood and drawers of water' of the rest and 'the greatest parte of the Nation bee enslav'd'. Sexby argued that the soldiers had ventured their lives but 'had little propriety in the Kingdome'. Taking up that theme Rainsborough 'would fain know what the soldier hath fought for all this while? He hath fought to inslave himself, to give power to men of riches, men of estates, to make him a perpetual slave'. Sexby said, if this were going to be the case, 'Itt had been good in you to have advertis'd us of itt, and I believe you would have fewer under your command'.[30]

There was further talk of widening the franchise without making it universal. This has been much discussed by historians although it was a very secondary and fragmented part of the discussion. Ireton and Cromwell were both willing to admit that the franchise could be 'better than it is' without endangering private property. Maximillian Petty admitted in one brief remark that he supposed that servants and those dependent on others might be excluded from the vote. But the main axis on which debate turned was whether there should be an extensive broadening of the franchise, premised on the principle of popular sovereignty, or whether the principle of popular sovereignty was mistaken because only a severely restricted franchise would be an effective bulwark for property.[31]

As the debates moved toward a conclusion on their second day, more pressing strategic questions began to reassert themselves. Lieutenant Chillenden, Robert Everard and Captain Audley all urged that debate be concluded else 'every man dispute till wee have our throats cut'. The fear of the king's return was now once more at the centre of debate. Petty spoke 'against the Kinges vote and the Lords' as 'both the power of the Kinge and the Lords was ever a branch of Tyranny'. Wildman feared the destructive role of the king, but Ireton said they had agreed not to take away the power of the Lords and that if an agreement could be reached with the king that secured the rights of the people then 'his Rights may be consider'd soe farre as may consist with the Rights of the people'. Wildman leapt on this saying, 'in these very words . . . you doe now say the Legislative power to be partly in him'. And, concluded Wildman, 'There's his Restoration'.[32]

The following day, Saturday 30 October, a committee came up with a set of proposals that favoured the Levellers. It concluded that 'all freeborne Englishmen, or persons made free denizons of England, who have served the Parliament in the late warre for the liberties of the Kingdome' or who have financially assisted the war effort would be given the vote. This approached the notion of 'a democratic government of the Revolution' rather than a universal franchise which, in the political circumstances then obtaining, would have endangered the Revolution. But it was not a property qualification of any kind. On Sunday 31 October, while the council was in recess, Thomas Rainsborough visited John Lilburne, 'unto whom he professeth much friendship', for two hours in the Tower. The two men found common ground in their distrust of Cromwell although Rainsborough, according to Sir Lewis Dyve, seemed concerned that the anti-monarchist sentiment of the radicals might outpace what the army as a whole was feeling. Dyve, ever the optimist about the Royal cause, transmitted this news to the king, who, having had his own experience with the colonel, told his follower not to trust Rainsborough.[33]

When the council reconvened on 1 November anti-monarchist sentiment was on the rise. Agitator William Allen claimed that their work was
to eradicate the negative voice of the Lords and the king. Captain Carter
said he could no longer find it in his heart to pray for the king. Cromwell
argued that though the negative voice might be removed, still the 'Kinge
was the Kinge by contract', and that unless there were some visible show
of mass support for the *Agreement* the Parliament was still the supreme
legislature, for 'if they be noe Parliament they are nothing, and we are
nothing likewise'. Allen and Sexby objected that this was to 'sett uppe the
power of Kinges, some part of itt, which God will destroy'. Captain Bishop
insisted that the reason why they were being unsuccessful in rescuing the
Kingdom from the 'dying condition in which itt is' was because they were
laboring to 'preserve that Man of Bloud, and those principles of tyranny
which God from Heaven by his many successes hath manifestly declared
against'. As the debate continued the direction of the room started to turn
in the Levellers' favour, and on the following day, 2 November, the
committee passed a proposal which reproduced much of the *Agreement
of the People*.[34]

On 5 November, as Cromwell attended the Commons, Rainsborough
moved that the council write to Parliament stating its opposition to any
further addresses to the king. Ireton, unable to defeat this proposal, stormed
out of the meeting, saying 'he would act no more with them' unless they
recalled the letter. But the letter was sent anyway.[35] No doubt this was the
cause of Cromwell's attack against the *Agreement* on 8 November when he
returned to Putney. He repeated the claim that widening the franchise
would 'tend very much to Anarchy'. But he was answered in a 'longe speech'
from Captain William Bray, an army veteran from Robert Lilburne's regiment, and a confederate of Edward Sexby and John Lilburne.[36] Sadly by this
time Clarke was no longer making a substantial record of the debates so we
do not have an account of all that Bray had to say. It was clear, however, that
supporters of the *Agreement* commanded a majority on the General
Council, an unacceptable situation to Cromwell and Ireton. Accordingly,
Cromwell moved a resolution that the Agitators be sent back to their regiments and that a rendezvous of the army be called at which the agreed
propositions would be presented for assent. Clarke's notes are clear in
describing the rendezvous in the singular. This was the understanding of
the Agitators as well, though it was subsequently a much-disputed issue.[37]

The following day was to be a watershed. Fairfax informed the
Commons there was to be an army rendezvous. Meanwhile the Commons

voted that the *Agreement of the People* was 'destructive to the Being of Parliaments, and to the fundamental Government of the Kingdom'. But Parliament was not alone in its concern about developments in the army. The king was also alarmed at the growing radicalism of the army, so much so that he fled from Hampton Court to the protection of Colonel Robert Hammond on the Isle of Wight. He claimed to be in fear for his safety and possibly his life. Rumours were abroad that the Levellers planned to assassinate the king. These were given weight by the fact that they were spread by John Lilburne's very much more conservative brother Henry, soon to defect to the royalists. Charles, in a pamphlet that contained the first printed naming of the Levellers, also seemed to endorse the rumour. The Levellers, among them William Eyre, William Bray and William Thompson, protested to Fairfax. Bray thought the whole story was aimed at trying to get the 'Cavalrie to joyn to destroy the Levellers'. But if ever there was a case of a lie circling the world while the truth was still getting to its feet, this was it.[38]

What really happened at Ware?

The Council of the Army in Putney concluded that there would be a single rendezvous of the army. When the Grandees called three separate rendez-vous, the first to be at Corkbush Field near Ware on 15 November, the Levellers were suspicious. When the officers prepared *A Remonstrance from his Excellency Sir Thomas Fairfax* as a replacement for the *Agreement of the People* those suspicions were confirmed. The events at Ware were in part a powerful elemental revolt by the troops, but it was successfully given political shape by the involvement of the Levellers.

These events did not happen in isolation. They were part of a wider wave of agitation around the *Agreement. Mercurius Rusticus* complained of peti-tions 'framed in Army and sent abroad by the Agitators into those Counties and Cities', where they were taken up by the Sectaries.[39] Agitators in Ireton's regiment organised their own rendezvous on 8 November, where five out of six troops signed the *Agreement of the People*. The Agitators then sent one of their number to report to 'the Convention of Agents residing in London' and to remain there as their representative. Their letter speaks of Agitators in Hampshire and 'other counties', encouraging 'the City and County Agitators' to write to the 'souldiery at Southampton' and the inhab-itants of Bristol, Weymouth, Exeter and Gloucester.[40]

On 10 November, Leveller Tobias Box was arrested carrying important papers from a meeting in the Mouth at Aldersgate, a well known radical meeting place. The papers may have related to the army for they were sent by the Commons to Fairfax.[41] The next day a report from the Agitators about the proceedings of the General Council at Putney were scattered in the streets in London. It appeared in two versions, one of which was printed by John Harris and was signed by a number of Agitators, including Tobias Box.[42] All this indicates a standing organisation of Agitators centred on London and the existence of civilian as well as army Agitators. Again on 11 November the twenty-three Agitators of Twistleton's regiment declared in favour the *The Case of the Army* and the *Agreement*.[43] John Rede was made governor of Poole on the same day and, in the early stages of his tenure, enjoyed considerable local support.[44] About the same time 150 weavers met at the Mouth. They spoke of coordinated action with the army. One of them suggested they follow the example of Naples, where, he understood, 'if any Person stand up for Monarchie there, he is immediately hanged at the Doore'.[45]

In response the Commons ordered a committee to investigate the business of the 'London agents' who had 'fomented and abetted' unrest in the army, 'thus indicating their belief that the London Levellers and the Agitators were connected'.[46] There were meetings held in Mile End and papers 'dispersed upon and down the city' to gather weavers to march to Ware in support of the Leveller cause, though these plans were thwarted.[47] There were bills posted up 'in many Churches, and upon severall Gates and Ports throughout the City, inciting the People to rise as one Man, and free themselves from the Tyranny of their Task-Masters at Westminster'. Meanwhile Henry Marten was on his feet in the Commons defending those involved in the protests. He was also meeting with 'above a hundred desperate Sectaries in a House in London'.[48]

Civilian Levellers were closely implicated in the events at Ware. Royalists alleged that Henry Marten and Thomas Rainsborough were meeting together at this time.[49] Lilburne was now on bail from the Tower and we know, because William Clarke reported it to Parliament, that 'Lieut. Col. John Lilburne came this day to Ware', although he did not come on to Corkbush Field itself but waited for news nearby.[50] Some reports also claim that Richard Overton was at Ware.[51] And it was said that Thomas Lambe had a hand in producing the papers worn in the soldiers' hats at the Ware Mutiny that bore the legend 'England's Freedoms, Soldiers Rights'.[52] Samuel Chidley was at Ware promoting the *Agreement of the People* among the mutinous troops.[53] It was a commonplace in the newsbooks and pamphlets that the Agitators were 'begotten of Lilburne (with Overtons help) . . . counselled by Walwin' and 'patronisd by Mr Martin'.[54] But it was, of course, the army Levellers who were directly involved in the events on Corkbush Field.

Captain William Bray, last seen defending the *Agreement of the People* against Cromwell at Putney, was battling to win the hearts and minds of soldiers of Robert Lilburne's regiment, of which he was a member. His account of the mutiny, which began at Dunstable sometime before the Ware rendezvous, confirms that it was in part a spontaneous action by the troops. An attempt by loyal officers sent to stem the mutiny resulted in a fight in which two lives were lost and a lieutenant and had his hand sliced off. Bray's account demonstrates that he had to contend with a strand of popular royalism among some soldiers in the first days of the revolt by Lilburne's regiment. But his appeal to the authority of the Agitators managed to give the revolt a different direction. Bray suggested to the mutinying troops that 'the way to get the Regiment to march, was to send a faire letter to the Agents from the five Regiments of Horse, and to get an Order from them'.[55] This shows not only a connection with the Leveller-influenced new Agitators, but also the political shape that could be given to such elemental revolts by Leveller activists. Bray stuck with the mutineers and brought them to Ware. He was immediately arrested as the mutinous regiment appeared on Corkbush Field. Bray was the only officer still with the regiment. He obviously enjoyed support among the troops, who, on a later occasion in 1649, petitioned for his release, citing their support for the Levellers.[56]

Colonel William Eyre was another key Leveller figure at Ware. Eyre was a returning New Englander and, as we have seen earlier, rallied retreating troops at Edgehill, fought at Brentford, and had been made a captain in Cromwell's regiment. He was also an ally of Henry Marten. Fairfax's official report records that as he came onto Corkbush Field, 'Col. Eyers, Major Scot, and others, were observed to be insinuating divers seditious Principles into the Soldiers, and incensing them against the General and General Officers'. As a result Eyre and Scot were immediately arrested.[57] Thomas Rainsborough then 'rode from division to division exhorting the men to stand firm'. Rainsborough and some others presented a petition and the *Agreement of the People* to Fairfax.[58] But Fairfax had no intention of presenting such a document to the troops.

Fairfax read his own declaration at the head of the regiments. This directly blamed the Agitators, 'guided by divers private persons that are not of the army', for spreading 'falsehoods and scandals . . . in Print' about the army high command. Fairfax threatened to resign his commission if the revolt was not ended. But he was also careful to try and take the sting from Leveller propaganda by announcing that he might still call together one general rendezvous of the army, that army declarations would be adhered to, that 'constant pay', arrears, indemnity, 'freedom from pressing', care for injured soldiers and compensation for apprentices who had left their craft to serve would all be addressed. General political demands were also to be met: there would be 'a period set for this present Parliament', there would be 'freedome and equality of Elections thereto', and the army would 'mediate' with Parliament 'for the redresse of the common grievances of the people'.[59] The Grandees' tactic seemed to have simultaneously defeated the organisation of the Agitators by force while draining its political impetus by adopting many of its demands.

Fairfax confronted the troops. Harrison's regiment and Robert Lilburne's regiment, 'the most mutinous Regiment in the Army', according to William Clarke, were the core of the revolt.[60] Harrison's troops had papers in 'their Hats with this Motto on the outside in capital Letters, England's Freedom, and Soldiers Rights', but Fairfax persuaded the men to remove them.[61] Robert Lilburne's cavalry replied to demands that they 'take those papers from your hats' by shouting 'No, no'. Major Gregson tried to intercede but a private soldier, Bartholomew Symonds, called out, paradoxically, that the major was 'against the king' and the major was promptly stoned by the mutineers. At some point in the proceedings

> the Generall . . . came to them, attended them with his Officers, who commanded them to pull their papers out of their Hats, but they refused. Whereupon some Officers rode in among them, and plucked out the papers of some that were most insolent, and then the rest began to submit.[62]

Contrary to some accounts, Cromwell *was* present on the field. Clarke reports, 'The Soldiers of this Regiment crying out, That they were abused by their Officers, and being told by the Lieutenant General, That they should have Justice against them, were very much satisfied, sensible of their error, and promised conformity to the Generals Commands for the future'.[63]

In the immediate aftermath a Council of War was called in the field and 'eight or nine' ringleaders were singled out.[64] Then 'three of them were tryed and condemned to death, and one of them (whose turn it fell to by lot) was shot to death at the Head of the Regiment, and the others are in hold to be tried'.[65] Private Richard Arnold was the man shot by his two fellow soldiers, who escaped with their lives. Parliament asked MP John Evelyn to write to Fairfax congratulating him on the execution of Arnold and encouraging him to 'bring such guilty Persons as he shall think fit to condign and exemplary Punishment'.[66]

After the mutiny, the Levellers continued to petition the Commons on their main programme and in defence of those punished for their part in the Ware Mutiny but they paid a price for the defeat on Corkbush Field. Richard Arnold had lost his life and Leveller agitation after Ware insisted to the Commons, 'Especially that you will make inquisition for the blood of that Soldier, viz. Richard Arnall of Col Lilburne's Regiment, which was shot to death neare Ware'.[67] We do not know what role Major John Cobbett, an Agitator and Leveller supporter, played at Ware. But, whatever it was, he was arrested for it. Bray and Eyres were already in prison. At the same time, Thomas Rainsborough's appointment as vice admiral was immediately blocked by the Commons. And when the Levellers petitioned on 23 November the Commons put Thomas Prince and Samuel Chidley in the Gatehouse prison, and Jeremiah Ives, Captain Thomas Taylor and William Larner in Newgate.[68] Chidley's sojourn behind bars was brief because in January 1648 he was active in promoting the Levellers' Smithfield petition. On 11 December Samuel Oates, then in London, was ordered arrested for his part in propagating the *Agreement*. Oates escaped to his old stamping ground in Rutland and, after two more arrest orders were issued, he eventually considered himself acquitted when his accusers failed to present sufficient evidence at assizes in Rutland. Nevertheless, after Ware the Grandees faced no more opposition at the two remaining army rendezvous.[69]

In reply to the Levellers' petition Cromwell told the Commons that 'he gave way to dispute about it at the Counsell of war, partly to perswade them out of the unreasonableness' that the London Agents had encouraged. But when he could no longer discount 'this drive at a levelling parity', and when he discovered their plan for a broad franchise, he saw the 'dangerous consequences' of allowing them to gain the support of 'many honest officers'. He therefore thought it 'high tyme to suppress such attempts' and so put an end to the 'calumnies raised upon the Army . . . from that partie'.[70] The Levellers, undaunted, returned to Parliament on both 25 and 29 November to demand that those imprisoned for their part in the Ware mutiny and those imprisoned for petitioning on their behalf be freed. The numbers were so great that the lord mayor offered to guard the Commons with the

City militia. Parliament vowed that in the light of 'the Dangers and Mischiefs that may be brought upon the Kingdom' by the London Agents, they would enforce the 'Punishment and Suppression of such Persons as shall be found spreading of Papers, or writing of Books, or procuring Subscriptions to Petitions, or any other way active in promoting so destructive a Design'.[71]

An uncomfortable truth was, however, soon to impose itself on the Grandees: they could not afford to finally dispense with the radical wing of the Revolution while the threat of the restoration of the king remained. Late in the year John Wildman's *Putney Projects* provided a lengthy review of recent developments with just such a warning at its core. It reviewed the Grandees' embrace of the Agitators and the radicals when they were threatened by the Holles–Stapleton coup and denounced their volte-face when they felt themselves secure. It blamed Cromwell and Ireton for their compromises with the king and the danger that this would feed popular royalism, asking, 'Did not many Regiments at Ware cry out, for the King and Sir Thomas?' It denounced Cromwell for allowing Lilburne to suffer in jail and for preventing Rainsborough from being appointed to command of the navy. But the vast majority of its forty or more pages were dominated by argument against granting powers to the king.[72] Charles, ever willing to fulfil the worst expectations of his critics, was busy negotiating with the Scots and so exposing the pointlessness of Cromwell's policy of conciliation. And so it was when the army held an all-day prayer meeting at Windsor on 22 December, although Rainsborough and others involved in the mutiny at Ware expressed contrition and declared for the unity of the army, it was not only, as it is sometimes said, the radicals who were having to adjust their stance. So too were Cromwell and the Grandees. Pardons were issued to mutineers and the army again advocated Rainsborough's appointment as vice admiral, though the Lords remained obstinate. Major John Cobbett and Captain William Bray were released and returned to the army. Less than a week later the king and the Scottish commissioners signed a provisional agreement that a Scottish army would come south to aid Charles.[73]

The Levellers and the army

The Levellers could not have made the connections that they did with the revolt in the army unless their general reputation as radicals had spread through the ranks. But, more than this, some Levellers were *of* the army themselves, not external to it. John Lilburne's military exploits were well known and he and others continued to use his military rank even after he left the army. Indeed, when the Lords failed to refer to Lilburne using his military rank in the year after he left the army Overton reproved them in print.[74] Other Levellers also saw military service: William Larner, Thomas Prince, John Harris, Major Tulidah, John Cobbett, John Rede and Tobias Box, to name only some. Thomas Rainsborough, his brother William, Agitator Edward Sexby and army chaplains Jeremiah Ives and Edward Harrison supported the Levellers. So did leading figures in the mutinies at Ware, Captains William Eyre and William Bray. Captain William Thompson was already active at the time of Putney and was to become one of the central figures in the Burford revolt. Early in the Civil War Henry Marten had raised his own force in Berkshire, but perhaps more telling is the cipher that appears to date from 1647 that was later found in Marten's papers which mostly contains the names of Levellers involved with the army and their allies.[75]

The Levellers' actions throughout 1647 significantly increased both the audience for their ideas in the army and the number of soldiers who were active in the movement. Loose adherents were drawn closer to them and they were obliged to codify their ideas into a short political programme—this, again, won them a wider audience in the army than ever before. There were many others who, with more or less intensity, were drawn into support for Leveller initiatives, including Bray's cornet Christopher Cheesman, Bray's quartermaster John Nayler, Captain John Clarke, Henry Denne, John Pitchford (whose troop was filled with 'anabaptists and Levellers of the worst sort', according to Baxter), Captain Edward Scotten, Miles Sindercombe, Baptist John Spencer, James Thompson, Captain Francis White, Captain Stephen Winthrop, Judith Rainsborough's husband, and Robert Everard. Military service created bonds of comradeship and networks of influence that lasted well beyond the time that any particular individual spent in the army. This kind of influence did not create army radicalism. It took both immediate material grievances and a society-wide political crisis to do that. And these two elements, immediate grievance and general crisis, were never as far apart as some historians assume. To be purusing a limited grievance in the midst of a political crisis is not the same as pursuing that grievance in a time of political quietude. Lenin was to make the point that people become revolutionary when they have to fight the government for a crust of bread, but long before he did so the Agitators made the same point. They wrote that 'we finde by sad experience that there was no possibility of obtaining either' their 'constant pay' or 'our arrears' for as 'long as the settlement of the peoples freedoms was delaid'.[76]

An army revolt in the middle of an existential crisis of the state can never be divorced from politics. Even if the soldiers had only ever raised 'economic' demands the very fact that they did so by mutiny and the creation of their own autonomous network of elected representatives would have made their actions political in any case. But, more than this, a minority were politically active before the revolt of the army, and some of those were Levellers or influenced by Leveller ideas. What the organisation of the Agitators and the Levellers did was to help shape the exact direction and the organised form that such emerging radicalism took. The Ware Mutiny, as we have seen, arose in the midst of a wave of agitation around the *Agreement of the People* published on 3 November 1647. Fairfax's letter to the Commons after Ware directly attributed to the 'London agents' an important part in the mutiny in both Harrison's and Robert Lilburne's regiments. On this news the Lords ordered that 'a Committee shall examine who are the London Agents mentioned in the Generalls letter'.[77] As the revolt developed over 1647, as it became clear that a Presbyterian coup was real, this process accelerated. By the winter months the radicals were winning the political battle for hegemony, if not in numbers then in strategy and ideology, in the New Model Army. This is why the Grandees used all their authority up to and including military force to push them back, at least for a time.

CHAPTER 11

Counterrevolution

Within five days in February 1648 the House of Commons twice declared that £100 would be given to anyone who could identify the author or printer of 'the vile blasphemous' pamphlet that pretended to be the New Testament of the House of Commons and the supreme council of the New Model Army. In the second vote the House instructed the Sheriffs that the pamphlet was to be 'burnt by the Hands of the common Hangman the next Week, in three of the most publick Places of *London* and *Westminster*, upon a Market Day'.[1] At the same time the parliamentary press was outraged at this 'abomination', which, they imagined, was both atheistical and blasphemous:

> Good Lord, confound King Oliver,
> And all his holy crew.
> With Rainsborow, that leveller
> and Pride that precious Jew
>
> Let say once more, we do thee pray
> Into a saw-pit fall.
> Let Martin purge his pox away
> Within some hospital
>
> Let Hammon have his brains knock't out
> With his own bunch of keys.
> Let Walton and his zealous rout
> Visit the Hebridies

Let the two Houses fight and scratch
Like wives at Billingsgate;
And let them ne'er a peace up patch
Until it be too late

That so upon each House of clay
King Charles may mount his throne
Hear us (O Father) we thee pray:
Our hopes in thee alone.[2]

But perhaps what the parliamentary authorities were really concerned about was that the verse accurately captured the political situation. The poem revealed how the king hoped to use divisions among supporters of Parliament to regain his full authority. Moreover, it identified the main enemies of the king as 'that leveller' Thomas Rainsborough, republican and Leveller ally Henry Marten, Independent Thomas Pride, the king's jailer Robert Hammond, Cromwell's son-in-law and fellow Independent Valentine Walton and, of course, Cromwell himself. But in early 1648 relations between those at the radical end of the parliamentary camp were in flux and it was an open question whether or not they could maintain the forward momentum of the Revolution or be swept away by resurgent royalism.

The counterrevolution in 1648

In the dying days of 1647 Charles agreed with the Scots that they would invade England in his support and, in return, he would impose the authority of the Presbyterian Church upon the nation for a period of three years. This invasion would coincide with a series of royalist risings known as the Second Civil War. But there are a number of reasons why it is also useful to think of this war as a counterrevolutionary offensive. The king remained the prisoner of the New Model Army, garrisoned in a castle on the Isle of Wight. At the same time Presbyterians and other moderates in the parliamentary camp—in the City, at Westminster and in the army—were working to effect a Personal Treaty with the king, hoping to bring him to London and 're-inthrone' him.

In the first month of the New Year the advantage seemed to lie with those opposed to appeasement. Charles's duplicity had exhausted the patience of many and deprived the king's supporters of credible arguments in support of a treaty. A Vote of No Addresses, lost in the Commons the previous autumn when proposed by Marten and Rainsborough, was passed on 3 January by 141 votes to ninety-one. This ended further meetings with Charles and declared that the settlement of the nation would be made by Parliament alone. On 11 January the Army Council lent its support to the Vote of No Addresses. Six days later the Lords did likewise, but only after peers who favoured a treaty absented themselves. Only the Scottish commissioners in London registered objections. On 11 January Henry Marten was in print attacking the Scottish commissioners and the king in his sustained and closely argued *The Independency of England.*

There was, however, some opposition. On 9 January a crowd crying 'For the king and no plunder' rioted against taxes being levied to pay for the army. On 3 February a petition to the Lords and Commons in the name of 'many thousands' of 'knights, Gentlemen, Freeholders, Citizens and Tradesmen from severall Counties and Cities' called for the disbandment of the army. It also complained that Presbyterians had been 'totally deprived of all Offices and Commands'.[3] Four days later Henry Marten was again in print. *The Parliaments Proceedings Justified* defended the Vote of No Addresses, opposed a Personal Treaty, and castigated the Scottish commissioners for their willingness to accommodate a royalist revival.[4] At just this juncture the Levellers were preparing another petitioning campaign.

Leveller organisation in early 1648

The Levellers were now approaching the height of their powers. On 17 January 1648, George Masterson, a minister from Shoreditch parish, attended a Leveller meeting in Wapping. The sixty people in the room were addressed by both John Lilburne and John Wildman, promoting *The Earnest Petition of many Free-born People of this Nation.*[5] Lilburne had been invited to the meeting 'by some friends' in order to answer the scruples and objections that 'some honest people, in or about Wappin' had concerning the petition.[6] Masterson 'stood sneaking in a corner to heare what was said'. The following day the 'lying shepherd of Shoreditch', as the Levellers called him, denounced the meeting as a traitorous conspiracy to both the Lords and the Commons.[7] What Masterson unintentionally provided was a rare illumination of the wheels and pulleys that moved popular opposition to both royalism and those in the parliamentary camp who would compromise with the king.

Lilburne and Wildman then gave their version of the event at the bar of the House of Commons. A full House listened as both men defended themselves. Lilburne spoke for so long that he began to lose his voice. The Commons debated the issue until past nightfall but concluded by charging both Leveller leaders with treason. But Lilburne, never one to give up easily, had 100 supporters with him who challenged the sergeant-at-arms to produce a legal warrant when he attempted to arrest the Leveller leaders in the lobby of the Commons. The sergeant had to repair to the clerk's office to get the warrant, but by now the Speaker who was to sign the warrant had gone home. Lilburne promised to return the following morning. He did so with Coke's *Institutes* in his hand and demanded to address the Speaker. The sergeant called for his arrest. But after Lilburne addressed the soldiers of the guard they refused to hold him. It took the intervention of a Colonel Baxter at the head of another group of soldiers to enforce the order. And as the soldiers rushed the closely packed crowed Lilburne handed his books, staff and gloves to a friend and attempted to leave the hall. As he cried 'murder, murder!' the crowd joined in. Some of Lilburne's friends were knocked to the floor with the musket butts of Baxter's troops; other soldiers ran at Lilburne with swords drawn. Lilburne thought that one sally would have 'undoubtedly dispatched me' had not Elizabeth Lilburne 'stood betwixt me and them'. But in the end the soldier's overcame the Levellers' resistance and Lilburne was committed to the Tower, Wildman to the Fleet.[8]

It seems, however, that Lilburne and Wildman did not reach prison that night because the Commons had to reissue the order that they be jailed on the following day, 20 January. The motion noted angrily that 'some of their party had given out words that they should not go to prison'. The Commons was alarmed that 'there was to be a great meeting held at Dartford in Kent about their petition'. The Commons ordered the Kent committee to 'suppress all meetings upon that petition, and to prevent all tumults'. The London militia were also ordered to suppress both meetings and the petition. The Commons further ordered that a declaration 'to undeceive the people and to show them the dangerous consequences that will arise by such practices' should be issued to counter the Leveller's *Petition of many thousands of Freeborn people of England*.[9]

A pamphlet war exploded in the wake of the arrests. Wildman gave his account in *Truth's triumph, or Treachery anatomized*, published on 1

February. Ten days later Masterson shot back with *The Triumph Stain'd, being an Answer to Truths Triumph*. Lilburne joined in with *The People's Prerogative* at about the same time. The paper-bullets were flying thick and fast as Leveller John Harris replied to Masterson on 22 February with one of the most effective and most readable of the pamphlets, *A Lash for a Lyar, or The Stayner Stayned*. Then Lilburne was back in print with *A Whip for the present House of Lords*.[10] This remarkable series of pamphlets tells us about the political situation in early 1648, about the Levellers' response to it, and about the condition of Leveller organisation.

The last of these insights is the most interesting as we have relatively few snapshots of the Levellers at work. Lilburne and Wildman hotly contested Masterson's charge of treason but the picture that emerges from all the protagonists' accounts gives us our most detailed account of how the Levellers and their supporters organised.[11] It was an evening meeting held at the house of Mr Williams, a gardener, in Well-yard, Wapping. The purpose of the meeting was to promote the petition and, once enough signatories had been gained, to organise a demonstration in its support. Of the sixty at the meeting, nineteen of them later signed a letter contradicting Masterson's account of events.[12] At the meeting Lilburne and Wildman fielded questions about the petition and explained the methods by which it was to be promoted. Masterson records part of Lilburne's speech as saying,

> Lieutenant Colonel John Lilburn did then and there Affirm, That the People of London had appointed ten or twelve of their Commissioners (whereof he said that Lilburn was one) though he said likewise, that the honest Blades in Southwark did not like the word Commissioners. These Commissioners were appointed to promote the Petition, and send out Agents to every City, Towne, and Parish, (if they could possibly) of every County of the Kingdome, to inform the people of their Liberties and Priviledges.[13]

Masterson also gives us Lilburne's account of where and how often these commissioners met. Wapping seems to have been a base for Leveller activity:

> Lieutenant Col. Lilburne told them, That they (the Commissoners) had their constant meetings on Mondays, Wednesdays and Fridays in the evening at the Whalebone; and the other three days at Southwark, Wapping, and other places, with their friends; and that upon the next Lords day they were to meet at Dartfort in Kent, to receive an account of their Agents,

(from Gravesend, Maidstone, and the most choice Townes of the County) how they had promoted the business there.[14]

The Whalebone inn, to which Lilburne refers, was one of the regular meeting places of the Levellers. It was known as one of the Levellers' 'two new Houses of Parliament', located in Lothbury near the Royal Exchange in the City of London.[15] Lilburne continued his speech, according to Masterson, by 'drawing a Paper-Book from under his short Red Coat' and giving the meeting a summary of the letters that had been sent out to the 'well-affected' around the country encouraging them to promote the petition. Lilburne also reported to the meeting that 30,000 of the petitions were to come from the printing presses the following day. The Levellers' supporters were to distribute them, including friendly soldiers who would help get them around the country. One Lazarus Tindall of Colonel Barkstead's regiment was ready to take 1,000 copies for the use of the soldiers.[16] To fund this work, Lilburne told the meeting, money needed to be raised:

> That because the businesse needs must be a work of charge (there being thirty thousand Petitions to come forth in Print to tomorrow, and it would cost money to send their Agents abroad, though honest souldiers now at White Hall would save them something in scattering them up and down the Counties) they had therefore appointed Treasurers, namely Mr. Prince and Mr. Chidly, and others, and Collectors (whose names as I remember, he did not reade) who should gather up from those that acted for them, of some two pence, three pence, six pence, a shilling, two shillings, half a Crown a week: and thus promising to meet them the next night, he tooke leave.[17]

That 30,000 petitions were being printed is some indication of the scale on which the Levellers were operating at this time.[18]

Masterson's account of Lilburne's speech is corroborated by the letter that Lilburne, Wildman, John Davies and Richard Woodward sent to the 'well affected' of Kent. The letter is an encouragement to support the petition and it contains some fairly precise suggestions on the way the well affected of Kent should organise:

> for the more effectuall proceedings in this bussinesse, there is a Method and Order setled in all the Wards of London, and the out Parishes and Suburbs; they have appointed severall active men in every Ward and

Division, to be a Committee, to take speciall care of the busninesse, and to appoint active men in every Parish to read the Petition at set meetings for that purpose, and to take Subscriptions, and to move as many as can possibly, to goe in person when the day of delivering it shall be appointed; and that they intend to give notice of that time to all the adjacent Counties, that as many as possibly can, may also joyne with them the same day.[19]

The petitioning, and the assembly organised to present it to the Commons, were, the letter continued, to be promoted in the counties of Hertfordshire, Buckingham, Oxford, Cambridge and Rutland, among others. The Leveller leaders urged their supporters in Kent to use 'the same Method, as the best expedient for your union':

That you would appoint meetings in every Division of your County, and there select faithful men of publick spirits, to take care that the Petition be sent to the hands of the most active men in every Town, to unite the Town in those desires of common right, and to take subscriptions.[20]

Another source of information about Leveller organisation at this time is Lilburne's transcription of his own speech at the bar of the House of Commons on 19 January 1648. This transcript formed part of Lilburne's pamphlet *An Impeachment for High Treason against Oliver Cromwell and his son in law Henry Ireton Esquires* published eighteen months later, on 10 August 1649. Lilburne reported that

as soon as I and some of my true and faithful Comrades had caused some thousands of that Petition printed, I did the best I could to set up constant meetings in severall places in Southwark to promote the Petition; to which meetings all scruplers and objectors against any thing contained in the Petition, might repair for satisfaction.[21]

Lilburne confirms that he then set about appointing 'Trustees in every parish' to 'take especial care to promote the Petition effectually and vigourously'. Once this was done a coordinating committee was set up at a meeting at the Whalebone inn:

I labored the most I could to set up like meeting in London; and for that end, diverse cordial, honest, faithful noun substantive English-men met openly at the WHALEBONE behind the Exchange, where by common consent, we chuse out a Committee, or a certaine number of faithful under-standing men . . . to withdraw into the next roome, to forme a method, how to promote it in every Ward in the City, and out-parishes, and also in every County in the Kingdome.[22]

Lilburne goes on to confirm Masterson's information about the appoint-ment of treasurers and the collection of dues at rates of between twopence and half a crown a week. This was 'to pay for the Printing of the Petitions, and the bearing of the charges of those messengers we should have occa-sion to send downe into the Countries to our friends.' Lilburne also confirms that he sent a letter to friends in Buckinghamshire and Hertfordshire, as well as to Kent.

The letter to associates in Hertfordshire and Buckinghamshire is espe-cially interesting since it adds detail both about petitioning methods and about how the Levellers organised contact with supporters outside London. Lilburne urged his supporters to try and get the petition read 'on the first day of the week in the meeting house' and if this is not possible to have it read at 'as great a meeting of the people some other day'. The petition should be read and explained to the crowd and then 'select some active men as Trustees to take care of gaining subscriptions'. When this is done, Lilburne continued, a date will be chosen when the petition is to be delivered to Parliament and then, he tells his supporters, they should 'engage as many persons as you can to come to London with the petition an to cry very resolutely to the Parliament, Justice, Justice'. Finally Lilburne encourages the Leveller supporters in Hertford and Buckingham to choose 'an Agent to reside here at London constantly to give you constant intelligence of all affaires and to send you books for your information'. These books should be bought with publicly collected money entrusted to the agent.[23]

All this speaks of a widespread and relatively cohesive organisation with leaders capable of coordinating both their own efforts and those of their supporters. Certainly the pamphlets produced by Lilburne, Wildman and Harris all reference and mutually support one another. Pauline Gregg esti-mates that the Levellers and the Agitators produced some forty pamphlets in 1647, compared to just fourteen in 1645. And despite new laws passed in September 1647 that were meant to crack down on unlicensed or scandal-ous pamphlets, and which imposed stiffer sanctions on authors, printers, booksellers and hawkers, the Levellers produced about the same number again in 1648. In addition, as we shall see below, the first Leveller news-paper, *The Moderate*, began publication in June 1648. The picture of the

Levellers that emerges is one of sustained, widespread political organisation. No doubt the same methods were used again in July to gain the 10,000
names for the petition to free Lilburne from the Tower and, in August and
September, to gain 40,000 signatories for the Large Petition.[24]

The discussion at the Wapping meeting also reveals fascinating insights
about the political situation in early 1648. The politically sophisticated
audience raises questions to do with the disillusionment among supporters
of Parliament, and this speaks directly to the atmosphere in which the
Second Civil War was brewing. And there is also a discussion about the
reasons why Cromwell and his supporters chose to support the Vote of No
Addresses after advocating discussions with the king for so long.

In the meeting Lilburne is directly challenged by one member of the
audience who argues that there is no point petitioning Parliament because
they have turned a deaf ear to all previous attempts to influence them.
Another insists that pro-royalist sentiment is in the ascendency. Lilburne
replies that petitioning is still an important political tool and that it is the
only way that a movement can be built that might address the fundamental
root of growing royalism: disillusionment with Parliament's actions. As
Wildman insisted, 'there was no other visible Authority . . . which is
intrusted by the people with the power to redresse their grievances'.[25]

The second thread of discussion concerns the Vote of No Addresses.
Why had Cromwell changed his view on negotiations with the king? To
this Lilburne gives one answer that is unlikely to have been true, or at least
was only partially so: he suggests that a member of Parliament had sworn
to act the Felton (John Felton, who assassinated the duke of Buckingham in
1628) and 'dispatch Cromwell'. To this end he had 'charged a Pistoll, and
took a Dagger in his Pocket'. But the would-be assassin had been locked in
his chamber in Whitehall for a day by another MP who warned Cromwell.
Cromwell then, Lilburne argues, called a day of prayer to reunite the army,
a reference to the meeting in December, and then swung over to support
the Vote for No Addresses. This is less interesting as a credible explanation
of Cromwell's actions than it is about Lilburne's obviously close relations
with the MP in question. Lilburne refuses to name the MP, whom he calls
'our good friend', but describes him as one whose 'father was a parliament
man, and a Knight, but is dead, and this Gentleman his son is of his
Christian name'.[26] This is obviously Henry Marten, whose father was also
Henry Marten, also an MP, a knight, and died in 1641. Harris later accused
Masterson of naming Marten at the bar of the Commons and this is
substantiated by the diary of MP John Boys. Marten had to swiftly deny

involvement in any such plot but he did insist that he was not willing to 'stick to any government because its what we found, unles it be good, and for the safety of the people'.[27]

A more convincing argument for Cromwell's change of heart was given by Wildman. He accurately demonstrates that the Scots successfully 'out-bid' Cromwell by promising Charles a 'negative voice'. This left the Grandees high and dry, and not a little angry at the deceit involved. Consequently, 'the tenders of the Lieutenant General being rejected, hee was necessitated to ingage with this Honorable house in those Votes that there should neither be any addresses made further to him, nor any received from him'.[28]

Lilburne was more convincing in his presentation of the case that the seed of royalist rebellion lay in the unrealised promises that Parliament had made to its supporters and its inability to come to a settlement of the nation. Lilburne and Wildman were well aware of the worsening condition of the poor in the winter of 1647. Wildman had heard in the coaching inn where he lodged in the City of the plight of the Wiltshire clothiers who formally employed 100 people but now employed only a dozen. He also heard that the poor of the county were gathering on the roads in crowds of up to thirty and 'seized upon Corne as it was carrying to market, and divided it among themselves before the owners faces, telling them they could not starve'. Some in the audience were worried that this popular anger would turn against those that were called 'Round-heads' and 'Independents' for 'adhearing to Parliament'. Lilburne and Wildman argued that using the petition to show that they were on the side of the people would protect them better than having a 'Blew Ribbon in their hats, that being the Generals colours and the modern badge of protection'.[29]

Lilburne told the meeting that the poor 'doted implicitly on the King as a fountain of peace' because 'their burdens are now greater than before, and are likely to continue without any redresse'. The people have spent blood and treasure but still do not have their liberty and freedom. Instead the Parliament had encouraged the people to fight the king, yet still maintained that the king 'can do no wrong'. This, said Lilburne, was 'riddle upon riddle, and mystery upon mystery, which did even confound and amaze the people, and put them into Woods, and Wilderness, that they could not see or know where they are, or what to think of themselves, or of the Parliament'.

All this was a fairly accurate diagnosis of the mood that soon erupted into a Second Civil War. Indeed Wildman told his listeners at Well-yard, 'I conceived no other possible way of preventing a new warre with the Scots . . . but by uniting the people in the principles of common right and freedome'.[30] To this end Lilburne advocated a settlement based on the *Agreement of the People*. All this agitation and action shows that the Levellers were far from simply being proclaimers of abstract notions of liberty and democracy, but were a vitally engaged political movement attempting to understand a complex and fast-changing political moment.

The persistence of Leveller influence in the army

The defeat of the rising at Corkbush Field, Ware, in November 1647 had certainly been a reverse for the Levellers. But it did not end their influence in the army, nor did it stem the tide of army radicalism. Two incidents in the first half of 1648 testify to the ongoing struggle for the hearts and minds of the soldiers. At almost exactly the same time as Lilburne and Wildman were addressing the Well-yard meeting in Wapping a remarkable meeting of army officers took place in the Cotswold town of Broadway.

Here some eighty officers gathered for a meeting that seems to have lasted the best part of a week. They came from four regiments: those of Colonels Kempson, Herbert, Cooke and Eyre. They were promised assistance from Colonel Laugharne's regiment stationed in south Wales. The plan was to surprise Gloucester by night and sieze the 300 barrels of powder stored there. The officers hoped that Hartlebury Castle would be delivered to them by Colonel Turton and, if not, that would be taken as well. There was also talk of taking towns the length of the Welsh Marches: Bewdley, Shrewsbury, Hereford and Ludlow. London citizens were reported to be organising to provide them with both money and armour.[31]

The plan, unsurprisingly, caused division among the officers with twenty or so opposed to the undertaking. The meeting broke up without decision but it was assumed that 'the rest that were for it will meete again, or have met sometime the beginning of this week'. The letter containing an eyewitness account of the discussions was sent from Gloucester on 19 January and read in the Commons on 24 January. Fairfax wrote to the County Committees in Worcester, Gloucester and Hereford demanding the arrest of soldiers who 'continue any longer in bodies together to the oppression and terror of the country'. The Commons also took the threat seriously and sent loyal troops into the West Country and made plans for paying arrears and disbanding regiments.[32]

We last saw Colonel William Eyre being arrested at Ware. He faced a court martial but, in the spirit of forgiveness that broke out between Independents and Levellers in the army in December 1647, he was allowed to return to his regiment quartered in Worcestershire. Eyre's regiment was not part of the New Model Army and faced disbandment, part of a wider programme of decommissioning regiments with radical associations. In the wake of the discovery of the Broadway meeting all the regiments involved were disbanded the following month. Eyre certainly blamed Cromwell for this injustice and it is hard to imagine that he was not one of the most vocal in urging action. Soon after the disbandment he enlisted with the 'Leveller regiment' raised by his Berkshire neighbour, Henry Marten.[33]

The second flash of army militancy came in April at St Albans. Like the Broadway meeting this too involved representatives from several regiments. But this time it was not just officers who represented the men but elected Agitators on the Putney model. These Agitators met to propagate a new petition whose demands were closely modelled on the *Agreement of the People*.[34] Conscious of the dangerous gulf opening between the army and the civilian population, the petition and the text accompanying it were an appeal to civilians by the army rank and file. It asks them join together to throw off the rule of the Grandees in both army and Parliament and to settle the nation along the lines of the *Agreement*. It retells the history of the Agitators and their struggle to win the people's freedom in the teeth of opposition from the officers. It concludes that at Ware 'the Grand Officers wresting all power out of the Agitators hands, this settlement of your Freedoms, and the removal of your grievances hath been prevented'.[35]

In order to promote the petition 'some soldiers of severall regiments of horse . . . met at St Albans about 24 April, and Colonell Riches Regiment chose one of every Troop to meet there and give them an account of their proceedings'.[36] Nicolas Lockyer, one of the most active Agitators, was from Rich's regiment and was clearly attempting to revive Agitator organisation. As the meeting was taking place some 'Officers rushed violently into the place, where they were met, and imprisoned all their persons.' These were three captains—Brown, Gladman and Packer—from Fairfax's horse. John Gladman was originally from Cromwell's own troop of horse and had the previous year belatedly become an Agitator but now had changed sides. The soldiers were taken to Windsor as prisoners. The organisation they were part of was nevertheless sufficiently strong to reproduce the petition and to attach a second petition from soldiers in Rich's regiment demanding that their Agitators be freed from prison. These documents use the now familiar Leveller technique of quoting the previous declarations of Parliament and the army that upheld the right to petition against those now trying to deny that same right to the soldiers. In particular it reminds its readers of the senior officers' willingness to see soldiers petition, and the officers' defence of the right to do so, when, the previous year, such petitioners were declared 'enemies of the state' by the Presbyterian majority in the Commons. These themes were forcefully reiterated in the Leveller-sympathetic pamphlet *Windsor Projects*. But whatever the logical strengths of this case might be, and however desirous the Grandees were of re-establishing army unity after Ware, they were not about to tolerate the re-emergence of Agitator organisation in the ranks. The two messengers that brought the final petition to Fairfax were cross-questioned about their organisation but refused, even when threatened with execution, to divulge their accomplices. Ultimately Rich's troopers took action themselves and managed to free some of their compatriots.[37]

William Eyre was not the only Leveller back in action in early 1648. Another Leveller released after arrest at Ware, Captain Bray, was also in military service once more. As troops were being raised in Kent to meet the threat of a royalist rising, Bray joined the regiment of Colonel John Reynolds, then an officer with a radical reputation. Bray's troop was to become a centre of Leveller radicalism. His cornet, Christopher Cheeseman, had already played a brief part in the Putney debates and was a former sequestration agent in Berkshire. And Bray's quartermaster, John Naylor, was soon to prove equally radical in his views. They were willing 'to gird our Swords to us againe', said Naylor, because they saw that they were about to be 'brought to Slavery by the . . . prevailing party'. And in Bray they saw an officer they were willing to fight under because he would defend the proposition 'That the People under God, are the Original of all just Power'. They thought that he would not, as other of their 'old Machiavellian Adversaries' had done before, 'backslide from Principles of Righteousness'.[38]

The counterrevolution and Thomas Rainsborough

Royalist rebellion broke out in Wales in March, just as the Scottish Parliament was preparing to invade England. Colonel Poyer declared for the king in Pembroke, an act preceded by a petition resisting disbandment and demanding back pay. On 22 March a petition from Essex marked the start of a widespread campaign in favour of a Personal Treaty. This was led by the Essex Grand Jury and the lower estimate of signatures was 20,000. Those names took nearly two months to collect in spite of a Commons attempt to supress the petition. In early April monarchist riots hit London, and Norwich, Berwick and Carlisle were taken for the king. On 1 May Cromwell was ordered to Wales to suppress the growing royalist threat before heading north to confront the Scottish invasion. A day later Parliament received notification that Surrey petitioners were going to gather at Leatherhead. They had collected 5,000 signatures and started to march towards the capital, arriving in mid-May with the accompaniment of pipes, trumpets and fiddles. When they reached Westminster fighting broke out between them and 500 soldiers. Some eight petitioners and two soldiers were killed. Lieutenant Colonel Cobbett reported the events to the Commons, still bleeding from his wounds. In the same month rioters in Bury St Edmunds, Suffolk, gathered on the pretext of traditional May festivities at their maypole or May bush, assaulted soldiers of Fairfax's cavalry and drove them from the town. Resistance was also to be seen in Worcester, Plymouth, Exeter, Nottingham, Lincoln, Huntingdon, Leicester, Warwick, Hertford and Cambridge. But the centres of counterrevolution most dangerously close to London were in Kent and Essex. On 9 May some 2,000 petitioners delivered the Essex petition to Westminster calling for the return of the king and the disbandment of the army. They were warmly welcomed as they came through the City. On 11 May a petition from Kent, subscribed at the Grand Jury hearings in Canterbury, demanded a Personal Treaty with the king and the disbandment of the New Model Army. The Kent petition was said to have over 20,000 subscribers. In all, between March and August, some thirty-six conservative petitions arrived at Westminster, an overall majority of the total of the fifty-six petitions delivered in this period. The mass petitioning campaign was the soil out of which armed counterrevolution grew.[39]

The Leveller Thomas Rainsborough was right at the heart of the developments in Kent. Rainsborough came from a seafaring family. His father, William Rainsborough, had been a senior adviser on naval affairs and the commander of a raid on the Barbary pirates in 1637 that had won him popular and royal acclaim. Thomas Rainsborough had a powerful desire to command Parliament's navy and he was named vice admiral by the Lords and Commons on 1 October 1647. But Rainsborough's support for the Levellers at Putney and his participation in the Ware mutiny in November 1647 had led the army Grandees, the Commons and the Lords to block him from taking up his command.[40] However, relations between Independents and Levellers had been partially repaired, at least in the army.[41] The sense of a rising threat from Presbyterians within the parliamentary camp and royalist opposition had created conditions in which recomposing army unity was a pressing necessity. Rainsborough and others professed regret for the divisions at Ware and Cromwell and the Independents rescinded their opposition to Rainsborough's appointment as vice admiral. As early as 22 December 1647 Fairfax was urging Parliament to confirm Rainsborough as vice admiral.[42]

This was part of a wider push by the Independents to secure key appointments for figures they could trust, and the navy was a crucial area of contention. The royalist news-sheet *Mercurius Pargamaticus* reported that the army Independents had replaced William Batten with Rainsborough to 'make sure at Sea that as well as Lande' they retained control of the armed forces.[43] Nevertheless it was not until 1 January 1648 that the Commons, having failed to win over the Lords to agree Rainsborough's appointment, pushed ahead without the peers' consent.[44] Batten, the man Rainsborough replaced, was certainly an opponent of the radicals. He was for a treaty with the king and opposed the Vote of No Addresses. He had been reported to the Lords for saying that the army would not deal fairly with the king and, possibly, that they would 'take off his head'.[45] He was a supporter of the most outspoken moderate Presbyterians in the Commons and in the army. Batten had already enabled the flight overseas of six of the eleven members excluded from the Commons by the army. Rainsborough and Henry Marten were both members of the Independent-dominated Admiralty committee, which met three times in September 1647 to examine Batten over his part in the operation. Batten, in response, was deeply unhappy that he had been displaced by 'a Committee at the Head-quarters at Putney with the advice of their Adjutators' in favour of Rainsborough when, in Batten's opinion, 'that man should hold no command who openly professed himself to be a Leveller'.[46] According to spies, Batten had been meeting with royalist agents in the Hoop tavern in Leadenhall, where he 'plotted and contrived' a revolt of the fleet even before he defected to their cause.[47]

The rebel petitioners in Kent had made contact with the seamen of the navy then in the Downs, the sheltered anchorage off the Kent coast. A crucial contact between the Kent petitioners and the seamen was Samuel Kem. Kem was a preacher who had fought with Parliament in the First Civil War as an officer in his own right. Royalists then claimed that he preached in the morning and plundered in the afternoon, 'a saint in the pulpit and a devil out of it'. He preached before Charles when he accompanied the parliamentary commissioners to meet the king in Oxford in late 1644. Kem was assigned to the navy in 1646 and became chaplain to William Batten when he was vice admiral. He acted as Batten's agent with the Scots in 1647 and again preached before the then captive king. The sermon pleased Charles but led to accusations that Kem was in touch with royalist agents. By this time he was certainly a Presbyterian moderate hostile to lay preaching and Independency. He became a parson in Deal and assisted Batten in organising the flight of the Presbyterian MPs in August 1647. Seamen trying to prevent the flight of the MPs were 'threatened' and 'reviled against by parson Major Kem'. As the Kent rising took shape Kem was secretly visiting every ship promoting mutiny. Seamen Lisle, Lendal and Mitchell of Batten's old flagship, now Rainsborough's command, the *Constant Reformation*, had already been selected as leaders of the revolt. Rainsborough suspected Kem and wrote to the Commons as early as 18 February 1648 to remind them of an earlier promise to remove 'the Parson to some other living'. The warnings went unheeded.[48]

Kent was already aflame in May when a remarkable incident took place that, though entirely accidental, nevertheless acted as the trigger for events of great consequence. On 20 May, as Rainsborough himself reported, a man 'in mean dress' stepped ashore from a ship that had come in from the West. His name was Cornelius Evans. But in a performance of incredible bravado he claimed that he was the Prince of Wales. He held court for some days at the Bell tavern in Sandwich and even when challenged by a royalist courtier who knew the real Prince of Wales by sight he had his accuser arrested and imprisoned. As long as the mock-prince's reign lasted he became a rallying point for royalist revolt. Some of the crew of the *Providence* joined in the popular enthusiasm and Sandwich, Faversham and Rochester all declared for the imposter. Rainsborough was ordered to arrest Evans and recapture Sandwich but, he replied, he was barely able to do so because revolt was spreading in the fleet. He had already dispatched the *Providence* and the *Convertine* north because he could not trust that they would not mutiny if they remained off Kent. 'The present distemper of this county is such', wrote Rainsborough, 'as hath put as sad a face on things as ever England saw; and it hath got distemper in the fleet'. The 'greatest motive to the disturbance of the seamen, is, that these part's are wholly for the King'. If 'this gathering be not . . . speedily supressed', warned Rainsborough, it 'will be of as dangerous a consequence as any one thing besides'.[49]

Rainsborough was about the very business of supressing the rising when the mutiny of the fleet took place. He was ashore attempting to stem the conflagration that had already lost Sandwich and was about to engulf all the castles facing the Downs. He was inspecting the defences of Deal castle where he and his family were quartered when, according to one royalist witness, he heard the shouts of the mutinying sailors taking over the ships at anchor off the coast. Rainsborough stood on the roof of the castle and saw Kem and other royalists marching past. Rainsborough was 'waving his Sword over his head in a threatening defyance to them'.[50] But Kem got aboard the ships and distributed money to the sailors. Not two hours before at a Council of War the captains had all sworn loyalty to Rainsborough, but they were now arrested and locked below decks. When Rainsborough reached the ships the seamen refused to let him aboard, saying that 'they were now upon other designes then they knew he would lead them on . . . and had declared themselves for the King and the Gentlemen of Kent'. Seaman Lendall was declared vice admiral. The mutineers' primary demands were in fact a direct reproduction of the Kent petition: the king should be brought to London and a Personal Treaty concluded with him; the New Model Army should be disbanded. Some declarations indicate a personal dislike of Rainsborough's pride and 'insolancy'. But beneath this lies the more fundamental hostility to the army's attempt to take the navy under its control and objections to Rainsborough's politics. The navy, the mutineers said, was being put into the hands of men who were 'not only enemies of the king and kingdom, but of the monarchy itself'. Commissions, they said, were now only given out in the name of Parliament and the army, 'leaving out the King's name'. 'Colonel Rainsborough' was, they complained, 'a man of the most destructive principles both in religion and policy and a known enemy to peace and the ancient government of this kingdom'. Some accounts have the mutineers exchanging threats with Rainsborough but others have the sailors admitting that Rainsborough had been 'a loving and Courteous Colonell to them' and assuring him he would suffer no injury. But they refused him a pinnace to take him to London and so Rainsborough, his wife Margaret, his sister Judith, his brother William's wife Margery, and an assortment of children had to escape from Deal in a Dutch fly-boat.[51]

It was a black day for the parliamentary cause and certainly Rainsborough's worst day in military service. Rainsborough's letter to Speaker Lenthall describing the mutiny began, 'My last was sad, this most sad'. And so it was. A substantial part of the fleet had sailed to Holland to serve royalist masters. The City had petitioned to have Batten restored to command even as Batten himself was working with royalist agents to spread the mutiny to Portsmouth. Rainsborough was replaced as vice admiral by the earl of Warwick, who had resigned as lord admiral under the Self-Denying Ordnance in 1645. Warwick, assisted by Captain Penrose of the *Satisfaction*, bent every effort to return the ships to parliamentary command but Samuel Kem managed to stiffen the resolve of the mutineers and keep them in the royalist camp. The events in Kent were not, however, to be the last of Rainsborough's dealings with the royalist rising in the South East. The rebels in Kent were rapidly defeated and chased out of the county by Fairfax. They crossed the Thames to land in the east of Tower Hamlets, aiming to join forces with the royalist rising in Essex. They were pursued through Bow and Stratford before joining with their allies in Essex. The whole force was eventually reluctantly admitted to Colchester, where they were besieged by Fairfax. Rainsborough, renowned for his abilities as a siegemaster, was Fairfax's second in command.[52]

Henry Marten's 'Leveller regiment'

As the counterrevolution flared into a Second Civil War, Henry Marten left London for his Berkshire estate and began to raise a military force. Its significance to the military conflict was small, in part because royalist forces in the West never came close enough to London for Berkshire to be contested as it had been in the First Civil War. But as an example of radical, popular military mobilisation, Marten's regiment holds considerable interest. Marten's aim was to raise a force that would fight 'on behalf of the people of England for the recovery of their freedom and for common justice against tyranny and oppression whatsoever'.[53] Indeed, the mysterious phrase, at least to the royalist newsbook that reported it, 'For the People's Freedom against all tyrants whatsoever' embellished the colours of the regiment.[54] William Eyre, the Leveller veteran of Ware, whom we last met at the meeting planning mutiny at Broadway in January, was organising the regiment with Marten. Eyre held lands in Pusey, Oxfordshire, which bordered Marten's estates and so both men would have known the locality and its people.[55]

Marten had been active in raising forces in his county in the First Civil War and in early June 1648 he returned home with the same aim in mind.

The County Committee first raised a regiment of foot in Reading but these were quickly sent to participate in the siege of Colchester and to garrison Wallingford and Windsor. Parliament regarrisoned Reading but instructed Marten to desist from further recruitment himself. Marten and Eyre ignored this command and proceeded to raise a regiment of horse. Another former Agitator, John Waldron, became a captain in the regiment.[56] The regiment was horsed by the simple expedient of requisitioning from the stables of the local gentry. Landowners like Lord Craven of Hampstead Marshall, Charles Garrard of Lambourne and William Jones of Welford were raided. When Garrard asked Eyre on whose authority he acted, Eyre 'laying his hand on his sword' replied, 'the same was his authority', and he took horses 'by the same authority that this informant and his father did take tithes of the parish'. Marten's regiment swiftly became notorious. In early June one newsbook reported that 'Henry Marten hath drawn to himself from the city into Berkshire and bids defiance to the House and all their messages'.[57] This was certainly true. Marten and Eyre refused all attempts by Parliament even to get them to come and account for their actions, let alone disband the regiment. By August the regiment had become even more infamous in the royalist press. *Mercurius Elenticus* reported that 'Henry Marten is resolved to level all of Berkshire . . . the greatest part of the Agitators of the Army and such others as stand for the doctrine of levelling are come unto him so that within 8 days he is wonderfully increased, being nigh 1,500 strong already'.[58]

Meanwhile Marten was practising the egalitarian ideology that he preached at this time. In his capacity as a Justice of the Peace he told jurors to refuse to take their hats off in the presence of the judges at the summer quarter sessions because 'they were the supreme authority and majesty of England'. This refusal of hat honour so impressed John Lilburne that he cited it in his treason trial the following year. William Walwyn was similarly impressed, as his later pamphlet *Juries Justified* shows. Here he praised Marten as 'a true Englishman . . . always . . . most zealous in affection of his Countries liberties', and recalled that 'upon the Bench at Redding' he desired the jury 'not to stand bare any longer, but to put on their hats, as became them, and not to under-value their Countrey, which virtually they were'. And a few weeks later Marten told the tenants of Lord Craven to refrain from paying homage to their landlord since to do so was to acknowledge 'slavery' and represented 'a badge of Norman Conquest'.[59] Professions of equality rarely go down well with the press, especially when directed to those who stand most in need of it. *Mercurius Pragmaticus* exploded that 'some thousands are become his proselytes' and they are 'well pleased as long as he tells them of the high prerogative of the people not to stand bare to him or anyone else. Thus he makes them believe they shall be kings and princes'. Marten was described, rather uninventively, as 'a right Jack Cade in declaring against king, lords, gentry, Parliament, the army all clergymen and lawyers'.[60]

Marten was, of course, well able to express his own views. And, if the Presbyterian Clement Walker is correct in attributing the pamphlet *Englands Troublers Troubled* to Marten, then he never did so more forcefully or passionately.[61] This pamphlet came out in August and is a magnificent polemic delivered in the name of 'the plaine-men of England against the rich and mightie'. It illuminates in arresting prose the condition of England in the Second Civil War and is unsparingly radical in its solutions. Basing itself on an account of the history of the Revolution from the outbreak of the Civil War, it concludes, as the Leveller pamphlets about the Well-yard meeting had done in January, that counterrevolution can only be avoided if the post-war disappointment with Parliament is addressed. There are in Parliament 'too many wolves and foxes in sheeps cloathing getting in amongst some honest men'. The Presbyterians, and Waller, Essex and Manchester, are named as responsible for the continuance of the wars because they plan to 'erect the power of the King and Lords, above that of the people in the house of Commons':[62]

> To this end, a universal rising is contrived, together with the revolting of the Navy, the Scots invasion, and the engagement at London, all at one instant, and all expressly for the same things, chiefly a Personall Treaty, and the disbanding of the Army.[63]

The disappointment with Parliament was combining with economic hardship to provide the grounds for a royalist revival. But the pamphlet rejects this perspective:

> ye think we will be so mad as to . . . joyne with such desparate enemies of God and all goodness as Goring, Rupert, Maurice or with such apostates as the Scots, to bring ourselves and our posterity into bondage and beggary . . . we look for no grapes from such thornes, nor figs from such thistles.[64]

Instead *Englands Troublers Troubled* proposes some far-reaching political measures. Until treating with the king stops, scandalising the army ceases, the Scots are withdrawn, 'the revolted Ships come be in', and trade is recovered, 'ye must hold us excused for paying any of you either rents, debts, or interest, and all enclosures of fens and Commons, ye must expect to be laid open'.[65] This was essentially a programme for economic warfare against the rich. But still more was intended:

we shall make bold with our Servants and Families to visit your rich houses, barns, butteries, cupboards and tables, with whatever else may supply our necessities, and that not by way of felony, or robbery, but in the just and usuall way of free quarter, as too many of our selves have given, both to the Kings Armies and yours . . . even for years and half years . . . so farre above our power as to make us so much unable to maintain our Families at this time.[66]

This was essentially to recommend as 'reasonable and equitable' the actions of the Wiltshire poor that Wildman had described at the Well-yard meeting and the requisitioning being carried out by Marten's regiment at precisely the moment *Englands Troublers Troubled* appeared in print.

Anticipating a hostile response, ringing prose declares, 'If ye think us too bold with you, and that the burden will be too heavy for you, then think what it is for us to be this extreamly necessitated by your malitious wilfulness, and for your own sake make an end the sooner', or else 'we shall be enforced to take a more effectual course with you'. This course of action was required because 'Ye are so rich, fat and swoln with wealth, that ye esteem far lesse of plaine men then you do of your horses or dogs which ye feed and pamper, whilst by your means such as we are enforced to starve or begg'. The pamphlet concludes by rounding on Presbyterian sympathy for the king in his 'sad and miserable condition', saying that this 'condition is too good for him, considering so many thousands and ten thousands honest people have been destroyed by his obstinate tyrannous disposition'.[67] This remarkable text, with its accurate diagnosis of popular discontent, its radical proposals for economic and political action, and its stirring and direct appeals to plebeian class instinct, was precisely the kind of ideology that was guiding the actions of Marten's Leveller regiment.

The press, especially the royalist press, was less impressed with Marten's views and his actions. *Mercurius Pragmaticus* reported in June that Marten 'preaches to the holy Tribe of Levellers, and in the Army, Come out of her my people', and so the 'smocks' to come in 'Thousands against King and Parliament, to scourge the members for their hypocrisy in voting a

King'. Marten proclaims 'No King, No Lords, No Tithes', and would that 'every mountain be brought low, and laid level with a dunghill, and all creatures as well as things, be in common'.[68] In August *Mercurius Pragmaticus* was reporting that Marten was seizing between two and fifteen horses from 'stable and plough' alike. The Commons was said to be receiving 'whole packets' of letters from Berkshire complaining about the actions of Marten's regiment, which had raised a 'Standard and Colours . . . and glorified it with the learned motto For the People; and one Major Eyre is joined with him as his partner and Privie-Councellor'.[69]

Interestingly, even the hostile press had to concede that Marten 'wanted not Advocates enough in the House' even while the Commons majority demanded that 'he and Eyre should come up to the House' and agree to disband the regiment and return the requisitioned horses. But Marten and Eyre refused and continued 'perfecting the Design according to the new-model of the Levelling Reformation'. Later the same week there were 'fresh complaints against Harry Marten' for robbing the highway and plundering Sir Humphrey Foster's house. The raid on Sir Humphrey Foster's house was conducted by Eyre, who first withdrew his force of about a dozen troopers when Sir Humphrey showed him Fairfax's order that his house be protected. But later Eyre returned with between sixty and eighty men and, with swords and pistols drawn, interrupted a dinner party then in progress, injuring the bulter. Eyre took eight horses and equipment and quartered half his troop at the hall overnight. He also treated the dinner party to 'uncivil speeches towards the Parliament'.[70]

Nor was it denied that Marten had some popular support. *Mercurius Elencticus* warned, 'I promise you the People are much taken with the Hinges he moves on'. And it saw his activities as a direct riposte to the negotiations with the king taking place at Newport on the Isle of Wight: 'whatever is done at Newport: Harry Marten is resolved to levell all Berkshire'.[71] *Mercurius Pragmaticus* thought Marten could raise 'six score thousand men for the maintenance of these principles'.[72] *Mercurius Melancholicus* mocked Marten as the 'Generalissmo of all the Smock petticoats in his new erected Empire of Berkshire' and as 'a Proselite of the new translation, which is to say a Leveller'. But it also saw the threat of popular mobilisation, saying that Marten's opponents in Parliament, 'the mighty Bashawes of Basileopolis', seeing the 'dangerous consequences' that 'their power would be fly-blown and so shortly corrupt and stink in the noistrills of the people . . . hath sent forth certaine Troops of their Janisaries' to take on Marten's regiment. But Marten is resolved 'to spit defiance in the teeth of all Authority, rather than desert the glorious worke of the Levell-Reformation'.[73]

This force of janissaries was sent by the Common's executive body, the Derby House committee, on 21 August under the command of Major Fincher.[74] Derby House told the committees of the surrounding counties that Marten, Eyre and Waldron had committed 'great outrages' and that they were to provide additional troops for Fincher. These were commanded 'to proceed to the suppression of those forces under Col. Marten and the rest. The horses you take from them, which they have taken from the country, you are to see restored to their former owners'.[75] Fincher, however, was at first unable to make contact with Marten's regiment because they had left Berkshire heading north. But on Monday 31 August an engagement did take place in which Marten's troops came off worst.[76] The *Perfect Weekly Account* reported, 'Major Fincher hath dispersed and taken above 100 men under Col. Martin and Col. Ayres and hopes to give a good account of the rest, there not being fifty left of them in a body'.[77] But the hopes of Marten's opponents were being raised too soon.

The next day Fincher pursued Marten's forces into Leicestershire, but here 'Col. Martin fell upon his forces, routed them and took some prisoners, but rallying again, did some execution on Major Fincher's men'.[78] Marten's troops then moved towards Market Harborough, 'which put the Market people into great fear, some running one way, and some another'. But, 'upon the Levellers perceiving this, made a Proclamation neer the Swan, and at the Crosse, That no violence or wrong should be executed upon any, neither would they in the least disturb or hinder the Market'. Even a hostile report from ejected minister William Turvil had to admit that the Leveller regiment 'deport themselves with far more civility than formerly'. This was a result of Marten's orders that 'no souldier whatsoever shall care to plunder or use violence against any, but they behave themselves civilly, executing nothing contrary to order'. And on this basis, Turvil warned, they would 'grow very numerous, if not timely suppressed', because their 'new design of levelling' had 'by their strange, politick, and subtill delusions' found its way into 'the hearts of divers people to ingage with them, especially, amongst those who are of desperate fortune, and mean condition, the basest and vilest of men'.[79]

Meanwhile the unlucky Fincher seems to have been getting into difficulties with both his supposed allies and his masters in Derby House. Lieutenant Colonel Kelsey at Oxford refused to send troops to aid Fincher without a direct order from Fairfax, earning him a stinging rebuke from the Derby House committee.[80] An only slightly less intemperate reprimand was handed out to Fincher himself, who seems to have lost track of the forces under Eyre:

> We . . . understand that Col. Eyre and his troop are gone out of the counties to which you were sent. It was not intended that you should stay there to defend the country against him but to suppress him wherever you should find him; but seeing he has escaped thence and you know not where he is, so after three or four days carrying there, if you have no further news of him or of his return thither, we desire you then to return hither to your charge.[81]

This was not going well, at least from the government's point of view. Some allies were unresponsive, Fincher's forces had won one engagement but lost another, and now Eyre's troops had escaped into a not wholly unsupportive countryside. By October Fincher had been reassigned to other duties.[82] In fact Marten's regiment was never suppressed and never disbanded. The Commons voted to amalgamate it into the New Model Army in early 1649 and Marten was recompensed for the cost of raising it. Richard Overton thought that this was a manoeuvre to end the regiment's radical influence. If so, it was a ploy that failed, for in April 1649 the Wiltshire committee were still complaining of the 'ill-carriage of Coll. Martins Regiment in this County' and the 'greate oppression and outrages' that these troops were committing in Whitchurch and the area around. Within weeks of this letter being sent, Marten's troops, including William Eyre, were to join the Leveller-inspired Burford mutiny.[83]

The Moderate

The impact of Leveller organisation was significantly increased by the appearance of weekly newsbooks strongly supportive of their cause. This was new, not just for the Levellers but also for the history of radical political organisation as a whole. The Levellers has already mastered the arts of the printed pamphlet and the printed petition over the course of the last six years, but until mid-1648 they did not have a regular weekly publication.

Before the Long Parliament newspapers were restricted to reporting foreign news and even these were banned by the Star Chamber in 1632. This order was revoked in 1638 when two booksellers, Nicholas Bourne and Nathaniel Butter, who had previously produced these 'corantos', were licensed to produce newsbooks once more.[84] In November 1641, as censorship broke down, the first eight-page, weekly newsbook containing domestic stories appeared. The snappily named *Heads of Severall Proceedings* was made up of news from both Houses of Parliament.[85] This was new, indeed shockingly radical. Many other newsbooks—royalist, Presbyterian and Independent—followed.

In 1643 Parliament made one of its more determined efforts to check unlicensed printing. This restriction had more effect on those producing weekly publications than it did on printers of one-off pamphlets. It is a difficult task to produce an illegal pamphlet, but it is much more difficult to produce an illegal regular weekly newspaper. As a result, most newsbooks registered their title to comply with the new rules. John Dillingham's *Parliamentary Scout* was the first to do so, but others soon followed. This may be an important part of the reason why the Levellers were relatively slow to produce a weekly newspaper, as the origins of *The Moderate* proved.

It seems to have been a conflict over licensing that first allowed *The Moderate* to publish. Licensing was a battleground throughout the Revolution. From 1645 to 1646 the Presbyterians seemed to have had 'a tyranny over the press'.[86] In the midst of the post-war battle for supremacy between king, Presbyterians and Independents in March 1647 Parliament revoked their delegation of newsbook censorship from the army, where it had been in the hands of Thomas Fairfax's secretary John Rushworth and his assistant Gilbert Mabbot. In September 1647, as Royalist material flourished, Fairfax protested and Mabbot was reinstated.[87] But the flood of royalist mercuries continued as the Second Civil War loomed.

By 1648 John Dillingham was producing a title called the *Moderate Intelligencer*. Dillingham, previously associated with Oliver St John's Middle Group, expressed sentiments sympathetic to John Lilburne. Mabbot refused to licence Dillingham and in the interim a counterfeit *Moderate Intelligencer* appeared, using Dillingham's printer Robert White, with whom he was also in dispute. Dillingham protested to the Lords and they upheld his complaint. Dillingham moved to another printer and continued to publish the *Moderate Intelligencer*. Meanwhile, White continued to publish his counterfeit under the abbreviated title *The Moderate*. It was a misnomer that so offended one early reader that he amended his copy so that it read 'im*Moderate* rogue'.[88] It is a joke that has run for some centuries and seems in no danger of extinction. Out of this tangled web, and possibly only out of such a tangled web, a Leveller newsbook was born.

Mabbot is often cited as the editor of *The Moderate*, but the evidence is not conclusive.[89] While it is true that Mabbott was sympathetic to radicals in his licensing policy and had allowed the publication of the *Agreement of the People*, these are positions that are compatible with radical Independency as well as with Levellerism.[90]

The Moderate cultivated its personality through a series of attention-grabbing front-page editorials. From the outset it campaigned against the monarchy and in favour of bringing the king to trial. It reproduced the petitions that sought to destroy the prospects of a Personal Treaty, and thus reinforced the mass petitioning campaign both in the counties and in the army aimed at preventing the king from being taken to London. In this it reflected the joint aims of the Leveller–Independent bloc which emerged as the vehicle for a radical solution to the political crisis in the second half of 1648. After the victory of this project *The Moderate* sided with the Levellers against the Independents in early 1649. *The Moderate* was cowed by the Leveller defeats of mid-1649 and ceased publication in September 1649.[91]

From the moment of its launch *The Moderate* was an explicit organ of the Leveller movement and was recognised as such by contemporaries. One saw it as 'a friend of the Levellers, and not to Cromwell'.[92] It began, like the *Moderate Intelligencer*, with twelve pages and much foreign news. After three issues it reoriented, beginning again with a new issue 1 which was cut back to eight pages and it moved its publication date from Thursday to Tuesday. In its sixth issue it introduced its characteristic Leveller editorial. These editorials would often start with an arresting aphorism designed to draw in the reader. 'There is nothing so secretly hid, but time and truth will reveal it', readers were told in issue 7; 'Opportunities neglected are manifest tokens of folly', they learnt in issue 9; 'Where the peoples judgements are rectified, the Traytors purposes are prevented', argued the opening line of issue 11; number 19 opened with 'No man lives happily if he want the freedom of liberty, because slavery is the greatest evil'; number 20 was more direct: 'All Governments come originally from the People, and are mutable at their pleasure'.[93]

The paper really found both editorial and campaigning focus with the launch of the Levellers' Large Petition in September. The movement thus provided the paper with its rationale rather than the other way round. *The Moderate* printed the entirety of the petition and many of the subsequent county and army petitions that were based on it. Its editorials were relentless in pursuing the themes, already familiar from Leveller material in 1648, that the political crisis would result in victorious royalism if the needs of the poor and the disappointments of Parliament's best supporters were not met with a sustained radical solution involving bringing the king to justice and settling the nation along the lines of the Large Petition, itself an extensive reformulation of the *Agreement of the People*.[94] The editorial of issue 20 described hereditary monarchy as 'against the law of God, nature and reason'. The 'arbitrary power of the King', argued the editorial in issue 19, 'was first gained, and since maintained by the sword'. Issue 17's editorial argued that 'never any law was granted for the advantage of the people of this Nation, but when their Prince was forced to grant it by the sword . . . or for some advantage to himself'.[95]

The Moderate spoke in the name of, and to, the 'well affected', of which the Levellers were the most forward element. It spoke against the 'chiefest Peers' and the 'Popish and Royal Faction' who for 'fifteen years together vassalize and enslave the people by Monopolies, Ship-money' and other taxes. These enemies keep the people in ignorance by enforcing the Book of Common Prayer, using the bishops to 'silence Preaching Minsters' and to 'Preach down Puritans'. More generally the Scots and all those in favour of a treaty were enemies. This included 'all the Kings party that consists of Rebels, Papists, Monopolizers, Dammee Cavaliers, Whoremasters, Drunkards, Villains, &c. besides many of the Episcopall and Presbyterian Clergy'.[96]

If *The Moderate* had a watchword during this period it was *Salus Populi Suprema Lex*, the safety of the people is the highest law.[97] 'What earthly Principalities or Powers which the people have chosen for their own good, can injoyn them to obedience in things destructive and unlawful? Is not *Salus populi Suprema Lex*, the peoples safety the Supreme Law?'[98] The same motto, accompanied by the picture of a severed monarch's head, appeared on the battle flag of the troop captained by Leveller William Rainsborough, Thomas's brother. For *The Moderate* this maxim applied to Parliament as well as to the monarch if the people's representatives breached their trust.[99]

No other paper launched anything like this attempt to get across a programmatic message, or backed it up with relentless editorial support. By the late summer and autumn of 1648 *The Moderate* was regarded as *the* radical news-sheet.[100] It best reflected the actions of the Levellers, Sectaries and radicals in the army but, like any newspaper, it had a readership outside both its geographical and its social heartlands. It is perhaps a sign of how seriously its ideas, and those of the movement to which it was aligned, were taken that it was read by enemies as well as friends. Sir John Gell sent newspapers to his family in Derbyshire with the explicit recommendation that 'Sir Cornelius see the *Moderates*'. The earl of Bath read *The Moderate*. The earl of Leicester was a regular reader, though he thought it should 'not be tolerated in any Christian state, nor even amongst the heathen'.[101]

Some historians have argued,'The political thought of the *Moderate* is neither startling nor original in many of its aspects. Much of what the paper had to say about government, the people, God, and their mutual relations was built on political commonplaces'.[102] But that is not how contemporaries saw it. The earl of Leicester railed that *The Moderate* 'endevours to invite people to overthrow all propriety, as the original cause of sin; and by that to destroy all government, magistracy, honesty, civility, and humanity'.[103] Of course the earl was scaremongering. But that is not the usual reaction to something that one finds 'neither startling nor original'. Even *The Moderate's* more conservative formulations would have led the writers to the Tower, if not Tyburn, a mere eight years since. In 1648 people were still fighting and dying in every corner of the country over precisely these issues. Further, *The Moderate* was primarily intended as a popular intervention aiming to alter the course of a fast-developing political crisis.[104] And the use of a newsbook for these purposes by a defined political organisation was both startling and original.

In the midst of a Presbyterian-inspired and popular demand for a Personal Treaty with the king, *The Moderate* aimed to rally the forces of the Revolution in a moment of crisis. With less reservation than some Leveller leaders it campaigned for Charles to be brought to justice and for some kind of popular rule to replace the existing state. Of course no newspaper could exactly sum up the Leveller movement in the dynamic environment of the Revolution. And a newspaper must, in a way that an individual pamphlet or petition does not have to, pay attention to a wider spectrum of views among its intended audience. It can, and *The Moderate* did, reflect the alliances that the Levellers made as well as their programmatic statements. But, even when all this is taken into account, *The Moderate* was of a piece with the entire direction of Leveller political activity in the critical months of 1648.

The counterrevolution in mid-1648

Looking back, some historians have been inclined to dismiss the threat of counterrevolution in 1648, seeing it a series of isolated military risings in which royalist forces were weaker than in the First Civil War. And of course the counterrevolution was ultimately defeated. But this cannot have been how it appeared to those living through these events in the middle of 1648. And neither can the eventual defeat of the royalist thrust be taken to mean that its defeat was inevitable. Certainly, viewed from the middle months of the year the prospect of imminent defeat hung over the parliamentary cause.

It is not just that Parliament faced military risings in Wales, Kent, Essex and the North. The Scots had invaded and a substantial part of the navy had revolted and gone over to the royalists. London was at boiling point and dangerously close to, and linked with, the revolts in Kent, Essex and other home counties. Fairfax's supply trains to Colchester had to avoid London after one of them was attacked. Some Londoners had made their way to Colchester to fight for the royalist cause. As one news-sheet noted, all eyes were on London.

And beneath all this lay a deep war-weariness amongst the population at large and a profound disappointment amongst some of Parliament's most active supporters over the failure to settle the nation on a more democratic basis. And beneath all that lay an economic crisis and a 'decay of trade', the ceaseless complainants about which echoed from every broadsheet, newssbook and petition, whether parliamentarian or royalist. The most popular immediate cure for this condition was the end of free quarter and wartime taxation which often reduced itself to the demand to disband the New Model Army. Some disbandment had taken place in the early part of the year, leaving forces depleted when the Second Civil War broke out.

The end of the war did not lessen the political danger. Parliament remained under Presbyterian control and the clamour for a Personal Treaty with the king was sustained into the late summer and autumn. Moderate domination of Parliament, exhaustion in victory and remaining popular discontent kept the prospect of the return of the king very much alive. Vacillation among the parliamentary grandees in the Commons and in the Army meant that a more radical solution was still far from inevitable, despite the increasing anger at 'the man of blood' among the army militants and the plebeian radicals. It was at this critical juncture that the Leveller organisation, which, against the grain of national politics, had strengthened itself and sustained its links with the army militants, began a new campaign greater than any that had gone before. And at just this moment John Lilburne, imprisoned alongside John Wildman for their part in the Well-yard meeting since January, now walked free from the Tower.

CHAPTER 12

Revolution

In a political sense the Second Civil War divided the nation more than the first, even though the military conflict was much shorter. It was in essence a counterrevolution. As the Scots invaded, making common cause with royalists in the North; as the Kentish rebels crossed the Thames and sheltered in besieged Colchester; and as the mutinous ships came under Prince Charles's command—the Revolution was in danger. In addition to the military threat was a political threat in the capital that made the situation more dangerous for the parliamentary cause than at any time since Naseby.

Presbyterians sympathetic to the Scots programme of Church government, without toleration of dissent, and who favoured the disbandment of the army and peace with the king were powerful in the Commons. The House of Lords was dominated by a peace party and, as the expelled Presbyterian MPs like Denzil Holles and William Waller returned over the summer, their co-thinkers gained further ascendency in the Commons as well. As a result the City felt confident enough to withhold taxes from the army and again attempted to wrest control over the Trained Bands and the Tower into their own hands. By mid-summer the Common Council elected staunch Presbyterians as sheriffs while the high Presbyterian and royalist sympathiser Francis West was commander of the Tower.[1]

In the heart of the City open recruitment for royalist forces was being carried out in front of the Royal Exchange with, at least, the seeming forbearance of the City government. This muster provided a stream of young men, organised by royalist agents like Sir Thomas Lunsford, to reinforce centres of resistance in Maidstone, Kingston, Colchester and

Pontefract. In July, when a detachment of horse was sent to arrest the royalist recruiters at the Exchange, a large crowd gathered and managed to free four of the seven that were in custody. A man suspected of being a New Model soldier had to run for his life as a crowd chased him into his inn. Soldiers were derided in the streets as 'King Fairfax' bastards'.[2] Parliamentary forces were attacked within the walls. An ammunition train was overturned in Walbrook and another supply train attacked by apprentices in Cheapside. After that Fairfax's supply wagons avoided the City. Some sixty officers from the Trained Bands demanded that the king be brought to London and that they be given the power to raise their own cavalry.[3]

Resistance to the counterrevolution came from the Derby House committee, the Commons executive, and the radicals in the Commons and the army. Major General Phillip Skippon was charged with leading the parliamentary opposition to the forces of reaction. He laboured long and hard through the summer and autumn of 1648 to disrupt royalist recruitment, subdue counterrevolutionary plots and keep Fairfax supplied.[4]

Skippon's actions increasingly had to mobilise the plebeian supporters of Parliament inside the City. The City elders accused the major general of enlisting servants and apprentices in 'a clandestine way at unseasonable times in the night . . . tending to the raising of tumults'. It was claimed that he was enlisting religious Sectaries like Coleman Streeter John Goodwin and the Independent ally of the Levellers Mark Hildesley. At the same time, a thousand men from Aldgate, Bishopsgate, Whitechapel and Shoreditch, where the radicals were strong, petitioned Skippon to be allowed to appoint their own officers to command them.[5] It was at this point that Lilburne was freed from the Tower to rejoin the fray.

The struggle begins

On 1 August 1648 the Levellers delivered to Parliament a petition for the release of John Lilburne from the Tower, signed by 10,000 people.[6] On the day, 'The House being informed, that divers Citizens, and others, were at the Door', the petition was read after the petitioners withdrew. The House then voted that 'the Order of Restraint of Colonel John Lilbourne be taken off, and discharged'. In the wake of this most immediately effective of all the Leveller petitions the Lords agreed the following day and Lilburne walked free.[7]

The Presbyterians in Parliament had their reasons for freeing Lilburne. They thought, given his animosity towards Cromwell, that his liberty would work to their advantage.[8] *Mercurius Pragmaticus* praised Lilburne's 'late moderation', which had convinced the 'moderate party of both houses' to join 'together against Cromwell's Faction' and so voted for Lilburne to be freed. *Pragmaticus* predicted that 'seeing honest John is got loose 'twill not be long ere Mr Speaker and Nol Cromwell be both brought to the stake, I can tell you; for he means to have bout with them to some purpose'.[9] On Lilburne's own account, he was 'earnestly solicited to it again and again, and might have had money to boot', if he had joined the attack against Cromwell.[10]

But the Presbyterians and *Pragmaticus* had read Lilburne wrong. Sensible of what was at stake in the war, he 'scorned' attacking Cromwell and 'rather applied my hand to help him up again'. Leveller and Agitator Edward Sexby was sent north to Cromwell, then facing the invading Scottish army, with a letter that Lilburne wrote on 3 August. He wrote that if he had 'desired revenge for an hard imprisonment', he could 'of late had the choice of twenty opportunities to have payd you to the purpose'. But, he continues, he is 'no staggerer from my first principles that I engaged my life upon' and would not attack Cromwell 'when you are low'. Sexby reported to Lilburne that Cromwell found the letter 'not a little welcome'.[11] The exchange opened a period of uneasy but effective cooperation between the Levellers and the radical Independents. This became more intense as the Second Civil War drew to a close and with the increasing threat that the moderate majority in the Commons would conclude a treaty with the king.

The New Model Army's victory at Preston between 16 and 18 August marked the beginning of the end of the Second Civil War. William Rainsborough, Thomas's younger brother, fought at Preston and Edward Sexby was sent by Cromwell to bring news of the victory to the House of Commons. Just as the war had been as bitterly divisive a struggle as the First Civil War, so the contest for political power that followed was correspondingly hard-fought. The Levellers were in the van of those demanding there be no treaty with the king and that the nation be settled in 'a democraticall spirit' based on the view that 'the supreme power is seated in our selves', as one critic of the Levellers put it.[12] Lilburne turned his hand to agitation against the appeasers:

> being at liberty, not liking in the least the several juglings of divers great ones in reference to a personall Treaty, and that there was nothing worth

praising . . . by the Parliament in reference to the Peoples Liberties or Freedoms . . . I was compelled in conscience to have a hand in that most
excellent of Petitions of 11 of Septermb. 1648.[13]

This was the so-called Large Petition or, to give it its full title, the *Humble
Petition of divers wel affected Persons inhabiting the City of London,
Westminster, the Borough of Southwark, Hamlets and places adjacent.*
Probably written by John Lilburne and William Walwyn, it compressed
into a single document an analysis of the threats to the Revolution
combined with the demands of the *Agreement of the People.* In many ways
the petition is as comprehensive an account of what the Levellers stood for
as anything they ever wrote. When it was presented to Parliament it was
said to have gathered 40,000 signatures. To force the message home the
Levellers organised a demonstration to attend its presentation at
Westminster. And on 13 September the crowd that gathered outside
Parliament 'became so bold as to clamour at the very Door against such
Members as they conceived cross to their Designs; and said they resolved
to have their large petition taken into consideration before a Treaty [with
the king]; that they knew no Use of a King or Lords any longer'. The Large
Petition was the great original on which pattern were drawn many of the
subsequent petitions from localities and from the army that countered the
pro-treaty petitions over the coming months.[14]

The Second Civil War had radicalised the army and the Levellers were
again drawing closer to those Independents who had opposed them at the
Putney debates and the rendezvous at Ware. The Large Petition was therefore better disposed to the army while remaining harshly critical of the
Parliament that had now withdrawn the Vote of No Addresses and was
attempting to conclude a treaty with the king. The petition insisted that 'the
safety of the People is above the law' and that 'most of the oppressions of
the Common-wealth have in all times bin brought upon the people by the
King and Lords'. And it held Parliament responsible because,

to our exceeding grief, we have observed that no sooner God vouchsafeth
you victory . . . but according as ye have bin accustomed, passing by the
ruine of the Nation, and all the bloud that hath bin spilt by the King and his
Party, ye betake your selvs to a Treaty with him.[15]

The petition went on to outline the Levellers' political demands, repeating
the democratic demands enshrined in the *Agreement of the People*

presented at Putney the previous year. The petition also included a considerable number of economic demands: an end to monopolies, abolition of excise, the laying open of recent land enclosures, relief for those imprisoned for debt, measures to relieve beggars and abolition of tithes, while making sure to allay fears that they intended to level all property. Towards the end of the Large Petition the authors return to its opening theme, calling for the trial of the king. The petitioners expected of the Commons,

> That you would have done Justice upon the Capitall Authors and Promoters of the former or late Wars, many of them being under you power: Considering that mercy to the wicked, is cruelty to the innocent: and that all your lenity doth make them more insolent and presumptuous.[16]

In the wake of the success of the Large Petition the Levellers mounted their largest-ever campaign to drive the course of national politics away from a treaty with the king and towards the adoption of the *Agreement of the People*.[17]

The Levellers were not alone in their fears of the restoration of the king or in pushing for a radical political outcome.[18] By early September the radical Independent Colonel Ludlow had already visited Ireton at the siege of Colchester to encourage him to act against the king. It is possible that Rainsborough, who was also at Colchester, was at least aware of the meeting. But the fulcrum of Cromwell and Ireton's influence was the Council of Officers of the New Model Army. And this body, unlike the Levellers, was divided over whether to make a treaty with the king. Even Ireton, at the time he met with Ludlow, did not want to act before a treaty was concluded between Parliament and the king. Ludlow records,

> I went to Commissary General Ireton . . . we both agreed that it was necessary for the army to interpose in this matter, but differed about time; he being of the opinion, that it was best to permit the King and Parliament to make an agreement, and to wait till they had made full discovery of their intentions, whereby the people becoming sensible of their own danger, would willingly join to oppose them.[19]

Although much work has been done to illuminate the ways in which Ludlow's manuscript was rewritten by his editors, there seems little that directly throws doubt on this incident.[20] Certainly the views attributed to Ireton by Ludlow are congruent with other accounts of his outlook at this time.

By 27 September, however, Ireton had become convinced that action was necessary to prevent the restoration of the king. On that day he wrote a long letter to Fairfax expressing this view.[21] But Fairfax was opposed to any radical action. In response, Ireton withdrew from the army headquarters to Windsor and, subsequently, tendered his resignation (a 'pretended' resignation, said Lilburne[22]). According to *Mercurius Pragmaticus*, It was the negotiations between Parliament and the king that were 'the true cause, why Ireton left the Head-Quarters, and retired to Windsor'.[23]

Although his resignation was not accepted, Ireton could find no way forward. Instead he began work on the document that would become the *Remonstrance of the Army* during his stay in Windsor even though he knew it would be rejected by Fairfax and the high command of the New Model Army. Only pressure from below on the Council of Officers and on MPs could radically change this situation. The Levellers were invaluable in such a campaign.

The demands within the Large Petition were now being reproduced in letters and petitions that began to flow into army headquarters. They, in turn, were reprinted in the Leveller press. Agitators reappeared in at least two regiments and they were demanding that the Council of the Army be recalled. By late October 'most regiments were in a dangerous political condition', according to Ian Gentles.[24] And, at about the same time as Ireton was writing to Fairfax, Sexby was heading north for another meeting with Cromwell. On Sexby's report to Lilburne, Cromwell was 'begging with tears in his eyes a conjunction of the honest nicknamed Levellers once again, and he would never oppose more the honest things they stood for, but adhear to them; and in the North at this time laid them to his very bosome'.[25]

Gradually, with Cromwell's blessing, Ireton moved towards cooperation with the Levellers. In January Ireton had called for a settlement that included the king; now he moved to enact one without the consent of the monarch. To accomplish this he needed to rebuild the links with the Levellers that had been severed at Putney and Ware. He had little choice given that he was caught between the Leveller-assisted pressure from the army remonstrances and the opposition of the officers of the army.[26]

Over the next few months the Levellers were crucial to the defeat of the counterrevolution's last political offensive. They were capable of playing a decisive role for two reasons. First, their political judgement of the threats and possibilities inherent in the situation was largely accurate. Second, they commanded sufficient organisation of a kind that no other political actor possessed and which was capable of acting effectively. Indeed, in mid-summer 1648 the Levellers were probably stronger than they had ever been. Soon the existing Leveller news-sheet, *The Moderate*, was joined by another, *Mercurius Militaris, or the Army's Scout*.

Mercurius Militaris, or the Army's Scout

Mercurius Militaris was even sharper in tone and more militant in rhetoric, but shorter-lived, than *The Moderate*. It appeared five times at the very height of the Revolutionary crisis between October and November 1648 and it was edited by John Harris, who had been the operator of the army's secret press in the previous year and had also been a pamphleteer in the Leveller cause.[27] Perhaps it was Harris's former employment as an actor which gave the *Mercurius Militaris* its sense of timing, because it certainly made its entrance just at the moment when the tide for a Personal Treaty needed turning.[28]

Mercurius Militaris was, unlike *The Moderate*, unlicensed—and so was its prose. The humour was mocking and the phrases were memorable. Its first issue explained to readers that news of soldiers was still important because 'now their lives are secured they are to attend to their Work, which we may all remember was, *To Set the People Free*'. Harris was virulently anti-monarchical. This characteristic satire of both King Charles and Denzil Holles is simultaneously a precise picture of the political dilemma facing radicals in late 1648 and proof positive that Harris's previous profession as an actor made him the master of the 'Leveller style':

> What virtue unknown is in his subscription Carolus Rex? Why is this name adored more then another? Write that and Denzil Hollis together, is it not as fair a name? Sound them, doth it not become the mouth as well? Weigh them, is it not as heavy? Conjure with them, Denzil Holles will start a spirit as soon as the name Carolus Rex; and yet this meer puff of breath, this powerless name King Charles set so high in the vulgars hearts, that what would be vice in others, his name like richest Alchemy, change to vertue and worthiness; and the subscribing of his name to that which he can neither promote nor hinder, must set him above his Masters and Conquerors, and permit him to bestride this narrow world like a Colossus, when you victors must walk like petty slaves, and peep about under his huge legs to find your selves dishonourable graves.[29]

Mercurius Militaris was scathing about the monarchy. Harris could see the father's likeness in the son since both James I and Charles I believed in the principle 'no bishop, no king'. But he still doubted that James 'begot' Charles because 'I cannot tell how King Charles could be so sober'. It was also consistent in sustained opposition to the Personal Treaty as the last hope of the defeated cavaliers: "Their strength is spent, now, now, they cry, / Hold Treaty, hold, or else we dye."[30] Harris was as happy to insult Presbyterians as Independents. Commenting on the continuing stand-off between the revolted ships under Prince Charles and the parliamentary navy under Rainsborough's replacement the earl of Warwick, Harris wrote,

> Methinks it puts me in mind of two London Cheats that must pretend to fight, yet are glad that any will interpose, and yet they rage desperately to make the Croud bigger, that their third fellow may the better cut a purse.[31]

Readers might guess what was ahead when the second issue asked on its first page, 'Didst ever know a Tyrant or a King, that was content the people's eyes should be opened? It's against their interest; if the horse his eyes be not blinded, he will never grind the mill'.[32] When the Lords voted that the king should come to London in safety to negotiate a treaty *Militaris* wrote, 'this makes me think the King is an Alchemist and the Lords are his Mercury . . . he can make them dance the Philosophical circle four or five times an hour, like an Ape through a hoop, or a Dog in a wheel'.[33] *Militaris* cried out at the apostates in the parliamentary camp and called directly for the king's blood.[34] Parliaments were in any case 'but a delegated or entrusted power themselves, and therefore cannot delegate or transmit their power over to another'—and certainly not to the king, who was 'a Traytor, and a Murderer and Robber of the People'.[35]

In addition to news, the pages contained petitions supportive of the Levellers from Wiltshire, Gloucester, Oxford, Suffolk, York, Newcastle and Somerset. A successful revolt of soldiers against disbandment in Wiltshire was retold, as was a small mutiny in Ireton's regiment.[36] Wildman and Lilburne's exploits were reported, particularly Lilburne's clash with Prynne in defence of the poor of Wiltshire, which was covered both with glee and in some detail.[37] *Militaris* loved to pillory its royalist rivals *Mercurius Pragmaticus*, or *Prag* in the conventional shorthand used by Harris, and *Mercurius Elencticus*. *Militaris* delighted in telling *Elencticus* that 'his poor Majesty cannot find a Cabs noddle dark enough to hammer the Chain in for the people'.[38] 'Cabs' was a widespread demeaning contraction of 'cavalier' and Harris used it practically without exception. 'Noddle' was a favourite Harris term for the heads of those he thought dim-witted, be they royalist or Independent. In *Mercurius Militaris* we hear most clearly echoing down the centuries the voice of the troopers, apprentices and small masters, the 'well affected' and radical preachers, the mercury women and the poor of the counties, who looked to the Levellers. We hear how they talked of their enemies and what they thought of their sometime allies. Polished by a highly skilled writer certainly, but still authentic.

It could not last. Royalist opponents reported that in the last 'weeke there were no lesse then twentie State-Beagles Hunting after' Harris[39] In verse Harris agreed that the beagles numbered twenty but in prose he allowed it might only be ten. But whatever the number they caused him to miss a week in publication before the final edition came out. He knew the game was up, as he described in verse across the front page,

> Who ever dares discover Knaves in power,
> Must not enjoy his next succeeding hour;
> The Crimes of State, if any, Crimes dare call,
> He but prepares for his own funeral.
> Last week even twenty Beagles from the State,
> Pursued this Mercury with mortal hate.
> Where's that Rogue (said they) who dare speak Reason,
> When Cries for justice are voted Treason?[40]

John Harris fought on after the closure of *Militaris* in November 1648. In a remarkably apposite political moment he was present at the very event that *Militaris* had long argued was a necessity. On the day that Charles I was executed, John Harris, with a half-pike in hand, served with fellow radical Richard Rumbold as a guard on the scaffold.[41] Perhaps it was *Mercurius Militaris*'s statement that the 'children of kings are all born with crowns upon their heads and the people with saddles on their backs' that Richard Rumbold was recalling when, thirty-seven years later, he said on his own gallows 'none comes into the world with a saddle upon his back, neither any booted and spurred to ride him'.

Thomas Rainsborough's last fight

Once again, but for the last time, Thomas Rainsborough was at the heart of political developments. Royalist animosity towards Rainsborough was at an all-time high as a result of events at the end of the siege of Colchester. Fairfax's victorious troops entered the Essex city on 28 August. The besieged royalists inside the walls had previously dismissed three offers of quarter. As a result Fairfax's council of war, which included Commissary General Henry Ireton, Colonel Whalley and Rainsborough, met and decided that two royalist commanders, Sir Charles Lucas and Sir George Lisle, should be executed. When the city fell, Rainsborough acted as one of the commissioners who agreed the articles of surrender.[42] Whalley, Ireton and Rainsborough were charged with ensuring that the verdict of the council of war be carried out, although it was Ireton who seems to have been most closely associated with the actual execution, involving himself in a lengthy argument with Lucas about the judicial basis of the execution.[43] The royalists instantly claimed Lucas and Lisle as martyrs. Fairfax and Rainsborough were demonised for their part in the killings.

The first attempt on Rainsborough's life took place only a month after the executions at Colchester, possibly in an act of vengeance. At this time the New Model Army headquarters had moved to St Albans, and shortly before he went north with orders to take over the siege of Pontefract Rainsborough was riding between London and St Albans, accompanied only by a captain. En route he was attacked by royalists.[44] On this occasion Rainsborough's bravery prevailed and he saw off his attackers. The execution of Lucas and Lisle and the attempted murder of Rainsborough were a microcosm of the banking up of hostility in the wider society.[45]

Cromwell's victory at Preston and the victory of Fairfax and Rainsborough at Colchester left Pontefract Castle the last remaining royalist stronghold in England. This important garrison had changed hands twice in the Civil War already and it was hotly contested because it was the key to the North. A siege by parliamentary forces began in July. It was commanded by Sir Edward Rodes and Sir Henry Cholmley. Cholmley was certainly not an enthusiastic parliamentarian. A year before he began the siege of Pontefract, on 8 July 1647, he wrote to the Speaker of the House of Commons outlining the problems, as he saw them, of the parliamentary cause in Yorkshire. He wrote that the Parliament had more enemies than friends in the area and that the common soldiers were 'so well agitated' by Lilburne that they were in the same condition as the soldiers in the South. He urged peace between Parliament and the army. 'Otherwise', Cholmley warned, 'Clubbs and Clouted Shoes will in the end be too hard for them both.'[46]

Cholmley's military conduct of the siege of Pontefract was of a piece with these political sentiments. Royalist raiding parties ranged far and wide through the local countryside, virtually unimpeded by Cholmley's troops. All the while Cholmley remained on the friendliest terms possible with those he besieged. *The Moderate* reported,

> The siege is managed very absurdly, if not treacherously, for the enemies horse within have increased lately from 60 to six score; besides last Friday the enemy upon a sally ruined one of the besiegers Troops, killed 8, and took the Capt. Lieut. and severall other prisoners, the 14 upon another killed 10 in the place, and carried many prisoners. They ramble out daily 8 and 10 miles into the Country, and bring in the Gentry thereof Prisoners, and other Booty, without opposition.[47]

An anonymous letter from York to Parliament, dated 28 October, gives an even more astonishing picture.

> They . . . make a Fair of their Horses near the Castle, sell them to Sir Henry Cholmleys Troopers, and in the Cessation they drink to one another, Here is to thee Brother Roundhead, and I thank thee Brother Cavalier: They have and do take much Salt, Corn; Beans, and Horses from the Country: They prepare for a better Seige.[48]

Given the condition of the siege it is not surprising that Fairfax ordered the New Model Army's foremost siegemaster to travel north to take matters in hand.[49] Rainsborough duly arrived in Doncaster, a few days after his regiment, on 14 October 1648. He immediately ran into a rearguard action, not from the royalists but from Cholmley. Rainsborough was too young, Cholmley wrote to the Speaker of the House, complaining that 'his Excellency the Lord Fairfax had given a Commission to Col. Rainsborough to command in chief before Pontefract-Castle, and that the disparagement was great to him'.[50]

The Moderate's report from Pontefract on 28 October, probably based on the York letter, brings together the themes of Cholmley's disastrous conduct of the siege and opposition from Rainsborough and soldiers to a treaty with the king:

The Inhabitants of this county say that they are worse by Sir Henry Cholmley three hundred thousand pounds . . . Sir Henry and his men buy the Oxen, Horses and plundered goods daily from the Rogues, and keep a market by the Castle . . . Sir Henry Cholmleys house but six miles off have lost nothing, though they have plundered all fifteen or twenty miles around.[51]

The following paragraph then moves immediately to this account of growing opposition within the army to a treaty with Charles:

The forces in the West, say they will not suffer themselves to be enslaved by this Malignant and Bugbear Treaty, and therefore they have already begun to draw up their desires, in relation to the freedome of the People, the good of the Kingdome, and to bring all Delinquents (without exception) to condigne punishment . . .

The report goes on to tell of similar moves in other regiments, including Rainsborough's, and of their efforts to coordinate their actions.[52] Cholmley's conduct of the siege and his antipathy to Rainsborough were known about in the high command of the army, in Parliament and in the London press. For many who were opposed to the treaty with the king, Cholmley appeared as an example of what disasters could be caused by attempting to placate the royalists or by not prosecuting action against them with sufficient zeal. Therefore one could read in the relations between Cholmley and Rainsborough a microcosm of relations between pro-treaty moderates and anti-treaty radicals.

The death of Rainsborough

Thomas Rainsborough was killed early in the morning of Sunday 29 October. He died at his lodgings in the centre of Doncaster, where he was staying while waiting for the disputed command of Pontefract's besieging forces to be resolved by Parliament. His killers were from a twenty-two-strong royalist raiding party who, with the help of a spy in Doncaster, tricked the guard placed at the entrance to the town and gained access to Rainsborough's quarters. Reports of the murder were carried in the press, especially the Leveller press.

The Moderate gave an account of events immediately before and after the killing. It claimed that the officer in charge of the guard, Captain John

Smith, was at a brothel in Doncaster all night when he was supposed to be on duty. Smith immediately fled the regiment for London, although he strongly contested the allegation in the pamphlet *The Innocent Cleared*.[53] The Commons received letters from Pontefract on 4 November which told of Cholmley's 'Horse permitting the Enemy . . . to return back again at Noon-time of the Day, and not a Pistol fired at them.'[54] *The Moderate* report repeated the news that the raiding party returned through the lines of Cholmley's forces without challenge. It went on to tell of a letter sent by the royalist governor of Pontefract to Cholmley saying 'that he had now decided the controversie about the Command for his men had left Rainsborough dead in Doncaster street'. Cholmley, said the report, 'very much laughed and rejoyced'.[55]

The mood among supporters of the Levellers may be judged from *The Moderate*. In the issue that preceded Rainsborough's funeral it was pouring out its ire on Cholmley for his 'publikely declared' view that the invading Scots army 'were his friends' 'before we routed them' and that 'this Armie his enemies . . . and that the next work they were to go upon, was to destroy this Army'. 'Therefore judge', concluded *The Moderate*, 'if the Governour and he did not lay the design to murder gallant Rainsborough'.[56] Combining opposition to a treaty with Charles and a desire for revenge on Rainsborough's killers, the issue concluded with verse:

> The Treaty's now effected, all's agreed;
> Draw, draw for Freedome, or we're slaves indeed;
> The King's upon escape, looke, looke about you,
> You'r all betry'd, and how the Cabbs then flout you.
>
> Now Cholmley laugh, and let Malignants grin,
> Yet know from hence your reckoning shall begin:
> Up then stout souls, born for the peoples good,
> Mount him to his grave, and next revenge his blood.
> For though intomb'd with Honour Rainsborow lies,
> Yet still his dust for satisfaction cries.

The call to arms in the face of imminent danger and the desire for revenge are fused into a single urgent message in this verse. *Mercurius Militaris* seems to have caught the mood most forcefully in a direct call for the execution of the king:

Shall not his bloud be doubly avenged upon the heads of such barbarous worse than brutish villaines? But the misery is there is no bloud amongst the Cabs worthy to be named in the same day the head of that crew, even his bloud, as to gallant Rainsbroughs bloud, is not better than asses; yet he being the original cause of this butchery, Upon his head the guilt must rest, no way expiated.

It was only his transcendent gallantry for his Countries freedom that caused his bloud to be thirsted after and no bloud fit to answer it, as that of the head of the Tyrants.[57]

One of the letters that brought the news of Rainsborough's death to the Houses of Parliament also contained news of the reaction of the soldiers of the New Model Army to the loss of one of their best-known and most radical officers. Dismissing the idea that the assassination of Rainsborough could be mitigated as revenge for the death of Lucas and Lisle at Colchester, the letter says,

the whole Souldiery with us lay this businesse much to heart, and although the losse of such an instrument as he, cannot be small: yet we are confident that we have this gain, that the hearts of all the well affected party in the Kingdome will be more firm in conjunction with each other . . . And as for those that are such implacable enemies to peace, and fiercely thirst after the blood of such as would live quietly in the Land, we hope care will be taken to preserve us from their malice, and to bring those to condign punishment which do justly deserve it, that they may be a terror to others from running into like mischiefs.[58]

Thus the death of Rainsborough occasioned some of the most direct calls for the execution of the king. From the first Rainsborough's death gave new force to demands that justice be served on the fomenters of the Civil War. When the Commons heard of the death of Rainsborough it immediately sent a message to Cromwell instructing him to make 'a strict and exact scrutiny of the manner of the horrible murder of Colonel Rainsborough and to certify the same to the House'.[59]

Rainsborough's death took place amidst a wider climate of fear. Accompanying the letters bringing news of Rainsborough's death was 'A List of the chiefe of the members of both Houses of Parliament, and Officers of the Army, against whom the design is discovered to take away their lives'. The plot was said to threaten the lives of eighty parliamentary leaders, including Fairfax, Cromwell, Lord Say and Sele, and Colonels Hammond, Pride, Rich, Hewson and Okey. A vote was moved to bring up an additional regiment of horse and foot to secure the House, but it was not passed because the regiments already doing the work were 'thought more fit'.[60] A few days later, however,

> The Commons spent much Time in the Debate of the Report concerning the Guarding of the House, which was clearly and unanimously concluded to be in great Danger by reason of the malignant Party, who flock up to London, and as is conceived, upon some dangerous Design at the Breach of the Treaty, most of them having Daggers and Pistols in their Pockets.[61]

Given the highly polarised politics in London at this time, the concerns of Parliament were real enough.

Royalists rejoiced at the death of Rainsborough. The following year, after the execution of Charles I, royalists were still imagining Rainsborough being tormented in hell.[62] One broadsheet pictured a dialogue held on the day of his murder between Rainsborough and Charon, the ferryman to Hades. It concluded with a justification of Rainsborough's murder based on revenge for his actions at Colchester: 'Feare not Colchesterian Dames, left Lucas 'rife; / Veng'ance is fully paid; Here Rainsb'rough lies.'[63]

The political situation after the murder of Rainsborough

A week after Rainsborough's death Cromwell was at Knottingly in Yorkshire on his way to take control of the siege of Pontefract. W. C. Abbott, the editor of Cromwell's *Writings and Speeches*, notes, 'The death of Rainsborough deepened the hatred of the army toward the King; and while Cromwell was busy with the siege of Pontefract, that idea spread from the Levellers, who had long advocated it to more moderate men.'[64] Abbott's general point is right, but he suggests that Cromwell was more passive than was in fact the case.

On 6 November Cromwell wrote to Colonel Robert Hammond, the king's chief jailer on the Isle of Wight. He urged Hammond to think on the events that Cromwell had recently witnessed in Scotland. There, said Cromwell, 'A lesser party of Parliament hath made it lawful to declare the greater part a faction'. It then dissolved Parliament by force and called a new one. 'Think of the example', urged Cromwell, 'and let others think of it too'. Cromwell also explicitly addresses Hammond's fear of an alliance with the Levellers. Hammond worried that the Levellers would destroy the nobility and was therefore sympathetic to a treaty with the king. Cromwell wrote, 'How easy it is to find arguments for what we would have; how easy to take offence at things called Levellers, and run into an extremity on the other hand, meddling with accursed things'.[65] At about the same time Cromwell met Henry Marten at York and Lilburne in Knottingly itself. Lilburne found Cromwell 'savoured more of intended self-exalting' than he was interested in 'the Liberties and Freedoms of the Nation'.[66] But Lilburne persisted in trying to coordinate the actions of the Levellers with the radical Independents. There was every need to do so because Ireton was still not able to get his *Remonstrance* past the army Grandees.

On 7 November 1648 Fairfax called a council of officers, though not the Council of the Army, thus excluding the Agitators. Meeting at St Albans, it considered Ireton's first draft of the *Remonstrance* on 10 November. Fairfax spoke against the *Remonstrance* and it was rejected. The logjam remained. On his return to London Lilburne wrote again to Cromwell, now arrived at Pontefract, to the effect that 'to our knowledge, God had caused him [Cromwell] to understand the principles of just Government, under which the glory of God may shine forth by an equall distribution unto all men' and that 'obtaining this was the sole intended end of the Warre: and that the Warre cannot be justified on any other account'. Cromwell replied by directing the Independents to meet with the Levellers, 'some of whom appointed a meeting at the Nags-head Tavern by Blackwell-Hall, and invited M. Wildman and my self, &c. thither'. This first meeting was divided over whether to 'cut off the Kings head . . . and force and thoroughly purge, if not dissolve Parliament'. Nor could it agree on whether a constitutional settlement should be decided before any action was taken, as the Levellers wanted. After debate it was agreed matters would be decided at a second meeting of representatives from both sides.[67] But this meeting would only take place after Thomas Rainsborough's funeral procession.

Rainsborough's funeral

The funeral of Thomas Rainsborough was a planned, political demonstration of the Leveller movement.[68] It was a symbolic moment of resistance against a treaty with the king. The day before the funeral a single-sided sheet, *An Elegie Upon the Honourable Colonel Thomas Rainsborough*, explicitly argued that Rainsborough's death should be understood as a providential warning against such a course:

> What if Heaven purpos'd Rainsborough's fall to be
> A prop for Englands dying Libertie?
> And did in Love thus suffer one to fall
> That Charles by Treaty might not ruine all?
> For who'l expect that Treaty should doe good
> Whose longer date commenc't in Rainsborough's blood?[69]

The verse went on to tell 'noble Fairfax' and 'bold Cromwel' that if they were to 'Conclude a peace with Charles' they would end up riding in 'robes of Scarlet' dyed in 'your own dearest blood' because 'instead of Gold' Charles would 'pay you all with steel'.

It was in this atmosphere that the date and time of Rainsborough's funeral were announced in advance in the Leveller press. *Mercurius Militaris* gave an account of the murder. Following the description of the murder it argued that 'until right be done upon his adversaries',

> I desire right may be done to his corps in rememberance that such a noble soul once possessed it; to that end I desire all in whom any sparkd of this brave soul dwel, even all the lovers of their Country, may take notice that on Tuesday next, being the 14 of Nov. about ten a clock at the latest, his honourable Corps is to be met at Tatnam-high-cross, two miles beyond Kings-land, within five miles of London, to be attended honourably into London.

Following this public call to attend the funeral, *Mercurius Militaris* sought to stir its readers with a poem extolling Rainsborough's virtues. The last lines of the poem read,

> Oh thou unkindest Fate!
> To play the Tyrant and subvert the State,
> Of setled Goddnes: Who shall hence forth stand,
> A pure example to enforme the Land
> Of her true Freedome? Who shall countercheck
> The wanton pride of Greatnes? And direct
> The Soldiers in the true, magnifck way,
> To bring the Land its long expected day?

Oh that speak forth your losse in mournfull mood,
And keen your spirits to avenge his blood.[70]

The Moderate also gave an account of Rainsborough's death, ending it with this call to arms:

Can the soldiery of this Kingdom be silent, and not revenge the barbarous murder of their incomparable Commander, the like for sea and land service never came out of the bowels of this Nation. The Lord stir up your hearts to be avenged of these bloody enemies.

And then made a public appeal to all the 'well-affected' to join the funeral procession.[71] The scale of the procession must have exceeded the Levellers' expectations, although the most detailed accounts of the funeral itself come from sources hostile to the Levellers. *Mercurius Elencticus* described Rainsborough's funeral as the event that 'crowned the day':

[Rainsbourgh's] sacred corps convayed from Doncaster, came this day to London, being met and attended on by a great number of the well affected of all Professions, Will: the Weaver, Tom the Tapster, Kit the Cobler, Dick the Doore Sweeper, and many more Apron youths of the City, who trudg'd very devoutly both before and behind this glorious Saint, with about 100 she-votresses crowded up in Coaches, and some 500 more of the better sort of Brethern mounted on Hackney beasts.[72]

Apart from conveying the scale of the procession, this account is immediately striking for the unmistakably note of snobbery that pervades the piece, giving us a glimpse of the force of class feeling engendered by the Revolution. It is also notable for the particular reference to 'she-votresses' which exhibits hostility to the participation of women in politics. The account in *Mercurius Elencticus* does, however, give us a detailed account of the route of the funeral procession:

The Body came in by way of Islington, and so through Smithfield, (where they should have burnt it) thence along Old Baily (in defiance of Newgate and the Sessions house) and under Ludgate, not through Pauls [for there the Organs stood, but on the backside of the church and so along Cheap-side. Sure they were aware of the Ground whereon the crosse was founded] and through Cornwall, in great pompe, and with a variety of sad postures;

at length they arrived at Wapping chappell, where they bestowed this precious peece of Mortality, as nigh as might be to the tombe of the Honourable and expert Skuller his father, where the Godly Party (with their hands in their pockets) lamented his untimely Grave.[73]

As a mark of official respect the cannon at the Tower were fired as the funeral took place.[74] A single-sheet poem by Thomas Alleyn, *An Elegie on the Death of that Renowned Heroe Col Rainsborrow*, was collected by Thomason on the day of the funeral itself, 14 November.[75] *Mercurius Elencticus* used Rainsborough's seafaring career as basis of a poem that celebrated how great a loss Rainsborough was to the Godly Party and how shipwrecked their project was without him. Marchmont Nedham's *Mercurius Pragmaticus* managed to combine seafaring allusion with class snobbery: 'the carkasse of Rainsborough was attended by a regiment of horse, all the tag-rags of the faction that were able to hire horses, entered at Wapping among his fellow-swabbers and skippers'.[76]

The scale of the procession was impressive. The *Moderate Intelligencer* reported, 'This day came through London the Corps of Col. Rainsborough, accompanied with very many Coaches, and neer 1,500 horse.'[77] *Mercurius Militaris* estimated the demonstration to be larger still, claiming 'fifty or sixty Caroches, and near three thousand Gentlemen and Citizens on horse-back'.[78] For the Levellers' supporters the size of the procession was not the only remarkable element of the day. The inscription on Rainsborough's tombstone at the family church in Wapping told its own story:

> He that made King, Lords, Commons, Judges shake,
> Cities, and Committees quake:
> He that fought nought but his dear Countreys good,
> And seal'd their right with his last blood.
> Rainsborow the just, the valiant, and the true,
> Here bids the noble Levellers adue.[79]

This inscription is not just testimony to the connection between Rainsborough's radical politics and the Levellers. It is also noticeable for the positive use of the term 'Leveller' by the movement itself.[80]

Another moment of symbolism from the day of the funeral also became identified with the movement: the adoption of the sea green colour as an identification of the Leveller movement. 'Azure and black' were the Rainsborough's colours. As Ian Gentles records, 'from the time of his funeral his personal colours, green and black, were adopted as the badge of the Leveller movement'.[81] A satirical attack on the Levellers in the single sheet *The Gallant Rights, Priviledges, Solemn Institutions of the Sea-Green Order* in print thirteen days after Rainsborough's funeral confirms this. Throughout the text there is great play on the novelty of the Levellers being known as the 'Sea-Green Order'. It refers to the 'Fundamental Right of the Sea-Green Order'; it tells readers that the Levellers have chosen 'deep Sea Green . . . our Flag and Colours, and do hereby ordain and authorize it to be worn as the lively badge of Constancy, Sufferance and Valour in grain, the cognizance of Justice, and the mark of Freedom and Deliverance'.[82]

In what seems likely to be a direct reference to the practice at Rainsborough's funeral, this sheet also says that 'every one so wearing our Colours in hatband, cuff, garment, bridle, mayn, or sail . . . shall hence forth, according to our Noble Order, be intitled the Free born Assistant of Justice'.[83] The practice of wearing sea green to denote association with the Leveller cause seems to have become widespread. It was worn again at the funeral of Leveller Robert Lockyer in April 1649. In May *Mercurius Militaris* was describing 'the brave Blades of the sea-green order honest Johns Lifeguard' and the 'bonny Besses, In the Sea-green dresses', who strike fear into 'Nol and his asses.'[84] And in July Richard Overton was himself writing to 'my Brethren of the Sea green Order'.[85]

This symbolism was being mobilised in pursuit of a political objective. Six days after the funeral another broadsheet was collected by Thomason. *A New Elegie in Memory of the Right Valiant, and most Renowned Souldier, Col. Rainsborough* warned of the dangers of concluding a treaty with Charles.[86] The political messages that emerged from Rainsborough's funeral were simple: no treaty, no 'apostasy' in Parliament, the king and the royalists must be brought to justice. At the family church in Wapping, which Rainsborough's father had helped to found and where he was buried, Thomas Brooks preached a sermon that reinforced these points. Brooks had been chaplin to Rainsborough's father and to Thomas himself.[87] His sermon follows the theme of what the godly must do in order to appear glorious in the sight of God. Brooks also reflects some of Rainsborough's egalitarian sentiment. He compares Rainsborough to David in his battle with Goliath. And he praises Rainsborough for persisting where others fell by the wayside:

> So men turn off the worke, it is too hard saith one, it is too high, it is too rough, it is too dangerous say others. Now to doe gloriously is to doe that

that others refuse to doe, and that others have not the heart to doe. And in this respect this thrice-honoured Champion hath done gloriously. The mountains that he hath gone over, the difficulties he was engaged in are known to thousands in this Kingdom.

And Brooks lambasted those Parliament men who were resiling from support for the radical saints. When David battled Goliath, said Brooks,

> They did not stand disputing, wee have estates to loose, and if Saul know that wee joyne with David . . . we shall lose our heads and lose our estates. The politicians of our times are wise, they will say, they wish the Saints well, but they dare not, they will not side with them. Ah wretches, God will save his Glory . . . and will deliver the righteous . . .
>
> So, if Parliament-men, and those that have power, do not side with the Saints, deliverance will come another way, but they, and their fathers house may perish.

And at a time when Rainsborough's death was being used as a justification for the trial and possible execution of the king, Brooks used his sermon to hammer home the importance of justice being done to high and low alike: 'to do gloriously, is to do Justice impartially, upon high, and low, honoura-ble, base, father, and sonne, kinsman, and brother, and that one is great, and the other is too meane for Justice; this is inglorious'.[88] The sermon was printed, Brooks tells us, because 'many precious soules' 'besieged me so strongly' that he consented although he 'had not the least thought to put it to the Presse'. No doubt some of its sentiments were common enough in sermons preached by radical independents or those sympathetic to the Levellers. But on this day, to this audience, at this particular moment in the English Revolution, it will have had a special force. After the funeral anti-royalist rioting lasted for two days.[89]

The petition war

Many of the political conflicts alluded to in Brooks's funeral sermon were stated more directly in the *Remonstrance of the regiment of the late Col. Rainsborough to his Excellency, for the revenge of their Colonells death.* This remarkable document was produced just six days after Rainsborough's funeral and it was of a piece with the wider mood in the New Model Army.

It was reprinted in *The Moderate*.[90] The regiment's remonstrance moves almost immediately to the broadest political concerns about the possibility of a treaty with the king: 'we feare we are deluded into the hopes of a safe peace, by the expectation of an unsafe Treaty'. The case against a treaty with Charles is expressed with force and brevity:

> That if the utmost purchase of the losse of so much pretious and declared righteous bloud, be onely a liberty to Treat with out Capitall Enemy, whether with his dissembled consent we shall enjoy these liberties, that the sword of the Lord, and the sword of his people have wrung from his bloudy hands, we are consigned to the most fruitless imployment, to be alwayes fighting for what we can never obtaine; Armies can subdue powers but not change minds.[91]

The *Remonstrance* goes on to announce that the regiment is 'much perplexed' that the 'late resolutions of Parliament' engaged them to 'fight with an enraged enemy' and now try to persuade them that 'all our differences can be wrapped up in the sweet compliance of a Treaty':

> And when it was declared to us, that because the King has so often attempted to inslave the Nation, by raising Armies contrary to many Protestations, he was no more to be trusted, nor no more addresses to be made unto him, and when they signified the truth of that Declaration by confederate risings of all his active parties in the Kingdome of England and Scotland, we doe much wonder from thence, there should arise any reason to invite them to new addresse.

Rainsborough's regiment calls for 'impartiall Justice to be done upon the eminent undertakers of this second war' in order that 'cruell mercies showed to our implacable enemies, might not indanger the lives of our dearest friends'.[92] The response of the House of Commons on 25 November was to order that 'the Tower regiment, late under the command of Colonel Rainborough, be forthwith disbanded'.[93] In fact Fairfax did not disband Rainsborough's regiment but instead gave it to another commander, one of the returning New Englanders, George Cook.[94]

The petition of Rainsborough's regiment was a part of an ongoing petition war. Robert Ashton has argued that an organised petitioning campaign began with the Presbyterian reaction against the army and the radical Independents in 1647. Petitions were seen by many on all sides in politics as manipulation of popular forces by the elites. MP Clement Walker, for instance, thought that the September 1648 petitions were 'all penned by the enraged party of the House and the Army and sent abroad by Agitators to get subscriptions'.[95]

Ashton examines the well over a hundred petitions that were received by Parliament between the Vote of No Addresses in January 1648 and Pride's Purge in December 1648. He records that 'during the spring and summer, if there is one theme which predominates and characterises more petitions than any other, it was the request for a Treaty with the king with a view to a final settlement of the kingdom'. But by the autumn the tide was beginning to turn and both army and civilian petitions against the treaty became more numerous.[96] The Levellers' Large Petition was important in turning the tide. Its influence on other petitions was considerable. As Ashton notes,

> Beginning with the radical petition of 11 September from some self-styled well-affected persons of London and finding further expression on 13 September in the Oxfordshire petition denouncing those who "cry *Peace, Peace*, but seek after *Blood*", and those in October from Leicestershire, Newcastle-upon-Tyne, York and Somerset, the petitions now holding the stage are those seeking to abort the Treaty and demanding the bringing of delinquents to justice.[97]

In early October, *Mercurius Pragmaticus* recorded of one group of petitioners,

> It being resolved by them (all as one man) to come and petition their friends in the House, in persuance of the Levellers Large Petition; as appears by severall Petitionary Letters (preparatory to their design) which they have sent up out of the North to the Generall, to invite him to joyne with them, and another gratulatory Letter to the presenters of the Large Petition.[98]

Norah Carlin's systematic analysis of the sixty-four surviving petitions for this period makes some important points.[99] She notes that the sixty-four which survive are far from uniform, though many state their support for the London Levellers' 11 September petition and this is widely recognised as having inspired the others. Nevertheless, they often express this agreement in general terms or select their own preferred demands, often adding local or regional issues.[100] This indicates both a degree of national coordination by Independent and Leveller leaders in London, in Parliament and in the army, but it also indicates that the 'honest', 'godly' or 'well affected' in the localities, and the officers and soldiers of the New Model Army, were not merely instruments of the London leaders.[101]

This is to be expected if we adopt the dialectical model of the relationship between a radicalising constituency and a radical organisation. The mainspring of radicalisation was the incompatibility of the forces contending the Second Civil War, not the subjective agitation of the Levellers or the Independents. But this agitation did shape the way in which this incompatibility was resolved. It gave the radical views based on experience a particular ideological shape and an organised political form. And in doing so it assisted in making these views, rather than those that wanted or would have acquiesced in a treaty with the king, ascendant.

Both Ashton and Carlin point to the novelty of many petitioners, civilian as well as military, addressing themselves to the army rather than to Parliament.[102] This was certainly the case with the petition from Rutland, published by William Larner, and presented to Fairfax on 24 November. It complained of the danger of a personal treaty and raised the fear that 'we are like to be massacred in our beds, or as our beloved Rainsborough was, whose death addeth to the life of our sorrows'.[103] This marked a breakdown in the belief that Parliament could or would remedy the petitioners' concerns. In practice it was a recognition that there was a situation of 'dual power' in the country with two incompatible institutions seen by different sections of the population as legitimate bodies to which appeals might be made over the settlement of the nation.

Carlin argues that the soldiers' petitions are not primarily about bread-and-butter issues. Their priority is bringing the king and others to justice. It might be added that even where the petitions do deal with 'bread-and-butter issues' these are directly connected with the largest political questions facing the nation. So the issue of 'free quarter' that was raised again and again in regimental petitions was seen by petitioners not just as important in itself. They were also concerned that Parliament was using the issue to turn the general population against the army. The petition of Hewson's regiment saw 'a renewed design upon this Army, by forcing us to free quarter, still to make us the contempt and hissing of the people'.[104] Similarly on the issue of arrears: the sentiment of the petitions no longer seemed to be simply that Parliament must address this issue, but reflected a growing mood that this issue would not be addressed until there was a fundamental transformation in the political situation which involved a final settlement of the nation. The sentiment among many soldiers was that the most elementary of demands would not be gained without a fundamentally different political regime in place.

Carlin sees 'circumstantial evidence for a significant level of political awareness' in the fact that thirteen of the sixteen regiments petitioning had been involved in the army agitation of 1647 and five were to take part in the disturbances of 1649. Some eleven of the soldiers' petitions are supportive of the Levellers' Large Petition.[105] Looking at the shorter time period of 10 October until mid-November (that is, the from the period immediately before Rainsborough's murder until the days immediately following his funeral), Gentles finds that army headquarters received petitions from nine New Model Army regiments, the Northern Brigade and 'several regiments' in the West of England; 'Five of these petitions explicitly supported the Leveller programme'.[106] And at least one petition, although it does not explicitly mention support for the Levellers' Large Petition, reproduces its demands so extensively that it is likely that it was influenced by it.[107]

The Levellers' influence over the petitioning process was extended by the existence of their own press. The Leveller press was a unique method of reproducing petitions, thus broadening their reach and deepening support for the views they expressed. Reproducing the petitions in *The Moderate* was a way of 'double petitioning'—once when the petition was collected, twice when its presentation and subsequent fate were reported.

We should also note, and neither Carlin nor Ashton lay enough emphasis on this, that a very large percentage of the petitions direct their anger at the apostates in Parliament. That is, they are an intervention in the debate taking place on the parliamentary side about what is an acceptable settlement of the nation. In the petition of Fleetwood, Whalley and Barkstead's regiments, for instance, this issue is directly connected with the murder of Rainsborough:

> this we humbly conceive they [the royalists] are more imboldened unto, because of the prevelancy of some in greatest authority, that will not let Justice be executed upon the grand fomenters, contrivers, and actors, in the first and late Warre . . . so that their bloudy intentions against the wel-affected in this Nation, doth begin to manifest itself, both against the

Parliament, and the Army, as is apparent by that most desperate and inhuman murthering of Col. Rainsborough.[108]

Carlin finds that some petitions made a direct call for Charles to pay for the blood spilt in the Civil War, but she makes a different argument than that made by Patricia Crawford in her widely cited article 'Charles Stuart, That Man of Blood'. Crawford argues,

The question was no longer how to compel the king to assent to peace terms; it was what should be done about the Lord's evident wrath for the nation's blood guiltiness. Thus blood guilt could be used both as a moral imperative to compel people to action, and as an excuse for action, as a respectable device in propaganda for convincing people that something had to be done about Charles.[109]

But only a minority of petitions raise the question of blood split in this manner. More frequently one finds references in the context of 'suffering than in that of guilt', as in the case of Fleetwood's regiment, who expected 'some satisfaction for their services and former losses, and the settlement of this Kingdom in their Birth-rights and privileges, as the purchase of so much blood and treasure'.[110] This was also the tenor of the petition from Fleetwood, Whalley and Barkstead's regiments.[111]

But however we interpret the demand for blood vengeance it was at this stage inextricably linked with the notion of bringing justice to those who had caused the Second Civil War. *The Moderate* reprinted the petition of Overton's regiment, then garrisoned at Berwick. It declared,

First, we desire that a diligent inquisition may be had for the innocent blood shed in the late warre, and that all the Contrivers, Actors, or Abettors may be brought to exemplary Justice:

That in the distribution of Justice, neither King, Lords, or any such persons be exempted from being proceeded against according to their demerits, knowing that many whoredomes, and witchcrafts of Jesabell hindered the peace of Israell, and Princes judging for reward, and the Priest teaching for hire, caused Sion to be plowed up as a field, and Jerusalem to become an heap.[112]

And after Rainsborough's murder his death was added to the list of crimes for which account must be given. Indeed the army sent a petition to the king on the Isle of Wight expressing their 'exceeding great sense of the losse of Colonell Rainsborough' and telling him that they 'thought fit that an inquiry should be made about that wicked murder, and that justice should be done therein'.[113] But from the moment of Rainsborough's death most regimental petitions contained a fresh demand: vengeance against his murderers.

The road to revolution

On the day after Rainsborough's funeral there was a dramatic parting of the ways between the radicals and Parliament. On that day, 15 November, Parliament voted that the king should be brought to London 'with freedom, safety, and honour, so soon as the Concessions of the Treaty are concluded and agreed'.[114] Army officers at St Albans, too, concurred when they met on the same day.

Meeting on the same day at the Nags Head near Blackwall Hall, an old Leveller meeting place, Lilburne and Ireton could not have been further from Parliament's resolution or the sentiments of the officers at St Albans. With the enormous prestige of the Rainsborough funeral procession behind them the Levellers quickly concluded with the Independents a joint version of Ireton's *Remonstrance* with enough of the *Agreement of the People* in it to content them. Lilburne recorded that this was sent straight to the army headquarters at St Albans:

> Which Agreement of ours (as I remember) was immediately sent away to the Head Quarters in St. Alban's by Mr Hiland of Southwark, where (as it was afterwards told to us) it was very well accepted and approved by the great ones there.[115]

The following day, 16 November, the council of officers sent the king proposals for a permanent constitutional settlement. No one thought he would accept it and indeed he did not.

When Cromwell had written to Hammond on 6 November recommending a purge of Parliament he said nothing of the fate of the king. But by 20 November, when he forwarded a collection of four regimental petitions to Fairfax, he wrote,

> I find a very great sense in the officers . . . for the sufferings of the poor kingdom, and in them all a very great zeal to have impartial justice done

upon offenders; and I must confess I do in all, from my heart, concur with them, and I verily think and am persuaded they are things which god puts into our hearts.[116]

One of the petitions that Cromwell sent to Fairfax was from his own regiment. It demanded that 'impartial Justice may be done upon them [the contrivers of the late rebellions], according to the many Petitions to that purpose, especially that large Petition of Sept. 11 1648'. The petitions from the other three regiments—Harrison's, Pride's and Deane's—also contained explicit statements of support for the Levellers' Large Petition.[117] In all, between 20 November and the end of the year, Fairfax received twenty-one more petitions from thirteen regiments, more than twenty-five garrisons, the Northern Brigade and the county forces of Northumberland. Some tweve of these declared support for the Leveller programme. Some thirty petitions are recorded as reaching army headquarters in the last three months of 1648, testimony to the extensive organisational capacity of the army radicals and the Levellers.[118]

There followed a flurry of meetings between the Levellers and the radical Independents to conclude the final formulations of the *Remonstrance*. A large meeting of Leveller agents agreed it in London. Lilburne and Henry Marten were in conference with Ireton and other Independents at the Garter inn in Windsor. Then, on 20 November, *A Remonstrance or Declaration of the Army* was presented to the House of Commons by Colonel Ewer and six other colonels and captains, the same day that the *Remonstrance* from Rainsborough's regiment appeared. Its first demand, printed on its cover, was 'that King Charles, as the Capitall Grand Author of the late troubles, may be speedily brought to Justice'.[119] When it was presented to the House, reported *Mercurius Militaris*,

> the very reading of it sweld the spleens of most of the House, and it was even white with the foaming of their indignation, their countenance and their brains run too and fro like shutters, but what Cobwebs they will weave, either to cover their shame, or hide themselves from Justice.[120]

The *Remonstrance* was to open the final act of the Revolution and it was a result of cooperation between Independents and the Levellers. On 6 December Colonel Thomas Pride took a detachment of soldiers to the Commons and, with a list of MPs to be excluded in his hand, prevented the House from voting a treaty with the king.[121]

The Levellers and the Revolution

The period between the freeing of Lilburne from the Tower in August 1648 and Pride's Purge marks the period of closest effective cooperation between the Levellers and the radical Independents. Before this moment, at Putney and Ware in 1647, for instance, Levellers and radical Independents had been more sharply opposed. After this moment, with the arrest of Lilburne, Overton, Walwyn and Prince in the spring of 1649, they were diametrically opposed. But this four-month period marks a high tide of Leveller activity and of their capacity to alter the course of the Revolution. The same period also covers the death and funeral of Rainsborough, which carries its own significance.

In the first place, Rainsborough's death added fuel to the argument that Charles and his party were irreconcilable. To those opposed to a treaty with Charles, it furnished an additional reason why no such agreement could or should be reached. The Levellers were the practical party most opposed to an agreement with Charles, whatever Lilburne's tactical reservations about the execution of the king. Without the weight of the Levellers cast into the balance it is unlikely that Ireton could have carried the day among the officers to break with the king and to open the road to Pride's Purge. Leveller agitation, both generally and within the army, added significant social weight and political clarity to the cause of the radical wing of the Revolution. Rainsborough's funeral procession was an impressive physical manifestation of this fact. And it occurred at the absolutely critical moment when the future development of the Revolution hung in the balance.

Leveller organisation was substantial at the start of 1648 and their strength grew over the course of the year. In January they had no press but by mid-year both *The Moderate* and *Mercurius Militaris* were propagating Leveller ideas, strategy and organisation. Pamphlet production was as great as it had ever been. As the presentation of the Large Petition showed, the Levellers' activity on this front was more effective than ever. Demonstrations in favour of the petition, and the great demonstration at Rainsborough's funeral, are evidence of the effect of such organisation. The development of the sea green emblem caught the imagination of supporters and opponents alike.

The political crisis of 1648 provided a unique correlation of forces within which Leveller organisation could affect the course of national politics. The increasingly bitter divisions of the Second Civil War, the consequent mounting hostility to the king among radical supporters of Parliament, the antipathy of these same forces to a treaty with the king and to those attempting to foster one, and the impasse of the senior radical officers in the New Model Army, all created conditions in which Leveller organisation could play a critical role.

The cooperation between the Levellers and the radical Independents could never be easy. As the Putney debates had shown, two significantly different views of the Revolution were held on each side of that divide. To make cooperation possible it was probably Ireton who had moved furthest, although this was as much under the pressure of events as it was a result of Leveller argument. But the Levellers had also been willing to accommodate to Ireton's cautious, less democratic instincts in order to reach consensus.

The Levellers and the radical Independents fashioned at this period a working alliance without which the revolution of Pride's Purge and the execution of the king would not have happened. The alliance was the joint work of, for different reasons, Cromwell, Ireton, Lilburne and the Leveller leadership. Forging this alliance required considerable effort on both sides. Its results were not what either side imagined they would be—but without this alliance the probability must be that events would have turned in a direction that neither side wanted: the 're-inthroning' of the king. Leveller activity was essential in avoiding the counterrevolution that threatened through much of 1648. The revolution that did happen was to a significant degree a result of their activity.

In the event the revolution that did take place was significantly less democratic than either Ireton or the Levellers had imagined. The army's purge of Parliament made them, like it or not, the effective power in the land. But the army's determination to cover this naked fact with the inadequate cloth of the Rump Parliament threw away the chance of a renewed, constitutional settlement. Ireton had said such an arrangement would be a 'mock parliament'. Lilburne now took up the phrase. Ireton was content to serve the 'mock power'. The Levellers were not.

CHAPTER 13

Defeat in Victory

Henry Marten and Oliver Cromwell walked into the Commons side by side after Pride's Purge. It was a fitting expression of the fact that an alliance between Cromwellian Independents and Levellers had at last banished the prospect of the return of the king. In the weeks that preceded the purge a fair prospect seemed to open up before the Levellers. The cooperation that had developed during the autumn of 1648 and had resulted in the meeting at the Nags Head on the day after Rainsborough's funeral had become more systematic. Ahead of that first meeting the representatives of the army were already driving at the execution of the king as the first order of business. Lilburne's response to this call set the whole direction of Leveller policy for the coming months. He agreed that king was an evil man and a tyrant who could no longer to be trusted. He also agreed that the Parliament were 'as bad as they could make them'. Yet 'there being no balancing power in the Kingdome against the Army, but the King and Parliament, it was our interest to keep up one Tyrant to balance another, till we certainly know what that Tyrant that pretended fairest would give us as our Freedom'. Lilburne's fear, real enough given the Levellers' experience at Putney and Ware the previous year, was that once the Grandees had defeated the king and the pro-treaty Parliament they would rule by the sword. Lilburne was certainly not against either the dissolution of the Parliament or the trial of the king—as long as the *Agreement of the People* was adopted first, giving a constitutional and legal basis for these acts rooted in a popularly approved settlement.[1]

At the first Nags Head meeting this strategy won wider approval among the Independents. It was this plan that was sent to army headquarters and became the basis of the declaration of the army drawn up by Ireton, who was even prevailed upon to remove some 'lashes' that tacitly criticised the Levellers. As a consequence Lilburne, John Wildman, Maximillian Petty and Colonel Wetton journeyed to army headquarters at Windsor to pursue their advantage. The first meeting between this delegation and Ireton, attended by 'a whole Train of Officers', at the Garter inn almost fell apart. Ireton wanted restrictions on liberty of conscience and to retain Parliament's right to prosecute where no law existed. The Levellers, on the other hand, would have neither.

The meeting broke up without agreement and the Levellers were set to return to London. Colonel Thomas Harrison, who had supported them in the meeting, prevailed on them to stay, and raised again the army plan to move swiftly to London and so prevent Parliament concluding a treaty with the king. A treaty, said Harrison, would mean 'you will be destroyed as well as we'. In a wide-ranging discussion the Levellers convinced Harrison of the necessity of adopting the *Agreement of the People* before such action since the army had 'broke their promise once already'. From this discussion emerged a committee of sixteen to draw up a new constitutional proposal. This committee was to be composed of four radical MPs, four army nominees, four Independents, and four Levellers, and was widely approved. Harrison and the Levellers finally made their way to Ireton's lodgings in Windsor Castle while he was still in bed with his wife. Harrison conveyed the scheme to Ireton, who approved it, though there was later some controversy about what had been agreed regarding the process by which the plan would be approved before it was circulated for popular assent.[2]

Ireton, hardly a daring thinker, exercised his special talent of taking the demands thrown up by the Levellers and others and draughting them into a form that, shorn of their more radical meaning, became acceptable to the more moderate Independents. This had been his method since the start of the army revolt in 1647 and he was still practising it. But the events of the intervening year had also changed Ireton, hardening his attitude against the king and making him more mindful of the need for a fundamental resettlement of the nation. He seems to have been genuinely committed to the strategy agreed with the Levellers.[3] At all events the committee got to work with Lilburne, Walwyn, Wildman and Petty as the Leveller representatives. They will have been encouraged that Henry Marten was one of the nominated MPs. Indeed it was these five that initially thrashed out the new edition of the *Agreement*.[4]

It was at this point that the army advanced to London, an action much opposed by Walwyn. This proved a fateful moment inside the Revolutionary alliance, as well as between it and the pro-treaty forces. Ireton and Harrison, true to the understanding they had reached with the Levellers, were opposed to the mere purging of Parliament. They argued that Parliament as whole had forfeited its trust and that if it were merely purged only a 'mock-parliament' would remain. At this moment and like the Levellers, they wanted a more complete reformation of the political system, the dissolution of Parliament and a new election. The irremovable obstacle to this plan was the army's allies among the MPs who set their face against a total dissolution and in favour of merely purging their opponents in the Commons. In a confrontation 'in a chamber near the Long Gallery' in Whitehall Ireton derided the MPs as 'mock-power' and a 'pretended Parliament', but to no avail. The Rump, as the post-purge Parliament was known, stuck to their seats. So it was that Colonel Thomas Pride purged the Commons on 6 December, standing at the door of the House and arresting those MPs who had backed a treaty with the king. An important chance to found a republic on wider consent among the Revolution's supporters had been lost.[5]

The committee of Levellers and Independents nevertheless continued to do its work. It sent its draft of the *Agreement of the People* to the council of officers on 11 December, and the officers called together a wider assembly in Whitehall to discuss it, beginning on 14 December. In order to bring pressure on those debating at Whitehall, Lilburne immediately published the committee's existing draft as *The Foundations of Freedom: or an Agreement of the People*. In the Whitehall debates some 160 officers of every rank and civilians spoke. We can assume that the total attendance was greater, perhaps considerably. This was the largest and most representative meeting there would ever be of the Independents and Levellers that had made the Revolution. Lilburne, Overton, Wildman and Walwyn were all present. So too were the Independent chaplains Hugh Peter, John Goodwin, Thomas Collier and, from the Dissenting Bretheren, Philip Nye. The Seeker William Erbury spoke on six occasions. Fairfax was in the chair and Ireton and Harrison were the highest-profile, but not the only, representatives of the army command.[6]

The *Agreement* was read out from a long scroll and debated clause by clause. On the first day, the only day for which there is a substantial record of the debate, there was still wrangling between the Levellers and Ireton over the extent of liberty of conscience and over the power of Parliament to inflict punishment where no law existed. Yet it was not the content of the argument that exasperated Lilburne most but the procedure by which the finished document would be agreed. Lilburne thought he had Ireton's agreement that once the committee had agreed the document it would immediately be sent to the Council of War, then to the regiments of the army, and finally 'all over the Nation' for subscription. But now he found it committed to a lengthy process of review by meetings of officers, soldiers and civilians. For Lilburne this looked too much like the procrastination and evasion he had seen at Putney, and which the committee of sixteen had deliberately been designed to avoid. He walked out after the first day and never returned. Other Levellers stayed on, however. As it turned out they were right because Ireton was often defeated in the debates that followed. And, in any case, it was unrealistic to assume that the committee's draft could simply be sent out for subscription to the nation without some wider debate involving more than sixteen people, however representative they might be of broader forces. But in a timescale longer than a few weeks Lilburne was right to fear for the fate of the new *Agreement*.[7]

The first day's lengthy debate on liberty of conscience was only resolved by the appointment of a representative committee that included Wildman. Ireton lost the vote to give the state final judgement in moral matters by twenty-seven votes to seventeen. He did, however, successfully keep religion out of the reserved powers of the *Agreement* by thirty-seven votes to twelve. In the end it was resolved that the state might recommend, but could not compel, forms of religious observance, although toleration did not extend to prelacy or popery. This was a genuine compromise. But Ireton lost out entirely in the discussion on whether the state had the power to prosecute in cases where no law was already on the statute. Here the Leveller position prevailed. The *Agreement* that emerged from the Whitehall debates was by far the most detailed attempt to write a constitution for the Commonwealth that came from those who had defeated the counterrevolution. If it had prevailed it would have provided a mechanism for mobilising popular support for the Revolutionary regime. It would not have been a fully democratic constitution because the Revolutionary minority were unlikely to prevail over combined forces ranged against them at this juncture. But it would have been a way in which the whole of the 'well affected' and their political representatives, both Independent and Leveller, could have shifted the balance of the regime away from military rule and towards a system of constitutionally reinforced political hegemony.[8]

The document that emerged from the Whitehall debates was a compromise, but the evidence is of a compromise that both Independents and Levellers could support, for the moment. Lilburne's later account of its genesis has proven factually correct.[9] But, perhaps inevitably given it was written after Lilburne was made a prisoner in the Tower, his account attributes bad faith to Ireton and magnifies the Levellers' fears of the Independents' intentions. But if we examine statements made on both sides while the debate was taking place a different picture emerges. Ireton, in the course of debate, gave testimony to the degree of consensus in the committee of sixteen that drew up the original draft. Replying to Overton's motion that the debate move on and the *Agreement* be approved by a vote, Ireton defends the necessity of the debate they were then engaged in at Whitehall. But he notes, referring to the committee of sixteen, that there 'was little difference in those that drew this up'.[10]

The Levellers were lobbying for the best version of the *Agreement* that they could get. On the night of 28 December Lilburne delivered his objections to the officers' *Agreement* 'to the General's own hands at the Mews'. He was accompanied by a considerable delegation of Levellers, including Richard Overton, John Harris, Thomas Prince, Major Robert Cobbet (brother of John Cobbett arrested at Ware), Thomas Daffren, Edward Tench and Samuel Blaicklock. This new document was quickly printed by Larner.[11] The following day the council was presented with these objections from the Levellers. This revealed how 'very much statisfied' the Levellers had been that Ireton's *Remonstrance* recommended the *Agreement* and acknowledged how 'much more satisfactory it was, that you allowed us to chuse certain friends from amongst us, to be joined with you in the drawing up of the Agreement of the People'. This revived their hopes and 'our confidence was great'. The main complaints about the Whitehall debates were procedural: the disputes are 'tedious', points remain still 'in suspence', the speeches go on 'at length'—this last probably a swipe at Ireton, who certainly never made a short speech where he could make a long one. It recommends the expedition of debate by limiting the number of times a speaker could address any one issue, that the debate should be better chaired, that senior officers should not overawe their juniors. Substantively the message was that if decisions are not made swiftly 'you be entangled in such perplexities, that when you would, it shall not be in your power to help yourselves, or to free this Common-wealth from misery and bondage'. Additionally there should be no disbandment of the army until this work was done.[12] The Levellers were wary certainly, but they were committed to seeing the draft of the *Agreement* concluded. Indeed, even after they were later imprisoned, the collective statement by Lilburne, Overton, Walwyn and Prince stated,

> The agreement of the People which was presented by his Excellency and the
> Officers of the Army to the Right Honourable the Commons in Parliament,
> although in many things short (according to our apprehension) of what is
> for the good of the Common-wealth, and the satisfaction of the People . . .
> yet, had it been put into execution, we should scarcely have interrupted
> the proceedings thereof, since therein contained many things of great
> importance and concernment to the Common-wealth.[13]

The *Agreement* was presented to Parliament on 20 January, the first day of
the king's trial. The MPs acknowledged it, ordered it printed, and set it
aside for future discussion.[14] But that moment never came. The political
logic of the king's trial overrode the constitutional debate, as Lilburne had
warned that it would. More importantly, the MPs of the Rump were happy
to see the *Agreement* shelved. They had resisted dissolution of Parliament
when Ireton argued for it in December and, by the same token, they had
no interest in subjecting themselves to biennial elections by an expanded
electorate or any of the other limitations on their power. If there was to be
a republic they preferred a narrower dictatorship rather than the 'democratic dictatorship' of the well affected that was in essence what the
Agreement represented. Finally, the army high command was not likely to
break with the MPs in favour of the Levellers when class and political
conservatism spoke against any such move.

England did indeed become a republic, executing the king on a scaffold
outside the Banqueting House in Whitehall on 30 January 1649. This was a
political earthquake of unprecedented proportions. It had simply never
been the case in the entire history of kings, kaisers, caesars or emperors
that a democratically driven movement of the people had publicly tried
their monarch for treason and put him to death. It was, as Thomas Harrison
said at the trial of the Regicides, 'not a thing done in a Corner, I believe the
sound of it hath been in most Nations'.[15] In short order the House of Lords
was abolished as 'dangerous and useless'—or 'useless but not dangerous', as
Henry Marten quipped. Nonetheless, the political bloc that had accomplished the Revolution's victory shattered on the rock of its own success. In
the national state of shock that followed the king's execution an essentially
military regime controlled by the Silken Independents moved to eradicate
any attempt to construct a more radical alternative. A Council of State was
elected as an executive of the Rump.[16]

All this had a deeply disorienting effect on the Levellers. They had lived to
see the destruction of so much that they had fought against for a decade,

coming close, perhaps closer than they ever thought they would, to seeing the *Agreement of the People* adopted as the constitutional framework for the settlement of the nation. But at the same instant power was now in the hands of their reluctant allies—an essentially military regime—whom they had cajoled at every step of the way. Some among them were attracted by the gravitational pull of the new republic: Henry Marten signed the king's death warrant and now served on the Council of State, John Wildman disappeared from Leveller circles as quickly as he had appeared, Edward Sexby now oriented to the regime and was swiftly promoted in the army. Even those who were not supportive of the regime were paralysed: Walwyn withdrew from activity; Lilburne, having refused to serve as a commissioner at the king's trial, left London for County Durham, attempting to make good on the long-delayed reparations awarded him by Parliament. For the first time in over a decade presses associated with Lilburne, Overton and Larner ceased to print.[17]

Only an external shock brought the Levellers back to activity. Such a jolt was forthcoming because the regime found itself the target of both royalists and pro-treaty parliamentarians, and its own radical supporters. The nation was at the end of its economic tether, and the disbandment or transportation to Ireland of the army remained unresolved. New currents were also now emerging among radicals that sought to address the unprecedented crisis. Some, either religiously transported by the epoch-making events of which they were a part, like the Fifth Monarchists, or religiously and socially sensitised to the prospects of a fundamentally different society, like the Diggers and Ranters, added to a febrile political atmosphere. These brilliant sparks showered forward from the arrested development of the Revolution and raised political and ideological issues that could only be addressed, as their proponents thought, by God, or by direct action under God. But unlike the Levellers they lacked either a practical political programme or a movement to demand it.[18]

Since December Lilburne had been in a deeply uncharacteristic depression. In 'a kinde of deep muse with myself' he resolved to 'wholly devote my self to provide for the future well being of my wife and children'. He thought of going to Holland but feared for his safety from exiled cavaliers enraged by the king's execution. Lilburne felt like 'an old weather-beaten ship, that would fain be in some harbour of ease and rest'. He no longer attended meetings and his friends thought he 'was become like all the rest of the world, and so there was an end of me'.[19] His friends need not have worried, for Lilburne was the first back into print. *Englands New Chaines Discovered* was in the streets on 26 February 1649.

The first into action, however, were Captain Bray and his troop. Since they had joined the parliamentary forces fighting in Kent during the Second Civil War, Bray's troop had guarded the king while he was a prisoner at Hurst Castle and then been quartered in the West Country. Now they faced disbandment, in part because their colonel, John Reynolds, and the Grandees found them too radical. Bray protested first at the Council of War, where he defended the troops right to petition. This got him excluded from the council so he raised his complaints in a petition against Fairfax which he delivered to the Commons himself on 19 March. The House examined Bray and then declared the petition tended 'to stir up Sedition in the People' before imprisoning him in Windsor castle.[20]

But Bray enjoyed considerable support for his Leveller ideas among his own troop. They petitioned on his behalf with over seventy-five of their names attached. His quartermaster, John Nayler, and his cornet, Christopher Cheeseman, both wrote impassioned pamphlets detailing the troop's parliamentary service and demanding that Bray receive justice. Bray himself repeatedly petitioned and wrote pamphlets in his own defence. In May one such appeal was taken from Bray at Windsor and presented to Parliament by Christopher Cheeseman. He appeared at the bar of the Commons to make his plea and then withdrew into Westminster Hall. As he was walking through the Hall an extraordinary scene unfolded. The Speaker entered the Hall after the House had risen and Cheeseman approached him to see if anything had been done about Bray's case. The Speaker had barely told him that nothing had been decided when Cromwell approached the cornet and asked him if his name was Cheeseman. As soon as Cheeseman told him it was, Cromwell called a guard of halberdiers who 'came running very greedily like so many Lions to their prey, pulling and punching of me'. Cheeseman 'gave them fair words, beseeching them as Gentlemen not to punch me'. But Cromwell 'cryed out, very vehemently, Do punch him, punch him on'. Cheeseman was arrested and held in jail for seventeen days before release. The incident highlights the sheer animosity that now existed between the Levellers and the Silken Independents.[21]

On 21 March the Grandees were under literary assault in the magnificently titled pamphlet *The Hunting of the Foxes from Newmarket and Triploe-Heaths to Whitehall, By five small Beagles (late of the army)*. The foxes were the Silken Independents, the locations were the first rendezvous of the army revolt and the current home of the Grandees, and the five small beagles were the soldiers lately court-martialled. The prose was likely from

Overton. This was followed by *The second part of Englands New-Chaines Discovered* on 24 March. A nervous and isolated regime reacted by moving against the Leveller leaders with great force. On 27 March the Commons voted them guilty of high treason, declaring that Lilburne's book was 'highly seditious, and destructive to the present Government; as it is now declared and settled by Parliament; tends to Division and Mutiny in the Army, and the Raising of a new War in the Commonwealth, and to hinder the present Relief of Ireland; and to the Continuing of Free Quarter'. The specific offence was that 'Lt. Colonell Lilburne did read the Book called Englands new Chains discovered on Sunday last at Winchester House, before a great multitude of people and perswaded Subscriptions to it, and endeavoured to answer objections made against it'.[22]

The following day an armed detachment between 100 and 200 strong arrested Lilburne from his bed in an early-morning raid. He was marched through the streets to the guard house at St Pauls. Thomas Prince was surprised at his shop by 200 troops under Lieutenant Colonel Daniel Axtell. When he walked out in the lane to go with them he laughed at the numbers sent to detain him and told the officer that one man with a warrant would have been enough but, he supposed, since his name was Prince, 'it was usual for Princes to have a great attendance'. Lilburne and Prince met each other at the St Pauls guardhouse, where they had just embraced each other and began to talk when they saw Walwyn brought up by another party of soldiers. Lilburne had not seen Walwyn at Leveller meetings for some months and was surprised he had been arrested. Lilburne, Walwyn and Prince were taken by river to Westminster.

Meanwhile Axtell was arresting Overton in a similar manner, a story told with comic incredulity in *A Picture of the Councel of State*. Axtel accuses Overton of believing in the 'community of wives'. Overton challenged him to name one of the Levellers who thought this. Axtel said that it might be that Overton was of that opinion. To which he got the reply 'it might be that he was of that opinion, and that my may be was as good as his May be'. Axtel told Overton he was a 'sawsey fellow'. Overton too was marched off under heavy guard via St Pauls to Whitehall, where he found Lilburne, Walwyn and Prince already detained. They were examined by John Bradshaw and members of the Council of State, Prince and Lilburne with their hats firmly clamped on their heads. A now-familiar scene followed: the prisoners refused to incriminate themselves. While they waited on judgment outside the room, Lilburne could hear Cromwell talking very loudly to the council: 'I tel you Sir, you have no other way to deale

with these men but to break them in pieces'. Thumping the table he continued, 'if you do not break them, they will break you; yea, and bring all the
guilt and blood and treasure shed and spent in this Kingdome upon your
heads and shoulders, and make voide all that Worke'. They would, Cromwell
told his fellow council members, be a low-spirited generation if they
allowed themselves to be routed by such 'despicable contemptible' men.
Colonel Ludlow pleaded that the Levellers should be bailed, but it was not
to be. *The Moderate* reported Cromwell's outburst; the Leveller leaders
were committed to the Tower.[23]

The arrests were part of a concerted campaign against the Levellers and
it provoked a breach between them and the gathered churches from which
they had previously drawn support.[24] There were many things that drew
the churches to support the Levellers, but by far the most important was
freedom of worship. Under the republic, however, this was now obtained,
and as a result many of the leaders of the churches, the Particular Baptists
most notably, swung behind mainstream Independency and away from the
Levellers. This became apparent after Leveller agents attended churches on
25 March, as they had many times before, to read out and muster support
for *The Second Part of Englands New-Chaines Discovered*. Samuel Rutherford
visited the Leveller leaders in the Tower on behalf of the churches but failed
to get them to back down. The following Sunday the Particular Baptist
pastors brought their own petition to their congregations denouncing the
Levellers. The day following, Lilburne's long-time ally, William Kiffin,
presented it in the name of seven churches to the Commons. The Speaker
assured them they were guaranteed 'liberty and peace'.[25]

The Leveller leaders were convinced, no doubt rightly, that MPs had
connived in the presentation of the Particular Baptists' petition. Notably, in
the version presented to Parliament the clause calling for clemency for the
Levellers had been deleted. There were other causes for the split as well.
Very broadly, Particular Baptism's emphasis on the saving of the few elect
had an elitist cast at variance with the popular and democratic bent of
Leveller thought. More specifically, Walwyn's rationalist religion had always
had its enemies, notably John Price in Goodwin's church. Earlier in 1649
Walwyn had published *The Vanitie of the Present Churches* and this gave his
enemies the chance to reply. They did so with a wholesale attack, *Walwins
Wiles*. Among the signatories were William Kiffin and Edmund Rosier,
both long-standing Lilburne supporters. Lilburne stuck with Walwyn, calling *The Vanitie of the Present Churches* 'one of the shrewdest books that
ever I read in my life'. Walwyn replied with *Walwyn's Just Defence*. The

breach with the Particular Baptist leaders was now open, bitter and permanent. Daniel Axtell, the officer who arrested Overton and Prince, was a member of William Kiffin's church.

The petitions of the Leveller women

Leveller organisation now sprang into operation with surprising resilience. On 2 April Leveller supporters presented a petition on behalf of their four leaders in the Tower, reported to be signed by 10,000 hands. But the Commons ordered that prosecution go ahead.[26] The Levellers responded with another petition on 18 April, again rejected with 'a sharp reproof', reported *The Moderate* when it reproduced the petition.[27] Two more petitions, one from London and another from Essex, followed on 2 May.[28] These petitions had thousands of supporters. Then came the *Humble Petition of divers wel-affected Women*, calling for the freedom of the four prisoners in the Tower, Captain Bray at Windsor, and William Sawyer held in Newgate. This petition was the result of a subscription campaign that asked supporters to deliver copies to 'the women which will be appointed in every Ward and Division to receive the same' and then to 'meet at Westminster Hall' on 23 April between eight and nine in the morning to present it.[29] As the royalist *Mercurius Pragmaticus* had it, 'the lusty lasses of the levelling party are drawing to a general Rendezvous at Westminster' and intended to 'cock their Petticoats' as their 'Brethren do their Pistolls'. For the Leveller's *Mercurius Militaris* they were the 'bonny Besses, In the Sea-green dresses', who strike fear into 'Nol and his asses'. Some 500 women were at the protest and there were said to be 10,000 names on their petition. The women's petition argued that circumstances had obliged 'the weaker vessel' to step 'beyond our compass' and no longer be 'bounded in the custom of our sex'. They claimed 'an equal share and interest with the men in the Common-wealth, and it cannot be laid waste (as it now is) and not we be the greatest & most helpless suffers therein'. It went on to draw inspiration from the fact that 'God hath wrought many deliverances for severall Nations, from age to age by the weake-hand of women'. And for examples it pointed out that 'by the British women this land was delivered from the tyranny of the Danes' and 'the overthrow of Episcopall tyranny in Scotland was first begun by the women of that Nation'.[30]

On the day of presentation some twenty women got into the lobby of the Commons despite troops drawing pistols on them. One MP told them to go home and wash their dishes, to which one of the petitioners replied, 'Sir, we scarce have any dishes left to wash'. When another MP remarked that it was strange to see women petitioning he was told, 'It was strange that you cut off the King's head, yet I suppose you will justify it'. Cromwell tried to mollify them by saying that their husbands would have a fair trial. One of the 'sea-green sisters' said, 'if you take away their lives or the lives of any, contrary to the law, nothing shall satisfy us, but the lives of them that do it'. Eventually the sergeant-at-arms told them the issue was 'of an higher concernment than you understand' and that the House had already given 'an answer to your husbands, and therefore that you are desired to go home and meddle with your housewifery'.[31]

But on 5 May the women returned, sea green ribbons pinned to their breasts, with a second petition, probably written by Katherine Chidley. It complained to the MPs that the women 'should appear so despicable in your eyes as to be thought unworthy to petition' and went onto ask,

> Have we not an equal interest in the Kingdome with the men of this nation in those liberties and securities contained in the *Petition of Right*, and other good laws of this land? Are any of our lives, limbs, liberties or goods to be taken from us more than from men, but by due process of law and conviction of twelve sworn men of the neighbourhood? And can you imagine us to be so sottish or stupid as not to perceive, or not to be sensible when daily those strong defences of our peace and welfare are broken down and trod underfoot by force and arbitrary power?[32]

As before, this petition was reprinted in *The Moderate*. The women were not acting in isolation. Also in May apprentices in the Cripplegate Without ward issued a broadsheet calling on apprentices in other parts of the City to do as they had and to 'speedily choose out from among yourselves in your several and respective Wards four or six . . . cordial and active young men to be Agitators for you. And that you forthwith appoint Meetings in your several wards for better carrying on of this work'.[33] This immediately drew an anti-Leveller broadsheet from apprentices in the City's Bridge Within ward claiming that Lilburne, Walwyn, Prince and Overton were 'engaging in a fresh Party without any the least colour of Authority whatsoever'. In response the Cripplegate apprentices compared the Leveller leaders to Korah, Dathan and Abiram, 'who took unto them what party they could procure among the families of Israel, (as these do among the Regiments of the Army, and elsewhere)'.[34] It seems as if, even in retreat, the Levellers were capable of reaching out to and mobilising new constituencies on a scale commensurate with some of their strongest campaigns in the past. The figure of 20,000 that Lilburne gives for the print runs of the Leveller leaders' joint defence, A *Manifestation*, and for the final and fullest *Agreement of People*, with the compromises made the previous December rescinded, underline this point.[35]

The Levellers and Ireland

As the Levellers entered their first month in the Tower a new series of mutinies in the army began over disbandment, pay arrears and service in Ireland. Disbandment of the army and Ireland were issues that were always closely interwoven for the radicals of the Revolution. The issue was complex. The rebellion in Ireland and the massacre of the Protestants had been a central issue in the case against Strafford and the king at the outbreak of the Revolution. Essentially the opposition's case was that the Court had allowed Protestants to be butchered, were incapable of repressing the rebellion, and were risking invasion of England, and all this because of secret sympathy for popery. During the course of the war Charles's willingness to call on Irish Catholic troops reinforced these sentiments. The necessity of reducing Ireland was therefore part of parliamentarian ideology. This was reinforced by economic considerations since many soldiers were awarded land in Ireland as part of their arrears or had previously owned land or been involved in settler projects. This was true of the Rainsboroughs, for instance, and of William Eyre.

However, the Presbyterians' excuse of raising troops for Ireland as a way of disbanding the New Model Army in 1647 had introduced a cross-cutting argument into radical discourse. While not in principle against an expedition to Ireland the Agitators and radicals began argue that this was not possible until a secure settlement of their rights was achieved at home. In this context some of the extreme sceptics as regards the intentions of the Grandees in the army began to develop a stronger and more principled opposition to an Irish expedition. The Leveller leaders were among this group. Henry Marten is a case in point. In Parliament he had challenged the use of force against the Irish.[36] And while Leveller publications often excused themselves from the accusation that they were trying to obstruct the relief of Ireland, in *The English Souldiers Standard* the Levellers had this to say:

> To what end should you hazard your lives against the Irish: have you not been fighting these seven years in England for Rights and Liberties, that you are yet deluded of? . . . and will you go on stil to kil, slay and murther men, to make them as absolute Lords and Masters over Ireland as you have over them over England? or is it your ambition to reduce the Irish to the happiness of Tythes upon trebble dammages, to Excise, Customs and Monopolies in the Trades? or to fill their Land with swarms of beggers; to enrich their Parliament-men, and to impoverish their people; to take down Monarchical Tyranny, and set up Aristocratical Tyranny . . .

Settle matters at home, the pamphlet urged, and then approach the Irish with a good platform in your hands so that 'you might overcome them by just and equal offers, then by strength and force'.[37] And Leveller John Cobbett is the likely author of the pamphlet printed in Bristol in 1649 called *The Souldiers Demand*, which argues that the Grandees should be asked,

> What have we to do with Ireland, to fight, and murther a People and a Nation (for indeed they are set upon cruelty, and murthering poore people, which is all they glory in) which have done us no harm, only deeper to put our hands in bloud with their own? we have waded fare in that Crimson streame (already) of innocent and Christian bloud.[38]

This seems to have become something of the settled view among Leveller leaders. Thomas Prince, although he was an Irish investor, wrote in *The Silken Independents Snare Broken* that if England were settled on the lines the Levellers suggested then the Irish would be willing to change their 'condition of bondage for freedom'. John Harris's *Mercurius Militaris* struck a similar but more direct pro-Irish note. The Levellers did not have a settled or entirely unambiguous attitude to Ireland, but some of them reached the most advanced ideological conclusions that any radicals in the English Revolution attained on the Irish issue.[39]

The Bishopsgate mutiny

The first major army mutiny of 1649 happened on 24 April. It was led by a twenty-three-year-old trooper named Robert Lockyer. At sixteen he had undergone adult baptism in Bishopsgate, where he had been brought up. He served in Cromwell's Ironsides and followed them into Colonel

Whalley's regiment of the New Model. Like Rainsborough and Sexby, he was a veteran of Naseby. Like Rainsborough he had been at Ware and fought at the siege of Colchester. Whalley's regiment, with Lilburne's encouragement, re-elected more radical Agitators in September 1647.[40]

Lockyer's regiment was stationed around Bishopsgate when it was ordered out of London, part of a strategy by army commanders 'to move some troops to . . . where they would be less subject to Leveller propaganda'.[41] But the soldiers were owed arrears and in response Lockyer and about thirty other troopers went to the Four Swans inn in Bishopsgate Street, seized the colours and took them to the Bull inn, also in Bishopsgate Street. When their captain arrived they told him, 'They were not his colours carriers' and that 'they, as well as he, had fought for them'.[42]

The mutiny lasted into the following day, when the officers provided some of the back pay. Then a general rendezvous of the regiment was called at Mile End Green with the intention of getting the troopers out of the city. But the mutineers stayed fast, and 'put themselves into a posture of defence in Galleries of the Bull Inn, with their swords and pistols, standing upon their guard'.[43] There was another unsuccessful attempt to take the colours, then loyal troopers and more senior officers of the regiment were brought down to the Bull to confront the mutineers. This, too, proved unsuccessful. 'And all the while they thus capitulated with their Officers, they stood drawn up in Galleries and Windows with their Swords and Pistols, as if they were treating with an enemy, and did not submit' and 'cryed out for the Liberties of the people'.[44] Finally Thomas Fairfax and Oliver Cromwell arrived on the scene just as 'the yard was clearing, to make way for the Horse and Foot to force them' to surrender.[45] Lockyer and fourteen others were taken into custody. Some other mutineers were punished, but only Lockyer eventually faced the death penalty.[46]

Some accounts of the mutiny sympathetic to the Leveller cause claimed that Fairfax and Cromwell singled out Lockyer because he had participated in the Ware mutiny.[47] Certainly, in reply to demands for clemency, Fairfax said that he would not pardon Lockyer because of the volatile situation in the City and the army.[48] Cromwell and Fairfax were, as we have seen, facing more than Lockyer's mutiny during these days in late April. John Lilburne and Overton petitioned Fairfax for mercy for Lockyer from their cells in the Tower. Cromwell had been inclined to leniency but Fairfax insisted on execution. Lockyer was taken to St Paul's Churchyard, where he faced a firing squad. After saying his farewells to friends and family he refused a blindfold and addressed the soldiers. He said,

Fellow soldiers, I am here brought to suffer in behalf of the People of England, and for your Privileges and Liberties, and such as in conscience you ought to own and stand to: But I perceive that you are appointed by your officers to murder me; and I did not think that you had such heathen-ish and barbarous principles in you . . . when I stand up for nothing but what is for your good.

Colonel Okey, in charge of the detail, accused Lockyer of still trying to 'make the soldiers mutiny'. Lockyer told the firing squad that they should shoot when he raised both his hands. And so they did.[49]

Lockyer's funeral procession began in Smithfield and went by way of the City to Moorfields, where he was buried in the new churchyard. Seven trumpeters 'sounded before the Corpse'. Lockyer's horse, draped in black and led by a footman, followed the coffin that was draped in rosemary branches dipped in blood and had Lockyer's sword laid on it.[50] The ritual elevated the ordinary trooper to the status of a 'chief commander'. Some 4,000 to 5,000 were in the original procession, among them an estimated 300 soldiers and some discharged men. A company of women brought up the rear of the cortège. When the procession reached its destination, the marchers were joined by more of the 'highest sort' who stayed aloof from the controversial progress through the City.[51] Black mourning ribbons and sea green ribbons were widely worn among the mourners.[52] There were eulogies but no sermon in the new churchyard. The speeches advocated the Leveller programme and aimed criticism at the new government. One of the army's defenders complained that the Levellers are 'pleased to canonize' Mr Lockyer as 'a Martyr since his death'.[53] Some thought that Lockyer's mourners outnumbered those for Charles I.[54]

Lockyer's funeral was, if anything, even larger than Rainsborough's. And it served the same function of rallying Leveller support, though this time in a moment of retreat. Rainsborough's funeral occurred at the high point of Leveller–Independent joint endeavour to prevent the re-enthronement of Charles I. The Rainsborough procession was Leveller-inspired and organ-ised but it had the character of a broad Revolutionary front against the spectre of restoration. Lockyer's procession was a Leveller-only affair held at a political moment when the mutinies in the army were afoot, the Leveller leaders were in the Tower and their erstwhile Independent allies were persecuting them. The iconography is important in this context. Lockyer's funeral had all the pomp that was traditionally associated with the cortège of individuals of much higher rank when he was of 'no higher quality than a Trooper'.[55] Perhaps this was an attempt to elevate the Levellers' standing at a moment of relative political isolation. Certainly it was an attempt to project their cause to a wider audience. Ian Gentles believes that Lockyer's funeral confirmed the fears of Cromwell and the Grandees that Leveller agitation in the army and in London could threaten the new regime. And he notes that the funeral is a reminder that 'the use of mourning for a martyred popular hero as a vehicle of political protest was invented long before its contemporary exploitation in South Africa and Northern Ireland'.[56]

On Saturday 5 May 1649, two other troopers were punished for their part in the Bishopsgate mutiny:

> two Troopers of Captain Savages Troop, according to the sentence passed upon them, rid the Wooden Horse, with two Muskets tyed to their legs in the Palace yard at Westminster, like true Champions of the Wooden Horse; mounted with much courage and valour, one of them said, he had served the parliament on a better horse, and that he had bestowed much money that way, and this was an exchange; but if he consider, it is better then his fellow Lockiers was.[57]

The business of Burford

The 'Burford mutiny' is shorthand for a series of connected revolts by troops across the West Country in May 1649. They began in Salisbury on 1 May 1649 among Scroop's regiment. Their petition was carried in *The Moderate* immediately following the paper's reprint of a London petition in support of Lilburne, Walwyn, Overton and Prince. The mutineers were joined at a rendezvous at Old Sarum by Ireton's regiment, where they issued a joint declaration on 11 May.[58] This objected to forced disbandment for those who refused to go to Ireland but framed these issues in general political terms. The soldiers objected to being deprived of 'our Native Liberties', and to the army commanders departing from the engagement at Triploe Heath; demanded the recall of the General Council with 'Two Souldiers, chosen out of every Regiment'; referred back to the debates at Putney; and appealed to soldiers and civilians to support them. They reassured their readers, in the manner often used by the Levellers, that they did not aim at 'Levelling your Estates (as may be suggested)'. The soldiers declared that they were unwilling to be sent to Ireland before they had seen the 'Freedom and Liberty' for which they had fought established in England.[59] The royalist *Mercurius Pragmaticus* reported that the forces 'in Wiltshire upon the Plaines of Salisbury' were 'a competent number and cry out violently for revenge, Professing to have the Blood of those who had the blood of Lockyer'.[60] The mutinous forces moved north through Marlborough, reaching Wantage on 13 May. The following day a rendezvous was held at Abingdon.[61] They were joined by more mutineers that included a troop from Harrison's regiment led by Captain Winthrop, Thomas Rainsborough's kinsman. Colonel Reynolds's regiment called a rendezvous at their headquarters in Banbury. This was joined by Captain Smith's county troop and most of Henry Marten's regiment.[62] Captain William Thompson, the leader at Banbury, was a Leveller and a supporter of the *Agreement of the People* with a personal connection to Lilburne and Leveller printer John Harris.[63] Thompson had already tried to raise a revolt at Towcester and at Coventry, where he found the city gates closed against him.[64]

As soon as the revolt occurred Cromwell called a review of his and Fairfax's regiment in Hyde Park before heading west to confront the mutineers. Some appeared with the sea green ribbon in their hats and many announced they would not fight fellow soldiers. Cromwell railed against the Levellers but had to promise that any who did not want to fight could leave with their arrears. Most discarded the sea green emblems and were reduced to obedience.[65] In all Cromwell left London with five regiments, two of horse and three of foot.[66] But even by the time Cromwell called a further rendezvous of his and Fairfax's troops at Andover on 12 May he had to address them again promising to 'live and die with them' in fighting 'against those Revolters which are now called Levellers'. Some of his troops were still saying 'they would not fight against their friends'.[67]

Forces under Colonel John Reynolds caught up with the Leveller troops near Newbridge and prevented them from crossing the Thames, forcing them to a ford higher up the river. There was an initial skirmish between 100 horse and '200 of the Levellers, and after a sharp conflict, the Levellers declining engagement, retreated towards Oxford'. Events reached their climax at Burford.[68] Major Francis White, who had been sent by Cromwell to negotiate with the mutineers at the beginning of the revolt, was with them drawing up documents to be taken to Cromwell in the following morning when, at midnight, a body of horse under Cromwell drew up at the north end of Burford and attacked.[69] The only resistance came from troops with Colonel William Eyre, whom we have seen as a key Leveller figure at Ware: 'there was only one centre of resistance—the Crowne Inn, in the centre of town, where Sheep Street joins the High Street. Here Colonel William Eyre led a desperate little resistance, during which one man was killed and two wounded, before himself being taken prisoner'.[70] Eyre declared that if only ten men had stepped forward for the cause, he would have made the eleventh. Cromwell expressed 'much dissatisfaction' with White when the major told him the violence was unnecessary.[71] Some 300 captured mutineers were kept overnight in Burford church, where one of them, Anthony Sedley, carved his name and the words '1649. Prisner' into the stone font, where it can still be seen. Cromwell had three of the mutineers—Corporal Perkins, Corporal Church and Cornet Thompson—shot in Burford churchyard.[72] Cornet James Thompson was the brother of William Thompson. Thompson himself briefly took refuge in Northampton, where he seized the magazine and distributed money to the poor. But in the wake of the Burford defeat he and a small band of followers were hunted down and he was killed while resisting capture. Eyre, because he was not formally commissioned at the time, was sent to Oxford castle 'to be proceeded against at Common Law'.[73]

Cromwell claimed he was dealing with a widespread Leveller rising. He wrote that the Levellers planned to raise their 'standard of Sea-green Colours' in York, Oxford, Bristol, Gloucester 'and many other places in the West of England' and that they had actually made proclamations 'throughout the Counties of Oxford, Gloucester and Worcester'. He also noted Leveller claims to have 'great influence in divers Regiments of the Army' and that action had been taken against Leveller influence in the regiments of Scroop, Harrison and 'divers others'.[74] Certainly one contemporary report claimed, 'The Agitators are now again in every regiment, and they carry out their designs dayly'.[75] There are grounds for these claims.

The Burford mutinies took place in the direct aftermath of Lockyer's execution and while protests were taking place by Leveller supporters in London to have their leaders freed from the Tower. The edition of *The Moderate* that reported the mutiny at Salisbury also reported a petition of Leveller women calling for the freedom of the prisoners in the Tower and denouncing the death of Lockyer as 'the blood of War . . . shed in time of Peace'.[76] In response the Commons ordered that the troops guarding the Tower be supplemented with loyal units and that the Leveller leaders be denied visitors and access to pen and paper. Cromwell was reported as saying that unless 'Lilburn and Walwyn were by some means or other taken out of the way they could not carry on their design'.[77] The Burford mutiny had been preceded by the mutiny in Captain Bray's troop. Colonel

Hewson's regiment mutinied in late April and it was news of this that triggered the original revolt by Scroop's regiment at Salisbury. In South Wales, eighty troopers from Horton's regiment set off to join the Salisbury revolt but turned back when they heard of the defeat at Burford. Three companies of Skippon's foot marched to Salisbury led by a Leveller major, but when they arrived they did not join the revolt, though they pledged not to fight against it.[78] Rainsborough's old regiment attempted to mutiny at Minehead before embarkation for Ireland.[79] On 27 April there was news from Haverford that 'the Levelling party, so called, are very active in these parts . . . the people and some of the souldiery comply with them, saying they hold out essential points for Freedom and Liberty, and desire to Center and Acquiesse in their proposals'. From Barnstaple it was reported on 5 May, 'These parts complain much of want and misery. Much discontents amongst the Souldiery, who are so possest with the Levellers rational doctrines, that its feared, it will ere long . . . tell the Nation their affectionate thoughts thereof'.[80] In Portsmouth and the Isle of Wight the army had to 'fight with the Levellers'. There were reports that Captain, previously Cornet, Joyce was leading a revolt. Joyce, it was said, had 'sweld . . . from a Taylor to a Cornet, and from a Cornet to a grand Segnior amongst the Levellers, able in his thoughts to conquer Parliament and Army, with no longer a weapon than a Spanish Needle'.[81] In Poole Lieutenant Colonel John Rede was accused of supporting the Levellers at the 'time of great danger when the Levellers rose in actual arms against the State'.[82]

It may be, of course, that Cromwell was exaggerating the threat of the Levellers. It may be that he genuinely thought it to be greater than it was. Or it may be that the revolt, and the potential for the revolt, was indeed considerable and that this is what required the deployment of sizable military force led by Cromwell himself. Richard Baxter thought the Levellers at Burford alone commanded about 1,500 men and that Cromwell had only just caught them in time before they could 'get their numbers together' and so 'the Levellers War was crush't in the Egg'. The best estimate is that the total number involved in the Leveller mutinies was over 2,500 men. Cromwell and Fairfax's force dispatched from London to confront the Burford mutiny was not twice that size.[83] Certainly the elaborate titles and awards showered on Cromwell and his fellow officers in thanksgiving ceremonies in both Oxford University and Westminster seem to indicate that the traditional elites thought that a real threat had been defeated.[84]

The Oxford mutiny

The regiment of twenty-eight-year-old Richard Ingoldsby was at the heart of the last Leveller mutiny in Oxford. Ingoldsby was from the Buckinghamshire gentry and his mother was Oliver Cromwell's sister, but his men were of a different nature. They were considered one of the most radical regiments in the New Model Army: they had, with Rainsborough's regiment, seized the parliamentary artillery train at Oxford two years previously. They were one of the first regiments to petition against a personal treaty and in favour of bringing the king to justice. And they were sympathetic to the Burford mutineers, though unable to join them after the force under John Reynolds pushed the Salisbury rebels westward away from Oxford. William Eyre had been imprisoned in Oxford after Burford, but was moved to Warwick Castle for fear of the effect he was having on the troops. They were a ready audience for Lilburne's *The Outcry of the Youngmen and Apprentices* when it appeared in early September 1649 with its call for the soldiers to re-elect their Agitators.[85]

Lilburne himself gave copies of *The Outcry* to soldiers in Fairfax's life-guard, and in Oxford, John Radman, first elected Agitator of Ingoldsby's regiment at Triploe Heath, was distributing copies of this and other radical material. In the first week of September anger within the regiment exploded into the open. Major John Mills wrote to Fairfax reporting 'Great discontents and disturbances' in the ranks. While both Ingoldsby and his lieutenant colonel were away from Oxford, the remaining officers called a rendezvous in order to 'undeceive them' about the 'scandalous Papers' and to offer them a declaration drawn up by the officers. Yet the men were not easily placated. They 'would not be satisfyed with any thing but what some men chosen by them should present'. Mills told them that he would not tolerate the re-election of Agitators and that 'my Lord General, and a General Council of the Army, had formerly dissolved such kinde of things'. The officers were nevertheless 'forced to suffer some particular souldyers to prepare and represent their desires to us, which this they did, by which we gather they drive for a Court of Agitators, the performance of the engagement at Triploe Heath, and the Agreement of the people'. The rendezvous ended peaceably enough with the Agitators agreeing to consider the officers' declaration.[86]

The next morning the Agitators rejected the officers' declaration and enclosed their own proposal that called for the reinstatement of the Council of the Army and support for the declarations of Newmarket and Triploe Heath. The two sides met to discuss their demands. The Agitators were wary given the previous breaking of engagements by officers but a joint petition was debated from Thursday to Saturday. Ultimately the Agitators' demands were too much for the officers and they refused to back them. The main areas of disagreement were over the recall of the Army Council, the removal of tithes, and the demand for arrears to be paid within six months. The revolt now broke into open mutiny. The Agitators marched a company to New College, where the magazine was kept, and took control of it. A Captain Wagstaff was taken prisoner as he tried to leave Oxford that evening. Mutineers broke into their major's lodging at midnight and with 'naked swords' forced him from his bed. He and all the other officers were rounded up and brought to New College.[87]

This was now a full-scale revolt involving hundreds of troops. Ingoldsby's regiment were joined by part of Colonel Tomlinson's regiment of 600 horse. The *Moderate Intelligencer* reported on 8 September

> they have the Magazine in their possession, and their Officers whom they detain as prisoners at large, according to the usual mode; they expect the Levellers from London, and other parts, and to be 500 horse in a few days, there come in daily to them, and they brag now Col. Reynolds and Major Shelborns rude Blades are in Ireland, there will not be so many of the army against them as for them.

London Levellers did come to join them. The university was in uproar. 'The scholars at the first beginning of the Mutiny declared themselves so much against it, as they offered the officers to assist them with six hundred men armed to adventure themselves against the mutineers'. The central government was no less alarmed and the Council of State ordered Fairfax to redouble efforts to suppress distempers in other regiments and to dispatch Colonel Lambert to put down the Oxford revolt. Lambert began to assemble a force comprising Colonel Cox's regiment and seventeen other companies drawn from the regiments of Fairfax and Pride and Okey's dragoons.[88]

Colonel Ingoldsby arrived back in Oxford in the early hours of Sunday morning. The Agitators allowed him to stay at an inn in the town but placed a guard on him that included John Radman. On Sunday morning the mutineers brought all the regiments' colours to New College and mounted artillery at the college gates. About midday they sent drummers out into the city and a proclamation was read calling on all the regiment to join them or else leave the city. But events were about to take another turn. Early on Monday morning the captured officers at New College confronted their guards in the courtyard of the college. They prevailed on them to allow them to leave, despite some soldiers shouting 'No' as they forced their way out of the gates. They made their way towards the inn where Ingoldsby was being held, stopping off at a cutler's shop to arm themselves with swords. When they reached the inn the guard set by the Agitators stood their ground with swords drawn and pistols at the ready. The loyal officers were forced out of the inn yard but they then closed the gate, trapping the rebels inside. Meanwhile one of the officers ran into the inn to talk to Ingoldsby, but he was confronted by John Radman commanding the guard. Ingoldsby was now alert to the situation and, still being armed, forced his way through the guard and reasserted his authority over some of the soldiers. In the ensuing struggle one Agitator who had arrived on horseback had his horse wounded. It fell under him in the street and Ingoldsby's loyal soldiers chased him down the road. He killed one soldier who tried to prevent his escape, but he got away successfully. John Radman also made good his escape. Ingoldsby took the force he had won over, made the Agitators his prisoner, and set guards at the East Gate of the city. He then headed for New College, picking up more loyal soldiers as he went. Before long the rebels at New College were overpowered.[89]

The state's retribution was swift. On Saturday 15 September a court martial at Oxford presided over by Lambert, Robert Lilburne, Ingoldsby and the governor of Wallingford sentenced three private soldiers, Piggen, Biggs and Hoyden, to death. Seven others were cashiered and Captain Shrimpton, Ensign Scot and another marshal in the regiment were sentenced to run the gauntlet because they had refused to join Ingoldsby in suppressing the rebellion. Hoyden was pardoned for joining with Ingoldsby when he moved against the mutiny. On Tuesday 18 September Piggen and Biggs were shot outside the city walls near the castle. Piggen was 'very resolute, and not at all fearful of death, saying that he died for what he acted for the good and ease of the people, who were now under great oppression and slavery, and some such like expressions of penitency. Mr Biggs likewise died very pertinently', according to one witness.

In contrast the victors were entertained by the university vice chancellor and other dignitaries, as they had done Cromwell and his officers after the suppression of the Burford mutiny. Lambert was presented with 'a pair of rich gloves'. Other loyal officers also received gloves. The royalist news-sheet *Mercurius Pragmaticus* thought the whole event was staged just to get Lambert 'another Thanksgiving-Dinner out of the Wise-men of Guildhall'. It also reported the relief of MPs in the Commons, where 'up went the eggs of their eyes like a Wash-ball in a Barbars bason', as John Bradshaw denounced *The Outcry*. The Commons ordered the trial of the author of *The Outcry* and the civilians involved in the Oxford mutiny under the recently passed Treason Act. A new Act to suppress the printing and sale of anti-regime pamphlets was brought forth.[90]

But even now, in the midst of the final defeat of the Leveller mutinies, there were signs that the movement could command active support. In Windsor a party of Levellers had broken in the prison doors and freed some soldiers imprisoned for using 'many incivilities' to the mayor of Wickham. There were 'commotions' concerning Levellers at Lichfield. In Carlisle 'Some of the Levelling party hearabout, do much storm at the shooting of their friends at Oxford . . . And likewise that there should be any thought of bringing Lieutenant Colonel John Lilburne, and other true Assertors of Englands Freedom to Tryal'. A letter to *The Moderate* from Bristol, where Major John Cobbett was stationed, claimed, 'We find that the Levellers Interest have very large influence, not only upon these parts but we hear upon most Counties of the Nation'.[91] Henry Parker, employed as one of Cromwell's penmen, still thought that Lilburne had between 10,000 and 20,000 supporters, although he dismissed the greatest part of these 'turbulent Levellers' as consisting of 'women, boyes, Mechanicks, and the most sorid sediment or our Plebians'.[92]

What some modern historians who tend to dissolve Leveller organisation into the wider spectrum of radical parliamentarianism fail to explain is not the Levellers at their height when they had a hegemonic relationship with other constituencies around them but their continued strength even at the moment of their defeat. Shorn of Independent support and of much support from the gathered churches, with some members of their leadership departed and their main leaders imprisoned, the Levellers could still produce pamphlets with a coherent analysis, could petition and protest repeatedly on a mass scale, and could be at the root of three successive mutinies in the army. It is some indicator of what must have been the reach of the organisation at its height if this was the scale of its activity when reduced to its narrowest base.

The trial of John Lilburne

By the autumn of 1649 the Leveller movement had sustained a series of heavy blows. A section of its support among the gathered churches had moved into open opposition; its main leaders were prisoners in the Tower; the Bishopsgate, Burford and Oxford mutinies had all been defeated; and their prime movers had been shot or jailed. For John Lilburne personally things were worse still. Elizabeth Lilburne had been ill with smallpox and narrowly escaped death. Two of their three children, both boys, were not so lucky and died of the same illness, leaving only a daughter. It was at this moment that the regime enacted a long-considered plan to put Lilburne on trial for his life. The charge was treason. Though the trial had been long considered it was the publication of *The Outcry of the Youngmen and Apprentices of London* and its role in igniting the Oxford mutiny that propelled the government into action. The Levellers petitioned against the trial. Both Lilburne's brother Robert and his wife Elizabeth petitioned Parliament to drop the trial. Lilburne himself would have preferred to avoid open battle, in part because Elizabeth was understandably distraught at the prospect of losing her husband as well as two children. He offered to settle the charges in front of four MPs, two of which his accusers would choose and two of which, probably Henry Marten and Alexander Rigby, Lilburne would nominate. He even offered to go into voluntary exile. It was all to no avail. Clement Walker, the chronicler of the trial, wrote that the rejection of these pleas 'very much confirme me in the belief of that common report, that he was judged and condemned before he was tryed or heard'. And so it was that in these inauspicious circumstances on 24 October 1649 the trial began at the Guildhall.[93]

This was certainly a show trial and, for that reason, very large crowds were allowed to fill the Guildhall, some of them standing on scaffolding, for the duration of the trial. The judges, for the same reason, wanted it to be seen that Lilburne had a fair chance to conduct his defence. Lilburne had thought that he might be brought to trial for consorting with royalists, partly because there had recently been a plan to entrap him into writing an appeal to Prince Charles.[94] But Lilburne had had none of that and, in any case, the prosecution must have thought that this was an unlikely gambit. In the end the regime settled for a straightforward prosecution based on the accusation that Lilburne was agitating to overthrow the state, particularly by appeals directed to soldiers in the New Model Army. Their evidence relied very heavily on citation from Lilburne's published works: *The Outcry,*

The Impeachment of High Treason against Oliver Cromwell, A Salva Libertate, The Legall and Fundamental Liberties, A preparative to a Hue and Cry after Sir Arthur Haselrig, and the *Agreement of the People.*

This combination of factors produced a deeply unsatisfactory mood inside the Guildhall, at least from the prosecution's point of view. Lilburne made long and sustained interventions that even the eight judges struggled to control. When Lilburne was not actually speaking himself the clerk was frequently asked by the prosecuting attorney, Edmund Prideaux, to read out long extracts from the offending pamphlets. When Lilburne spoke his words were met with warm approval by the overwhelmingly sympathetic crowd and the extracts from the pamphlets 'pleased the People as well as if they had acted before them one of Ben Jonson's plays'.[95] At one point Lilburne himself had to quieten the crowd just to hear what was being said by his accusers. Lilburne eschewed for the most part rhetorical flights, even though the prosecution both accused him of doing so; he played a dead-bat defence. Much of the first day of the trial was taken up with argument about whether the court was a proper court, whether the trial could proceed when the laws were in Latin and French, and whether the judges would allow Lilburne legal counsel. Lilburne refused even to swear his name or to plead unless they agreed to grant him a lawyer. Ultimately the judges ruled he could have counsel if any issue of legal interpretation arose. On this basis Lilburne agreed to plead, although subsequently the judges both refused counsel and refused to allow him time to prepare his case. Then Lilburne relied on retelling his service to Parliament since it first challenged the king. The point was clear: how could the judges accuse the victim of the Star Chamber, the hero of Brentford, the man who faced down the cavalier court at Oxford, of undermining the Commonwealth? Lilburne resorted to this stratagem so often that Justice Keeble had to remind him that they were there to hear him defend himself, 'not to hear you tell the story of all your life'. Finally, and probably least effectively, Lilburne simply refused to say that he was the author of any of the pamphlets, even the ones with his name on them. It was up to the court to prove that they were his and he would not assist them by incriminating himself, he told them. Christ had preached to all that he was the son of God, but when challenged to say so by Pilate he refused. So Freeborn John would not admit to his accusers that the books were his, no matter what might be said elsewhere.[96]

Only on the second day of the trial, and not without contention, was the jury impanelled. Even before Lilburne managed to disable some jurors that he did not like the look of, they seemed a promising dozen citizens drawn from Smithfield, Cheapside and Friday Street, long known as centres of radicalism. One of their number, John Hinde, took down the trial in short-hand and this was probably one source of Walker's account.[97] For historians the interest in the examination of witnesses is less about the courtroom drama and more about what it tells us about Leveller organisation and the state's fears about it. The whole drive of the government's case was that Lilburne was fomenting rebellion systematically. They needed to implicate Lilburne directly in this work. What emerges is one of the single most detailed accounts of Leveller organisation since George Masterson gave his evidence about the Wapping meeting at the bar of the Commons some twenty months earlier.

Burford, and the threat of its repetition, was at the forefront of Attorney Prideaux's concerns. He is interested in the printing of Lilburne's pamphlets and distribution, especially to soldiers. Printer Thomas Newcombe was called to give evidence about the printing of *The Outcry*. Newcombe had been arrested for this work but released to give evidence against Lilburne. Prideaux argued that *The Outcry* 'hath a very dangerous Title, and in the Direction especially to the Souldiers of the Army', not least in its defence of 'the Rebels at Burford' who are 'Mr. Lilburns deare friends'. Additionally *The Outcry* was intended 'for a dangerous end, Which was to stir up the great mutiny that was in the City of Oxford'. Newcombe gave evidence that Lilburne and a Captain Jones arrived at his printshop with only the last sheet of *The Outcry* and he did not know where the rest of the book was printed. Jones agreed a price and Lilburne returned later with a proof of the work. Lilburne and Jones returned a third time to correct the printing errors. Apart from Samuel Chidley's report of Lilburne correcting proofs we have no better report of Lilburne's close personal attention to the process of pamphlet production.[98]

The next three witnesses were all soldiers, John Tooke, John Skinner and Thomas Lewis. Seven weeks previously, on 6 September, they had been at dinner with a fourth soldier, John Smith, after their duties at the guardhouse near St Pauls. And as they were walking after they had eaten in Ivy Lane near St Pauls they met Lilburne. Thomas Lewis already knew Lilburne and had previously visited him in the Tower. Lilburne asked them to go for a beer in the Red Crosse tavern in Newgate market. After some conversation Lilburne asked if they had seen *The Outcry* and Thomas Lewis said he had heard of it and was hoping to buy one as he had heard they were for sale at around the Exchange. Lilburne said he had just been given a single copy and passed it on to Lewis, who thanked him for saving him the penny to buy it. Lewis told Lilburne he 'might buy some more of them' and Lilburne directed him to an address in Martin's Lane. Lewis conveniently forgot the name of the contact Lilburne gave him.[99] The prosecution then moved on to examine Thomas Daffren, one of those who accompanied Lilburne on the delegation that presented his objections to the officers' *Agreement* the previous December. Daffren testified that he had met Lilburne on London Bridge on 12 August and accompanied him back to his home in Winchester House, Southwark. Daffren told Lilburne he was going to Warwickshire the next day. Lilburne knew that Eyre had been transferred from Oxford jail to Warwick Castle to prevent him propagandising among the troops. He asked Daffren to take a copy of *The Impeachment of High Treason* to Eyre, which he did. Unfortunately it found its way into the hands of the castle's governor and from there to Lilburne's prosecutors.[100]

This testimony was important to the prosecution because they wished to focus on Lilburne's organised relationship with his supporters. The passages that the clerk was required to read out, from *The Impeachment*, for instance, are those that stressed organisation:

> write to your friends in every Country of England, to chuse out from among themselves and send up some Agents to you, (two at least from each County, with money in their pockets to bear their charges) to consider with your culled and chosen Agents of some effectual course speedily to be taken . . .

Prideaux damned Lilburne for having 'blown the Trumpet for all to come in, he hath set up his Center, he would have it be a Standard for all his friends to flock to him'.[101] Citing reports from *The Moderate*, Prideaux accused Lilburne of being 'closely joyned' with 'open Traytors and Rebels' to promote the *Agreement of the People* by overthrowing the existing state 'by force and Arms'. Damning Cromwell for executing Private Arnold at Ware and defending the Burford mutineers were also brought in as evidence of this scheme.[102]

This mountain of evidence did not achieve what the prosecution hoped. Luck remained with Lilburne. As he was pleading yet again to be allowed more time to withdraw and consult his books, and being refused once again by Justice Keeble, Lilburne, 'in a mighty voice', called out to God:

> I appeale to the righteous God of heaven and earth against you, where I am sure, I shall be heard and find access, and the Lord God Omnipotent, and a

mighty Judge betwixt you and me, and requier and requite my bloud upon the heads of you and your posterity, to the third and fourth generation.

At this exact point the scaffolding on which some of the crowd were standing collapsed into the hall with 'a great noise and some confusion by reason of the peoples tumbling'. Some spectators were hurt and it took almost an hour to restore order, during which the 'terrifyed and unjust Judges . . . did nothing but stare one upon another'. When the court resumed Lilburne was found making good use of the interruption to study his books and papers. It was a brave juryman who could ignore such direct divine intervention, and a humourless one who could put out of his mind Lilburne's next piece of theatre. Barred from leaving the court to relieve himself, Lilburne demanded a chamber pot be brought to him at the bar. And while it was being brought Lilburne was again consulting his notes. When it arrived 'he made water, and gave it to the Foreman'.[103]

Lilburne's most powerful argument, and the one that angered the judges the most, was that the jury were judges of law as well of the facts of the case. That is, they were to say not only whether the letter of the law had been transgressed but whether the law itself was just. In a powerful oration towards the end of the trial Lilburne addressed 'my honest Jury and Fellow-Citizens, who I declare by the law of England, are the Conservators and sole Judges of my life, having inherent in them alone, the juridical power of the law, as well as fact', and described 'you Judges that sit there' as 'being no more, if they please, but Ciphers to pronounce the Sentence, or their Clerks, to say Amen to them, being at the best, in your Original, but Norman Conquerours, Intruders'. To which the crowd called out 'Amen, Amen'. The atmosphere in the court was such that Major General Skippon brought up three more companies of foot to add to the guard.[104]

At five o'clock on 26 October the jury retired to consider their verdict. By six o'clock they were back in court. The cryer asked the foreman of the jury if John Lilburne were 'guilty of the Treasons, charged upon him: or any of them, or not guilty?' The foreman replied, 'Not guilty of all of them'. The clerk seemed disconcerted and asked again, 'Nor of all the Treason, or any of them that are layed to his charge?' And the foreman again replied, 'No, of all, nor any one of them'. Clement Walker recorded that 'immediatly the whole multitude of the People in the Hall, for joy at the Prisoners acquittall gave such a loud and unanimous shout, as is believed, was never heard in the Yeeld-hall'. The cheering lasted for half an hour without a break, 'which made the Judges for fear, turne pale, and hange down their heads'. The judges left quickly 'for fear the People should pull them off their seats of Justice by the eares'. As they passed through the streets they 'were scoff'd, mock'd and derided by Men, Women and Children'. Lilburne 'stood silent at the Barre, rather more sad in his countenance then he was before'. Relief and exhaustion, no doubt, were his dominant sensations. In spite of the verdict Skippon was ordered to take him back to the Tower. The 'extraordinary acclamations' and 'loud rejoycings' carried on outside the Guildhall were 'the like of which hath not been seen in England'. The cheering crowds followed Lilburne to the gates of the Tower. Even the soldiers in the guard were cheering. That night bells rang and bonfires blazed in the streets. Later no less than three versions of a commemorative medal were struck in silver, copper gilt and copper with Lilburne's profile on one side and a list of the jurors' names on the other. Another smaller version was also cast with a small ring at the top so that it could be worn around the neck. And yet there was still no release from captivity. It was only when 'the People wondered and began to grumble' that Henry Marten, Edmund Ludlow and other sympathetic MPs managed to ensure that, on 8 November, John Lilburne, Richard Overton, William Walwyn and Thomas Prince walked from the Tower.[105]

Henry Parker, the regime amanuensis, thought Lilburne had flattered the jury by telling them they were judges of law as well as of fact, and 'lest these gentle stroaklings should not sufficiently win upon them, you place some hundreds of your Myrmidons behind in ambuscade, who are ready to break forth with mighty hums, and acclamations, at the closing of your defence'. The jury were susceptible to such techniques, 'half of them being congregated out of Chicklane, Pickt-hatch, and other suburbs of Smithfield, without one Butcher amongst them'. This, for Parker, was all one with Lilburne's doctrine that 'the Flower of the Nation must subject to the bran, or else Libertie cannot prosper: the Gentleman must be order'd at the pezants direction, the Judge must do the mean office of the Clerk, and cry Amen to the Juryman'. 'How', opined Parker, 'Levelling therefore should stand Liberty amongst men, when it stands not with that more perfect Order which is amongst the Angels, I cannot see'.[106] Lilburne and Parker were polar opposites on the spectrum of the Revolution. Parker was legally trained and had acted in the role of intellectual private secretary to the earl of Essex, John Pym, Henry Ireton and Cromwell. While secretary for the Merchant Adventurers' Company he defended them against the Levellers and had worked with Thomas May, another parliamentary critic of Lilburne. His overriding political concern was that the general interests of the state triumph over lesser sectional interests, even to the extent that state interest might override the law. Lilburne's defenders were as alive to this division as were his enemies. A reply to Parker by John Jones said that there were no grounds for abusing the jurors simply because they worked with their hands, for 'I conceive writing is but an handi-craft taught a Lawyer' and that 'the meanest handicrafts man, when he growth rich, turns Merchant, that he may live Lazier', and so there was no reason why 'Plow men . . . which are the best kinde of free men in England' should not be jurors who judged law and fact. This, in essence, was the cleavage that now separated Independents and Levellers: the interests of the established state elite versus any notion of popular sovereignty.[107]

There had been divisions in the Revolutionary camp before, but the bloc had previously been recomposed on successively more radical grounds under the threat of counterrevolution. That threat removed, the bloc fractured irretrievably. In a year that saw a rupture in the Levellers' relationship with some gathered churches; the arrest of their leaders; and the defeats of Bishopsgate, Burford and Oxford, Lilburne's victory at the Guildhall was not enough to turn the tide. After his release Lilburne was elected to the Common Council, but the election was quashed by the state. His very presence in England was too much for the new masters of the state. He was forced into exile and told that, if he should return, he would be tried once more for his life. This was the end of the Levellers as an effective political movement.

CHAPTER 14

Lieutenant Colonel John Rede's Last Stand

The brilliant splinters of the Leveller movement were scattered across the political landscape after the defeats of 1649. Many Levellers continued to be politically active, but they were no longer a collective leadership or an effective movement. They charted their different courses, sometimes by accommodation, sometimes in opposition, to the new regime. John Lilburne was exiled on pain of death, despite the victory in his treason trial. He returned nevertheless, was tried again for his life, and was again victorious. Still too dangerous to be released, in 1654 Cromwell had him interred in Jersey, where the writ of habeas corpus did not run. In 1657, shortly after he became a Quaker, he died while on bail in Eltham in Kent and was buried in the new churchyard in Bishopsgate. William Walwyn retired to private life, writing books on medicine. Richard and Mary Overton spent time in the Netherlands, dabbled a little and inconclusively with royalist opponents of Cromwell, and then disappeared from view. Henry Marten retained his sympathy with the Levellers and his friendship with Lilburne. He was expelled with the Rump and branded a 'whoremaster' by Cromwell, probably the only man to be so called by both the late king and the new Protector. As a Regicide Marten was lucky to escape with his life at the Restoration, deploying Lilburne-like tactics at his trial. He spent the remainder of his life in jail at Chepstow Castle. Both Sexby and Wildman accommodated to and plotted against the new regime, directly implicated in an attempt to kill Cromwell. Sexby famously defended this course of action in the pamphlet *Killing Noe Murder*. He was imprisoned in the Tower, where he died in 1658. William Bray was eventually released from prison in 1651 and was still writing pamphlets in defence of the Leveller cause in the brief radical revival that came between Cromwell's death and Charles II's enthronement. Samuel Chidley and William Larner continued as radical critics of the republic, the former pushing for greater legislative reform, the latter keeping his press busy printing in defence of the Good Old Cause.[1]

There are many such stories that could be told which show how the political waters closed over the heads of the Levellers in the 1650s, and demonstrate the social forces that combined against them. Perhaps the most obvious histories would be found at the centre of power, in London, where the leaders of the Leveller movement confronted their opponents. But, unlikely as it may seem, one of the most powerful illustrations of the fate of the Leveller movement can be found in the Dorset port of Poole, where a little-known Leveller ally was military governor. Far from London and far from the heart of the Leveller movement a drama was played out which illuminated how the local elite of both Presbyterian and Independent persuasions closed ranks in the face of political and religious radicalism. This was in many ways a microcosm of national events, partly because the local elites had, and could not do without, powerful national political allies.

Before this final confrontation took place, the events in Poole also show how Leveller influence travelled far from the capital and how alliances between Levellers and other radicals were formed. And after the final scenes in Poole came to their close we can see one of the ways in which Leveller supporters dealt with defeat and how the radical legacy fed into the underground Nonconformist tradition for decades to come. But first let us meet the figure at the heart of these events, Wiltshire yeoman Lieutenant Colonel John Rede.[2]

John Rede lived a long life and thus gives us a chance to see how his political affiliations altered with the changing times. Rede was a radical parliamentarian and an Independent. But he also falls within the circle of Leveller allies. He was a separatist in religion and these views clearly made him sympathetic to the Levellers. In addition he was a supporter of the radical political programme associated with the Levellers and only the most radical of the Independents in 1649. And in the great division within the victorious parliamentarian camp that year his sympathy was with the Levellers to the degree that he took the dangerous step of sheltering John Radman, one of the leaders of the last Leveller armed mutiny in Oxford. This gave his Presbyterian and moderate Independent enemies the chance to successfully move against him, part of a wider pattern of removing Leveller sympathisers from positions of trust within the army and the state.

John Rede of Porton

John Rede was born in 1615 and died ninety-five years later in 1710.[3] There seems little doubt that Rede was a charismatic figure. It was long remembered that 'when young he could lay his hand on the saddle of the 1st troopers horse & vault unto that of the fourth' and that he never 'took a dose of physick in his life'. This rude health was sustained by a diet that included 'his usual food' of 'a breakfast of milk porridge with 1 pound of butter: roast or boild beef' with which he 'drank ale at little supper'. But as well as being physically robust he was 'a man of learning for those times particularly in the Hebrew language'. At the age of ninety he used 'to ride over to a clergyman at Salusbury' from his farm at Porton in the south of Wiltshire to converse with him in Hebrew. Rede married three times, to widow Ann Errington of Purbeck; Elizabeth Baynton, the daughter of Nicholas Baynton of New Sarum; and Sarah Bernard, also a widow. He married Sarah at the age of seventy-eight. A loss of appetite singled his approaching death and he took it as a signal to make his will.[4] He was still recalled as 'a violent Republican & independent' after his death.[5]

We know little of Rede's life between his marriage to Ann Errington in 1636 and the civil war. It is equally difficult to trace Rede's early military career, partly because there were many Redes in the army.[6] But John Rede of Porton was appointed on 1 July 1644 to the Militia Committee for Wiltshire, sitting alongside Denzil Holles, Sir Edward Hungerford, Sir Edward Baynton, radical Independent Edmund Ludlow, and others. Rede disappears from the committee fifteen days later, possibly because he was now in military service under Ludlow, whose task it was to secure Wiltshire for Parliament during the First Civil War.[7]

A few months later, in the dead of winter 1644, Rede was engaged in the battle for the county town, Salisbury. Ludlow's forces were caught in a night battle with overwhelmingly superior royalist attackers. In the snow-covered streets of the town Ludlow charged the enemy in the hope that the darkness would hide the fact he was outnumbered. At first the ruse worked. But soon the royalists realised the odds were in their favour and took the town.[8] When Ludlow had entered Salisbury he had made the belfry of the cathedral, then a free-standing structure in the Close, into a strong point. Ludlow had left Rede to hold the belfry. As the battle turned Ludlow was forced to escape alone, pistolling one of his pursuers as he fled. As soon as he was safe he 'endeavoured to procure some force for the relief of those poor men that were left in the belfry at Salisbury'. But while he was about this task he heard of their fate:

> after vigorous resistance for the most part of that day, the enemies had forced a collier to drive a cart, loaden with charcoal, to the door of the belfry, (where he lost his life) and burnt down the door, which in a day's time we should have secured by a breast-work; but for want thereof Lieu-tenant-Colonel Read was forced to yield the place to the enemy upon such terms as he could get, which were, to have their lives, and to be prisoners of war.[9]

Rede may have been one of those prisoners who escaped when a handful of the local citizens confronted the royalist guards and put them to flight. Or he may have been freed a little later when Ludlow organised an exchange of the parliamentary prisoners for royalists held at Southampton.[10] He may have been at the council of war held in May 1647 at Bury St Edmunds alongside the army Agitators Edward Sexby, Nicholas Lockyer, William Allen and Tobias Box. The record simply names 'Lieu. Col. Read', so this could either be John Rede or Lieutenant Colonel Thomas Reade, with whom John Rede is sometimes confused.[11] But John Rede was definitely named in the parliamentary ordinance of July 1647 as one of those respon-sible in Wiltshire for raising funds for the New Model Army. The next sighting of Rede was at the Putney debates. It is probable that it was John Rede who spoke in the Putney debates on 28 October 1647. The interven-tion is in the debate on the franchise and its sentiments are certainly in line with Leveller sympathies. He told the meeting, 'I suppose itt's concluded by all, that chusing a Representative is a priviledge; now I see noe reason why any man that is a native ought to bee excluded that priviledge, unless from volunatarie servitude'.[12]

Rede's radical sympathies seem to have been fully developed by this point. His signature appears on the front page of his copy of prophetess Mary Cary's 1647 pamphlet *A Word in Season to the Kingdom of England*. This is a spirited defence of the right of lay preaching and of separatist congregations. It takes up the cudgels against Presbyterian heresy hunter and anti-Leveller controversialist Thomas Edwards.[13] Cary was later to be a defender of the regicide and a Fifth Monarchist.[14] This association, and the attempt to appoint Baptist John Gardner as preacher in Poole, examined below, suggest that Rede was an example of the coming together of radical religious sentiment and Leveller sympathy.[15]

The governor and his opponents

On the last day of the Putney debates, 11 November 1647, Rede was made governor of Poole by Sir Thomas Fairfax.[16] The fact that this commission was issued on the last day of the debates increases the likelihood that Rede was at Putney. There had previously been an attempt to appoint Leveller John Wildman to the governorship of Poole but this had been blocked by Fairfax.[17] Nevertheless, Rede's appointment was part of the takeover of key garrisons that followed the army's entry into London in August 1647.[18] Rede's connections with the Levellers are first apparent in a letter written to Rede on 25 January 1648 by William Clarke, Fairfax's secretary, detailing the fate of the Levellers in London. The letter specifically refers to the arrest of John Lilburne and John Wildman, at the Levellers' Well-yard meeting in Wapping in early January 1648.[19] Clarke goes on to report another event in which Levellers were involved: the meeting attended by William Eyre and some eighty other army officers in Broadway, Worcestershire, which planned a widespread rising in the West of England. The letter contains a postscript asking that Rede pass on greetings from Clarke to a Mr Lockyer, with whom Rede was clearly on good terms.[20]

Rede initially commanded considerable support in Poole. Some 150 townspeople and worthies, including former MP George Skutt, later Rede's nemesis, petitioned in his support.[21] This was soon after Rede's initial appointment when the threat of the return of the king made mainstream parliamentarians sensitive to the need to secure the gains of the Revolution. But as the execution of the king and the proclamation of a republic banished that immediate fear, debate increasingly turned on what the religious and political settlement of the nation would look like. It was not long before these issues brought Rede into conflict with the local elite.

Rede also seems to have taken on duties additional to his governorship of Poole in the midst of the crisis caused by the Second Civil War. Parliament ordered Wiltshire to be put in a state of defence at the request of Edmund Ludlow, Rede's old commander. Ludlow named Rede as one of the commissioners responsible for raising the militia. But moderate parliamentarians were quick to object on the grounds that 'this Reid (for his part) had often declared himself against Kingly power, saying, he thought this Kingdome might be governed better without a King'. It was also objected in a long debate that Ludlow's appointments were all 'base, meane fellowes, Sectaries, and such as are against Monarchy'. Ludlow, it was said, was 'setting up base fellowes, to trample down the Gentry'. The royalist press also reported that Rede was accused of being merely 'a servingman' and that his fellow commissioners 'were of no Estates in the County'. Of course he was not a serving man and this is simply routine royalist abuse, but it is true that Rede was a yeoman farmer and a long way from being one of the leading county families.[22] Similar accusations of political radicalism and sectarian religious affiliation, underpinned by social elitism, were about to play their part in the conflict in Poole.

Perhaps we can see the conflict in Poole emerging in July 1648 when Rede wrote to the Derby House committee complaining of the need to repair and reinforce Brownsea Castle. The letter is not preserved but it was read in the Commons.[23] The committee then wrote a letter to the Dorset committee demanding action, lest the 'dissatisfaction of the people' and the threat of the 'revolted ships' should 'be put upon design of seizing the garrisons'.[24] The Dorset committee that were being told so abruptly to put their house in order and supply Rede with the necessary materials for the defence of the port numbered among their members MPs Denzil Holles and Denis Bond, George Skutt and Colonel John Bingham.[25] These were some of the most powerful figures in the local elite.

At the heart of the opposition to Rede were two families, the Skutts of Poole and the Bonds of Dorchester. George Skutt Senior was one of the wealthiest merchants in the town, a brewer and owner of the ships *Desire*, *Seaflower*, *Primrose* and *Susanna*, and joint owner of the *Jeane*. Skutt had married the daughter of Thomas Robarts, returned as Poole's MP in 1604, and was four times the mayor of the town. Robarts was a wealthy merchant who further boosted his income in 1626–7 through a joint privateering venture with his son-in-law George Skutt.[26] Skutt himself became mayor of Poole four times before he became the town's MP in 1645, replacing the ejected royalist William Constantine. Skutt profited from the sequestered lands of local royalist George Carew. His son, George Skutt Junior, became mayor in 1652.[27]

William Skutt, George's eldest son and business partner, owned the most expensive house in Poole and was a colonel of the volunteer regiment for Parliament in the Civil War. William Skutt had been a previous governor of Poole in March 1647.[28] He was mayor of Poole in 1646 and again in 1657. His intials, 'WS', are carved with the date 1646 on the Poole corporation silver mace in the place where the royal arms were removed, possibly by Skutt himself. Depite this he provided a 'stately banquet' at his house for Charles II when the king visited Poole in 1665. During this visit Charles II attempted to appoint Skutt mayor but the burgesses ignored this attempted exercise of prerogative power.[29]

George Skutt's time as an MP was short-lived. He left the Commons, possibly ejected in Pride's Purge, but probably earlier in 1648. In his twenty-six-page *A Letter from an Ejected Member of the House of Commons to Sir Jo. Evelyn*, Skutt reveals his deep antipathy to the course the Revolution has taken.[30] The content of Skutt's pamphlet is Presbyterian with a pronounced sympathy for the king. Its tone is vituperative to a degree that might have given Thomas Edwards pause for thought. Any engagement of MPs with a wider public, either through the printing of parliamentary speeches or by accepting petitions, was roundly condemned as destructive populism. The Vote of No Addresses was abhorred, the return of the king recommended. Those royalists promoting the Second Civil War were excused. The Scots were lauded and Parliament's failure to keep faith with them was derided. Above all, what Skutt finds obnoxious is the radicalisation of the parliamentary camp under the pressure of events. For Skutt it all began to go wrong after 1643. 'Passionate orators' keen to 'tickle the attention of the Houses' would speak up for turbulent spirits like 'Lilburne, Burton, Prin and Bastwick'. And yet, argues Skutt, it was no wonder that these men and their defenders fell out with the king and his bishops since 'when now being all at liberty, they could not agree among themselves. For Prin was become a State-Presbyter, and Bastwick an Ecclesiaticall, Burton an Independent and Lylburne a Leveller'. A list of some thirty-nine MPs are branded 'Traytors and Rebels', including Cromwell, Ireton and Thomas Rainsborough. Especial vitriol is reserved for 'that rhapsody of all villiany' Henry Marten. Alongside the routine sexual innuendo to which he was habitually subject (Skutt describes him as a 'legislative Priapus'), Marten is castigated 'because though he be not for the Parliament in all things, yet he be against the King in all things'.[31] Skutt despairs of a Parliament that is 'neither just, free, not compos mentis'.[32]

The Skutts were soon to have support in London from influential Dorchester MP Denis Bond. Denis Bond, unlike Skutt, was a central figure of Cromwellian Independency. Bond was a wealthy clothier and former mayor of Dorchester. He came from a rich Puritan trading family who had narrowly escaped the St Bartholomew's Day Massacre in Rouen in 1572. He was a New England investor. Denis Bond's eldest son John served in the

Westminster Assembly of Divines from 1643. Unlike Skutt, he admired the Puritan martyrs Burton, Bastwick and Prynne. Denis was first elected for the town alongside Denzil Holles in 1640. He became a friend of Cromwell, an enemy of religious toleration and a member of the Council of State in 1648, and was shortly to become its president.[33] He was appointed a commissioner to try the king, but did not serve. Both Bond's brother Elias and son Samuel were admitted as burgesses in Poole in 1650, just before the attempt to remove Rede began.[34] Samuel became MP for Poole in 1659 and Elias became MP for Wareham and later an Admiralty judge under the restored monarchy.

Colonel John Bingham was another key ally of the Skutts. He commanded a parliamentary regiment in Poole during the Civil War and was instrumental in preventing the garrison being betrayed in a royalist plot. He was Poole's governor immediately before Rede was appointed. Bingham served on the committee appointed for the defence of the port alongside George and William Skutt and future mayor William Williams. He was a recruiter MP for Shaftesbury from 1645. Bingham married the daughter of John Trenchard, the influential MP for Wareham and a fellow member of the Dorset committee. He was in the business of making money from the sale of dean and chapter lands and one of his business associates, from whom he borrowed money, was George Skutt. He also amassed a considerable fortune from compounding royalist assets.[35] Bingham, in the midst of the crisis of John Rede's term of office, became governor of the last royalist stronghold to be captured, the island of Guernsey. On 9 April 1651, on the basis of Denis Bond's report from the Council of State, the Commons transferred companies from Colonel James Heane's regiment, who had served in the taking of Jersey, to Bingham's command.[36]

The crisis of Rede's governorship

John Rede's political views could not have been at greater variance with those of George Skutt. Rede was one of forty-eight officers from the south coast who, in January 1649, signed the *Humble Petition and Representation of the Officers and Souldiers of the Garrisons of Portsmouth*.[37] Even in a period when there were numerous remarkable petitions, many generated in the first instance by the Leveller's Large Petition of 11 September 1648, this petition commands special attention. It comes late in the petition war that began to turn the tide against a Personal Treaty with the king during the autumn of 1648. But, perhaps for this reason, it is one of the most comprehensive broadsheets dealing with what the new republic could look like.

It is a strikingly well-thought-out and well-presented petition. After a brief preamble the document sets out six grievances and, following each, a proposed remedy. The first specific grievance, again a common theme in such petitions, is that 'Justice is not executed upon the Grand Delinquents and Authors of our miseries, bloud-shed and calamities'. Its first remedy is that the 'King and all the other Grand Contrivers . . . be brought to speedy Triall'.

The rest of the five grievances and remedies are concerned with the 'settlement of this Nation'. The first of these concerns the 'intollerable burden of Free Quarter' and 'the great oppression by Tithes'. The remedy: the abolition of both, the abolition of the excise, plus the provision of constant pay. This was not just a practical matter, for radicals at this time feared that free quarter was being deliberately prolonged to sow dissension between the common people and soldiers. Money was instead to be found from 'Crowne, Bishops Lands, Deanes and Chapters Lands, Compositions of Delinquents, and Sequestrations'. The second grievance concerns the squandering of 'great summes of money' by officers and the failure to account for money raised in taxation. The remedy was for 'all publique moneys to be brought into one common Treasury'. At the end of every six months a public account would be issued, for 'we conceive it is of right due to the Commons of England'.

The fourth remedy was to streamline government so that soldiers and others were not kept waiting for unacceptable lengths of time for Commons committees to discuss their claims. The solution was to appoint committees at county level and root out the corrupt committee members. The fifth grievance railed against monopolies as a restraint on trade, 'especially to the poor'. The remedy was the abolition of monopolies. The sixth and final grievance was the 'vast expense' of the common law. This, the petition says, is a complaint 'of long continuance and universally knowne and felt'. The cost of the law feeds 'the corrupt interests of . . . Locusts and Catepillers' who will, if they are not prevented, 'devour the Common-wealth'. The remedy is the direct election every six months of twelve able and impartial men in each hundred or division to administer justice.

These were themes that were are at the core of Leveller agitation. The concentration on the abolition of tithes and monopolies, the cost of the common law, and support for the elective principle are hallmark Leveller notions. And indeed the concluding remarks of the petition call for support for measures in both the remonstrance of the army and the Levellers' 'Petition of the 11th September last'. If these measures are adopted, the petitioners argue, it will mean 'a happy beginning of the establishment of the Peoples Freedom'. The petition claimed to be signed in the names of 'many thousands of public-spirited persons'. The final lines of the petition say that the signatories have been 'impowered to agitate' on behalf of the soldiers under their command, as well as their 'Neighbours and fellow Commoners'.

John Rede's name appeared on the petition alongside two others who were to be central to the unfolding drama of the south coast radicals, George Joyce and James Heane.[38] On 17 January 1649 the Commons was informed that 'divers Officers and Soldiers of the Garrison of Portesmouth, South-sea Castle, Southampton and other Places, were at the Door'. They were called in and Captain Baskett presented the petition to the House. A committee of twenty-five MPs was appointed to consider it, although the quorum for the committee was set at five. The committee included Cromwell, Ireton, Thomas Scott, Ludlow and Marten.[39]

The first open conflict with the local elite came in December 1650 after Rede reported Presbyterian minister John Haddesley to the government for not taking the Engagement. Haddesley was removed from his position by the government and imprisoned. The core of the dispute was Rede's subsequent attempt to promote his own pastor, John Gardner, a soldier and religious radical. Immediately before he was involved in events in Poole Gardner had been promoted captain in the regiment of radical Independent Robert Overton.[40] He also seems to have become a chaplain in the army and immediately after the events in Poole to have served in both the Newcastle garrison and in Scotland. In Newcastle he met woman preacher Jane Turner. Jane's husband John Turner may have been the prisoner of the same name whose cause John Lilburne publicised in 1645.[41] Four years after the events in Poole, Gardner provided a second of two prefaces to Jane Turner's *Choice Experiences of the Kind Dealings of God*.[42] The first preface was provided by Particular Baptist and founder of an early gathered church John Spilsbury, who counted John and Elizabeth Lilburne among his congregation.[43] The pamphlet was printed by Leveller and Baptist Henry Hills, a close associate of both Edward Sexby and John Lilburne.[44]

Gardner was cashiered from the army in 1654 for 'some unhandsome miscarriages' and two years later, in May 1656, he turned up in Swan Alley in Coleman Street preaching with a ferocity that brought him to the notice of the authorities. He spoke, said an informant, to 'a great concourse of people', telling them that their time of deliverance from the apostate 'hypocritical government' was near. He preached from Deuteronomy: 'If I whett my glittering sword, and mine hand take hold on judgment, I will render vengeance to mine enemyes, and will reward them that hate me'. Another congregant who spoke after Gardner

> observed much to the same purpose as the former, and expressed himselfe, that . . . he had known many godly and religious men of the army heretofore, but that since they had soe fully employed themselves in possessing them of the bishops and king's lands, that they had much altered from what they were, and are now become tyrannous by taxing and rating the nation.[45]

Rede's attempt to appoint Gardner in Haddesley's place in late 1650 brought a sharp reaction from the Poole elite. George Skutt, his son, and Thomas Cromwell, no relation to Oliver, submitted a petition signed by six score and twelve hands to the mayor, William Williams. It objected to the 'designe of our military governour to impose Mr Gardiner to be the pastor or teacher over us'. Significantly it asserted that it was both the 'judgement of Presbyterians and independents' that there was 'much to object against the said Mr Gardiner both in poynts of practice and doctrine'. The petition concluded by calling on the mayor to stop Rede appointing Gardiner.[46]

The petition got a sympathetic hearing from Mayor Williams and he added his name to that of two Skutts and two others in a letter to Rede. This demanded that Rede 'forebeare any farther to prosecute the designe of haveing Mr Gardiner our pastor and teacher'. It warned Rede to 'forebeare by force to impose him' and that they were 'resolved to oppose the sayd Mr Gardner to the uttmost of our power'.[47]

Confronted with this onslaught, Rede chose to retreat. He replied to the letter from the mayor saying that he had never thought to impose a preacher by force and had only asked Gardner to preach because the mayor had failed to appoint a replacement for Haddesley after he was removed by special order. But he still defended Gardner, saying, 'yet in my judgement (whatever you or others doe yet imagine) God is much to be admired for the gift of knowledge and utterance he hath bestowed upon that man, if we consider seriously the meane and low condition out of which he hath brought him'.[48]

Rede's retreat over the appointment of Gardner did not appease Skutt and his allies. Three months later, in March 1651, they mounted a full-scale attack on Rede designed to remove him from his post and have him replaced by Colonel John Bingham. They wrote to the Council of State complaining of Rede supporting 'exhorbitant Levellers and Ranters, those great enemies to just liberty, civility and godliness'. The letter was signed by Mayor William Williams, Thomas Cromwell, George Skutt Senior, George Skutt Junior, William Skutt and seven others.[49] It was accompanied by a much longer charge sheet of eleven 'Articles exhibited against John Rede'.[50] The articles included that 'being disaffected to the present Government he promoted the designs of the Levellers against the State, not only in his command but in the County of Dorset and elsewhere'. And 'that in March and April 1648, being a time of great danger when the Levellers rose in actual arms against the State, he did absent himself from Poole'. They said that after the defeat of 'the Levellers, he was angry and fell out with Captain Lillingston (then commander in the said Garrison well-affected to the present Government, and of known integrity) for apprehending some of the Leveller party (who had been active in the designs and fled to the Garrison for protection)' and that Rede had given 'shelter to Levellers and raises them to places of great trust'. Rede had 'in a time of eminent danger . . . disarmed the Mayor and other inhabitants of the Garrison, because they would not join with him in his levelling design'.

The articles go on to specifically accuse Rede of sheltering Agitator and Leveller John Radman after the suppression of the Leveller-inspired rising in Oxford in 1649. In reference to the Gardner appointment it said, 'he with a high hand did endeavour to impose one Gardiner, a soldier and dipper, to be pastor and lecturer of Poole in opposition to the orthodox divines and well-affected ministers as were provided by the magistracy of Poole'. And it ends with an account of an incident that shows how far relations between Rede and the Poole elite had degenerated:

> by force he caused William Williams, Mayor of Poole, a man well-affected to be brought before him as a delinquent, in a disgraceful manner by a Sergeant and Musketeers with lighted matches; which might have proved of dangerous consequence had not the Mayor quietly submitted himself, and suffered this ignominious reproach and affront.

The first nine of these eleven charges all have to do with Rede's support for the Levellers, the Ranters or the Baptists. Only the final two are more general charges of misgovernence. This hardly supports Henry Reece's contention that the town worthies were simply larding up their complaints against Rede with convenient accusations of Levellerism and political and religious radicalism.[51] Indeed, almost the entire substance of the complaint is about Rede's Levellerism. *The Moderate* certainly printed reports from Poole. On 5 April 1649 it reported on the distress of the poor in Poole. In the next issue it reported on the townspeople's petition in support of Rede. Perhaps their informant was Rede himself or other sympathisers. Reports to *The Moderate* also came at the same time from nearby Weymouth, where James Heane was governor, and from Portland, where Edward Sexby and then George Joyce were governors.[52]

We do not know where Rede was in his crucial period of absence from Poole during the mutinies of 1649. But it is possible that he travelled to the rendezvous at Old Sarum which began the Burford mutiny, a mere five miles from his home at Birdlymes Farm in Porton, and even closer to Rede's involvement in the battle of Salisbury. In 1649 at Portsmouth there was 'more talk of the Levellers then of all the Princes Fleete at sea'. It was reported that a party of horse was sent to Portsmouth and the Isle of Wight to 'fight with the Levellers'. There were also reports that Joyce was leading a revolt. Joyce, it was said, had 'sweld . . . from a Taylor to a Cornet, and from a Cornet to a grand Segnior amongst the Levellers'.[53]

Rede's willingness to shelter Radman is a sign of considerable commitment to the Leveller cause. Both the man and the moment posed considerable dangers. Radman was a long-time Agitator, first elected at Triploe Heath in 1647. He was a central figure in the Leveller-inspired Oxford mutiny which began with the distribution of a Lilburne pamphlet. The demands of the Oxford mutineers are strikingly similar to those in the petition Rede signed earlier the same year. This was the last of the mutinies of 1649, which began with the Bishopsgate mutiny led by Robert Lockyer. Two of Radman's fellow Oxford mutineers had already been shot. Two other Oxford mutineers had already escaped to Poole in the hope of enlisting with Rede's garrison. They had both signed the declaration that began the mutiny. Rede had little choice but to detain them and send them to London when requested to do so by Fairfax.[54] It may have been over this incident that Rede 'fell out with Captain Lillingston . . . for apprehending some of the Leveller party'.

Henry Reece has questioned whether John Radman reached Poole. But if other Oxford mutineers reached Poole, and with two contemporary newsbooks reporting that Radman was captured at Poole, the evidence suggests he did. And the rest of the specific allegations in the articles against Rede are, so far as we know from other evidence, entirely accurate.[55] In short, what seems likely is that Radman and other mutineers sought refuge in Poole. The reporting on these events for *The Moderate* also suggests that other Levellers were active in Poole.

Interestingly, when Rede contested the attempt to remove him as governor in a letter to Cromwell, then serving in Scotland, he did not disavow any of the accusations of Levellerism made against him, nor did he refute the claim that he had sheltered Radman. Indeed, in one of the few directly political points in the letter, he says that he has been the victim of 'a most deep design of the Scotified clergy in these parts to gain not only the power of Poole garrison into their hands but the command and interest of all of this country [i.e. county] if the proud armed enemy could in any way prevail over you and your army'. Rede writes that the scandals urged against him will vanish like mist if he is given a hearing to contest them and that they are 'invented by clergy because they could not cast [me] in their Scottish mould'.[56]

But before Rede wrote his letter to Cromwell, the Council of State replaced him as governor of Poole with George Skutt on 15 April 1651.[57] By 23 April 1651 Skutt was in Weymouth demanding that its governor, Colonel James Heane, come to Poole with him to relieve Rede of his command. Skutt had a commission and a letter from Dorchester MP Denis Bond. But Heane was an old ally of Rede's and a co-signatory of the 1649 petition. He refused to go with Skutt. When Skutt arrived at Rede's house in Poole he was in for another shock. Rede demanded to see his commission. After reading it and the letter from Bond, Rede told Skutt, 'If that be all you have to show, we are not parting yet'. Rede demanded a specific order requiring rendition of the garrison and told Skutt 'he durst not deliver up the same as being bound in duty and conscience not to resign the said Garrison without a special order'. 'Then' said Skutt, 'you will not deliver it upon sight of this commission?' Rede simply replied, 'No'.

Rede then told his captain, Richard Bamford, to secure the garrison. Two companies were drawn up in a 'field near the town gates'. Rede addressed them and told them what had taken place. He had already drawn up a counterpetition to the Council of State the night before, having received advance warning of Skutt's appointment from James Heane. He then set out to ride to London to present his petition. But in the street he overtook Skutt heading towards where the two companies were drawn up. Skutt read his commission and Bond's letter to the troops. Rede then asked him if he had done. Skutt replied, 'Yes', and Rede then addressed his troops, calling on their loyalty. Upon which the soldiers cast up their hats, shouting, 'The Lord bless you, Governor, and grant you return speedily to your trust with honour, peace, and safety'.[58]

But after Rede left for London Skutt attempted to win the troops once more. 'Finally he spake to this effect, saying: "All ye that are for me declare yourselves"'. But the companies stood silent; so he called out again, saying: 'Declare yourselves, or else you little think the danger etc'. One of the companies then declared for Skutt. Then so did Captain Bamford. Skutt and Bamford then tried to get the companies to march away, but some at least refused under the influence of a Lieutenant Waterhouse.[59] This was, all legalistic devices set aside, and as Rede and Heane must have known, mutiny. And initially it succeeded.

The Council of State backtracked in the face of Rede's counterpetition. It refused to appoint Skutt, making Lieutenant Colonel Joseph Junkins care-taker governor in May 1651 until the competing petitions of Rede and Skutt could be heard. The conflict remained unresolved in July. Finally, after both Rede and the Council of State had failed to engage Cromwell in settling the dispute it was sent to Colonel John Desborough for decision. But even Desborough did not seem to have the time to settle the issue. Only in December 1651 do we learn that at some earlier point Skutt had finally replaced Rede.[60]

George Joyce, now Lieutenant Colonel Joyce, governor of Portland Castle, was caught in a similar dispute at the same time. In July 1651 he printed long a defence of his conduct against those he accused of plotting against him. This he saw as more than a personal vendetta and he included a three-page postscript defending John Rede against those attempting to remove him as governor of nearby Poole.[61]

This defence of Rede argues that he has not been given a fair trial. And it puts the attack on Rede in the wider context of a London-led design to get the whole of the West Country out of the hands of the radicals, just as Rede had done in his letter to Cromwell. This included the removal of Joyce himself from Portland and the appointment of a new governor of Guernsey. James Heane had been in command of the force that reduced the last royal-ist stronghold, the island of Jersey, and became its governor in 1651. Colonel Bingham, previously in charge of Poole garrison, who had been promoted by Skutt to replace Rede, was now appointed to the command of Guernsey. Joyce accurately records the transfer of troops out of Heane's regiment and into Bingham's. He also reports that James Heane thought Bingham's appointment was to 'envite an enemy thither' and that Bingham had opposed the execution of the king. Heane was in a position to know

Bingham. He had served under him as a captain in 1643. Joyce also notes that Denis Bond had promoted his son as recorder of Poole. Like Rede in his letter to Cromwell, Joyce blames a 'Scotish Presbyterian faction' for conspiring against him and for promoting Bingham and reducing Heane's regiment. He cites Rede's replacement as their chosen tool.[62]

Printed at the end of this pamphlet is a note, originally a private letter, addressed to 'his honoured Friend Lieut. Col, Joyce at London'. The note is a brief expression of solidarity and appreciation written in circumspect and coded language. It clearly indicates close political collaboration in a repressive atmosphere. It is signed with the initials 'JR'. There seems little doubt that this is John Rede.[63]

On this evidence there seems to have been a Leveller-inclined network in this area of the south coast. Joyce was given command of Southsea Castle in early 1648, shortly after John Rede became governor of Poole. In 1650 Edward Sexby became governor of Portland, about twenty-five miles from Poole, having previously been engaged in searching the post at Dover. Joyce then succeeded Sexby as governor of Portland. He and Sexby had been partners in a land deal in Portland. Joyce later bought his partner out.[64] Edward Sexby was being court-martialled at exactly the same time as the crisis was unfolding in Poole, in June 1651. Interestingly, Cromwell distanced himself from both cases. One of the few times that we hear of Leveller leader Richard Overton outside London is Sexby's evidence at his own court martial, where he says that Richard Overton joined his forces on the march possibly in Scotland, but possibly earlier on the south coast.[65]

What happened on the south coast is that local Presbyterian elites combined with mainstream 'Cromwellian' Independents to remove radical Independents and Leveller allies from positions of influence. Rede, Heane, Joyce and Sexby formed one axis, while the Skutts and their allies, Bingham, MP Denis Bond and his relations on Poole council acted against them. The original complaint against Rede's appointment of Gardner had stressed that the objection was raised in the name of Presbyterians and Independents. This alliance, cemented by common backgrounds and family ties in the local elite, overwhelmed Rede and his radical allies. The old elite had stood in need of radical allies in the moment of danger created by royalist resurgence in 1648. Events from the crushing of the Leveller mutinies in 1649 to the removal of Rede in the following year showed that a new alignment of forces had come into play.[66]

Rede's career up to 1650 is interesting precisely because he was *not* at the organised heart of the Leveller movement. But the fact that his political thought and political responses were, nevertheless, shaped by Leveller ideas is some testimony to the reach of this idealogy. Moreover, Rede was clearly an influence on other radicals, religious, military and political, who were not Levellers. And so we see here how a Leveller sympathiser might influence political action beyond the ranks of the Levellers themselves. In part this was because Rede, like other Levellers, was not *only* a Leveller. He was also a Baptist, and therefore influenced other religious radicals like John Gardner. And Rede was of the army, not simply a civilian agitating the troops. He therefore had the ability to draw on support from, and to influence, other army officers like Heane and Joyce, as well as his own troops.

Ultimately the radical coalition of which Rede was a part did not withstand the combined Presbyterian and 'Silken Independent' forces brought against it. Interestingly though, this was not simply a question of the solidity of the local county community to which some historians have pointed.[67] It was in fact an alliance between local elites and their allies in London government which, just, enabled them to unseat Rede. This tends to suggest not only a more complex picture of how power worked in the republic, but also the enduring influence of the radicals even in the aftermath of the crushing of the Leveller rebellions in 1649.

After the Revolution: the Porton Baptist church

John Rede survived his dismissal as governor of Poole to emerge as an active militia and sequestration commissioner and a Justice of the Peace in the 1650s.[68] As early as 1651 Rede was back at his home in Birdlymes Farm, in the Porton tything of Idmiston parish near Salisbury.[69] He was engaged in work that would last the rest of his life: building Porton Particular Baptist church.[70] In his role as JP, Rede was charged with raising money for maimed soldiers and sailors and funds for a hospital at Salisbury. The Idmiston parish records numerous marriages conducted by Rede as a JP between 13 March 1654 and 20 May 1658.[71]

Porton was one of the earliest Baptist churches in Wiltshire. On 3 April 1653, '85 brethren and sisters met as a Church of Christ at Porton'. Two years later a total of 111 people from some twenty Wiltshire and Hampshire villages met again in the large hall of Birdlymes Farm. That the congregation came from twenty villages suggests a preaching circuit that pre-dates the formation of the Porton church. An early historian of the church notes, 'some kind of organised bond of union must have existed before this time, for these persons who were assembled came from places widely separated, taking in a circuit of about 40 miles'.[72] Rede's father, Edward, had left twenty shillings to 'the Church at Porton' some fifteen years before his son gave it a permanent home.[73] Indeed the church was formed in part from congregants who had been worshipping in exile in Amsterdam during the reign of Charles I. The church was well organised and disciplined. The congregation worshipped every week on a Sunday and 'The Manner of Worship' is recorded as 'Some brother to be appointed at each meeting to exercise his gift at the next meeting, by way of doctrine and exhortation'. The places of worship took in a wide geographical area. Those who did not attend, even if they pleaded the long distances that they were required to travel, were cut off from the church.[74]

The 1660 Restoration enforced a clampdown on both republicanism and the dissenting churches. Rede was imprisoned in the Tower in 1661. He had taken care to stay within the law but had been accused nevertheless. He demanded to confront his accuser and pleaded conformity. The official record of his examination says, 'John Rede, prisoner in the Tower. To be speedily confronted with his accuser, who has taken an unjust oath against him; has been faithful and obedient since the passing of the Act of Indemnity, and has taken the Oath of Allegiance before justices of the peace in Wiltshire'.[75] The Clarendon Code made life for Porton's Baptists even more difficult. As a result of the 1662 Act of Uniformity some 2,000 preachers lost their livings because they did not accept the use of the Book of Common Prayer. In 1664 the Conventicle Act banned meetings of more than five dissenters—exactly the kind of meeting that had been taking place in John Rede's Birdlymes Farm for the preceding decade. In 1665 the Five Mile Act prevented dissenters from preaching in towns and cities.

Unsurprisingly in this environment, Rede was again in trouble with the authorities. In September 1665 he was examined by Lord Arlington in connection with a planned insurrection. He denied all knowledge of the plot and the plotters. But when it was put to him that he 'was governor of Poole in the late rebellion' he would 'not say whether he is sorry for it'. Neither would he say whether greater numbers of people than that law allowed had come to his house to worship.[76] Rede clearly thought that he had been too defiant in this exchange and soon after wrote from Porton to Lord Arlington saying he wished to 'recant every syllable of his examination' as 'not consistent with one willing to submit to the present government'. He again insisted that he 'was no plotter'. But he did in the same letter return to a consistent theme of his life: the right to worship free of restraint. Rede went so far as to suggest 'a plan to prevent the necessity of restraining persons of their liberty for conscience sake'. He complained that 'some are taken for plotting at conventicles to stir up insurrections, the very name of which he abhors, yet knows many good people, who do not think it right to attend their parish church nor will be compelled by persecution'. He went on to insist that 'men should not be allowed to attack these at their devotions and take them to prison, except by warrant' and that such peaceable worshippers 'may not be hindered from meeting, nor disturbed in their devotions'.[77]

Rede's plea fell on deaf ears. But the dissenters continued to meet, and continued to be persecuted. The quarter sessions held at Marlborough in 1671 paint a remarkable picture. A depositon by Sir Edward Hungerford tells of a dissenters' meeting held on 25 September the previous year, 1670. Hungerford recounts

> about the number of 2000 at an unlawful meeting & Conventicle held in a Wood called and known by the name of Brockers Wood in the p[ar]ish of North Bradley ... under the colour and pretence of Religious Worship. And a person whose name & habitation unknown did then reach and preach to the People contrary to Statute ... for which their offences I have imposed and fined each of them.[78]

The scale of this conventicle is staggering but it was a long-standing practice of this church dating back decades. The North Bradley church had links with the Porton church since its earliest days and some of its congregants seem to have been related to the Rede family.[79] In this single incident some thirty worshippers were fined between five and ten shillings. Two, possibly the organisers of the meeting, were fined ten pounds each. In separate cases a man in nearby Westbury was fined forty pounds for teaching at a conventicle and another was fined twenty pounds for holding a conventicle in his barn at Dilton. In all that year 100 people in the county were fined for attending conventicles.[80]

Even when the 1672 Act of Indulgence lifted the Clarendon Code, Rede's initial request for a license to worship at Birdlymes Farm was turned down. John Haddesley's request for one in New Sarum was approved, at some point before 20 April 1672.[81] Haddesley was Rede's old adversary from Poole in 1649. A month later, in May 1672, Rede was also granted a license.[82]

Rede had already been elected a minister in the Porton church in 1671, alongside Walter Penn and Thomas Long.[83] Through the 1670s Porton church rebuilt its strength after the persecution visited on it during the years of the Clarendon Code. On 24 January 1675 the church met to consider a letter from churches in London calling a general assembly. Porton sent John Rede as its messenger carrying a letter 'concerning the state of the church and its ministry'. Late the same year Porton church elected John Rede, Walter Penn, Henry Penn of Chalk, John Kent of Wallop and Thomas Long of Amesbury as elders, though only Rede, Walter Penn and Long were finally ordained at a meeting on 19 April 1679. Porton was now a strong organising centre for Baptists across the West Country, sending out emissaries as far afield as Andover, Basingstoke and Devizes. Records for money paid for the rent of a meeting house in Sarum exist in 'an almost unbroken line from 1657 to 1679'.[84]

The 1680s saw a return of political instability. The succession crisis produced the Rye House plot in 1683, involving old Levellers in an attempt to assassinated Charles II, and the Monmouth rebellion centred on the West Country in 1685, as the major indicators of the unrest. In Wiltshire at the Warminster quarter sessions, 12 July 1681, several people living in Mere were presented 'as being reputed Anabaptists'. The following year at Marlborough Henry Dent of Ramsbury and William Hughes of Marlborough were presented for holding conventicles. But popular resistance to this kind of repression meant that several jurymen were also presented for refusing to report a conventicle at Alderbury. It was 'the humble desier of the Grand Inquest that the Lord Bishop and Deane of the Diocesse may . . . proceed to an Excommunication against all sorts of dissenters'.[85] Rede himself was the particular object of a splenetic outburst from the authorities at the same quarter sessions. They recalled his record of opposition and demanded that he be 'disarmed'. They had, they said, 'been informed that John Reade of Porton Esq . . . and sevall Dissenters from the Church of England doe refusse to appeare at the Assizes or Sessions to answere to their seval Indictments or presentments'. They desired that

> this Court will order the Clarke of the Peace of this County or his deputy to proceed against all such dissenters (under what name soe ever they doe call themselves) . . . to the end they may be brought to obiedience to the Kinge and his Lawes both in Church and State, for we may finde by more then Twenty yeares experience that noething but the severity of the law will reclaime such men, and that all the Indulgencies, Tollerations & conniveances makes them more redy to rebell.

To prevent rebellion the Court was to 'request [the] speedie . . . disarmeing of all sorts of dissenters as men very dangerous to the peace of this Kingdome and allsoe to the life & being of the best of the kings whom God longe preserve'.[86]

The message was, at least in part, acted upon in Porton itself. In 1683 the churchwardens of Porton reported to the bishop in Salisbury 'Thomas Bebis excommunicated for not Baptizing his children' and that the wife of Henry Perin had been presented for not coming to church. At the same presentment the churchwardens of Idmiston parish reported 'George Rumboll and his wife for not coming to the Parish church these twelve months or neare upon'.[87] Three years later another Porton parishioner was reported for non-attendance and for refusing to renew his sacrament. In the same year one Richard Overton of St Edmonds parish in Salisbury, the same parish in which John Rede's future third wife, Sarah Bernard, was living, was indicted for refusing to bring his children to the parish church to be baptised. Overton's wife was presented for refusing to give thanksgiving for the delivery of their children and for not attending and not renewing the sacrament at the parish church.[88]

But the Porton church survived this latest onslaught. Thomas Long died in 1681, leaving Rede and Penn to carry on until 1690. They seem to have overcome an earlier disagreement and steered the church through the turbulent 1680s. But as the new decade dawned, on 10 September 1690, the church divided in a 'very Christian and friendly manner' between those in Sarum who had Penn as pastor and the Porton church with Rede as pastor. Around the turn of the century Rede seems to have gone to live in Devizes, a town with a long history of dissenting religion stretching back to the days of Lollardy. In June 1699 he drafted the first of five documents, the last of which is dated 1 January 1703, in which he made a bequest of £100 plus interest to the Baptist cause. Baptist churches in Southampton and Devizes are specifically mentioned as recipients. Rede appointed a series of trustees, all of whom were to be Baptists. These included John Eyles, MP for the borough in 1679–81, and James Webb. There had been two Baptist groups meeting in Devizes from the late 1660s, one of which was 'reckoned to be Fifth Monarchist, at the house of Thomas Okey, a woolbroker'. These two merged by 1672. James Webb inherited this congregation and took a leading part in the London General Assembly in 1689. He and other trustees, two of whom seem to be from Webb's family, maintained Rede's bequest.[89]

Rede had married his third wife, widow Sarah Bernard, on 18 February 1693. John was seventy-eight and Sarah was thirty-four. They almost immediately had a daughter named Sarah Cartaret Rede, but she died just before her seventh birthday in December 1700. Sarah Rede wrote *A Token for Youth*, an emotionally intense tract recording her daughter's religious devotion during her short life.[90] Sarah Rede herself died in 1708 in Devizes, aged forty-nine. Both mother and daughter were buried in the Baptist burial ground at Porton. Rede had two more years of his long life remaining.[91] In 1710 he was buried, if the provisions of his will were respected, in the dissenters' graveyard at his home in Birdlymes Farm beside his three wives.[92]

The last Leveller

Where does John Rede stand on the spectrum of seventeenth-century radicalism? In comparison with James Heane, best seen as a radical Independent, Rede stood closer to the Levellers. Even compared with George Joyce, who could be said to be an Independent with some Leveller sympathies, Rede stood closer to the Levellers during the crucial years of crisis, 1647–50. Unlike Particular Baptist preacher John Gardner, Rede's political sympathies ran beyond the promotion of religious radicalism. But Rede was not, however, in any sense a key organiser of the Leveller movement, nor one of its spokesmen, as Edward Sexby or John Radman can be thought to be.

As interesting as the placing of these figures in the appropriate concentric circle of Leveller organisation is the fact of their cooperation. Heane, Joyce, Sexby, Gardner and Rede were clearly all part of a radical bloc. They recognised themselves as allies and their opponents saw them as a common enemy at a crucial political juncture. This last point is important. Political movements and the alliances they construct are always in part determined by the actions of their enemies. This was true of the Levellers as a whole, and true of Rede in particular. Radicals, Leveller and non-Leveller, banded together in the face of the threat of a Personal Treaty with the king in 1648. On a national level a similar coalition of forces had been critical in the Revolutionary resolution of the political crisis of 1648. Then it broke apart on the rock of what a post-Revolutionary state should look like. Rede and his associates were fighting a rearguard operation in the wake of Burford, and this they lost as the centre and Silken Independents, to use the Levellers' term, and Presbyterians united against them.

These, however, are judgements that only hold good for the critical high point of the Revolution, and Leveller influence within it, during the

1647–50 period. After that moment all the radicals, Leveller or not, had to find ways of accommodating to the new regime. As the Revolutionary tide ebbed it was Rede's Baptist affiliation that came to dominate his life. There is no sign, however, that Rede explicitly rejected his Leveller associations, either in 1649 when many Particular Baptists did, or later.[93] He worked with the regime as a reluctant sequestrator, but it was the building of Porton Baptist Church that became his life's work.

This was, of course, a political stance as well as a merely theological choice. It landed Rede in the Tower at the Restoration. He and his church were persecuted and his Revolutionary past, for which he refused to apologise, was still getting him into trouble with the authorities in the 1680s. In John Rede we can see one channel through which the Revolutionary fervour of the 1640s flowed into the dissenting tradition which played such a large part in British radicalism for hundreds of years after his death. Before Rede died in 1710 he was, so far as we know, the last man living to have been known as a Leveller during the Revolutionary era. Now, in that quiet corner of the dissenters' churchyard in Porton village in Wiltshire, still lies the last Leveller.

CHAPTER 15

The Levellers and the English Revolution

There is a significant body of historians who do not accept that the Levellers were an identifiable or effective political organisation, although this has not prevented them writing extensively about them. Mark Kishlansky long ago complained that 'recent historiography has raised the Levellers to fantastic heights', and he sought to reject the view that they were the 'deus ex machina in explanations of the Revolution'.[1] John Walter regrets 'the attention devoted to the seductive developments' of the later 1640s 'with the emergence of radical groups, whose status as "vanguard *political parties*" has undoubtedly been exaggerated'.[2] Jonathan Scott argues that 'any notion of a "Leveller party" is misleading' and that the 'movement never established a large-scale organisation of its own'.[3] Diane Purkiss says, 'The term "Leveller movement" used by historians is misleading . . . the Levellers were not a party or a group . . . they did not have any kind of simple programme'.[4] Michael Braddick is sceptical of the Levellers' 'practical significance to the events of the 1640s'.[5]

This revisionist case was contested from the moment it originated in the late 1970s. Austin Woolrych's *Soldiers and Statesmen* deployed close argument to conclude that Kishlansky's case was 'surely implausible'.[6] Ian Gentles's work has done much to reassert the importance of the politicisation of the New Model Army, pointing out that 'there is considerable evidence of receptiveness, between 1647 and 1649, within the army, to Leveller ideas'.[7] Barbara Taft, Clive Holmes and Rachel Foxley have all pointed to the critical phase of cooperation between the Levellers and the Independents in the culminating months of the Revolution.[8] Blair Worden argues that 'when Cromwell and Ireton moved against Charles I in late 1648 and early 1649 they were finally accepting the position which the Levellers had urged on them in the autumn of 1647'.[9] But the high tide of revisionism has now passed and a more open historical debate about the Levellers has begun. It is time to make a renewed case about their contribution to the English Revolution.

The Levellers did not, because no movement does, emerge fully formed. They had a prehistory. Before the Levellers became an identifiable movement, and certainly before they were given a name, the leading figures had a considerable record of political activism. Moreover, this activism was not simply that of isolated individuals. It was the kind of political activity that required a degree of collective political organisation. In the densely packed streets of the walled City of London, in the artillery fields that lay beyond, in the gathered churches and in the ale houses and taverns, networks and oppositional currents formed within which the Leveller movement incubated. These networks were perhaps more widespread and more radical than some historians have accepted. They were not, in the early phases of the Revolution, politically differentiated in the way they became in the mid-1640s. But they did provide an early form of association for those who were to become Levellers. Moreover, these patterns of work and association lasted into the period in which the Levellers emerged as a distinct political formation. These were a more or less permanent foundation on which the movement rested. So it is possible to describe a number of circles within which the future leaders of the Levellers made contact with one another, including the streets, taverns, gathered churches and the apprentice networks of the City of London. But it would take more than physical proximity and common meeting places to transform individual activists into a recognisable collective entity.

Illegal printing was a critical close circle of cooperation that led in this direction. In the first phase of the Revolution individuals who were later to be prominent in the Leveller movement were running illegal printing presses, circulating petitions and organising protests. It was printing that brought John Lilburne and his supporters together in specifically organised relationships long before they became known as Levellers. John Lilburne, William Larner and Henry Hills, Richard Overton, Katherine and Samuel Chidley, Thomas Paine and William Walwyn were all active in this milieu. Each one of them knew some or all of the others from the underground print networks of the early days of the Revolution.[10] It is from such contact that the embryo of an organisation emerged. This kind of early contact between future Leveller leaders required a degree of trust essential to running a secret press because sustaining an illegal press was a complex enterprise needing collective organisation.[11]

Printing petitions deepened and made public this collective activity. Petitions must be formulated, written and delivered, and the support of backers organised.[12] Multiple copies must be circulated, often distributed in the streets at night, given away at Westminster or pinned to church doors.[13] Thus from an early stage petitioning was linked to popular mobilisation. Indeed the very signing of petitions was a mass activity in some cases, for instance at Blackheath, Southwark and St George's Fields.[14] This was work carried out on a considerable scale. In January 1648 it was claimed that 30,000 copies of a Leveller petition were being printed for widespread distribution.[15] The same year opponents of the Levellers were complaining of Leveller plans to print 3,000 copies of a petition.[16] *The Remonstrance of Many Thousands of the Free-People of England . . . and those called Levelers* claimed that this 'is already signed by 98064 hands, and more to be added daily'.[17] Lilburne claimed that two publications in 1649, the *Manifestation* and the *Agreement of the People* of 1 May, had a print run of 20,000, which were sent 'gratis all over England'.[18] In March 1649 *The Humble Petition of Divers wel-affected Women*, a plea to free Lilburne, Walwyn, Prince and Overton from their imprisonment in the Tower, collected 10,000 names using women ward organisers.[19] All this speaks of a high degree of organisation and coordination, both in the presentation of the petitions and in their subsequent printing and distribution.[20] Needless to say, the Levellers did not invent and were not alone in undertaking this kind of activity but they are significant in being an organised current that could repeatedly mass-petition on this scale over a relatively long period.

As this was happening the dynamic of the Revolution posed new problems, dissolving some political alliances and making others possible. The future Levellers began political activity as part of the broad parliamentary alliance, became advocates of the win-the-war party, became allies of the Independents and, as new conditions arose, became more ideologically and organisationally distinct until they were so recognisable that their opponents gave them a name. Lilburne himself commented on the successive phases of development within the Revolutionary camp in *The Innocent Man's Second Proffer*.[21] As these stages of Revolutionary activity arose, the originally separate strands of activity by future Levellers began to merge. Lilburne, Overton and Larner cooperated from the early 1640s. Lilburne and Walwyn came together in 1645 when the Salters' Hall group met with Lilburne's supporters in the Windmill tavern. Wildman and Rainsborough were working with Lilburne around the time of the Putney debates. These are only some of the strands and connections that formed the Levellers. These individuals did not all know each other at first. But they came to, and they came to cooperate openly.

The war opened up both political challenges for the radicals and new fields of activity. How the future Levellers reacted to the rise of the peace party and of Presbyterianism helped define them as a recognisable political force. This could and did happen while they were still part of the wider current of Independency. It was not necessary for them to be in opposition to the Independent leaders before they were seen as a distinct current with its own ideas, methods of work and audience. This was compatible with, but distinct within, the Independent alliance in the initial period.

The army and the Levellers

The army provided a new field of operation for future Levellers but the extent of Leveller influence in the army is one of the most hotly contested issues in the history of the movement. John Morrill long ago argued that the army was more interested in bread-and-butter issues than it was in radical politics. Mark Kishlansky has drawn a more or less absolute distinction between radicalisation of the army and the Levellers: the army 'was insulated from the Leveller programme by its determination not to meddle in matters of state and developed its own unique set of grievances and desires'. He went on to argue that there was no mutiny at Ware and that nothing occurred which seriously discomfited the Grandees. More recently John Morrill and Philip Baker have noted that in certain important cases Leveller influence may have been less than previously thought and the roots of radicalisation were independent of their influence.[22] This 'revisionist' interpretation has been challenged by Austin Woolrych, Ian Gentles and Brian Manning, among others. All produced studies which insisted on the scale and effectiveness of the Agitator movement and of the Levellers' links with it. More recently Jason Peacey has argued that it was at the time of the Ware mutiny that the Levellers 'honed their technique for reaching out to, and securing support from, the political nation beyond London, and far beyond their natural support base'. Rachel Foxley has suggested a continually renewed alliance of army radicalism and Leveller organisation that 'reverses the picture painted by standard revisionist historiography'.[23]

Part of the problem with the revisionist case is the artificial separation of 'experience derived' grievance and 'external' agitation, and a related separation between 'economic' and 'political' grievances. Of course no agitation succeeds unless it reflects genuine grievance. Morrill in fact produced some crucial evidence of the politicised nature of these griev-ances, although he drew the opposite conclusion. He appended to his article on the army revolt of 1647 a table listing the issues raised by the regiments at Saffron Walden. This showed forty-eight instances of regi-ments raising economic issues such as arrears, pensions, post-service apprenticeships and indemnity. But it also shows thirty-four instances of regiments raising political issues such as the right to petition, calls for a purge of royalists, demands for freedom of religion, law reform and resist-ance to service in Ireland. This hardly looks like an army only interested in bread-and-butter issues. And that is before we address the question whether an army refusing a parliamentary order to disband, even if it were over exclusively economic issues, is behaving politically or not.[24]

But internally generated unrest frequently requires political expression and often finds it in forms that have been pre-developed and articulated by broader political forces in society at large. And, in any case, it is not true that the Levellers were completely 'external' to the army. In some senses they were internal to and shaped army radicalism. Some Levellers already had military experience, and some of the leaders of the army revolt quickly asso-ciated with the Levellers even if they were not connected to them previously. Moreover, there is a significant amount of evidence that Leveller pamphlets and petitions circulated widely and parts of the army had adopted these ideas as their own. Richard Baxter complained that long before Putney,

> A great part of the mischief they did among the soldiers was by pamphlets which they abundantly dispersed; such as R. Overton's *Martin Mar-Priest*, and more of his, and some of J. Lilburne's, who was one of them; and divers against the King, and against the ministry, and for liberty of conscience, &c. And soldiers being usually dispersed in their quarters, they had such books to read when they had none to contradict them.[25]

Baxter's observation has often been misused, sometimes to assert that the majority of the army were Leveller-influenced, sometimes as a straw man whose demolition proves Leveller influence to be negligible. Closer acquaintance with Baxter's own account would help this discussion. The context for his remark was an analysis that insisted that most soldiers were *not* Levellers, but that the radicals in the army, including Levellers, were exercising influence beyond their numbers because they were organised, not least in the distribution of printed material. This is exactly what we might expect: an organised minority struggling, and sometimes but not always succeeding, to exercise a wider hegemony. So the Levellers were not the 'God outside the machine', as Kishlansky has it, rather they were an organised machine among the godly. But how should we best define exactly what kind of organisation the Levellers were?

Movement, party and organisation

The Levellers at best seen as a movement rather than a political party. This accords with the modern distinction between highly organised, member-ship-based organisations and looser campaigning organisations that may not have the same ideological homogeneity or structured internal deci-sion-making processes as a party. It is perhaps this sense of political movement that is captured by John Harris when he writes of 'Robin Hood and his Levellers' are resolved to wipe Cromwell's nose 'with the *Agreement of the People*.'[26] But before the later nineteenth century it is unclear that there was such a rigid distinction between 'movement' and 'party'. In 1848 Marx and Engels, for instance, used the term 'party' in the *Communist Manifesto* in a much more general sense, meaning a group or current in broad support of a relatively defined ideological position. What they did *not* mean was the kind of party that the German Social Democrats were to become in the last quarter of the nineteenth century with their mass-circu-lation newspapers, membership structure, electoral campaigns and array of cultural and sporting associations. So, paradoxically, what modern usage means by the term 'movement' may actually be closer to what, before the later nineteenth century, was meant by 'party'.

It is therefore worth considering whether in this looser sense the Levellers can be thought of as a political party. The way in which people in the seventeenth century most frequently used the term 'party' in a political sense is one of the definitions still included in modern dictionaries: 'a person or people forming one side in an agreement or dispute'. This usage, especially in the heightened and divided political context of the English Revolution, already contains some elements of a more modern political usage. It assumes some ideological agreement. It assumes some level of organisational cooperation.[27] But it does not assume stable membership and structure, close programmatic unity or long-lasting organisation as modern usage does.[28]

The Levellers had some characteristics that approximate to this kind of political organisation because, over and above the notion of 'party' in its seventeenth-century definition, the Levellers did require at the peak of their organisational development that their supporters make regular payments to appointed treasurers. They met regularly with their supporters in public and in committees to carry on the business of the organisation. Office holders were chosen from such meetings. They issued joint declarations in the names of their leading figures, indicating a higher-than-usual degree of publicly declared cooperation. They came to identify themselves by the name their enemies gave them, sometimes with qualification, sometimes neutrally or approvingly. They organised secret presses and produced prodigious amounts of ideologically coherent material in leaflet, petition, pamphlet and newspaper form. Historian Murray Tolmie notes that even in

> the earliest phase of the Leveller movement William Walwyn, John Lilburne, and Richard Overton made brilliant use of the unlicensed press to provide an articulate defence of religious toleration . . . This phase was essentially one of pamphleteering and propaganda, but each man had a distinct range of contacts among the London radicals and was able to make an organisational contribution to the inner core of the Leveller party. It is at this organizational level that much about the history and ultimate fate of the Leveller movement in London becomes clearer.[29]

There is something of this sense of the Levellers in some seventeenth-century usage. In his memoirs Denzil Holles referred to 'the Leveller party'.[30] In 1655 a correspondent of Charles II wrote of 'the party of Levellers'.[31] In 1649 the mercury *The Kingdomes faithfull and Impartiall Scout* referred to the 'further proceedings of Leuit. Col J, Lilburn, and his party'.[32] In a later edition the same publication referred more directly to several agents of 'John Lilburns party' who were said to be gathering subscriptions in Hertfordshire, Buckinghamshire, Bedfordshire and 'other parts'.[33] In 1645 John Bastwick was worried should Lilburne's 'party grow a little stronger'.[34] Some of this usage is hostile. It uses the term 'party' as a synonym for 'faction', meaning those causing unnecessary division. Henry Denne in his recantation of his role in the Burford mutiny, *The Levellers Designe Discovered*, says 'I joined with that Party, deviding from the army'.[35] John Lilburne referred to his Presbyterian opponents as a 'trayerous Party'.[36] But even here if we subtract the judgemental aspect of the usage we are left with the fact that those who used the term are identifying a recognisable and organised body of political activists. Thomas Edwards used the term 'party' at least five times in the twelve pages of the Epistle which opens *Gangraena*, Part I. Elsewhere in the same work Edwards refers to 'the Independent party', the 'Court party', the 'Malignant party', the 'well-affected party'. The Sectaries are routinely referred to as a party.[37] The 1647 *A true account of the character of the times* gives a brief history of the entire Revolution almost exclusively in terms of the conflicts between the king's, Parliament's, the Presbyterians' and the Independents' 'parties'.[38]

But not all usage was hostile. Indeed, when the Levellers replied to Denne's accusations in the pamphlet *Sea-Green and Blue*, they repeat the word 'party' but with a neutral usage.[39] *The Moderate* refered to 'the Levelling party' at the end of April 1649.[40] And in the following issue it complained of those who 'exasperate their spirits against that party, called the Levellers'.[41] Pro-Leveller apprentices compared the Leveller leaders to Korah, Dathan and Abiram, 'who took unto them what party they could procure among the families of Israel, (as these do among the Regiments of the Army, and elsewhere)'.[42] In his account of the Burford mutiny Francis White referred to the mutineers as 'our party' and more generally addressed debates that might mean that 'our own party . . . may be taken into union'.[43] A 1659 defence of the Levellers talked of 'a party of levellers'.[44]

All this may still fall short of the modern notion of a political party, but it certainly conforms to the definition of a political movement: 'a group of people working together to advance their shared political, social, or artistic ideas'.[45] And since even political movements exist on a spectrum ranging from loose and temporary single-issue campaigns at one end to more party-like multiple-issue stable alliances at the other, we can say that the Levellers were at the more party-like end of that range.

Alliances and constituencies

Revolutions, almost by definition, are a dynamic and fluid political environment. For any group the allies of one phase can become opponents in another phase. Every political grouping will seek support and alliances beyond its own core of adherents. This is true of modern political parties as well as of early modern political groupings. Even today's more monolithic and independent political parties ultimately depend at least in part on alliances and relationships that stretch for a considerable distance beyond their core membership. If we think of the modern Labour Party and its relations with the trade union movement, the cooperative movement and single-issue campaigns like CND we can see this process at work.

In the history of the Levellers we can see them emerge as a distinct group from a network of such relationships, and seek new constituencies in response to the development of the Revolution. The gathered churches provided one broad stratum from which the Levellers emerged. It was a constituency from which they continued to draw support until a rupture at the very end of the Revolutionary decade of the 1640s. The apprentices of the City, whose mobilisation was an essential part of the popular dimension of the Revolution, also provided a constituency from which the Levellers drew support. Within this broad stratum the 'puritan underground' of secret presses was a far narrower, necessarily more organisationally formed set of relationships within which the future Leveller leaders cooperated.

The divisions arising from the prosecution of the war produced other alliances. As the 'win-the-war' party emerged the future Levellers were part of this radicalised group, forming relations that would be maintained throughout the decade. Later the revolt in the army provided a chance for the Levellers to connect with radicals in the New Model Army in the organised network of Agitators. It is unwise to assert either that the radicals in the army were the simple tools of the Levellers or that they acted without Leveller influence at all. Yet the radicalisation of the army was not *caused* by the Levellers but by the far wider conflict between the Presbyterians and the New Model. The Levellers located themselves within this conflict with considerable agitational skill and accrued support accordingly. This support then influenced the further development of the Revolution.

Jason Peacey makes a valuable point when he says, 'That Lilburne and Wildman were seeking to create something resembling a "party" structure has distracted historians from the fact that they were eliciting much broader support'.[46] This is true, and is a point that cuts in both directions. Only something that is itself a distinct current can create alliances and solicit support from other political forces. There has to be a 'something' that is conducting an alliance with others. Rachel Foxley, while appreciative of some recent scholarship that has located the Levellers in the broader spectrum of radicalism in the gathered churches, the parliamentary opposition and the army, makes the point that this should not lead us to 'dissolve them into an undifferentiated part of that complex political world'.[47] This is a critical methodological point. The approach that Foxley criticises runs the risk of producing what the philosopher Hegel described as 'a night in which all cows are black', meaning that it is impossible to differentiate the object of study from its background.

Seeing the Levellers both as a distinct organisation and as part of a wider network of alliances enables us to appreciate that all such political alliances were subject to the wider stresses of a revolutionary process. The long-standing relationship with London's gathered churches was breached at the peak of the Revolution. The degree of support among the soldiers rose and fell according to the course of the wider conflicts and the success of Leveller organisation. The critical alliance with the political Independents, from whose camp the Levellers sprang in the first place, was broken at Putney and Ware, rebuilt in 1648, and shattered irrevocably in 1649. What I have attempted to do is to properly and carefully delineate what the Levellers owed to their background but at the same time to demonstrate the ways in which they combined their influences in unique patterns and with a specific, original organisation that made an essential contribution to the outcome of events in the 1640s.

The shape of the English Revolution

The impact that the Levellers had on the course of the English Revolution cannot be settled by simply identifying them as a political organisation. Nor can it be settled by calculating the degree of support for the Levellers as an organisation, important though it is to accomplish this task as well. It can only be decided by examining the constellation of political forces in the English Revolution and then calibrating the impact of the Levellers within this overall situation. It is often the case, particularly in revolutionary crises, that a relatively small social weight can have a decisive political impact.

Since much historical debate has revolved around a critique of Marxist accounts of the Levellers it is worth outlining the foundational elements of Marx and Engels's view of the English Revolution. The first important element to grasp is that Marx and Engels believed that modern revolutions under capitalism and those that arose as the system was first establishing itself have fundamentally different dynamics. Capitalism produces both a simplified social structure and the necessity of accomplishing at the same time a revolution in the economic sphere and a political seizure of power. Early modern revolutions have a more complex social structure in which the system can be transformed at an economic level over a long period while the political overthrow of the existing state is still a temporally contracted moment.

Unlike workers' revolutions, Marx and Engels believed that 'all previous movements were movements of minorities, or in the interests of minorities'.[48] It could hardly be otherwise since, in Marx and Engels's view, these early modern revolutions established a new ruling class in power whose interests were opposed to those of the mass of the population. And yet there was a paradox, since these revolutions could not triumph against the old order simply by relying on the forces that the new exploiting class could bring onto the field itself. It therefore engages other plebeian classes in the battle on its side:

> had it not been for [the] yeomanry and for the plebeian element in the towns, the bourgeoisie alone would have never fought the matter out to the bitter end, and would never have brought Charles I to the scaffold. In order to secure even those conquests of the bourgeoisie that were ripe for gathering at the time, the revolution had to be carried considerably further—exactly as in 1793 in France and 1848 in Germany . . . upon this excess of revolutionary activity there necessarily followed the inevitable reaction which in its turn went beyond the point where it might have maintained itself.[49]

The assault on the old order was therefore carried out under universalist demands which, though they resulted in the triumph of a minority, still held meaning for the plebeian forces mobilised in the conflict:

> side by side with the antagonism of the feudal nobility and the burghers (who claimed to represent all the rest of society), there was the general antagonism of exploiters and exploited, of the idlers and the toiling poor. It was precisely this circumstance that enabled the representatives of the bourgeoisie to put themselves forward as the representatives not of one special class but of the whole of suffering humanity. Still more . . . although, on the whole, the burghers in their struggle with the nobility could claim to represent at the same time the interests of the different working classes of that period, in every great bourgeois movement there were independent outbursts of that class which was the more or less developed forerunner of the modern proletariat. For example . . . in the great English Revolution, the Levellers.[50]

As Christopher Hill long ago noted, Marx and Engels were careful not to overstate the degree of working-class development:

In both revolutions [the English and the French] the bourgeoisie was the class which found itself effectively at the head of the movement. The proletarians and those fractions of the burgher class that did not belong to the bourgeoisie either still had no interests separate from the bourgeoisie or still did not form independent evolved classes or sub-classes.[51]

Nevertheless, the necessary 'excess of revolutionary activity' imparted to the movement is what makes victory possible. But then a contrary dynamic takes over:

It is the fate of all revolutions that this union of different classes, which in some degree is always the necessary condition of any revolution, cannot subsist long. No sooner is the victory gained against the common enemy than the victors become divided among themselves into different camps, and turn their weapons against each other.[52]

Or, as Engels elaborated,

As a rule, after the first great success, the victorious minority split; one half was satisfied with what had been gained, the other wanted to go still further, and put forward new demands, which, partly at least, were also in the real or apparent interest of the great mass of the people. In isolated cases these more radical demands were actually forced through, but often only for the moment; the more moderate party would regain the upper hand, and what had been won most recently would wholly or partly be lost again; the vanquished would then cry treachery or ascribe their defeat to accident. In reality, however, the truth of the matter was usually this: the achievements of the first victory were only safeguarded by the second victory of the more radical party; this having been attained, and, with it, what was necessary for the moment, the radicals and their achievements vanished once more from the stage.[53]

One of the virtues of this account is that it provides the basis for answering the question that Ariel Hessayon and David Finnegan ask: 'if canonical radicalism was as popular as Marxists and their fellow-travellers maintained, then why did so much of the ancient regime survive the English Revolution, why was there a restoration of the monarchy, what happened afterwards to the defeated radicals . . . ?'[54] Part of the answer is that, on Marx's account, long-term social changes were being incorporated into society in a way which did not require *social* revolution. And part of the answer lies in the fact that in the *political* revolution that did take place the radicals were always a minority working to gain only enough popular support to overwhelm their opponents. Once this was achieved both the solidity of the social and economic structure and the minority status of the radicals resulted in their rapid marginalisation.

This approach also allows us to resolve some methodological problems posed by revisionism. Glenn Burgess summarises the revisionist critique of Marxism by arguing that it sees Marxism as social determinism ('whig history with statistics'), aims at a holistic account, and is reductionist:

> This point is a simple one: if it is accepted that politics can never be 'reduced' to something else or explained totally in terms of some other thing, then it becomes necessary to treat it, at least in part, on its own terms with its own irreducible patterns and structures.[55]

There is a lot to unpack here. First, the casual identification of Marxism with social determinism is contested, indeed rejected, by the intellectually dominant currents in the Marxist tradition.[56] Second, the claim is incoherent in its own terms. Either politics is 'irreducible' to other social structures or it is 'in part' explicable by a relation to other structures, but it cannot be both. Third, Burgess violates his own method by going on to explain politics in terms of religion, which is to reduce it to another social structure. If it was a fault of some Marxist interpretations to 'write the social history of politics (politics with the politics left out, all too often)', as Burgess claims, then it must be a fault to write a religious history of politics with the politics left out.[57] Finally, what Burgess seems to be aiming for is an account which allows politics to have its own autonomy but to still trace its relations with other elements of the social structure; that is, to see politics as shaped by but not reducible to other social structures. Ironically this is exactly the kind of account which many Marxist interpretations aim to provide. The technical term in Marxist philosophy is a 'mediated totality' in which the relatively autonomous spheres of religion, politics, art, science and so on are seen as interconnected, but not reducible to one another. In this account I have tried to use such a framework to analyse what the political alternatives were that confronted the radicals of the English Revolution and how the activities of the Levellers made a certain resolution of these dilemmas possible, rather than others.

The scope of this book has not enabled me to deal with debates about the class structure of early modern England or the way in which these classes were politically represented. But, leaving these issues aside, this outline of the *political dynamic* between the radical wing of the Revolution and its mainstream representatives is helpful in locating the position of the Levellers within the general pattern of development in the English Revolution.

The role of the Levellers

In the first place the preceding analysis suggests that we should not be surprised to find a constantly shifting pattern of alliance and conflict between the Levellers and the Independents. Some historians have assumed only conflict, and Philip Baker has issued a timely corrective to this view.[58] But we should be wary of exaggeration in either direction. The dynamic of the Revolution in its crucial phase was produced by a relationship of conflict *and* collaboration between the Levellers and the Independents.

Second, the critical role of the Levellers does not depend on an argument that they actively represented a majority current in society. The nature of the revolution that emerges from Marx and Engels's analysis is one in which we would expect to find a great deal of neutralism, where the Clubman phenomenon or popular royalism, for instance, should come as no surprise. The leaders of the Revolution had to struggle with these opponents to convince a wider audience that they had a stake in the outcome of the war. The Levellers and other representatives of subaltern groups did not need to command majority support for their role in this project to be of importance. As Hill put it, 'the radicals owed their brief period of significance to the political function they performed rather than to their own inherent strength in the country'.[59] Nevertheless, this point, too, can be overstated. The Levellers needed to have a degree of popular support and capacity to mobilise it, or their 'political function' could not have been exercised.

Third, the balance of forces at the peak of the Revolution magnified the importance of the Levellers. As Murray Tolmie has noted,

The Levellers were the most important gainers on the radical side in the wake of the polarization over toleration. With astonishing boldness, and with equally astonishing success, they were able to seize the initiative in organizing what Walwyn called 'the generality of the congregations' to respond to the conservative threat in London. At its most successful moments, in the spring of 1647 and the autumn of 1648, this movement was able to deflect the course of the revolution in England.[60]

In the second of the periods referred to by Tolmie, after the Second Civil War, the Independents were confronted by a political stalemate. The obstinacy of Charles I and his Presbyterian allies in the parliamentary camp threatened a counterrevolution. Popular discontent might feed this, or it might feed the drive for a more radical solution, especially in the ranks of the New Model Army. Ireton and Cromwell wished to be neither pushed back nor forced forward. The Levellers provided a vital forward impetus. With their participation this deadlock could be broken. The Levellers brought an essential element of popular drive to the final phase of the Revolution that defeated the king and the moderate parliamentarians. After this they became, for Cromwell, the danger that had to be faced down. If these be the times, then this was the organisation that was equal to them. But once that time had passed the Levellers could make no progress alone.

Finally, we should be wary of reducing the Levellers to epiphenomena of the Independents' strategy. It was by their own efforts that they created a popular base, alliances with the gathered churches and support among the ranks of the New Model Army. They made their own arguments and developed novel practical and ideological interventions. They were a force in their own right. Like any movement they were weaker when alliances failed and they were isolated. But they knew how to seize a political moment and re-created their strength on more than one occasion. It is widely accepted that the Levellers bequeathed us a dramatic ideological heritage of democratic ideas. But they were also pioneers of revolutionary political organisation. What radical movements or parties today do not still petition and write pamphlets, hold meetings and collect subscriptions? In authoritarian regimes they still do so illegally and are often imprisoned for their pains. The communications revolution of our age has not made these forms redundant but given them new life. The fruit of the Levellers' organisation, the establishment of the republic, was a revolution that would not have been made without them, but it was not the revolution the Levellers wanted to make. The revolution that they helped to create turned out to be one they could only half-accept. But they only failed after it was victorious.

Notes

For the ease of readers in following endnotes I have preferred fuller citations and have minimised the use of abbreviations.

Abbreviations regularly used are as follows:

BL: British Library
Bod.: Bodleian Library
CJ: Journals of the House of Commons
CSPD: Calendar of State Papers Domestic
CSPV: Calendar of State Papers Venetian
DWL: Dr Williams Library
LJ: Journals of the House of Lords
HLMP: House of Lords Main Papers
HMC: Historical Manuscripts Commission
LMA: London Metropolitan Archive
MECW: Marx–Engels Collected Works
ODNB: *Oxford Dictionary of National Biography*
PRO: Public Records Office
STC: Short Title Catalogue. A. Pollard and G. Redgrave, *A Short-Title Catalogue of Books Printed in England, Scotland and Ireland, and of English Books Printed Abroad 1475–1640*.
STC (2nd edn): *A Short-Title Catalogue of Books Printed in England, Scotland and Ireland, and of English Books Printed Abroad 1475–1640*, 2nd edn, revised and enlarged, begun by W. Jackson and F. Fergusson, completed by K. Pantzer
TNA: The National Archive

Wing: D. Wing, *A Short-Title Catalogue of Books Printed in England, Scotland, Ireland, Wales, and British America and of the English Books Printed in Other Countries, 1641–1700* (1945–51)

The numerical codes that follow the title of original pamphlets and broadsides refer to entry numbers in the Catalogue of the Thomason Tracts in the British Library, unless otherwise stated.

Introduction

1   *An Exact and Impartial Accompt of The Indictment, Arraignment, Trial . . . of Twenty Nine Regicides* (London, 1679), p. 57.

2   C. Carlton, *Going to the Wars: Experience of the British Civil Wars, 1638–51* (London: Routledge, 1992), p. 214. The only possible rival being the Wars of the Roses.

3   *The Speech of Major John Harris* (London, 1660), E1043[3], p. 3. See also C. V. Wedgewood, *A King Condemned: The Trial and Execution of Charles I* (London: Tauris Parke, 2011), p. 189. R. Clifton, 'Richard Rumbold', *ODNB*.

4   H. N. Brailsford, *The Levellers and the English Revolution* (ed. C. Hill) (Nottingham: Spokesman, 1961). Henry Brailsford died just before he completed his work, which was then edited and prepared for publication by Christopher Hill. The most notable of recent work is Rachel Foxley's outstanding study of Leveller ideology *The Levellers: Radical Political Thought in the English Revolution* (Manchester: Manchester University Press, 2013). The only book-length studies of the Levellers before Brailsford are T. C. Pease, *The Leveller Movement* (Gloucester, MA: Peter Smith, 1965), which was first published in 1916; and J. Frank, *The Levellers: A History of the Writings of Three Seventeenth-Century Social Democrats: John Lilburne, Richard Overton, William Walwyn* (Cambridge, MA: Harvard University Press, 1955). For a fuller account of Leveller historiography see J. Rees, 'Leveller Organisation and the English Revolution' (PhD thesis, Goldsmiths, University of London, 2014), Ch. 1.

5   J. Peacey, *Politicians and Pamphleteers: Propaganda during the English Civil Wars and Interregnum* (Aldershot: Ashgate, 2004), pp. 7–8.

6   H. Denne, *The Levellers Designe Discovered* (London, 1649), p. 8. For one modern account taking this view see R. Howell Jr. and D. E. Brewster, 'Reconsidering the Levellers: The Evidence of the Moderate Author(s)', *Past and Present*, 46 (February 1970), pp. 69–70.

7   The introduction to P. Baker and E. Vernon (eds.), *The Agreements of People, the Levellers and the Constitutional Crisis of the English Revolution* (Basingstoke: Palgrave Macmillan, 2012), contains an overview of recent debate; see pp. 2–27. Another review of recent literature is contained in the introduction to Rachel Foxley's *The Levellers: Radical Political Thought in the English Revolution* (Manchester: Manchester University Press, 2013), pp. 1–19.

8   *Sea Green and Blue* (London, 1649), E559[1], p. 2.

9   I. Gentles, 'London Levellers in the English Revolution: The Chidleys and Their Circle', *Journal of Ecclesiastical History*, 29 (1978), p. 282.

10   In the words of Murray Tolmie, see 'Thomas Lambe, Soapboiler, and Thomas Lambe, Merchant, General Baptists', *Baptist Quarterly*, 27.1 (Jan. 1977), p. 6.

11   I have dealt with some of this history in an analytical form elsewhere: J. Rees, *Leveller Organisation and the English Revolution*, Ch. 1.

12   J. Rees, *The Algebra of Revolution: The dialectic and the classical Marxist tradition* (London: Routledge, 1998), pp. 6–8. R. Levins and R. C. Lewontin, *The Dialectical Biologist* (Cambridge, MA, Harvard University Press, 1987), for instance p. 277. See also R. C. Lewontin, *The Doctrine of DNA* (London: Penguin, 1993).

1. 'The Maddest Christmas That Ever I Saw'

1   B. Morgan, 'Sir Thomas Lunsford', *ODNB*. HMC, *De L'Isle and Dudley Manuscripts*, Vol. 6, 1626–98 (London: HMSO, 1966), p. 192.

2   House of Lords MS, HP/PO/JO/1/18. F. 268–9. I agree with Robert Brenner that the final name on this manuscript copy of the Londoner's petition appears to be 'Rich. Overton'. The transcribed copy in the *LJ* has this as 'Ric. Turner'. See R. Brenner, *Merchants and Revolution: Commercial Change, Political Conflict, and London's Overseas Traders, 1550–1653* (Cambridge: Cambridge University Press, 1993), pp. 398, 364; and *LJ*, Vol. 4, 23 December 1641 (London, 1767–1830), pp. 486–8. I do not, however, follow Brenner in seeing Overton as a signatory of the following day's London petition.

3   *CJ*, Vol. 2, 1640–3, 23 December 1641. J. Rushworth, *Historical Collections of Private Passages of State*, Vol. 4, 1640–2 (London, 1721), pp. 436–71. *Diurnal Occurences of the heads of Severall proceedings in both Houses of Parliament*, 20 December 1641–27 December 1641 (London, 1641), E201[4]. *Diurnal Occurences of the heads of Severall proceedings in both Houses of Parliament*, 27 December 1641–3 January 1642 (London, 1641), E201[5]. *The Journal of Sir Simonds D'Ewes* (ed. W. H. Coates) (Hamden:

Archon Books, 1970), pp. 336, 345. HMC, Montague MS (1900), p. 137.

4 *The Scots Loyaltie* (London, 1641), E181[16]. *Diurnal Occurences of the heads of Severall proceedings in both Houses of Parliament*, 27 December 1641–3 January 1642 (London, 1641), E201[5]. HMC, Montague MS (1900), p. 137.

5 *A Bloody Masacre* (London, 1641), E181[9]. *The Scots Loyaltie*, E181[16]. *Diurnal Occurences of the heads of Severall proceedings in both Houses of Parliament*, 27 December 1641–3 January 1642 (London, 1641), E201[5]. Rushworth, *Historical Collections of Private Passages of State*, Vol. 4, pp. 436–71. J. Lilburne, *Innocency and Truth Justified* (London, 1645), E314[22], pp. 14–15. J. Lilburne, *The Legal Fundamental Liberties* (London, 1649), E560[14], p. 22. J. Lilburne, *The Copy of a Letter sent by Lieutenant Colonell John Lilburne to a friend* (London, 1645), E296[5], pp. 3–4. *England's Weeping Spectacle* (1648), E450[7], p. 3. J. Lilburne, *Liberty Vindicated Against Slavery* (London, 1646), E351[2], pp. 18–19. S. Chidley, *The Dissembling Scot* (London, 1652), E652[13], p. 5. HMC, Montague MS (1900), p. 138.

6 Rushworth, *Historical Collections of Private Passages of State*, Vol. 4, pp. 436–71. *A Petition of the Mayor, Aldermen, and Common-Councell of the Citie of London* (London, 1642), p. 10. HMC, Cowper MS, Vol. 2 (1888), p. 302. B. Whitelocke, *Memorials of the English Affairs*, Vol. 1 (Oxford: Oxford University Press, 1853), pp. 148–9.

7 G. Williams, *The Discovery of Mysteries* (1643), E60[1], p. 23. HMC, Hastings MS, Vol. 2 (1930), p. 83, Rushworth, *Historical Collections of Private Passages of State*, Vol. 4, pp. 436–71. *A Bloody Masacre*, p. 6. HMC, Montague MS (1900), pp. 137–8. *Londons Teares* (London, 1642), 669.f.4[46]. *The Journal of Sir Simonds D'Ewes*, p. 358 n. 14. *Persecutio Undecima* (London, 1648), E470[7], p. 65.

8 *The Apprentices Lamentation* (London, 1642), 669.f.4[45].

9 K. Chidley, *The Justification of the Independent Churches* (London, 1641), Wing C3832; and J. Lilburne, *The Christian Mans Triall* (London, 1641), E181[7], were both printed by William Larner.

10 *By the King* (London, 1641), 669 f.3 [96]. *CSPD*, Charles I, 1641–3, 28 December 1641.

11 *Mr Smith's Speech in Parliament* (London, 1641), E119[46], pp. 3–4.

12 HMC, Hastings MS, Vol. 2 (1930), p. 83. HMC, Montague MS (1900), p. 138. HMC, Cowper MS, Vol. 2 (1888), p. 302. *CSPD*, Charles I, 1641–3, 30 December 1641. *Diurnal Occurences of the heads of Severall proceedings in both Houses of Parliament*, 27 December 1641–3 January 1642 (London, 1641), E201[5].

13 *Diurnal Occurences of the heads of Severall proceedings in both Houses of Parliament*, 27 December 1641–3 January 1642 (London, 1641), E201[5].

HMC, Hastings MS, Vol. 2 (1930), p. 83. HMC, 5th Report, House of Lords MS (1876), p. 4. B. Manning, *The English People and the English Revolution*, 2nd edn (London, Bookmarks, 1991), p. 147.

14 Manning, *The English People and the English Revolution*, p. 147. *A True Relation* (London, 1641), Wing V191, pp. 4–5.

15 *CSPD*, Charles I, 1641–3, 30 December 1641. *The Journal of Sir Simonds D'Ewes*, p. 361.

16 Rushworth, *Historical Collections of Private Passages of State*, Vol. 4, pp. 436–71. *The Journal of Sir Simonds D'Ewes*, p. 365.

17 D. Holles, *Densell Hollis Esquire, His worthy and learned Speech in Parliament* (London, 1641), HMC, Montagu MS (1900), p. 139. *The Journal of Sir Simonds D'Ewes*, pp. 367–8. Manning, *The English People and the English Revolution*, pp. 147, 150–1. *Diurnal Occurences of the heads of Severall proceedings in both Houses of Parliament*, 27 December 1641–3 January 1642 (London, 1641), E201[5]. HMC, Cowper MS, Vol. 2 (1888), p. 302. *CSPD*, Charles I, 1641–3, 30 December 1641.

18 *CSPD*, Charles I, 1641–3, 30 December 1641 and 6 January 1642.

19 *CSPD*, Charles I, 1641–3, 30 December 1641.

20 *A Common Councell held at Guild-hall* (London, 1642), E131[12].

21 *CSPD*, Charles I, 1641–3, 3 January 1642. *The Two Petitions of the Buckinghamshire Men* (London, 1641 [1642]), Wing (2nd edn) T3501A, pp. 1–2. *Diurnal Occurences of the heads of Severall proceedings in both Houses of Parliament*, 2–10 January 1642 (London, 1641), E201[6], pp. 2–3. Rushworth, *Historical Collections of Private Passages of State*, Vol. 4, pp. 473–94.

22 *The Journal of Sir Simonds D'Ewes*, pp. 379, 398, 398 n. 4.

23 *To the honourable the Knights, Citizens and Burgesses Of the House of Commons in Parliament assembled . . .* (London, 1642), Wing T1470.

24 *To the honourable the Knights, Citizens and Burgesses Of the House of Commons.*

25 *To the honourable the Knights, Citizens and Burgesses Of the House of Commons.*

26 R. J. Blakemore, 'Thinking Outside the Gundeck: Maritime History, the Royal Navy, and the Outbreak of the British Civil War, 1625–1642', *Historical Research*, 87.236 (May 2014), pp. 251–74. J. Cox, *Old East Enders: The History of Tower Hamlets* (Stroud: The History Press, 2013), pp. 179–80.

27 *CSPV*, Vol. 25, 1640–2, ed. Allen B. Hinds (London, 1924), pp. 267–86.

28 Rushworth, *Historical Collections of Private Passages of State*, Vol. 4, 473–94. Whitelocke, *Memorials of the English Affairs*, Vol. 1, pp. 153–4. B.

Morgan, 'Sir Thomas Lunsford', *ODNB*. *The Journal of Sir Simonds D'Ewes*, pp. 381–2, 393. *Diurnal Occurences of the heads of Severall proceedings in both Houses of Parliament*, 2–10 January 1642 (London, 1641), E201[6], pp. 2–4, 6. *A True Relation of the unparaleled Breach of Parliament by his Majesty* (London, 1641). *The Two Petitions of the Buckinghamshire Men*, p. 2. HMC, Montague MS (1900), p. 141.

29 *The Journal of Sir Simonds D'Ewes*, p. 384. Rushworth, *Historical Collections of Private Passages of State*, Vol. 4, pp. 473–94.

30 Rushworth, *Historical Collections of Private Passages of State*, Vol. 4, pp. 473–94. *CSPD*, Charles I, 1641–3, 6 January 1642.

31 *CSPD*, Charles I, 1641–3, 6 January 1642.

32 *CSPD*, Charles I, 1641–43, 4–6 January 1642. *The Humble Petition of the Mayor, Aldermen and Commons of the Citie of London* (London, 1642), E84[14]. *The Journal of Sir Simonds D'Ewes*, p. 387. Rushworth, *Historical Collections of Private Passages of State*, Vol. 4, pp. 473–94. HMC, Montague MS (1900), p. 141. Whitelocke, *Memorials of the English Affairs*, Vol. 1, p. 155.

33 *CSPD*, Charles I, 1641–3, Thomas Smith to Sir John Pennington, 7 January 1642.

34 *The Journal of Sir Simonds D'Ewes*, p. 392. *CSPD*, Charles I, 1641–3, Thomas Smith to Sir John Pennington, 7 January 1642. *CSPV*, Vol. 25, 1640–2, entry for 10 January 1642. HMC, Cowper MS, Vol. 2 (1888), p. 303.

35 Rushworth, *Historical Collections of Private Passages of State*, Vol. 4, Saturday 8 January 1642, 'Examinations taken touching words spoken by Captain Hide'.

36 HMC, Cowper MS, Vol. 2 (1888), p. 303. *CSPD*, Charles I, 1641–3, 8 January 1642. Rushworth, *Historical Collections of Private Passages of State*, Vol. 4, pp. 473–94. Whitelocke, *Memorials of the English Affairs*, Vol. 1, p. 157.

37 Rushworth, *Historical Collections of Private Passages of State*, Vol. 4, pp. 473–94. *The Journal of Sir Simonds D'Ewes*, pp. 400–1.

38 *CSPV*, Vol. 25, 1640–2, entry for 24 January 1642.

39 *CSPV*, Vol. 25, 1640–2, entry for 24 January 1642.

40 *A True Relation of the unparaleled Breach of Parliament by his Majesty*, p. 5. *The Two Petitions of the Buckinghamshire Men*, p. 5. *The Journal of Sir Simonds D'Ewes*, p. 401 n. 22. Rushworth, *Historical Collections of Private Passages of State*, Vol. 4, pp. 473–94. *CSPV*, Vol. 25, 1640–2, entry for 24 January 1642.

41   *CSPV*, Vol. 25, 1640–2, entry for 24 January 1642.

42   *A Speech made by Sr. Thomas Lunsford* (London, 1642). B. Morgan, 'Sir Thomas Lunsford', *ODNB*. By June Lunsford was free and had joined the King in York. HMC, Cowper MS, Vol. 2 (1888), p. 303.

43   Williams, *The Discovery of Mysteries*, p. 20. *A Complaint to the House of Commons, and a Resolution taken up by the free Protestant Subjects of the Cities of London and Westminster . . .*, E244[31], pp. 13, 15.

44   *CSPV*, Vol. 25, 1640–2, entry for 10 January 1642.

45   *A Declaration of The valiant Resolution of the Famous Prentices of London . . .* (London, 1642), E109[5], p. 1.

46   Rushworth, *Historical Collections of Private Passages of State*, Vol. 4, pp. 473–94.

47   Williams, *The Discovery of Mysteries*, pp. 20–4.

48   *A Discoverie of Six women preachers* (1641), E166[1].

49   *The Brothers of the Separation* (London, 1641), *LJ*, Vol. 4, 1629–42 (1767– 1830), pp. 134–5. M. Tolmie, *The Triumph of the Saints* (Cambridge: Cambridge University Press, 1977), pp. 12–27. K. Lindley, *Popular Politics and Religion in Civil War London* (Aldershot: Scolar, 1997), pp. 79–83.

50   S. Wright, *The Early English Baptists 1603–1649* (Woodbridge: Boydell, 2006), pp. 92, 93 n. 65.

51   Williams, *The Discovery of Mysteries*, p. 22.

52   *A Complaint to the House of Commons, and a Resolution taken up by the free Protestant Subjects of the Cities of London and Westminster*, p. 13.

53   *CSPV*, Vol. 25, 1640–2, 10 January 1642.

54   Lindley, *Popular Politics and Religion in Civil War London*, p. 35. Manning, *The English People and the English Revolution*, p. 158.

55   Brenner, *Merchants and Revolution*, pp. 368–9.

56   *To the Right Honourable The House of Peeres Now Assembled in Parliament* (London, 1642), Wing T1638, italics in the original.

57   *To the Honourable The House of Commons Assembled in Parliament . . .*, 669 f.4[54].

58   J. Wildman, *Truths Triumph* (London, 1648), E.520[33], p. 17.

2. The First Leveller, John Lilburne

1   J. Lilburne, 'Letter to apprentices', 10 May 1639, reprinted at the end of J. Lilburne, *A Prisoners Plea for Habeas Corpus* (London, April 1647), E.434[19].

2   N. Carlin, 'Liberty and Fraternities in the English Revolution: The Politics of the Artisans' Protests, 1635–1659', *International Review of Social History*, 39.2 (August 1994), pp. 223–54. P. Earle, *The Making of the English Middle Class* (London: Methuen, 1989) Ch. 3.

3   See Earle, *The Making of the English Middle Class*, Ch. 3. L. Schwarz, 'London Apprentices in the Seventeenth Century: Some Problems', available at www.localpopulationstudies.org.uk/PDF/LPS38/LPS38_1987_18 -22.pdf; and P. Wallis and C. Minns, 'Apprenticeships in Early Modern London: Economic Origins and Destinations of Apprenticeships in the 16th and 17th Centuries', paper given at Gresham College, 26 January 2012, available at www.gresham.ac.uk/lectures-and-events/apprenticeship -in-early-modern-london-the-economic-origins-and-destinations-of.

4   Wallis and Minns, 'Apprenticeships in Early Modern London: Economic Origins and Destinations of Apprenticeships in the 16th and 17th Centuries'.

5   R. Brenner, *Merchants and Revolution* (Cambridge: Cambridge University Press, 1993), p. 70, where the cost of a Levant Company apprenticeship before 1640 is given as between £200 and £300. Similar amounts were expected by the Merchant Adventurers.

6   Earle, *The Making of the English Middle Class*, pp. 94–5.

7   S. R. Smith, 'Almost Revolutionaries: The London Apprentices during the Civil Wars', *Huntington Library Quarterly*, 42.4 (Autumn 1979), p. 316. Although Smith is exaggerating when he says that the social composition of apprentices 'was as broad as that of the entire kingdom' (pp. 313, 324), since not only the greater nobility but also the poor, labourers and servants were unlikely to be apprentices.

8   B. Manning, *The English People and the English Revolution*, 2nd edn (London, Bookmarks, 1991), p. 281.

9   Smith, 'Almost Revolutionaries'.

10 N. Carlin, 'Liberty and Fraternities in the English Revolution: The Politics of the Artisans' Protests, 1635–1659', *International Review of Social History*, 39.2 (August 1994), pp. 252–4. Smith, 'Almost Revolutionaries', p. 327.

11 J. Lilburne, *Legal and Fundamental Liberties* (London, 1649), E567[1], pp. 20–2. J. Lilburne, *Christian Mans Triall* (London, 1641), E181[7], p. 2.

12 J. Lilburne, *Legal and Fundamental Liberties* (London, 1649), E567[1], pp. 20–2. M. Tolmie, *The Triumph of the Saints: The Separate Churches of London 1616–1649* (Cambridge: Cambridge University Press, 1977), pp. 36–7.

13 J. Lilburne, *The Poor Mans Cry* (London, 1639), p. 5.

14 J. Taylor, *The Booke of Martyrs* (London, 1639).

15 J. Taylor, *The Booke of Martyrs*, 'The Second Booke' (London, 1639), n.p.

16   M. A. Gibb, *John Lilburne, The Leveller* (London: Lindsay Drummond, 1947), pp. 39–40.

17   J. Lilburne, *Innocency and Truth Justified* (London, 1646), E314[22], p. 7.

18   *CPSV*, Vol. 24, 1636–9 (1923), 'Venice: July 1637', pp. 234–50.

19   Tolmie, *The Triumph of the Saints*, p. 36.

20   J. Lilburne, *A Coppy of a Letter Written . . . to the Wardens of the Fleet* (London, 1640), p. 10.

21   J. Lilburne, *Christian Man's Triall* (London, 1641), p. 1.

22   Lilburne, *Christian Man's Triall*, pp. 6–8.

23   Rushworth, *Historical Collections of Private Passages of State*, Vol. 2, pp. 461–81.

24   J. Lilburne, *The Worke of the Beast* (Amsterdam, 1638), p. 5.

25   Rushworth, *Historical Collections of Private Passages of State*, Vol. 2, 1629–38, pp. 461–81. Lilburne, *A Coppy of a Letter Written . . . to the Wardens of the Fleet*, pp. 13–15. J. Lilburne, *Innocency and Truth Justified* (London, 1645), E314[22], p. 73.

26   Rushworth, *Historical Collections of Private Passages of State*, Vol. 2, 1629–38, pp. 461–81. Lilburne, *A Coppy of a Letter Written . . . to the Wardens of the Fleet*, pp. 20, 23. Lilburne, *Innocency and Truth Justified*, p. 73.

27   Lilburne, *The Worke of the Beast*, pp. 5–24. Lilburne, *A Coppy of a Letter Written . . . to the Wardens of the Fleet*, p. 24.

28   Rushworth, *Historical Collections of Private Passages of State*, Vol. 2, 1629–38, pp. 461–81. In the same passage Rushworth drew attention to the Lilburne family's gentry status, a point designed to make his treatment all the more unacceptable.

29   J. Lilburne, *A true relation of the material passages of Lieut. Col. John Lilburne's sufferings* (London, 1645), E324[9]. Lilburne, *A Coppy of a Letter Written . . . to the Wardens of the Fleet*, pp. 9–10. P. Gregg, *Free-Born John: A Biography of John Lilburne* (London: Dent, 1961), pp. 64–7.

30   Lilburne, *A true relation of the material passages of Lieut. Col. John Lilburne's sufferings*. Lilburne, *The Poor Mans Cry*, pp. 4, 8, 10–13. Lilburne, *Innocency and Truth Justified*, p. 73.

31   'Petition of Katherine Hadley, 21 Dec. 1641', HMC, *Fourth Report* (1874), pp. 33–34, which confirms Lilburne's account of his imprisonment. Lilburne, *A Coppy of a Letter Written . . . to the Wardens of the Fleet*, pp. 2–6. Gregg, *Free-Born John*, pp. 69–70. Possibly indicating that he was not under 'close imprisonment' for the whole time. Gibb, *John Lilburne, The Leveller*, p. 57.

32 This letter of 10 May 1639 is reprinted at the end of Lilburne, *A Prisoners Plea for Habeas Corpus*. See also Lilburne, *Innocency and Truth Justified*, pp. 74–5.

33 J. Rushworth, *Historical Collections of Private Passages of State*, Vol. 3, 1639–40 (London, 1721), 'Historical Collections: 1639, March–June', pp. 885–946. Gregg, *Free-Born John*, pp. 77–8.

34 Lilburne, *A Prisoners Plea for Habeas Corpus*. Gregg, *Free-Born John*, pp. 77–8.

35 *CSPV*, Vol. 25, 1640–2, 'Venice: May 1640', pp. 40–9. K. Lindley, *Popular Politics and Religion in Civil War London* (Aldershot: Scolar, 1997), pp. 5–7. V. Pearl, *London and the Outbreak of the Puritan Revolution* (Oxford: Oxford University Press, 1961), pp. 107–8.

36 *CSPD*, Charles I, 1640, 11–18 May 1640, pp. 145–81. Smith, 'Almost Revolutionaries', p. 314.

37 *CSPD*, Charles I, 1640, 11–18 May 1640, pp. 145–81. *CSPV*, Vol. 25, 1640–2, 'Venice: May 1640', pp. 40–9.

38 O. Cromwell, 'Speech to the First Protectorate Parliament, 4 September 1654', in *Oliver Cromwell's Letters and Speeches* (ed. T. Carlyle), Vol. 3 (London: J. M. Dent, 1908), p. 39. On Cromwell's background see J. Morrill, 'The Making of Oliver Cromwell', in J. Morrill (ed.), *Oliver Cromwell and the English Revolution* (London: Longman, 1990) Ch. 2.

39 *Oliver Cromwell's Letters and Speeches* (ed. T. Carlyle), Vol. 1 (London: J. M. Dent, 1908), pp. 89–91. A. Fraser, *Cromwell, Our Chief of Men* (London: Mandarin, 1989), p. 64. Gregg, *Free-Born John*, p. 84. Lilburne, *Innocency and Truth Justified*, p. 74.

40 Manning, *The English People and the English Revolution*, pp. 51–5. Lindley, *Popular Politics and Religion in Civil War London*, pp. 13–15. Gregg, *Free-Born John*, p. 84.

41 HMC, 10th Report, Appendix, Pt VI, Braye MSS, pp. 140–41. T. W. Strafford, *A Briefe and Perfect Relation . . .* (London, 1647), p. 87. Manning, *The English People and the English Revolution*, pp. 63–4.

42 *LJ*, Vol. 4, 1629–42 (1767–1830). Lilburne, *Innocency and Truth Justified*, pp. 74–5.

43 *CJ*, Vol. 2, 1640–3 (1802), pp. 133–4.

44 K. Thomas, 'Women and the Civil War Sects', *Past and Present*, 13 (April 1958), p. 44.

45 P. Higgins, 'The Reactions of Women, with Special Reference to Women Petitioners', in B. Manning (ed.), *Politics, Religion and the English Civil War* (London: Arnold, 1973), pp. 220–1. J. Eales, *Puritans and Roundheads: The*

Harleys of Brampton Bryan and the Outbreak of the English Civil War (Cambridge: Cambridge University Press, 1990).

46   Higgins, 'The Reactions of Women', pp. 192, 201–6.

47   I. Gentles, 'London Levellers in the English Revolution: The Chidleys and Their Circle', *Journal of Ecclesiastical History*, 29 (1978), pp. 281–2, *Katherine Chidley: The Early Modern Englishwoman, Series II, Printed Writings, 1641–1700, Part 4* (ed. K. Gillespie) (Farnham: Ashgate, 2009), p. ix.

48   P. Studley, *The Looking-Glasse of Schisme* (London, 1634), p. 269, STC (2nd edn) 23403.

49   Tolmie, *The Triumph of the Saints*, pp. 21–2.

50   K. Chidley, *The Justification of the Independent Churches* (London, 1641) Wing C3832., p. 64,

51   Gentles, 'London Levellers in the English Revolution', p. 283.

52   S. Chidley, *The Dissembling Scot* (London, 1652), E652[13], p. 4. I. J. Gentles, 'Samuel Chidley', *ONDB*.

53   Chidley, *The Justification of the Independent Churches*. J. Lilburne, *The Christian Man's Triall* (London, 1641), E181[7].

54   Chidley, *The Justification of the Independent Churches*, pp. 22, 44.

55   Chidley, *The Justification of the Independent Churches*, p. 26.

56   *Katherine Chidley, The Early Modern Englishwoman, Series II, Printed Writings, 1641–1700, Part 4*, pp. 216–33.

57   Preface to T. Edwards, *Gangraena* (London, 1646), Part III. References are to the facsimile reprint by The Rota/University of Exeter (1977).

58   M. Nevitt, *Women and the Pamphlet Culture of Revolutionary England, 1640–1660* (Aldershot: Ashgate, 2006), p. 27.

59   *The Humble Petition of divers wel-affected Women* (London) 5 May 1649, p. 5, 669.f.14 [27]

60   Gentles, 'London Levellers in the English Revolution', p. 294.

61   R. Trubowitz, 'Female Preachers and Male Wives: Gender and Authority in Civil War England', in J. Holstun (ed.), *Pamphlet Wars: Prose in the English Revolution* (London: Frank Cass, 1992), pp. 115–20.

62   As Jordan Downs has argued; see his 'Mobilising the Metropolis', paper given to the Institute for Historical Research's Early Modern Britain seminar. I'm grateful to the author for allowing me to see this unpublished paper.

63   As Rushworth noted, 'Three years Imprisonment till the Parliament released him, and might otherwise have been for ever'. J. Rushworth, *Historical Collections of Private Passages of State*: Vol. 2: 1629–38, pp.

461–81. 'Cath. Hadley discharged out of Bridewell', *LJ*, Vol. 4, 1629–42 (1767–1830), pp. 113–14.

64   As D. Alan Orr has noted; see his 'Law, liberty and the English Civil War: John Lilburne's Prison Experience, the Levellers and Freedom', in M. J. Braddick and D. L. Smith, *The Experience of Revolution in Stuart Britain and Ireland* (Cambridge: Cambridge University Press, 2011), p. 155. Orr, p. 155, argues that 'Lilburne's view of liberty derived increasingly from the actual experience of being constrained behind prison walls'.

3. London, The First Leveller

1   V. Pearl, *London and the Outbreak of the Puritan Revolution* (Oxford: Oxford University Press, 1961), Ch. 1.

2   R. Weinstein, 'London at the Outbreak of the Civil War', in S. Porter (ed.), *London and the Civil War* (London: Macmillan, 1996), pp. 33–8. L. German and J. Rees, *A People's History of London* (London: Verso, 2012), pp. 45–6.

3   Pearl, *London and the Outbreak of the Puritan Revolution*, pp. 23–37.

4   Pearl, *London and the Outbreak of the Puritan Revolution*, pp. 50–68.

5   See D. Cressy, *Dangerous Talk* (Oxford: Oxford University Press, 2010) Chs. 7 and 8.

6   See, for instance, accounts in Pearl, *London and the Outbreak of the Puritan Revolution*; B. Manning, *The English People and the English Revolution*, 2nd edn (London, Bookmarks, 1991); K. Lindley, *Popular Politics and Religion in Civil War London* (Aldershot: Scolar, 1997); M. Tolmie, *The Triumph of the Saints: The Separate Churches of London 1616–1649* (Cambridge: Cambridge University Press, 1977).

7   *Persecutio Undecima* (London, 1648), E470[7], pp. 64–5.

8   J. Coffey, *John Goodwin and the Puritan Revolution* (Woodbridge: Boydell, 2006), p. 44.

9   Coffey, *John Goodwin and the Puritan Revolution*, p. 45.

10   B. Capp, *The World of John Taylor the Water Poet* (Oxford: Clarendon, 1994), p. 178.

11   D. A. Kirby, 'The Radicals of St. Stephen's, Coleman Street, London, 1624–1642', *Guildhall Miscellany*, 3.2 (April 1970), pp. 101–8. D. A. Kirby, 'The Parish of St. Stephen's, Coleman Street, London: A Study in Radicalism, c.1624–1664' (B.Litt., Oxford University, 1969). Another account of Coleman Street can be found in A. Johns, 'Coleman Street', *Huntington Library Quarterly*, 71.1 (March 2008), pp. 33–54.

12 Coffey, *John Goodwin and the Puritan Revolution*, pp. 48–9.

13 Kirby, 'The Radicals of St. Stephen's', pp.103–4, 111–13.

14 Kirby, 'The Radicals of St. Stephen's', p. 114.

15 Confusingly there are two Baptist preachers, both with Leveller associations, with the same name, though sometimes with variant spellings. Thomas Lambe was a soap boiler and preacher in the Spitalfields/ Whitechapel area, originally from Colchester. Thomas Lamb was a merchant from Coleman Street. The former was an important Leveller activist, although both had an association with William Walwyn. See M. Tolmie, 'Thomas Lambe, Soapboiler, and Thomas Lambe, Merchant, General Baptists', *Baptist Quarterly*, 27.1 (Jan. 1977), pp. 4–13. G. F. Nuttall, 'Thomas Lambe, William Allen and Richard Baxter: An Additional Note', *Baptist Quarterly* 27.3 (July 1977), pp. 139–40. See also *ODNB* entries for Thomas Lambe and Thomas Lamb.

16 T. Edwards, *Gangraena* (London, 1646), Part I, pp. 92–93.

17 Edwards, *Gangraena*, Part I, p. 84.

18 A. Hessayon, 'Attaway, Mrs.', *ODNB*.

19 Kirby, 'The Radicals of St. Stephen's', p. 113. Johns, 'Coleman Street', p. 43.

20 Edwards, *Gangraena*, Part I, pp. 79–80. Kirby, 'The Parish of St. Stephen's', p. 185. K. Lindley, 'Whitechapel Independents and the English Revolution', *Historical Journal*, 41.1 (March 1998), pp. 283–91.

21 *LJ*, Vol. 4, 1629–42 (1767–1830), pp. 134–5. Although the Lords also told ministers to forbear from introducing rites and ceremonies beyond what was approved.

22 TNA: PRO, SP 18/74 f.132.

23 *Persecutio Undecima*, pp. 56, 58.

24 *A Letter from Mercurius Civicus to Mercurius Rusticus* (1643), Wing B6324, p. 4.

25 G. A. Raikes, *The Ancient Vellum Book of the Honourable Artillery Company* (London, 1890), pp. vii–viii, xiv.

26 Raikes, *The Ancient Vellum Book*, pp. xii, 45, 46, 58, 68. Though Raikes's claim that the John Milton who became a member in 1635 is the poet is untrue. This John Milton was from St Dunstan's in the East, a captain in the White Regiment taken prisoner at Cheriton. *Cromwell Association Directory of Army Officers* (British History Online, forthcoming). I am very grateful to Tim Wales for allowing me pre-publication access to this material.

27 *Cromwell Association Directory of Army Officers*.

28 *Cromwell Association Directory of Army Officers*.

29 P. N. Hardacre, 'William Allen, Cromwellian Agitator and 'Fanatic'', *Baptist Quarterly*, 19.2 (July 1962), p. 292.

30 G. Goold Walker, *Honourable Artillery Company 1537–1986*, 3rd edn (London: Honourable Artillery Company, 1986), p. 45.

31 A. Tinniswood, *The Rainborowes: Pirates, Puritans and a family's Quest for the Promised Land* (London: Jonathan Cape, 2013), p. 90.

32 S. Hardman Moore, *Pilgrims, New World Settlers and the Call of Home* (New Haven: Yale University Press, 2007), pp. 64–6, 71, 234 n. 52. Tinniswood, *The Rainborowes*, pp. 149–50, 153.

33 J. Everard, *The arriereban: a sermon preached to the company of the military yarde at St. Andrewes Church in Holborne at St. Iames his day last. By Iohn Everarde student in Diuinity, and lecturer at Saint Martins in the fields* (London: printed by E. G[riffin] for Thomas Walkley, and are to be sold at his shop at the Eagle and Childe in Brittaines Burse, 1618); W. Gouge, *The dignitie of chiualrie set forth in a sermon preached before the Artillery Company of London, Iune xiii. 1626. By William Gouge, B. of Diuinity and preacher of Gods Word, in Black-friers London* (London: Printed by George Miller, 1626).

34 Raikes, *The Ancient Vellum Book*, p. 64.

35 Kirby, 'The Radicals of St. Stephen's', pp. 111–13. Kirby, 'The Parish of St. Stephen's', pp. 55–8.

36 R. Symonds, *The Kings Army 1643*, 'The Ensignes of the Rigiments in the Citty of London, both Trayned Bands and Auxiliries', British Library, Harley MSS. 986, pp. 21–2. W. Lovell, *Ensignes of the Regiments in the Rebellious Citty of London, Both of Trayned Bands and Auxilieries* (1643), pp. 21, 31, National Army Museum, Accession No. 6807-53. G. A. Raikes, *The History of the Honourable Artillery Company* (London, 1878), pp. 102, 112–13, 128, 135–9. Goold Walker, *Honourable Artillery Company 1537–1986*, pp. 54, 56, 63–4. H. Foster, *A true and exact relation of the marchings of the two regiments of the trained-bands of the city of London* (London, 1643) final page. For an explanation of the relationship between the Symonds and Lovell manuscripts see H. A. Dillon, 'On a MS. List of Officers of the London Trained Bands in 1643', *Archaeologia*, 52 (January 1890), pp. 129–44.

37 Symonds, *The Kings Army 1643*, p. 33. *Cromwell Association Directory of Army Officers.*

38 Symonds, *The Kings Army 1643*, pp. 66–7.

39 Pearl, *London and the Outbreak of the Puritan Revolution*, p. 234.

40 *Cromwell Association Directory of Army Officers.*

41 A. Everitt, 'The English Urban Inn, 1560–1760', in A. Everitt (ed.), *Perspectives in Urban History* (London: Macmillan, 1973), pp. 104, 106, 110, 113–14.

42   P. Clark, 'The Alehouse and the Alternative Society', in D. Pennington and K. Thomas, *Puritans and Revolutionaries* (Oxford: Oxford University Press, 1978), pp. 47–72.

43   See Cressy, *Dangerous Talk*, pp. 135, 139–40, 147, 149, 151, 153–4, 165.

44   W. Rowley, *A Match at Midnight*, at http://www.letrs.indiana.edu/cgi-bin /eprosed/eprosed-idx?coll=eprosed;idno=P1.0204. K. Rodgers, *Signs and Taverns round and about Old London Bridge* (London: Homeland Association, 1937), pp. 47, 143, 145. Among other Nags Heads, Rodgers mentions one 'at Leadenhall/Bishopsgate Street, entrance between 153 and 155 Leadenhall Street', which sounds very much like Rowley's Nags Head.

45   H. Wilkinson, *Miranda, Stupenda* (London, 1646), E345[7], p. 26. C. Hill, *The World Turned Upside Down* (London: Pelican, 1972), p. 198. Clark, 'The Alehouse and the Alternative Society', p. 67.

46   *Persecutio Undecima*, p. 55.

47   Cressy, *Dangerous Talk*, p. 189.

48   TNA: PRO, SP 16/486 f.85. The transcript reads 'Canning Street' but may be 'Cannon Street'.

49   *Persecutio Undecima*, p. 60.

50   Pearl, *London and the Outbreak of the Puritan Revolution*, pp. 233–4.

51   *The Vindication of the Cobler* (London, 1640).

52   J. Taylor, *A Swarme of Sectaries and Schematiques* (London, 1642), E158[1]. Taylor was a bitter opponent of the lower orders preaching and, later, of the Levellers. See, for instance, J. Taylor, *A three-fold discourse betweene three neighbours, Algate, Bishopsgate, and John Heyden the late cobler of Hounsditch, a professed Brownist* (London, 1642), and *The Levellers directory for private preaching new vamp'd. In which, certaine formes are warranted (by the agitators) . . .* (London, 1648). Also B. Capp, *The World of John Taylor the Water Poet* (Oxford: Clarendon, 1994), p. 178, for Taylor's attack of Henry Marten.

53   'To the Reader', in S. How, *The Sufficiency of the Spirits Teaching* (Glasgow, 1794), p. 11. William Kiffin, Postscript, in S. How, *The Sufficiency of the Spirits Teaching* (London, 1683), Wing (2nd edn) 2953, pp. 41–2.

54   *The Sufficencie of the Spirits Teaching* was issued in 1639, 1640, 1644, 1655, 1683 and 1689. The bibliographical information in STC attributes the 1640 edition to the Cloppenburg press, of which more below. How's pamphlet contained one of the revolution's more amusing printer's descriptions—'Seen, Allowed and Printed, by us &c.'—in the 1639, 1640 and 1644 editions. John Lilburne's early pamphlet *A Light for the Ignorant* came out

the year before the first edition of *The Sufficiencie of the Spirits Teaching* and also contains the tag 'Seene and allowed'. STC (2nd edn) 15591. The Larner edition of 1655 included the tag that it 'was first printed by some friends of the Author', which may possibly mean that Larner himself was involved with the earlier editions. The single sheet *The Vindication of the Cobler* (1640) was printed by Richard Oulton, an associate of Larners.. The 1683 edition contains a contemporary verse from *The Vindication of the Cobler* inserted at the end of How's preface which is signed with the intials 'R.O.', presumably Richard Oulton.

55   Kirby, 'The Radicals of St. Stephen's', pp. 114–15.

56   J. Lilburne, *A Coppy of a Letter written . . . to the Wardens* (London, 1640), p. 7. Kirby, 'The Parish of St. Stephen's', p. 184.

57   W. Walwyn, *Walwyns Just Defence*, in *The Writings of William Walwyn* (ed. J. R. McMichael and B. Taft) (Athens: University of Georgia Press, 1989), p. 418.

58   *An Order from the High Conrt* [sic] *of Parliament which was read on Sunday last in every church . . .* (London, 1641).

59   L. Claxson [Clarkson], *The Lost Sheep Found* (London, 1660), pp. 28–9. Unfortunately those arresting Clarkson found his almanac with the names of those who distributed his pamphlets recorded in it.

60   See I. Gentles, 'Parliamentary Politics and the Politics of the Street: The London Peace Campaigns of 1642–3', *Parliamentary History*, 26.2 (2007), p. 143.

61   B. Lillywhite, *London Signs* (London: Allen and Unwin, 1972), p. 661, entries 16599 and 16600.

62   B. Whitelocke, *Memorials of the English Affairs*, Vol. 1 (Oxford: Oxford University Press, 1853), p. 49. J. Rushworth, *Historical Collections of Private Passages of State*, Vol. 1, 1618–29 (1721), pp. 610–27.

63   T. Edwards, *Gangraena* (London, 1646), Part I, p. 96. A claim contested by Lilburne and his allies.

64   P. Gregg, *Free-Born John: A Biography of John Lilburne* (London: Dent, 1961), p. 116. J. Lilburne, *Innocency and Truth Justified* (London, 1645), E314[21], p. 4.

65   *The Charity of Churchmen*, in W. Haller and G. Davies, *The Leveller Tracts* (Gloucester, MA: Peter Smith, 1964), p. 343.

66   *Walwyns Just Defence* in Haller and Davies, *The Leveller Tracts*, p. 369.

67   M. Tolmie, *The Triumph of the Saints: The Separate Churches of London 1616–1649* (Cambridge: Cambridge University Press, 1977), pp. 146–50. W. Walwyn, *Englands Lamentable Slaverie* (London, 1645), E304[19]. See

also *The Writings of William Walwyn* (ed. J. R. McMichael and B. Taft) (Athens: University of Georgia Press, 1989), pp. 20–5.

68   I. Gentles, *The New Model Army* (Oxford: Blackwell, 1992), p. 220.

69   *Cobbett's State Trials*, Vol. 5 (London, 1810), pp. 445–50. M. A. Gibb, *John Lilburne, The Leveller* (London: Lindsay Drummond, 1947), p. 322.

70   William Hitchcock is recorded in the pre-1700 Honourable Artillery Company list of members.

71   W. Lovell, *Ensignes of the Regiments in the Rebellious Citty of London, Both of Trayned Bands and Auxilieries* (1643), pp. 21–2, National Army Museum, Accession No. 6807-53. See also *The London Trained Bands Mustered in Finsbury Fields, 26 September 1643*, National Army Museum, at www.cgsc.edu/CARL/nafziger/643IAB.pdf, accessed 28 May 2013. This latter document is a typescript condensation of the officers' names and ranks and the descriptions of their backgrounds as they appear under Lovell's original paintings of the flags. The original book in the archives is listed under the name 'Lovell' but the typescript is attributed to 'Lovett'; however, there is no doubt they refer to the same document. I am grateful to Dr Alastair Massie at the Templer Centre of the National Army Museum for allowing me access to Lovell's original book.

72   R. Overton, *Overton's Defyance* (London, 2 July 1649), pp. 6–7. R. Overton, *The Baiting of the Great Bull of Bashan* (London, 9 July 1649), p. 2.

73   J. Lilburne, *To all the Affectors and Approvers in England of the London petition of the eleventh of September 1648* (London, 1649).

74   *Mercurius Pragmaticus* (London) 9–16 November 1647, p. 66, 69–70. Gregg, *Free-Born John*, p. 229.

75   *Mercurius Pragmaticus* (London) 8–15 May 1649, E555[14], pp. 26–27.

76   *Perfect Weekly Account* (London) 10–17 November 1647. J. P. de Castro, *A Dictionary of the Principal London Taverns since the Restoration*, LMA MS. 3110/2. There are references to inns before the Restoration in this work, as in the case of the Mouth. John Towill Rutt suggests, 'The Mouth was probably a sign of Boulogne mouth, or harbour, which is supposed to have produced the corruption of "Bull and Mouth Street", partly on the basis it was near Petit France with its population of French speakers. T. Burton, *Diary of Thomas Burton, Esq. Member in the Parliaments of Richard and Oliver Cromwell, From 1656 to 1659* (ed. John Towill Rutt) (London: Henry Colburn, 1828). See editor's note, Vol. 3, pp. 507–8.

77   Z. Grey, *An Impartial Examination of the Third Volume of Mr. Daniel Neal's History of the Puritans* (London, 1737) Appendix, pp. 129–30. Gentles, *The New Model Army*, p. 221.

78 *Mercurius Politicus*, 27 August–3 September 1657, E505[18], pp. 1597–8. *The Publick Intelligencer*, 31 August–7 September 1657, E505[19], pp. 1874–5. Pauline Gregg gives the number of mourners as 400, but her source, *London Past and Present*, gives the figure as 4,000. See Gregg, *Free-Born John*, p. 347. Burton, *Diary of Thomas Burton*, Vol. 3, pp. 507–8.

79 J. Peacey, 'The People of the *Agreements*: The Levellers, Civil War Radicalism and Political Participation', in P. Baker and E. Vernon (eds.), *The Agreements of the People, the Levellers and the Constitutional Crisis of the English Revolution* (Basingstoke: Palgrave Macmillan, 2012), p. 53.

80 See J. Wildman, *Truth's Triumph, or Treachery anatomized* (London, 1648), p. 5, for his description of the Saracen's Head as 'my Inn'. And for Lilburne's reference to Wildman's lodgings at the Saracen's Head see *A Declartation of Some Proceedings*, in Haller and Davies, *The Leveller Tracts*, p. 100.

81 *The Case of the King Stated* (dated 18 November 1647), pp. 15–16.

82 *LJ*, Vol. 9, 1646–7 (1767–1830), pp. 529–31.

83 *Persecutio Undecima*, p. 60.

84 Merchant Taylors company archives held at Guildhall Library, MS. 34100/29. The 1669 deed replaces one of 1656 which in turn replaces one of 1634, although this last is not preserved. The deeds may be of the adjoining house that fronts onto Friday Street, but the sketch map gives us some idea of the proportions of the Saracen's Head. The Plan Book of 1680 gives a more detailed view, and since the City worked to keep the outline of the building unchanged after the Great Fire we can assume the Saracen's Head would have looked like this in the 1640s. See MS 34216, p. 2. I am grateful to Stephen Freeth, archivist of the Merchant Taylors, for information on this issue.

85 'Sandy's Row—Savage's Rents', in H. A. Harben, *A Dictionary of London* (1918). J. P. de Castro, *A Dictionary of the Principal London Taverns since the Restoration*, LMA MS. 3110/3. See also the useful digest of coaching inns at www.turnpikes.org.uk/Inn%20Summary.htm.

86 J. Taylor, *The carriers cosmographie or A briefe relation, of the innes, ordinaries, hosteries, and other lodgings in, and neere London, where the carriers, waggons, foote-posts and higglers, doe usually come* (London, 1637), STC 23740.

87 TNA: PRO, SP 16/492 f.49.

88 Wildman, *Truth's Triumph*, pp. 3–5.

89 As Elliot Vernon has suggested, private communication, 27 April 2013.

90 As Blackwell Hall and Coleman Street are essentially the same place. Rodgers, *Signs and Taverns round and about Old London Bridge*, p. 145. C.

H. Firth (ed.), *Clarke Papers*, Vol. 2 (London: Royal Historical Society, 1894), p. 256. There were other Nags Heads which 'stood a little to the East of Harp Lane on the North side of Thames Street in a court called Wilson's yard', and at 'at Leadenhall/Bishopsgate Street, entrance between 153 and 155 Leadenhall Street'. See Rodgers, *Signs and Taverns round and about Old London Bridge*, pp. 47, 143. And another Nags Head is recorded at 'Cheapside, without Temple Bar'; see John Taylor, the Water Poet, *An Alphabet of English Inn Signs*, p. 24.

91   Walwyn, *Walwyn's Just Defence*, in *The Writings of William Walwyn*, p. 886, D. M. Wolfe, *Leveller Manifestoes of the Puritan Revolution* (New York: Frank Cass, 1967), p. 344. Kirby, 'The Parish of St. Stephen's, pp. 118, 134–5. W. L. Sachse (ed.), *The Diurnal of Thomas Rugg 1659–1661*, Camden Third Series, Vol. 91 (London: Royal Historical Society, 1961), p. 118.

92   M. Ashley, *John Wildman* (London: Jonathan Cape, 1947), pp. 103, 119, 145, 176–7.

93   *An Order from the High Conrt* [sic].

94   Edwards, *Gangraena*, Parts I, II and III. A. Hughes, *Gangraena and the Struggle for the English Revolution* (Oxford: Oxford University Press, 2004).

95   *Persecutio Undecima*, p. 57.

96   I. Waters, *Henry Marten and the Long Parliament* (Chepstow: F. G. Comber, 1973), p. 36.

97   *CJ*, Vol. 2, 1640–3 (1802), pp. 54–5.

98   H. Overton, *An order made to a select committee chosen by the whole house of Commons to receive petitions touching ministers* (London, 1640).

99   *Persecutio Undecima*, pp. 19–20, 54.

100   *The Brothers of the Separation* (London, 1641), *LJ*, Vol. 4, 1629–42 (1767– 1830), pp. 134–5; Tolmie, *The Triumph of the Saints*, pp. 12–27. Lindley, *Popular Politics and Religion in Civil War London*, pp. 79–83.

101   S. Wright, *The Early English Baptists 1603–1649* (Woodbridge: Boydell, 2006), pp. 92, 93 n. 65.

102   W. Prynne, *A Fresh Discovery . . .* (London, 1645), pp. 13–14.

103   'Index of Notable Baptists before 1850', *Transactions of the Baptist Historical Society*, Vol. 2 (London: Baptist Union, 1920–1) p. 223. Kirby, 'The Parish of St. Stephen's', p. 102.

104   J. Lilburne, *The Legall Fundamental Liberties* (London, 1649), E560[14], p. 19. See also Edwards, *Gangraena*, Part I, p. 55. Wright, *The Early English Baptists*, pp. 231–5.

105   Tolmie, *The Triumph of the Saints*, pp. 67, 147. Johns, 'Coleman Street', p. 44.

106   E. Vallance, 'Oaths, Covenants, Associations and the Origins of the *Agreements of the People*: The Road to and from Putney', in Baker and Vernon, *The Agreements of the People, the Levellers and the Constitutional Crisis of the English Revolution*, pp. 28–49.

107   'William Allen, Cromwellian Agitator and "Fanatic"', *Baptist Quarterly*, 19.7 (July 1962), pp. 292–308.

108   S. Wright, 'Thomas Lambe', *ODNB*; S. Wright, *The Early English Baptists*, pp. 191–4.

109   A. Laurence, *Parliamentary Army Chaplains: 1642 –1651* (Woodbridge: Boydell, 1990), p. 52.

110   *A Bloody Independent Plot Discovered* (1647), E419[2]. *To the Supream Authority of England, the Commons in Parliament Assembled . . .* (London, 1647). Tolmie, 'Thomas Lambe, Soapboiler, and Thomas Lambe, Merchant, General Baptists' p. 8.

111   A. Southern, *Forlorn Hope: Soldier Radicals of the Seventeenth Century* (Lewes: The Book Guild, 2001), pp. 73–7.

112   *The Triall of Lieut.Collonell John Lilburne* (London: Henry Hils, 1649), E584[9].

113   Tolmie, 'Thomas Lambe, Soapboiler, and Thomas Lambe, Merchant, General Baptists', p. 6. As Tolmie's article makes clear, there were two Thomas Lambes in London in the 1640s and, even more confusingly, both were Baptists. More confusingly still, both knew William Walwyn. They were then and are now conventionally distinguished by description as either 'soap boiler' or 'merchant'. The Leveller Thomas Lambe is the soap boiler.

114   S. Wright, 'Thomas Lambe', *ODNB*.

115   *LJ*, Vol. 4, 1629–42 (1767–1830), 19 January and 21 January 1641, pp. 135, 138. S. Wright, 'Thomas Lambe', *ODNB*.

116   Tolmie, 'Thomas Lambe, Soapboiler, and Thomas Lambe, Merchant, General Baptists', pp. 6–7. Wright, *The Early English Baptists*, p. 176. Edwards, *Gangraena*, Part I, p. 92.

117   Edwards, *Gangraena*, Part I, pp. 92–4.

118   T. Lambe, *A Treatise of Particular Predestination* (London, 1642), Wing L212A.

119   *The humble Petition of sundry of ye Ministers of ye Countie of Rutland & ye Parts adiacent*, in A. Betteridge, 'Early Baptists in Leicestershire and Rutland, I, Original Documents: Samuel Oates in Rutland, 1647–1648', *Baptist Quarterly*, 25.5 (January 1973), p. 207. *Tub-preachers overturned* (London, 1647), E384[7]. This printed letter associates Lambe, Ives,

Tulidah and Oates, as well as other preachers from sectarian churches. Wright, *The Early English Baptists*, p. 204.

120   Edwards, *Gangraena*, Part I, pp. 92–4. Wright, *The Early English Baptists*, pp. 143–5. S. R. Gardiner, *History of the Great Civil War*, Vol. 2 (London: Windrush, 1987), pp. 192–3.

121   Edwards, *Gangraena*, Part II, pp. 17–18.

122   *The Summe of a conference at Terling* (London, 1644), Wing S6166. Edwards, *Gangraena*, Part III, pp. 30–31. Wright, *The Early English Baptists*, pp. 155, 160. Tolmie, 'Thomas Lambe, Soapboiler, and Thomas Lambe, Merchant, General Baptists', p. 8.

123   Walwyn, *Walwyns Just Defence*, in Haller and Davies, *The Leveller Tracts*, pp. 355–6.

124   *The Writings of William Walwyn* (ed. J. R. McMichael and B. Taft) (Athens: University of Georgia Press, 1989), pp. 286, 390. J. Lilburne, *Rash Oathes Unwarrantable* (London, 1647), E393[39], pp. 35, 40.

125   Tolmie, 'Thomas Lambe, Soapboiler, and Thomas Lambe, Merchant, General Baptists', p. 9. S. Wright, 'Thomas Lambe', *ODNB*.

126   Walwyn, *Walwyns Just Defence*, in *The Writings of William Walwyn*, p. 409. See also p. 374.

127   T. Lamb, *Absolute freedom from sin* (London, 1656), Wing L208.

4. Levelling by Print

1   On the distinction between different forms of censorship see A. Hessayon, 'Incendiary Texts: Book Burning in England, *c.*1640–*c.*1660', *Cromohs*, 12 (2007), pp. 1–25, esp. point 14, available at www.cromohs.unifi.it/12_2007 /hessayon_incendtexts.html.

2   W. Prynne, *A Speech made in the House of Commons* (London, 1648), Wing P4013, p. 28. D. Cressy, *England on Edge: Crisis and Revolution 1640–1642* (Oxford: Oxford University Press, 2006), pp. 281–4. C. Hill, 'Censorship and English Literature', in C. Hill, *Writing and Revolution in 17th Century England* (Brighton: Harvester, 1985), p. 37.

3   J. Lilburne, *The Christian Man's Triall* (London, 1641), E181[7], p. 1.

4   *Vox Borealis* (1641), E177[5]. See Hill, 'Censorship and English Literature', p. 39, for the date of writing. In the same pamphlet Overton also complains about censorship in the theatre. See M. Heinemann, 'Popular Drama and Leveller Style', in M. Cornforth (ed.), *Rebels and Their Causes: Essays in Honour of A. L. Morton* (London: Lawrence and Wishart, 1978), p. 76.

5   TNA:PRO, 'Information furnished to Dr. John Lambe, stating the doctrines held by and names of the followers of several Separatist sects . . .', SP 16/250 f.126.

6   D. F. Mckenzie, 'Printing and Publishing 1557–1700: Constraints on the London Book Trades', in J Barnard, D F McKenzie, et al. (eds), *The Cambridge History of the Book in Britain* (Cambridge: Cambridge University Press, 2002), p. 567.

7   G. Kemp and J. McElligott, 'General Introduction', in G. Kemp, J. McElligott, C. S. Clegg and M. Goldie (eds.,) *Censorship and the Press*, Vol. 1 (London: Pickering and Chatto, 2009), p. xxvii.

8   Kemp and McElligott, 'General Introduction', p. xxvi.

9   A. Hessayon, 'Incendiary Texts', paras. 10, 11, 12. C. Nelson and M. Seccombe, 'The Creation of the Periodical Press 1620–1695', in J Barnard, D F McKenzie, et al. (eds), *The Cambridge History of the Book in Britain*, especially the graph on p. 785. Cressy, *England on Edge*, p. 292. Hill, 'Censorship and English Literature', p. 39.

10 D. Como, 'Print, Censorship, and Ideological Escalation in the English Civil War', *Journal of British Studies*, 51.4 (October 2012), pp. 822–3. Cressy, *England on Edge*, pp. 303–9. See also J. Peacey, *Politicians and Pamphleteers: Propaganda during the English Civil Wars and Interregnum* (Aldershot: Ashgate, 2004), p. 137.

11 A. Hessayon, 'Incendiary Texts', points, 16, 17, 18, 19, 20.

12 Cressy, *England on Edge*, p. 303.

13 *The Humble Remonstrance of the Company of Stationers* (London, 1643), E247[23].

14 *The Humble Remonstrance of the Company of Stationers*, pp. 1–2. Pagination is irregular and so I give them as they appear or as they can be counted from those pages that are numbered.

15 *The Humble Remonstrance of the Company of Stationers*, p. 3.

16 *The Humble Remonstrance of the Company of Stationers*, p. 6.

17 *The Humble Remonstrance of the Company of Stationers*, pp. 3–4.

18 *LJ*, Vol. 6, 1643, pp. 95–7. See also Como, 'Print, Censorship, and Ideological Escalation in the English Civil War', pp. 823–5.

19 D. Como, 'Secret Printing, the Crisis of 1640 and the Origins of Civil War Radicalism', *Past and Present*, 196 (Aug. 2007), pp. 37–82.

20 Como, 'Secret Printing', p. 41–4.

21 *Vox Borealis* (1641), E177[5].

22 Como, 'Secret Printing', p. 69.

23 H. Marten, *The Independency of England* (London, 1648), E422[16].

24 Como, 'Secret Printing', p. 52.

25   S. Chidley, *The Dissembling Scot* (London, 1652), E652[13], pp. 7–8.

26   P. Baker, 'William Larner', *ODNB*. *A true relation of all the remarkable Passages and Illegal Proceedings, and Illegall Proceedings of some Sathannical or Doeg-like Accussers of their Brethern Against William Larner, A Freeman of England* (London, 1646), E335[7], p. 11.

27   W. Kiffin, *Certaine Observations on Hosea* (London, 1642), Wing (2nd edn) K423A. J. Lilburne, *The Christian Man's Triall* (London, 1641), E181[7]. H. Knollys, *The Rudiments of Hebrew Grammar* (London, 1648), Wing (2nd edn) K724A. T. Goodwin, *A Glimpse of Sion's Glory* (London, 1642), E175[5]. For Lilburne's early relationship with Kiffin see S. Wright, *The Early English Baptists 1603–1649* (Woodbridge: Boydell, 2006), Appendix 2.

28   *To the honourable the Knights, Citizens and Burgesses of the House of Commons* (London, 1642), Wing T1470.

29   *The Apprentices Lamentation* (London, 1642), 669. f.4[45]. *To the Honourable The House of Commons . . . the humble Petition of many thousand poore people* (London, 1641), Wing (2nd edn) T1437.

30   *A true relation of all the remarkable Passages and Illegal Proceedings*, p. 8. *To the Supream authority of England, the Commons in Parliament assembled . . .* (London, 1647), 669 f.11[98].

31   J. Bothumley, *The Light and Dark Sides of God* (London, 1650), E1353[2]. T. Pride, *The Beacons Quenched* (London, 1652), E678[3]. H. Barrow, *The Relief of the Poore* (London, 1656), Wing B924. S. Fisher, *Baby-Baptism meer Babism* (London, 1653), Wing F1055. T. Lamb, *Absolute Freedom from Sin by Christs Death* (London, 1656), Wing L208. P. Baker, 'William Larner', *ODNB*.

32   Como, 'Secret Printing', pp. 75, 81–2.

33   J. Lilburne, *The Christian Man's Triall* (London, 1641), E181[7]. In January 1641 Larner also had printed the remarkable *To the Honourable The House of Commons Assembled in Parliament . . .*, 669 f.4[54]. K. Chidley, *The Justification of the Independent Churches* was printed by William Larner in 1641. See also P. R. S. Baker, 'William Larner', *ODNB*. K. Lindley, *Popular Politics and Religion in Civil War London* (Aldershot: Scolar, 1997), pp. 393–4.

34   Como, 'Print, Censorship, and Ideological Escalation in the English Civil War', p. 831.

35   This was a work by Thomas Devenish, John Lilburne's landlord and a member of Goodwin's church. David Como's careful work has revealed Dexter as the printer of the second edition of Milton's divorce tract. Como notes Dexter's connections with Thomas Paine and the circles within which William Walwyn was moving, but does not mention this early connection with Larner. Yet it may be this connection which explains why

Milton moved from Paine to Dexter for the second printing of the divorce pamphlet. See Como, 'Print, Censorship, and Ideological Escalation in the English Civil War', pp. 829–36. The 1641 pamphlet by Dexter and his business partner Richard Oulton that they printed 'for William Larnar' is T. Devenish, *Certraine Observations on Concerning the Duty of Love . . .* E142[21]. Kirby, 'The Parish of St. Stephen's,' pp. 118–19.

36   *A view of part of the many Traiterous, Disloyal and Turn-about Actions of H. H. Senior* (1684), Wing (CD-Rom) V359. I. Gadd, *ODNB*. R. L. Greaves and R. Zaller, *Biographical Dictionary of British Radicals in the Seventeenth Century*, Vol. 2 (Brighton: Harvester, 1984), pp. 91–2. 'Henry Hills, Official Printer', *Baptist Quarterly*, 6.5 (January 1932), pp. 215–16.

37   See M. Mendle, 'Putney's Pronouns: Identity and Indemnity in the Great Debate', in M. Mendle (ed.), *The Putney Debates of 1647* (Cambridge: Cambridge University Press, 2001), pp. 126–33. *A view of part of the many Traiterous, Disloyal and Turn-about Actions of H. H. Senior*. 'Henry Hills, Official Printer', p. 216.

38   Chidley, *The Dissembling Scot*.

39   *Alas Pore Parliament how Art thou Betrai'd?*, E21[9]. D. R. Adams, 'The Secret Publishing Career of Richard Overton the Leveller, 1644–46', *Library*, series 7, 11.1 (March 2010), p. 56.

40   *The Humble Remonstrance of the Company of Stationers*, p. 3.

41   Cressy, *England on Edge*, p. 300.

42   T. Edwards, *Gangraena* (London, 1646), Part II, pp. 155–6. Edwards was so outraged that the ballad features again in *Gangraena*, Part III, p. 230.

43   Como, 'Secret Printing' p. 56.

44   *LJ*, Vol. 8, 1645–7, pp. 256–8.

45   *LJ*, Vol. 8, 1645–7, pp. 244–5.

5. Civil War

1   J. Lilburne, *Legal and Fundamental Liberties* (London, 1649), E567[1], pp. 26–7.

2   J. Lilburne, *Innocency and Truth Justified* (London, 1646), E314[22], p. 59.

3   *Three Speeches Spoken in the Guildhall . . . Two of them spoken by the Lord Brook* (London, 1642), E126[44], pp. 7–8. Lilburne, *Innocency and Truth Justified*, p. 40.

4   Lilburne, *Innocency and Truth Justified*, pp. 40–1. S. Porter and S. Marsh, *The Battle for London* (Stroud: Amberley Publishing, 2011), p. 72.

5   J. Rushworth, *Historical Collections of Private Passages of State*, Vol. 5, 1642–5 (London, 1721), pp. 52–77. *Special passages And certain Informations*, 8–15 November 1642 (London, 1642), E127[12], p. 119.

6   Rushworth, *Historical Collections of Private Passages of State*, Vol. 5, pp. 52–77. *A Copie of a Letter . . . Containing a true Relation of his Majesties Army* (1642), Wing C6139. *A continuation of certain Special and Remarkable passages*, 12–17 November 1642 (London, 1642), E242[14], p. 1. *A Exact and True Relation of the Battell Fought on Saturday last at Acton* (London, 1642), E127[8], p. 3. B. Whitelock, *Memorials of the English Affairs*, Vol. 1 (Oxford: Oxford University Press, 1853), p. 190. W. Eyre, *The Serious Representation of Col. William Eyre* (London, 1649), E394[5A], p. 2.

7   Lilburne, *Innocency and Truth Justified*, p. 41. Porter and Marsh, *The Battle for London*, p.75.

8   Lilburne, *Innocency and Truth Justified*, p. 41.

9   Lilburne, *Innocency and Truth Justified*, pp. 39–41. T. Varax (Clement Walker), *The Triall of Lieu. Colonell John Lilburne* (London, 1649), E584[9], pp. 36, 137. C. Carlton, *Going to the Wars: Experience of the British Civil Wars, 1638–51* (London: Routledge, 1992), p. 55. Porter and Marsh, *The Battle for London*, pp.73–4.

10   Lilburne, *Innocency and Truth Justified*, p. 41. *A Copie of a Letter . . . Containing a true Relation of his Majesties Army. A continuation of certain Special and Remarkable passages*, 12–17 November 1642, p. 7. *Special passages And certain Informations*, 8–15 November 1642, p. 121. S. R. Gardiner, *History of the Great Civil War*, Vol. 1 (London: The Windrush Press, 1997), p. 57.

11   *Walter Yonge's Diary of Proceedings in the House of Commons 1642–1645*, Vol. 1 (ed. C. Thompson) (Wivenhoe: Orchard Press, 1986), p. 111. Gardiner, *History of the Great Civil War*, Vol. 1, p. 55.

12   J. Milton and others, *John Milton: Poems* (Oxford: Oxford University Press, 1991), Sonnet 8, p. 35. The original manuscript has the title 'On his door when the City expected an assault'. This is later crossed out and replaced with the title 'When the assault was intended on the City'. It is dated 1642 in Milton's hand.

13   B. Whitelocke, *Memorials of the English Affairs*, Vol. 1 (Oxford: Oxford University Press, 1853), p. 192. D. North, *A Narrative of some passages in or relating to the Long Parliament* (London, 1670), Wing N1285, pp. 36–8. *A continuation of certain Special and Remarkable passages*, 12–17 November 1642, pp. 2–3. J. Rushworth, *Historical Collections of Private Passages of State*, Vol. 5, pp. 52–77. *Walter Yonge's Dialry*, Vol. 1, p. 133. Gardiner, *History of the Great Civil War*, Vol. 1, pp. 58–60. A. Woolrych, *Battles of the English Civil War* (London: Pimlico, 1991), pp. 16–19.

14   *The Diary of John Evelyn* (ed. W. Bray) (London: W. W. Gibbings, 1890),
     p. 39. Clarendon, *The History of the Rebellion and Civil Wars in England*
     (Oxford: Oxford University Press, 1843), p. 320. Gardiner, *History of the
     Great Civil War*, Vol. 1, pp. 53, 57. Porter and Marsh, *The Battle for
     London*, p. 82.

15   J. Lilburne, *A Whip for the present House of Lords* (London, 1647), E431[1],
     p. 4. J. Lilburne, *The Free-mans Freedome Vindicated* (London, 1646),
     E341[12], p. 9. J. Lilburne, *A Letter sent from Captaine John Lilburne to
     divers of his friends in London* (London, 1643), p. 4, E84[5]. *A true and
     most sad Relation of the The hard usage* . . . (London, 1643), p. 4, E89[13].

16   J. Lilburne, *Legal and Fundamental Liberties* (London, 1649), E567[1],
     pp. 25–6. J. Lilburne, *L Colonel John Lilburne Revived* (1653), E689[32],
     p. 3.

17   Rushworth, *Historical Collections of Private Passages of State*, Vol. 5, pp.
     77–102. *A true and most sad Relation of the The hard usage*, pp. 4–5,
     E89[13]. K. Maslan, *The Life of Francis Freeman of Marlborough (c1600–
     1671)* (Woking: Rosemary Cleaver, Pyford Press, 1994), pp. 10–11. J.
     Waylen, *A History, Military and Municipal, of the Town (Otherwise Called
     the City) of Marlborough* (1854, reprinted London: Forgotten Books,
     2013), pp. 180–3. *Marleborowes Miseries, or, England turned Ireland*
     (1643), E245[8]. N. Smith, *A Collection of Ranter Writings: Spiritual Liberty
     and Sexual Freedom in the English Revolution* (London: Pluto Press, 2014),
     pp. 19, 30. Maslan argues that Freeman escaped capture but, unless there
     was a second Francis Freeman captured at Marlborough, the pamphlet
     that Freeman cosigned with Lilburne and others from Oxford jail suggests
     otherwise. 'Conies' is an archaic term for rabbits.

18   Lilburne, *A Letter sent from Captaine John Lilburne to divers of his friends
     in London*. Lilburne, *The Copy of a Letter sent by Lieutenant Colonell John
     Lilburne to a friend* (London, 1645), E296[5], p. 7. *A true and most sad
     Relation of the The hard usage*.

19   Lilburne, *Innocency and Truth Justified*, p. 65.

20   J. Lilburne, *Legal and Fundamental Liberties* (London, 1649), E567[1],
     p. 70.

21   Lilburne, *Legal and Fundamental Liberties*, p. 71. Lilburne, *A Whip for the
     present House of Lords*, p. 4.

22   *The Examination and Confession of Captaine Lilbourne and Captaine
     Viviers* (London, 1642), Wing F665. Varax, *The Triall of Lieu. Colonell John
     Lilburne*, pp. 33–4, 38–9. Rushworth, *Historical Collections of Private
     Passages of State*, Vol. 5, pp. 77–102.

23   *The Speech spoken by Prince Robert* (London, 1642), Wing R2308. The pamphlet is 'Printed for JH and Richard Crosby'. JH may be John Harris, the future Leveller printer who came from Oxford.

24   *A Copie of a Letter . . . Containing a true Relation of his Majesties Army.* Lilburne, *A Letter sent from Captaine John Lilburne to divers of his friends in London*, p. 7.

25   Varax, *The Triall of Lieu. Colonell John Lilburne*, pp. 38–9. Rushworth, *Historical Collections of Private Passages of State*, Vol. 5, pp. 77–102. *CJ*, Vol. 2, 1640–3 (London, 1802), pp. 892–3.

26   J. Lilburne, *England's Weeping Spectacle* (London, 1648), E450[7], pp. 4–5. Lilburne, *A Whip for the present House of Lords*, p. 5. Rushworth, *Historical Collections of Private Passages of State*, Vol. 5, pp. 77–102. Varax, *The Triall of Lieu. Colonell John Lilburne*, p. 39. Clarendon, *The History of the Rebellion and Civil Wars in England*, p. 802. M. A. Gibb, *John Lilburne, The Leveller* (London: Lindsey Drummond, 1947), p. 94.

27   Lilburne, *Innocency and Truth Justified*, p. 41.

28   J. H. Hexter, *The Reign of King Pym* (Cambridge, MA: Harvard University Press, 1941), esp. Chs. II and IV. I. Gentles, 'Parliamentary Politics and the Politics of the Street: The London Peace Campaigns of 1642–3', *Parliamentary History*, 26.2 (2007), pp. 139–59. J. Downs, 'Mobilising the Metropolis', paper given to the Institute for Historical Research Early Modern Britain seminar. I am grateful to the author for allowing me to see this unpublished paper.

29   *The True and Originall Copy of the first Petition* (London, 1642), Wing W1061.

30   Anon, *The Humble Petition and Remonstrance of Divers Citizens . . .*, E83[22].

31   *The True and Originall Copy of the first Petition.*

32   *The Humble Petition of The Major, Aldermen, and Commons of the Citie . . . With His Majesties Gracious Answer* (London, 1643), Wing H3557A. *Mercurius Aulicus*, 4 January 1643, in *The English Revolution Newsbooks 1, Oxford Royalist* (London: Cornmarket Press, 1971).

33   *CJ*, Vol. 2, 1640–3 (London, 1802), pp. 922–5.

34   *The Writings of William Walwyn* (ed. J. R. McMichael and B. Taft) (Athens: University of Georgia Press, 1989), pp. 1–51. B. Taft, 'William Walwyn', *ODNB*.

35   W. Walwyn, *A whisper in the eare of Mr Thomas Edwards minister* (London, 1646), pp. 3–4. R. Brenner, *Merchants and Revolution: Commercial Change, Political Conflict, and London's Overseas Traders, 1550–1653* (Cambridge:

Cambridge University Press, 1993), pp. 372, 398–9. W. Walwyn, *Some Considerations Tending to the Undeceiving of Those, Whose Judgements are Misinformed*, in *The Writings of William Walwyn*, p. 75.

36   The only full biography of Marten is S. Barber, *A Revolutionary Rogue: Henry Marten and the English Republic* (Stroud: Sutton, 2000). Other valuable but shorter modern accounts of his life can be found in I. Waters, *Henry Marten and the Long Parliament* (Chepstow: F. G. Comber, 1973); C. M. Williams, 'The Anatomy of a Radical Gentleman: Henry Marten', in D. Pennington and K. Thomas, *Puritans and Revolutionaries* (Oxford: Oxford University Press, 1978), pp. 118–38; and A. L. Rowse, *Four Caroline Portraits* (London: Duckworth, 1993).

37   A. Wood, *Athenae Oxoniensis*, Vol. 3 (London, 1813–20) pp. 1237–8. J. Aubrey, *Brief Lives* (Bath: The Folio Society, 1975), pp. 197–8. J. Forster, *The Statesmen of the Commonwealth of England*, Vol. 3 (London, Longman, Green, Longman, and Roberts, 1862), p. 357.

38   Clarendon, *The Life of Edward earl of Clarendon*, in Clarendon, *The History of the Rebellion and Civil Wars in England*, p. 937.

39   Wood, *Athenae Oxoniensis*, Vol. 3, p. 1240. Aubrey, *Brief Lives*, p. 198.

40   *Walter Yonge's Dialry*, Vol. 1, p. 98. *Special Passages And certain Informations from severall places* (1642), E126[26], p. 111. *Mercurius Aulicus*, 16 July 1643 (London, 1643), p. 375, E63[2].

41   *Walter Yonge's Dialry*, Vol. 1, p. 79.

42   Aubrey, *Brief Lives*, p. 200. *A Proclamation warning all His majesties good Subjects* . . . (Oxford, 1643), Wing C2716.

43   For instance, two single-sheet verses printed dated 10 and 20 March 1643 respectively: *The Sence of the House* (Oxford, 1643), 669.f.6.117; *The City* (Oxford, 1643), Wing C4352.

44   Aubrey, *Brief Lives*, p. 198.

45   J. Maynard, 'Speech in answer to Mr Martyn', manuscript, E.422[32].

46   BL, Add. MS 71533, 'Letter from John Lilburne to Council of State from Bruge 8 Sept 1652'. Lilburne's remark in G. Masterson, *A Declaration of Some Proceedings* (London, 1647), E427[6]. The code is in BL, *Henry Marten Papers*, Add. MS. 71532, f. 23. Most of the cipher refers to general terms ('Ammunition', 'Troops') or named regiments. On Maximillian Petty's inclusion see *ODNB*. Williams, 'The Anatomy of a Radical Gentleman', p. 121. The only document that seems to suggest that Marten was not a supporter of the Levellers, which is entered in the BL catalogue of the Henry Marten Papers as a 'Tract against the Levellers' (BL, Add. MS 71532, ff. 14, 14v.), is in fact on close inspection

a tract in defence of the Levellers, albeit expressed in circumlocutory language.

47   Aubrey, *Brief Lives*, pp. 198–200. Wood, *Athenae Oxoniensis*, Vol. 3, pp. 1237–42. J. Rushworth, *Historical Collections of Private Passages of State*, Vol. 2, 1629–38 (London, 1721), pp. 461–81. E. Bernstein, *Cromwell and Communism* (Nottingham: Spokesman, 1980), pp. 134 n. 1, 162. J. Frank, *The Levellers: A History of the Writings of Three Seventeenth-Century Social Democrats: John Lilburne, Richard Overton, William Walwyn* (Cambridge, MA: Harvard University Press, 1955), pp. 236–7 and n. 76. Lilburne repeats Marten's joke in *The Just Defence of John Lilburne*; see W. Haller and G. Davies, *The Leveller Tracts 1647–53* (New York: Peter Smith, 1944), p. 451. North, *A Narrative of some passages in or relating to the Long Parliament*, pp. 96–7.

48   *Remonstrans Redivivus* (London, 1643), pp. 2–4, 6, E61[21]. Walwyn, *A whisper in the eare of Mr Thomas Edwards minister*, p. 4. This pamphlet was printed by Thomas Paine. I identify Paine as the printer of *Remonstrans Redivivus* on the basis that at about the same time 'T. Pain and M. Simons' are identified as the printers of *A Declaration of the Proceedings of the Honourable Committee of the House of Commons at Merchant-Taylors Hall* (London, 1643), E63[10]. This is the Committee for the General Rising in which Henry Marten and William Walwyn played a leading role, as we shall see below. Paine used his initials as identification when he later printed William Walwyn's pamphlets, and he and Simmons were still working together in the 1650s.

49   K. Lindley, *Popular Politics and Religion in Civil War London* (Aldershot: Scolar, 1997), pp. 306–7.

50   Lilburne, *Innocency and Truth Justified*, p. 40.

51   Walwyn, *A whisper in the eare of Mr Thomas Edwards minister*, p. 4.

52   *A Declaration and Motive of the Persons trusted, usually meeting at Salters Hall in Breadstreet* (London, 1643), 669.f.7[10]. This was printed by R. Oulton and G. Dexter. David Como notes Dexter's connections with Thomas Paine and the circles within which William Walwyn was moving, but does not mention an early connection with Larner. See D. Como, 'Print, Censorship, and Ideological Escalation in the English Civil War', *Journal of British Studies*, 51.4 (October 2012), pp. 829–36. The 1641 pamphlet by Dexter and his business partner Richard Oulton that they printed 'for William Larnar' is T. Devenish, *Certraine Observations on Concerning the Duty of Love . . .*, E142[21]. Thomas Devenish was John Lilburne's landlord and a member of John Goodwin's church.

53   *Peace and plenty comming unto us* (London, 1643), E102[12], p. 6.

54   Lindley, *Popular Politics and Religion in Civil War London*, p. 312.

55   V. Pearl, *London and the Outbreak of the Puritan Revolution* (Oxford: Oxford University Press, 1961), p. 268.

56   *A Declaration and Ordinance of the Commons and Lords assembled in Parliament for the seizing and sequestrating of the estates* . . . (London, 1643), Wing (2nd edn), E1301A, pp. 3, 11, 15. *CJ*, Vol. 3, 6 April 1643 (London, 1802), pp. 31–3. *Mercurius Aulicus*, 2–9 April 1643 (London, 1643), pp. 176–7, E97[10]. *CJ*, Vol. 3, 25 March 1643 (London, 1802), pp. 17–19.

57   *A Briefe relation of The Remarkable occurrences in Northern parts* . . . (London, 1642), Wing H1686, p. 3. The queen's impeachment was discussed by radicals, including Pennington, at the Merchants Taylors' Hall, see *Mercurius Aulicus*, 16 July 1643 (London, 1643), p. 376, E63[2]. North, *A Narrative of some passages in or relating to the Long Parliament*, p. 47.

58   *CJ*, Vol. 3, 1643–4 (London, 1802), pp. 17–19, 23–7, 30–1, 36–8. *Mercurius Aulicus*, 2–9 April 1643 (London, 1643), pp. 172–3, E97[10]. Later in June, troops under Marten's command entered Westminster Abby and 'smashed an epitaph because it gave the title of Majesty to the queen' and 'broke the organs and choir stalls as not being in keeping with Puritanism', according to the Venetian ambassador, *CSPV*, Vol. 26, 1642–3 (London, 1925), pp. 278–91.

59   *A Letter from Sir John Hotham* (London, 1643), Wing R1164. *CJ*, Vol. 3, 4 April 1643(London, 1802), pp. 28–30.

60   *LJ*, Vol. 5, 6 and 7 April 1643 (London, 1830), pp. 695–9.

61   *CJ*, Vol. 3, 18 April 1643 (London, 1802), pp. 49–52. *LJ*, Vol. 6, 18 April 1643 (London, 1767–1830), pp. 9–11.

62   *CJ*, Vol. 3, 3 May 1643 (London, 1802), pp. 67–9. *LJ*, Vol. 6, 3 May 1643 (London, 1767–1830), pp. 28–30. *Mercurius Aulicus*, 8 May 1643, in *The English Revolution Newsbooks 1, Oxford Royalist*, p. 238.

63   *CJ*, Vol. 3, 1643–4 (London, 1802), pp. 112–14. *CSPV*, Vol. 26, 1642–3 (London, 1925), pp. 278–91. Wood, *Athenae Oxoniensis*, Vol. 3, pp. 1237–8. For Wither see C. Hill, 'George Wither and John Milton', in C. Hill, *Writing and Revolution in 17th Century England* (Brighton: Harvester Press, 1985), pp. 133–56.

64   W. Lithgow, *The Present Survey of London and Englands State* (London, 1643), Wing (2nd edn) L2543. Lithgow had travelled to many Mediterranean countries and was imprisoned in Malaga. He claimed

compensation on his return and, when the Spanish ambassador accused him of lying, Lithgow punched him. He was jailed until the ambassador had left England. The nickname 'Lying Lithgow' stuck, but there is no suggestion that his description of the lines of communication is inaccurate. See *Somers Tracts*, Vol. 4 (London: T. Cadwell and W. Davies, 1810), p. 535.

65   *CSPV*, Vol. 26, 1642–3, ed. Allen B. Hinds (London, 1925), pp. 247–59. V. Smith and P. Kelsey, 'The Lines of Communication: The Civil War Defences of London', in S. Porter (ed.), *London and the Civil War* (London: Macmillan, 1996), p. 121.

66   Lithgow, *The Present Survey of London and Englands State*. *Mercurius Civicus*, 4–11 May, 11–18 May, 25 May-1 June, 8–16 June 1643, S. F. Jones (ed), *Mercurius Civicus, London's Intelligencer: The Original 1643 Text Transcribed and Annotated* (Tyger's Head Books 2013), pp. 11, 16, 29, 44. Smith and Kelsey, 'The Lines of Communication, p. 123.

67   Lithgow, *The Present Survey of London and Englands State*. *Mercurius Civicus*, 25 May–1 June 1643; Jones, *Mercurius Civicus, London's Intelligencer*, p. 27.

68   Lithgow, *The Present Survey of London and Englands State*. *CSPV*, Vol. 26, 1642–3, ed. Allen B. Hinds (London, 1925), pp. 267–78. Although there was some payment both by well-off supporters of Parliament and by the City; see *Mercurius Civicus*, 11–18 May 1643; Jones, *Mercurius Civicus, London's Intelligencer*, pp. 17–18; and Smith and Kelsey, 'The Lines of Communication, pp. 142–3.

69   Pearl, *London and the Outbreak of the Puritan Revolution*, pp. 265–7.

70   *Mercurius Aulicus*, 16 July 1643 (London, 1643), p. 375, E63[2].

71   *Mercurius Aulicus*, 16 July 1643 (London, 1643), p. 385, E63[2]. Hexter, *The Reign of King Pym*, pp. 118–19. Williams, 'The Anatomy of a Radical Gentleman, p. 123.

72   *The Humble Petition of thousands of well-affected Inhabitants of the Cities of London and Westminster, and the Suburbs thereof*. . . (London, 1643), Wing (CD rom) T1650. Walwyn, *A whisper in the eare of Mr Thomas Edwards minister*, p. 4. W. Walwyn, *The Power of Love* (London, 1643), E1206[2].

73   *All sorts of well-affected Persons*. . . (London, 1643), E61[3]. Typographically this anonymous leaflet appears to have come from the same press that Peter Cole used to produce the main petition for the committee of the general rising. J. Spelman, *The case of our Affaires in Law* . . . (Oxford, 1643), Wing S4935, pp. 36. *Mercurius Civicus*, 13–20 July

1643; Jones, *Mercurius Civicus, London's Intelligencer*, p. 58. I. Gentles, 'Parliamentary Politics and the Politics of the Street', pp. 150–2.

74   *The Humble Petition of thousands of well-affected Inhabitants of the Cities of London and Westminster, and the Suburbs thereof.* Spelman, *The case of our Affaires in Law*, p. 36. This report is repeated in *A Letter from Mercurius Civicus to Mercurius Rusticus* (1643), Wing B6324, p. 31. *CJ*, Vol. 3, 1643–4 (London, 1802), pp. 175–7. *Mercurius Aulicus*, 25 July 1643, in *The English Revolution Newsbooks 2, Oxford Royalist* (London: Cornmarket Press, 1971), pp. 419–20.

75   *Three Speeches delivered at a Common-hall* (London, 1643), Wing T1119, pp. 3–4, 6–7, 9–10, 12, 13, 15. 17.

76   *Three Speeches delivered at a Common-hall*, pp. 17–18.

77   *A declaration of the proceedings of the honourable committee of the House of Commons at Merchant-Taylors Hall* (London, 1643), E63[10]. *Mercurius Aulicus*, 16 July 1643 (London, 1643), pp. 398–400, E63[2].

78   Downs, 'Mobilising the Metropolis'. *Mercurius Aulicus*, 31 July and 11 September 1643, in *The English Revolution Newsbooks 2, Oxford Royalist*, pp. 43–4. Pearl, *London and the Outbreak of the Puritan Revolution*, p. 271, italics in the original.

79   BL, D'Ewes Diary, Harley MS 165, ff. 145–7. *Mercurius Aulicus*, 10 and 12 August 1643, in *The English Revolution Newsbooks 2, Oxford Royalist*, pp. 455–8. *Mercurius Civicus*, 3–11 August, in Jones, *Mercurius Civicus, London's Intelligencer*, pp. 81–2. Gentles, 'Parliamentary Politics and the Politics of the Street', pp. 153–7. Lindley, *Popular Politics and Religion in Civil War London*, pp. 317–20.

80   *A Declaration of the Proceedings of the Honourable Committee at the Merchant-Taylors Hall* (London, 1643) esp. pp. 6–7, E63[10]. This was printed by Thomas Paine. Hexter, *The Reign of King Pym*, pp. 127–8. Pearl, *London and the Outbreak of the Puritan Revolution*, esp. pp. 272–3. *Mercurius Aulicus*, 6 August, 8 August 1643, in *The English Revolution Newsbooks 2, Oxford Royalist*.

81   *Mercurius Aulicus*, 6 August 1643, in *The English Revolution Newsbooks 2, Oxford Royalist*. Gentles, 'Parliamentary Politics and the Politics of the Street', p. 157. C. M. Williams, 'Extremist Tactics in the Long Parliament, 1642–1643', *Historical Studies*, 15.57 (1971), p. 149.

82   *Walter Yonge's Dialry*, p. 226. B. Whitelock, *Memorials of the English Affairs*, Vol. 1 (Oxford: Oxford University Press, 1853), p. 208. See Hexter, *The Reign of King Pym*, p. 148.

83   J. Forster, *The Statesmen of the Commonwealth of England*, Vol. 3 (New

York, 1846), pp. 356–7. *CJ*, Vol. 3, 1643–4 (London, 1802), pp. 206–8, 206 n. 2. *Mercurius Civicus*, 11–17 August 1643, in Jones, *Mercurius Civicus, London's Intelligencer*, p. 88.

84 BL, Harley MS 165 f.152. Waters, *Henry Marten and the Long Parliament*, p. 24.

85 Hexter, *The Reign of King Pym*, pp. 125–6, this despite the reference to the Roman tradition that anyone making a proposal to alter the state should do so wearing a noose in case it did not find favour. And Marten's 'disregard of marriage' hardly seems a relevant criticism.

86 Hexter, *The Reign of King Pym*, pp. 133, 142.

87 Gentles, 'Parliamentary Politics and the Politics of the Street', pp. 151–3, 159.

88 Pearl, *London and the Outbreak of the Puritan Revolution*, esp. pp. 250–75. Lindley, *Popular Politics and Religion in Civil War London*, esp. pp. 317–20.

89 See Barber, *A Revolutionary Rogue*, p. 8.

90 Pearl, *London and the Outbreak of the Puritan Revolution*, pp. 262–5. For the order to close shops and enlist in the Trained Bands see 669. f.7[33] and *Walter Yonge's Diary*, Vol. 1, p. 83.

91 T. Prince, *The Silken Independents Snare Broken* (London, 1649), E560[24], p. 3. P. Baker, 'Thomas Prince', *ODNB*. H. Foster, *A true and exact relation of the Marchings of the Two Regiments of the Trained Bands . . .* (London, 1643), Wing (2nd edn) F1625A. G. A. Raikes, *The History of the Honourable Artillery Company* (London, 1878), pp. 136–9.

92 Spelman, *The case of our Affaires in Law*, p. 37.

93 Williams, 'Extremist Tactics in the Long Parliament', p. 150. Walwyn, *A whisper in the eare of Mr Thomas Edwards minister*, p. 4.

94 D. Wootton, 'From Rebellion to Revolution: The Crisis of the Winter of 1642/3 and the Origins of Civil War Radicalism', *English Historical Review* (July 1990), p. 654.

95 G. Alymer, 'Gentlemen Levellers?', *Past and Present*, 49 (Nov. 1970), pp. 120–5.

6. The War, the Church and the State

1 C. Firth and G. Davies, *The Regimental History of Cromwell's Army*, Vol. 1 (Oxford: Clarendon Press, 1940), pp. 1–2.

2 S. R. Gardiner, *Oliver Cromwell* (Ilkley: The Scolar Press, 1976), p. 31.

3 See Gardiner, *Oliver Cromwell*, pp. 28–9.

4   B. Whitelocke, *Memorials of the English Affairs*, Vol. 1 (Oxford: Oxford University Press, 1853), p. 209. Firth and Davies, *The Regimental History of Cromwell's Army*, Vol. 1, p. 5.

5   At this time half a dozen county associations were set up as organisations of defence against royalism. Only the Eastern Association of Norfolk, Suffolk, Essex, Cambridgeshire, Hertfordshire and, in May 1643, Huntingdonshire, sustained itself.

6   J. Bruce and D. Masson, *The Quarrel between the Earl of Manchester and Oliver Cromwell* (London: Camden Society, 1875), p. xiii.

7   J. Lilburne, *Legall and Fundamental Liberties* (London, 1649), E567[1], p. 27. A. Hughes, 'Elizabeth Lilburne', *ODNB*.

8   Firth and Davies, *The Regimental History of Cromwell's Army*, Vol. 1, pp. 6–15. The best short account of Cromwell's work at this time remains C. Hill, *God's Englishman* (London: Penguin, 1970), Ch. 3.

9   Firth and Davies, *The Regimental History of Cromwell's Army*, Vol. 1, pp. 11–12. A. Woolrych, 'Cromwell as a Soldier', in J. S. Morrill (ed.), *Oliver Cromwell and the English Revolution* (London: Longman, 1990), pp. 94–6.

10   T. Carlyle, *Oliver Cromwell's Letters and Speeches*, Vol. 1 (London: J. M. Dent and Sons, 1908), pp. 134–5.

11   Carlyle, *Oliver Cromwell's Letters and Speeches*, Vol. 1, p. 141.

12   Carlyle, *Oliver Cromwell's Letters and Speeches*, Vol. 1, p. 146. Bruce and Masson, *The Quarrel between the Earl of Manchester and Oliver Cromwell*, p. xxiv.

13   Carlyle, *Oliver Cromwell's Letters and Speeches*, Vol. 1, pp. 148, 150. Firth and Davies, *The Regimental History of Cromwell's Army*, Vol. 1, p. 12. 'Narrative of the Earl of Manchester's Campaign', in Bruce and Masson, *The Quarrel between the Earl of Manchester and Oliver Cromwell*, p. 9.

14   W. Eyre, *The Serious Representation of Col. William Eyre* (1649), E394[5A], pp. 1–3. Firth and Davies, *The Regimental History of Cromwell's Army*, Vol. 1, p. 5. P. Gregg, *Free-Born John: A Biography of John Lilburne* (London: Dent, 1961), 222.

15   E. Clarendon, *History of the Rebellion and Civil Wars in England* (Oxford: Oxford University Press, 1843), p. 858. Firth and Davies, *The Regimental History of Cromwell's Army*, Vol. 1, pp. 61–2. D. F. Lawson, '"Upon Dangerous Design": The Public Life of Edward Sexby, 1647–1657' (PhD thesis, University of Alabama, 2011), Ch. 1. G. E. Aylmer, 'Gentlemen Levellers?', *Past and Present*, 49 (November 1970), pp. 120–1.

16   J. Lilburne, *Innocency and Truth Justified* (London, 1646), E314[22], pp. 41–2. Modern accounts which stress the alliance between Cromwell and

Lilburne during this phase of the Revolution can be found in P. Baker, '"A Despicable Contemptible Generation of Men"? Cromwell and the Levellers', in P. Little (ed.), *Oliver Cromwell: New Perspectives* (Basingstoke: Palgrave Macmillan, 2008), Ch. 4, and J. Peacey, 'John Lilburne and the Long Parliament', *Historical Journal*, 43.3 (2000), pp. 625–45.

17   C. Holmes, 'Colonel King and Lincolnshire Politics, 1642–1646', *Historical Journal*, 16.3 (September 1973), pp. 452–8. C. Holmes, *The Eastern Association in the English Civil War* (Cambridge: Cambridge University Press, 2007), pp. 198–9.

18   J. Lilburne, *The Just Mans Justification*, 2nd edn (London, 1647), E407[26], pp. 5, 20. J. Lilburne, *Innocency and Truth Justified* (London, 1646), E314[22], pp. 41–2.

19   Lilburne, *Innocency and Truth Justified*, pp. 41–2. Lilburne, *The Just Mans Justification*, p. 6.

20   Whitelocke, *Memorials of the English Affairs*, Vol. 1, p. 248. Bruce and Masson, *The Quarrel between the Earl of Manchester and Oliver Cromwell*, pp. xlviii–xlix.

21   Whitelocke, *Memorials of the English Affairs*, Vol. 1, p. 248.

22   Lilburne, *The Just Mans Justification*, p. 7. Whitelocke, *Memorials of the English Affairs*, Vol. 1, p. 248.

23   Lilburne, *The Just Mans Justification*, p. 7. Lilburne, *Innocency and Truth Justified*, pp. 25, 65, 67. Whitelocke, *Memorials of the English Affairs*, Vol. 1, p. 249. K. Lindley and D. Scott (eds.), *The Journal of Thomas Juxon, 1644–1647* (ed. K. Lindley and D. Scott, Cambridge: Royal Historical Society and Cambridge University Press, 1999), p. 49.

24   S. R. Gardiner, *The Constitutional Documents of the Puritan Revolution, 1625–1660* (Oxford: Clarendon Press, 1906), pp. 137–44.

25   *LJ*, Vol. 6, 1643, pp. 95–7. See also D. Como, 'Print, Censorship, and Ideological Escalation in the English Civil War', *Journal of British Studies*, 51.4 (October 2012), pp. 823–5. Gardiner, *The Constitutional Documents of the Puritan Revolution, 1625–1660*, pp. 267–75.

26   Lilburne, *The Just Mans Justification*, p. 9. Lilburne, *Innocency and Truth Justified*, pp. 24, 41–3. A. Laurence, *Parliamentary Army Chaplains: 1642–1651* (Woodbridge: Boydell, 1990), pp. 92–3, 129–30.

27   'A Statement by an Opponent of Cromwell', in Bruce and Masson, *The Quarrel between the Earl of Manchester and Oliver Cromwell*, p. 72. E. King, *A Discovery of the Arbitrary, Tyrannical, and illegal Actions of some of the Committee of the County of Lincoln* (London, 1647), E373[3], p. 16.

28   Holmes, 'Colonel King and Lincolnshire Politics', pp. 463–8.

29   Lilburne, *Innocency and Truth Justified*, p. 46.

30   C. H. Firth, *Cromwell's Army: A History of the English Soldier during the Civil Wars, the Commonwealth, and the Protectorate*, 3rd edn (London, Greenhill Books, 1992), pp. 125–6. Gregg, *Free-Born John*, pp. 109–10. Bruce and Masson, *The Quarrel between the Earl of Manchester and Oliver Cromwell*, pp. xliii–xliv. Holmes, 'Colonel King and Lincolnshire Politics', 466.

31   'A Statement by an Opponent of Cromwell', pp. 9, xxxi, lxi. Holmes, *The Eastern Association in the English Civil War*, pp. 204–5.

32   Lilburne, *Innocency and Truth Justified*, pp. 22–3.

33   Lilburne, *Innocency and Truth Justified*, pp. 23–4.

34   Manchester to the Committee of Both Kingdoms, 27 July 1644, in Bruce and Masson, *The Quarrel between the Earl of Manchester and Oliver Cromwell*, p. 2.

35   Lilburne, *Innocency and Truth Justified*, pp. 24–5. Lilburne, *Legall and Fundamental Liberties*, p. 27.

36   S. R. Gardiner, 'A Letter from the Earl of Manchester to the House of Lords Giving an Opinion of the Conduct of Oliver Cromwell', *Camden Miscellany*, 8 (1883). Bruce and Masson, *The Quarrel between the Earl of Manchester and Oliver Cromwell*, p. lx.

37   *The Journal of Thomas Juxon*, pp. 63–4. Holmes, *The Eastern Association in the English Civil War*, pp. 195–6.

38   Holmes, *The Eastern Association in the English Civil War*, pp. 205–8.

39   *The Journal of Thomas Juxon*, p. 67.

40   'Cromwell's Narrative', in Bruce and Masson, *The Quarrel between the Earl of Manchester and Oliver Cromwell*, p. 79.

41   'Narrative of the Earl of Manchester's Campaign', pp. 80–1. *CSPD*, Vol. 503, November 1644, ed. William Douglas Hamilton (London, 1890), pp. 87–170. *The Journal of Thomas Juxon*, p. 67.

42   Gardiner, 'A Letter from the Earl of Manchester'. *CSPV*, Vol. 27, 1643–7, ed. Allen B. Hinds (London, 1926), pp. 156–67. *The Journal of Thomas Juxon*, p. 67.

43   *CJ*, Vol. 3, 1643–4 (London, 1802), pp. 704–5.

44   'Cromwell's Narrative'; 'Notes of Evidence Against the Earl of Manchester', in Bruce and Masson, *The Quarrel between the Earl of Manchester and Oliver Cromwell*, pp. 93, 99. *The Journal of Thomas Juxon*, p. 63. C. Hill, *God's Englishman*, p.69. Lilburne, *Legall and Fundamental Liberties*, p. 30.

45   *The Journal of Thomas Juxon*, p. 68. B. Whitelocke, *Memorials of English Affairs* (London: Nathaniel Ponder, 1882), pp. 111–13. R. Spalding (ed.),

The Diary of Bulstrode Whitelocke (Oxford: Oxford University Press, 1990), pp. 160–1. Bruce and Masson, *The Quarrel between the Earl of Manchester and Oliver Cromwell*, pp. lxxviii–lxxix.

46   *The Journal of Thomas Juxon*, pp. 69–70. Holmes, *The Eastern Association in the English Civil War*, pp. 210–11. *CSPV*, Vol. 27, 1643–7, ed. Allen B. Hinds (London, 1926), pp. 156–67. Whitelocke, *Memorials of English Affairs*, p. 114. S. R. Gardiner, *History of the Great Civil War, 1642–1649*, Vol. 2 (London: Weidenfeld & Nicolson, 1987), p. 90. Lilburne, *Legall and Fundamental Liberties*, p. 30.

47   Holmes, *The Eastern Association in the English Civil War*, p. 202. T. Edwards, *Gangraena* (ed. M. M. Goldsmith and Ivan Roots) (Exeter: Imprint Academic, United Kingdom, 2008), Part III, pp. 17–18.

48   *CSPV*, Vol. 27, 1643–7, ed. Allen B. Hinds (London, 1926), pp. 156–67.

49   W. Lithgow, *The Present Surveigh of London* (London, 1643), Wing (2nd edn) L2543. *CSPV*, Vol. 27, 1643–7, ed. Allen B. Hinds (London, 1926), pp. 156–67.

50   *CSPV*, Vol. 27, 1643–7, ed. Allen B. Hinds (London, 1926), pp. 156–67.

51   J. Milton, *Areopagitica, and Other Political Writings of John Milton* (Indianapolis: Liberty Fund, 1999), pp. 7, 8, 26, 28, 32–3, 40,

52   D. R. Adams, 'The Secret Publishing Career of Richard Overton the Leveller, 1644–46', *Library*, series 7, 11.1 (March 2010), pp. 33–9, 56. *CJ*, Vol. 3, 1643–4 (London, 1802), p. 721.

53   *Alas Pore Parliament how Art thou Betrai'd?*, E21[9].

54   *CSPV*, Vol. 27, 1643–7, ed. Allen B. Hinds (London, 1926), pp. 156–67. *LJ*, Vol. 7, 1644 (London, 1767–1830), pp. 91–2, 96–100, 116–17. Adams, 'The Secret Publishing Career of Richard Overton the Leveller', p. 39.

55   W. Walwyn, *A New Petition of the Papists*, in *The Writings of William Walwyn* (ed. J. R. McMichael and B. Taft) (Athens: University of Georgia Press, 1989), pp. 55–61.

56   W. Walwyn, *Some Considerations Tending to the Undeceiving of Those, Whose Judgements are Misinformed*, in *The Writings of William Walwyn*, pp. 62–77.

57   W. Walwyn, *The Compassionate Samaritane*, in *The Writings of William Walwyn*, pp. 97–130.

58   Walwyn, *The Compassionate Samaritane*, pp. 105, 106, 117, 119, 121, 122.

59   R. Overton, *Articles of High Treason Exhibited against Cheap-side Crosse* (London, 1642), E134[23].

60   R. Overton, *New Lambeth Fayre* (London, 1642), Wing O631A.

61   R. Overton, *Mans Mortalitie* (London, 1644), Wing (2nd edn) O629E. *CJ*, Vol. 3, 1643–4 (London, 1802), pp. 606–8. J. Frank, *The Levellers: A History*

of the Writings of Three Seventeenth-Century Social Democrats: John Lilburne, Richard Overton, William Walwyn (Cambridge, MA: Harvard University Press, 1955), pp. 40–1.

62   Baker, '"A Despicable Contemptible Generation of Men"?'; Peacey, 'John Lilburne and the Long Parliament'.

63   Bruce and Masson, *The Quarrel between the Earl of Manchester and Oliver Cromwell*, p. xxxvii.

64   Walwyn, *The Compassionate Samaritane*, p. 101–2, 123.

65   Gardiner, 'A Letter from the Earl of Manchester'.

66   Gregg, *Free-Born John*, p. 109. T. Prince, *The Silken Independents Snare Broken* (London, 1649), E560[24], p. 3. P. Baker, 'William Larner', *ODNB*.

7. The Coming of the Levellers

1   *CSPV*, Vol. 27, 1643–7, ed. Allen B. Hinds (London, 1926), pp. 156–67.

2   J. Peacey, 'John Lilburne and the Long Parliament', *Historical Journal*, 43.3 (2000), p. 629. C. Holmes, 'Colonel King and Lincolnshire Politics, 1642–1646', *Historical Journal*, 16.3 (September 1973), p. 460.

3   D. Como, 'Print, Censorship, and Ideological Escalation in the English Civil War', *Journal of British Studies*, 51.4 (October 2012), pp. 823–5.

4   A. Hughes, *Gangraena and the Struggle for the English Revolution* (Oxford: Oxford University Press, 2004), pp. 35–6, 44.

5   K. Chidley, *A New Yeares-Gift or a Brief Exhortation to Mr. Thomas Edwards* (London, 1645), Wing C3833. K. Chidley, *A Good Counsell, to the Petitioners for Presbyterian Government* (London, 1645), 669.f.10[39].

6   D. R. Adams, 'The Secret Publishing Career of Richard Overton the Leveller, 1644–46', *Library*, series 7, 11.1 (March 2010), p. 22.

7   W. Prynne, *Truth Triumphing* (London, 1645), E259[1]. J. Goodwin, *Innocencies Triumph* (London, 1644), Wing G1174.

8   J. Lilburne, *A Copie of a Letter Written by John Lilburne Leut. Colonell. To Mr. William Prinne Esq.* (London, 1645), E24[22]. *A Review of a certain Pamphlet under the name of one John Lilburne* (London, 1645), E278[4], pp. 2–3.

9   HLMP, HL/PO/JO/10/1/180. f. 144, 146. *LJ*, Vol. 7, 1644 (London, 1767–1830), pp. 142–3. H. R. Plomer, 'Secret Printing during the Civil War', *Library*, series 2, 5 (1904), pp. 376–81. Adams, 'The Secret Publishing Career of Richard Overton', p. 12. Hughes, *Gangraena and the Struggle for the English Revolution*, p. 147.

10   R. Overton, *The Arraignment of Mr Persecution* (London, 1645), E276[23]. R. Overton, *A Sarcred Decretall* (London, 1645), E286[15]. R. Overton, *Marten's Eccho* (London, 1645), E290[2]. R. Overton, *The Nativity of Sir John Presbyter* (London, 1645), E290[17]. Adams, 'The Secret Publishing Career of Richard Overton the Leveller', p. 12.

11   Overton, *The Arraignment of Mr Persecution*, pp. 10, 22–3, 27, 32.

12   Overton, *A Sarcred Decretall*, pp. 7–8.

13   Overton, *A Sarcred Decretall*, pp. 13–14.

14   Overton, *A Sarcred Decretall*, pp. 16–17. Overton, *The Nativity of Sir John Presbyter*, p. 11.

15   Overton, *Marten's Eccho*, p. 7.

16   Overton, *Marten's Eccho*, pp. 18–19].

17   J. Lilburne, *The Copy of a Letter from Lieutenant Colonell John Lilburne to a Friend* (London, 1645), E296[5], pp. 6–9. J. Lilburne, *Innocency and Truth Justified* (London, 1646), E314[22], pp. 63–4, 67–8. W. Prynne, *The Lyar Confounded* (London, 1645), E267[1], pp. 3–5. J. Lilburne, *A More full Relation of the great Battell fought betweene Sir Tho: Fairfax, and Goring* (London, 1645), E293[3]. For the 'Savile affair' links with royalists see J. Rushworth, *Historical Collections of Private Passages of State*, Vol. 6, 1645–7 (London, 1722), pp. 141–228. Peacey, 'John Lilburne and the Long Parliament', pp. 629–31.

18   W. Prynne, *A Fresh Discovery of some New Wandering-Blazing-Stars and Firebrands* (London, 1645), E261[5], pp. 3, 10–11, 17, 40, 43. A second edition of *A Fresh Discovery* came out on 16 December; see E267[3]. Plomer, 'Secret Printing during the Civil War', pp. 387, 394. I think Plomer is right in identifying Larner's central part here, as opposed to D. R. Adams's otherwise excellent account which rather sidelines Larner's role in printing. Adams's attempt to relocate the Goodman's Field press to a Southwark location near Overton's lodging rests on too slender evidence of a confusion of spelling. This is turn makes it less likely that Overton controlled this press rather than Larner. And although conclusive evidence is difficult to find, the examination of Larner and other witnesses by Manchester in the Lords in 1646 makes it clear that Larner was involved in buying a press. Adams, 'The Secret Publishing Career of Richard Overton'. W. Larner, *A true relation of all the remarkable Passages and Illegal Proceedings, and Illegall Proceedings of some Sathannical or Doeg-like Accussers of their Brethern Against William Larner, A Free-man of England* (London, 1646), E335[7], pp. 14–15.

19   B. Whitelocke, *Memorials of English Affairs* (London: Nathaniel Ponder, 1882), p. 160. On 26 August a petition in favour of Lilburne's release was rejected by the Speaker, but the House voted £100 subsistence for Lilburne.

20 J. Bastwick, *A Just Defence of John Bastwick* (London, 1645), E265[7].

21 Bastwick, *A Just Defence*, p. 20.

22 Bastwick, *A Just Defence*, p. 32. Pagination is erratic, so that pp. 32–3 come before a sheet of two pages numbered 20 and 17.

23 Bastwick, *A Just Defence*, pp. 16–17.

24 As Jason Peacey has argued in 'John Lilburne and the Long Parliament', .

25 Bastwick, *A Just Defence*, pp. 21–2.

26 Bastwick, *A Just Defence*, p. 33.

27 W. Walwyn, *Strong Motives* (London, 1645), E304[15]. D. Como, 'An Unattributed Pamphlet by William Walwyn: New Light on the Prehistory of the Leveller Movement', *Huntington Library Quarterly*, 69.3 (2006), pp. 353–82. Cromwell's original, censored, report was officially published on 11 September; see E301[18]. A single-sheet version of the redacted final paragraph was reproduced and scattered in the streets on 22 September; see *The Conclusion of Lieuten: Generall Cromwell's Letter* (London, 1645), 669.f.10[38].

28 J. Lilburne, *Englands Birth-Right Justified* (London, 1645), E304[17], pp. 17–18, 31–2, 44. D. M. Wolfe, *Leveller Manifestoes of the Puritan Revolution* (New York: Frank Cass, 1967), pp. 5–6. Como, 'An Unattributed Pamphlet by William Walwyn'.

29 W. Walwyn, *England's Lamentable Slavery* (1645), E304[19], pp. 6–7. Lilburne, *Englands Birth-Right Justified*, p. 37. Como, 'An Unattributed Pamphlet by William Walwyn', p. 356.

30 Walwyn, *England's Lamentable Slavery*, p. 8.

31 Prynne, *The Lyar Confounded*.

32 Prynne, *The Lyar Confounded*, pp. 6–7.

33 J. Hunscot, *The humble petition of Joseph Hunscot Stationer . . .* (London, 1646), E340[15], pp. 3–7.

34 Hunscot, *The humble petition of Joseph Hunscot Stationer*, pp. 3–7. Lilburne, *Englands Birth-Right Justified*, pp. 10–11, 42–43.

35 Adams, 'The Secret Publishing Career of Richard Overton', p. 45.

36 Hunscot, *The humble petition of Joseph Hunscot Stationer*, pp. 3–7. Plomer, 'Secret Printing during the Civil War', pp. 386–7, 393–4.

37 *The Journal of Thomas Juxon, 1644–1647* (ed. K. Lindley and D. Scott, Cambridge: Royal Historical Society and Cambridge University Press, 1999), pp. 101–14.

38 *CJ*, Vol. 4, 1644–6 (London, 1802), pp. 397–8. S. Barber, *A Revolutionary Rogue: Henry Marten and the English Republic* (Stroud: Sutton, 2000), pp. 10–13.

39   T. Edwards, *Gangraena* (London, 1646), Part II, p. 29, and Part III. 'A
      Relation . . .' is unpaginated but is placed immediately before the main
      text.

40   Edwards, *Gangraena*, Part III, pp. 155, 197, and Part I, p. 53, where the
      Arraingment of Mr Persecution and *Martin's Eccho* are said to be Lilburne's.
      For a discussion of the importance of Overton and the emergence of the
      Levellers as a target for Edwards see Hughes, *Gangraena and the Struggle
      for the English Revolution*, p. 364.

41   P. Baker, 'William Larner', *ODNB*. The Chidleys were living in a house at St
      Botolphs without Bishopsgate, although by the early 1650s they seem to
      have moved to 'the sign of the Chequers in Bow Lane'; see I. Gentles,
      'London Levellers in the English Revolution: The Chidleys and Their
      Circle', *Journal of Ecclesiastical History*, 29 (1978), pp. 283 n. 12, 305.

42   Edwards, *Gangraena*, Part III, p. 170.

43   Edwards, *Gangraena*, Part I, pp. 79–80, and Part III, p. 170. References are
      to the facsimile reprint by The Rota and the University of Exeter (1977).

44   J. Lanseter, *Lanseter's Lance for Edwards'es Gangrene* (London, 1646),
      E354[17]. A. L. Morton, *The World of the Ranters* (London: Lawrence and
      Wishart, 1970), pp. 24–36.

45   G. K. Fortescue, *British Museum Catalogue of Thomason Tracts 1640–1652*,
      Vol. 1 (London, 1908), January–June 1646.

46   Lilburne, *Innocency and Truth Justified*. J. Lilburne, *A true Relation of the
      material passages of Lieut. Col. John Lilburne* (London, 1646), E324[9]. W.
      Walwyn, *A Whisper in the Eare of Mr. Thomas Edwards* (London, 1646),
      E323[2]. W. Walwyn, *A Word More to Mr. Thomas Edwards* (London,
      1646), E328[20].

47   *The Last Warning to the Inhabitants of London* (London, 1646), E328[24].
      The Presbyterian reply to Overton is G. Smith, *An Alarum to the last warn-
      ing* (London, 1646), E339[6], pp. 3–4

48   *LJ*, Vol. 8, 1645–1647 (London, 1767–1830), pp. 241–5. Anon., *A True
      Relation of all the Remarkable Passages and Illegall Proceedings. Every Mans
      Case*, 669 f.10[52].See *A Vindication of every Free-mans libertie . . .*, which
      contains *To the Right Honourable, the Lords . . . the humble petition of
      Hellen Larner . . .* (note that Ellen Larner's first name is given as 'Hellen' in
      this second petition), Wing L445A. Adams, 'The Secret Publishing Career
      of Richard Overton', p. 49.

49   Hunscot, *The humble petition of Joseph Hunscot Stationer*, pp. 3–7.

50   *LJ*, Vol. 8, 1645–7 (London, 1767–1830), pp. 241–5, 256–8, 273–5. *A true
      relation of all the remarkable Passages and Illegal Proceedings*. W. Larner, *A

Vindication of Every Free-mans Libertie (London, 1646), Wing L445A. 'Warrants', in *CSPD*, Interregnum, 1649–50 (ed. Mary Anne Everett Green) (London, 1875), p. 529. *CSPD*, Interregnum, 1653–4 (ed. Mary Anne Everett Green) (London, 1879), p. 198. Baker, 'William Larner'. J. Frank, *The Levellers: A History of the Writings of Three Seventeenth-Century Social Democrats: John Lilburne, Richard Overton, William Walwyn* (Cambridge, MA: Harvard University Press, 1955), p. 66.

51 HLMP, HL/PO/JO/10/1/211. f. 79. *Every Man's Case*, E337[5], p. 8. The single-sheet version of *Every Man's Case* does not include the postscript. *An Alarum to the House Of Lords*, E346[8], p. 11.

52 *A Word In Season*, E337[25].

53 *A Word In Season*, E1184[3].

54 M. Tolmie, *The Triumph of the Saints: The Separate Churches of London 1616–1649* (Cambridge: Cambridge University Press, 1977), pp. 66, 147. A. Johns, 'Coleman Street', *Huntington Library Quarterly*, 71.1 (March 2008), p. 44.

55 Edwards, *Gangraena*, Part I, pp. 79–80, and Part III, p. 170.

56 Tolmie, *The Triumph of the Saints*, p. 147.

57 H. Knollys, *Christ Exalted, A Lost Sinner Sought and saved by Christ* (London, 1645), E322[33].

58 B. Coke, H. Knollys and W. Kiffin, *A Declaration Concerning The Publike Dispute* (London, 1645), E313[22], pp. 3–5.

59 Tolmie, *The Triumph of the Saints*, p. 76.

60 Overton, *A Sarcred Decretall*, pp. 16–17. Overton, *The Nativity of Sir John Presbyter*, p. 11.

61 Edwards, *Gangraena*, Part I, p. 84. A. Hessayon. 'Attaway, Mrs', *ODNB*. Tolmie, *The Triumph of the Saints*, p. 81.

62 Edwards, *Gangraena*, Part III, p. 30. S. Wright, 'Jeremiah Ives', *ODNB*.

63 Edwards, *Gangraena*, Part I, pp. 92, 120, Part. II, pp. 161, 146–8, and Part III, pp. 105–6. A. Bettridge, 'Early Baptists in Leicestershire and Rutland, Part 1', *Baptist Quarterly*, 25 (1973–4). A. Betteridge, 'Early Baptists in Leicestershire and Rutland, Part 2', *Baptist Quarterly*, 25 (1973–4), pp. 357–8. S. Wright, 'Samuel Oates', *ODNB*, pp. 204–11.

64 Whitelocke, *Memorials of English Affairs*, p. 212.

65 Whitelocke, *Memorials of English Affairs*, p. 213.

66 *Walwyns Just Defence*, in W. Haller and G. Davies, *The Leveller Tracts 1647–53* (New York: Peter Smith, 1944), p. 352.

67 J. Lilburne, *Jonah's Cry* (London, 1647), E400[5], pp. 5–6.

68 *Walwyns Just Defence*, p. 393. T. C. Pease, *The Leveller Movement* (Gloucester, MA: 1965), pp. 122–3. On the City petition see R. Ashton,

Counter Revolution: The Second Civil War and Its Origins, 1646–8 (New Haven: Yale University Press 1994), p. 133. K. Lindley, *Popular Politics and Religion in Civil War London* (Aldershot: Scolar, 1997), pp. 367–70.

69   Tolmie, *The Triumph of the Saints*, p. 230 n. 22.

70   W. Walwyn, *A Word in Season* (London, 1646), E1184[3], is the edition containing the reference to Lilburne.

71   *LJ*, Vol. 8, 10–11 June, 1646 (London, 1767–1830), pp. 368–71. J. Lilburne, *The Free-mans Freedome Vindicated* (London, 1646), E341[12]. Lilburne, *Innocency and Truth Justified*, p. 27. Pease, *The Leveller Movement*, pp. 125–31.

72   Lilburne, *The Freemans Freedom Vindicated*. J. Lilburne, *A coppy of a letter sent by Lieu. Col. John Lilburne to Mr. Wollaston* (London, 1646), 669.f.10[62]. W. Walwyn, *The Just Man in Bonds* (London, 1646), E342[2]. W. Walwyn, *A Pearle in a Dounghill* (London, 1646), E342[5]. On 19 June the first edtion of *Vox Populi or the Peoples Cry Against the Clergy* (London, 1646), E351[7], was published. A second came out in August. Haller attributed *Vox Populi* to Walwyn, but McMichael and Taft make a strong case that this is unlikely; see *The Writings of William Walwyn* (ed. J. R. McMichael and B. Taft) (Athens: University of Georgia Press, 1989), pp. 529–30.

73   Walwyn, *The Just Man in Bonds*.

74   *LJ*, Vol. 8, 11 July 1646 (London, 1767–1830), pp. 432–3.

75   *LJ*, Vol. 8, 11 July 1646 (London, 1767–1830), pp. 432–3. *LJ*, Vol. 8, 10 July 1646 (London, 1767–1830), pp. 426–31. J. Lilburne, *Liberty Vindicated Against Slavery* (London, 1646), E351[2], pp. 21, 23. J. Lilburne, *Londons Liberty in Chains Discovered* (London, 1646), E359[17], p. 26. Pease, *The Leveller Movement*, pp. 125–31.

76   Whitelocke, *Memorials of English Affairs*, pp. 216, 227. Lilburne, *Londons Liberty in Chains Discovered*, pp. 33–4. Elizabeth Lilburne's petition is reprinted in *Londons Liberty in Chains Discovered*, pp. 65–70. J. Lilburne, *Regall Tyrannie Discovered* (London, 1647), E370[12], p. 71. Pease, *The Leveller Movement*, pp. 125–31.

77   *A Remonstrance of Many Thousand Citizens, and other Free-born People of England* (London, 1646), E343[11].

78   *A Remonstrance of Many Thousand Citizens*, pp. 3–7.

79   *A Remonstrance of Many Thousand Citizens*, pp. 8–9.

80   *A Remonstrance of Many Thousand Citizens*, p. 14.

81   *A Remonstrance of Many Thousand Citizens*, pp. 6, 11–12, 15–19 .

82   Peacey, 'John Lilburne and the Long Parliament', p. 633.

83   Larner, *A Vindication of Every Free-mans Libertie*, p. 2.

84   H. N. Brailsford, *The Levellers and the English Revolution* (ed. C. Hill) (Nottingham: Spokesman, 1961), p. 109. G. E. Aylmer, 'Gentlemen Levellers?', *Past and Present*, 49 (November 1970) pp. 120-125. J. Peacey, 'The Struggle for *Mercurius Britanicus*: Factional Politics and the Parliamentarian Press, 1643–1646', *Huntington Library Quarterly*, 68.3 (September 2005), pp. 517–43.

8. Petitions and Prison

1   *The Journal of Thomas Juxon, 1644–1647* (ed. K. Lindley and D. Scott, Cambridge: Royal Historical Society and Cambridge University Press, 1999), pp. 106, 116, 137. R. Brenner, *Merchants and Revolution: Commercial Change, Political Conflict, and London's Overseas Traders, 1550–1653* (Cambridge: Cambridge University Press, 1993), pp. 496–7. V. Pearl, 'London's Counter-revolution', in G. E. Aylmer (ed.), *The Interregnum: The Quest for a Settlement 1646–1660* (London: Macmillan, 1972), pp. 29–38. K. Lindley, *Popular Politics and Religion in Civil War London* (Aldershot: Scolar, 1997), pp. 357–67. R. Ashton, *Counter Revolution: The Second Civil War and Its Origins, 1646–8* (New Haven: Yale University Press 1994), p. 133.

2   Pearl, 'London's Counter-revolution', pp. 29–38.

3   Pearl, 'London's Counter-Revolution', pp. 29–44.

4   *The Journal of Thomas Juxon*, pp. 61, 116–17.

5   R. Brenner, *Merchants and Revolution*, pp. 498–508.

6   R. Overton, *An Alarum to the House of Lords* (London, 1646), E346[8], pp. 4, 5, 11.

7   'The humble petic[i]on of Robert Eles', HLRO Main Papers, 13 August 1646. R. Overton, *A Defiance Against All Arbitrary Usurpations* (London, 1646), E353[17], pp. 8–9, 11. M. Overton, *The humble Appeale and Petition of Mary Overton* (London, 1647), E381[10], p. 3. See also D. R. Adams, 'The Secret Publishing Career of Richard Overton the Leveller, 1644–46', *Library*, series 7, 11.1 (March 2010), p. 55.

8   Overton, *A Defiance Against All Arbitrary Usurpations*, pp. 13–14.

9   *LJ*, Vol. 8, 1645–7 (London, 1767–1830), p. 457. Overton, *A Defiance Against All Arbitrary Usurpations*, p. 13–14, 17, 24–5. R. Overton, *The Commoners Complaint* (London, 1647), E375[7], pp. 2–3, 7, 13.

10   J. Lilburne, *Regall Tyrannie Discovered* (London, 1647), E370[12], p. 1. *Regall Tyrannie* may have been written by Overton and Lilburne did deny authorship, but I have maintained the standard retribution here. *LJ*, Vol. 8, 5–6

January 1647 (London, 1767–1830), pp. 645–9. Overton, *The Commoners Complaint*, pp. 16–19. Overton, *The humble Appeale and Petition of Mary Overton*, pp. 6–7. Mary Overton says that she, 'with Thomas Overton her husbands brother', was brought to the Lords' 'Prerogative-Barre'. Richard also confirms that it was his brother who was brought before the Lords and that his brother-in-law escaped capture (see Overton, *The Commoners Complaint*, p. 16).The only two people brought before the Lords were Mary and Thomas Johnson. This suggests that Thomas Johnson is Thomas Overton. Lilburne reproduces Thomas Johnson's tract attacking monopolies and defending Lilburne in his *The Charters of London* (London, 1646), E366[12], pp. 37–52. B. J. Gibbons, 'Richard Overton', *ODNB*, accepts that it was Overton's brother who was brought to the Lords with Mary Overton.

11   Overton, *The Commoners Complaint*, pp. 16–19. Overton, *The humble Appeale and Petition of Mary Overton*, pp. 6–7.

12   For an overview of the Levellers' relationship with the City see P. Baker, '*Londons Liberty in Chains Discovered*: The Levellers, the Civic Past, and Popular Protest in Civil War London', *Huntington Library Quarterly*, 76.4 (2013), pp. 559–87.

13   J. Lilburne, *Londons Liberty in Chains Discovered* (London, 1646), E359[17], pp. 8–9, 21. Lindley, *Popular Politics and Religion in Civil War London*, p. 387.

14   *The Journal of Thomas Juxon*, p. 113. K. Lindley, 'Thomas Adams', *ODNB*. B. Coke, H. Knollys and W. Kiffin, *A Declaration Concerning The Publike Dispute* (London, 1645), E313[22], pp. 3–5. *LJ*, Vol. 8, 1645–7 (London, 1767–1830), pp. 241–5. Lilburne describes 'Major Wansie, a Watch-maker in Cornhill (a man that in these late wars, hath freely and gallantly adventured his life for the preservation of the present Parliament, and Englands Liberties)'. Lilburne, *Londons Liberty in Chains Discovered*, p. 21. For Wansey's military service see TNA, SP 46/95/fo24. TNA, SP 46/95 f.16. TNA, SP 46/95 f.20. Wansey was originally from Warminster in Wiltshire, where he was also described as a watchmaker. One of his sons was also called Henry, also fought for Parliament, and was a member of the clock-maker's guild. Lindley, *Popular Politics and Religion in Civil War London*, pp. 168–9, 394–8, 402. T. Maclachlan, *The Civil War in Wiltshire* (Salisbury: Rowanvale Books 1997), pp. 177–8.

15   Lilburne, *Londons Liberty in Chains Discovered*, pp. 27–32. J. Lilburne, *The Charters of London* (London, 1646), E366[12]. Baker, '*Londons Liberty in Chains Discovered*', 578–9.

16   Baker, '*Londons Liberty in Chains Discovered*', pp. 559–587.

17   R. Overton, *To the right honourable, the betrusted . . .*, 669 f.10[115]. This petition is dated old-style as 1646. J. Lilburne and R. Overton, *Out-Cryes of oppressed Commons* (London, 1647), E378[13], pp. 9–12. *CJ*, 9 March 1647, Vol. 5, 1646–8 (London, 1802), pp. 108–9.

18   W. Walwyn, *Walwyn's Just Defence*, in W. Haller and G. Davies, *The Leveller Tracts 1647–53* (New York: Columbia University Press, 1944), pp. 351–8. M. Tolmie, *The Triumph of the Saints: The Separate Churches of London 1616–1649* (Cambridge: Cambridge University Press, 1977), pp. 144–55.

19   D. Wolfe, *Leveller Manifestoes of the Puritan Revolution* (New York: Frank Cass, 1967), pp. 135–41.

20   W. Walwyn, *Gold Tried in the Fire . . .*, E392[19]. Also available in *The Writings of William Walwyn* (ed. J. R. McMichael and B. Taft) (Athens: University of Georgia Press, 1989), pp. 275–93. *CJ*, Vol. 5, 1646–8 (London, 1802), p. 112. J. Lilburne, *Rash Oaths Unwarrantable* (London, 1647), E393[39], p. 29.

21   *CJ*, Vol. 5, 1646–8 (London, 1802), pp. 114–16, 125–6. Lilburne, *Rash Oaths Unwarrantable*, pp. 29, 36–7, 40. S. Gardiner, *History of the Great Civil War*, Vol. 3, 1645–7 (London: Weidenfeld Nicolson, 1987), p. 256. Although Tulidah did eventually get to make his case to Leigh's committee with Stapleton and Holles in attendance; see *CJ*, 4 May 1647, Vol. 5, 1646–8 (London, 1802), pp. 160–2. Two days later his bail was annulled.

22   *CJ*, 4 May 1647, Vol. 5, 1646–8 (London, 1802), pp. 160–2. *CJ*, 20 May 1647, Vol. 5, 1646–8 (London, 1802), pp. 178–80. *CJ*, 2 June 1647, Vol. 5, 1646–8 (London, 1802), p. 195. Lilburne, *Rash Oaths Unwarrantable*, pp. 43–7. W. Walwyn, *Gold Tried in the Fire* (London, 1647), in A. L. Morton, *Freedom in Arms* (London: Lawrence and Wishart, 1975), p. 116. The original is in the Thomasson Tracts at E.392[19]. D. Wolfe, *Leveller Manifestoes of the Puritan Revolution* (New York: Frank Cass, 1967), p. 134. R. Overton, *An Appeale From the degenerate Representative Body the Commons of England* (London, 1647), E398[28], p. 14.

23   Lilburne, *Rash Oaths Unwarrantable*, pp. 2, 4–5, 55. J. Lilburne, *A Copy of a Letter Written to Collonel Henry Marten* (London, 1647), 669 f.11[46]. J. Lilburne, *The Juglers Discovered* (London, 1647), p. 5 on Marten being negligent, E409[22]. H. Marten, *Rash Censures Uncharitable*, BL Add. MS 71532, ff. 7–8.

24   R. Overton, *An Arrow Against All Tyrants* (London, 1646), E356[14], p. 19, reproduced in A. Sharp (ed.), *The English Levellers* (Cambridge: Cambridge University Press, 1998), p. 71. *An Arrow* was itself written in the form of a letter to Marten. Lilburne, *Rash Oaths Unwarrantable*, p. 6.

25   Overton, *An Appeale From the degenerate Representative Body the*

Commons of England, p. 8. Walwyn, *Walwyn's Just Defence*, p. 356. R. Brenner, *Merchants and Revolution*, pp. 508–10.

26   Lilburne, *Rash Oaths Unwarrantable*, pp. 50–6.

9. Agitators

1   This is one of the most contentious periods of the English Revolution among modern historians. For the period before the Putney debates in October 1647 the case of the revisionist historians which tends to downplay both the radicalism of the New Model Army and the role of the Levellers within it can be found in M. Kishlansky, 'The Army and the Levellers: The Roads to Putney', *Historical Journal*, 22.4 (December 1979); M. Kishlansky, *The Rise of the New Model Army* (Cambridge: Cambridge University Press, 1979); M. Kishlansky, *A Monarchy Transformed: Britain 1603–1714* (London: Penguin, 1996); and J. Morrill and P. Baker, 'The Case of the Armie Truly Re-stated', in M. Mendle (ed.), *The Putney Debates of 1647* (Cambridge: Cambridge University Press, 2001). Contrary views can be found in I. Gentles, 'The Politics of Fairfax's Army, 1645–9', in J. Adamson, *The English Civil War* (Basingstoke, 2009); I. Gentles, *The New Model Army in England, Ireland and Scotland, 1645–1653* (Oxford: Oxford University Press, 1992); A. Woolrych, *Soldiers and Statesmen: The General Council of the Army and Its Debates* (Oxford: Oxford University Press, 1987); and R. Foxley, *The Levellers: Radical Political Thought in the English Revolution* (Manchester: Manchester University Press, 2013). J. Holstun, *Ehud's Dagger: Class Struggle in the English Revolution* (London: Verso, 2000). Analogous discussions about the Putney debates and the Ware mutiny are referenced in the next chapter.

2   V. Pearl, 'London's Counter-Revolution', in G. E. Aylmer (ed.), *The Interregnum: The Quest for a Settlement 1646–1660* (London: Macmillan, 1972), pp. 44–56.

3   *To the parliament: the petition of the Lord Mayor and Common Council* (London, 1647), E381[2]. R. Baillie, *The Letters and Journals of Robert Baillie*, Vol. 2 (Edinburgh: Alex Lawrie and Co., 1841), p. 512. R. Ashton, *Counter Revolution: The Second Civil War and Its Origins, 1646–8* (New Haven: Yale University Press 1994), pp. 170–1, 132–3, 276. *The Journal of Thomas Juxon, 1644–1647* (ed. K. Lindley and D. Scott, Cambridge: Royal Historical Society and Cambridge University Press, 1999), pp. 150–1.

Pearl, 'London's Counter-Revolution', pp. 44–5. K. Lindley, *Popular Politics and Religion in Civil War London* (Aldershot: Scolar, 1997), pp. 375–77 .

4   Pearl, 'London's Counter-Revolution', pp. 45–46. Baillie, *The Letters and Journals of Robert Baillie*, Vol. 2, p. 16.

5   W. Walwyn, *The Poore Wise-mans Admonition* (London, 1647), in A. L. Morton, *Freedom in Arms* (London: Lawrence and Wishart, 1975), pp.119–34. The original is in the Thomasson Tracts at E.392[4].

6   Walwyn, *The Poore Wise-mans Admonition*.

7   *The Petition of the Officers and Souldiers in the Army* (London, 1647), E383[12]. S. Gardiner, *History of the Great Civil War*, Vol. 3, 1645–7 (London: Weidenfeld Nicholson, 1987), pp. 222–6.

8   Gardiner, *History of the Great Civil War*, Vol. 3, p. 222. *The Journal of Thomas Juxon*, pp. 157–8. J. Lilburne, *Jonah's Cry Out of the Whales belly* (London, 1647), E400[5], pp. 2–5.

9   *CJ*, Vol. 5, 1646–8 (London, 1802), pp. 127–32. *LJ*, Vol. 9, 1646 (London, 1767–1830), pp. 110–16. J. Rushworth, *Historical Collections of Private Passages of State*, Vol. 6, 1645–7 (London, 1722), pp. 444–75. Rushworth records a letter from Saffron Walden on 3 April denying that any force was used in gaining names for the petition, the charge of which Pride stood accused, but asserting, 'For that charge of Mutiny; I can assure you there was no such thing, the Petition being generally approved of, and whole Regiments unanimously subscribing it'. Gardiner, *History of the Great Civil War*, Vol. 3, pp. 225–9, 231, 231 n. 3. Lilburne's letter to Cromwell, dated 25 March 1647, is reprinted in Lilburne, *Jonah's Cry Out of the Whales belly*, pp. 2–5. *A Declaration of Parliament* (London, 1647), 669.f.9 [84]. I. Gentles, *The New Model Army in England, Ireland and Scotland, 1645–1653* (Oxford: Oxford University Press, 1992), p. 151.

10   J. Rushworth, *Historical Collections of Private Passages of State*, Vol. 6, 1645–7 (London, 1722), pp. 444–75. *A New Found Stratagem* (London, 1647), E384[11], pp. 5, 8–11. *A New Found Stratagem* may be the work of Overton. It is certainly his writing style and the crude dropped capital surrounded by small printers' devices at the start of the main text is the same as that used on his earlier pamphlets, for instance *The Nativity of Sir John Presbyter*. The identical figure also appears on the first page of J. Lilburne, *The Resolved Mans Resolution* (London, 1647), E387[4]. *CJ*, Vol. 5, 1646–8 (London, 1802), pp. 154–5. Gentles, *The New Model Army*, p. 159.

11   HMC, *Portland MSS*, Vol. 3 (London: HMSO, 1894), pp. 155–6. Gardiner, *History of the Great Civil War*, Vol. 3, pp. 237, 245, 257. C. H. Firth, *The Clarke Papers: Selections from the Papers of William Clarke, Volumes I & II*

in One Volume (London: Royal Historical Society, 1992), pp. 3–5, 5 n. a, 92. See Lilburne's letter to Goodwin of 13 February reproduced in Lilburne, *Jonah's Cry Out of the Whales belly*, pp. 5–6. *CJ*, Vol. 5, 1646–8 (London, 1802), pp. 154–5. Gentles, *The New Model Army*, p. 153.

12   Firth, *The Clarke Papers*, pp. 112–13.

13   Firth, *The Clarke Papers*, pp. 65–7, 96. J. Rushworth, 15 May 1647, in *Historical Collections of Private Passages of State*, Vol. 6, *1645–47* (London, 1722), pp. 475–500.

14   *CJ*, Vol. 5, 1646–8 (London, 1802), pp. 157–58. Firth, *The Clarke Papers*, pp. 430–1. Gentles, *The New Model Army*, pp. 160–1.

15   *A Perfect and True Copy of the Severall Grievances of the Army* (London, 1647), E390[3].

16   William Constable to Lord Fairfax, 24 May 1647, in R. Bell (ed.), *Memorials of the Civil War: Comprising the Correspondence of the Fairfax Family* (London: Richard Bentley, 1849), p. 345.

17   Clarke MSS. 100 ff.30–1 is a letter dated 17 May, the same day as Sexby's letter concerning the need for a press to be set up in the army. It concerns the meeting at Walton and is signed by Sexby, Agitator William Allen and others listing the Agitators chosen and an account of the meeting. Its central demands concern pay, disbandment and deployment to Ireland. At the same time was sent a 'Letter from the Agitators of Horse to the Horse in the North'. See Clarke MSS. 100 ff.48–9.

18   Clarke MSS. 110 f.53. The large asterisk with a small 's' next to it in Sexby's text seems to be a coded reference to an individual, perhaps Harris. Sexby signs the letter with a similar asterisk but without the small 's' adjacent.

19   W. Clarke, *The Clarke Papers*, Vol. 1 (London: Royal Historical Society, 1992), p. 86. See also M. Mendle, 'Putney's Pronouns: Identity and Indemnity in the Great Debate', in M. Mendle (ed.), *The Putney Debates of 1647* (Cambridge: Cambridge University Press, 2001), pp. 126–33.

20   A. Woolrych, *Soldiers and Statesmen: The General Council of the Army and Its Debates 1647–1648* (Oxford: Oxford University Press, 1987), p. 93 n. 7.

21   Woolrych, *Soldiers and Statesmen*, p. 133.

22   Mendle, 'Putney's Pronouns', pp. 126–33. Mendle's account is diminished by his attempt to exaggerate Harris's royalist sympathies. While it is true that Harris's wife Susanna did have such sympathies and was eulogised on her death by Sir George Wharton (*In Memorie of that Lively Patterne of True Pietie, and unstained Loyaltie* . . . (1649), 669 f.15.1), it is also the case that Wharton attacked *Mercurius Militaris*. In his *Mercurius Impartialis* he called Harris a 'rogue', a 'rebel' and a 'Mad-man', E476[3],

pp. 2–3. Mendle does not mention *Mercurius Militaris* and its pronounced hostility to the king.

23   *A Declaration of Master William Lenthall* (Oxford, 1647), Wing L1072; *A Letter Sent from the Agitators of the Army*, Wing L1605; *The Resolutions of the Agitators of the Army*, E405[22].

24   *A view of part of the many Traiterous, Disloyal and Turn-about Actions of H. H. Senior* (1684), Wing (CD-Rom) V359. I. Gadd, *ODNB*. R. L. Greaves and R. Zaller, *Biographical Dictionary of British Radicals in the Seventeenth Century*, Vol. 2 (Brighton: Harvester, 1984), pp. 91–2. 'Henry Hills, Official Printer', *Baptist Quarterly*, 6.5 (January 1932), pp. 215–16. See Mendle, 'Putney's Pronouns'.

25   C. H. Firth (ed.), *Clarke Papers*, Vol. 1 (London: Royal Historical Society, 1992), pp. 22–24, 111–13.

26   E. Kitson and E. K. Clark, 'Some Civil War Accounts, 1647–1650', *Thoresby Society Publications*, Vol. 2, Miscellanea IV (Leeds, 1904), pp. 137–235. The payment to Rede is for troops in Poole and may not be directly related to Agitator activity. Some sense of the value of the amounts paid can be got by comparing them with the multiple other payments listed, like the six pounds paid to the tent-keeper for two months work on 10 October 1648. Jason Peacey, private communication, suggests that this payment to Hill is for printing the Officers' Agreement.

27   R. W. Stent, 'Thomas Rainsborough and the Army Levellers' (M.Phil, University of London, 1975), Vol. 2, pp. 252–349.

28   *The Copies of the Papers from the Armie* (London, 1647), Wing C6273B. Rushworth, *Historical Collections of Private Passages of State*, Vol. 6, pp. 500–45. Firth, *The Clarke Papers*, pp. xxi–xxiv.

29   W. Walwyn, *Walwyns Just Defence* (London, 1649), in *The Writings of William Walwyn* (ed. J. R. McMichael and B. Taft) (Athens: University of Georgia Press, 1989), pp. 391–2. C. Hill, *God's Englishman* (London, 1970), pp. 84–5.

30   J. Harris, *The Grand Designe* (London, 1647), E419[15]. This pamphlet is signed with John Harris's anagrammatic pseudonym 'Sirrahniho', the second 'i' standing for 'j' as often in seventeenth-century typography. Joyce later claimed that Cromwell wanted him to publically refute the account given by Harris; see G. Joyce, *A True Narrative of the Occasions and Causes of the late Lord Gen. Cromwells Anger and Indignation against Lieu. Col. George* Joyce (London, 1659), p. 1, 669.f.21[50]. W. Walwyn, *Gold Tried in the Fire* (London, 1647), in A. L. Morton, *Freedom in Arms* (London: Lawrence and Wishart, 1975), p. 117. The original is in the Thomasson Tracts at E.392[19]. Gardiner, *History of the Great Civil War*,

Vol. 3, p. 275. Rushworth, *Historical Collections of Private Passages of State*, Vol. 6, pp. 500–45.

31   *Two Speeches* (London, 1647), E391[13]. Firth, *The Clarke Papers*, p. 113. The rest of this account is based on Joyce's own report of the events, 'A true Impartial Narration, concerning the Armies Preservation of the King', in Rushworth, *Historical Collections of Private Passages of State*, Vol. 6, pp. 500–45.

32   *A true Impartial Narration, concerning the Armies Preservation of the King* in Rushworth, *Historical Collections of Private Passages of State*, Vol. 6, pp. 500–45.

33   Rushworth, *Historical Collections of Private Passages of State*, Vol. 6, pp. 500–45. *Two Speeches.* John Rushworth to Lord Fairfax, 9 June 1647, in Bell, *Memorials of the Civil War*, p. 353. G. Joyce, *A True and impartiall Narration, concerning the Armies Preservation of the King* (London, 1647), E393[1].

34   One of the best-reasoned discussions of Cromwell's attitude to Joyce's actions remains Gardiner, *History of the Great Civil War*, Vol. 3, pp. 266–8 n. 1, 272–3 n. 1. See also Firth, *The Clarke Papers*, pp. xxvi–xxxi for Firth's complementary analysis, 118–20 for Joyce's letters sent as events unfolded at Holmby. Hill, *God's Englishman*, pp. 84–6.

35   *An humble Representation of the Dissatisfactions of the Army* and *A Solemn Engagement of the Army*, in Rushworth, *Historical Collections of Private Passages of State*, Vol. 6, pp. 500–45. Also *A Solemn Engagement of the Army* (London, 1647), Wing S4436. *A Solemn Engagement* was followed nine days later by the explanatory text *A Declaration of the Army*, reproduced in W. Haller and G. Davies, *The Leveller Tracts 1647–1653* (Gloucester, MA: Peter Smith, 1964), pp. 51–63. Also see Woolrych, *Soldiers and Statesmen*, pp. 117–22; and Gentles, *The New Model Army*, pp. 173–6.

36   *A Declaration of the Army*, p. 55.

37   *A Copie of a Letter Sent From the Agitators* (London, 1647), E393[33], p. 8. Bell, *Memorials of the Civil War*, pp. 356–7.

38   *His Excellency Sir Thomas Fairfax . . . Answer to the Scots Declaration* (London, 1647), E392[23]. Bell, *Memorials of the Civil War*, pp. 354–5, 370–71.

39   Walwyn, *Walwyns Just Defence*, p. 393. *The Heads of Charges* (London, 1647), E397[11]. Bell, *Memorials of the Civil War*, pp. 360–4, 370, 372. 'Letter from the Agitators of Horse to the Horse in the North', pp. 89–92.

40   *Plaine Truth without Feare or Flattery* (London, 1647). The 'Amon Wilbee' edition is E516[7], the edition signed 'JL' is Wing L2157. Pauline Gregg followed Thomason in attributing the pamphlet to Lilburne. I am more inclined to Don Wolfe's view that it is not a Lilburne pamphlet. See P. Gregg, *Free-Born John: A Biography of John Lilburne* (London: Dent, 1986),

p. 399. D. Wolfe, *Milton and the Puritan Revolution* (New York: Thomas Nelson and Sons, 1941), p. 473. Neither mention Overton's comments in *An Appeale From the degenerate Representative Body the Commons of England* (London, 1647), E398[28], p. 15.

41 *A Cleere and Full Vindication of the late Proceedings of the Armie* (London, 1647), E397[21]. *The Grand Informer* (Oxford, 1647), E398[18].

42 *The Humble Petition of Many Thousands of young men and Apprentices* (London, 1647), E398[9]. The Presbyterian counterpetition is *To the Lords and Commons. The Petition of Young Men and Apprentices* (London, 1647), E398[23]. J. Harris, *The Antipodes or Reformation with its Heeles Upward* (Oxford, 1647), Wing H42.

43 Lilburne, *Jonah's Cry Out of the Whales belly*, p. 9. W. Prynne, *The Totall and Finall Demands already made by . . . the Agitators and Army* (London, 1647), E399[9].

44 Overton, *An Appeale From the degenerate Representative Body the Commons of England*, pp. 7, 10–12, 27, 30–1.

45 'The Representation of the Agitators', Firth, *The Clarke Papers*, pp. 170–2, 171 n. b. John Rushworth to Lord Fairfax, 20 July, in Bell, *Memorials of the Civil War*, pp. 369–71.

46 Firth, *The Clarke Papers*, pp. 173–84, 203–8, 210. John Rushworth to Lord Fairfax, 20 July, in Bell, *Memorials of the Civil War*, pp. 369–71. *The Just Request* (1647), Wing J1238A. The note continues, 'but the temper of the army is well changed and it is to be hoped such fellowes will now no more be either defended or encouraged'. There is no indication when this note was added or by whom. It seems likely to have been within a few years of publication.

47 Baillie, *The Letters and Journals of Robert Baillie*, Vol. 2, pp. 9–10. *The Journal of Thomas Juxon*, p. 161.

48 W. Lenthall, *A Declaration of Master William Lenthall* (Oxford, 1647), Wing L1072. *The Journal of Thomas Juxon*, p. 162. John Rushworth to Lord Fairfax, 27 July 1647, in Bell, *Memorials of the Civil War*, pp. 379–81. *CSPV*, Vol. 28, 1647–52, ed. Allen B. Hinds (London, 1927), pp. 5–12. Firth, *The Clarke Papers*, p. 218.

49 *The Journal of Thomas Juxon*, pp. 162–8. Firth, *The Clarke Papers*, p. 220.

50 Baillie, *The Letters and Journals of Robert Baillie*, Vol. 2, pp. 16–17.

51 For the one early appeal by Sexby, Allen and Shepherd designed to bring pressure to bear on Fairfax, Skippon and Cromwell to 'beare us witness', without which 'we are likely to be wholly ruined', see *For our faithful and ever honoured commanders* (London, 1647), 669.f.11[9]. Firth, *The Clarke Papers*, p. 112.

52   *The Journal of Thomas Juxon*, pp. 167–8. *A Perfect and True Copy of the Severall Grievances of the Army* (London, 1647), E390[3], point 10. A *Declaration and Remonstrance of the present engagement of the Kingdome of Scotland* (Edinburgh, 1647), E402[14], pp. 5–6. G. Wither, *A mode the cities profound policie, in delivering themselves, their city, their vvorks and ammunition, into the protection of the Armie* (London, 1647), 669.f.11[69]. Also in August 1647 Lilburne again appeared in verse in the broadsheet *A Loyall Song of the Royall Feast, kept by the Prisoners in the Tower* (London, 1647), 669.f.11[82]. Earlier in the year a pamphlet had announced Lilburne's recantation of his beliefs. It was entirely fake but it demonstrated an accurate knowledge of his life and views; see *The Recantation of John Lilburne* (London, 1647), E386[19]. Lilburne and Overton's freedom was also demanded in the equally fake but nevertheless politically astute *A Coppie of a Letter sent from one of the Agitators in the Army to an Agitator in the Citie* (London, 1647), E399[29], p. 6. Firth, *The Clarke Papers*, pp. xix, 72. John Rushworth to Lord Fairfax, 20 July 1647, in Bell, *Memorials of the Civil War*, p. 369.

10. Putney Church and Corkbush Field

1   J. Rushworth, *Historical Collections of Private Passages of State*, Vol. 7: *1647–48* (London, 1721), pp. 801–29, 830–58. *CSPD, Charles I, 1645–7*, ed. William Douglas Hamilton (London, 1891), pp. 567–70. *CSPV*, Vol. 28, 1647–52, ed. Allen B. Hinds (London, 1927), pp. 17–24.

2   H. G. Tibbutt, 'The Tower of London Letter-Book of Sir Lewis Dyve, 1646–47', in *The Publications of the Bedfordshire Historical Record Society*, Vol. 38 (Streatley: Bedfordshire Records Society, 1957), p. 77.

3   Accounts of Rainsborough's life can be found in E. Peacock, 'Notes on the Life of Thomas Rainborowe', *Archaeologia*, 46 (1880); E. Peacock, 'Transcripts and Notes Largely Concerning Thomas Rainborowe' (John Rylands University Library, Civil War Collections); H. R. Williamson, *Four Stuart Portraits* (London: Evans Brothers, 1949); L. S. Jones, *Colonel Thomas Rainsborough: Wapping's Most Famous Soldier* (History of Wapping Trust, n.d.). W. R. D. Jones, *Thomas Rainborowe (c.1610–1648): Civil War Seaman, Siegemaster and Radical* (Woodbridge: Boydell, 2005). A. Southern, *Forlorn Hope: Soldier Radicals of the Seventeenth Century* (Lewes: The Book Guild, 2001). A. Tinniswood, *The Rainborowes: Pirates, Puritans and a Family's Quest for the Promised Land* (London: Jonathan Cape, 2013).

4   Jones, *Thomas Rainborowe*, pp. 48–50. Tibbutt, 'The Tower of London Letter-Book of Sir Lewis Dyve, pp. 84–5.

5   Tibbutt, 'The Tower of London Letter-Book of Sir Lewis Dyve, pp. 89–90. Rainsborough was confirmed as vice admiral by the Commons on 24 September; see J. Rushworth, *Historical Collections of Private Passages of State: Vol. 7, 1647–48* (London, 1721), pp. 801–29. S. R. Gardiner, *History of the Great Civil War: 1645–47*, Vol. 3 (London: Weidenfeld Nicolson, 1987), p. 367.

6   Tibbutt, 'The Tower of London Letter-Book of Sir Lewis Dyve, pp. 85–8, 93–5. The following day the Commons did resolve to hear Lilburne's case, perhaps through Cromwell's intervention, but the business was then put off. It returned on 14 September but 'upon long Debate thereof, the House ordered that the Business should be re-committed, to find out some Precedents of this nature and to report to the House'. He was then called to the committee on Friday, 15 October. On 1 November the Commons 'appointed many Members of the House to be added to the Committee concerning Lieutenant-Colonel John Lilburn's Business', presumably to increase the likelihood of his release. On 9 November it was ordered that Lilburne be released during the day but return to the Tower each night. See Rushworth, *Historical Collections of Private Passages of State: Vol. 7, 1647–48*, pp. 801–29, 830–58, 858–922. B. J. Gibbons, 'Richard Overton', *ODNB*.

7   Tibbutt, 'The Tower of London Letter-Book of Sir Lewis Dyve, pp. 90–5. M. A. Gibb, *John Lilburne, The Leveller* (London: Lindsay Drummond, 1947), pp. 209–10. *Mercurius Pragmaticus*, 28 September–6 October and 9–16 October 1647. 'John a Leyden' was a familiar derogatory term deployed by heresy hunters such as Thomas Edwards.

8   Rushworth, *Historical Collections of Private Passages of State: Vol. 7, 1647–48*, pp. 801–29, 830–58. In another paper of the same day protesting at accusations that they were trying to divide the army the Agitators asked, 'Distractions increase daily; some blame one, some another? there are Seeds of Division daily sown; and hath not the King his Agents in all our Quarters to kindle and blow up the Coals of Heart-burnings and Divisions?'

9   *CSPV*, Vol. 28, 1647–52, ed. Allen B. Hinds (London, 1927), pp. 24–30.

10   M. Ashley, *John Wildman, Plotter and Postmaster* (London: Jonathan Cape, 1947). Also see the review of Ashley by Christopher Hill, 'A 17th-Century Democrat', *The Listener*, 1 May 1647, p. 676. G. E. Aylmer, 'Gentlemen Levellers?', *Past and Present*, 49 (November 1970), p. 123.

11   S. R. Gardiner, *History of the Great Civil War: 1645–47*, Vol. 3, p. 380.

12   'Shorthand manuals (which proliferated in the 1640s and 1650s) were targeted at conscientious sermon attenders', notes Ann Hughes, 'Preachers

and Hearers in Revolutionary London', paper given at the North American Conference on British Studies, Montreal, November 2012.

13   A. Woolrych, 'Preface to the 1992 edition', in C. H. Firth, *The Clarke Papers: Selections from the Papers of William Clarke, Volumes I & II in One Volume* (London: The Royal Historical Society 1992).

14   Firth, *The Clarke Papers*. A. S. P. Woodhouse (ed.), *Puritanism and Liberty: Being the Army Debates (1647–49) from the Clarke Manuscripts*, 3rd edn (London: Everyman, 1986). C. B. MacPherson, *The Political Theory of Possessive Individualism* (Oxford: Oxford University Press, 1962). A. L. Morton, *Leveller Democracy: Fact or Myth?* (London: Communist Party Historians Group, 1968). K. Thomas, 'The Levellers and the Franchise', in G. Aylmer (ed.), *The Interregnum: The Quest for Settlement 1646–1660* (Basingstoke: Macmillan, 1972). J. Morrill, 'The Army Revolt of 1647', in A. C. Duke et al. (eds.), *Britain and the Netherlands* (The Hague: Martinus Nijhoff, 1977), pp. 54–78. M. Kishlansky, 'The Army and the Levellers: The Roads to Putney', *Historical Journal*, 22.4 (December 1979) pp. 795-824. C. Thompson, 'Maximilian Petty and the Putney Debate on the Franchise', *Past and Present*, 88 (August 1980) pp. 63-69. A. Woolrych, *Soldiers and Statesmen: The General Council of the Army and Its Debates 1647–1648* (Oxford: Oxford University Press, 1987). I. Gentles, *The New Model Army in England, Ireland and Scotland, 1645–1653* (Oxford: Blackwell, 1992), Ch. 7. M. Mendle (ed.), *The Putney Debates of 1647: The Army, the Levellers and the English State* (Cambridge: Cambridge University Press, 2001). P. Baker and E. Vernon (eds.), *The Agreements of the People, the Levellers and the Constitutional Crisis of the English Revolution* (Basingstoke: Palgrave Macmillan, 2012). P. Baker, 'The Franchise Debate Revisited: The Levellers and the Army', in G. Tapsell and S. Taylor (eds.), *The Nature of the English Revolution Revisited: Essays in Honour of John Morrill* (Woodbridge, The Boydell Press 2013).

15   Rushworth, *Historical Collections of Private Passages of State*, Vol. 7, 1647–48, pp. 830–58.

16   *An Agreement of the People* (London, 1647), E412[21].

17   Firth, *The Clarke Papers*, pp. 227–8. Studs are the load-bearing uprights in a lath and plaster wall.

18   Firth, *The Clarke Papers*, p. 228.

19   Firth, *The Clarke Papers*, pp. 229–30.

20   Firth, *The Clarke Papers*, pp. 232–6. The Agitators' defence against charges of splitting the army are not given in the Clarke Papers but are available in part in *More Papers from the dissenting Agitatators to clear their Under*

takings; see Rushworth, *Historical Collections of Private Passages of State*, Vol. 7, 1647–8, pp. 830–58.

21   Firth, *The Clarke Papers*, pp. 244–7.

22   Firth, *The Clarke Papers*, pp. 247.

23   W. Walwyn, *The Poore Wise-mans Admonition* (London, 1647), in A. L. Morton, *Freedom in Arms* (London: Lawrence and Wishart, 1975), pp. 119–34. The original is in the Thomasson Tracts at E.392[4]. Firth, *The Clarke Papers*, pp. 260, 260 n. a, 264, 265.

24   Firth, *The Clarke Papers*, pp. 268, 273, 276, 279.

25   *A Call to all the souldiers of the Armie* (London, 1647), E412[10]. This anonymous pamphlet is often attributed to Wildman, but the dropped capital at the start of the text and the printer's decorations are identical to Overton's earlier productions, including the Marpriest pamphlets.

26   *A Call to all the souldiers of the Armie.*

27   Firth, *The Clarke Papers*, pp. 300–1.

28   Firth, *The Clarke Papers*, pp. 319, 323, 342. Following a suggestion from Ariel Hessayon I believe that this is Lieutenant Colonel John Rede, not Lieutenant Colonel Thomas Reade. No Christian name is given by Clarke. Both men had their names spelt 'Reade' and 'Rede', so this is not decisive. John Rede was appointed governor of Poole on the last day of the Putney debates, which increases the likelihood of his being present. And the sentiments expressed here are for an inclusive franchise, which accords with John Rede's later Leveller sympathies. Gentles, *The New Model Army*, p. 212, reads this remark differently and does not discuss this issue of the speaker's identity, but assumes that it is Thomas Reade.

29   Firth, *The Clarke Papers*, pp. 301–2, 306.

30   Firth, *The Clarke Papers*, pp. 320, 323, 325, 330 .

31   Firth, *The Clarke Papers*, pp. 324, 328, 342. Earlier Petty had defended more universalist propositions; see pp. 335–6, 351–2.

32   Firth, *The Clarke Papers*, pp. 338, 339, 355–8, 362.

33   Firth, *The Clarke Papers*, p. 366. Tibbutt, 'The Tower of London Letter-Book of Sir Lewis Dyve, p. 96.

34   Firth, *The Clarke Papers*, pp. 367, 368, 369, 376, 377, 383.

35   Firth, *The Clarke Papers*, p. 441. *CJ*, Vol. 5, 6 November 1647 (London, 1802), pp. 351–2. Woolrych, *Soldiers and statesmen*, pp. 259–60.

36   Firth, *The Clarke Papers*, p. 411. W. Bray, *A Representation to the Nation* (London, 1648). W. Bray, *A Letter to the General* (London, n.d., but probably 1649), pp. 4–6. W. Bray, *Innocency and the Blood of the slain Souldiers*

(London, 1649), pp. 11, 17. W. Bray, *A Letter to His Excellencie Sir Thomas Fairfax* (London, 1647), p. 3.

37   Firth, *The Clarke Papers*, pp. 412–13, 440.

38   Firth, *The Clarke Papers*, pp. 412–13, 418–19. Rushworth, *Historical Collections of Private Passages of State:* Vol. 7, 1647–8, pp. 858–922. *CJ*, Vol. 5: 9 November 1647 (London, 1802), pp. 353–4. Bray, *Innocency and the Blood of the slain Souldiers*, p. 11. On the rumours of a plot to kill the king see *Mercurius Melancholicus*, 13–20 November 1647, p. 69. *Mercurius Elencticus*, 12–19 November 1647 (London), E416[13], p. 17. *His Majesties Most Gracious Declaration* (1647), E413[15]. I. Gentles, *The New Model Army*, p. 220.

39   *Mercurius Rusticus* (London, 1647), E414[5]. This edition contains no printed date but is annotated by Thomason as 12 November 1647.

40   'A Copy of a Letter from Com.Gen. Regiment, to the Convention of Agents residing at London', Worcester College, Oxford, Clarke Papers, MS. AA1.19 /145. I am very grateful to Elliot Vernon for making his transcript of this letter available to me. Also see Woolrych, *Soldiers and Statesmen*, pp. 263–4.

41   *CJ*, Vol. 5, 13 November 1647 (London, 1802), pp. 357–9.

42   The Harris printed version signed by Tobias Box is *A Copy of a letter from Several Agitators* (London, 1647), E414[8] and it is reproduced in A. S. P. Woodhouse, *Puritanism and Liberty* (London: Dent, 1938), pp. 452–3. The variant that Thomason notes as scattered in the streets is *A Copy of a letter Sent by the Agents of Several Regiments* (London, 1647), E413[18]. Woolrych, *Soldiers and Statesmen*, p. 277. Gentles, *The New Model Army*, p. 221.

43   Woolrych, *Soldiers and Statesmen*, p. 264.

44   'A commission from General Fairfax', in H. Ellis and F. Douce (eds.) *A Catalogue of the Lansdowne Manuscripts in the British Museum* (London: Record Commission, 1819), p. 222, Stowe MS. 189 f.44, petition signed by about 150 people: 'We the Mayor, Justices, Burgesses, Townsmen and Natives, and Inhabatiants of the towne and county of Poole, doe unanimously, singly, and voluntarily, adhere to, assist, maintaine and joyne with the present Governour Leit. John Rede, his Officers and souldiers in the preservation of this Garrison, and castle of Brownsea, against all opposition, treachery, open force and violence whatsoever'.

45   Z. Grey, *An Impartial Examination of the Third Volume of Mr. Daniel Neal's History of the Puritans* (London, 1737), Appendix, pp. 129–30. Gentles, *The New Model Army*, pp. 220–1.

46   *Perfect Occurrences*, 12–19 November 1647 (London) , p. 318. *Mercurius Elencticus*, 12–19 November 1647 (London), E416[13], p. 24. P. Gregg, *Free-Born John: A Biography of John Lilburne* (London: Dent, 1961), p. 224.

47   *A New Declaration from Eight Regiments in the Army* (London, 1647), pp. 2–3. MPs were also meeting with the weavers about their grievances at the same time; see *Perfect Occurrences*, 12–19 November 1647 (London), p. 317.

48   *Mercurius Elencticus*, 12–19 November 1647 (London), E416[13], pp. 20–1.

49   Tinniswood, *The Rainborowes*, p. 256.

50   W. Clark, prefatory note to *A full relation of the proceedings . . .* (1647), p. 6.

51   *Mercurius Pragmaticus*, 16–22 November 1647 (London), p. 73.

52   S. Wright, 'Thomas Lambe', *ODNB*; S. Wright, *The Early English Baptists 1603–1649* (Woodbridge: Boydell, 2006), pp. 191–4.

53   *To the Supream authority of England, the Commons in Parliament assembled . . .* (London, 1647).

54   *The Character of an Agitator*, dated 11 November 1647, p. 7. See also *Mercurius Melancholicus*, 13–20 November 1647, p. 73.

55   *The Justice of the Army . . .* (London, 1649), p. 4.

56   J. Naylier, *The Foxes Craft Discovered* (London, 1649), pp. 6–7.

57   W. Clark, prefatory note to *A full relation of the proceedings*, p. 5.

58   *To the Supream authority of England, the Commons in Parliament assembled*. Clark, prefatory note to *A full relation of the proceedings*, p. 6. *Kingdomes Weekly Intelligencer*, 16–23 May 1647 (London), p. 734.

59   *A Remonstrance From His Excellency Sir Thomas Fairfax* (London, 1647).

60   Clark, prefatory note to *A full relation of the proceedings*, p. 5.

61   Clark, prefatory note to *A full relation of the proceedings*, p. 6. J. Rushworth, 'Proceedings in Parliament, November 1st–December 4th, 1647', *Historical Collections of Private Passages of State*: Vol. 7: 1647–8 (1721), pp. 858–922. *Mercurius Pragmaticus*, 16–22 November 1647 (London), p. 74.

62   Rushworth, *Historical Collections of Private Passages of State*, Vol. 7, 1647–48, pp. 923–52. *The Justice of the Army*, p. 6.

63   Clark, prefatory note to *A full relation of the proceedings*, pp. 5–6. R. Scrope and T. Monkhouse (eds.), *Clarendon State Papers* (Oxford, 1767–86), Vol. 2, Appendix, p. xlii. The seemingly eyewitness and certainly contemporary account in the Clarendon State Papers is definitive about Cromwell's role.

64   *The Justice of the Army*, p. 6.

65   Clark, prefatory note to *A full relation of the proceedings*, pp. 5–6. *Mercurius Elencticus*, 12–19 November 1647 (London), E416[13], p. 19.

66   *CJ*, Vol. 5: 1646–8 (1802), pp. 366–8.

67   *To the Supream authority of England, the Commons in Parliament assembled*.

68   *CJ*, Vol. 5, 23 November 1647 (London, 1802), pp. 366–8.

69   *To the Supream authority of England, the Commons in Parliament assem-bled*. Gentles, *The New Model Army*, p. 223. A. Bettridge, 'Early Baptists in Leicestershire and Rutland, Part 1', *Baptist Quarterly*, 25 (1973–4), pp. 209–11. A. Betteridge, 'Early Baptists in Leicestershire and Rutland, Part 2', *Baptist Quarterly*, 25 (1973–4), p. 357. S. Wright, 'Samuel Oates', *ODNB*.

70   D. Underdown, 'The Parliamentary Diary of John Boys, 1647–8', *Historical Research*, 39 (1966), pp. 152–3.

71   Gregg, *Free-Born John*, p. 224. *CJ*, Vol. 5, 25 November 1647 (London, 1802), pp. 368–9.

72   J. Lawmind (Wildman), *Putney Projects* (London, 1647), E421[19], pp. 2, 7–10, 27, 40, 44. Pagination is absent after page 39.

73   J. Rushworth, 18 December and 24 December 1647, in *Historical Collections of Private Passages of State*, Vol. 7, 1647–8 (London, 1721), pp. 923–52.

74   R. Overton, *An Alarum to the House of Lords* (London, 1646), E346[8], p. 3.

75   BL, *Henry Marten Papers*, Add. MS. 71532. f.23.

76   *A Copy of a letter Sent by the Agents of Several Regiments* (London, 1647), E413[18].

77   *Perfect Weekly Account*, 10–17 November 1647 (London), final page.

11. Counterrevolution

1   *CJ*, Vol. 5, 19 February 1648 and 23 February 1648.

2   'Ecce! Or the New testament of our lords and Saviours, the house of Commons and the Supreme Councel at Windsor' (Somers Tracts, 7.61), in E. Peacock, 'Transcripts and Notes largely concerning Thomas Rainborowe' (John Rylands University Library, Civil War Collections, English MS 235). *The Kingdomes Weekly Account*, 16–23 February 1647 (1648), E429[16], p. 52.

3   *To the right honourable, The Lords and Commons . . . The earnest and passionate Petition* (London, 1648), E425[10], p. 3. H. Marten, *The Independency of England Endeavored to be Maintained* (London, 1648), Wing M822. I. Gentles, *The New Model Army in England, Scotland and Ireland, 1645–1653* (Oxford: Blackwell, 1994), p. 237.

4   H. Marten, *The Parliaments Proceedings Justified . . .* (London, 1648), E426[2].

5   J. Lilburne, *An Impeachment for High Treason against Oliver Cromwell and his son in law Henry Ireton Esquires* (London, 1649), E568[20]. D. Underdown, 'The Parliamentary Diary of John Boys, 1647–8', *Historical Research*, 39

(1966), p. 157. W. Haller and G. Davies, *The Leveller Tracts 1647–53* (New York: Columbia University Press, 1944), pp. 88, 106–15, 126–9.

6   Lilburne, *An Impeachment for High Treason.*

7   J. Norris (John Harris), *A Lash for a Lyar, or The Stayner Stayned* (London, 1648), p. 8, E. 428[8]. Haller and Davies, *The Leveller Tracts 1647–53*, pp. 88–9.

8   Underdown, 'The Parliamentary Diary of John Boys', pp. 157–8. J. Lilburne, *A Whip for the present House of Lords* (London, 1648), E431[1], pp. 21–6. B. Whitelocke, *Memorials of the English Affairs*, Vol. 2 (Oxford: Oxford University Press, 1853), p. 263.

9   Whitelocke, *Memorials of the English Affairs*, Vol. 2, p. 264.

10 For the printed material of the main protagonists see Haller and Davies, *The Leveller Tracts 1647–53*, pp. 88–9. See also N. Carlin, 'Leveller Organization in London', *Historical Journal*, 27, 4 (1984), pp. 955–60. J. Wildman, *Truth's triumph, or Treachery anatomized* (London, 1648), E520[33]. G. Masterson, *The Triumph Stain'd, being an Answer to Truths Triumph* (London, 1648), E426[18]. J. Lilburne, *The People's Prerogative* (London, 1648), E427[4]. Norris, *A Lash for a Lyar*. Lilburne, *A Whip for the present House of Lords.*

11 See Norah Carlin's excellent exposition, 'Leveller Organization in London', especially pp. 958–60.

12 Underdown, 'The Parliamentary Diary of John Boys', p. 157. Masterson, *The Triumph Stain'd*, p. 6. Norris, *A Lash for a Lyar*, p. 13.

13 *A Declaration and Some Proceedings*, E427(6); and also Haller and Davies, *The Leveller Tracts 1647–53*, p. 98.

14 *A Declaration and Some Proceedings*; Haller and Davies, *The Leveller Tracts 1647–53*, p. 100.

15 See P. Gregg, *Free-Born John* (London: Dent, 1986), p. 229. The Mouth in Aldersgate was the other.

16 P. Gregg, *Free-Born John*, p. 231.

17 *A Declaration and Some Proceedings*; Haller and Davies, *The Leveller Tracts 1647–53*, pp. 100–1.

18 The figure of 5.2 million is for 1646. See E. A. Wrigley and R. S. Schofield, *The Population History of England 1541–1871* (Cambridge, 1989) Table 7.8, pp. 208–9.

19 *A Declaration and Some Proceedings*; Haller and Davies, *The Leveller Tracts 1647–53*, p. 103.

20 *A Declaration and Some Proceedings*; Haller and Davies, *The Leveller Tracts 1647–53*, p. 103–4.

21   Lilburne, *An Impeachment for High Treason*. See also N. Carlin, 'Leveller Organisation in London', *Historical Journal*, 27.4 (1984), pp. 959–60

22   Lilburne, *An Impeachment for High Treason*.

23   The letter is reproduced in Lilburne, *The People's Prerogative*.

24   J. Frank, *The Levellers: A History of the Writings of Three Seventeenth-Century Social Democrats: John Lilburne, Richard Overton, William Walwyn* (Cambridge, MA: Harvard University Press, 1955), p. 167.

25   Wildman, *Truth's triumph*, p. 5.

26   Masterson, *The Triumph Stain'd*, p. 9.

27   Norris, *A Lash for a Lyar*, p. 6. Underdown, 'The Parliamentary Diary of John Boys', p. 158.

28   Wildman, *Truth's triumph*, pp. 7–8.

29   Wildman, *Truth's triumph*, p. 5. Norris, *A Lash for a Lyar*, p. 13.

30   Wildman, *Truth's triumph*, p. 5.

31   *Two Letters Read in the House . . . of a Great Bloody Plot* (London, 1648), E423[20], pp. 1–2. J. Rushworth, 'Proceedings in Parliament: January 3rd–29th, 1648', in *Historical Collections of Private Passages of State*, Vol. 7, 1647–8 (London, 1721), pp. 953–79; and 'Proceedings in Parliament: February 28th–April 1st, 1648', pp. 1010–45, BL, Stowe MS. 189.f.39–40.

32   J. Rushworth, 'Proceedings in Parliament: January 3rd–29th, 1648', in *Historical Collections of Private Passages of State*, Vol. 7, 1647–8 (London, 1721), pp. 953–79; and 'Proceedings in Parliament: February 28th–April 1st, 1648', pp. 1010–45. Gentles, *The New Model Army*, p. 231.

33   W. Eyre, *The Serious Representation of Col. William Eyre* (London, 1649), Wing E3945A, pp. 2–3. P. Hardacre, 'William Eyre', *ODNB*. J. Rushworth, *A True Relation of the Disbanding of Supernumerary Forces* (London, 1648), E429[10]. Gentles, *The New Model Army*, p. 231. *The Kingdomes Weekly Post*, 22 February–1 March 1648, E430[6], p. 65.

34   Anon., *The Armies Petition or A New Engagement of the Army, Who are yet Faithfull to the People . . .* (collected by Thomason, 3 May 1648), E438[1]. *Perfect Weekly Account*, 26 April–3 May 1648, E438[1], pp. 58–9.

35   Anon., *The Armies Petition or A New Engagement of the Army*, pp. 2–3.

36   Anon, *The Armies Petition or A New Engagement of the Army*, p. 8.

37   Anon, *The Armies Petition or A New Engagement of the Army*, pp. 7, 8. *Windsor Projects and Westminster Practices* (London, 1648), E442[10], pp. 4–6. R. W. Stent, 'Thomas Rainsborough and the Army Levellers' (M.Phil, University of London, 1975), Vol. 2, pp. 261–2, 339. Gentles, *The New Model Army*, p. 245. Gladman was later involved in the suppression of the Diggers and he and Packer were involved in land deals together in Hertfordshire in the 1650s.

38   J. Naylier, *The Foxes Craft Discovered* (London, 1649), pp. 4–6. J. Naylier, *The New made Colonel* (London, 1649), E552[10]. C. Cheeseman (or Chisman), *The Lamb Contending with the Lion* (London, 1649), E563[10]. For more on Cheeseman see J. Peacey, *Print and Public Politics in the English Revolution* (Cambridge: Cambridge University Press, 2013), pp. 293–4.

39   R. Ashton, *Counter Revolution: The Second Civil War and Its Origins, 1646–8* (New Haven: Yale University Press 1994), pp. 139–58. Gentles, *The New Model Army*, pp. 241–2, 246. M. Carter, *A Most True and exact Relation of That as Honourable as Unfortunate Expedition of Kent, Essex, and Colchester* (1650), Wing C662, pp. 11–13. See Underdown, 'The Parliamentary Diary of John Boys', pp. 159–60, for a contemporary account of the beginnings of counterrevolutionary action in Kent nominally in defence of the right to celebrate Christmas.

40   J. R. Powell and E. K. Timings, *Documents Relating to the Civil War 1642–1648* (London: Navy Records Society and, Spottiswoode, Ballantyne and Co., 1963), pp. 291, 295–6.

41   Gentles, *The New Model Army*, p. 230. R. D. Jones, *Thomas Rainsborough (c.1610–1648): Civil War Seaman, Siegemaster and Radical* (Woodbridge: Boydell Press, 2005), pp. 99–100.

42   Powell and Timings, *Documents Relating to the Civil War 1642–1648*, pp. 296–7.

43   *Mercurius Pargamaticus*, 28 September–6 October 1647, E410[4].

44   *CJ*, Vol. 5, 1646–8 (London, 1802), pp. 413–15.

45   Powell and Timings, *Documents Relating to the Civil War 1642–1648*, p. 288.

46   *CJ*, Vol. 5, 1646–8 (London, 1802), pp. 297–300. W. Batten, *A Declaration of Sir William Batten* (London, 1648), Wing B1152, pp. 2–5.

47   Powell and Timings, *Documents Relating to the Civil War 1642–1648*, p. 389. A. Tinniswood, *The Rainborowes: Pirates, Puritans and a Family's Quest for the Promised Land* (London: Jonathan Cape 2013), p. 256. Whitelocke, *Memorials of the English Affairs*, Vol. 2, pp. 198–9.

48   Powell and Timings, *Documents Relating to the Civil War 1642–1648*, pp. 285, 315, 343. B. Donagan, 'Samuel Kem', *ODNB*. A. Laurence, *Parliamentary Army Chaplains: 1642 – 1651* (Woodbridge: Boydell, 1990), p. 241. Jones, *Thomas Rainsborough* , p. 102. Tinniswood, *The Rainborowes*, pp. 254, 258. Kem continued his erratic political career by defecting to the royalists, spying for Parliament, returning to serve the parliamentary army and then conforming at the Restoration.

49 Powell and Timings, *Documents Relating to the Civil War 1642–1648*, pp. 302–3, 329–30.

50 Carter, *A Most True and exact Relation of That as Honourable as Unfortunate Expedition*, Wing C662, p. 52.

51 Carter, *A Most True and exact Relation of That as Honourable as Unfortunate Expedition*, pp. 52–4. Powell and Timings, *Documents Relating to the Civil War 1642–1648*, pp. 330–4, 354–5. Tinniswood, *The Rainborowes*, p. 257.

52 Carter, *A Most True and exact Relation of That as Honourable as Unfortunate Expedition*, p. 155. Powell and Timings, *Documents Relating to the Civil War 1642–1648*, pp. 336, 338–9, 352–3.

53 'A Commission issued by Henry Marten', in C. H. Firth (ed.), *The Clarke Papers: Selections from the Papers of William Clarke*, Vol. 2 (London: Royal Historical Society, 1992), p. 56. C. Durston, 'Henry Marten and the High Shoon of Berkshire: the Levellers in Berkshire in 1648', *Berkshire Archaeological Journal*, 70 (1979), p. 88. 'Shoon' is an archaism for fool.

54 *Mercurius Pragmaticus*, 22–9 August, quoted in Firth, *The Clarke Papers*, Vol. 2, pp. 56–7.

55 S. Barber, '"A Bastard Kind of Militia": Localism and Tactics in the Second Civil War', in I. Gentles, J. Morrill and B. Worden (eds), *Soldiers, Writers and Statesmen of the English Revolution* (Cambridge: Cambridge University Press, 2007), p. 139.

56 Barber, 'A Bastard Kind of Militia', pp. 138–9, 140, 140 n. 31. Firth, *The Clarke Papers*, Vol. 2, pp. 56–7 n. b.

57 *Mercurius Pragmaticus*, 6–13 June 1648, E447[5]. Durston, 'Henry Marten and the High Shoon of Berkshire', p. 91.

58 *Mercurius Elencticus*, 23–30 August 1648, E461[20].

59 W. Walwyn, *Juries Justified* (London, 1651), E618[9], p. 3. *Mercurius Pragmaticus*, 15–22 August 1648, E460[21]. A. L. Morton, *The World of the Ranters* (London: Lawrence and Wishart, 1970), pp. 191–2. Durston, 'Henry Marten and the High Shoon of Berkshire', p. 92. Firth, *The Clarke Papers*, pp. 56–7 n. b.

60 *Mercurius Pragmaticus*, 15–22 August 1648, E460[21].

61 *Englands Troublers Troubled* (London, 1648), E459[11]. I. Waters, *Henry Marten and the Long Parliament* (Chepstow: F. G. Comber, 1973), p. 41.

62 *Englands Troublers Troubled*, pp. 1, 3.

63 *Englands Troublers Troubled*, pp. 4–5.

64 *Englands Troublers Troubled*, p. 5.

65 *Englands Troublers Troubled*, p. 7.

66 *Englands Troublers Troubled*, p. 8.

67   *Englands Troublers Troubled*, p. 9–11.

68   *Mercurius Pragmaticus*, 6–13 June 1648, E447[5].

69   *Mercurius Pragmaticus*, 15–22 August 1648, E460[21].

70   *Mercurius Elencticus*, 23–30 August 1648, E461[20]. Durston, 'Henry Marten and the High Shoon of Berkshire', p. 91. Whitelocke, *Memorials of the English Affairs*, Vol. 2, p. 382.

71   *Mercurius Elencticus*, 23–30 August 1648, E461[20].

72   *Mercurius Pragmaticus*, 15–22 August 1648, E460[21]. Durston, 'Henry Marten and the High Shoon of Berkshire', p. 91.

73   *Mercurius Melancholicus*, 28 August–4 September 1648, E462[7], pp. 163–4.

74   *CJ*, Vol. 5, 21 August 1648 (London, 1802), pp. 675–7.

75   *CSPD: Charles I, 1648-9* (London, 1893), pp. 226–62.

76   *Kingdomes Weekly Intelligencer*, 29 August–5 September 1648, E462[10], pp. 1067, 1072.

77   *Perfect Weekly Account*, 30 August–6 September 1648, E462[13]. *Kingdomes Weekly Intelligencer*, 29 August–5 September 1648, E462[10], p. 1072.

78   *Terrible and bloudy Newes from the disloyall Army in the North* (London, 1648), E462[28], p. 2.

79   *Terrible and bloudy Newes*, pp. 2–3.

80   *CSPD, Charles I, 1648-9*, 5 September 1648 (London, 1893), pp. 262–94.

81   *CSPD, Charles I, 1648-9*, 5 September 1648 (London, 1893), pp. 262–94.

82   *CSPD, Charles I, 1648-9* (London, 1893), pp. 294–315.

83   *CJ*, Vol. 6, 2 February 1649 (London, 1802), pp. 129–30. Firth, *The Clarke Papers*, Vol. 2, pp. 212–13, also 213 n. Durston, 'Henry Marten and the High Shoon of Berkshire', p. 94. H. N. Brailsford, *The Levellers and the English Revolution* (ed. C. Hill) (Nottingham: Spokesman, 1961), p. 343.

84   F. Dahl, *A Bibliography of English Corantos 1620–1642* (London: Bibliographical Society, 1952), pp. 19, 22. C. Nelson and M. Seccombe, 'The Creation of the Periodical Press 1620–1695', in J Barnard, D F McKenzie, et al. (eds), *The Cambridge History of the Book in Britain*, pp. 538–41.

85   J. Raymond, *The Invention of the Newspaper: English Newsbooks 1641–1649* (Oxford: Oxford University Press, 1996), pp. 13, 20.

86   Raymond, *The Invention of the Newspaper*, p. 47.

87   Raymond, *The Invention of the Newspaper*, pp. 53–4.

88   Peacey, *Print and Public Politics in the English Revolution*, p. 93.

89   Brailsford, *The Levellers and the English Revolution*, pp. 402–3. J. Diethe, 'The Moderate: Politics and Allegiances of a Revolutionary Newspaper', *History of Political Thought*, 4.2 (Summer 1983), pp. 251–4.

90   Indeed the *The Moderate* itself scotched contemporary rumours that Mabbot was involved: 'As for one Mabbot that thou barkest at so violently, I professe I know him not, nor to my knowledge ever saw him'. Of course this may have been a ruse. Brailsford supports the theory of Mabbot's involvement but, more plausibly if we are to rely on style of expression, sees the hand of Overton in the writing. Given the lack of evidence, however, there is only so far we can go in attributing authorship and so it may be better to trace the evolution of *The Moderate* in terms of the political challenges that it and the Levellers faced in 1648 and 1649. *The Moderate*, 12, 26 September–3 October 1648, E465[25]. See F. Henderson, 'Gilbert Mabbot', *ODNB*. Raymond, *The Invention of the Newspaper*, pp. 65–6. Brailsford, *The Levellers and the English Revolution*, pp. 402–3. J. Peacey, *Politicians and Pamphleteers: Propaganda during the English Civil Wars and Interregnum* (Aldershot: Ashgate Publishing, 2004), pp. 157–8.

91   Diethe, 'The Moderate, pp. 248–51.

92   HMC, *De L'Isle and Dudley Manuscripts*, Vol. 6, 1626–98 (London: HMSO, 1966), p. 594. Peacey, *Print and Public Politics in the English Revolution*, p. 119.

93   *The Moderate*, 7, 22–9 August 1648; 9, 5–12 September 1648; 11, 19–26 September 1648; 15, 17–24 October 1648; 16, 24–31 October 1648; 19, 14–21 November 1648; 20, 21–8 November 1648.

94   See, for instance, *The Moderate*, 11, 19–26 September 1648.

95   *The Moderate*, 17, 31 October–7 November 1648; 19, 14–21 November 1648; 20, 21–8 November 1648.

96   *The Moderate*, 11, 19–26 September 1648; 10, 12–19 September 1648.

97   *The Modertate*, 19, 14–21 November 1648; 14, 10–17 October 1648.

98   *The Moderate*, 16, 24–31 October 1648.

99   *The Moderate*, 14, 10–17 October 1648; 16, 24–31 October 1648.

100   Diethe, 'The Moderate', p. 248.

101   HMC, *De L'Isle and Dudley Manuscripts*, Vol. 6, 1626–98 (London: HMSO, 1966), pp. 590–1. Peacey, *Print and Public Politics in the English Revolution*, pp. 69, 109.

102   R. Howell Jr and D. E. Brewster, 'Reconsidering the Levellers: The Evidence of the Moderate Author(s)', *Past and Present*, 46 (February 1970), pp. 68–86. See the critique of Howell and Brewser in Diethe, 'The Moderate, pp. 262–4.

103   HMC, *De L'Isle and Dudley Manuscripts*, Vol. 6, 1626–98 (London: HMSO, 1966), pp. 590–1. Raymond, *The Invention of the Newspaper*, p. 67.

104   *The Moderate*, 12, 26 September–3 October 1648, E465[25]. *The Moderate*, 13, 3 October–10 October 1648, E467[15]. *The Moderate*, 14, 10 October–17 October 1648, E468[2].

12. Revolution

1   I. Gentles, 'The Struggle for London in the Second Civil War', *Historical Journal*, 26.2 (June 1983), pp. 291–2.

2   *The Moderate*, 4, 1–8 August 1648.

3   Gentles, 'The Struggle for London in the Second Civil War', pp. 290, 293–6.

4   Gentles, 'The Struggle for London in the Second Civil War', pp. 291–2.

5   Gentles, 'The Struggle for London in the Second Civil War', pp. 296–8.

6   *To the Honourable the Commons of England assembled in parliament. The Humble petition of divers thousands of wel-affected Citizens, and others in behalf of Lieutenant Collonel John Lilburne, Prisoner of the Tower of London* (London 1648), E457 (19). The frontispiece of this petition records that it was 'presented the first of August 1648, with above 10,000 hands thereunto subscribed'. See also J. Frank, *The Levellers: A History of the Writings of Three Seventeenth-Century Social Democrats: John Lilburne, Richard Overton, William Walwyn* (Cambridge, MA: Harvard University Press, 1955), pp. 163 and 314 n. 85. See also H. Brailsford, *The Levellers and the English Revolution* (ed. C. Hill) (Nottingham: Spokesman, 1961), p. 345.

7   *CJ*, Vol. 5, 1 August 1648, pp. 654–7. *LJ*, Vol. 10, 2 August 1648, pp. 406–14.

8   *Mercurius Pragmaticus*, 1 August–8 August 1648, E457[11].

9   *Mercurius Pragmaticus*, 1–8 August 1648, E457[11].

10   J. Lilburne, *Legall and Fundamental Liberties* (London, 1649), E567[1], reproduced in W. Haller and G. Davies, *The Leveller Tracts 1647–53* (New York: Peter Smith, 1944), p. 414.

11   Lilburne, *Legall and Fundamental Liberties*, in Haller and Davies, *The Leveller Tracts 1647–53*, p. 414.

12   A.P., *An Appendix to the Agreement of the People Published for the Satisfaction of Tender Consciences* (London, January 1648), Wing P2, p. 7.

13   Lilburne, *Legall and Fundamental Liberties*, in Haller and Davies, *The Leveller Tracts 1647–53*, p. 415.

14   See B. Manning, *1649: The Crisis of the English Revolution* (London: Bookmarks, 1992), p. 19.

15 *The Humble Petition of divers wel affected Persons inhabiting the City of London, Westminster, the Borough of Southwark, Hamlets and places adjacent* (hereafter I refer to this as the Large Petition even though, confusingly, the Leveller petition of March 1647 is also sometimes referred to in the same way), in A. L. Morton, *Freedom in Arms* (London, 1975), pp. 186–7.

16 The Large Petition, in Morton, *Freedom in Arms*, pp. 192–3.

17 S. R. Gardiner, *History of the Great Civil War*, Vol. 4 (London: Weidenfeld Nicholson, 1987), p. 226. See also *Packets of Letters*, E469[21], pp. 5–6.

18 The term 're-inthrone' comes from a petition of Ireton's regiment. See 'A True Copy of a Petition . . . by the Officers and Soldiers of the Regiment under the Command of Commissary General Ireton', E.468[18].

19 E. Ludlow, *The Memoirs of Edmund Ludlow* (Oxford, 1894), pp. 203–4.

20 See B. Worden, *Roundhead Reputations: The English Civil Wars and the Passions of Posterity* (London: Penguin, 2001) esp. Ch. 2. S. R. Gardiner's judgment on this passage was that 'Ludlow can never be trusted about dates, but I do not think he would have written that he went to Colchester if his visit had been at a later time when the army was some other place. If he did go to Colchester his visit cannot have been later than about Sept. 6, as it was known in London on the 8th that Ireton was no longer there'. Gardiner, *History of the Great Civil War*, Vol. 4, p. 213 n. 1.

21 D. Farr, *Henry Ireton and the English Revolution* (Woodbridge: Boydell, 2006), p. 130.

22 Lilburne, *Legall and Fundamental Liberties*, in Haller and Davies, *The Leveller Tracts 1647–53*, p. 417.

23 See Farr, *Henry Ireton*, p. 130. See also R. M. Ramsey, *Henry Ireton* (London: Longmans, Green and Co., 1949), pp. 110–14. F. Henderson, 'Drafting the Officer's *Agreement of the People*, 1648–49: A Reappraisal', in P. Baker and E. Vernon (eds.), *The Agreements of the People, the Levellers and the Constitutional Crisis of the English Revolution* (Basingstoke: Palgrave Macmillan, 2012), p. 165.

24 I. Gentles, *The New Model Army in England, Ireland and Scotland, 1645–1653* (Oxford: Oxford University Press, 1992), p. 269.

25 Lilburne, *Legall and Fundamental Liberties*, E567[1], p. 32. *Mercurius Elenticus*, 4 October 1648. See Brailsford, *The Levellers and the English Revolution*, p. 361.

26 Farr, *Henry Ireton*, p. 132. See also I. Gentles, 'The Politics of Fairfax's Army, 1645–9', in J. Adamson, *The English Civil War* (Basingstoke: Palgrave Macmillan, 2009), pp. 191–2.

27 The title was used once more the following year by the Levellers, although

the same title was used once before by a royalist and once in 1649 by an anti-Leveller journalist.

28 See J. Peacey, 'The Hunting of the Leveller: The Sophistication of Parliamentarian Propaganda, 1647–53', *Historical Research*, 78.199 (February 2005) pp. 15–42.

29 *Mercurius Militaris*, 1, 10 October 1648, E467[34]. It is Margot Heinemann's path-breaking 'Popular Drama and Leveller Style', in M. Cornforth (ed.), *Rebels and Their Causes: Essays in Honour of A. L. Morton* (London: Lawrence and Wishart, 1978), for instance at pp. 69–93, that argues the Richard Overton and Harris developed this particular theatrical form of address. In this quote Harris uses the line 'bestride this narrow world like a Colossus' directly from Shakespeare's *Julius Caesar*.

30 *Mercurius Militaris*, 1, 10 October 1648, E467[34].

31 *Mercurius Militaris*, 1, 10 October 1648, E467[34].

32 *Mercurius Militaris*, 2, 10–17 October 1648, E468[35].

33 *Mercurius Militaris*, 3, 24–31 October 1648, E469[10].

34 *Mercurius Militaris*, 4, 31 October–8 November 1648, E470[14].

35 *Mercurius Militaris*, 2, 10–17 October 1648, E468[35]. *Mercurius Militaris*, 3, 24 October–31 October 1648, E469[10].

36 *Mercurius Militaris*, 1, 10 October 1648, E467[34]. *Mercurius Militaris*, 2, 10–17 October 1648, E468[35]. *Mercurius Militaris*, 3, 24–31 October 1648, E469[10].

37 *Mercurius Militaris*, 3, 24–31 October 1648, E469[10]. *Mercurius Militaris*, 5, 14–21 November 1648, E470[14]. Lilburne's clash with Prynne was also reported in *The Moderate*, 18, 7–14 November 1648.

38 *Mercurius Militaris*, 5, 14–21 November 1648, E470[14].

39 G. Wharton, *Mercurius Impartialis*, E476[3], p. 2.

40 *Mercurius Militaris*, 5, 1421 November 1648, E470[14].

41 *The Speech of Major John Harris* (London, 1660), E1043[3], p. 3. See also C. V. Wedgewood, *A King Condemned: The Trial and Execution of Charles I* (London: Tauris Parke, 2011), p. 189. R. Clifton, 'Richard Rumbold', *ODNB*.

42 Lucas had been in charge of Berkeley Castle, Gloucestershire, at the end of the First Civil War when Rainsborough commanded the siege. Rainsborough summoned Lucas to surrender and, ironically given that starvation had reduced the royalists in Colchester to eating their horses, Lucas replied, 'I will eat horseflesh before I will yield, and when that is done, man's flesh'. Rainsborough stormed the outworks and three days later he took Lucas's surrender. Lucas returned to fight the New Model in the last engagement of the First Civil War. Rainsborough might not have felt that lenient terms were appropriate a second time. J. Sprigge, *Anglia*

Rediviva: England's Recovery, Being the History of the Motions, Actions and Successes of the Army under the Immediate Conduct of His Excellency Sir Thomas Fairfax, KT (Oxford, 1854), pp. 136–7. J. Rushworth, 'Historical Collections: The Proceedings of Fairfax's Army', *Historical Collections of Private Passages of State*, Vol. 6, 1645–7 (1722), pp. 89–116. Also see W. R. D. Jones, *Thomas Rainborowe (c.1610–1648): Civil War Seaman, Siegemaster and Radical* (Woodbridge: Boydell, 2005), pp. 39–40. Hugh Ross Williamson, *Four Stuart Portraits* (London, 1949), pp. 115–16.

43   W. Clarke, *Clarke Papers*, Vol. 2 (Royal Historical Society, 1992), pp. 31–9. Gardiner, *History of the Great Civil War*, Vol. 4, p. 203. B. Donagan, *War in England 1642–1649* (Oxford: Oxford University Press, 2010), pp. 364–6.

44   J. Rushworth, 'Proceedings in Parliament: September 1st–October 2nd 1648', *Historical Collections of Private Passages of State*: Vol. 7: 1647–8 (1721), pp. 1248–80.

45   For other reports of royalist attacks on parliamentarians see *Mercurius Pragmaticus*, Tuesday 26 September to 3 October 1648, E465[19].

46   See A. Southern, *Forlorn Hope: Soldier Radicals of the Seventeenth Century* (Lewes: The Book Guild, 2001), p. 67. Tanner Manuscripts, 58.f. 346.

47   *The Moderate: Impartially communicating the Martial Affaires to the Kingdom of England* (hereafter *The Moderate*), 15, Tuesday 17–Tuesday 24 October (London, 1648), E468[24]. This report is taken directly from the letter written from Pontefract on 20 October and printed as *A Bloudy Fight at Pontefract Castle in Yorkshire* (1648), E469[4].

48   Rushworth, 'Proceedings in Parliament: October 2nd–November 1st, 1648', pp. 1281–1314. The story is also told in *A Full Relation of the Horrid Murder committed upon the body of Col. Rainsborough, the persons that did it, and the cause thereof* (London, 1648), E470[4]. See also E. Peacock, 'Notes on the Life of Thomas Rainborowe', *Archaeologia*, 46 (1880), p. 40.

49   Some contemporaries and some modern historians have speculated that Rainsborough was sent north by Fairfax and/or Cromwell in order to keep him away from his radical political allies in London and, possibly, to deliberately endanger his life. Both may be true, but there is no direct evidence for either. In any case the choice of Rainsborough for the task of besieging Pontefract was so obvious that no other reason needed to be advanced. For a summary of these arguments see H. R. Williamson, 'The Assassination of Colonel Rainsborough, 29 October 1648', in H. R. Williamson, *Who Was the Man in the Iron Mask?* (London, 2002), pp. 173–91.

50   Rushworth, 'Proceedings in Parliament: October 2nd–November 1st, 1648', pp. 1281–1314.

51   *The Moderate*, 16, Tuesday 24–Tuesday 13 October (London, 1648), E469[16]. The date on this edition is presumably a mistake. The final date should be 31 October when issue 17 of *The Moderate* begins. *The Moderate* report is drawn from *Packets of Letters*, E469[21], p. 6.

52   *The Moderate*, 16, Tuesday 24–Tuesday 13 October. *Packets of Letters*, E469[21], p. 6.

53   J. Smith, *The Innocent Cleared: or a Vindication of Captaine John Smith* (Amsterdam, 1648), E472[25]. Smith's previous service under Ludlow and Marten might make him seem an unlikely accessory to Rainsborough's murder. But there is no proof whether or not he was deliberately (or indeed accidentally) negligent.

54   J. Rushworth, 'Proceedings in Parliament from November 1 to December 1, 1648', *Historical Collections of Private Passages of State*: Vol. 7: 1647–8 (1721), pp. 1281–1314.

55   Williamson, 'The Assassination of Colonel Rainsborough, p. 182.

56   *The Moderate*, 18, Tuesday 7–Tuesday 14 November (London, 1648), E472(4). 'Cabbs' or 'Cabs' is a nickname for cavaliers, from the Spanish for horseman, 'Caballero'.

57   *Mecurius Militaris* or *The Armies Schout* [Scout], 4, Tuesday 31 October–Tuesday 8 November (London, 1648), E470[14].

58   *A Full Relation of the Horrid Murder committed upon the body of Col. Rainsborough.*

59   See Williamson, 'The Assassination of Colonel Rainsborough', pp. 189–90.

60   Attached as an appendix to *A Full Relation of the Horrid Murder committed upon the body if Col. Rainsborough*. See also *The Moderate Intelligencer*, 189, Thursday 26 October–Thursday 2 November 1648 (London), E470[1].

61   Rushworth, 'Proceedings in Parliament from November 1 to December 1, 1648', pp. 1281–1314.

62   See *The Life and Death of Philip Herbert, the late infamous Knight of Barkshire, once Earle of Pembrock, Montgomerie, &c, who departed from this life to another January 23, 1649. Having by his Degenerate basenesse betrayed his Nobilite, and entered himselfe a Commoner, among the vere Scum of the Kingdom* (London, 1649), E592[1]. Also see *The Famous Tragedie of King Charles* (London, 1649), in which the deaths of Lucas and Lisle at the siege of Colchester are connected to the death of Charles and blamed on, among others, 'the Leveller Rainsborough'. The play contains a scene that portrays the death of Rainsborough.

63   *An Ironicall Expostulation with Death and Fate . . . also a brief Discourse*

held Octob. 29 between Col. Rainsborough and Charon at their Meeting (1648), E472[18].

64   W. C. Abbott, *Writings and Speeches of Oliver Cromwell*, Vol. 1, 1599–1649 (Cambridge, MA: Harvard University Press, 1937), p. 674.

65   See Brailsford, *The Levellers and the English Revolution*, p. 362. See Abbott, *Writings and Speeches of Oliver Cromwell*, Vol. 1, p. 676.

66   Lilburne, *Legall and Fundamental Liberties*, E567[1], p. 32, also in Haller and Davies, *The Leveller Tracts 1647–53*, p. 415.

67   Lilburne, *Legall and Fundamental Liberties*, E567[1], p. 33, also in Haller and Davies, *The Leveller Tracts 1647–53*, p. 415–16. Sean Kelsey brings out the degree of indecision among some of those who tried the King over whether he should be executed. Kelsey does not, however, discuss this account by Lilburne which provides evidence that some army officers were intent on execution at least by early November 1648. See S. Kelsey, 'The Death of Charles I', *Historical Journal*, 45, 4 (2002), pp. 727–54.

68   I. Gentles, 'Political Funerals during the English Revolution', in S. Porter (ed.), *London and the Civil War* (London: Macmillan, 1996), p. 207.

69   J.T., 'An Elegie Upon the Colonel Thomas Rainsborough, butchered at Doncaster Sunday the 29 Octob. 1648', 669 f.13[48].

70   *Mecurius Militaris* or *The Armies Schout*, 4, Tuesday 31 October–Tuesday 8 November (London, 1648).

71   *The Moderate*, 17, Tuesday 31 October–Tuesday 7 November (London, 1648), E470[12].

72   *Mercurius Elencticus*, 52, Wednesday 15–Wednesday 22 November (London, 1648), E473[9].

73   *Mercurius Elencticus*, 52.

74   *Mercurius Elencticus*, 52.

75   T. Alleyn, 'An Elegie on the Death of that Renowned Heroe Col Rainsborrow', 1648, 669.f.13[41].

76   *Mercurius Pragmaticus*, 14–21 November (London, 1648), E473[7]. See also Gentles, 'Political Funerals during the English Revolution', p. 218.

77   *Moderate Intelligencer*, Thursday 9–Thursday 16 November (London, 1648), E472[11].

78   *Mecurius Militaris*, 14–21 November 1648 (London), E473[8]. See also Peacock, 'Notes on the Life of Thomas Rainborowe'.

79   'In Memoriam Thomas Rainsborough, Pro Populo, & Parliamento' (London, 14 November 1648), 669 f.13 40. Reprinted in the *The Moderate*, 18, Tuesday 7–Tuesday 14 November (London, 1648), E472[4].

80 Although Lilburne himself used the term in a more neutral way when he described his supporters as 'we that were nick-named Levellers', in Lilburne, *Legall and Fundamental Liberties*, in Haller and Davies, *The Leveller Tracts 1647–53*, p. 420. The Quakers also appropriated a name that was first used pejoratively.

81 Gentles, 'Political Funerals during the English Revolution', p. 217.

82 'The Gallant Rights, Christian Priviledges, Solemn Institutions of the Sea -Green Order', 1648, 669.f.13[48].

83 The sheet was then reprinted with minor alterations as an eight-page pamphlet under the title *The Levellers Institutions for a Good People and Good Parliament*. Thomason dates his acquisition of this version as 30 November. See *The Levellers Institutions for a Good People and Good Parliament* (London, 1648), E474[4].

84 *Mercurius Militaris*, 8 May 1649, E554[13]. 'Nol' was a nickname for Cromwell. See also Jones, *Thomas Rainborowe*, p. 136.

85 Richard Overton, *The Baiting of the Great Bull of Bashan*, in Morton, *Freedom in Arms*, p. 287.

86 *A New Elegie in Memory of the Right Valiant, and most Renowned Souldier, late Admirall of the narrow Seas* (London, 1648), 669 f.13[45].

87 Southern, *Forlorn Hope*, p. 71. T. Brooks, *The Glorious Day of the Saints Appearance* (London, 1648), E474[7].

88 Brooks, *The Glorious Day of the Saints Appearance*.

89 L. S. Jones, *Colonel Thomas Rainsborough, Wapping's Most Famous Soldier* (History of Wapping Trust, n.d.), p. 15.

90 *The Moderate*, 19, Tuesday 14–Tuesday 21 November 1648, E473[1].

91 *Remonstrance of the regiment of the late Col. Rainsborough to his Excellency, for the revenge of their Colonells death* (London, 1648), E473[3].

92 *Remonstrance of the regiment of the late Col. Rainsborough*.

93 *CJ*, Vol. 6, p. 87. See also Jones, *Thomas Rainborowe*, p. 135.

94 C. Firth and G. Davies, *Regimental History of Cromwell's Army* (Oxford: Oxford University Press, 1940), pp. 577, 579.

95 R. Ashton, *Counter Revolution: The Second Civil War and its Origins, 1646–8* (New Haven: Yale University Press, 1994), pp. 122–3.

96 Ashton, *Counter Revolution*, pp. 132–9.

97 Ashton, *Counter Revolution*, p. 157.

98 *Mecurius Pragmaticus*, 28, 3–10 October 1648, E.466[11].

99 N. Carlin, 'Petitions and Revolution in England, September 1648–January 1649'. I am extremely grateful to Norah Carlin for letting me read this unpublished study.

100   Carlin, 'Petitions and Revolution in England', pp. 7–8.

101   Carlin, 'Petitions and Revolution in England', p. 8.

102   Ashton, *Counter Revolution*, pp. 128–32. Carlin, 'Petitions and Revolution in England, p. 11.

103   *To His Excellency The Lord Fairfax . . . The Humble Petition or remonstrance of the Well affected Inhabitants of the County of Rutland* (London, 1648), 669.f.13[47].

104   *Two petitions Presented to His Excellency the Lord Fairfax . . . by the Officers and Soldiers commanded by Colonel Hewson* (London, 1648), E473(23).

105   Carlin, 'Petitions and Revolution in England', p. 20. Although it is not clear whether this figure of eleven petitions supportive of the Levellers relates to the total of sixteen regimental petitions or to the total of twenty-nine regimental and garrison petitions. Either way it does not seem to justify Carlin's passing remark that Leveller agitation 'had a limited role in politicizing the army at this stage', especially as not all influence will have resulted in explicit declarations of support in petitions.

106   Gentles, *The New Model Army*, pp. 271, 267–8.

107   *The Declarations and Humble representations of the Officers and Soldiers in Colonel Scroops, Colonel Sanders and Col. Wautons Regiment* (London 1648), E475(24), pp. 4–5. The petition of Wauton's (Walton's) regiment is the one which reproduces the demands of the Levellers' petition.

108   *A Petition From Severall Regiments of the Army . . .* (London, 1648), E470[32].

109   See P. Crawford, 'Charles Stuart, That Man of Blood', *Journal of British Studies*, 16.2 (Spring 1977), p. 45.

110   Carlin, 'Petitions and Revolution in England', p. 18.

111   *A Petition From Severall Regiments of the Army . . .* (London, 1648), E470[32], reproduced in *The Moderate*, 18, Tuesday 7–14 November (London, 1648).

112   *The humble Petition of the Officers of Colonell Overtons Regiment, now in the garrison of Berwick* (London, 1648), E473[3]. See also *The Moderate*, 19, Tuesday 14–Tuesday 21 November 1648.

113   A. Brady, 'Dying with Honour: Literary Propaganda and the Second Civil War', *Journal of Military History* 70 (January 2006), p. 27.

114   Rushworth, 'Proceedings in Parliament from November 1 to December 1, 1648', pp. 1281–1314.

115   Lilburne, *Legall and Fundamental Liberties*, in Haller and Davies, *The Leveller Tracts 1647–53*, p. 417.

116   *Several Petitions Presented to his Excellency the Lord Fairfax ... together with Lieut. Gen. Cromwels Letter to his Excellency concerning the same* (1648), E474[5]. Also see S. R. Gardiner, pp. 250–1.

117   *Several Petitions Presented to his Excellency the Lord Fairfax ... together with Lieut. Gen. Cromwels Letter to his Excellency concerning the same* (1648), E474[5] pp. 3, 6, 7.

118   See Gentles, *The New Model Army,* p. 268.

119   *A Remonstrance or Declaration of the Army: presented to the House of Commons on Munday Novemb.20.1648* (London), E473[3].

120   *Mecurius Militaris,* 14–21 November 1648 (London), E473[8].

13. Defeat in Victory

1   The best account of the purge remains D. Underdown, *Pride's Purge* (Oxford: Oxford University Press, 1971), esp. Ch. 9.

2   D. Underdown, *Pride's Purge* (Oxford: Oxford University Press, 1971), pp. 150–1. J. Lilburne, *Legall and Fundamental Liberties* (London, 1649), E567[1], pp. 33–4.

3   Lilburne, *Legall and Fundamental Liberties,* pp. 34–7.

4   Lilburne's account of these events in *Legall and Fundamental Liberties* was written later in 1648, after the final breach with the Independents, and it reads Ireton's actions through this lens. But at the time Lilburne, though wary of the Grandees because of previous experience, was more accepting of the good faith of Ireton and other senior officers. On this argument see F. Henderson, 'Drafting the Officer's *Agreement of the People,* 1648–49: A Reappraisal', in P. Baker and E. Vernon (eds.), *The Agreements of the People, the Levellers and the Constitutional Crisis of the English Revolution* (Basingstoke: Palgrave Macmillan, 2012), pp. 163–95; and B. Taft, 'The Council of Officers' *Agreement of the People,* 1648/9', *Historical Journal,* 28.1 (March 1985), pp. 169–85.

5   The other MPs were Alexander Rigby, Thomas Chaloner and Thomas Scot, although only Marten seems to have attended. The Independents were Robert Tichborne, John White, Danial Taylor and Richard Price from Goodwin's church. The army would send any four of Ireton, Colonel (and MP) William Constable, Colonel Matthew Tomlinson, Colonel John Barkstead, Lieutenant Colonel Thomas Kelsey, and Captain William Packer. See Lilburne, *Legall and Fundamental Liberties,* pp. 37–8.

6   Lilburne, *Legall and Fundamental Liberties,* pp. 38–9. Underdown, *Pride's Purge,* pp. 140–1, and generally Ch. 6.

7   Taft, 'The Council of Officers' *Agreement of the People*', pp. 173–4. B. Taft, 'From Reading to Whitehall: Henry Ireton's Journey', in M. Mendle (ed.), *The Putney Debates of 1647: The Army, the Levellers and the English state* (Cambridge: Cambridge University Press, 2001), pp. 191–2. Henderson, 'Drafting the Officer's *Agreement of the People*', p. 163.

8   A. S. P. Woodhouse (ed.), *Puritanism and Liberty: Being the Army Debates (1647–49) from the Clarke Manuscripts*, 3rd edn (London: Everyman, 1986), pp. 125–78. Henderson, 'Drafting the Officer's *Agreement of the People*', p. 169. Lilburne, *Legall and Fundamental Liberties*, pp. 38–9.

9   Taft, 'The Council of Officers' *Agreement of the People*', pp. 177–8.

10   Henderson, 'Drafting the Officer's *Agreement of the People*'. C. Polizzotto, 'What Really Happened at the Whitehall Debates? A New Source', *Historical Journal*, 57.1 (2014), pp. 33–51.

11   Woodhouse, *Puritanism and Liberty*, p. 148.

12   Lilburne, *Legall and Fundamental Liberties*, pp. 39–40. J. Lilburne, *A Plea for Common-Right* (London, 1648), E536[22].

13   Taft, 'The Council of Officers' *Agreement of the People*', pp. 178–9.

14   J. Lilburne, R. Overton, W. Walwyn and T. Prince, *A Manifestation*, in A. L. Morton, *Freedom in Arms: A Selection of Leveller Writings* (London: Lawrence and Wishart, 1975), p. 258.

15   *CJ*, Vol. 6, 20 January 1649 (London, 1802), p. 122.

16   *An Exact and Impartial Accompt of The Indictment, Arraignment, Trial . . . of Twenty Nine Regicides* (London, 1679), p. 57.

17   *CJ*, Vol. 6, 7 February, 14 February 1649 (London, 1802), pp. 133, 141.

18   *The Writings of William Walwyn* (ed. J. R. McMichael and B. Taft) (Athens: University of Georgia Press, 1989), p. 37. H. N. Brailsford, *The Levellers and the English Revolution* (ed. C. Hill) (Nottingham: Spokesman, 1961), pp. 159–60.

19   For more on these groups see, for instance, J. Gurney, *Gerrard Winstanley: The Digger's Life and Legacy* (London: Pluto, 2013); J. Gurney, *Brave Community: The Digger Movement in the English Revolution* (Manchester: Manchester University Press, 2012); N. Smith, *A Collection of Ranter Writings: Spiritual Liberty and Sexual Freedom in the English Revolution* (London: Pluto Press, 2014); B. Capp, *The Fifth Monarchy Men* (London: Faber, 1972). A. Hessayon, 'Early Modern Communism: The Diggers and the Community of Goods', *Journal for the Study of Radicalism*, 3.2 (2009), pp. 1–50.

20   Lilburne, *Legall and Fundamental Liberties*, p. 46.

21   *CJ*, Vol. 6, 19 March 1649 (London, 1802), pp. 167–9. *CSPV*, April 1649, Vol. 28 (London, 1927), pp. 93–7. W. Bray, *Innocency and the Blood of the Slain Souldiers* (London, 1649), E568[12], pp. 11–16.

22   W. Bray, *Appeal for Justice*, in H. Cary, *Memorials of the Great Civil War*, Vol. 2 (London: Henry Colburn, 1842), pp. 141–8. C. Cheeseman (or Chisman), *The Lamb Contending with the Lion* (London, 1649), E563[10]. J. Naylier, *The Foxes Craft Discovered* (London, 1649), pp. 5–8. J. Naylier, *The New made Colonel* (London, 1649), E552[10].

23   *CJ*, Vol. 6, 27 March 1649 (London, 1802), TNA: PRO, SP25/62 f.125, pp. 174–5.

24   T. Varax (Clement Walker), *The Triall of Lieu. Colonell John Lilburne* (London, 1649), p. 11. J. Lilburne, R. Overton and T. Prince, *A Picture of the Councel of State* (London, 1649), E550[14], pp. 1, 2–3, 15, 26–33, 49, 51.Overton's narrative is available in Morton, *Freedom in Arms*, pp. 199–225. *The Moderate*, 17–24 April 1649.

25   M. Tolmie, *The Triumph of the Saints: The Separate Churches of London 1616–1649* (Cambridge: Cambridge University Press, 1977), Ch. 8.

26   Tolmie, *The Triumph of the Saints*, pp. 181–3. J. Lilburne's postscript in *A Picture of the Councel of State* (London, 1649), E550[14], p. 24.

27   *CJ*, Vol. 6, 2 April 1649 (London, 1802), pp. 177–8. *CJ*, Vol. 6, 11 April 1649 (London, 1802), pp. 183–4. *Mercurius Pragmaticus*, 17–14 April 1649. Brailsford, *The Levellers and the English Revolution*, p. 486.

28   *The Moderate*, 17–24 April 1649. *CJ*, Vol. 6, 18 April 1649 (London, 1802), pp. 188–90.

29   The lengthy London petition was reproduced in *The Moderate*, 1–8 May 1649, which claimed that 'several Counties' presented petitions in Lilburne's favour on 2 May, although the Commons Journal records petitions from London and Essex. See *CJ*, Vol. 6, 2 May 1649 (London, 1802), pp. 199–200.

30   *The Humble Petition of divers wel-affected Women* (London, 1649), E551[14], p. 8.

31   *Mercurius Pragmaticus*, 17–14 April 1649. *Mercurius Militaris*, 8 May 1649, E554[13]. *The Humble Petition of divers wel-affected Women* (London, 1649), E551[14], pp. 4–5. A. Plowden, *In a Free Republic* (Stroud: Sutton, 2006), p. 49.

32   Brailsford, *The Levellers and the English Revolution*, p. 487.

33   *Petition of the Women, Affectors and Approvers of a Petition of Sept. 11, 1648* (London, 1649), 669.f.14[27]. Available in Woodhouse, *Puritanism and Liberty*, pp. 367–9. Brailsford, *The Levellers and the English Revolution*, p. 317

34   *The thankfull acknowledgement . . .* (London, 6 May 1649).

35   *The Resolved Apprentices . . .* (London, 17 May 1649), 669.f.14[32] The biblical reference is to Numbers 16, in which Korah leads a revolt against Moses.

36   *The Moderate*, 1–8 May 1649. J. Lilburne, *Apologetical Narration*

(Amsterdam, 1652), Wing L2083, p. 71; Lilburne, Walwyn, Prince and Overton, *A Manifestation*, pp. 248–59.

37   D. Underdown, 'The Parliamentary Diary of John Boys, 1647–8', *Historical Research*, 39 (1966), p. 153.

38   *The English Souldiers Standard*, in Morton, *Freedom in Arms*, p. 239.

39   *The Souldiers Demand* (Bristol, 1649), pp. 12–13.

40   T. Prince, *The Silken Independents Snare Broken* (London, 1649), E560[24], p. 7. N. Carlin, 'The Levellers and the Conquest of Ireland in 1649', *Historical Journal*, 30.2 (June 1987), pp. 269–88, esp. p. 278 on Harris's views.

41   A. Southern, *Forlorn Hope: Soldier Radicals of the Seventeenth Century* (Lewes: The Book Guild, 2001), pp. 73–7.

42   I. Gentles, *The New Model Army in England, Ireland and Scotland, 1645–1653* (Oxford: Oxford University Press, 1992), p. 326.

43   *A True Narrative of the late Mutiny made by several Troopers of Captain Savage's Troop* (London, 1649), E552[18], p. 4.

44   *A True Narrative of the late Mutiny*, p. 6.

45   *The Impartiall Intelligencer*, 29, 25 April–2 May (London, 1649), E529[29], p. 69.

46   *The Justice of the Army* . . . (London, 1649), E558[14], p. 13. *Impartiall Intelligencer*, 29, 25 April–2 May, p. 69.

47   *A True Narrative of the late Mutiny*, p. 8–11.

48   *The Army's Martyr, or a more ful relation of the barbarous and illegall proceedings of the court martial at Whitehall on Mr Robert Lockier* (London, 1649), E552[11], p. 5.

49   'To his Excellency Thomas Lord Fairfax Generall of the English Forces', in *The Army's Martyr*, p. 13.

50   *The Army's Martyr*, p. 10.

51   *A Perfect Diurnall*, 30 April–7 May 1649 (London), p. 2469. *The Moderate*, 24 April–1 May 1649 (London).

52   *The Moderate*, 24 April–1 May 1649 (London). *Impartiall Intelligencer*, 29, 25 April–2 May 1649 (London), E529[29], p. 72.

53   *The Moderate*, 24 April–1 May 1649 (London). I. Gentles, 'Political Funerals during the English Revolution', in S. Porter (ed.), *London and the Civil War* (Basingstoke: Palgrave Macmillan, 1996), pp. 219–21.

54   *The Justice of the Army*, p. 11.

55   Gentles, *The New Model Army*, p. 326.

56   *The Moderate*, 24 April–1 May 1649 (London).

57   Gentles, *The New Model Army*, pp. 328–9.

58   *A Modest Narrative of Intelligence* . . ., 5–12 May 1649 (London, 1649), p. 42. The wooden horse was a triangular wooden spar mounted

horizontally, like a builder's trestle. Those being punished were forced to sit astride it, so inflicting maximum pain to the genitals.

59   *The Moderate*, 1–8 May 1649. *The Leveller's (falsly so called) Vindicated* (London, 1649), E571[11], pp. 3–4.

60   *The Unanimous Declaration of Colonel Scope's and Commissary Gen. Ireton's Regiments* (1649), E555[4]. *The Moderate*, 1–8 May 1649 (London).

61   *The Moderate*, 8–15 May 1649 (London). *Mercurius Pragmaticus*, 8–15 May 1649 (London). Gentles, *The New Model Army*, p. 330.

62   F. White, *A true relation of the proceedings in the businesse of Burford* (London, 1649), E574[26], p. 2.

63   *A Modest Narrative of Intelligence*, 5–12 May 1649 (London), pp. 45, 47. B. Manning, *The Far Left in the English Revolution* (London: Bookmarks, 1999), pp. 92–3.

64   W. Thompson, *A True and Impartial Relation . . .* (London, 1647[1648]), p. 7. W. Thompson, *Englands Standard Advanced* (London, 1649).

65   *A Modest Narrative of Intelligence*, 5–12 May 1649 (London), p. 47.

66   *The Leveller's (falsly so called) Vindicated*, p. 4. *The Moderate*, 8–15 May 1649 (London). P. Gregg, *Free-Born John*, pp. 278–9. Also *England's Standard Advanced*, E553[2]; and *A Modest Narrative of Intelligence*, 5–12 May 1649, E555[8].

67   *Mercurius Pragmaticus*, 8–15 May 1649.

68   *The Declaration of Lieutenant-Generall Crumwell Concerning the Levellers* (London, 1649), E555[12], pp. 1–2.

69   *The Declaration of Lieutenant-Generall Crumwell*, p. 3. S. R. Gardiner, *History of the Commonwealth and Protectorate*, Vol. 1, 1649–1650 (Aldestrop: Windrush, 1988), p. 53.

70   White, *A true relation of the proceedings in the businesse of Burford*, p, 7.

71   *Kingdomes Weekly Intelligencer*, 15–22 May 1649 (London), p. 1363. Oxfordshire Record Office (Oxford), MS D.D.Par. Burford, c.1, Burford parish register of baptisms, marriages and burials, 1612–1715. This records 'a soldier slaine at yᵉ Crowne buried yᵉ 15°of May' (15 May 1649). I am grateful to Ariel Hessayon for this reference. R. L. Greaves and R. Zaller, *Biographical Dictionary of British Radicals in the Seventeenth Century* (Brighton: Harvester, 1984), 'Eyres, William'. Gregg, *Free-Born John*, pp. 280–1.

72   White, *A true relation of the proceedings in the businesse of Burford*, p. 8.

73   Oxfordshire Record Office (Oxford), MS D.D.Par. Burford, c.1, Burford parish register of baptisms, marriages and burials, 1612–1715. This records 'three soldiers shot to death in Burford churchyard buried May 17 (1649). I am grateful to Ariel Hessayon for this reference.

74   *Perfect Occurrences*, 18–25 May 1649 (London), pp. 1053–5.

75   *The Declaration of Lieutenant-Generall Crumwell Concerning the Levellers* (London, 1649), pp. 4–6.

76   *A Modest Narrative of Intelligence*, 5–12 May 1649 (London), p. 45.

77   *The Moderate*, 1–8 May 1649 (London).

78   *Mercurius Pragmaticus*, 8–15 May 1649 (London), E555[14], pp. 27, 29–30.

79   B. Manning, *1649: The Crisis of the English Revolution* (London: Bookmarks, 1992), pp. 201–7.

80   C. H. Firth and G. Davies, *Regimental History of Cromwell's Army* (Oxford: Clarendon, 1940), pp. 579–80.

81   *The Moderate*, 24 April–1 May 1649 (London).*The Moderate*, 1–8 May 1649 (London).

82   *Perfect Occurrences*, 18–25 May 1649 (London), p. 1064. J. Hackluyt, *Mercurius Militaris*, 22–9 May 1649 (London), p. 8.

83   BL, Stowe MS. 189 f.53, 'Articles against Rede exhibited by Poole, 29 March 1651'. See also in A. R. Bayley, *The Great Civil War in Dorset* (Taunton: Wessex Press, 1910), pp, 343–5. H. Reece, *The Army in Cromwellian England 1649–1660* (Oxford: Oxford University Press, 2013), pp. 129–30. D. Underdown, *Revel, Riot and Rebellion* (Oxford: Oxford University Press, 1985), p. 235.

84   R. Baxter, *Reliquiae Baxterianae* (London, 1696), Wing B1370, p. 61. Gentles, *The New Model Army*, p. 346.

85   *Perfect Occurrences*, 18–25 May 1649 (London), pp. 1063–4.

86   *Kingdomes Weekly Intelligencer*, 18–25 September 1649. *A Perfect Summary of Exact Passages of Parliament*, 17–24 September 1649, E533. R. W. Stent, 'Thomas Rainsborough and the Army Levellers' (M.Phil, University of London, 1975), Vol. 2, p. 342. C. H. Firth, 'The Mutiny of Col. Ingoldsby's Regiment at Oxford in September, 1649', *Proceedings of the Oxford Architectural and Historical Society*, new series, 30 (1884), pp. 235–7.

87   Firth, 'The Mutiny of Col. Ingoldsby's Regiment', pp. 238, 241.

88   *The Moderate*, 11–18 September 1649. Firth, 'The Mutiny of Col. Ingoldsby's Regiment', p. 242.

89   *The Moderate Intelligencer*, 6–13 September 1649.

90   *The Moderate*, 11–18 September 1649, carried Captain Wagstaff's long report to the Commons, the most detailed account of the mutiny. See also Firth, 'The Mutiny of Col. Ingoldsby's Regiment', pp. 239–41, 243–4, 246. *CJ*, Vol. 6, 11 September 1649 (London, 1802), p. 293.

91   *The Moderate*, 18–25 September 1649. *Perfect Weekly Account*, 19–26 September 1649, pp. 611–12. Firth, 'The Mutiny of Col. Ingoldsby's Regiment', 244–5. *CJ*, Vol. 6, 11 September 1649 (London, 1802), p. 293. *Mercurius Pragmaticus*, 10–17 September, 1649, pp. 3–4.

92   *The Moderate*, 4–11 September 1649. *Perfect Weekly Account*, 19–26 September 1649, p. 613. *The Moderate*, 18–25 September 1649. *The Moderate*, 11–18 September 1649.

93   H. P. (Henry Parker), *A Letter of Due Censure and Redargution* (London, 1650), E603[14], p. 39. Interestingly, given Parker's attempts throughout this pamphlet to portray Lilburne as in league with royalists, he admits here that there are a few Lilburne supporters in that camp.

94   Varax, *The Triall of Lieu. Colonell John Lilburne*, pp. 13, 154–67. P. Gregg, *Free-Born John: A Biography of John Lilburne* (London: Dent, 1986), p. 283.

95   On the regime's plot to entrap Lilburne and its fears of Leveller–royalist cooperation, see J. Heron, 'The Trial of John Lilburne October 1649: A New Perspective' (MA thesis, Canterbury Christchurch University, 2013), pp. 24, 33–4.

96   J. Lilburne, *Truths Victory over Tyrants* (London, 1649), E579[12], p. 4. Gregg, *Free-Born John*, p. 295.

97   Varax, *The Triall of Lieu. Colonell John Lilburne*, pp. 1–4, 22, 27–8, 38, 41–7, 98 (sequentially this is p. 114, but the pagination become irregular at this point), E584[9].

98   Lilburne, *Truths Victory over Tyrants*, p. 1. Heron, 'The Trial of John Lilburne', pp. 27–48. The dispute with the jury was both over objections to some of its members by Lilburne and separately over the misrepresenta-tion of the jury's views by one of the judges in court. See *The Second Part of the Triall of Lieu. Col. John Lilburn* (London, 1649/1650), E598[12]. This contains the material also published separately as *The First Dayes Proceedings at the Tryal of Lieu. Col. John Lilburne* (London, n.d.), Wing F975. John Hinde used his notes to prove to Judge Jermyn that he had misrepresented the jurors' views in court.

99   Heron, 'The Trial of John Lilburne', p. 54. Varax, *The Triall of Lieu. Colonell John Lilburne*, pp. 70–2.

100 Varax, *The Triall of Lieu. Colonell John Lilburne*, pp. 72–6.

101 Varax, *The Triall of Lieu. Colonell John Lilburne*, pp. 78–80.

102 Varax, *The Triall of Lieu. Colonell John Lilburne*, pp. 101–2, 106.

103 Varax, *The Triall of Lieu. Colonell John Lilburne*, pp. 101–11.

104 Lilburne, *Truths Victory over Tyrants*, p. 6. Varax, *The Triall of Lieu. Colonell John Lilburne*, p. 120.

105   Varax, *The Triall of Lieu. Colonell John Lilburne*, pp. 141–1. Clement
        Walker's note cites Henry Marten's words to the jurors of Berkshire as the
        precedent for this elevation of the jury's powers; see p. 123.

106   Lilburne, *Truths Victory over Tyrants*, pp. 6–8. Varax, *The Triall of Lieu.
        Colonell John Lilburne*, pp. 150–3. Gregg, *Free-Born John*, p. 302.

107   H. P., *A Letter of Due Censure and Redargution*, pp. 23, 37.

108   M. Mendle, 'Henry Parker', *ODNB*. T. May, *An Anatomy of Lieut. Col. John
        Lilburne's Spirit and Pamphlets* (London, 1649), E575[21]. J. Jones, *Jurors
        Judges of Law and Fact* (London, 1650), E1414[2], pp. 60, 65, 93.

14. Lieutenant Colonel John Rede's Last Stand

1   On the later careers of some Levellers see P. Gregg, *Free-Born John: A biog-
      raphy of John Lilburne* (London: Dent, 1986) Chs. 26–9; *The Writings of
      William Walwyn* (ed. J. R. McMichael and B. Taft) (Athens: University of
      Georgia Press, 1989), pp. 43–9; B. J. Gibbons, 'Richard Overton', *ODNB*; S.
      Barber, *A Revolutionary Rogue: Henry Marten and the English Republic*
      (Stroud: Sutton, 2000), pp. 26–46; M. Ashley, *John Wildman, Plotter and
      Postmaster: A Study of the English Republican Movement in the Seventeenth
      Century* (London: Jonathan Cape, 1947). J. Holstun, *Ehud's Dagger: Class
      Struggle in the English Revolution* (London: Verso, 2000), Ch. 8; P. Baker,
      'William Larner', *ONDB*. W. Bray, *A Plea for the Peoples Fundamental
      Liberties* (London, 1659), Wing B4306; W. Bray, *A Plea for the Peoples
      Good Old Cause* (London, 1659), Wing (2nd edn) B4307.

2   This chapter is based on my earlier study of John Rede. See J. Rees,
      'Lieutenant-Colonel John Rede: West Country Leveller and Baptist
      Pioneer', *Seventeenth Century*, 30.3 (2015), pp. 317–37.

3   There has previously been no accurate dating of John Rede's life. His date
      of birth here is based on his marriage license to Ann Errington in 1636 at
      the age of twenty-one, giving his date of birth as 1615. See Wiltshire
      County Archives, Marriage Licence Allegations, 1632–1636, D1/62/1/7.
      The date of his death is taken from two sources. The first is John Rede's
      will, which is not lost, as some accounts contend, but which was made in
      1708 and went to probate in 1710. See TNA, PRO, prob. 11/517. The
      second is the record on Rede's burial in the Register of the Parish of
      Idmiston (Wiltshire County Archives, R1098/3). The entry for Rede's
      burial in November 1710 is recorded on the first blank page of the register
      and not in the main chronological record. This is presumably because

Rede was a dissenter. The transcribed record incorrectly records this as the death of the wife of John Rede. See Wiltshire Family History Society, 'The Parish Registers and Bishops Transcripts, Idmiston including Porton, Baptisms 1584–1837 and Burials 1577–1837', p. 71. But examination of the original parish register clearly shows that this burial is in fact of John Rede himself. The transcribed record has now been corrected. I am grateful to Margaret Moles, Wiltshire County archivist, for verifying this change.

4   BL, Stowe MS 189 f.53: 'An Abridgement of M. Scott's Confession and Discovery of his Transactions made immediately after the Restoration in 1660'. This key source is a little mysterious. It is a handwritten note at the end of the transcription of Thomas Scot's testimony. But it cannot be from Scot since he died at the Restoration and the material on Rede contains information about him from immediately before his death in 1710. All we can say is that it is clearly written by someone who knows Rede well and is accurate about his dates and politics as far as we know from other sources. It was clearly included in the Scot confession because, like his material, it too contained information about a republican and radical.

5   BL, Stowe MS 189 f.53. C. Reade and R. Reade Macmullen, *A record of the Redes of Barton Court, Berks, with a Short Précis of Other Lines of the Name* (Hereford: Jakeman and Carver, 1899), p. 127. Elizabeth may have been a member of the Baynton family of (unreliable) parliamentarian MP Sir Edward Baynton, for whom see A. Hooper, *Turncoats and Renegades* (Oxford: Oxford University Press, 2012), p. 52. Rede served as a JP with Edward Baynton in the 1650s; see I. Slocombe (ed.), *Wiltshire Quarter Sessions Order Book, 1642–1654* (Salisbury: Wiltshire Record Society, 2014), p. 322.

6   There was, for instance, more than one John Rede (or Read or Reade) in the army. John Rede is sometimes confused with Thomas Reade, also a lieutenant colonel and also with Anabaptist sympathies. To add to the confusion there is also a Captain Robert Reade, possibly a relative of John, in the same regiment as Thomas Reade. Firth and Davies have shown that a Major Read was appointed to Aldrich's, soon to be Lloyd's, regiment of foot by the Lords on 18 March 1645. Sprigge cites a Major Read, later lieutenant colonel, as serving in Lloyd's regiment and records that he was injured at Taunton. This was in the action around Taunton in 1644–5 when it was held by Robert Blake for Parliament. This is Thomas Reade according to Firth and Davies, and this seems likely as it was Thomas, not John as some accounts claim, who was with this regiment in Wales spreading the Baptists message. See C. Firth and G. Davies, *Regimental History of Cromwell's Army* (Oxford: Clarendon Press, 1940), pp. 384–7. *LJ*, , Vol. 7: 1644 (1767–1830), pp.

277–9. P. Young and R. Holmes, *The English Civil War* (London: Eyre Methuen, 1974), pp. 251–2. J. Sprigge, *Anglia Rediviva: Englands Recovery* (Oxford: Oxford University Press, 1854, originally 1647), p. 329. The 'John Rede of Devizes' who, in a bequest originally dated 1699, left £100 to Devizes Baptist Church is the same as John Rede of Porton, as can be seen from later discussion of this document below. See also E. Crittall (ed.), 'The Borough of Devizes: Religious and Cultural History', *A History of the County of Wiltshire*, Vol. 10 (Victoria County History, 1975), pp. 285–314.

7   J. H. P. Pafford (ed.), *Accounts of the Parliamentary Garrisons of Great Chalfield and Malmesbury, 1645–1646* (Devizes: Wiltshire Record Society, 1940), p. 15.

8   *Baptist Quarterly*, 11.1–2, January–April 1942. This article confuses John Rede and Colonel Thomas Rede. See also T. Maclachlan, *The Civil War in Wiltshire* (Salisbury: Rowan Books, 1997), pp. 203–6.

9   C. H. Firth (ed.), *The Memoirs of Edmund Ludlow*, Vol. 1 (Oxford: Clarendon Press, 1894), pp. 112–13. Blair Worden has shown that much religious material was excised from Ludlow's memoirs by later editors, but this does not throw any doubt on Ludlow's account of his military engagements. B. Worden, *Roundhead Reputations* (London: Penguin, 2011) Chs. 1–4.

10   Firth, *The Memoirs of Edmund Ludlow*, Vol. 1, pp. 112–13.

11   *Two Letters of his Excellencie Sir Thomas Fairfax* (London, 1647).

12   *An Ordinance of the Lords and Commons . . . For the Raising of Moneys* (London, 1647), Wing E2020A, p. 31. W. Clarke, *The Clarke Papers* (London: Royal Historical Society, 1992), pp. 341–2. I am grateful to Ariel Hessayon for the suggestion that it may have been John Rede who spoke at Putney. The entries in the Clarke Papers all refer only to Lieutenant Colonel Read or Reade, but both John and Thomas Rede held this rank. Both John and Thomas often had their names rendered as 'Reade' so nothing can be assumed from this.

13   M. Cary, *A Word in Season to the Kingdom of England* (London, 1647), Friends Meeting House Library, London, see pp. 5, 6, 7, 11.

14   See B. Capp, 'Mary Cary', *ODNB*; and C. Gheeraert-Graffeuille, 'Tyranny and Tyrannicide in Mid-Seventeenth-Century England: A Woman's Perspective?' (2009), available at etudes-episteme.org/2e/?tyrants-and-tyrannicide-in-mid, accessed 11 November 2014.

15   A connection well established in M. Tolmie, *The Triumph of the Saints: The Separate Churches of London 1616–1649* (Cambridge: Cambridge University Press, 1977); and S. Wright, *The Early English Baptists 1603–1649* (Woodbridge: Boydell, 2006). Although the fact that Rede was a Particular Baptist and not a General Baptist runs counter to Tolmie's view

that it was General Baptists who were more sympathetic to the Levellers and more likely to sustain Leveller sympathies after 1649.

16   BL, A Catalogue of the Lansdowne Manuscripts, Landsdowne MS, Vol. 155 f.270, p. 222.

17   I. Gentles, *The New Model Army in England, Scotland and Ireland, 1645–1653* (Oxford: Blackwell Publishers 1994), p. 198.

18   H. Reece, *The Cromwellian Army in England 1649–1660* (Oxford: Oxford University Press, 2013), p. 111.

19   G. Masterson, *A Declaration of Some Proceedings of Lt. Col. John Lilburne . . .*, E427[6], p. 40, BL, Stowe MS. 189. ff. 39–40. I am grateful to Frances Henderson for pointing out that only the last paragraph of the letter is written in Clarke's own hand, including, perhaps significantly, the message for Lockyer.

20   BL, Stowe MS. 189. ff. 39–40. It is possible that this is Leveller ally Nicolas Lockyer, an early advocate of sectarian congregations and one of the most active Agitators in the army, although it is equally possible it might be the Independent preacher of the same name. It is highly unlikely that it is Robert Lockyer the Leveller shot for his leadership of the Bishopsgate mutiny in 1649. R. W. Stent, 'Thomas Rainsborough and the Army Levellers' (M.Phil, University of London, 1975), Vol. 2, p. 339.

21   BL, Stowe MS. 189. f. 44.

22   *Mercurius Pragmaticus*, 1–8 August 1648, E457[11]. *Mercurius Pragmaticus*, 8–15 August 1648, E458[24].

23   *CJ*, 1646–8, Vol. 5, 12 August 1648.

24   C. Van Raalte, *Brownsea Island* (London: A. L. Humphreys, 1906), pp. 46–7. Van Raalte says that the committee's reply was to the previous governor, William Skutt, but this is a mistake. Rede had been governor since 1647 and the *Commons Journal* confirms that the correspondence is with Rede. *CJ*, 1646–8, Vol. 5, 12 August 1648.

25   *LJ*, 1648–9, Vol.10, 6 September 1648.

26   A. Thrush and J. P. Ferris (eds.), 'Robarts, Thomas (1568–1633), of Poole, Dorset', in *The History of Parliament: The House of Commons 1604–1629* (Cambridge: Cambridge University Press, 2010).

27   J. Sydenham, *The History of the Town and County of Poole* (London: Whittaker & Co., 1839), pp. 236–7. H. P. Smith, *The History of the Borough and County of the Town of Poole*, Vol. 2 (Poole: J. Looker, 1951), p. 142.

28   *CJ*, 1646–8, Vol. 5, 13 March 1647. Sydenham, *The History of the Town and County of Poole*, p. 128. Smith, *The History of the Borough and County of the Town of Poole*, Vol. 2, pp. 142–4.

29   Sydenham, *The History of the Town and County of Poole*, pp. 133, 199, 237. Smith, *The History of the Borough and County of the Town of Poole*, Vol. 2, p. 144.

30   G. Skutt, *A Letter from an Ejected Member of the House of Commons to Sir Jo. Evelyn* (London, 1648), E643[18]. The letter, dated 16 August 1648, is signed with the initials GS, and is attributed to George Skutt. Skutt is said to have been ejected at Pride's Purge, but clearly the letter is dated three months earlier. Skutt was not one of the eleven members secluded by the army in 1647, so the exact circumstances of his ejection remain unclear.

31   Skutt, *A Letter from an Ejected Member*, pp. 6, 24.

32   Skutt, *A Letter from an Ejected Member*, pp. 11, 14.

33   'Denis Bond', *ODNB*. L. M. G. Bond, 'A Transcript of "A Private Chronology of Denis Bond Esqre of Lutton in the Isle of Purbeck Made AD 1636 and 1640" with Notes by Thomas Bond' (1919), Dorset History Centre, D/53/1, pp. 30-1. Also see D. Underdown, *Fire from Heaven* (London: HarperCollins, 1992) in which the Bond family play a central role. G. Joyce, *A Letter or Epistle to all the well-minded People in England, Ireland, Wales and Scotland* (London, 1651), E637 [3], for Joyce's accurate allegation that Denis Bond's son was the recorder in Poole.

34   L. M. G. Bond, 'A Transcript of "A Private Chronology"', pp. 13, 21. Dorset History Centre, 'The Old Record Book', Admittance of Burgesses 11th day of March 1650, DC/PL/B/1/1/1, f. 119.

35   *CJ*, Vol. 6, 23 May 1649 (1802), pp. 214-16. *CJ*, Vol. 6, 2 June 1649 (1802), pp. 222-3. *LJ*, 1648-9, Vol. 10, 6 September 1648. C. R. B. Barrett (ed.), *Memoirs of the Binghams* (London: Spottiswoode, 1915), see Appendix, 'Colonel John Bingham', pp. 175-8. Smith, *The History of the Borough and County of the Town of Poole*, Vol. 2, pp. 148-50.

36   *CJ*, Vol. 6 (1802), pp. 557-8.

37   *Humble Petition and Representation of the Officers and Souldiers of the Garrisons of Portsmouth, Southsea Castle . . .* (1649), 669.f.13 [71]. Also see Reece, *The Cromwellian Army in England*, pp.111.

38   *Humble Petition and Representation of the Officers and Souldiers of the Garrisons of Portsmouth, Southsea Castle.*

39   *CJ*, 1648-51, Vol. 6, 17 January 1649.

40   Dorset History Centre, 'The Old Record Book', ff. 117-18. See also Sydenham, *The History of the Town and County of Poole*, pp. 303-5. Smith, *The History of the Borough and County of the Town of Poole*, Vol. 2, pp. 158-9. Tolmie, *The Triumph of the Saints*, p. 158.

41   J. Lilburne, *A Copy of a Letter . . . to a Friend* (London, 1645), E296[5], p. 15.

42   J. Turner, *Choice Experiences of the Kind Dealings of God . . .* (London, 1653), Wing T3294. See the preface by Jane Turner herself as well as Gardner's introduction. Also see A. Laurence, *Parliamentary Army Chaplains 1642–1651* (Woodbridge: Boydell, 1990), p. 128. Firth and Davies, *Regimental History of Cromwell's Army*, pp. 354–8. Captain John Turner, Jane's husband, was a Baptist and provided a third preface to her pamphlet. See Tolmie, *The Triumph of the Saints*, p. 158.

43   Wright, *The Early English Baptists*, pp. 92, 93 n. 65.

44   J. Turner, *Choice Experiences of the Kind Dealings of God . . .* (London, 1653), Wing T3294. Another possible link between Rede and Gardner exists if the army officer Robert Reade is the same Robert Reade who is related to John. Both fought in the West Country; both were Particular Baptists. Robert Reade's wife circulated Baptist pamphlets in the army and he was stationed in Newcastle where John Gardner met Jane Turner and her husband Captain John Turner. Robert Reade and John Turner were partners in a land deal in Cumberland in 1651. See the will of John Rede's father, Edward Rede, for the existence of Robert Rede, Edward's brother and John's uncle, at TNA/PRO B11/169/484. But it also appears from the will of Robert Rede of Stratford-sub-Castle, Salisbury, dated February 1675 (TNA/PRO 11/354/32), that John Rede also had a brother called Robert. In this will Robert left John Rede land in Poole. John's brother Robert Rede was a member of the Church of England when he wrote his will. Robert Rede the army officer rose from a captain to a lieutenant colonel. See Firth and Davies, *Regimental History of Cromwell's Army*, Vol. 1, pp. 388–9, 396. Wright, *The Early English Baptists*, pp. 188–9.

45   'The information of George Morris of the tower of London gent. taken the 26th day of May 1656', *A Collection of the State Papers of John Thurloe, Volume 5, May 1656 - January 1657*, ed. Thomas Birch (London, 1742), pp. 60–72.

46   Dorset History Centre, 'The Old Record Book', ff. 117–18. See also Sydenham, *The History of the Town and County of Poole*, pp. 303–4.

47   Dorset History Centre, 'The Old Record Book', ff. 117–18. Sydenham, *The History of the Town and County of Poole*, p. 304.

48   Sydenham, *The History of the Town and County of Poole*, p. 305.

49   BL, Stowe MS. 189. f. 52. See also the account in F. Henderson (ed.), *The Clarke Papers*, Vol. 5, pp. 21–6, 38–43.

50   BL, Stowe MS. 189. f. 53.

51   H. Reece, *The Army in Cromwellian England 1649–1660* (Oxford: Oxford University Press, 2013), pp. 130–1.

52   The report on local support for Rede is in *The Moderate*, 40, 10–17 April 1649, E550[28]. The report on poverty in Poole in in *The Moderate*, 39, 3–10 April 1649, E550[10]. In all there are some eighteen editions of *The Moderate* which contain reports from the south coast. A. R. Bayley, *The Great Civil War in Dorset* (Taunton: The Wessex Press, 1910), pp. 339–42.

53   *A Moderate Intelligence*, 1, 17–24 May 1649, *Perfect Occurrences*, 18–25 May 1649 (London), p. 1064. J. Hackluyt, *Mercurius Militaris*, 22–9 May 1649 (London, 1649), p. 8. From this it seems G. E. Alymer was mistaken in saying that Joyce had no part in the mutinies of 1649 in his *ODNB* entry for George Joyce.

54   *The Moderate*, 62, 11–18 September 1649, E574[4]. *The Moderate*, 63, 18–25 September 1649.

55   *Kingdomes Weekly Intelligencer*, Tuesday 18–Tuesday 25 September 1649, E574[23]. *A Perfect Summary of Exact Passages of Parliament*, Monday 17–Monday 24 September 1649, E533. *The Moderate*, 62, Tuesday 11–Tuesday 18 September 1649 (London). C. H. Firth, 'The Mutiny of Ingoldsby's Regiment at Oxford in September, 1649', *Proceedings of the Oxford Architectural and Historical Society* (Oxford, 1884), pp. 241, 243, 245–6. Stent, 'Thomas Rainsborough and the Army Levellers', Vol. 2, p. 342. H. Reece, *The Army in Cromwellian England 1649–1660*, pp.121–32.

56   Henderson, *The Clarke Papers*, Vol. 5, pp. 16–17, 37–9.

57   TNA, SP 25/96 f.123. See Henderson, *The Clarke Papers*, Vol. 5, pp. 21–6, 38–43.

58   Bayley, *The Great Civil War in Dorset*, pp. 345–8. Smith, *The History of the Borough and County of the Town of Poole*, Vol. 2, pp. 160–2.

59   Bayley, *The Great Civil War in Dorset*, pp. 345–8.

60   *CJ*, Vol. 5, 12 August 1648 (1802), pp. 668–9. CSPD, 1651, pp. 171, 173, 195, 211, 220, 231, 264–5, 294. *CSPD*, 1651–2, p. 74.

61   G. Joyce, *A Letter or Epistle to all the well-minded People in England, Ireland, Wales and Scotland* (London, 1651), E637 [3].

62   Joyce, *A Letter or Epistle*, pp. 8–9. Firth and Davies, *Regimental History of Cromwell's Army*, p. 718.

63   Joyce, *A Letter or Epistle*, p. 10.

64   A. Marshall, 'Edward Sexby', *ODNB*. G. E. Alymer, 'George Joyce', *ODNB*.

65   Sexby's evidence at his court martial. See Henderson, *The Clarke Papers*, Vol. 5, p. 31. I am grateful to Frances Henderson for pointing out the similarity of Cromwell's attitude to the Rede and Sexby cases.

66   The Baptist influence in Poole continued after Rede's removal. Quaker founder George Fox visited Poole in 1655 and met with several Baptists, one of whom, William Bayly, became one of the most committed and effective Quakers. Fox visited Poole again in 1656, 1658 and 1675. Smith, *The History of the Borough and County of the Town of Poole*, Vol. 2, p. 169.

67   A. M. Everitt, *The Local Community and the Great Rebellion* (London: Historical Association, 1969). J. Morrill, *Cheshire 1630–1660: County Government and Society during the 'English Revolution'* (Oxford: Clarendon Press, 1974). The approach taken here has more in common with Underdown, *Fire from Heaven*.

68   Slocombe, *Wiltshire Quarter Sessions Order Book, 1642–1654*, p. 322. M. A. E. Green, *Calender of Proceedings of the Committee of Compounding, 1643–1660* (London, 1889–92) pp. 755–60, 762.

69   A tything is an historic administrative area, originally one-tenth of a hundred, which is itself an archaic term for ward. Wapentake has the same meaning.

70   E. Compton, *A History of the Baptist Church, Broughton, Hampshire, from the year 1653 to the Present Time* (Leicester: Winks and Son, 1878), p. 5. Wiltshire County Archive 3319/75.

71   Slocombe, *Wiltshire Quarter Sessions Order Book, 1642–1654*, entries 860, 918, 751, 905. See also wiltshire-opc.org.uk/Items/Idmiston/Idmiston%20 -%20Marriages%201577-1812.pdf, accessed 6 August 2014.

72   Compton, *A History of the Baptist Church*, p. 7.

73   Will of Edward Rede, TNA/PRO, prob. 11/169/484.

74   Compton, *A History of the Baptist Church*, pp. 8–9.

75   TNA, SP 29/48 f.36.

76   TNA, SP 29/132 f.2. CSPD: Charles II, 1664–5 (1863), pp. 545–64.

77   CSPD: Charles II, 1664–5 (1863), pp. 545–64.

78   B. Howard Cunnington, *Records of the County of Wilts, Being Extracts from the Quarter Session Rolls of the Seventeenth Century* (Devizes: George Simpson and Co., 1932), p. 247.

79   'Porton and Broughton Church Book', Angus Library, Regents College Oxford, document B1/1. The Porton church book records: '1655, Nicholas Frowde and his wife . . . of North Bradley'. Also 'Louise Frowde wife to James Frowde being a member of the Church at North Bradley (Southwick) stand now as related to us at Amesbury'. The Frowdes may have been related to the Rede family. W. Doel, *Twenty Golden Candlesticks! or A History of Baptist Nonconformity in Western Wiltshire* (Trowbridge

and London: B. Landsdown & Sons and George Rose, 1890), pp. 9, 17–18, 20, 222.

80   Howard Cunnington, *Records of the County of Wilts*, pp. 247–8.

81   TNA, SP 29/330. f. 133.

82   TNA, SP 29/320 f.237.

83   Compton, *A History of the Baptist Church*, p.11.

84   Compton, *A History of the Baptist Church*, pp.11–12.

85   Howard Cunnington, *Records of the County of Wilts*, pp. 265–8.

86   Howard Cunnington, *Records of the County of Wilts*, pp. 268–9.

87   Wiltshire County Archives, Amesbury-Chalke Presentments, D1/54/10/4.

88   Wiltshire County Archives, Amesbury-Chalke Presentments, D1/54/11/4. On Sarah Bernard see Wiltshire County Archives, Marriage Licence Bonds 1693, D1/62/4/28. It is tempting to think that this might be the Leveller leader Richard Overton, based on his Baptist sympathies. But there is no reason to think that Overton was in Salisbury at this time, although there is so little known of his life after 1663 that this is not impossible. But it is also unlikely that he was having children forty years later than his original family with Mary Overton in the mid-1640s. On the latest estimate of his birth he was the same age as John Rede and this would make him seventy -one years old in the year of the report to the bishop of Salisbury. B. J. Gibbons, 'Richard Overton', *ODNB*.

89   Wiltshire County Archives, 1215/24. This is a series of six documents, starting in 1699. The bequest was still being administered by trustees in 1791. E. Crittall (ed.), , *A History of the County of Wiltshire*, Vol. 10 (Victoria County History, 1975), pp. 285–314. This account confuses Rede's will with the letters of attorney of this bequest. Neither are lost as this account suggests. Nor is the bequest to Southampton and Devizes in the name of Sarah Reade. These are in fact the details of John Rede's bequest.

90   S. Rede, *A Token for Youth* (London, 1760). Although not published until 1760 the pamphlet is clearly written in the immediate aftermath of Sarah Cartaret Rede's death by her mother.

91   A. Tucker, 'Porton Baptish Church, 1655–85', at biblicalstudies.org.uk/pdf /tbhs/01-1_056.pdf.

92   The Baptist burial ground in Porton remains, although the Rede family table tomb was broken by contractors who were 'restoring' the graveyard in 1976. The remains of the tomb are kept in Porton Baptist Church. The church Rede founded met at Porton for the last time in 1710, the year of his death. The church was then located at Broughton under Henry Steele,

a scion of the Porton church who had been baptised there on 10th October 1680, and who took over from Rede. Compton, *A History of the Baptist Church*, pp. 13–14.

93   Tolmie, *The Triumph of the Saints*, pp. 182–7.

15. The Levellers and the English Revolution

1   M. Kishlansky, *The Rise of the New Model Army* (Cambridge: Cambridge University Press, 1979), p. x.

2   J. Walter, 'Politicising the Popular? The "Tradition of Riot" and Popular Political Culture in the English Revolution', in N. Tyacke (ed.), *The English Revolution c.1590–1720: Politics, Religion and Communities* (Manchester: Manchester University Press, 2007), p. 96, italics in the original.

3   J. Scott, *England's Troubles: Seventeenth-Century English Political Instability in European Context* (Cambridge: Cambridge University Press, 2000), p. 270. Scott claims that the Levellers depended for support on groups wider than their own immediate periphery (pp. 270–1). But even many much more strictly defined modern political parties share this characteristic.

4   D. Purkiss, *The English Civil War: A People's History* (London: HarperCollins, 2006), p. 476. Both Scott, see note above, and Purkiss, however, go on to treat the Levellers as if they *were* a coherent group despite the generalisations with which they open their analyses.

5   M. Braddick, *God's Fury, England's Fire: A New History of the English Civil War* (London: Penguin, 2008), p. 444.

6   A. Woolrych, *Soldiers and Statesmen: The General Council of the Army and Its Debates 1647–1648* (Oxford: Oxford University Press, 1987), p. 20.

7   For the full account of the history of the New Model Army see I. Gentles, *The New Model Army in England, Ireland and Scotland, 1645–1653* (Oxford: Oxford University Press, 1992); and for a discussion of Leveller influence see I. Gentles, 'The Politics of Fairfax's Army, 1645–9', in J. Adamson (ed.), *The English Civil War* (Basingstoke: Palgrave Macmillan, 2009), pp. 173–201, esp. pp. 186–94.

8   B. Taft, 'The Council of Officers' Agreement of the People, 1648/9', *Historical Journal*, 28.1 (March, 1984), p. 171. C. Holmes, *Why Was Charles I Executed?* (London: Hambledon Continuum, 2006), pp. 116–17. P. Baker, 'Rhetoric, Reality and Varieties of Civil War Radicalism', in Adamson, *The English Civil War*, p. 214. R. Foxley, *The Levellers: Radical Political Thought in the English Revolution* (Manchester: Manchester University Press, 2013), pp. 150–94.

9   B. Worden, *Roundhead Reputations: The English Civil Wars and the Passions of Posterity* (London: Penguin, 2001), p. 338.

10 J. Lilburne, *The Christian Man's Triall* (London, 1641), E181[7]. In January 1641 Larner had also printed the remarkable *To the Honourable The House of Commons Assembled in Parliament . . .*, 669 f.4[54]. K. Lindley, *Popular Politics and Religion in Civil War London* (Aldershot: Scolar, 1997), pp. 393–4. K. Chidley's *The Justification of the Independent Churches* was printed by William Larner in 1641. See also P. R. S. Baker, 'William Larner', *ODNB*. S. Chidley, *The Dissembling Scot* (London, 1652), E652[13], p. 4. I. J. Gentles, 'Samuel Chidley', *ODNB*. D. Como, 'Print, Censorship, and Ideological Escalation in the English Civil War', *Journal of British Studies*, 51.4 (October 2012), p. 831. *A view of part of the many Traiterous, Disloyal and Turn-about Actions of H. H. Senior* (1684), Wing (CD-Rom) V359. I. Gadd, *ODNB*. R. L. Greaves and R. Zaller, *Biographical Dictionary of British Radicals in the Seventeenth Century*, Vol. 2 (Brighton: Harvester, 1984), pp. 91–2. M. Mendle, 'Putney's Pronouns: Identity and Indemnity in the Great Debate', in M. Mendle (ed.), *The Putney Debates of 1647* (Cambridge: Cambridge University Press, 2001), pp. 126–33.

11 D. Como, 'Secret Printing, the Crisis of 1640 and the Origins of Civil War Radicalism', *Past and Present*, 196 (August 2007), p. 52.

12 Bod., Tanner MSS, Vol. 67, ff. 193, 194.

13 See G. K. Fortescue, Preface, *British Museum Catalogue of Thomason Tracts 1640–1652*, Vol. 1 (London: British Museum, 1908), p. xxiii.

14 Sir Thomas Aston, the Collector to the Reader in 'A Collection of Sundry Petitions . . .', E150[28].

15 G. Masterson, *A Declaration of Some Proceedings of Lt. Col. John Lilburne . . .*, E427[6], p. 17.

16 G. Masterson, *A Declaration and some Proceedings . . .* Also see D. Zaret, 'Petitions and the "Invention" of Public Opinion in the English Revolution', *American Journal of Sociology*, 101.6 (May 1996), p. 1526.

17 *The Remonstrance of Many Thousands of the Free-People of England . . . and those called Levelers*, E574[15], p. 8. Although the figure of nearly 100,000 signatories is very high given a national population figure of less than 6 million.

18 J. Lilburne, *Apologetical Narration* (Amsterdam, 1652), p. 71.

19 Anon., *To the Supream Authority of this Nation . . . The Humble Petition of Divers wel-affected Women*, E551[14].

20 *The Humble Petition of the Well Affected Young Men and Apprentices of the City of London*, E399[2].

21 J. Lilburne, *The Innocent Man's Second Proffer* (London, 1649).

22 J. Morrill, 'The Army Revolt of 1647', in A. C. Duke et al. (eds.), *Britain and the Netherlands* (The Hague, Martinus Nijhoff, 1977). M. A. Kishlansky, 'The Army and the Levellers: The Roads to Putney', *Historical Journal*, 22.4 (December 1979), p. 824. M. Kishlansky, 'What Happened at Ware?', *Historical Journal*, 25.4 (December 1982). M. Kishlansky, 'Consensus Politics and the Structure of Debate at Putney', *Journal of British Studies* 20 (1981) pp. 50–69. J. Morrill and P. Baker, 'The Case of the Armie Truly Re-stated', in M. Mendle (ed.), *The Putney Debates of 1647* (Cambridge: Cambridge University Press, 2001), pp. 103–25.

23 Woolrych, *Soldiers and Statesmen*. Gentles, *The New Model Army*. J. Peacey, 'The People of the Agreements: The Levellers, Civil War Radicalism and Political Participation', in P. Baker and E. Vernon (eds.), *The Agreements of the People, the Levellers and the Constitutional Crisis of the English Revolution* (Basingstoke: Palgrave Macmillan, 2012) pp. 50–75. Foxley, *The Levellers*, p. 158 and generally Ch. 5.

24 Morrill, 'The Army Revolt of 1647', p. 78.

25 R. Baxter, *Reliquiae Baxterianae* (London, 1696), Wing B1370, p. 61. A. S. P. Woodhouse, *Puritanism and Liberty* (London: Dent, 1938), p. 389.

26 J. Harris, *Mercurius Militaris*, 17–24 October 1648, p. 26.

27 We catch something of the transition between these two uses in the trial of royalist John Penruddock in 1655. In his defence Penruddock first uses the term 'party' in the legal sense, saying, 'No man can be a Judge where he is a Party in the same cause'. But he then also goes on to use it in a more general sense: 'Colonel Dove, the reverend Sheriff of Wilts, who that the Jury might be sufficiently incensed, complaining of the many incivilities (he pretended) were offered him by our party'. This refers to events during the rising for which Penruddock was facing trial and it indicates organised political activity by an identifiable group. 'The Triall of the honourable Colonel John Penruddock of Compton in Wiltshire' (1655), Wiltshire County Archives, MS 332/265.

28 'A formally constituted political group that contests elections and attempts to form or take part in a government'. This definition is a little restrictive since not all political parties can or do take part in elections, and others would not see it as a primary activity. Oxford Dictionaries Online, at oxforddictionaries.com/definition/english/party.

29   M. Tolmie, *The Triumph of the Saints: The Separate Churches of London 1616–1649* (Cambridge: Cambridge University Press, 1977), p. 144.

30   See M. Ashley, *John Wildman* (London: Jonathan Cape, 1947), p. 54.

31   R. Scrope and T. Monkhouse (eds.), *Clarendon State Papers* (Oxford, 1767–86), Vol. 3, p. 273.

32   *Kingdomes faithfull and Impartiall Scout*, 2–9 March 1649, pp. 41, 46.

33   *Kingdomes faithfull and Impartiall Scout*, 16–23 March 1649, pp. 57, 60.

34   J. Bastwick, *A Just Defence of John Bastwick* (London, 1645), E265[7], pp. 21–2.

35   H. Denne, *The Levellers Designe Discovered* (London, 1649), E556[11], p. 4.

36   J. Lilburne, *Plaine Truth without Feare or Flattery* (London, 1647), Wing L2156, pp. 4, 20.

37   T. Edwards, *Gangraena* (London, 1646), Part I, Epistle, and Preface (first page), pp. 49, 50, 52, 63, 68. And elsewhere in *Gangraena*, Part I, pp. 56, 57, 60, 75. See also A. Hughes, *Gangraena and the Struggle for the English Revolution* (Oxford: Oxford University Press, 2004), p. 315.

38   N. LL. (John Hall) *A true account of the character of the times* (London, 1647), E401[13].

39   *Sea Green and Blue, see which speaks true* (London, 1649), E559[1], p. 10.

40   *The Moderate*, 24 April–1 May 1649 (London) p. 484.

41   *The Moderate*, 1–8 May 1649 (London).

42   *The Resolved Apprentices . . .* (London, 17 May 1649). The biblical reference is to Numbers 16, in which Korah leads a revolt against Moses.

43   F. White, *A True Relation of the Proceedings in the Businesse of Burford* (London, 1649), pp. 8–9.

44   *The Leveller; or, the principles and maxims concerning government and religion, which are asserted by those that are commonly called Levellers* (London: Thomas Brewster, 1659), in the *Harleian Miscellany*, Vol. 7 (London: Robert Dutton, 1810), p. 45.

45   Oxford Dictionaries Online, at oxforddictionaries.com/definition/english /movement?q=movement.

46   Peacey, 'The People of the Agreements', p. 53.

47   Foxley, *The Levellers*, p. 6.

48   K. Marx and F. Engels, *The Communist Manifesto*, in A. P. Mendel (ed.), *Essential Works of Marxism* (New York, Bantam, 1971), pp. 23–4.

49   F. Engels, Introduction to the English edition (1892) of *Socialism: Utopian and Scientific* (Peking: Foreign Languages Press, 1975), p. 27.

50   F. Engels, *Anti-Dühring* (Peking: Foreign Languages Press, 1976), pp. 20–1.

51   K. Marx and F. Engels, quoted in C. Hill, 'The English Civil War Interpreted by Marx and Engels', *Science and Society*, 12 (1948), p. 145.

52   F. Engels [and K. Marx], *Revolution and Counter-revolution in Germany* (London: Lawrence and Wishart, 1933), p. 41.

53   F. Engels, Introduction to K. Marx, *The Class Struggles in France 1848 to 1850*, MECW, Vol. 27, see pp. 506–24.

54   A. Hessayon and D. Finnegan, 'Reappraising Early Modern Radicals and Radicalism', in A. Hessayon and D. Finnegan (eds.), *Varieties of Seventeenth - and Early Eighteenth-Century English Radicalism in Context* (Farnham: Ashgate, 2011), p. 21....

55   G. Burgess, 'On Revisionism: An Analysis of Early Stuart Historiography in the 1970s and 1980s', *Historical Journal*, 33.3 (September 1990), pp. 609–10.

56   There is not the space to rehearse this argument here but strong anti-determinist statements can be found in all the writers in the classical Marxist tradition: Marx and Engels, Luxemburg, Lukacs, Lenin, Trotsky, Gramsci. Deterministic formulations are most often found in the work of the revisionists (in the turn-of-the-twentieth-century Marxist sense) like Edward Bernstein and Karl Kautsky or in the Stalinist tradition. See, among much other work, F. Jakubowski, *Ideology and Superstructure in Historical Materialism* (London: Pluto, 1976); J. Larraine, *A Reconstruction of Historical Materialism* (London: Allen and Unwin, 1986); E. P. Thompson, *The Poverty of Theory* (London: Merlin, 1978); P. Anderson, *Considerations of Western Marxism* (London: Verso, 1976); R. Dunayevskya, *Marxism and Freedom*, 4th edn (London: Pluto, 1975); G. Lukacs, *History and Class Consciousness* (London: Merlin, 1971); A. Callinicos, *Making History* (Oxford: Polity, 1987); T. Eagleton, *Why Marx Was Right* (New Haven: Yale, 2011); J. Rees, *The Algebra of Revolution* (London: Routledge, 1998).

57   Burgess, 'On Revisionism, pp. 612, 627. Burgess writes, 'I am not suggesting that I have "proved" that religion is absolutely the explanation for the Civil War. But religious explanations do seem to have an integrative capacity not available to other approaches'. And although he hopes 'that those historians who have recognized the importance of religion do not fall prey to the seemingly innate human tendency to turn a good idea into a monocausal explanation', he provides no other and so the reader is left with only one cause with which to explain events.

58   P. Baker, '"A Despicable Contemptible Generation of Men"? Cromwell and the Levellers', in P. Little (ed.), *Oliver Cromwell: New Perspectives* (Basingstoke: Palgrave Macmillan, 2009), pp. 90–116.

59   C. Hill, 'The English Civil War Interpreted by Marx and Engels', p. 147.

60   Tolmie, *The Triumph of the Saints*, p. 144.

Select Bibliography

Included here are the primary and secondary sources most immediately relevant to the history of the Levellers and of most use to general readers. More detail on manuscript sources, unpublished articles, the titles of newsbooks and online sources can be found both in the endnotes and in J. Rees, 'Leveller Organisation and the Dynamic of the English Revolution' (doctoral thesis, Goldsmiths, University of London, 2014).

Primary sources

Petitions, pamphlets and newsheets by unnamed or anonymous authors

Anon., *The Armies Petition or A New Engagement of the Army, Who are yet Faithfull to the People* . . . (1648), E438[1].

Anon., *The Humble Petition and Remonstrance of Divers Citizens* . . . (London, 1642), E83[22].

An Agitator Anotomiz'd (London, 1648), E434[6].

An Elegie Upon the Colonel Thomas Rainsborough, butchered at Doncaster Sunday the 29 Octob. 1648, 669 f.13.[48].

Alas Pore Parliament how Art thou Betrai'd? (1644), E21[9].

All sorts of well-affected Persons . . . (London, 1643), E61[3].

The Apprentices Lamentation (London, 1642), 669 f.4[45].

A Bloody Independent Plot Discovered (London, 1647), E419[2].

A Call to all the souldiers of the Armie (London, 1647), E412[10].

The Character of an Agitator (1648), E434[6].

A Cleere and Full Vindication of the late Proceedings of the Armie (London, 1647), E397[21].

The Coblers Threed is cut (London, 1640), STC (2nd edn) 13855.2.

A Copie of a Letter Sent From the Agitators (London, 1647), E393[33].

The Copies of the Papers from the Armie (London, 1647), Wing C6273B.

A Coppie of a Letter sent from one of the Agitators in the Army to an Agitator in the Citie (London, 1647), E399[29].

A Copy of a letter from Several Agitators [London, 1647), E414[8].

A Copy of a letter Sent by the Agents of Several Regiments (London, 1647), E413[18].

A Declaration and Motive of the Persons trusted, usually meeting at Salters Hall in Breadstreet (London, 1643), 669 f.7[10].

The Declaration of Lieutenant-Generall Crumwell Concerning the Levellers (London, 1649), E555[12].

A Declaration of the Proceedings of the Honourable Committee of the House of Commons at Merchant-Taylors Hall (London, 1643), E63[10].

A Discoverie of Six women preachers (London, 1641), E166[1].

Ecce! Or the New testament of our lords and Saviours, the house of Commons and the Supreme Councel at Windsor (Somers Tracts 7. 61), in E. Peacock, 'Transcripts and Notes Largely Concerning Thomas Rainborowe' (John Rylands University Library, Civil War Collections, English MS 235).

England's Standard Advanced (London, 1649), E553[2].

Englands Troublers Troubled (London, 1648), E459[11].

England's Weeping Spectacle (London, 1648), E450[7].

Every Man's Case (London, 1646), E337[5].

An Exact and Impartial Accompt of The Indictment, Arraignment, Trial . . . of Twenty Nine Regicides (London, 1679).

The Examination and Confession of Captaine Lilbourne and Captaine Viviers (London, 1642), Wing F665.

Fellow Apprentices . . . (1647), E384[12].

Four petitions to his Excellency Sir Thomas Fairfax . . . (London, 1647), E393[7].

A Full Answer to the Levellers Petition . . . (Lodnon, 1648), Wing F2343.

A Full Relation of the Horrid Murder committed upon the body of Col. Rainsborough, the persons that did it, and the cause thereof (London, 1648), E470[4].

A Full Relation of the Proceedings at . . . Corkbush Field (London, 1647), E414[13].

The Gallant Rights, Christian Priviledges, Solemn Institutions of the Sea-Green Order (London, 1648), 669 f.13[48].

The Humble Petition and Remonstrance of Divers Citizens . . . (London, 1642), E83[22].

Humble Petition and Representation of the Officers and Souldiers of the Garrisons of Portsmouth, Southsea Castle . . . (London, 1649), 669 f.13 [71].

The Humble Petition of divers wel affected Persons inhabiting the City of London, Westminster, the Borough of Southwark, Hamlets and places adjacent (London, 1648), E464[5].

The Humble Petition of divers wel-affected Women (London, 1649), E551[14].

The humble Petition of the Officers of Colonell Overtons Regiment, now in the garrison of Berwick (London, 1648), E473[3].

The Humble Petition of the Well Affected Young Men and Apprentices of the City of London (London, 1647), E399[2].

The Humble Petition of thousands of well-affected Inhabitants of the Cities of London and Westminster, and the Suburbs thereof . . . (London, 1643), Wing (CD-ROM) T1650.

In Memoriam Thomas Rainsborough, Pro Populo, & Parliamento (London, 1648), 669 f.13 40.

The Interest of England Maintained (London, 1646), E340[5].

A Letter sent from Several Agitators of the Army to their Respective Regiments (London, 1647), E414[8].

A Letter Sent from the Agitators of the Army (Oxford, 1647) Wing L1605.

The Levellers Institutions for a Good People and Good Parliament (London, 1648), E474(4).

The Levellers Remonstrance (London, 1649), E555[2].

London's Teares (London, 1642), Wing (2nd edn) L2952.

Match me these two: or the convicition [sic] *of Bitannicus and Lilburne* (London, 1647), E400[9].

A New Declaration from Eight Regiments in the Army (London, 1647), E416[35].

A New Elegie in Memory of the Right Valiant, and most Renowned Souldier, late Admirall of the narrow Seas (London, 1648), 669 f.13[45].

A New Found Stratagem (London, 1647), E384[11].

Outcry of the Young Men and Apprentices of London (London, 1649).

A Perfect and True Copy of the Severall Grievances of the Army (London, 1647), E390[3].

Persecutio Undecima (London, 1648), E470[7].

A Petition From Severall Regiments of the Army . . . (London, 1648), E470[32].

The Petition of the Citizens of London . . . (London, 1641), 669 f.4[13].

The Petition of the Officers and Souldiers in the Army (London, 1647), E383[12].

Petition of the Women, Affectors and Approvers of a Petition of Sept. 11, 1648 (London, 1649), 669 f.14[27].

Plaine Truth without Feare or Flattery (London, 1647), Wing P2371.

The Recantation of John Lilburne (London, 1647), E386[19].

A Remonstrance From His Excellency Sir Thomas Fairfax (London, 1647), Wing (2nd edn) F227A.

The Remonstrance of Many Thousands of the Free-People of England . . . and those called Levelers (London, 1649), E574[15].

Remonstrance of the regiment of the late Col. Rainsborough to his Excellency, for the revenge of their Colonells death (London, 1648), E473[3].

A Remonstrance or Declaration of the Army: presented to the House of Commons on Munday Novemb.20.1648 (London), E473[3].

Remonstrans Redivivus (London, 1643), E61[21].

The Resolutions of the Agitators of the Army (London, 1647), E405[22].

The Resolved Apprentices . . . (London, 1649), Wing R1170.

A Review of a certain Pamphlet under the name of one John Lilburne (London, 1645), E278[4].

The Scots Loyaltie (London, 1641), E181[16].

The Second Part of the Triall of Lieu. Col. John Lilburn (London, 1649/50), E598[12].

Sea Green and Blue (London, 1649), E559[1].

Several Petitions Presented to his Excellency the Lord Fairfax . . . together with Lieut. Gen. Cromwels Letter to his Excellency concerning the same (1648), E474[5].

The Souldiers Demand (Bristol, 1649), E555[29].

The Speech of Major John Harris (London, 1660), E1043[3].

The Speech spoken by Prince Robert (London, 1642), Wing R2308.

The Summe of a conference at Terling (London, 1644), Wing S6166.

Terrible and bloudy Newes from the disloyall Army in the North (London, 1648), E462[28].

Three Speeches delivered at a Common-hall (London, 1643), Wing T1119.

To the Honourable the Commons of England assembled in parliament. The Humble petition of divers thousands of wel-affected Citizens, and others in behalf of Lieutenant Collonel John Lilburne, Prisoner of the Tower of London (London 1648), E457[19].

To the Honourable The House of Commons Assembled in Parliament . . . (London, 1642), 669 f.4[54].

To the Honourable The House of Commons . . . the humble Petition of many thousand poore people (London, 1641), Wing (2nd edn) T1437.

To the honourable the Knights, Citizens and Burgesses of the House of Commons (London, 1642), Wing T1470.

To the Honourable, the Supreame Authority of this Nation . . . (London, 1649), 669 f.13[89].

To the parliament: the petition of the Lord Mayor and Common Council (London, 1647), E381[2].

To the Right Honourable The House of Peeres Now Assembled in Parliament (London, 1642), Wing T1638.

To the Right Honourable, the Supreme Authority of this Nation . . . (London, 1649), 669 f.13[73].

To the Supream authority of England, the Commons in Parliament assembled . . . (London, 1647), 669 f.11[98].

To the Supream Authority of this Nation . . . *The Humble Petition of Divers wel-affected Women*, (London, 1649), E551[14].

The Triall of Lieut.Collonell John Lilburne (London, 1649), E584[9].

The Triall of the honourable Colonel John Penruddock of Compton in Wiltshire (1655), Wiltshire County Archives, MS 332/265.

The True and Originall Copy of the first Petition (London, 1642), Wing W1061.

A True Copy of a Petition . . . *by the Officers and Soldiers of the Regiment under the Command of Commissary General Ireton*, (London, 1648), E468[18].

A True Narrative of the late Mutiny made by several Troopers of Captain Savage's Troop (London, 1648), E552[18].

A True Relation of all the Remarkable Passages, and Illegall Proceedings of some Sathannical or Doeg-like Accussers of their Brethern Against William Larner, A Free-man of England (London, 1646), E335[7].

Tub-preachers overturn'd . . . (London, 1647), E384[7].

Two Letters of his Excellencie Sir Thomas Fairfax (London, 1647), E391[2].

Two Letters Read in the House . . . *of a Great Bloody Plot* (London, 1648), E423[20].

Two Petitions From the City of London . . . (London, 1647), E410[20].

The Two Petitions of the Buckinghamshire Men (London, 1641 [1642]) Wing (2nd edn) T3501A.

Two Speeches (London, 1647), E391[13].

The Unanimous Declaration of Colonel Scroope's and Commissary Gen. Ireton's Regiments (Salisbury?, 1649), E555[4].

A view of part of the many Traiterous, Disloyal and Turn-about Actions of H H Senior (1684), Wing (CD-ROM) V359.

The Vindication of the Cobler (London, 1640), STC (2nd edn) 13855.4.

Vox Borealis (1641), E177[5].

Windsor Projects and Westminster Practices (London, 1648), E442[10].

You that are Subscribers to the Apprentices Petition . . . (London, 1643), E83[46].

Works by named authors

Alleyn, T., *An Elegie on the Death of that Renowned Heroe Col Rainsborrow* (London, 1648), 669 f.13[41].

Aston, Sir Thomas, *A Collection of Sundry Petitions . . .* (London, 1642), E150[28].

Bastwick, J., *A Just Defence of John Bastwick* (London, 1645), E265[7].

Baxter, R., *Reliquiae Baxterianae* (London, 1696), Wing B1370.

Bell, R. (ed.), *Memorials of the Civil War: Comprising the Correspondence of the Fairfax Family* (London: Richard Bentley, 1849).

Birch, T. (ed.), *A Collection of the State Papers of John Thurloe*, Vol. 1, 1638–53 (London, 1742).

Bothumley, J., *The Light and Dark Sides of God* (London, 1650), E1353[2].

Bray, W., *Appeal for Justice*, in H. Cary, *Memorials of the Great Civil War*, Vol. 2 (London: Henry Colburn, 1842).

Bray, W., *Innocency and the Blood of the slain Souldiers* (London, 1649), E568[12].

Bray, W., *A Letter to His Excellencie Sir Thomas Fairfax* (London, 1647), E421[27].

Bray, W., *A Letter to the General* (London, nd, but probably 1649), E522[6].

Bray, W., *A Representation to the Nation* (London, 1648), E422[27].

Brooks, T., *The Glorious Day of the Saints Appearance* (London, 1648), E474[7].

Brooks, T., *Gods Delight in the Progresse of the Upright* (London, 1649), E536[6].

Burton, T., *Diary of Thomas Burton, Esq. Member in the Parliaments of Richard and Oliver Cromwell, From 1656 to 1659*, edited by J. Towill Rutt (London: Henry Colburn, 1828).

Carter, M., *A Most True and exact Relation of That as Honourable as Unfortunate Expedition of Kent, Essex, and Colchester* (London, 1650), Wing C662.

Cary, M., *A Word in Season to the Kingdom of England* (London, 1647), Friends Meeting House Library, London.

Cheeseman, C. (or Chisman), *The Lamb Contending with the Lion* (London, 1649), E563[10].

Chidley, K., *Good Counsell, to the Presberterian Government, That they may declare their Faith before they build their Church* (London, 1645), 669 f.10[39].

Chidley, K., *The Justification of the Independent Churches* (London, 1641), Wing C3832.

Chidley, K., *A new-yeares-gift . . .* (1645), E23[13].

Chidley, S., *An Additional Remonstrance . . .* (London, 1653), E702[17].

Chidley, S., *The Dissembling Scot* (London, 1652), E652[13].

Chillenden, E., *Preaching without Ordination*, DWL: 12.46.2[5].

Clarendon, E., *History of the Rebellion and Civil Wars in England* (Oxford, 1843).

Clarke, W., prefatory note to *A full Relation of the Proceedings . . .* (London, 1647), E414[13].

Claxson [Clarkson], L., *The Lost Sheep Found* (London, 1660), Wing C5480.

Cobbett, W., *Cobbett's State Trials*, Vol. 5 (London, 1810).

Coppe, A., *A Fiery Flying Roll* (London, 1650), E587[13].

Cromwell, O., *The conclusion of Lieuten: Generall Cromwells letter* . . . London, 1645), 669 f.10[38].

Denne, H., *The Levellers Designe Discovered* (London, 1649), E556[11].

Edwards, T., *The Casting Down of the last Stronghold of Satan* . . . (London, 1647), E394[6].

Edwards, T., *Gangraena*, Parts I, II and III (London, 1646), references are to the facsimile reprint by the Rota/University of Exeter (1977).

Eyre, W., *The Serious Representation of Col. William Eyre* (London, 1649), E394[5A].

Fairfax, T., *The Declarations and Humble representations of the Officers and Soldiers in Colonel Scroops, Colonel Sanders and Col. Wautons Regiment* (London, 1648), E475[24].

Fairfax, T., *A New Declaration from Eight Regiments in the Army* (London, 1647), E416[35].

Fairfax, T., *A Petition From Severall Regiments of the Army* . . . (London, 1648), E470[32].

Fairfax, T., *A Remonstrance From His Excellency Sir Thomas Fairfax* (London, 1647), E414[14].

Fairfax, T., *Two petitions Presented to His Excellency the Lord Fairfax* . . . *by the Officers and Soldiers commanded by Colonel Hewson* (London, 1648), E473[23].

Freize, J., *The Levellers Vindication* . . . (London, 1649), E573[8].

Goodwin, J., *Innocencies Triumph* (London, 1644), Wing G1174.

GS (Skutt, George), *A Letter from an Ejected Member of the House of Commons to Sir Jo. Evelyn* (London, 1648), E643[18].

Harris, J., *The Antipodes, or Reformation with the Heeles Upward* (Oxford, 1647), E399[16].

Harris, J., *The Grand Designe* (London, 1647), E419[15].

Harris, J., *A Lash for a Lyar* . . . (London, 1648), E428[8].

Harris, J., *The Speech of Major John Harris* (London, 1660), E1043[3].

Holles, D., *Densell Hollis Esquire, His worthy and learned Speech in Parliament* (London, 1641).

How, S., *The Sufficiency of the Spirits Teaching* (Glasgow, 1794), and in the following edtions: 1640, STC (2nd edn) 13855; 1644, Wing H2951; 1655, Wing H2952; 1683 Wing (2nd edn) H2953; 1689, Wing H2954.

Hunscot, J., *The humble petition of Joseph Hunscot Stationer* . . . (London, 1646), E340[15].

Jones, J., *Jurors Judges of Law and Fact* (London, 1650), E1414[2].

Joyce, G., *A Letter or Epistle to all the well-minded People in England, Ireland, Wales and Scotland* (London, 1651), E637 [3].

Joyce, G., *A True and impartiall Narration, concerning the Armies Preservation of the King* (London, 1647), E393[1].

Joyce, G., *A True Narrative of the Occasions and Causes of the late Lord Gen. Cromwells Anger and Indignation against Lieu. Col. George Joyce* (London, 1659), 669 f.21[50].

Kiffin, W., *Certaine Observations on Hosea* (London, 1642), Wing (2nd edn) K423A.

King, E., *A Discovery of the Arbitrary, Tyrannical, and illegal Actions of some of the Committee of the County of Lincoln* (London, 1647), E373[3].

Knollys, H., *Christ Exalted, A Lost Sinner Sought and saved by Christ* (London, 1645), E322[33].

Knollys, H., *The Rudiments of Hebrew Grammar* (London, 1648), Wing (2nd edn) K724A.

Lamb, T., *Absolute Freedom from Sin by Christs Death* (London, 1656), Wing L208.

Lambe, T., *A Treatise of Particular Predestination* (London, 1643), Wing (2nd ed.) L212A.

Lanseter, J., *Lanseter's Lance for Edwards'es Gangrene* (London, 1646), E354[17].

Larner, W., *A Vindication of Every Free-mans Libertie* (London, 1646), Wing L445A.

Lawmind J. (John Wildman), *Putney Projects* (London, 1647), E421[19].

Lawrence, R., *The Justice of the Army Against Evill-Doers Vindicated . . .* (London, 1649), E558[14].

Lilburne, E., *To the Chosen and betrusted Knights, Citizens, and Burgesses . . .* (London, 1646), 669 f.10[86].

Lilburne, J., *Apologetical Narration* (Amsterdam, 1652), E659[30].

Lilburne, J., *The Christian Man's Triall* (London, 1641), E181[7].

Lilburne, J., *A Copie of a Letter Written by John Lilburne Leut. Colonell. To Mr. William Prinne Esq.* (London, 1645), E24[22].

Lilburne, J., *A coppy of a letter sent by Lieu. Col. John Lilburne to Mr. Wollaston* (London, 1646), 669 f.10[62].

Lilburne, J., *A Coppy of a Letter Written . . . to the Wardens of the Fleet* (London, 1640), STC (2nd ed.) 15597.

Lilburne, J., *A coppy of a letter . . .* (London, 1646), 669 f.10[62].

Lilburne, J., *The Copy of a Letter from Lieutenant Colonell John Lilburne to a Friend* (London, 1645), E296[5].

Lilburne, J., *A Copy of a Letter Written to Collonel Henry Marten* (London, 1647), 669 f.11[46].

Lilburne, J., *Englands Birth-Right Justified* (London, 1645), E304[17].

Lilburne, J., *England's New Chains Discovered* (London, 1649), E545[27].

Lilburne, J., *The Freemans Freedom Vindicated* (London, 1646), E341[12].

Lilburne, J., *An Impeachment for High Treason against Oliver Cromwell and his son in law Henry Ireton Esquires* (London, 1649), E568[20].

Lilburne, J., *Innocency and Truth Justified* (London, 1645), E314[22].

Lilburne, J., *The Innocent Man's First Proffer* (London, 1649), 669 f.14[83].

Lilburne, J., *The Innocent Man's Second Proffer* (London, 1649), Wing (CD-ROM, 1996) L2120.

Lilburne, J., *Jonah's Cry* (London, 1647), E400[5].

Lilburne, J., *The Juglers Discovered* (London, 1647), E409[22].

Lilburne, J., *The Just Defence of John Lilburne* (London, 1653), E771[10].

Lilburne, J., *L Colonel John Lilburne Revived* (Amsterdam?, 1653), E689[32].

Lilburne, J., *Legal and Fundamental Liberties* (London, 1649), E567[1].

Lilburne, J., *The Legall Fundamental Liberties* (London, 1649), E560[14].

Lilburne, J., *A Letter sent from Captaine John Lilburne to divers of his friends in London* (London, 1643), E84[5].

Lilburne, J., *Liberty Vindicated Against Slavery* (London, 1646), E351[2].

Lilburne, J., *A Light for the Ignorant* (Amsterdam, 1638), STC (2nd edn) 15591.

Lilburne, J., *Londons Liberty in Chains Discovered* (London, 1646), E359[17].

Lilburne, J., *A More full Relation of the great Battell fought betweene Sir Tho: Fairfax, and Goring* (London, 1645), E293[3].

Lilburne, J., *The Opressed Mans Opressions . . .* (London, 1647), E373[1].

Lilburne, J., *The People's Prerogative* (London, 1648), E427[4].

Lilburne, J., *Plaine Truth without feare or flattery . . .* (London, 1647), Wing L2156.

Lilburne, J., *A Plea for Common-Right* (London, 1648), E536[22].

Lilburne, J., *The Poore Man's Cry* (1639), STC (2nd ed.) 15598.

Lilburne, J., *Rash Oathes Unwarrantable* (London, 1647).

Lilburne, J., *Regall Tyrannie Discovered* (London, 1647), E370[12].

Lilburne, J., *The Resolved Mans Resolution* (London, 1647), E387[4].

Lilburne, J., *The Second Part of England's New Chaines Discovered* (London, 1649), E548[16].

Lilburne, J., *To all the Affectors and Approvers . . . of the London petition of the eleventh of September 1648* (London, 1649), Wing L2183A.

Lilburne, J., *A true and most sad Relation of the The hard usage . . .* (London, 1643), E89[13].

Lilburne, J., *A true Relation of the material passages of Lieut. Col. John Lilburne* (London, 1646), E324[9].

Lilburne, J., *A Whip for the present House of Lords* (London, 1647), E431[1].

Lilburne, J., *A Worke of the Beast* (Amsterdam, 1638), STC (2nd edn) 15599.

Lilburne, J. and Overton, R., *The Army's Martyr, or a more ful relation of the barbarous and illegall proceedings of the court martial at Whitehall on Mr Robert Lockier* (London, 1649), E554[6].

Lilburne, J., Overton, R. and Prince, T., *A Picture of the Councel of State* (London, 1649), E550[14].

Lovell, W., *Ensignes of the Regiments in the Rebellious Citty of London, Both of Trayned Bands and Auxilieries*, National Army Museum, Accession No 6807-53.

Ludlow, E., *The Memoirs of Edmund Ludlow* (Oxford, 1894).

Marten, H., *The Independency of England* (London, 1648), E422[16].

Marten, H., *The Parliaments Proceedings Justified* . . . (London, 1648), E426[2].

Marten, H., *Rash Censures Uncharitable*, BL Add. MS 71532, ff. 7–8.

Marten, H., *Three Speeches delivered at a Common-hall* (London, 1643), E63[8].

Marten, H., *A Word to Mr. Wil. Prynn Esq; and Two for the Parliament and the Army* . . . (London, 1649), E537[16].

Masterson, G., *A Declaration of Some Proceedings* (London, 1647), E427[6].

Maynard, J., *Speech in answer to Mr Martyn* (manuscript), E.422[32].

Naylier, J., *The Foxes Craft Discovered* (London, 1649), E549[7].

Naylier, J., *The New made Colonel* (London, 1649), E552[10].

Nickolls, J. (ed.), *Original Letters and Papers of State, Addressed to Oliver Cromwell; Concerning the Affairs of Great Britain*, from the Year MDCXLIX to MDCLVIII, found among the political collections of Mr John Milton (London, 1743).

Overton, H., *An order made to a select committee chosen by the whole house of Commons to receive petitions touching ministers* (London, 1640), STC (2nd edn) 7747.3.

Overton, M., *The humble Appeale and Petition of Mary Overton* (London, 1647), E381[10].

Overton, M., *To the right Honourable, the Knights, Burgesses, the Parliament of England* . . . (London, 1646), E381[10].

Overton, R., *An Alarum to the House of Lords* (London, 1646), E346[8].

Overton, R., *An Appeale From the degenerate Representative Body the Commons of England* (London, 1647), E398[28].

Overton, R., *The Arraignment of Mr Persecution* (London, 1645), E276[23].

Overton, R., *An Arrow Against All Tyrants* (London, 1646), E356[14].

Overton, R., *Articles of High Treason Exhibited Against Cheap-side Crosse* (London, 1642), E134[23].

Overton, R., *The Baiting of the Great Bull of Bashan* (London, 1649), E565[2].

Overton, R., *The Commoners Complaint* (London, 1647), E375[7].

Overton, R., *A Defiance Against All Arbitrary Usurpations* (London, 1646), E353[17].

Overton, R., *The Last Warning to the Inhabitants of London* (London, 1646), E328[24].

Overton, R., *Mans Mortalitie* (London, 1644), Wing (2nd edn) O629E.

Overton, R., *Marten's Eccho* (London, 1645), E290[2].

Overton, R., *The Nativity of Sir John Presbyter* (London, 1645), E290[17].

Overton, R., *New Lambeth Fayre* (London, 1642), Wing O631A.

Overton, R., *Overton's Defyance* (London, 1649), E562[26].

Overton, R., *A Remonstrance of Many Thousand Citizens* (London, 1646), E343[11].

Overton, R., *A Sarcred Decretall* (London, 1645), E286[15].

Overton, R., *To the High and Mighty States . . .* (London, 1646), 669 f.10[91].

Overton, R., *To the right honourable, the betrusted* (London, 1646), 669 f.10[115].

Parker, H. (HP), *A Letter of Due Censure and Redargution* (London, 1650), E603[14].

Paulden, T., *An Account of the Taking and Surrendering of Pontefract Castle* (Oxford, 1702).

Price, J., *A moderate reply to the citie-remonstrance* (London, 1646), E340[20].

Pride, T., *The Beacons Quenched* (London, 1652), E678[3].

Prince, T., *The Silken Independents Snare Broken* (London, 1649), E560[24].

Prynne, W., *A Fresh Discovery of some New Wandering-Blazing-Stars and Firebrands* (London, 1645), E261[5].

Prynne, W., *The Levellers Levelled . . .* (London, 1647), E428[7].

Prynne, W., *The Lyar Confounded* (London, 1645), E267[1].

Prynne, W., *A Speech made in the House of Commons* (London, 1648), Wing P4013.

Prynne, W., *The Totall and Finall Demands already made by . . . the Agitators and Army* (London, 1647), E399[9].

Prynne, W., *Truth Triumphing* (London, 1645), E259[1].

Rede, S., *A Token for Youth* (London, 1760).

Sexby, E., *A Copy of a Letter Sent by the Agents of severall Regiments* (London, 1647), E413[18].

Smith, G., *An Alarum to the last warning* (London, 1646), E339[6].

Smith, J., *The Innocent Cleared: or a Vindication of Captaine John Smith* (Amsterdam, 1648), E472[25].

Smith, W., *Mr Smith's Speech in Parliament* (London, 1641), E119[46].

Sprigge, J., *Anglia Rediviva: England's Recovery, Being the History of the Motions, Actions and Successes of the Army under the Immediate Conduct of His Excellency Sir Thomas Fairfax, KT.* (Oxford, 1854).

Symonds, R., *The Kings Army 1643*, 'The Ensignes of the Rigiments in the Citty of London, both Trayned Bands and Auxiliries', British Library, Harley MSS. 986.

Taylor, J., *The Booke of Martyrs* (London, 1639), STC (2nd edn) 23733.

Taylor, J., *The carriers cosmographie or A briefe relation, of the innes, ordinaries, hosteries, and other lodgings in, and neere London, where the carriers, waggons, foote-posts and higglers, doe usually come* (London, 1637), STC (2nd edn) 23740.

Taylor, J., *The Levellers directory for private preaching new vamp'd. In which, certaine formes are warranted (by the agitators)...* (London, 1648), Wing (2nd edn) L1880.

Taylor, J., *A Swarme of Sectaries and Schematiques* (London, 1642), E158[1].

Taylor, J., *A three-fold discourse betweene three neighbours, Algate, Bishopsgate, and John Heyden the late cobler of Hounsditch, a professed Brownist* (London, 1642), E145[3].

Thompson, W., *Englands Standard Advanced* (London, 1649), E555[7].

Thompson, W., *A True and Impartial Relation...* (London, 1647, [1648]), Wing T1870.

Turner, J., *Choice Experiences of the Kind Dealings of God...* (London, 1653), Wing T3294.

Varax, T. (Clement Walker), *The Triall of Lieu. Colonell John Lilburne* (London, 1649), E584[9].

Walwyn, W., *Englands Lamentable Slaverie* (London, 1645), E304[19].

Walwyn, W., *Gold Tried in the Fire...* (London, 1647), E392[19].

Walwyn, W., *Juries Justified* (London, 1651), E618[9].

Walwyn, W., *The Just Man in Bonds* (London, 1646), E342[2].

Walwyn, W., *A Pearle in a Dounghill* (London, 1646), E342[5].

Walwyn, W., *The Poore Wise-mans Admonition* (London, 1647), E392[4].

Walwyn, W., *The Power of Love* (London, 1643), E1206[2].

Walwyn, W., *Strong Motives* (London, 1645), E304[15].

Walwyn, W., *A Whisper in the Eare of Mr. Thomas Edwards* (London, 1646), E323[2].

Walwyn, W., *A Word in Season* (London, 1646), E1184[3] and variant E337[25].

Walwyn, W., *A Word More to Mr. Thomas Edwards* (London, 1646), E328[20].

White, F., *A true relation of the proceedings in the businesse of Burford* (London, 1649), E574[26].

Wildman, J., *Truth's Triumph* (London, 1648), E520[33].

Wood, J., *The Leveller's (falsly so called) Vindicated* (London, 1649), E571[11].

Secondary sources

Abbott, W. C., *Writings and Speeches of Oliver Cromwell*, Vol. 1, 1599–1649 (Cambridge, MA: Harvard University Press, 1937).

Adams, D. R., 'The Secret Publishing Career of Richard Overton the Leveller', 1644–46', *Library*, series 7, 11.1 (March 2010).

Alan Orr, D., 'Law, Liberty and the English Civil War: John Lilburne's Prison Experience, the Levellers and Freedom', in M. J. Braddick and D. L. Smith (eds.), *The Experience of Revolution in Stuart Britain and Ireland* (Cambridge: Cambridge University Press, 2011).

Anon., 'Henry Hills, Official Printer', *Baptist Quarterly* 6.5 (January 1932).

Ashley, M., *John Wildman, Plotter and Postmaster: A Study of the English Republican Movement in the Seventeenth Century* (London: Jonathan Cape, 1947).

Ashton, R., *Counter Revolution: The Second Civil War and Its Origins, 1646–8* (New Haven: Yale University Press, 1994).

Aubrey, J., *Brief Lives* (Bath: Folio Society, 1975).

Aylmer, G. E., 'Gentlemen Levellers?', *Past and Present*, 49 (November 1970).

Aylmer, G. E., 'George Joyce', *ODNB*.

Aylmer, G. E. (ed.), *The Levellers and the English Revolution* (London: Thames and Hudson, 1975).

Baker, P., '"A Despicable Contemptible Generation of Men"? Cromwell and the Levellers', in P. Little (ed.), *Oliver Cromwell: New Perspectives* (Basingstoke: Palgrave MacMillan, 2009).

Baker, P., '*Londons Liberty in Chains Discovered*: The Levellers, the Civic Past, and Popular Protest in Civil War London', *Huntington Library Quarterly*, 76.4 (2013).

Baker, P., 'Rhetoric, Reality and Varieties of Civil War Radicalism', in J. Adamson (ed.), *The English Civil War* (Basingstoke: Palgrave MacMillan, 2009).

Baker, P., 'Thomas Prince', *ODNB*.

Baker, P., 'William Larner', *ODNB*.

Baker, P. and Vernon E. (eds.), *The Agreements of the People, the Levellers and the Constitutional Crisis of the English Revolution* (Basingstoke: Palgrave Macmillan 2012).

Barber, S., *A Revolutionary Rogue: Henry Marten and the English Republic* (Stroud: Sutton, 2000).

Bayley, A. R., *The Great Civil War in Dorset* (Taunton: Wessex Press, 1910).

Berens, L. H., *The Digger Movement in the Days of the Commonwealth* (Monmouth: Merlin, 2007).

Bernstein, E., *Cromwell and Communism* (Nottingham: Spokesman, 1980).

Betteridge, A., 'Early Baptists in Leicestershire and Rutland', *Baptist Quarterly*, 25.5 (January 1973).

Betteridge, A., 'Early Baptists in Leicestershire and Rutland', *Baptist Quarterly*, 25.8 (October 1973).

Braddick, M., *God's Fury, England's Fire: A New History of the English Civil War* (London: Penguin, 2008).

Brady, A., 'Dying with Honour: Literary Propaganda and the Second Civil War', *Journal of Military History*, 70 (January 2006).

Brailsford, H. N., *The Levellers and the English Revolution* (ed. C. Hill) (Nottingham: Spokesman, 1961).

Bray, W. (ed.), *The Diary of John Evelyn* (London: W. W. Gibbings, 1890).

Brenner, R. L., *Merchants and Revolution: Commercial Change, Political Conflict, and London's Overseas Traders, 1550–1653* (Cambridge: Cambridge University Press, 1993).

Bruce, J. and Masson, D., *The Quarrel between the Earl of Manchester and Oliver Cromwell* (London: Camden Society, 1875).

Burgess, G. 'A Matter of Context: "Radicalism" and the English Revolution', in M. Caricchio and G. Tarantino (eds.), *Cromohs Virtual Seminars: Recent Historiographical Trends of the British Studies (17th–18th Centuries)*, 2006–7, 1–4, at www.cromohs.unifi.it/seminari/burgess_radicalism.html.

Burgess, G., 'On Revisionism: An Analysis of Early Stuart Historiography in the 1970s and 1980s', *Historical Journal*, 33.3 (September 1990).

Burton, T., *Diary of Thomas Burton, Esq. Member in the Parliaments of Richard and Oliver Cromwell, from 1656 to 1659* (ed. John Towill Rutt) (London: Henry Colburn, 1828).

Capp, B., *The World of John Taylor the Water Poet* (Oxford: Clarendon, 1994).

Carlin, N., *The Causes of the English Civil War* (Oxford: Blackwell, 1999).

Carlin, N., 'Leveller Organization in London', *Historical Journal*, 27.4 (1984).

Carlin, N., 'The Levellers and the Conquest of Ireland in 1649', *Historical Journal*, 30.2 (June 1987).

Carlin, N., 'Liberty and Fraternities in the English Revolution: The Politics of the Artisans' Protests, 1635–1659', *International Review of Social History*, 39.2 (August 1994).

Carlin, N., 'Marxism and the English Civil War', *International Socialism*, 10 (1980).

Carlyle, T. (ed.), *Oliver Cromwell's Letters and Speeches*, Vol. 1 (London: J. M. Dent, 1908).

Clifton, R., 'Richard Rumbold', *ODNB*.

Coates, W. H. (ed.), *The Journal of Sir Simonds D'Ewes* (Hamden: Archon Books, 1970).

Coffey, J., *John Goodwin and the Puritan Revolution* (Woodbridge: Boydell, 2006).

Como, D., 'Print, Censorship, and Ideological Escalation in the English Civil War', *Journal of British Studies*, 51.4 (October 2012).

Como, D., 'Secret Printing, the Crisis of 1640 and the Origins of Civil War Radicalism', *Past and Present*, 196 (August 2007).

Como, D., 'An Unattributed Pamphlet by William Walwyn: New Light on the

Prehistory of the Leveller Movement', *Huntington Library Quarterly*, 69.3 (2006).

Condren, C., *Argument and Authority in Early Modern England* (Cambridge: Cambridge University Press, 2006).

Cornforth, M. (ed.), *Rebels and Their Causes: Essays in Honour of A. L. Morton* (London: Lawrence and Wishart, 1978).

Crawford, P., 'Charles Stuart, That Man of Blood', *Journal of British Studies*, 16.2 (Spring, 1977).

Cressy, D., *Dangerous Talk* (Oxford: Oxford University Press, 2010).

Cressy, D., *England on Edge: Crisis and Revolution 1640–1642* (Oxford: Oxford University Press, 2006).

Dahl, F., *A Bibliography of English Corantos 1620–1642* (London: Bibliographical Society, 1952).

Davis, J. C., 'The Levellers and Christianity', in B. Manning (ed.), *Politics, Religion and The English Civil War* (London: Arnold, 1973).

Davis, J. C., 'The Levellers and Democracy', *Past and Present*, 40 (July 1968).

Dillon, H. A., 'On a MS. List of Officers of the London Trained Bands in 1643', *Archaeologia*, 52 (January 1890).

Donoghue, J., *Fire under the Ashes: An Atlantic History of the English Revolution* (Chicago: The University of Chicago Press, 2013).

Durston, C., 'Henry Marten and the High Shoon of Berkshire: The Levellers in Berkshire in 1648', *Berkshire Archaeological Journal*, 70 (1979).

Dzelzainis, M., 'History and Ideology: Milton, the Levellers and the Council of State in 1649', *Huntington Library Quarterly*, 68 (2005).

Eales, J., *Puritans and Roundheads: The Harleys of Brampton Bryan and the Outbreak of the English Civil War* (Cambridge: Cambridge University Press, 1990).

Earle, P., *The Making of the English Middle Class* (London: Methuen, 1989).

Engels, F., *Anti-Dühring* (Peking: Foreign Languages, 1976).

Engels, F., Introduction to K. Marx, *The Class Struggles in France 1848 to 1850*, MECW, Vol. 27.

Engels, F., Introduction to the English edition (1892) of *Socialism: Utopian and Scientific* (Peking: Foreign Languages, 1975).

Engels, F., *The Peasant War in Germany* (Moscow: Progress, 1977).

Engels, F., 'The Position of England, The Eighteenth Century', in K. Marx and F. Engels, *Articles on Britain* (Moscow: Progress, 1975).

Engels, F. [and Marx, K.], *Revolution and Counter-Revolution in Germany* (London: Lawrence and Wishart, 1933).

Engels, F., *Socialism: Utopian and Scientific* (London: Bookmarks, 1993).

Everitt, A., 'The English Urban Inn, 1560–1760' in A. Everitt (ed.), *Perspectives in Urban History* (London: Macmillan, 1973).

Everitt, A., *The Local Community and the Great Rebellion* (London: Historical Association, 1969).

Everitt, A. (ed.), *Perspectives in Urban History* (London: Macmillan, 1973).

Farr, D., *Henry Ireton and the English Revolution* (Woodbridge: Boydell, 2006).

Firth, C. H. (ed.), *Clarke Papers*, Vols. 1 and 2 (London: Royal Historical Society, 1992).

Firth, C. H.,'Ludlow , Edmund (1616/17–1692)', rev. Worden, B., first published 2004, *ODNB* Firth, C. H., 'The Mutiny of Col. Ingoldsby's Regiment at Oxford in September, 1649', *Proceedings of the Oxford Architectural and Historical Society*, new series, 30 (1884).

Firth C. H., *Cromwell's Army: A History of the English Soldier during the Civil Wars, the Commonwealth, and the Protectorate*, 3rd edn (London: Greenhill Books, 1992).

Firth, C. H. and Davies, G., *Regimental History of Cromwell's Army* (Oxford: Clarendon, 1940).

Firth, C. H. and Rait, R. S. (eds.) *Acts and Ordinances of the Interregnum* (London: HMSO, 1910).

Fletcher, A., *The Outbreak of the English Civil War* (London: Arnold, 1981).

Forster, J., *The Statesmen of the Commonwealth of England*, Vol. 3 (New York, 1846).

Foxley, R., 'John Lilburne and the Citizenship of "Free-Born Englishmen"', *Historical Journal*, 47.4 (2004).

Foxley R., *The Levellers: Radical Political Thought in the English Revolution* (Manchester: Manchester University Press, 2013).

Foxley, R., 'Problems of Sovereignty in Leveller Writings', *History of Political Thought*, 28.4 (Winter 2007).

Frank, J., *The Levellers: A History of the Writings of Three Seventeenth-Century Social Democrats: John Lilburne, Richard Overton, William Walwyn* (Cambridge, MA: Harvard University Press, 1955).

Fraser, A., *Cromwell, Our Chief of Men* (London: Mandarin, 1989).

Gardiner, S. R. (ed.), *The Constitutional Documents of the Purtian Revolution 1625–1660*, 3rd edn (Oxford: Oxford University Press, 1906).

Gardiner, S. R., *History of the Commonwealth and Protectorate*, 4 vols. (London: Windrush, 1987).

Gardiner S. R., *History of the Great Civil War, 1642–1649*, Vols. 1–4 (London: Windrush, 1987).

Gardiner, S. R., 'A Letter from the Earl of Manchester to the House of Lords Giving an Opinion of the Conduct of Oliver Cromwell', *Camden Miscellany*, 8 (1883).

Gardiner, S. R., *Oliver Cromwell* (Ilkley: The Scolar Press, 1976).

Gentles, I., 'London Levellers in the English Revolution: The Chidleys and Their Circle', *Journal of Ecclesiastical History*, 29 (1978).

Gentles, I., *The New Model Army in England, Scotland and Ireland, 1645–1653*, 1st edn (Oxford: Blackwell Publishers, 1994).

Gentles, I., 'Parliamentary Politics and the Politics of the Street: The London Peace Campaigns of 1642–3', *Parliamentary History*, 26.2 (2007).

Gentles, I., 'Political Funerals during the English Revolution', in S. Porter (ed.), *London and the Civil War* (London: Macmillan, 1996).

Gentles, I., 'The Politics of Fairfax's Army, 1645–9', in J. Adamson (ed.), *The English Civil War* (Basingstoke: Palgrave Macmillan, 2009).

Gentles, I., 'Samuel Chidley', *ODNB*.

Gentles, I., 'Soldiers, Levellers and the "Middle Sort" in the English Revolution', at pi.library.yorku.ca/ojs/index.php/lh/article/viewFile/5253/4449.

Gentles I., Morrill, J. and Worden, B. (eds.), *Soldiers, Writers and Statesmen of the English Revolution*, 1st edn (Cambridge: Cambridge University Press, 2007).

Gibb, M. A., *John Lilburne the Leveller: A Christian Democrat* (London: Lindsay Drummond, 1947).

Gibbons, B. J., 'Richard Overton', *ODNB*.

Gillespie, K. (ed.), *Katherine Chidley: The Early Modern Englishwoman*, Series 2, Printed Writings, 1641–1700, Part 4 (Farnham: Ashgate, 2009).

Glover, S. D., 'The Putney Debates: Popular versus Elitist Republicanism', *Past and Present*, 164 (1998).

Goldsmith, M., 'Levelling by Sword, Spade and Word: Radical Egalitarianism in the English Revolution', in C. Jones, M. Newitt and S. Roberts (eds.), *Politics and People in Revolutionary England* (Oxford: Blackwell, 1986).

Gooch, G. P., *The History of English Democratic Ideas in the Seventeenth Century* (Cambridge: Cambridge University Press, 1898).

Goold Walker, G., *Honourable Artillery Company 1537–1986*, 3rd edn (London: Honourable Artillery Company, 1986).

Greaves, R. L. and Zaller, R., *Biographical Dictionary of British Radicals in the Seventeenth Century*, Vol. 2 (Brighton: Harvester, 1984).

Gregg, P., *Free-Born John: A Biography of John Lilburne* (London: Dent, 1986).

Grey, Z., *An Impartial Examination of the Third Volume of Mr. Daniel Neal's History of the Puritans* (London, 1737).

Gurney J., *Brave Community: The Digger Movement in the English Revolution* (Manchester: Manchester University Press, 2012).

Gurney J., *Gerrard Winstanley: The Digger's Life and Legacy* (London: Pluto, 2012).

Haller, W. and Davies, G., *The Leveller Tracts 1647–53* (New York: Peter Smith, 1944).

Hardacre, P. H., 'William Eyre (fl. 1634–1675)', *ODNB*.

Hardacre, P. N., 'William Allen, Cromwellian Agitator and "Fanatic"', *Baptist Quarterly*, 19.2 (July 1962).

Heinemann, M., 'Popular Drama and Leveller Style', in M. Cornforth (ed.), *Rebels and Their Causes: Essays in Honour of A. L. Morton* (London: Lawrence and Wishart, 1978).

Henderson, F., *Further Selections from the Papers of William Clarke* (London: Royal Historical Society, 2006).

Henderson, F., 'Gilbert Mabbot', *ODNB*.

Hessayon, A., 'Attaway, Mrs.', *ODNB*.

Hessayon, A., 'Fabricating Radical Traditions', in M. Caricchio and G. Tarantino (eds.), *Cromohs Virtual Seminars: Recent Historiographical Trends of the British Studies (17th–18th Centuries)*, 2006–7, 1–6, at cromohs.unifi.it/seminari/hessayon2_radical.html.

Hessayon, A., *'Gold Tried in the Fire': The Prophet TheaurauJohn Tany and the English Revolution* (Aldershot: Ashgate, 2007).

Hessayon, A., 'Incendiary Texts: Book Burning in England, *c.*1640–*c.*1660', *Cromohs*, 12 (2007), pp. 1–25, available at cromohs.unifi.it/12_2007/hessayon_incendtexts.html.

Hessayon, A. and Finnegan, D. (eds.), *Varieties of Seventeenth- and Early Eighteenth-Century English Radicalism in Context* (Farnham: Ashgate, 2011).

Hexter, J. H., *The Reign of King Pym* (Cambridge, MA: Harvard University Press, 1941).

Higgins, P., 'The Reactions of Women, with Special Reference to Women Petitioners', in B. Manning (ed.), *Politics, Religion and the English Civil War* (London: Arnold, 1973).

Hill, C., 'Censorship and English Literature', in C. Hill, *Writing and Revolution in 17th Century England* (Brighton: Harvester, 1985).

Hill, C., *The Century of Revolution 1603–1714* (Wokingham: Van Nostrand, Reinhold, 1961).

Hill, C., *The Collected Essays of Christopher Hill*, 3 vols. (Brighton: Harvester, 1986).

Hill, C., 'The English Civil War Interpreted by Marx and Engels', *Science and Society*, 12 (1948).

Hill, C., *The Experience of Defeat: Milton and Some Contemporaries* (London: Faber, 1984).

Hill, C., *God's Englishman* (London: Pelican, 1970).

Hill, C., *Reformation to Industrial Revolution* (London: Pelican, 1967).

Hill, C., 'A 17th-Century Democrat', *The Listener*, 1 May 1647, p. 676.

Hill, C., 'Soviet Interpretations of the English Interregnum', *Economic History Review*, 8 (1938).

Hill, C., *The World Turned Upside Down* (London: Pelican, 1972).

Hill, C. and Dell, D. (eds.), *The Good Old Cause: The English Revolution of 1640–1660, Its Causes, Courses and Consequences* (London: Frank Cass, 1949).

Hill, C., James, M. and Rickword, E., *Three Essays in Interpretation: The English Revolution 1640* (London: Lawrence and Wishart, 1940).

Holmes, C., 'Colonel King and Lincolnshire Politics, 1642–1646', *Historical Journal*, 16.3 (September 1973).

Holmes, C., *The Eastern Association in the English Civil War* (Cambridge: Cambridge University Press, 2007).

Holmes, C., *Why Was Charles I Executed?* (London: Hambledon Continuum, 2006).

Holstun, J., *Ehud's Dagger: Class Struggle in the English Revolution* (London: Verso, 2000).

Holstun, J. (ed.), *Pamphlet Wars: Prose in the English Revolution* (London: Frank Cass, 1992).

Howard Cunnington, B., *Records of the County of Wilts, Being Extracts from the Quarter Session Rolls of the Seventeenth Century* (Devizes: George Simpson and Co., 1932).

Howell, R., Jr and Brewster, D. E., 'Reconsidering the Levellers: The Evidence of the Moderate', *Past and Present*, 46 (February 1970).

Hudson, W., 'Economic and Social Thought of Gerrard Winstanley: Was He a Seventeenth Century Marxist?', *Journal of Modern History*, 18.1 (March 1946).

Hughes, A., *The Causes of the English Civil War* (Basingstoke: MacMillan, 1991).

Hughes, A., 'Elizabeth Lilburne', *ODNB*.

Hughes, A., *Gangraena and the Struggle for the English Revolution* (Oxford: Oxford University Press, 2004).

Hughes, A., *Gender and the English Revolution* (London: Routledge, 2012).

Humber, L. and Rees, J., 'The Good Old Cause: An Interview with Christopher Hill', *International Socialism*, 56 (1992).

James, C. L. R. (writing as G.F. Eckstein), 'Ancestors of the Proletariat', *Fourth International*, 10.8 (September 1949), available at marxists.org/archive/james-clr/works/1949/09/english-revolution.htm.

James, C. L. R. (writing as G.F. Eckstein), 'Cromwell and the Levellers', *Fourth International*, 10.5 (May 1949), available at marxists.org/archive/james-clr/works/1949/05/english-revolution.htm.

Johns, A., 'Coleman Street', *Huntington Library Quarterly*, 71.1 (March 2008).

Jones, L. S., *Colonel Thomas Rainsborough: Wapping's Most Famous Soldier* (History of Wapping Trust, n.d.).

Jones, W. R. D., *Thomas Rainborowe (c1610–1648): Civil War Seaman, Siegemaster and Radical* (Woodbridge: Boydell, 2005).

Juxon, T., *The Journal of Thomas Juxon, 1644–1647* (ed. K. Lindley and D. Scott, Cambridge: Royal Historical Society, Cambridge University Press, 1999).

Kelsey, S., 'The Death of Charles I', *Historical Journal*, 45.4 (2002).

Kemp, G. and McElligott, J., 'General Introduction', in C. S. Clegg (ed.), *Censorship and the Press*, Vol. 1 (London: Pickering and Chatto, 2009).

Kirby, D. A., 'The Radicals of St. Stephen's, Coleman Street, London, 1624–1642', *Guildhall Miscellany*, 3.2 (April 1970).

Kishlansky, M., 'The Army and the Levellers: The Roads to Putney', *Historical Journal*, 22.4 (Dec., 1979).

Kishlansky, M., 'Consensus Politics and the Structure of Debate at Putney', *Journal of British Studies* 20 (1981).

Kishlansky, M., *A Monarchy Transformed: Britain 1603–1714* (London: Penguin, 1996).

Kishlansky, M., *The Rise of the New Model Army* (Cambridge: Cambridge University Press, 1979).

Kishlansky, M., 'What Happened at Ware?', *Historical Journal*, 25.4 (December 1982).

Kitson, E. and Clark, E. K., 'Some Civil War Accounts, 1647–1650', *Thoresby Society Publications*, Vol. 2, Miscellanea IV (Leeds, 1904).

Lake, P. and Pincus, S., 'Rethinking the Public Sphere in Early Modern England', in P. Lake and S. Pincus (eds.), *The Politics of the Public Sphere in Early Modern England* (Manchester: Manchester University Press, 2007).

Laurence, A., *Parliamentary Army Chaplains: 1642–1651* (Woodbridge: Boydell, 1990).

Lindley, K., *Popular Politics and Religion in Civil War* London (Aldershot: Scolar, 1997).

Lindley, K., 'Whitechapel Independents and the English Revolution', *Historical Journal*, 41.1 (March 1998).

Little, P. (ed.), *Oliver Cromwell: New Perspectives* (Basingstoke: Palgrave Macmillan, 2008).

Ludlow, E., *Memoirs of Edmund Ludlow* (Oxford, 1894).

Lukács, G., *History and Class Consciousness* (London: Merlin, 1971).

Macaulay, C., *History of England from James I to the Brunswick Line*, 8 vols. (London, 1763–83).

Mckenzie, D. F., 'Printing and Publishing 1557–1700: Constraints on the London Book Trades', in *The Cambridge History of the Book in Britain* (Cambridge: Cambridge University Press, 2002).

MacLachlan, A., *The Rise and Fall of Revolutionary England* (Basingstoke: MacMillan, 1996).

MacPherson, C. B., *The Political Theory of Possessive Individualism* (Oxford: Oxford University Press, 1962).

Manning, B., *Aristocrats, Plebeians and Revolution in England 1640–1660* (London: Pluto, 1996).

Manning, B. (ed.), *Contemporary Histories of the English Civil War* (London: Caliban, 2000).

Manning, B., *The English People and the English Revolution* (London: Heinemann, 1976).

Manning, B., *The Far Left in the English Revolution* (London: Bookmarks, 1999).

Manning, B., 'The Levellers and Religion', in J. F. McGregor and B. Reay (eds.), *Radical Religion in the English Revolution* (Oxford: Oxford University Press, 1984).

Manning, B. (ed.), *Politics, Religion and the English Civil War* (London: Arnold, 1973).

Manning, B., *Revolution and counter-revolution in England Ireland and Scotland 1658–60* (London: Bookmarks, 2003).

Manning, B., *1649: The Crisis of the English Revolution* (London: Bookmarks, 1992).

Marshall, A., 'Edward Sexby', *ODNB*.

Marx, K., *The Eighteenth Brumaire of Louis Bonaparte*, in D. Fernbach (ed.) *Surveys from Exile* (London: Penguin, 1973).

Marx, K., and Engels, F., *Articles on Britain* (Moscow: Progress, 1975).

Marx, K., and Engels, F., *The Communist Manifesto* (London: Verso, 1998).

Marx, K., and Engels, F., *Selected Correspondence* (Moscow: Progress, 1955).

Maslan, K., *The Life of Francis Freeman of Marlborough (c1600–1671)* (Woking: Rosemary Cleaver, Pyford Press, 1994).

Meiksins Wood, E., *Liberty and Property: A Social History of Western Political Thought from Renaissance to Enlightenment* (London: Verso, 2012).

Meiksins Wood, E., *The Pristine Culture of Capitalism* (London: Verso, 1991).

Meiksins Wood, E. and Wood, N., *The Trumpet of Sedition: Political Theory and the Rise of Capitalism 1509–1688* (London: Pluto, 1997).

Mendle, M. (ed.), *The Putney Debates of 1647: The Army, the Levellers and the English State* (Cambridge: Cambridge University Press, 2001).

Mervyn Himbery, D., 'The Religious Beliefs of the Levellers', *Baptist Quarterly*, 15.6 (April 1954).

Morrill, J., *Cheshire 1630–1660: County Government and Society during the 'English Revolution'* (Oxford: Clarendon Press, 1974).

Morrill, J., *The Nature of the English Revolution* (London: Routledge, 1993).

Morrill, J. (ed.), *Oliver Cromwell and the English Revolution* (London: Longman, 1990).

Morrill, J., *The Revolt of the Provinces* (London: Allen and Unwin, 1976).

Morrill, J. and Baker, P., 'The Case of the Armie Truly Re-stated', in M. Mendle (ed.), *The Putney Debates of 1647* (Cambridge: Cambridge University Press, 2001).

Morton, A. L., *Freedom in Arms: A Selection of Leveller Writings* (London: Lawrence and Wishart, 1974).

Morton, A. L., *The World of the Ranters* (London: Lawrence and Wishart, 1970).

Nelson, C. and Seccombe, M., 'The Creation of the Periodical Press 1620–1695', in *The Cambridge History of the Book in Britain* (Cambridge: Cambridge University Press, 2002).

Nevitt, M., *Women and the Pamphlet Culture of Revolutionary England, 1640–1660* (Aldershot: Ashgate, 2006).

Nuttall, G. F., 'Thomas Lambe, William Allen and Richard Baxter: An Additional Note', *Baptist Quarterly*, 27.3 (July 1977).

Orwell, G. and Reynolds, R. (eds), *British Pamphleteers*, Vol. 1, *From the Sixteenth Century to the French Revolution* (London: Allan Wingate, 1948).

Parker, D. (ed.), *Ideology, Absolutism and the English Revolution: Debates of the British Communist Historians* (London: Lawrence and Wishart, 2008).

Patterson, A., *Reading between the Lines* (Madison University of Wisconsin, 1993).

Peacey, J., 'The Hunting of the Leveller: The Sophistication of Parliamentarian Propaganda, 1647–53', *Historical Research*, 78.199 (February, 2005).

Peacey, J., 'John Lilburne and the Long Parliament', *Historical Journal*, 43.3 (September 2000).

Peacey, J., 'News, Politics and People, 1603–1714' (Cengage Learning EMEA Ltd, 2010).

Peacey, J., 'The People of the *Agreements*: The Levellers, Civil War Radicalism and Political Participation', in P. Baker and E. Vernon (eds.), *The Agreements of the People, the Levellers and the Constitutional Crisis of the English Revolution* (Basingstoke: Palgrave MacMillan, 2012).

Peacey, J., *Politicians and Pamphleteers, Propaganda during the English Civil Wars and Interregnum* (Aldershot: Ashgate, 2004).

Peacey J., *Print and Public Politics in the English Revolution* (Cambridge: Cambridge University Press, 2013).

Peacey, J., 'The Struggle for Mercurius Britanicus: Factional Politics and the

Parliamentarian Press, 1643–1646', *Huntington Library Quarterly*, 68.3 (September 2005).

Peacock, E., 'Notes on the Life of Thomas Rainborowe', *Archaeologia*, 46 (1880).

Peacock, E., 'Transcripts and Notes Largely Concerning Thomas Rainborowe' (John Rylands University Library, Civil War Collections).

Pearl, V., *London and the Outbreak of the Puritan Revolution* (Oxford: Oxford University Press, 1961).

Pease, T. C., *The Leveller Movement* (Gloucester, MA: Peter Smith, 1965).

Pennington, D. and Thomas, K. (eds.), *Puritans and Revolutionaries* (Oxford: Oxford University Press, 1978).

Pestana, C. G., 'William Rainborowe (fl. 1639–1673)', *ODNB*.

Petegorsky, D., *Left-Wing Democracy in the English Civil War* (London: Gollancz, 1940).

Plomer, H. R., 'Secret Printing during the Civil War', *Library*, 2.5 (1904).

Plowden, A., *In a Free Republic* (Stroud: Sutton, 2006).

Polizzotto, C., 'What Really Happened at the Whitehall Debates? A New Source', *Historical Journal*, 57.1 (2014).

Porter, S. (ed.), *London and the Civil War* (Basingstoke: Macmillan, 1996).

Porter, S. and Marsh, S., *The Battle for London* (Stroud: Amberley, 2011).

Powell, J. R. and Timings, E. K., *Documents Relating to the Civil War 1642–1648* (London: Navy Records Society and Spottiswoode, Ballantyne and Co., 1963).

Purkiss, D., *The English Civil War: A People's History* (London: HarperCollins, 2006).

Raikes, G. A., *The Ancient Vellum Book of the Honourable Artillery Company* (London, 1890).

Raikes, G. A., *The History of the Honourable Artillery Company* (London, 1878).

Ramsey, R. M., *Henry Ireton* (London: Longmans, 1949).

Raymond, J., *The Invention of the Newspaper: English Newsbooks 1641–1649* (Oxford: Oxford University Press, 1996).

Raymond, J., *Making the News: An Anthology of the Newsbooks of Revolutionary England* (Morton-in-Marsh, Windrush, 1993).

Reade, C. and Reade Macmullen, R., *A Record of the Redes of Barton Court, Berks; with a Short Précis of Other Lines of the Name* (Hereford: Jakeman and Carver, 1899).

Rees, J., *The Algebra Of Revolution: The Dialectic and the Classical Marxist Tradition* (London: Routledge, 1998).

Rees, J., 'Lieutenant-Colonel John Rede: West Country Leveller and Baptist Pioneer', *Seventeenth Century*, 30.3 (2015).

Rees, J., 'Revolution Denied', in L. German and R. Hoveman (eds.), *A Socialist Review* (London: Bookmarks, 1998).

Richardson, R. C., *The Debate on the English Revolution* (London: Methuen, 1977).

Richardson, R. C. and Ridden, G. M. (eds.), *Freedom and the English Revolution* (Manchester: Manchester University Press, 1986).

Robertson, G., *The Levellers: The Putney Debates* (London: Verso, 2007).

Robertson, G., *The Tyrannicide Brief: The Story of the Man Who Sent Charles I to the Scaffold* (London: Chatto & Windus, 2005).

Rodgers, K., *Signs and Taverns round and about Old London Bridge* (London: Homeland Association, 1937).

Round, J. H. , 'The Tower Guards', *Antiquary*, 10 (1884).

Rowse, A. L., *Four Caroline Portraits: Thomas Hobbes, Henry Marten, Hugh Peters, John Selden* (London: Gerald Duckworth & Co., 1993).

Schenk, W., *The Concern for Social Justice in the Puritan Revolution* (London: Longmans, 1948).

Scott, J., *England's Troubles: Seventeenth-Century English Political Instability in European Context* (Cambridge: Cambridge University Press, 2000).

Seaver, P., *Wallington's World: A Puritan Artisan in Seventeenth-Century London* (Stanford: Stanford University Press, 1985).

Sharpe, A. (ed.), *The English Levellers* (Cambridge: Cambridge University Press, 1998).

Sharpe, K., *The Personal Rule of Charles I* (New Haven, Yale University Press, 1996).

Shaw, H., *The Levellers* (London: Longmans, 1968).

Slocombe, I., (ed.), *Wiltshire Quarter Sessions Order Book, 1642–1654* (Wiltshire Record Society, Salisbury, 2014).

Smith, N., *A Collection of Ranter Writings: Spiritual Liberty and Sexual Freedom in the English Revolution* (London: Pluto Press, 2014).

Smith, N., 'Non-conformist Voices and Books', in *The Cambridge History of the Book in Britain*, Vol. 4, 1557–1695 (Cambridge: Cambridge University Press, 2002).

Smith, S. R. , 'Almost Revolutionaries: The London Apprentices during the Civil Wars', *Huntington Library Quarterly*, 42.4 (Autumn 1979).

Soboul, A., *The French Revolution 1787–1799* (London: Unwin Hyman, 1974).

Southern, A., *Forlorn Hope: Soldier Radicals of the Seventeenth Century* (Lewes: The Book Guild, 2001).

Taft, B., 'The Council of Officers' Agreement of the People, 1648/9', *Historical Journal*, 28.1 (March 1985).

Tapsell, G. and Taylor S. (eds.), *The Nature of the English Revolution Revisited: Essays in Honour of John Morrill* (Woodbridge: The Boydell Press, 2013).

Thomas, K., 'The Levellers and the Franchise', in G. Aylmer (ed.), *The Interregnum: The Quest for Settlement 1646–1660* (Basingstoke: MacMillan, 1972).

Thomas, K., 'Women and the Civil War Sects', *Past and Present*, 13 (April 1958).

Thompson, C., 'Maximilian Petty and the Putney Debate on the Franchise', *Past and Present*, 88 (August 1980).

Thompson, C. (ed.), *Walter Yonge's Dialry of Proceedings in the House of Commons 1642-1645*, Vol. 1 (Wivenhoe: Orchard Press, 1986).

Tibbutt, H. G., 'The Tower of London Letter-Book of Sir Lewis Dyve, 1646-47', *Publications of the Bedfordshire Historical Record Society*, Vol. 38 (Streatley: Bedfordshire Records Society, 1957).

Tinniswood, A., *The Rainborowes: Pirates, Puritans and a family's Quest for the Promised Land* (London: Jonathan Cape, 2013).

Tolmie, M., 'Thomas Lambe, Soapboiler, and Thomas Lambe, Merchant, General Baptists', *Baptist Quarterly*, 27.1 (January 1977).

Tolmie, M., *The Triumph of the Saints: The Separate Churches of London 1616-1649* (Cambridge: Cambridge University Press, 1977).

Trotsky, L., *Trotsky's Writings on Britain*, 2 vols. (London: New Park, 1974).

Underdown, D., *Fire from Heaven* (London: HarperCollins, 1992).

Underdown, D., *A Freeborn People* (Oxford: Oxford University Press, 1996).

Underdown, D., '"Honest" Radicals in the Counties, 1642-1649', in D. Pennington and K. Thomas (eds.), *Puritans and Revolutionaries* (Oxford: Oxford University Press, 1978).

Underdown, D., 'The Parliamentary Diary of John Boys, 1647-8', *Historical Research*, 39 (1966).

Underdown, D., *Pride's Purge: Politics in the Puritan Revolution* (Oxford: Oxford University Press, 1971).

Underdown, D., *Revel, Riot and Rebellion* (Oxford: Oxford University Press, 1985).

Vallance, E., 'Oaths, Covenants, Associations and the Origins of the *Agreements of the People*: The Road to and from Putney', in P. Baker and E. Vernon (eds.), *The Agreements of the People, the Levellers and the Constitutional Crisis of the English Revolution* (Basingstoke: Palgrave MacMillan, 2012).

Vallance, E., 'Reborn John? The Eighteenth-Century Afterlife of John Lilburne', *History Workshop Journal*, 74 (Autumn 2012).

W. T. W., 'Henry Denne', *Baptist Quarterly*, 11.3-4 (July-October 1942), p. 124.

Walwyn, W., *The Writings of William Walwyn* (ed. J. R. McMichael and B. Taft) (Athens: University of Georgia Press, 1989).

Waters, H., *The Rainborowe Family* (New York: privately printed, 1886).

Waters, I., *Henry Marten and the Long Parliament* (Chepstow: F. G. Comber, 1973).

Wedgewood, C. V., *A King Condemned: The Trial and Execution of Charles I* (London: Tauris Parke, 2011).

Whitley, W. T., 'General Ludlow's Baptist Comrades', *Baptist Quarterly*, 11.1–2 (January–April 1942).

Williams, C. M., 'The Anatomy of a Radical Gentleman: Henry Marten', in D. Pennington and K. Thomas, *Puritans and Revolutionaries* (Oxford: Oxford University Press, 1978).

Williams, C. M., 'Extremist Tactics in the Long Parliament, 1642–1643', *Historical Studies*, 15.57 (1971).

Williamson, H. R., *Four Stuart Portraits* (London: Evans Brothers, 1949).

Wintringham, T., *Mutiny: Mutinies from Spartacus to Invergordon* (London: Stanley Nott, 1936).

Wolfe, D. M., *Leveller Manifestoes of the Puritan Revolution* (London: Frank Cass, 1967).

Woodhouse A. S. P. (ed.), *Puritanism and Liberty: Being the Army Debates (1647–49) from the Clarke Manuscripts*, 3rd edn (London: Dent, 1986).

Woolrych A., *Battles of the English Civil War* (London: Pimlico 1991).

Woolrych, A., 'Cromwell as a Soldier', in J. S. Morrill (ed.), *Oliver Cromwell and the English Revolution* (London: Longman, 1990).

Woolrych, A., *Soldiers and Statesmen: The General Council of the Army and Its Debates* (Oxford: Oxford University Press, 1987).

Wootton, D., 'From Rebellion to Revolution: The Crisis of the Winter of 1642/3 and the Origins of Civil War Radicalism', *English Historical Review* (July 1990).

Wootton, D., 'Leveller Democracy and the Puritan Revolution', in J. H. Burns and M. Goldie (eds.), *The Cambridge History of Political Thought, 1450–1700* (Cambridge: Cambridge University Press, 1991).

Worden, B., *Roundhead Reputations: The English Civil Wars and the Passions of Posterity* (London: Penguin, 2001).

Wright, S., *The Early English Baptists 1603–1649* (Woodbridge: Boydell, 2006).

Zagorin, P., *A History of Political Thought in the English Revolution* (Bristol: Theommes, 1997).

Zaret, D., *Origins of Democratic Culture: Printing, Petitions, and the Public Sphere in Early-Modern England* (Princeton: Princeton University Press, 2000).

Zaret, D., 'Petitions and the "Invention" of Public Opinion in the English Revolution', *American Journal of Sociology*, 101.6 (May 1996).

Index

Abbot, Daniel, 192
Abbott, W. C., 264
Adams, Thomas, 143, 163 see also mayor of
    London
Admiralty committee, 235
Agitators, 50, 55, 57, 60, 172–97, 199,
    212–20
    Cromwell, 202, 203, 204
    new Agitators, 55, 205, 203, 215
Agreement of the People (pamphlet), 56–7,
    58, 63, 153, 235, 246, 279
    adoption, 280–6
    army, 213, 300
    Cromwell, 339
    imprisonment, 60, 73
    Lilburne, 231, 276, 280, 297, 305, 307,
        336
    Parliament, 212
    petitions, 165, 253
    print run, 336
    proposals, 205–6, 207
    Ware mutiny, 214–15, 220
Alas Pore Parliament how Art thou
    Betrai'd?, 75, 122, 123
Aldersgate, 43, 56, 214
Aldersgate Street, 80
Aldgate, 11, 43, 44, 136
Allen, Joan, 52
Allen, William, 50, 60, 179, 212, 314
Alleyn, Thomas, 268
    An Elegie on the Death of that Renowned
        Heroe Col Rainsborrow (Alleyn),
        268
Allhallows church, 50
Allin, William see Allen, William
Amsterdam, 46, 53
Lord Andover, 83
Andrews, Thomas, 92

The Antipodes or Reformation with its
    Heeles Upward, 189
Apologetical Narration, 124, 129
apprentices, 25, 35, 41, 58, 70, 86–7
    December Days, 4–8, 15, 16, 18, 73
    London, 21, 23, 24, 25, 32, 44, 45, 67
    riots, 33–4
apron youths, 26
Archer, John, 33
the Armada, 49
the army, xviii, 56, 65, 75, 78, 80, 101
    back pay, 177, 188, 233, 294
    The Case of the Army Truly Stated
        (pamphlet), 203, 204
    disbandment, 172, 174, 180, 181, 187,
        193, 232, 233–4, 240, 250, 287
    forced disbandment, 296
    An humble Representation of the
        Dissatisfactions of the Army
        (petition), 187
    Ireland, 286, 292
    The Just Request (petition), 192
    opposition, 196, 233, 257, 284
    petitions, 213
    Presbyterians, 235
    press, 65, 74–5, 180–2, 196, 256
    Representation of the Army (petition),
        179–80
    A Solemn Engagement of the Army,
        (petition), 187
    typhus, 73
    Ware, 213–18
army revolt (1647), 110, 170, 182–94, 196,
    220, 281, 287, 338
Arnold, Richard, 217
Artillery Garden, 48, 49
Ashe, Simeon, 113
Ashton, Robert, 271–3

Assembly of Divines, 113, 115, 124, 126, 131, 157, 318
  Cromwell, 118
  Independents, 129
  Manchester, 107
  petition, 135
Atkins, Thomas, 76, 90, 92, 104 see also mayor of London
Mrs Attaway, 146
Aubrey, John, 89, 90, 91
Captain Audley, 208, 211
Axtell, Daniel, 288, 290

Baillie, Robert, 63, 109, 174, 195
  Manchester, 116–17
  pamphlet, 196
  prisoners, 192–3
Baker, Philip, 164, 337, 347
Balfour, William, 2, 117
ballads, xvii, 28, 75, 168
Bamford, Richard, 324–5
Lady Bankes, 37
Banqueting House, xvii
baptism, 49, 61, 62, 147
Baptists, xix–xx, 11, 13, 40, 47, 60, 145, 322, 327–33
  Anabaptists, 20, 38, 109, 114, 118, 124, 146–7
  General Baptists, xx, 63, 130
  Particular Baptists, 60, 290
Barbary pirates, 234
Barebone, Praise-God, 19, 49
Colonel Barkstead, 226, 275
Barnardiston, Nathaniel, 47
Captain Baskett, 320
Bastwick, John, 27, 28, 29, 31, 47, 75, 128, 340
  book burning, 68
  ears, 29, 68
  Eastern Association, 136
  freedom, 35
  Gatehouse prison, 28, 30, 217
  A Just Defence of John Bastwick (Bastwick), 136
  the Letany (Bastwick), 30, 31, 32
  Lilburne, 135, 136–7
  Star Chamber, 29
earl of Bath, 248
Batten, William, 195, 199, 235, 236, 238
Baxter, Richard, 50, 60, 109, 219, 224, 299, 338
Bay Colony, 50
Baynton, Edward, 90
Captain Beaumont, 121
Dr Beeves, 82
Bell Alley, 47, 63, 64, 71, 30, 130, 146
Berkshire, 57, 88, 89, 90, 233
  Marten, 219, 232, 238, 239, 242, 243
Berry, James, 108

Berry, John, 111
Berwick, 234
Bethel, Christopher, 109, 112
Bethlem burial ground (New Churchyard), 56
the Bible, 26, 43, 53, 87
Bible carriers, 53
Bilbrowe, Mary, 19
Billingsgate, 96, 222
Bingham, John, 316, 318, 322, 325, 326
Colonel Birch, 188–9
Captain Bishop, 212
bishop of London, 44
bishops, 4, 5, 124 see also clergy
  books, 68, 125
  December Days, 8–9, 18, 19, 20, 12
  Latimer, 28
  Ridley, 28
Bishopsgate, 43, 44, 54, 56, 58, 76, 136, 141
Bishopsgate mutiny, 293–6, 323
bishops men, 11
Bishops' Wars, 1, 2
Blackfriars, 46
Blackheath, 336
Blackmoore, Edward, 144
Blackwell, Joseph, 123
Blackwell Hall, 58, 265
Blaicklock, Samuel, 284
Lord Blayny, 15
Bond, Denis, 316, 317–18, 324, 325
Bond, Elias, 318
Bond, John, 317–18
Bond, Samuel, 318
Book of Common Prayer, 125, 247
Book of Martyrs, 26
books, xix, 26, 28, 68
booksellers, xxi, 68, 72, 75, 139, 148, 244
Boroughside, 44
Boston, 52, 107, 111, 136
Bothumley, Ranter Jacob
  The Light and Dark Sides of God (Bothumley), 74
Bourne, Nehemiah, 50
Bourne, Nicholas, 244–5
Bow, 238
Bow Street, 58
Box, Tobias, 56, 214, 219, 314
Boye, Rice, 38, 47
  Rome's Ruin (Boye), 47
Boys, John, 166, 229
Boyse, Henry, 21
Braddick, Michael, 334
Bradley, John, 49
Bradshaw, John, 288
Brailsford, Henry, xix, 380n4
Brandiff, Henry, 165
Branford, 79

Bray, William, xx, 181, 212, 213, 215, 219, 287
imprisonment, 217, 218
Bread Street, 57, 92
Brenner, Robert, 21
Brentford, 73, 77, 79, 81, 84,
Eyre, 109, 127, 215
Lilburne, 78, 80, 83, 92, 112, 127, 305
Bridewell prison, 161
Bridgefoot, 148
Bright, Francis, 47
Bristol, 85, 137, 189, 199, 213, 293, 298, 303
broadsheets, xvii, 11, 28, 61, 72, 75, 149, 249, 264, 269
new republic, 319
royalists, 89, 249
Weekly Meal initiative, 92
Lord Brooke, 35, 77, 78, 79, 104
Brooks, Thomas, 269, 270
Browne, William, xxi, 139, 167, 178, 186
Brownists, 73, 114, 123, 126, 132, 133, 141, 147
Brownsea Castle, 316
duke of Buckingham 54, 55, 229
Buckinghamshire, 16
Captain Buller, 3
Bull tavern, 159
Alderman Bunce, 194
Bungie, Thomas, 11
Bunhill Fields, 49
Burford mutiny (1649), xx, 50, 63, 219, 244, 296–9, 323, 340
Burgess, Glenn, 345–7
Burroughs, Jeremiah, 11, 20
Burton, Henry, 28, 31, 47
book burning, 68
ears, 29, 68
London, 35, 58
Star Chamber, 29
Bury St Edmunds, 141, 179, 234, 314
Butter, Nathaniel, 245

Calamy, Edmund, 46, 129, 132, 145
Calvert, Giles, 76
Calvin, John, 26, 28, 111
Cambridge, 75, 186, 187, 227, 234
Cambridge University, 28, 204
Canne, John, 47
Canning Street, 53
Cannon Street, 23, 30
Canterbury, 234
archbishop of Canterbury, xvii, 27, 46
Capuchin friars, 93
Carew, George, 316
Carlin, Norah, 26, 272–4
Carlisle, 234
Carnarvon, 29
Captain Carter, 212

Cary, Mary, 314
A Word in Season to the Kingdom of England (Cary), 314
Catholic invasion, 1
Catholicism, 8, 27, 123
cavaliers, 11, 12, 121, 123, 143, 258, 305
Cromwell, 114
defeated, xviii, 257, 286
insult, 7, 18, 247, 260
Lunsford, 2, 4, 9
Cavendish, Charles, 108
censorship, xvii, 27, 67, 112–13, 124, 131, 137
army, 245
Committee of Examinations, 130
Edwards, 129
Milton, 122
Stationers' Company, 68–70, 130
Chalgrove Field, 105
Chandlers, Tallow, 26
Charing Cross, 7, 44
Charles I, xvii, 28, 35, 45, 89, 112, 135, 241–2, 348 see also monarchy
assassination, 213
bishops, 8
capture, 186, 195, 196, 197
censorship, 68, 69
Cromwell, 111, 201, 230
December Days, 9, 10, 11, 12, 14, 15, 17, 20
execution, 258, 262–4, 285, 286, 325
Lambe, John, 54–5
Lilburne, John, 36
London, 1, 5, 7, 17, 18, 34, 77, 78, 99
Lunsford, 2, 5, 6
mayor of London, 3, 6, 33
negotiations, 201, 205, 206
Parliament, 1, 2, 9, 10, 12–13, 33, 46, 85
Personal Treaty, 25, 76, 222, 234, 246, 249
reformation, 27
restoration, 218, 234, 255
Scotland, 140
speech to Commons, 19
earl of Strafford, 2
Tower of London, 1
treason, xvii, 288
treaty, 206, 252–4, 260–1, 265, 271–3, 279, 281, 282, 318 see also Personal Treaty
trial, 58, 285, 286
war, 77–81, 93
Charles II, 312, 317, 330, 340
Charles V, 54
Cheapside, 146, 251
Cheapside Cross, 124, 131, 306
Cheesman, Christopher, 219, 287
Chepstow castle, 311
Chidley, Daniel, 37

Chidley, Katherine, xx, 19–20, 36–41, 48, 61, 65, 74, 141
   Edwards, 39, 129
   family, 26
   Good Counsell to the Petitioners for Presbyterian Government (Chidley), 39
   The Justification of the Independent Churches (Chidley), 38, 39
   Lilburne, John, 27, 42
   A New-Yeares-Gift to Mr. Thomas Edwards (Chidley), 39, 129
   pamphlets, 6, 40, 72
   printing, 335
   role of women, 39, 40
   separatist church, 60, 145
Chidley, Samuel, xx, 36, 37, 39–40, 48, 65, 74, 75, 141
   imprisonment, 60, 217
   legislative reform, 312
   Lilburne, 27, 38, 42, 72
   printing, 335
   separatist church, 60, 145
   Ware, 214
children, 2, 5, 29, 34, 37, 62, 87, 123, 159–161, 237
   baptism, 49, 61, 62, 145, 147
Chillenden, Edmund, 30, 47, 48, 53, 60, 82, 191, 192, 211
Chilliburne, John, 30, 47, 48, 53, 191–2, 211
   separatist church, 60
Cholmley, Hugh, 93, 259–60
Christchurch, 58
Church of England, xvii, 27, 74
the City *see* City of London
City of London, 35, 48, 53, 58, 170, 250, 335
   aldermen, 85, 86, 147, 155
   Common Council, 10, 85, 86, 147, 193, 194, 250
   corporations, 24
   December Days, 1– 9, 11, 13, 14, 15, 17, 20
   government, 44, 45, 164
   petitions, 2, 85
   political organising, 18, 85
Civil War, 40, 41, 49, 77–105, 106–14, 152, 316, 318
   First Civil War, 39, 73, 235, 238, 248, 252
   outbreak, 9, 17, 18, 20
   printing, 70
   Second Civil War, 90, 222, 240, 245, 249–53, 273, 287, 315
      causes, 229, 230–1, 275
      divisions, 276
      Royalists, 317
      women, 37

earl of Clarendon, 35, 45, 51, 84, 88
Clarke, John, 192, 219
Clarke, William, 205, 212, 214, 216, 315
Clarke manuscripts, 180
Clarkson, Laurence, 54, 74
class, xix, 19, 24, 38–9, 133–4, 241, 345, 347
   army, 285
   ruling class, 344
   snobbery, 267–8
A Cleere and Full Vindication of the late Proceedings of the Armie (pamphlet), 189
clergy, 18, 27, 31, 46, 58, 131, 133, 324
   printing, 28, 68
Clink Liberty, 44
Clockmakers' Guild, 163
Cloppenburg Press, 71, 75, 97
cloth workers, 32, 57
Clotworthy, John, 176
Clubman phenomenon, 347
CND (Campaign for Nuclear Disarmament), 342
Cobbett, John 217, 218, 219, 234, 284
Cobbett, Robert, 284
Cobler's Sermon, 54
Cockcroft, Caleb, 50
Coke, Benjamin, 145
Coke, Thomas, 9, 15, 41
   Institutes, 41
Colchester, 61, 146, 238
   siege, 49, 239, 249, 250, 254, 259, 263, 264, 294
Cole, Peter, 55, 71, 105
   Committee for the General Rising (petition), 97, 100
Coleman Street, 6, 13, 18, 45–6, 47, 48, 53, 130, 320
   Bell Alley, 146
   Goodwin, 147, 183, 251, 320–1
   printing press, 63, 134
   separatist churches, 60, 63, 145, 147
   Trained Bands, 50
Coleson, William, 50
Colet, William, 163
Collier, Thomas, 282
Colony council, 47
Committee for the General Rising (petition), 88, 97–105, 153
Committee of Both Kingdoms, 107, 113, 116, 117
Committee of the House, 15
Committee of the House of Commons for Examinations, 70, 134, 136–7, 143, 165
Common Council, 10, 13, 14, 15, 18, 45, 140, 250
   petition, 85, 86, 100

Walwyn, 91
war, 97, 193, 194
Common Hall, 24, 45, 70, 98, 103, 104
the Commons *see* House of Commons
Commons Committee, 59, 90, 118, 168
the Commonwealth *see* Commonwealth of
    England
Commonwealth of England, xvii
Como, David, 71
Congregation of Saints, 58
conscription, 15
Convertine (ship), 236
Cook, George, 271
Corkbush field, 40, 213, 214, 215, 217
Cornhill, 76, 163
Council of Agitators, 192
council of officers, 254, 255, 265, 282
Council of State, 55, 285–6, 288, 301, 318
    Larner, 73
    Rede, 322, 324, 325
    the Rump, 282, 285
Council of the Army, 187, 191, 197, 199,
    223, 265, 300
    Agitators, 255
    Putney, 204, 205, 213
    *A Remonstrance from his Excellency Sir
        Thomas Fairfax* (pamphlet), 213
Council of War, 101, 191, 216, 237, 283,
    287
counterrevolution (1648), xix, 170, 172,
    221–49
County Committee, 239
Court of Aldermen, 45
Court of Requests, 4
Court of Wards, 4
Covent Garden, 44, 58, 86
earl of Coventry, 158
Crafts, Roger, 177
craftsmen, xix, 11
Cranham, 62
Lord Craven, 239
Crawford, Laurence, 109, 115–17
Crawford, Patricia, 275
Cray, Richard, 11, 12, 22
Creamer, Thomas, 200, 201
Cripplegate, 43
Cripps, Henry, 76
Cromwell, Margaret, 108
Cromwell, Oliver, 59, 90, 106, 126, 127,
    133, 140, 287
    army, 175, 180, 197, 199, 200
    Bond, 318
    Bristol, 137
    death, 312
    Denne, Henry, xx, 340, 341
    Drury Lane, 183, 184
    Fairfax, 110, 175, 178
    family, 108

Ironsides, 107, 109, 127, 293
Joyce, 186
king, 58, 111, 137, 201, 206, 212
Levellers, 217, 288–9f, 348
Lilburne, 34–5, 41, 84, 106–14, 154, 155,
    201–3, 288, 311–12
Long Parliament, 106
Marten, 280
Manchester, 114–20, 122, 128, 133, 138
prisoners, 192
Putney, 202, 206–9, 210, 211, 212, 215
Rainsborough, 200, 207–8, 235, 264–5
Scotland, 230, 234, 254
Wales, 234
Writings and Speeches (Cromwell), 264
Cromwell, Thomas, 28, 108, 320
Crowland Abbey, 113
the Crown, 14
Curie, Edward, 53

Daffren, Thomas, 284, 307
Dart, John, 19, 59
Davenport, John, 46, 47, 50
David and Goliath, 39, 269, 270
Davies, John, 226
Deal castle, 236, 237
December Days, 1–22, 95, 104, 112, 157
    strike, 8
Denne, Henry, xx, 60, 63, 64, 141, 219
Derby House committee, 243, 244, 251, 316
Derbyshire, 15, 248
Desborough, John, 325
Deuteronomy, 320
Devonshire, 97
Dexter, Gregory, 74
Lord Digby, 2
    December Days, 8, 17
Diggers, 286
Dillingham, John, 119, 245 *see also*
        Parliamentary Scout (newspaper)
Disbrowe, John, 108
Dissenting Brethren, 113, 115, 124, 129,
    282
Dolphin Inn, 165
Doncaster, 115, 261–2
Donnington Castle, 117
Dorchester, 317, 324
Dorman, Mary, 31
Dorset, 110, 312, 316, 318, 322
earl of Dorset, 2, 33
Dover, 52, 326
Lord Dover, 5
Downs, Jordan, 100
the Downs, 235, 237
drapers, 24, 55
Lord Dunsmore, 83
Dunstable, 203
Duppa, John, 37

Durham, 23, 286
Dyve, Lewis, 199, 200, 201, 202, 211,

Earle, Walter, 13, 167, 177
East Anglia, 107, 121
Easter, 61
Eastern Association, 110, 113, 153, 157
  Bastwick, 136
  Cromwell, 107
  Eyre, 127
  Lilburne, 127, 180
  Manchester, 111, 117
East Hoathly Church, 2
Ecclesiastical Commission, 47
Edgehill, 73, 77, 78, 81, 106, 109, 127, 215
Edwards, Thomas, 38, 39, 47, 48, 63, 75,
      121, 129, 158, 341
  Cary, 314
  Chidley, 39, 129
  Gangraena (Edwards), 38, 58–9, 129,
      140–2, 196, 341
  Lanseter, 141–2
  A New-Yeares-Gift to Mr. Thomas
      Edwards (Chidley), 39, 129
  The Power of Love, Good Counsell to All,
      Toleration Justified (Walwyn), 87, 97
  Reasons against the Independent
      Government of Particular
      Congregations (Edwards), 38
  A Whisper in the Eare of Mr. Thomas
      Edwards (Walwyn), 87
  Windmill Tavern, 55
  A Word in Season, A Still and Soft Voice
      from the Scriptures (Walwyn), 87
Eeles, Robert, 159–60
elites, xviii, 1, 20, 105
emergent properties, xxi
Engels, Fiedrich, 339, 343–5, 347
English Revolution xvii, xviii, xix, 26, 27,
      45, 205
  direct action, 59
  first phase, 32, 41, 65, 72, 123, 133
  leadership, 107, 161–2, 288
  outbreak, 52, 57, 59, 62
  petitioning, 59, 64, 65
  printed material, 67–76
  women, 37, 92, 96, 101–2
episcopalianism, 8
Erastian settlement, 157
Erbury, William, 282
Essex, 52, 63, 64, 101, 146, 234, 238, 249
earl of Essex, 77, 80, 82, 84, 91, 120, 122,
      123, 127
  letter, 97
  Overton, 159–60
  Personal Treaty, 233–4
  war, 100, 103 104, 106, 107, 177, 240

Essex Grand Jury
Essex petition, 177, 233–4
Evans, Cornelius, 236, 248
Evans, Hugh, 146
Eveling, Abraham, 159–60
Evelyn, John, 81, 216
Everard, John, 50, 211, 219
D'Ewes, Simonds, 10, 13, 101, 102
Exeter, 234
Eyre, William, xx, 78, 90, 109, 127, 213
  Cromwell, 232
  imprisonment, 217
  Marten, 239
  war, 242, 244
  Ware, 215, 219, 232, 238

Fairfax, Thomas, 90, 107, 172, 177, 220,
      231, 234, 315
  Agitators, 215–16
  army, 203, 204, 205, 212, 214, 216–17
  Council of War, 191, 287
  Cromwell, 110, 175, 178, 196, 207
  Eyre, 215
  Joyce, 186, 196
  Kent, 238
  king, 185, 196
  Levellers, 213
  Newmarket, 187
  New Model Army, 194, 197
  Oxford, 243
  Parliament, 188
  Rainsborough, 215, 235
  regiment, 181–2
  Tower, 198
  Whitehall, 282
farmers, 25, 35, 97, 99
Lord Faulconbridge, 5
Faversham, 236
Felton, John, 229
Fetter Lane, 52
Fifth Monarchists, 60, 286
Major Fincher, 243, 244
Finnegan, David, 345–6
Finsbury Fields, 44, 54
Firth, Charles, 180, 205
Fleet Bridge, 30
Fleet prison, 31, 32, 35, 62
Fleet river, 43
Fleet Street, 19, 54, 59
Fleetwood, Charles, 113, 179, 274, 275
Foster, Humphrey, 242
Founders' Hall, 54
Fowke, John, 86, 157
Foxe, John, 28
  Book of Martyrs (Foxe), 28
Foxley, Rachel, 334, 337, 342
France, 2, 317

Franklin, John, 82, 86
Freeman, Francis, 82
free speech, xviii
Friday Street, 46, 56, 57

Gainsborough, 108, 112
Gardiner, Samuel, xxi, 80, 81, 106, 177, 320
Gardner, John, 315, 320, 326–7
Garrard, Charles, 239
Alderman Garrett, 14
Gatehouse prison, 7, 27, 28, 30, 60
gathered churches, 19, 20, 39, 40, 47, 58,
        72, 74, 75
    arrests, 289
    attack, 145
    Cromwell, 109
    London, 28, 44, 59, 62, 67, 335, 343
    organisation, 61, 342
    petitions, 165
    taverns, 53–4
Gayre, John, 156
Gell, John, 247–8
Gentles, Ian, xx, 103, 268, 334, 337
German Social Democrats, 339
Justice Gibb, 62
Gloucester, 104
Gloucestershire, 72, 143
Glover, George, 130, 151
Glynn, John, 101, 166
Goat Alley, 19, 59
Colonel Goffe, 208
Goldsmith's Alley, 144
Goldsmiths' Company, 163
Goode, William, 113
Goodwin, John, 46, 39, 46, 47, 50, 58, 141,
        177, 251
    Anapologesiates Anapologias (Goodwin),
        39
    church, 45, 60, 147–8, 158, 165, 183, 289
    A Glimpse of Sion's Glory (Goodwin), 72
    How, Samuel, 53
    Innocencies Triumph (Goodwin), 129
    Lilburne, 147
    secret presses, 47–8
    Walwyn, William, 54
    war, 85
    Whitehall, 282
Major Goody, 183
Gouge, William, 46, 50
Grandees
    Agitators, 195, 196
    army, 199, 216, 218, 220, 232, 233,
        234–5, 249, 265, 287
    Cromwell, 197, 230, 296
    Independents, 154, 198
    Ireland, 292, 293
    Lilburne, 202

Parliament, 249
    Ware, 213, 217, 218, 234, 265, 337
Grand Remonstrance, 1, 18
Colonel Graves, 183, 186
Greenhill, William, 11, 20, 145
Greensmith, John, 53
Gregg, Pauline, 228
Major Gregson, 216
Colonel Grimes, 176
grocers, 26
Grocers' Company, 110
Grocers' Hall, 13, 15, 17, 98
Guernsey, 318, 325
Guildford, 64, 146
Guildhall, 10, 13, 18, 43, 46, 162–3
    war, 78, 81, 85, 193
Gundell, Anne, 86–7
Gunpowder Plot, 28

habeas corpus, 311
habedashers, 26, 50
Haberdashers Company, 37
Hackney, 44
Haddesley, John, 320
Hadley, Katherine, 32, 35, 41
    imprisonment, 35
    pamphlets, 42
Hales, Jane, 143
Hammersmith, 79
Colonel Hammond, 176, 200, 213, 264–5
Hampden, John, 10, 16, 41
    imprisonment, 86
    war, 79, 80, 89, 105, 106
Hampshire, 213
Hampstead Marshall, 239
Hampton Court, 17, 199, 213
Harley, Brilliana, 37
Harris, John, xviii, 75, 180–2, 189, 194, 197,
        214, 219, 256–8
    Levellers, 339
    Wapping, 225, 229
Harrison, Edward, 60
Harrison, Thomas, xvii, 74, 113, 181, 277,
        281
    army, 181, 219, 220, 297, 298
    Levellers, 282, 284
    trial, 285
    Ware, 216
    Whitehall, 282
Haselrig, Arthur, 10, 105
Hayman, Henry, 93, 98
Heads of Severall Proceedings (newsbook),
        245
Heane, James, 318, 320, 323–7, 332
Heath, Robert, 83, 84
Hebrew, 313
Hegel, Georg Wilhelm Friedrich, 342–3

Queen Henrietta Maria, 93
Henry VIII, 49
Hereford, 52, 189, 231
Hertford, 234
Hertfordshire, 75
Hessayon, Ariel, 69, 345–6
Hewson, Thomas, 23, 26, 27
Hexter, J. H., 103
Hide, David, 4, 12, 15
High Commission, 1, 31, 46, 47, 62, 152
   printing, 68, 70
Highland, Samuel, 60, 167
Hildesley, Mark, 58, 251
Hill, Christopher, 344
Hills, Henry, 60, 65, 69, 74, 181, 182, 189,
   320, 335
   Lenthall, 194
Reverend Hitch, 109
Hitchcock, William, 55, 56
Hobbes, Thomas, 125
Hobson, Paul, 203
Holland see Netherlands
earl of Holland, 33–4
Holles, Denzil, 8–9, 10, 41, 250, 256, 316, 318
   army, 50, 60, 100, 131
   Brentford, 78, 81, 109
   king, 184
   Levellers, 340
   peace party, 105, 156
   Presbyterians, 167
   Royalists, 135
   Stapleton, 190, 195, 218
   war, 110, 119, 173, 176, 177, 179, 189,
   313
Holmby House, 174, 182–4
Holmes, Clive, 334
Home Counties, 24
Honourable Artillery Company (HAC), 49,
   50, 56
Hotham, John, 17
House of Commons, 1, 57, 59, 60, 97, 130,
   218, 234
   bishops, 8, 112
   December Days, 7, 10, 11, 13, 15
   Lunsford, 2–3, 17
   Marten, 90, 91, 92–5, 126
   petitions, 21, 22, 73, 85
   Presbyterians, 119, 235
   single-chamber legislature, 22, 73
   Speaker, 12–13, 84, 135
House of Lords, xvii, 48, 62, 155
   abolition, 22, 90, 285
   bishops, 8, 112
   Cromwell, 118
   December Days, 8, 10, 12
   examinations, 76
   Lilburne, 149, 151

Lunsford, 3
Marten, 93–5
   petitions, 21, 57
   Speaker, 194
How, Samuel, 45, 47, 53, 54, 58
Hull, 17
Humble Petition of Many Thousands of
   young men and Apprentices
   (petition), 189
The Humble Petition of the Brownist
   (petition), 123
The Humble Remonstrance of the Company
   of Stationer (petition), 69, 70
Hunscot, Joseph, 139–40, 143–4
Lord Hunsdon, 159–60
Captain Hunt, 112
Huntingdon, 35, 107, 234
earl of Huntington, 7
Hurst Castle, 287
Hyde, Edward, 45, 88 see also earl of
   Clarendon
Hyland, Samuel, 48

Independent churches, 61, 140, 147
Independents, 39, 51, 58, 60, 91, 105,
   126–7, 136–7, 155
   Dissenting Brethren, 113, 124
   leadership, 199
   Levellers, 169, 183
   MPs, 194
   Presbyterians, 157–8
   Silken Independents, 287, 327
   strategy, 348
   war, 111, 112
infant baptism, 49, 61, 62, 145, 147
Ingoldsby, 184
Inns of Court, 9
Ireland, 2, 11, 50, 172, 175, 292
   invasion, 90
   Levellers, 292–3
   Protestants, 8
   rebellion, 1, 8, 21, 50
   relief, 21, 288
   troops, 8, 203
Ireton, Henry, 56, 64, 90, 108, 116, 176–9,
   187, 199
   Agitators, 213
   Cromwell, 212, 254, 255, 348
   Putney, 207, 209, 210, 211
   regiment, 257
   Remonstrance of the Army (Ireton), 255,
   265, 270–1, 277, 284
   Whitehall, 282–4
   Woburn, 200
Ironsides, 107, 109, 127, 293
Isle of Wight, 173, 213, 222, 242, 264, 275,
   299, 323

Israel, 341
Ives, Jeremiah, 60, 63, 64, 146–7, 181, 219
  imprisonment, 217

Colonel Jackson, 183
Jael, 39, 40
James I, 28, 257
James VI, 27
Jeffery, George, 123
Jersey, 182, 311, 318, 325
Jessey, Henry, 19, 27, 47, 49, 59
Jesus Christ, 53
Jews, 38, 90
Johnson, Thomas, 161
Jones, William, 239
Joyce, George, 49, 182, 184, 186, 196, 197,
    320, 323, 325
  Cromwell, 326
Junkins, Joseph, 325
Juxon, Thomas, 118, 120, 140, 156, 193,
    194, 196
  Charles I, 157
  Cromwell, 176

Colonel Kelsey, 243
Kem, Samuel, 235, 236, 237, 238
Kent, 64, 226, 227, 234, 249, 287
  petition, 234, 237
Kenton, battle of see Edgehill
Kiffin, William, 6, 20, 26, 28, 74, 145, 181,
    289–90
  Lilburne, 30, 72, 289
  Walwins Wiles (Kiffin/Rosier), 289
King see monarchy
King, Edward, 110, 111, 114, 128, 134, 135,
    148
King's Head, 52
Lord Kingston, 83
Kingston-on-Thames, 17, 101, 250
Kishlansky, Mark, 334, 337, 339
Knollys, Hanserd, 60, 72, 145
Knottingly, 264–5

Labour Party, 341–2
Lamb, Thomas, 391n149
Lambe, John, 54–5, 68
Lambe, Thomas, xx, 19, 47, 59, 60, 61–5,
    72, 130, 141, 146
  Absolute Freedom from Sin by Christs
    Death (Lambe), 74
  congregation, 166
  imprisonment, 62, 161
  Lamb, Thomas, 391n149
  minister, 145
  pamphlets, 123
Lambert, John, 188, 301, 302, 303
Lambeth, 33, 34

Lambeth fair, 124
Lambourne, 239
Lancaster, 29
Langham, John, 156
Langport, 135
Lanseter, John, 141–2
Large Petition, 164–75, 247, 253–4
  importance, 272, 278
  launch, 246
  London, 166
  petition war, 318
  reproduction, 255
  support, 229, 274, 277
Larner, Ellen, 73, 143
Larner, John, 143
Larner, William, xx, 6, 12, 58, 60, 65, 127,
    128, 152, 312
  The Apprentices Lamentation (Larner), 6
  arrest, 143, 148, 163
  Baby-Baptism meer Babism (Larner), 74
  Bishopsgate, 139–40, 141, 189
  broadsheet, 20
  Every Man's Case (Larner), 144
  Goodman's Fields, 136, 139
  illegal printing, 72, 335
  imprisonment, 73, 76, 141–4, 154, 158
  Lilburne, 30, 37, 38, 130
  military, 219
  parents, 143
  petitions, 12, 18, 19, 21, 22, 73, 74, 189,
    272
  printing, 6, 36, 19, 53, 72, 73, 76, 286
  raid, 139–40, 142
  The Relief of the Poore (Larner), 74
  secret press, 11, 19, 72, 134, 136, 139,
    141–3
  Stationers' Company, 69, 141–4
    A True Relation of all the Remarkable
      Passages, and Illegall Proceedings of
      some Sathannical or Doeg-like
      Accussers of their Brethren Against
      William Larner, A Free-man of
      England (Larner), 143, 144
The Last Warning to All the Inhabitants of
    London (pamphlet), 76, 143, 148,
    151
Laud, William, 1, 27, 30, 31, 46, 68, 110 see
    also Archbishop of Canterbury
  execution, 34
  Lambeth Palace, 33
  Laudian church, 28, 109, 113
  Lilburne, 32, 142
  riots, 32
  Tower, 35, 112
  treason, 35
Launceston, 29
Lavenham, 52

lawyers, 25, 29
Leadenhall, 235
Leatherhead, 234
Lee, Walter, 50, 51, 56
Bishop Lee, 113
Leicester, 234
earl of Leicester, 248
Leicestershire, 243
Admiral Lendall, 237
Lenin, Vladimir Ilich, 220
Lenthall, William, 135, 194, 237
Lichfield, seige of (1643), 105
Lilburne, Elizabeth, 19, 107, 149, 210, 224
    gathered churches, 59, 320
    illness, 304
    letter, 149
    pamphlets, 150
    petition, 164, 169
    pregnancy, 139
    prisoner exchange, 84
    Tower, 150, 249
    war, 77
Lilburne, Elizabeth (of Wapping), 19, 59
Lilburne, Henry, 213
Lilburne, John, xx, 4, 5, 19, 48, 58, 74,
        125–7, 144, 210
    An Answer to Nine Arguments
        (Lilburne), 130
    apprenticeship, 23, 26, 33
    arrests, 135, 288
    assassination attempt, 31
    Bastwick, 136–7
    Brentford, 78, 80, 83, 92, 112, 127, 305
    The Charters of London (Lilburne),
        163–4
    Christian Man's Triall (Lilburne), 32, 38,
        42, 72, 130, 151
    Come Out of Her My People (Lilburne), 32
    The Copy of a Letter from Lieutenant
        Colonell John Lilburne to a Friend
        (Lilburne), 136, 138
    counterrevolution (1648), 222–31
    Cromwell, 34–5, 106–14, 120, 134–5,
        154, 252, 288, 311
    A Cry for Justice (Lilburne), 32
    death, 30, 42, 54, 56, 311
    early career, 23–42, 83, 162
    Eastern Association, 127, 180
    Edwards, 142
    Englands Birth-Right Justified (Overton/
        Lilburne), 137, 138, 139, 144, 158,
        190
    Englands New Chaines Discovered
        (Lilburne), 286, 288, 289
    exile, 90, 311
    family, 23, 26, 111
    freedom, 195, 214, 251–2

The Freemans Freedom Vindicated
        (Lilburne), 149
gathered churches, 59
Goodwin, John, 48
Hadley, Katherine, 35
Hide, David, 4
House of Commons, 227
House of Lords, 149–50
An Impeachment for High Treason
        against Oliver Cromwell and his son
        in law Henry Ireton Esquires
        (Lilburne), 227
imprisonment, xviii, 26, 28, 29, 36, 41,
        53, 106, 135, 147, 158, 161
    Fleet prison, 31, 32, 35, 90
    Gatehouse prison, 30, 81
    illness, 82
    Newgate prison, 136, 138, 139, 149
    Oxford jail, 80, 81–4, 106
    release, 139
    solitary confinement, 31
    Star Chamber, 30, 31, 36, 60, 90, 106,
        134, 138–9
    Tower, 150–1, 162, 168, 190, 195, 199,
        211, 249, 251, 284, 336
Innocency and Truth Justified and A true
        Relation of the material passages of
        Lieut. Col. John Lilburne (Lilburne),
        142
The Innocent Man's Second Proffer
        (Lilburne), 336
The Just Mans Justification (Lilburne),
        148, 158
King, Edward, 114, 139
Lambe, Thomas, 64, 141
Larner, 42, 140
Laud, 33
leadership, 20–1, 22, 154
Large Petition (1647), 164–71
Londons Liberty in Chains Discovered
        (Lilburne), 163–4
Marten, 89–90, 151, 239
military, 219
Moorfields, 134
networks, 36, 42, 65, 74, 138, 154, 165
Newbury, battle of (1643), 73, 104
New Palace Yard speech, 31
Out-Cryes of oppressed Commons
        (Overton/Lilburne), 165
pamphlets, xxi, 6, 41–2, 61, 134, 139,
        148, 149, 151, 312
persecution, 23
petitions, 41–2
printing, 41–2, 67, 68, 138, 286, 335, 336
prisoner exchange, 84
protest (December 1641), 73
Prynne, 130, 139, 190, 257

Rash Oaths Unwarrantable (Lilburne), 168, 170
Regall Tyrannie Discovered (Lilburne), 160–1
Stationers' Company, 68
torture, 26, 29, 30, 31, 32
treason, 83, 84
The Triall of Lieut. Collonell John Lilburne, 61
trials, 30–32, 35, 40, 41, 62, 142, 148–9, 304–10, 311
Wansey, 163
Wapping, 223–4
war, 77–81, 105, 106–14, 128
Whalebone tavern, 56, 226–7
Whitehall, 282–4
Windmill tavern, 55
A Worke of the Beast (Lilburne), 32
Lilburne, Robert, 111, 113, 176
Putney, 212
Ware, 215, 216, 217, 220
Captain Lillingston, 322, 323
Limehouse, 11, 44
Lincoln, 110, 112, 234
Lincolnshire, 63, 107, 110, 111, 134, 136
Lincoln's Inn, 29
Lindley, Keith, 21, 103
Lisle, George, 259, 263
Lithgow, William, 95, 96, 121
women, 96
liverymen, 45
Lockyer, Robert, 60, 286, 314, 315, 323
Lollards, 28
London, xvii, 1, 2, 14, 17, 45, 72 *see also* mayor of London
army, 197, 198, 199
book trade, 43
chamberlain, 26
citizens, 4, 11, 26
the City, 1, 3
economy, 44
Great Fire of London (1666), 43
leadership, 21, 22
manufacturing, 44
May Day riots (1640), 33–4
monarchist riots, 234
pamphlets, 126–7
Paradise Lost (Milton), 122
political organisation, 18, 21, 34, 43, 46, 48, 56, 107
population, 43
retail, 44
secret churches, 44
shipbuilding, 44
suburbs, 10, 14, 25, 34, 37, 43, 45, 51, 70, 92, 97, 226, 309
war, 77–81, 95, 189

London Bridge, 43, 194
Londonstone, 23
Long Parliament, 45, 52, 87, 88, 110, 165, 244
beginning, 34,
censorship, 69
Lilburne, 41, 106,
lord mayor *see* mayor of London
the Lords *see* House of Lords
Lothbury, 46, 50, 54, 56, 226
Chancellor Loudoun, 119
Lovell, William, 56
Low Countries *see* Netherlands
Lucas, Charles, 259, 263, 264, 446n852
Ludgate, 43, 50
Ludlow, Edmund, 86, 163, 231, 254, 289, 309, 313–16, 320
De Luke, 94
Lunsford, Thomas, 1–6, 9, 12, 17, 36, 250
Luther, Martin, 26, 28

Mabbott, Gilbert, 177, 245–6
Machiavelli, Niccolò, 127, 153, 233
Magna Carta, 144, 160, 161
Maiden Lane prison, 161
Maidstone, 250
Mainwaring, Randall, 85, 86, 104
Lord Maltravers, 83
Countess of Manchester, 117
earl of Manchester, 10, 63, 94, 98, 122, 127, 128, 148, 158
Cromwell, 106–14, 114–20, 122, 128, 133, 138
Eastern Association, 111, 117
Larner, 143
Lenthall, 194
war, 240
Lord Mandeville, 10
Manning, Brian, 21, 337
Margery, Ralph, 109
mariners, 11, 16, 17, 175
Market Harborough, 243
Marlborough, 82
Marprelate, Martin, 131
Marpriest, Martin, 131–38, 190, 337 *see also* Overton, Richard
The Arraignment of Mr Persecution (Marpriest), 131
Lilburne, 138
Marten's Eccho (Marpriest), 131
The Nativity of Sir John Presbyter (Marpriest), 131
A Sacred Decretall (Marpriest), 131
Marston Moor, battle of, 103, 114, 115, 116, 117, 127
Marten, Henry, xviii, 3, 36, 55, 57, 68, 88–91, 127, 152

background, 88
Berkshire, 219
Committee for the General Rising
    (petition), 88, 97–105
Cromwell, 280
December Days, 9
Englands Troublers Troubled (Marten),
    240, 241
Eyre, 215
father, 68, 88, 229
House of Commons, 141, 214
imprisonment, 161
The Independency of England (Marten), 71
king, 286
Large Petition (1647), 164–71
Lilburne, 89–91, 151, 155
Overton, 160
protest, 59
Pym, 120, 126, 158
regiment, 238–44
Royalists, 93
war, 86, 93–4
Ware, 214
Martin, Anne, 147
Marx, Karl, 125, 339, 343–5, 347
    Communist Manifesto (Marx/Engels),
    339
Marxism, 343, 345–7
Masschusetts, 47
Massachusetts Artillery Company, 50
Massachusetts Bay Company, 47
Massey, Edward, 173, 177, 189, 194
Masterson, George, 223–5
May Day, 234
    May Day riots (1640), 33–4
Maynard, John, 89, 119
mayor of London, 24, 45, 86, 162, 193, 199,
    218
    December Days, 3, 5, 6, 9, 10, 14, 15
    Lambe, John, 55
    Lambe, Thomas, 64
    Lilburne, 32, 155, 163–4
McElligott, Jason, 68
Meldrum, John, 111
Merchant Adventurers Company, 26, 87,
    162, 164, 166
merchants, xix, 1, 3, 25, 87, 92, 96, 97
Merchants' Hall, 98
Merchant Taylors' Company, 57, 72
Merchant Taylors' Hall, 98, 107
Mercurius Aulicus (news-sheet), 93
Mercurius Britanicus (newspaper), 155
Mercurius Civicus (newsbook), 96
Mercurius Elencticus (news-sheet), 59, 239,
    242, 257, 267, 268
Mercurius Militaris (news-sheet), 256–8,
    262, 266, 269, 277, 278

Harris, John, 75, 180, 256–8, 293
    Ireland, 293
    Mercurius Pragmaticus (news-sheet), 235,
        242, 252, 255, 257, 272, 290, 297
    Burford mutiny, 302–3
    Lilburne, 56, 203
    Marten, 239, 241, 242
    Rainsborough, 235, 268
Mercurius Rusticus, 213
Mermaid Tavern, 7
Captain Merriman, 209
Meyrick, John, 119
earl of Middlesex, 34, 158
Captain Middleton, 185
Mile End, 214
Militia Committee, 51, 98, 163, 173, 174,
    194, 313
    Independents, 191, 193
    Lilburne, 78, 92
    Walwyn, 88
    war party, 86
militia companies, 44
Milton, John, xvii, 74, 80, 91, 123, 124, 125
    Areopagitica (Milton), 122, 126
    The Defence of the English People
        (Milton), xvii
    The Doctrine and Discipline of Divorce
        (Milton), 74, 125
    Paradise Lost (Milton), 122
The Moderate (news-sheet), 245–8, 256,
    267, 269, 275, 279, 289, 323
Moderate Intelligencer (newspaper), 245–8,
    268
monarchist riots, 234
monarchy, xvii, xviii, 17, 40, 95, 102, 142,
    209, 211
    the City, 45
    denunciation, 52
    loyalty, 18
    Parliament, 8, 21, 205–6
    Personal Treaty, 25, 76
Lord Montague, 186
Moor, Adwalton, 85
Moorfields, 22, 32, 35, 44, 53, 73, 87, 130
Moorgate, 43
Morrill, John, 337
Mouth Tavern, 55, 56, 214
mutineers, 2
    Leveller, xxi

Nags Head, 45, 53, 58, 265, 276, 280
Naples, 56, 214
Naseby, battle of (1645), 137–8, 140, 250,
    294
the navy, 207, 234, 235, 236, 237, 240, 249,
    257
Nayler, John, 219, 287

Nedham, Marchamont, 155, 268
Netherlands, xvii, 3, 32, 38, 238, 153, 238
  Lilburne, 30, 286
  Overtons, 311
  printing, 28, 53, 71
Newark, 111–12
Lord Newburgh, 10, 13
Newbury, battle of (1643), 50, 73
Newbury, battle of (second), 117, 127
Newcastle, 320
New England, 38, 50, 110, 215, 271, 317
New England Company, 47
New Fish Street, 52
Newgate prison, 2, 43, 136, 138, 139, 149, 160, 167, 217
New Haven, 47
New Jerusalem, 26
Newmarket, 182–7
New Model Army, 50, 58–9, 128, 133, 153, 155, 157–8, 425n578
  Agitators, 189
  council of officers, 254
  disbandment, 232, 234, 244, 249
  mutiny, 172–4, 342
  organisation, 187, 334, 348
  Preston, 252
  Putney, 205, 206
New Palace Yard, 13, 31, 149, 160
newsbooks, 68, 100, 103, 245–9
newsletters, 3, 14
newspapers, xvii, 245–8, 339
news-sheets, 53, 102, 247, 249, 256
Nonsuch House, 58
Norbury, John, 98
Normans, 41
North, Dudley, 80, 91
earl of Northampton, 83
Northamptonshire, 63, 75, 174
earl of Northumberland, 94, 101, 200
Norwich, 52, 108, 146, 234
Nottingham, 57, 115, 234
Null and Void Ordinance, 199
Nye, Philip, 282

Oates, Samuel, 63, 64, 146–7
  arrest, 217
Old Jewry, 54
Old Palace Yard, 101
Old Sarum, 323
oligarchy, 24, 26, 45
Overton, Henry, 46, 47, 49, 139, 148
  secret press, 59
  shop, 76
Overton, Mary, 159–62
  imprisonment, 161
  infant, 159–62
Overton, Richard, xviii, 2, 21, 48, 56, 65,

71–2, 97, 132–4, 141, 181, 269 see also Marpriest, Martin
An Alarum to the House Of Lords (Overton), 144, 158
Alas Pore Parliament how Art thou Betrai'd? (pamphlet), 122, 123, 126, 130
An Appeale From the degenerate Representative Body the Commons of England (Overton), 190
An Arrow Against All Tyrants (Overton), 169
arrests, 148, 290
Articles of High Treason Exhibited against Cheap-side Crosse (Overton), 124
Baptist, 60, 124
book burning, 68
Cloppenburg Press, 71, 97
Englands Birth-Right Justified (Overton/Lilburne), 137, 138, 139, 144, 158, 190
freedom, 195, 202
gathered churches, 59
illegal printing, 122–5, 138, 335
imprisonment, 160
infant, 159–62
Lambe's church, 64, 124
Large Petition (1647), 164–71
The Last Warning to the Inhabitants of London (Overton), 142
Lilburne, 138
Mans Mortalitie (Overton), 125
Marpriest, Martin, 131–38, 190
New Lambeth Fayre (Overton), 124
Out-Cryes of oppressed Commons (Overton/Lilburne), 165
printing, 286
raid, 159–62
  A Remonstrance of Many Thousand Citizens (Overton), 144, 151, 152, 153, 155, 158, 196, 336
secret press, xviii, 47, 53, 55, 63, 72, 129, 130, 134, 138
Sexby, 326
Stationers' Company, 69, 142
Ware, 214
Whitehall, 282, 284
Wilbee, Amon, 189 see also Lilburne, John
Overton, Robert, 320
Owen, Mathew, 11
Oxford, 88, 94, 112, 181, 189, 227, 243, 257, 297
  artillary train, 182, 184,
  castle, 298
  king, 86, 106, 135, 236
Oxford jail, 80, 81–4, 106

Oxford mutiny, 300–303, 312, 323
Oxfordshire, 52, 238
Oxford University, 28, 87, 88, 186, 205, 299

Packer, William, 109, 232
Paine, Thomas, 74, 91, 100, 105, 144, 148,
      335
   Hills, 181
   imprisonment, 168
pamphlets, xvii, xix, xx, 6, 19, 43, 74–6,
      122–5, 128–55
   army, 181
   illegal, xviii, 30, 70, 71, 126, 245–8
   Leveller, 147, 168, 205–6, 287
   Marpriest, 131–38
   pamphlet wars, 128, 136, 224
   taverns, 53
   women, 92
paper-bullets, 128, 225
papists, 11, 15, 21
Paris Garden, 44
Parker, Henry, 155
Parker, William, 58
Parliament, 54, 125
   army, 25, 57, 60, 77, 146, 185
   Bastwick, 136–7
   cause, xix, 79, 108, 138
   Charles I, 1, 2, 14, 46
   December Days, 12, 16, 18, 20
   London Petition, 86
   monarchy, 8
   petitions, 51, 72, 73, 100
   preaching, 64
   protest (1643), 101–2
   purge, 38
   Puritans, 11
   reform, 20
   separatists, 124
   split, 76
   Stationers' Company, 69
   war, 86, 106, 107, 111, 112
   women, 37
Parliamentary Archives, 149
Parliamentary Scout (newspaper), 119, 245
      see also Dillingham, John
peace party, 77, 81, 85, 250, 337
   defeat, 97, 99
   members, 94, 105, 156
   petition, 88
   protests, 25, 104
   opposition, 91, 92, 100, 101, 102, 103
   Scots, 102, 157
   victory, 86
Peacey, Jason, xix, 154, 337, 342
Pearl, Valerie, 103, 174
Pelham, Thomas, 2, 3
Pembroke, 233

Penruddock, John, 470n1158
Pennington, Isaac, 7, 11, 13, 18, 20, 21, 27,
      59, 157
   Coleman Street house, 46
   mayor, 46, 91–2
   Oxford, 82
   petition, 85, 98, 99
   treason, 86
   war, 89, 91, 104
   wife, 52
Pequot Native Americans, 50
Perfect Weekly Account (newspaper), 243
Persecutio Undecima, 48
Personal Treaty, 25, 76, 222, 233–4, 237,
      240, 246, 249
Peter, Hugh, 50, 58, 85, 141, 158, 282
petitions, 22, 139, 189, 246, 269
   burning, 174
   Committee for the General Rising
         (petition), 88, 97–105
   counterpetition, 189
   December Days, 11, 12, 16, 21
   Essex petition, 177, 233–4
   Large Petition (1647), 164–75, 247,
         253–4
   petition war, 270–9
   Representation of the Army (petition),
         179–80
   right to petition, 22
   subscriptions, 52–3
Petty, Maximillian, 26, 90, 211, 281
pillory *see* torture
Pitchford, John, 219
Plain Truth Without Feare or Flattery
         (Amon Wilbee), 189 *see also*
         Lilburne, John
Plymouth, 234
political organising, xviii, 20
   Leveller, xviii, xix, 65, 139
   London, 21, 74
   print, 67–76
Pontefract, siege of, 188, 250, 259, 261, 262,
      264, 265
Poole, Dorset, xxi, 93, 317, 318, 320
   conflict, 316
   Levellers, 312
   Rede, 214, 299, 315, 321–5, 327, 238,
      329
Poole, Neville, 102
the poor, 21, 24, 52
   working poor, xix
the Pope, 19
Popes Head Alley, 46, 76
popular sovereignty, 209–10
Portland, 323
Portland Castle, 325
Porton, 313, 323, 327–33

Portsmouth, 17, 64, 146, 182, 238, 299, 320, 323
Pottinger, H. A., 205
Poultry Counter, 143
powder plot *see* Gunpowder Plot
Poyntz, Sydenham, 188
Praise God Barebone, 19
preachers, 26
pregnancy, 14, 84
Prentice, Dorcas, 61
Presbyterians, 39, 51, 64, 74, 113, 125, 142, 250
  army, 235
  cause, 172–97
  censorship, 122, 124
  coup, 175, 176, 179, 187–97, 198–9
  Cromwell, 118
  government, 133, 140–1, 147, 153, 155, 235, 249
  press, 245
  war, 107, 112, 126, 140, 189, 240
  the press, 18–19, 27, 245–8
  freedom, 122
Preston, 252
Pretty, Henry, 64, 146
Price, Edward, 110
Price, John, 165, 183, 289
Pride, Thomas, 38, 49, 74, 176, 178, 282, 426n586
Pride's Purge (1648), 51, 272, 278, 280, 317
Captain Primrose, 84
Prince, Thomas, 26, 60, 73, 104, 127, 128, 219
  imprisonment, 217
  Levellers, 284–5, 288, 290
Prince Charles, 250, 257
Prince of Wales, 236
printing, xx, 67–76, 148
  December Days, 18
  illegal, xviii, 19, 40, 69, 70, 72, 74, 113, 122, 138, 335
  political organising, 67–76
  popular print, 18
  Puritan presses, 28
  secret presses, xviii, 19, 44, 46, 47, 65, 69, 72, 139, 256–8
Privy Council, 33, 69
Protestantism, 17, 28
Protestants, 124
  massacres, 1, 8
protests, 25, 34, 45, 59, 95, 96, 97
  December Days, 1–22
  mass demonstrations, 21, 40, 65, 80, 95
  national church, 45
  Turnham Green, 77, 80, 85, 95
Providence (ship), 236

Prynne, William, 28, 29, 31, 47, 75, 128, 136
  Agitators, 190
  book burning, 68
  ears, 29, 68
  A Fresh Discovery of some New Wandering-Blazing-Stars and Firebrands (Prynne), 135, 136
  gathered churches, 59
  Histrio-Mastix (Prynne), 29
  imprisonment, 29
  Larner, 143
  Lilburne, 134, 135, 138, 190
  London, 35
  The Lyar Confounded (Prynne), 138, 139
  Truth Triumphing (Prynne), 129
Puritanism, 13, 26
Puritan martyrs, 28, 68, 84, 128
Puritans, 11, 15, 18, 26, 36, 49, 73
  ministers, 52, 59
  petitions, 112
  shorthand, 205
  taverns, 53, 57
Purkiss, Diane, 334
Putney, 199, 204–13, 214, 234, 235, 254, 255
Putney debates, 76, 110, 204–13, 233, 314, 315, 337, 425n578
  A Call to all the souldiers of the Armie (pamphlet), 209
  Independents, 253, 279
  pamphlets, 204, 209
Pye, Robert, 178
Pym, John, 10, 11, 12, 41, 53, 91, 98
  death, 105
  Earl of Essex, 103, 120
  imprisonment, 86
  Marten, 126, 158
  war, 89, 94, 97, 99, 100, 101, 104–5

Radman, John, 300–2, 312, 322, 323, 324, 332
Rainsborough, Judith, 27, 219, 237
Rainsborough, Margaret, 237
Rainsborough, Margery, 237
Rainsborough, Martha, 27
Rainsborough, Thomas, 27, 47, 48, 50, 90, 113, 199, 201, 223
  Agitators, 188, 219
  army, 182, 200, 215, 218, 219, 259–261
  counterrevolution, 223–38
  Cromwell, 207, 208, 209, 211, 212, 235
  Deal castle, 237
  death, 261–5, 273, 274, 278
  An Elegie Upon the Honourable Colonel Thomas Rainsborough (pamphlet), 265–6

Fairfax, 215
family, 237
father, 234, 269
funeral, 265–70, 276, 278, 280, 295
Ireland, 292
Levellers, 127, 191, 217, 222, 247, 317
Lilburne, 135, 211, 214
New England, 113
New Model Army, 155, 194, 196
Parliament, 212
petition, 275
poems, 266–7, 268
Putney, 150, 207, 208, 209–12, 337
regiment, 182, 271, 277, 297, 299, 300
counterrevolution, 233–8
Sexby, 294
Ware, 214, 234, 235
Woburn, 200
Rainsborough, William, 50, 179, 188, 191,
    219, 247
Deal castle, 237
Ireland, 292
New Model Army, 155
war, 252, 254, 257
Ranters, 286
Ratcliffe, 19
Colonel Reade, 210, 314
Reading, 89, 93, 117, 188, 239
Red Coates, 79, 81
Rede, John, xxi, 163, 181, 214, 219,
    313–315, 321–33
Cromwell, 324
    Humble Petition and Representation of
    the Officers and Souldiers of the
    Garrisons of Portsmouth (petition),
    318–19
petitions, 318–20
Reece, Henry, 322, 323
Justice Reeves, 148
reformadoes, 2, 188, 193
the Reformation, 27
Reformed Church, 64
regicide, xvii, 47, 50, 56, 74, 163, 182
religious intolerance, 1
Remonstrans Redivivus (pamphlet), 91
republic, xvii, xviii
the Revolution see English Revolution
Reynolds, John, 287
Colonel Rich, 200
Richmond, 34
Rigby, Alexander, 98, 304
Earl Rivers, 83
Lord Robartes's, 73, 127, 143, 163
Robarts, Thomas, 316
Robinson, Henry, 135
Rochester, 236
Rodes, Edward, 259

Rolf, Edmund, 192
Rome, 27
the Root and Branch petition (1640), 112,
    113
Rosier, Edmund, 26, 27, 60, 289
    Walwins Wiles (Kiffin/Rosier), 289
Colonel Rossiter, 112
Rouen see St Bartholomew's Day Massacre
    (1572)
roundhead, 4, 7, 50, 51, 82, 166, 260
Roundway Down, 85, 100
Row, Paternoster, 86
Rowe, Nathaniel, 47
Rowe, Owen, 47
Rowley, William, 52
    A Match at Midnight (Rowley), 52
Royal Exchange, 33, 43, 56, 226, 250
Royalism, 347
    Royalists, 50, 51, 54, 286, 337
    army, 106, 111, 112
    artillery train, 117
    king, 241
    London, 77
    peace party, 92
    rebellion, 233
    war, 78, 82, 83, 84, 85, 97, 99
    women, 37, 82, 101
Rumbold, Richard, xviii, 258
Prince Rupert, 77–81, 83, 84, 111, 112, 114
Rushworth, John, 19, 31, 186, 191, 197,
    245, 426n586
Rutherford, Samuel, 289
Rutland, 63, 147, 217, 272

the Sabbath, 48, 61
Colonel Sadler, 177
Saffron Walden, 177, 178, 179, 338,
    426n586
Salisbury, 313–14
Salters' Hall committee, 92, 97, 103, 107,
    153, 336
    Walwyn, 88, 163, 336
    Weekly Meal initiative, 92
    women, 92
Saltmarsh, John, 102
Salus Populi, 111
Captain Sampson, 189
Sandwich, 236, 237
Saracen's Head, 46, 56–7
satirical pamphlets, 131, 132, 256, 269
satiric verses, 89, 124
Saunders, Robert, 177
Scotland, 74, 95, 102, 103, 104, 118, 152,
    320
    army, 107, 111, 112, 113, 121, 140, 218
    Bishops' Wars, 1
    Charles I, 188, 218

independent churches, 140
invasion, 233, 234, 240, 249, 262
Presbyterianism, 121, 140–1, 187–97, 198
Scott, Jonathan, 334
Scott, Peter, 7
Scotten, Edward, 219
Scottish Covenanters, 71
Lieutentant Scotto, 192
the Scriptures *see* the Bible
seamen, 16, 17, 21, 44, 175, 193, 235, 236–7
sailors, 4, 16
seamtresses, 75
Sectaries, 20, 47, 48, 58, 62, 111, 118, 247, 251, 341
Self-Denying Ordinance, 120, 122, 127, 238
separatist churches, 38, 60, 72
arrests, 38
Duppa church, 38
London, 26, 37–8, 154
separatists, 13, 19, 27, 40, 53, 54, 58, 59, 60, 124
toleration, 126
Severn, 62
Sexby, Edward, 26, 58, 60, 219, 323, 326
Agitators, 179, 188, 212, 314
Cromwell, 206, 207, 210, 252, 255
Killing Noe Murder (Sexby), 311
Levellers, 180–2, 206, 286, 320, 323, 332
pamphlets, 181, 212
Overton, 326
Portland, 326
Putney, 206, 207
war, 110, 127, 182, 183, 192, 294
Lady Seymour, 82
Lord Seymour, 82
Shaftesbury, 318
Shambrooke, William, 49, 51
Colonel Sheffield, 178, 179
Shepard, Thomas, 60, 179
sheriffs, 5, 14, 15
shoemakers, 96
Shoreditch, 11
shorthand, 19, 61, 205, 257
Shrewsbury, 37
Shropshire, 108
Simmons, Matthew, 91
Sindercombe, Miles, 219
Sion College, 156, 157
Skippon, Philip, 16, 50, 60, 309
war, 80, 110, 179, 251, 299, 308
Skutt, George, 315–18, 321, 322, 324, 325
A Letter from an Ejected Member of the House of Commons to Sir Jo. Evelyn (Skutt), 317
son, 316
Sleaford, 112

Slyngesbie, Robert, 9, 13
Smith, John, 261–2
Smith, Marshall, 81, 82
Smith, Thomas, 8
Smithfield, 94
petition, 217
soap boilers, 44, 47, 391
soldiers, 11, 64, 65, 85
court-martialled, 287
demobilised, 2, 4
Ireland, 2, 8
pay, 2, 3
reformadoes, 2, 188, 193
Solemn League and Covenant, 103, 113, 121, 131, 135,
Some Considerations Tending to the Undeceiving of Those, Whose Judgements are Misinformed (pamphlet), 123
Somerset House, 93
Southampton, 314, 320
Southsea Castle, 326
Southwark, 17, 18, 19, 25, 44, 48, 59, 336
army, 194
prisons, 33
raid, 159–62
regiment, 51
riots, 33–4
separatists, 60
Spelman, John, 104
Spencer, John, 219
Spilsbury, John, 19, 59, 320
Spitalfields, 44, 49, 64
St Albans, 177, 187
Stapleton, Philip, 119, 156, 167, 173, 174, 195
Holles, 179, 189, 190, 218
Star Chamber, 1, 50, 90, 244
censorship, 69
Lilburne, 30, 31, 36, 60, 90, 106, 134, 138–9, 152
Lunsford, 2
printers, 68, 70
Prynne, 29
Staresmore, Sabine, 38
Star Inn, 58
starvation, 82, 446n852
Stationers' Company, 68–70, 123, 128, 130, 135, 139, 144, 159
beagles, 142, 143
raids, 139–40
secret presses, 139
Stationers' Company petition (1643), 75
St Bartholomew's Day Massacre (1572), 317
St Bennet Gracechurch, 145
Steevens, Henry, 60

Stepney, 11, 12, 19, 48, 59, 145
St George's Fields, 33, 44, 51, 336
St Giles in the Fields, 19, 34,
Stilton, 52
St John, Oliver, 41, 154, 200, 245
St Katherines, 11
St Martins Lane, 15
St Mary's, Aldermanbury, 46
St Olave's, 44
Stoughton, Israel, 50
St Pauls cathedral, 43, 75, 144, 288
earl of Strafford, 1, 49
    execution, 2, 35, 150
    impeachment, 35
    imprisonment, 2
    trial, 35, 120
Strand, 44, 78, 119
Stratford, 238
Strode, William, 10, 13, 89, 93, 98, 100
    Marten, 105
St Saviour's, 19, 48, 59
St Stephens parish, 6, 13, 46, 47, 50, 58
Stuart government, 1
Studley, Peter, 37
    The Looking-Glasse of Schisme (Studley),
        37
Sturges, Richard, 48
Captain Styles, 177
Sub-committee for Volunteers, 92
Suffolk, 141, 145, 178, 234, 257
Sussex, 75
Captain Swallow, 108
Sweeting, John, 97–105
Symonds, Bartholomew, 216

Taft, Barbara, 334
Tate, Zouch, 118, 120
taverns, 52–8, 65
    political meetings, 45, 52–8
Taylor, John, 28, 46
    Booke of Martyrs (Taylor), 28
    imprisonment, 217
    separatists, 53
taxes
    excise, 104, 174, 254
    tithes, 131,132, 239
    abolition, 166, 254, 301
    compulsory, 27, 155
    opposition, 98, 142, 147, 177, 242, 319
Tench, Edward, 284
    Thames, 5, 17, 44, 78
    crossing, 43, 238, 250, 297
Thames Street, 87
Thickley Punchardon, 23
Thomasson, George, 142, 144, 151, 154,
        177, 189, 268, 269
Thompson, James, 219

Thompson, William, 213, 219
Three Horseshoes, 52
Tichborne, Robert, 49, 56, 198
Tickhill Castle, 115, 116, 118, 148, 149
Tindall, Lazarus, 226
Tolmie, Murray, 61, 340, 347–8
torture, 26, 29, 30, 31, 32
Tothill Fields, 34
Tower Hamlets, 11, 18, 25, 44, 238
Tower Hamlets Auxiliary Regiment, 49
Tower Liberty, 19, 59
Tower of London, 1, 2, 29, 43, 99, 198, 250,
        268
    Archer, John, 33
    bishops, 9, 112
    December Days, 10, 11, 12, 20, 40
    Levellers, 289, 336
    Liberties, 44
    Lilburne, 150–1, 162, 168, 190, 195, 199,
        211, 249, 251, 284, 336
    Lunsford, 3, 6
    the Mint, 1, 3
    moat, 11
    Tower Guards, 49
Towse, John, 92
To Your Tents, O Israel (Walker), 14
Trained Bands, 33, 34, 49, 50, 104, 250,
        251
    December Days, 5, 6, 10, 13, 15–16, 20
    protest (1643), 101–2
    war, 80, 92, 93, 95, 188
    Yellow Regiment, 56
treason, xvii, 1, 10, 12, 93
Treaty of Oxford, 85, 94, 104
Triploe Heath, 187, 296, 300, 301, 323
tub preachers, 14, 19, 38, 46, 159
Tue, Nicholas, 47, 63, 134, 161, 167, 168,
        209
    arrest, 130
    imprisonment, 130, 161
    Stationers' Company, 69
Tulidah, Alexander, 167, 168, 177, 181, 192,
        219
Turner, Jane, 320
    *Choice Experiences of the Kind Dealings
        of God* (Turner), 320
Turnham Green, 77, 80, 85, 95, 104, 106
Turvil, William, 243
Tweed, 107
Tyburn fields, 96
Tyndale, William, 28

Uxbridge, 187

Vane, Henry, 86, 117, 120, 143, 144, 154,
        200
Vaughan, Richard, 150

Venetian ambassador, 15, 16, 17, 18, 20, 29, 203–4
  military leadership, 120, 121, 123, 128
  prisons, 33
  riots, 34
  war, 95, 96, 203–4
Venn, John, 7, 18, 20, 21, 45, 49, 50
  treason, 86
  war, 89
Villiers, George see duke of Buckingham
Vote of No Addresses, 223, 235, 253, 272
  Cromwell, 201, 229
  Second Civil War, 229, 253, 317, 348

Walbrook, 51, 251
Waldron, John, 239, 243
Wales, 146, 233, 249
Walker, Clement, 240, 271
  Englands Troublers Troubled (Walker), 240
Walker, Henry, 14, 19
Waller, Edmund, 97, 99, 100, 101, 163, 167
  army, 176, 177
  war, 107, 240, 250
Wallingford, 239, 302
Wallington, Nehemiah, 21
Walter, John, 11, 334
Walton, Valentine, 108
Walton Hall, 127
Walwyn, William, 26, 47, 48, 54, 55, 58, 123, 125, 141
  army, 175, 188
  background, 86
  Cromwell, 183
  Committee for the General Rising (petition), 88, 97–105
  The Compassionate Samaritane, 124, 129, 130, 132, 196
  Declaration of the Army, 208
  Edwards, Thomas, 87, 142
  England's Lamentable Slavery, 137
  Gold Tried in the Fire, 167
  Juries Justified, 239
  Just Man in Bonds, 144, 149, 158, 196
  gathered churches, 60, 87, 165
  Lambe, Thomas, 64, 65
  Larner, 74
  Levellers, 135, 138, 147, 284–6
  Marten, 90, 239
  pamphlets, 91, 124, 142, 148
  Parliament, 91
  The Pearle in the Dunghill, 144, 149, 158, 196
  The Poore Wise-mans Admonition, 174
  The Power of Love, Good Counsell to All, Toleration Justified, 87, 97
  printing, 335

Salters' Hall committee, 92
  Some Considerations Tending to the Undeceiving of Those, Whose Judgements are Misinformed, 88
  Strong Motives, Or Loving and Modest Advice Unto the Petitioners for Presbyterian Government, 137
  The Vanitie of the Present Churches, 289
  Walwyn's Just Defence, 289
  A Whisper in the Eare of Mr. Thomas Edwards, 87, 142
Whitehall, 282
Windmill tavern, 55
  A Word in Season, A Still and Soft Voice from the Scriptures, 87, 144, 148
  A Word More to Mr. Thomas Edwards, 142
Wansey, Henry, 162–3
Wapping, 19, 44, 48, 50, 59, 268, 269, 306, 315
  meeting, 223, 225, 229, 231
Warcup, Robert, 48
Wareham, 318
Ware mutiny, 40, 55, 65, 213–18, 234, 235, 238, 253, 255
  petition, 217–18
  Royalism, 215
Warner, John, 50, 51, 92, 104, 156, 199
Warner, Samuel, 92
war party, 73, 81, 84, 86, 89, 91
  protests, 97, 101–102
  radical wing, 98, 100, 105
Warwick, Philip, 34–5
Warwick, 234
  earl of Warwick, 238, 257
Warwick castle, 300, 307
Warwickshire, 307
watermen, 44, 46, 96
Watling Street, 55
weavers, 56, 86, 87, 214
Weekly Meal initiative, 92
Welford, 239
Well Yard, 48, 57
  meeting, 240, 241, 249, 315
Wentworth, Peter, 86, 93
West, Francis, 250
West Country, 57, 287, 325
Westminster, 3, 5, 6, 30, 34, 44, 45
  December Days, 9, 10, 13, 15, 16, 17, 18, 20
  protests, 36, 73, 101–2
  war, 81, 86, 288
Westminster Abbey, 5, 9, 50, 56, 95, 113
Westminster College, 5
Westminster Hall, 4, 5, 100, 134, 144, 148, 287
Westminster Yard, 3–4, 5, 9, 18

Colonel Wetton, 281
Weymouth, 323, 324
Whalebone tavern, 46, 56, 225–7
Whalley, Edward, 60, 108, 259, 274, 275, 294
Wharton, John, 30
Wharton, Nehemiah, 57
White, Francis, 50, 201, 219
White, Robert, 245
Whitechapel, 11, 19, 44, 59
  Lambe, Thomas, 62, 63, 130
Whitechapel riot, 62
Whitecross Street, 19, 59
Whitefriars, 34, 52
Whitehall, xvii, 33, 229, 282, 285
  debates, 282–3
  December Days, 3, 5, 6, 9, 10, 12, 15
White Lion prison, 7, 33
White Lion tavern, 53
Whitelocke, Bulstrode, 119, 150
Wilbee, Amon, 189 see also Lilburne, John
Wildman, John, xx, 22, 46, 48, 56–8, 241, 249, 282, 311
  Cromwell, 230
  imprisonment, 249
  Levellers, 223–31, 257, 281, 282, 286, 337, 342
  Marten, 90
  Poole, 315
  pseudonym, 204
  Putney debates, 204, 206, 208, 210, 211
  Putney Projects, 218
  Truths Triumph, 22
  Whitehall, 283
  Wiltshire, 241
Wilkinson, Henry, 52
Williams, C. M., 105
Williams, William, 318, 320
Lord Willoughby, 111
Wilson, Aaron, 46
Wiltshire, 38, 57, 64, 89, 90, 146, 163, 241, 312, 328
  Anabaptists, 330
  clothiers, 230
  churches, xii, 327, 333
  committee, 244, 313
  New Model Army, 314

petitions, 257
poor, 241
revolt, 257
war, 146, 297, 313, 315
Wiltshire Protestation, 82
Winchester House, 288
Windmill Tavern, 46, 54–5, 56, 135, 147–8, 165, 337
Windsor, 97, 218, 232, 239, 255, 277, 281, 290, 303
Windsor Castle, 17, 287
Winstanley, Digger Gerrard
  The Beacons Quenched, 74
  England's Spirit Unfolded, 74
Winthrop, John, 47, 50, 219
Winthrop family, 27
Wiseman, Richard, 4, 5, 73
  death, 6
  funeral, 6
Wither, George, 95, 196
Woburn, 200
women, 19, 29, 37, 38, 39, 55, 59, 123, 139
  childbirth, 37
  Humble Petition of Divers wel-affected
    Women (petition), 336
  Leveller, 290–2
  organising, 92
  petitions, 40, 150
  preaching, 63, 146, 320
  protest (1643), 101–2
  public affairs, 40, 129
  voting, 63
  war, 96
Woodnett, 76
Woodstreet prison, 7–8
Woodward, Richard, 226
Woolrych, Austin, 205, 334, 337
Worcestershire, 86, 232, 315
Worden, Blair, 334–5
  working poor, xix
Wrighter, Clement, 141

Yonge, Walter, 81
York, 111
  archbishop of York, 5, 8, 9
Yorkshire, 24, 97, 115, 259
youngmen, 21